INTERNATIONAL LAW AND THE ADMINISTRATION OF OCCUPIED TERRITORIES

International Law and the Administration of Occupied Territories

Two Decades of Israeli Occupation of the West Bank and Gaza Strip

Edited by
EMMA PLAYFAIR

The proceedings of a conference organized by al-Haq in Jerusalem in January 1988

CLARENDON PRESS · OXFORD
1992

Oxford University Press, Walton Street, Oxford OX2 6DP
Oxford New York Toronto
Delhi Bombay Calcutta Madras Karachi
Petaling Jaya Singapore Hong Kong Tokyo
Nairobi Dar es Salaam Cape Town
Melbourne Auckland
and associated companies in
Berlin Ibadan

Oxford is a trade mark of Oxford University Press

Published in the United States
by Oxford University Press, New York

© Oxford University Press 1992

All rights reserved. No part of this publication may be reproduced, stored in a retrieval system, or transmitted, in any form or by any means, electronic, mechanical, photocopying, recording, or otherwise, without the prior permission of Oxford University Press

This book is sold subject to the condition that it shall not, by way of trade or otherwise, be lent, re-sold, hired out or otherwise circulated without the publisher's prior consent in any form of binding or cover other than that in which it is published and without a similar condition including this condition being imposed on the subsequent purchaser

British Library Cataloguing in Publication Data
Data available

Library of Congress Cataloging-in-Publication Data
International law and the administration of occupied territories: two decades of Israeli occupation of the West Bank and Gaza Strip/ edited by Emma Playfair.
Collection of essays originally presented at a conference held in Jan. 1988 in East Jerusalem.
Includes bibliographical references (p.   ) and index.
1. Law—West Bank. 2. Law—Gaza Strip. 3. West Bank—Politics and government. 4. Gaza Strip—Politics and government. 5. Israel—Arab War, 1967—Occupied territories. 6. Military occupation. 7. International law. I. Playfair, Emma.
KMM873.5.I58 1992   341.6'6'0956953—dc20   91-37464
ISBN 0-19-825297-8

Typeset by Best-set Typesetter Ltd., Hong Kong
Printed in Great Britain by Bookcraft Ltd.
Midsomer Norton, Avon

*This book is dedicated
to all those living under
the shadow of occupation*

Foreword

IN 1979, a group of Palestinian lawyers created an organization in the Israeli-occupied territories to monitor and document human rights violations by the occupiers under international law, and to promote the rule of law and respect for human rights in the Occupied Territories. They stuck closely to this task and avoided any participation in politics. The International Commission of Jurists was glad to accept them as an affiliated organization and gave them what help it could.

At first the organization was known as 'Law in the Service of Man', but later this was changed to 'al-Haq', which in Arabic signifies 'justice' and 'right'.

From its beginning, al-Haq has taken the utmost care to act within the law, that is to say both the domestic law in force at the time of the occupation, as amended or added to by Israel's military orders, and the international law relating to a military occupation. This has not been an easy task as the military orders are over 1,200 in number.

This book contains the report of a Conference organized by al-Haq in East Jerusalem in January 1988, in which al-Haq sought clarification of the provisions of international law relating to a military occupation. The participants were distinguished international lawyers with recognized expertise on various aspects of this body of law. Remarkably little writing exists on this subject, and what there is has related to short-term occupation. There is no precedent for Israel's occupation for over two decades.

I had the privilege of attending the Conference and can testify to its novelty and value. There is no need for me to attempt to describe the background to the Conference and the history of Israel's occupation, as this has been done brilliantly by the editor of this book, Emma Playfair, a former volunteer researcher with al-Haq. Her introduction contains a detailed account of the occupation which will give the reader all the information needed to bring to light the complexity of the subject dealt with by the authors.

NIALL MACDERMOT, CBE, QC,
*former Secretary-General of the
International Commission of Jurists*

Acknowledgements

THIS book was conceived in 1986 in one of al-Haq's weekly meetings. Facing yet again a problem of law to which we found no answer, Raja Shehadeh suggested appealing to the world's experts in the law of war for their help in clarifying the international laws governing Israel's administration of the West Bank and Gaza. My task as editor has been simply to co-ordinate the efforts of all those who responded to al-Haq's call. The real credit is due to all the staff and friends of al-Haq who enabled this project to be realized, and to the participants, who dedicated their time and effort to address a difficult and sensitive subject.

Raja Shehadeh has remained a central architect and advisor to both conference and book, neither of which would have happened without him. While every member of al-Haq contributed to this project, I am particularly grateful to Jacqueline Shahinian for her help in organizing the conference, and to Joost Hiltermann for his support as colleague, friend, and critic. Na'ila Hazboun, Paulein Natour, Nina Atallah, Riziq Shuqeir, Mona Rishmawi, Marty Rosenbluth, Lisa Taraki, Fateh Azzam, Randa Siniora, Charles Shammas, Abdel-Karim Kana'an, Ahmed Jaradat, Mervat Rishmawi, Judith Dueck, Lilia Bylos, Iyad al-Hadad, Maureen Khacho, and Sireen Hilele also played critical parts in assuring the success of the conference. Of al-Haq's friends, Roger Heacock, Andreas Kuhn, and David Kretzmer all offered valuable advice and suggestions in the planning stage, while Penny Johnson, Susan Rockwell, and Martha Moffett gave much help during the conference itself. Special thanks are due to Jay Winter and Adam Roberts, whose advice throughout the planning and realization of the research and conference and in relation to the publication has been invaluable, and to Richard Hart of Oxford University Press for steering me through the final stages.

I also wish to express thanks to my colleagues and friends in Cairo, especially to David Nygaard for his patience in allowing me time to work on this book, Robert Rubinstein who helped me overcome innumerable technical difficulties, and Cathy Costain who solved many bibliographical problems. For general support and encouragement, I am especially grateful to Catherine Essoyan in the early stages, to Necla Tschirgi and Abdullahi Ahmed an-Na'im towards the end, and to my family throughout.

Al-Haq, as always, is especially indebted to Niall MacDermot, the former Secretary-General of the International Commission of Jurists, of which al-Haq is an affiliate. His encouragement and support for al-Haq has been unflagging and has sustained the organization at times when frustration at the conditions described in this book seemed overwhelming. Finally, al-Haq gratefully acknowledges the continuing support and interest of funders which enabled it to undertake this project, including particularly the Ford Foundation, Oxfam, ICCO, IDRC, and the Church of Sweden Mission.

This work is thus the result of a collective effort by al-Haq, its members, and friends, though responsibility for any errors rests with me.

EMMA PLAYFAIR

Contents

LIST OF CONTRIBUTORS	xi
TABLE OF CASES	xiii
TABLE OF LEGISLATION	xix
TABLE OF INTERNATIONAL LEGISLATION, TREATIES, AND CONVENTIONS	xxv
PRINCIPAL ABBREVIATIONS	xxxv
NOTE ON TRANSLITERATION	xxxviii
MAPS	xl

Introduction
Emma Playfair — 1

PART ONE: INTERNATIONAL LEGAL FRAMEWORK

1. Prolonged Military Occupation: The Israeli-Occupied Territories 1967–1988 — 25
   Adam Roberts

2. The Application of International Law in the Occupied Territories as Reflected in the Judgments of the High Court of Justice in Israel — 87
   Mazen Qupty

3. The Relevance of International Law to Israeli and Palestinian Rights in the West Bank and Gaza — 125
   Richard A. Falk and Burns H. Weston

4. The Legislative Stages of the Israeli Military Occupation — 151
   Raja Shehadeh

5. The Destruction of Troy will not Take Place — 169
   Alain Pellet

6. Playing on Principle? Israel's Justification for its Administrative Acts in the Occupied West Bank — 205
   Emma Playfair

PART TWO: ADMINISTRATION OF OCCUPIED TERRITORIES

7. The Administration of Occupied Territory in International Law — 241
   Christopher Greenwood

8.	The Administration of the West Bank under Israeli Rule *Mona Rishmawi*	267
9.	The Right to Form Trade Unions under Military Occupation *John Quigley*	295
10.	Mass-based Organizations in the West Bank and Gaza: Offering Services Because of and Despite the Military Occupation *Joost R. Hiltermann*	313
11.	Taxation under Belligerent Occupation *Gerhard von Glahn*	341
12.	Financial Administration of the Israeli-Occupied West Bank *Hisham Jabr*	377
13.	Israel's Economic Policies in the Occupied Territories: A Case for International Supervision *Hisham Awartani*	399
14.	Powers and Duties of an Occupant in Relation to Land and Natural Resources *Antonio Cassese*	419
15.	Exploitation of Land and Water Resources for Jewish Colonies in the Occupied Territories *Ibrahim Matar*	443

PART THREE: ENFORCEMENT OF INTERNATIONAL LAW

16.	Enforcement of Human Rights in the West Bank and the Gaza Strip *John Dugard*	461
17.	Avenues Open for Defence of Human Rights in the Israeli-Occupied Territories *Jonathan Kuttab*	489
BIBLIOGRAPHY		505
INDEX		523

List of Contributors

Hisham Awartani, Assistant Professor of Economics, An-Najah National University, Nablus.

Antonio Cassese, Professor of International Law and Relations at the European University Institute, Florence, and Chairman of the Council of Europe's Steering Committee for Human Rights.

John Dugard, Professor of Law and Director of the Centre for Applied Legal Studies, University of the Witwatersrand, Johannesburg.

Richard Falk, Albert G. Milbank Professor of International Law and Practice, Princeton University.

Christopher Greenwood, Fellow of Magdalene College, Cambridge; Lecturer, Faculty of Law, University of Cambridge.

Joost Hiltermann, Sociologist, and volunteer researcher with al-Haq, 1985–90.

Hisham Jabr, Lecturer in Business Studies, An-Najah National University, Nablus.

Jonathan Kuttab, Palestinian lawyer practising in East Jerusalem, founder member of al-Haq.

Ibrahim Matar, Deputy Director of the American Near East Relief Agency, Jerusalem.

Alain Pellet, Professor of Law, l'Université de Paris Nord and l'Institut d'Études Politiques, Paris.

Emma Playfair, Lawyer and Program Officer for Human Rights in the Cairo office of the Ford Foundation; volunteer researcher with al-Haq, 1984–8.

John Quigley, Professor, College of Law, and Adjunct Professor, Department of Political Science, Ohio State University.

Mazen Qupty, Palestinian lawyer from Nazareth and Member of the Israeli Bar, practising in Israel and the Occupied Territories.

Mona Rishmawi, Palestinian lawyer, Legal Officer for the Middle East and North Africa with the International Commission of Jurists, former Executive Director of al-Haq.

Adam Roberts, Montague Burton Professor of International Relations, University of Oxford; and Fellow of Balliol College.

Raja Shehadeh, Palestinian lawyer practising in Ramallah, founder member of al-Haq.

Gerhard von Glahn, Professor Emeritus (Political Science), University of Minnesota-Duluth.

Burns Weston, Bessie Dutton Murray Professor of International Law, University of Iowa.

Table of Cases

ISRAELI HIGH COURT AND MILITARY COURT CASES
A'aryab v. The Appeal Committee HC 277/84; PD 40 [2] 57 91
Abu Aita et al. v. Military Commander of the Judea and
  Samaria Region; Kandil et al. v. Military Commander of the
  Gaza Strip Region HC 69/81 & HC 493/81; PD 37 [2] 197;
  summarized in IYHR 13 (1983) 348 . . . . 73, 91, 93, 96,
                                    98, 99, 119, 209, 213, 220, 372, 423
Abu Awad v. The Military Commander of the Judea and
  Samaria Region HC 97/79; PD 33 [3] 309, summarized
  in IYHR 9, 343 . . . . 91, 95, 110, 111, 249, 492
Abu el-Tin v. Minister of Defence et al. HC 500/72; 27 [1] PD 481
  excerpted in IYHR 5 (1975) 376 433
Advocate Tsemel et al. v. Commander of the Ansar Camp et al.
  HC 593/82; summarized in IYHR 13 (1983), 360 . . . . 39, 42
Al-Natshe et al. v. Minister of Defence et al. HC 175/81; PD 35
  [3] 361; summarized in IYHR 13 (1983) 359 230
Al-Nawar v. Minister of Defence et al. HC 574/82; PD 39 [3]
  449; summarized in IYHR 16 (1986) 321 437
Al-Nazir v. The Military Commander of the Judea and Samaria
  Region HC 285/81; PD 36 [1] 701; summarized in IYHR
  13 (1983) 368 91
Al-Talia Weekly Magazine v. Minister of Defence et al. HC
  619/78; PD 33 [3] 505; summarized in IYHR 10 (1980),
  333–5 . . . . 94, 95
Amar et al. v. Minister of Defence HC 774/83; PD 38 [4] 645;
  summarized in IYHR 15 (1985) 276 257
American European Beit El Mission v. Minister of Welfare HC
  103/67; PD 10 [3] 325 123
Amira et al. v. Minister of Defence et al. HC 258/79; PD 34 [1] 90;
  summarized in IYHR 10 (1980) 331–2 . . . . 229, 231, 233, 438
Ansar Prison Case. See Advocate Tsemel et al. v. Commander
  of the Ansar Camp et al.
Atiyah v. IDF Commander in the Gaza Strip HC 118/84; PD 38
  [3] 107; summarized in IYHR 15 (1985) 276 73
Attorney-General v. Eichmann Criminal Appeal 3364/1961,
  PD 16 2033 . . . . 89, 189
Ayyoub et al. v. Minister of Defence et al. HC 606/78; HC

610/78; PD 33 [2] 113 summarized in IYHR 9 (1979),
337–42; translated in Shamgar, *Military Government*,
371 & PYIL 2 (1985) 134–50 . . . . 46, 67, 71, 72, 90,
91, 95, 99, 105, 108–10, 227, 229,
233, 234, 433, 435–7, 455, 485

Beit El Case. *See* Ayyoub *et al. v.* Minister of Defence *et al.*

Ben Zion *v.* Military Commander of the Judea and Samaria
Region HC 369/79; PD 34 [1] 145; summarized in IYHR 10
(1980), 342 . . . . 104, 233

Burkan (Mohamed Sa'id) *v.* Minister of Finance *et al.* HC
114/78 494

Christian Society for the Holy Places *v.* Minister of Defence
HC 337/71; PD 26 [1] 574; summarized in IYHR 2 (1972)
354 . . . . 72, 73, 88, 91, 92, 94, 108,
206, 208, 212, 215, 219, 225, 349

Custodian of Abandoned Property *v.* Samara HC 25/55; PD 10
[3] 1825 115

Dweikat (Mustafa) *v.* State of Israel HC 390/79; PD 34 [1] 1;
summarized in IYHR 9 (1979) 345; translated in Shamgar,
Military Government, 404, and in PYIL 1 (1984) 134 . . . . . . 67, 71,
72, 91, 92, 99, 103, 104, 106, 110, 130,
210, 228, 234, 237, 433–5, 449, 455, 464,
485, 486, 495

Elon Moreh Case. *See* Dweikat *v.* State of Israel

First Jerusalem District Electricity Case. *See* Jerusalem District
Electricity Company Inc *v.* Minister of Defence

Frumer *v.* Military Appeals Court HC 69/85; PD 40 [2] 617 118

Ha'etzni (Elyakim) *v.* State of Israel HC 61/80; PD 34 [3]
595 . . . . 99, 103

Hilu Case. *See* Sheikh Suleiman Hussein Odeh Abu Hilu *et al.*
v. Government of Israel *et al.*

Hiram *v.* Minister of Defence *et al.* HC 69/80; PD 35 [4] 505 118

Jaber (Ramzi Hana) *v.* OC Central Command HC 897/86; PD 41
[2] 522 . . . . 91, 100, 107, 108, 122

Jerusalem District Electricity Company Inc *v.* Minister of
Defence HC 256/72; PD 27 [1] 124; summarized in IYHR 5
(1975) 381 . . . . 89, 91, 94,
202, 217, 222, 496

Jerusalem District Electricity Company Inc *v.* Minister of
Energy and Planning *et al.* HC 351/80; HC 764/80; PD 35 [2]
673; summarized in IYHR 11 (1981) 354 . . . . 73, 91, 210, 211,
259, 496

KLM *v.* Minister of Transportation HC 380/81 (Unreported) 115

Kandil Case. *See* Abu Aita *et al. v.* Military Commander of the

Judea and Samaria Region; Kandil *et al. v.* Military
Commander of the Gaza Strip Region
Kasrawi *et al. v.* Minister of Defence HC 454/85; PD 39 [3] 401;
  summarized in IYHR 16 (1986) 332 . . . . 110, 111
Mil. Pros. *v.* Suhadi S H Zuhad 47 IsLR (1974) 490 465
Morrar *v.* Minister of Defence HC 17/71; PD 25 [1] 141 109
Municipality of Hebron *v.* Abdel Jabber Siyouri Case 1351/83.
  Hebron Magistrates Court 291
Mustafa Yusef *et al. v.* Manager of the Judea and Samaria
  Central Prison HC 540-6/84; PD 40 [1] 567; summarized in
  IYHR 17 (1987) 309 74
Mustafa *et al. v.* Military Commander of the Judea and Samaria
  Region HC 629/82; PD 37 [1] 158; summarized in IYHR 14
  (1984) 313 . . . . 123, 433
Nazal *et al. v.* Military Commander of the Judea and Samaria
  Region HC 256/85; PD 39 [3] 645; summarized in IYHR 16
  (1986) 329 . . . . 110, 111, 113
Qawassmeh *et al. v.* Minister of Defence *et al.* HC 320/80; HC
  698/80; PD 35 [1] 617; PD 35 [2] 113 . . . . 100, 107–10,
                                                              113, 123, 496
Samara *et al. v.* Commander of the Judea and Samaria Region
  HC 802/79; PD 34 [4] 1 92
Second Jerusalem District Electricity Company Case. *See*
  Jerusalem District Electricity Company Inc *v.* Minister of
  Energy and Planning *et al.*
Shahin *et al. v.* Military Commander of the Judea and Samaria
  Region HC 13/86; HC 58/86; PD 41 [1] 197; summarized in
  IYHR 18 (1988) 241 . . . . 91, 109, 113, 123
Sheikh Suleiman Hussein Odeh Abu Hilu *et al. v.* Government
  of Israel *et al.* HC 302/72; PD 27 [2] 169; summarized in
  IYHR 5 (1975) 384 . . . . 88–90, 95, 99, 104, 109, 226, 233, 234
Tabib *et al. v.* Minister of Defence HC 202/81; PD 36 [2]
  622; summarized in IYHR 13 (1983) 364 . . . . 97, 98, 209, 210,
                                                        213, 214, 218, 219
Tamimi *et al. v.* The Minister of Defence *et al.* HC 507/85; PD 41
  [4] 57; summarized in IYHR 18 (1988), 248 . . . . 9, 305, 333
Teachers' Housing Cooperative Society *v.* Military Commander
  of the Judea and Samaria Region HC 393/82; PD 37 [4] 785;
  summarized in IYHR 14 (1984) 301 . . . . 74, 90, 91,
            97, 105, 106, 116, 202, 209, 210, 218, 222, 246, 250, 251,
                       260, 263, 421, 423, 426, 434, 440, 441
VAT Case. *See* Abu Aita *et al. v.* Military Commander of the
  Judea and Samaria Region; Kandil *et al. v.* Military
  Commander of the Gaza Strip Region

INTERNATIONAL CASES
Altstoetter, In re. (US Mil. Trib.) 365
Cession of Vessels and Tugs for Navigation on the Danube
  Case (1921) UN Reports of International Arbitral Awards,
  1, 107 421–2
Commune de Grace-Barleur v. Charbonnages de Gosson
  Lagasse et Consorts (1919) (Belgian Court of Cassation) 351
De Bataafsche Petroleum Maatschappij v. The War Damage
  Commission AJIL 51 (1957) 808 430
Flick, In re. (US Mil. Trib.) 430
Goering et al. Trial of Major War Criminals before the
  International Military Tribunal, Nuremburg 1947,
  1 (1947) 430
KNAC v. State of the Netherlands 16 Ann. Dig. 468 (Dist. Ct.,
  The Hague, 1949) 39
Kemeny v. Yugoslav State 4 Ann. Dig. 549
  (Hungarian-Yugoslav Trib.) 256
Krauch, In re. (US Mil. Trib.) 430
Krupp, In re. (US Mil. Trib.) 250, 430
List, In re. (US Mil. Trib.) 246

EUROPEAN HUMAN RIGHTS CASES
Cyprus v. Turkey (1975) (Nos. 6780/74 and 6950/75,
  Decision of 26 May 1975) 54, 56, 129
Cyprus v. Turkey (1978) (No. 8007/77, Decision of
  10 July 1978) 54, 56, 129, 234, 303, 307
Greek Case Report of 18 Nov. 1969, (1972) 311, 312
Hess (Ilse) v. United Kingdom (1975) 304, 307
Ismael Weinberger Communication No. R. 7/28 (1981) 300
Lawless Case Judgment of 1 July 1961 311
Rosario Pietraroia Communication No. R. 10/44 300–1
X v. United Kingdom Application No. 7990/77, Decision of
  11 May 1981 299

INTERNATIONAL COURT OF JUSTICE
Eastern Carelia Case PCIJ Reports, Ser B, No. 5 (1923) 469
Expenses Case ICJ Reports (1962) 151 463
FRG v. Denmark; FRG v. Netherlands. ICJ Reports (1969), 37,
  44, 71 189
Franco-Hellenic Lighthouse Case PCIJ Judgment, 17 Mar. 1934;
  Ser A/B No. 62 174
Genocide Case ICJ Reports (1951), 23 . . . . 307, 308

International Status of South-West Africa Advisory Opinion,
    ICJ Reports (1950), 128 . . . . 132, 470
Legal Consequences for States of the Continued Presence of
    South Africa in Namibia (South West Africa)
    notwithstanding Security Council Resolution 276 (1970)
    Advisory Opinion & Judgment 1971; ICJ Reports (1971),
    31. . . . . 31, 32, 129, 135,
                              185, 186, 424, 469–471, 473, 477, 479, 498
Military and Paramilitary Activities in and Against Nicaragua
    ICJ Reports (1986) 190, 300, 469, 472
Namibia Case. *See* Legal Consequences for States of the
    Continued Presence of South Africa in Namibia (South
    West Africa) notwithstanding Security Council Resolution
    276 (1970)
Nicaragua Case. *See* Military and Paramilitary Activities in and
    Against Nicaragua
North-Sea Continental Shelf Cases. *See* FRG *v*. Denmark; FRG
    v. Netherlands
Nuclear Tests Case. ICJ Reports (1974), 270 188
Ottoman Debt Arbitration (1925–6) 174
Voting Procedure Case ICJ Reports (1955) 115 481
Western Sahara Case ICJ Reports (1975) 12 469

SOUTH AFRICA
S *v*. Petane 1988 (3) SA 51(C). 485
S *v*. Tuhadeleni 1969 (1) SA 153 486
Winter *v*. Min of Defence 1940 AD 194 486

UNITED KINGDOM
Attorney-General *v*. BBC [1981] AC 303 (HL) 485
R *v*. Boundary Commission for England and Wales, *ex parte*
    Foot [1983] QB 600 264
R *v*. Chief Immigration Officer, Heathrow Airport, *ex parte*
    Salamat Bibi [1976] 3 All ER 843 (CA) 486
R *v*. Secretary of State for Home Affairs, *ex parte* Bhajan Singh
    [1976] QB 198 (CA) 486
Schiffahrt-Treuhand *v*. HM Procurator-General [1953] 1 All ER
    394 365

UNITED STATES
Aboitiz *v*. Price 99 F Supp 602 (D Utah 1951) 202, 203
Cobb *v*. US 191 F 2d 604 (9th Cir 1951) 191

Fernandez v. Wilkinson 505 F Supp 787 (1980) 485
Filartiga v. Pena-Irala 630 F 2d 876 (2nd Cir 1980); *Federal Reporter*, 630 (1980), 876 . . . . 299, 485
Lareau v. Manson 507 F Supp 1177 (1980) 485
Sterling v. Cupp 625 P 2d 123, Oregon 485

Table of Legislation

Israel and the Occupied Territories

Basic Law; Jerusalem Capital of Israel, 30 July 1980 . . . . 6, 41
   para. 15 494
   para. 17 494
Basic Law; Army
   art. 5 117
By-Law Concerning Fees and Excises on Local Goods (No. 31)
   (West Bank) 1976 383–4
Chamber of Advocates Law 1961 . . . . 163, 283
Court Law 1957
   s.7(b)(2) 90
Defence Services Law 1959 . . . . 163, 283
Emergency Labour Services Law 1967 163
Emergency Regulations 1967
   reg. 1 160
Emergency Regulations Extension (Registration of Equipment)
   Law 1981 163
Emergency Regulations 6B 1984 163
Entry into Israel Law 1952 . . . . 163, 283
General Staff Order No. 33.0133 of 20 July 1982 . . . . 106, 116, 118
General Staff Orders
   Appendix 61 117
Golan Heights Law, 14 Dec. 1981 . . . . 41, 82
Income Tax Ordinance Law 1961 283
Income Tax Ordinance 1980 . . . . 161, 163
Law and Administration Ordinance 1948
   s.9 160
Law of Return 1950 161
Local Councils Regional Councils Order (1958) 283
Military Jurisdiction (Amendment No. 12) Law 1978
   art. 2A 117, 118
Military Jurisdiction Law 1955 117
   art. 2(b) 119
   art. 3(a) 117–19
   art. 133 118
Municipalities Law 160
Municipalities Ordinance (Amendment No. 6) Law 1967 . . . . . 5–6, 41

Table of Legislation

National Insurance Law (Consolidated Version) 1968 . . . . . . 163, 283
Penal Code 1977
    art. 12 118
Population Register Law 1965 163
Psychologists Law 1968 163

ISRAELI MILITARY ORDERS IN THE OCCUPIED TERRITORIES

Proclamation No. 1 (Assumption of Control) 206
Proclamation No. 2 (Regulation of Administration
    and Law). . . . . 107, 151 *et seq.*, 271
    art. 2 . . . . 155, 271
Proclamation No. 3 (Concerning Security Regulations) 153
    art. 35 . . . . 119, 157, 188
Military Order 5 156
Military Order 7 (Closure of Banks and Financial Institutions)
  407
Military Order 9 152
Military Order 25 152
Military Order 31 . . . . 156, 157, 383
Military Order 34 (Closed Areas) 156
Military Order 39 155
Military Order 45 152
Military Order 47 (Prohibiting Exports without Permits) 152,
                                                                                                      155, 492
Military Order 49 152
Military Order 50 153
Military Order 58 (Absentee Property) 152, 492
Military Order 59 (State Land) 152, 157, 492
Military Order 65 . . . . 155, 165
Military Order 80 281
Military Order 89 (Fees for Entering Public Parks) 394
Military Order 92 . . . . 152, 157
Military Order 101 (Order Regarding Prohibition of Acts of
    Incitement and Hostile Propaganda) 153, 223, 327–9, 492
Military Order 103 154
  Preamble 156
  art. 1 156
Military Order 108 152
Military Order 109 381
Military Order 129 153
Military Order 144 . . . . 120, 188
Military Order 160 (Order on Interpretations) 492
Military Order 164 . . . . 153, 491

Table of Legislation

Military Order 191	152
Military Order 194	152
Military Order 215	152
Military Order 224	107
Military Order 255	152
Military Order 260	152
Military Order 291 (Suspending Procedures for Disputes over Land and Water)	492
Military Order 297	152
art. 11	164
Military Order 321	152
Military Order 324	152
Military Order 364	157
Military Order 378 (Order Concerning Security Regulations)	153, 223, 225, 327, 388
Military Order 384	155
Military Order 397	155
Military Order 398	155
Military Order 406	381
Military Order 412	155
Military Order 418	158, 221, 268, 290–2
art. 7	159
Military Order 419	158
Military Order 432	163
Military Order 437	152
Military Order 501	383
Military Order 505 (Fees for Land Registration)	383, 394
Military Order 509	381
Military Order 545	381
Military Order 569	158
Military Order 586	381
Military Order 604	292
Military Order 612	381
Military Order 636	381
Military Order 642 (Land Tax)	383, 394
Military Order 643	383
Military Order 671	383
Military Order 693 (Fees for Land Registration)	383, 394
Military Order 697	163
Military Order 725	381
Military Order 740	383
Military Order 746	383
Military Order 754	381

Military Order 770 381
Military Order 782 381
Military Order 783 (Establishing Four Jewish Regional Councils
   in the West Bank) 159, 282, 284, 446
Military Order 791 381
Military Order 808 (Court Fees) 395
Military Order 811 158
Military Order 816 381
Military Order 825 . . . . 326, 327
Military Order 835 381
Military Order 845 388
Military Order 846 158
Military Order 865 388
Military Order 873 381
Military Order 892 . . . . 160, 163, 282, 284
   art. 2(a) 282
Military Order 898 163
Military Order 900 381
Military Order 907 381
Military Order 920 381
Military Order 924 381
Military Order 943 381
Military Order 947 (Establishing a Civilian Administration) 161,
                                                                                                                    268, 275
   art. 2 276
   art. 3 277
   art. 5 278
   Sched. 1 277
   Sched. 2 277
Military Order 948 388
Military Order 952 . . . . 164, 165, 285
Military Order 958 381
Military Order 973 . . . . 165, 285
Military Order 974 285
Military Order 977 (Professional Licensing Fees) 383, 395
Military Order 978 381
Military Order 998 285
Military Order 1002 162
Military Order 1014 381
Military Order 1015 (Restriction on Planting of Grape-vines and
   Plum Trees) 162, 222
Military Order 1018 383
Military Order 1028 381

Military Order 1039 162
Military Order 1050 381
Military Order 1055 388
Military Order 1060 (Jurisdiction over Land Disputes) 455
Military Order 1062 381
Military Order 1071 388
Military Order 1084 381
Military Order 1094 381
Military Order 1098 381
Military Order 1106 381
Military Order 1133 165
Military Order 1140 164
Military Order 1141 164
Military Order 1142 (Tax on Imported Services) 395
Military Order 1149 164
Military Order 1150 (Vehicle Registration Fees) 395
Military Order 1167 162
Military Order 1180 (Amending Jordanian Banks Law) 165, 166
Military Order 1185 381
Military Order 1195 383
Military Order 1206 165
Military Order 1208 164
Military Order 1213 . . . . 165, 166
Military Order 1248 162

JORDAN
Jordan Constitution 1952 9
  art. 9(1) 107
  art. 33 120
    (1) 121
  art. 57 120
  art. 120 270
Customs and Excise Law (No. 1) 1962 379
Education By-Law (No. 1) 1956 383
Education Rules (No. 1) 1956 379
Income Tax Law (No. 25) 1964 381
  art. 8 378
  art. 24 379
  art. 25 378
Income Tax Law (No. 57) 1985
  art. 7 379
  art. 13 380
Labour Law (No. 21) 1960 317

    arts. 68–89 318
    art. 83(a), (b) 326
        (c) 327
Land Tax Law (No. 30) 1955 . . . . 379, 383
Law of Buildings and Lands Inside Cities (No. 11) 1954 379
Law for the Defence of East Jordan 1935 277
Law of Excises on Petroleum Products (No. 36) 1960 379
Law of Fees on Local Products (No. 16) 1963 . . . . 379, 384
Law of Land Registration Fees (No. 56) 1958 383
Law of Unification of Fees and Taxes Levied on Imported,
    Exported and Locally Manufactured Goods (No.
    25) 1952. 379
Municipal Law of 1955 160
    art. 105(a) 281
Nursery Law (No. 20) 1958 162
Penal Law of 1960 490
Planning Law (No. 79) 1966 . . . . 158, 290, 410
Prisons Law of 1953. 277
Profession Licensing Law (No. 89) 1966 . . . . 379, 383
Public Health Law (No. 43) 1966 383
Salt Law (No. 16) 1950 379
Tobacco Law (No. 32) 1952 379
Transport on Roads Law (No. 49) 1958 383
Village Guards Law of 1925. 277

Table of International Legislation, Treaties, and Conventions

African Charter on Human and Peoples Rights
  art. 10(1) 298
  art. 27(2) 310
American Convention on Human Rights
  art. 1 307
  art. 16 298
    (2) 310
  art. 27(1) 311
  art. 32(2) 310
Balfour Declaration 1917 132
Belgian Civil Code
  art. 526 431
British Mandatory Defence (Emergency) Regulations 1945 106
                              225, 234, 277, 492
  art. 3 107
  art. 108 . . . . 110, 224
  art. 112 . . . . 100, 107
  art. 119 . . . . 100, 107
British Manual of Military Law; The Law of War on Land
  para. 516 255
  para. 518 253
  para. 519 . . . . 248, 257
  para. 522 . . . . 248, 262
  para. 523 247
  para. 526 430
  para. 527 . . . . 350, 364
  para. 529 353
  paras. 532–4 247
  para. 544 251
  para. 614 438
Brussels Code of 1874 347
  art. 7 429
Convention Against Discrimination in Education (1960) 55
Covenant on the League of Nations (1919)
  art. 22 424–5

European Convention for the Protection of Human Rights and
    Fundamental Freedoms (1950) 485
   art. 1 . . . . 54, 303, 304
   art. 11(1) 297
       (2) 310
   art. 15 248
       (1) 311
European Social Charter
   art. 5 298
   art. 31(1) 310, 311
French Civil Code
   art. 2119 431
Geneva Conventions (1949) 44, 56
   art. 1 . . . . 58, 192, 196
   art. 2(2) 191
Geneva Convention (Fourth) Relative to the Protection of
    Civilian Persons in Time of War (1949) 5, 87, 128,
                                           157, 243, 342, 420, 461
   Pt. IV section III 37, 134, 171
   arts. 1–12 193
   art. 1 . . . . 468, 501, 502
   art. 2 . . . . 30, 46, 47, 51, 101, 102, 132, 133, 176, 195
       (2) 465
   art. 4 202
   art. 5 . . . . 62, 78
   art. 6 . . . . 176, 347
       (3) 36, 37, 76, 192
   art. 7(1) 40
   art. 27 . . . . 170, 193, 196, 199, 202, 224
   arts. 29–34 193
   art. 33 495
   art. 35 . . . . 119, 120
   art. 41 224
   art. 47 . . . . 137, 176, 192, 193, 202, 245, 264
   art. 48 . . . . 137, 193, 195
   art. 49 . . . . 62, 65–68, 78, 95, 97,
                    100, 109, 113, 130, 193, 200, 205, 220, 249, 495
       (1) 110
       (2) 198
       (6) 110, 431, 436
   art. 50 193
   arts. 51–3 193
   art. 51 256

Table of International Legislation, Treaties, and Conventions

art. 53	198
arts. 54–8	193
art. 54(1)	256, 261
(2)	255
art. 55	198, 200
art. 56(4)	202
art. 57	198
art. 58	202
art. 59	193
arts. 61–77	193
art. 62	199
art. 63	199
art. 64	170, 197, 199, 224
(1)	247, 261
art. 66	262
art. 68	62, 78
art. 73	195
art. 78	199, 224
(1)	57
art. 143	193, 198
art. 146	472
art. 147	472

Geneva Protocol I Additional to the Geneva Conventions of 12 Aug. 1949, and relating to the Protection of Victims of International Armed Conflict (1977) 35, 39, 44, 56, 76, 128, 137, 146, 185, 243, 342, 468, 485

Pt. IV section III	171
art. 1(1)	192
(4)	64
art. 3(b)	38
art. 4	176, 190, 244
art. 27(1)	192
art. 35	170
art. 48	170
arts. 48–79	137

Geneva Protocol II Additional to the Geneva Conventions of 12 Aug. 1949, and relating to the Protection of Victims of International Armed Conflict (1977) 128, 342

Hague Convention (Second) Respecting the Laws and Customs of War on Land (1899) 35

Hague Convention (Fourth) Respecting the Laws and Customs of War on Land (1907) and annexed Regulations 5, 30, 87, 128, 205, 242–3, 342, 420, 461

Preamble 376
art. 2(3) 189
art. 22 170
art. 23(g) 95, 170
arts. 42–56 137
art. 42 .... 39, 175
art. 43 .... 39, 40, 72, 81, 89, 92–8, 111, 121,
            172, 175, 197, 199, 200, 207, 208, 211, 213, 214, 223,
            224, 244–7, 255, 258, 305, 306, 343, 349, 352–4, 369, 372
art. 44 .... 134, 195
art. 45 .... 134, 195
art. 46 .... 95, 421, 134
  (2) 421
arts. 48–56 68
art. 48 .... 39, 40, 97, 342, 350, 351, 356, 365, 369, 430
art. 49 .... 39, 342, 343, 356, 369, 373–5, 430
art. 50 .... 246, 373
arts. 51–3 39
art. 51 .... 195, 342, 343, 369, 373
art. 52 .... 92, 95, 224, 226, 227, 373, 421, 430
  (1) 427
art. 53 .... 373, 421, 428, 430, 431
  (1) 427, 432
  (2) 421
art. 54 431
art. 55 .... 39, 246, 373, 421, 428–31, 434
art. 56 .... 246, 373, 430
  (1) 421
art. 58(2) 247
arts. 59–62 247
section III 171
Hague Convention and Protocol for the Protection of
  Cultural Property in the Event of Armed Conflict
  (1954) 35, 44, 128, 148
International Convention on Civil and Political Rights (1966) 302,
                                                                426, 470
art. 2(1) 307
art. 4 .... 54–5, 248
  (1) 310
  (2) 311
art. 19(2) 300, 301
art. 22(1) 297
  (2) 309

Table of International Legislation, Treaties, and Conventions xxix

International Convention on the Elimination of All Forms
    of Racial Discrimination (1966) 55, 129
International Court of Justice Constitution
    art. 38 113
International Court of Justice Statute
    art. 65 84
International Covenant on Economic, Social and
    Cultural Rights 470
    art. 1(2) 426
    art. 25 426
    art. 8(1) 309
        (a) 297
International Covenants on Human Rights 55, 56, 129, 148
International Labour Organisation Constitution (ILO)
    Preamble 296
    art. 7(1) 298
    art. 35 307
    Annex, 104 298
ILO Convention No. 87 concerning Freedom of Association
    and Protection of the Right to Organise Convention 337, 484
    art. 2 . . . . 298, 306
    art. 12 307
    para. 422 312
ILO Convention No. 111 concerning Discrimination in
    Respect of Employment and Occupation 337, 484
Islamic Shari'a Law 9
Italian Civil Code
    art. 812 431
Jordanian-Palestinian Accord (1985) 61
League of Nations Mandate for Palestine 1922 132
Nuremburg Charter
    art. 6(c) 130
Palestinian National Covenant 1968
    art. 2 49
Treaty of Peace, Israel-Egypt, 26 Mar. 1979
    art. II 42
Treaty of Versailles 358
Unification Act of the Hashemite Kingdom of Jordan 1950 181
Universal Declaration of Human Rights (1948) 52, 55, 88,
                             122, 123, 129, 148, 296, 302, 461, 470
    art. 13(1) 57
    art. 14 500
    art. 23(4) 297

art. 29(2) 309

UNITED STATES
AMG 22 Headquarters General Order No. 2 (13 Aug. 1943) 367
Comprehensive Anti-Apartheid Act 1986 462–3
United States Army Field Manual FM 27–10
   The Law of Land Warfare (Washington, 1956)
      para. 296 365
      para. 364 430
      para. 367 255
      para. 368 253
      paras. 369–71 247
      para. 371 . . . . 248, 257
      para. 374 . . . . 248, 262
      paras. 377–8 247
      para. 394(c) 438
      para. 426(a) 351
      para. 426(b) 353, 354
      para. 432 251

UNITED NATIONS
United Nations Charter 128, 243
   Ch. VII 462, 463, 480, 481
   Ch. XI 187, 466
   Preamble 148, 479
   art. 1 . . . . 183, 302
   art. 1(2), (3) 148
   art. 2 183
      (2) 479
      (4) 179, 479–81
   art. 13(1)(b) 148
   art. 25 476
   art. 39 462
   art. 46 479
   art. 51 179
   art. 55 . . . . 148, 183, 302
   art. 56 . . . . 148, 302
   arts. 73–85 51
   art. 80 471
   art. 96 84
   art. 103 482

GENERAL ASSEMBLY RESOLUTIONS
   No. 181 (II) (29 Nov. 1947) 139, 140, 470, 471

Table of International Legislation, Treaties, and Conventions

No. 217 (10 Dec. 1948)	297
No. 377 (V) 1950	463
No. 626 (VII) (21 Dec. 1952)	426
No. 217A (III) (10 Dec. 1948)	56, 148
No. 1514 (XV) (14 Dec. 1960)	183, 466
No. 1803 (XVII) 14 Dec. 1962	426
Preamble	426
No. 2131 (XX)	480
No. 2145 (XXI) (25 Oct. 1966)	31, 470, 471
No. 2200 (XXI) (19 Dec. 1966)	
art. 1	148
art. 2	148
No. 2252 ES-V (4 July 1967)	52, 190
No. 2253 ES-V (1967)	476
No. 2254 ES-V (1967)	476
No. 2372 (XXII) (12 June 1968)	31
No. 2403 (XXIII) (16 Dec. 1968)	32, 59
No. 2443 (XXIII) (19 Dec. 1968)	52, 56, 63, 461, 483
Preamble, para. 1	301
No. 2444 (XXIII) (19 Dec. 1968)	53
No. 2535B (XXIX) (10 Dec. 1969)	60, 182
No. 2546 (XXIV) (11 Dec. 1969)	56, 67, 483
No. 2625 (XXV) (24 Oct. 1970)	63, 179, 186, 477, 480
No. 2649 (XXV) (30 Nov. 1970)	183
No. 2672C (XXV) (8 Dec. 1970)	60, 182
No. 2675 (XXV) (9 Dec. 1970)	467
para. 1	301
No. 2727 (XXV) (15 Dec. 1970)	52, 56
No. 2763E (XXVII) (13 Dec. 1972)	182
No. 2765 (XXV)	461
No. 2792D (XXVI) (6 Dec. 1971)	182
No. 2851 (XXVI) (20 Dec. 1971)	190
No. 2871 (XXVI) (20 Dec. 1971)	31
No. 2949 (XXVII) (8 Dec. 1972)	184
No. 2994 (XXVII) (15 Dec. 1972)	426
No. 3005 (XXVII) (15 Dec. 1972)	52
No. 3021 (S-VI) 1 May 1974	
para. 4(e)	426
No. 3089D (XXVII) (7 Dec. 1973)	182
No. 3092A (XXVIII) (7 Dec. 1973)	45, 52
No. 3092B (XXVIII) (7 Dec. 1973)	184
No. 3166 (XXVIII) (14 Dec. 1973)	64
No. 3171 (XXVIII) (17 Dec. 1973)	426
No. 3175 (XXVIII) (17 Dec. 1973)	69

xxxii   *Table of International Legislation, Treaties, and Conventions*

No. 3210 (XXIX) (14 Oct. 1974) 182, 189
No. 3236 (XXIX) (22 Nov. 1974) 182, 475, 478
No. 3237 (XXIX) (22 Nov. 1974) 63
No. 3240 (XXIX) (29 Nov. 1974) 190, 483
No. 3240B (XXIX) (29 Nov. 1974) 52
No. 3281 (XXIX) (12 Dec. 1974)
   art. 2 426
No. 3314 (XXIX) (14 Dec. 1974)
   art. 5(3) 179
   Annex 63
No. 3340B (XXIX) (29 Nov. 1974) 45
No. 3379 (XXX) (10 Nov. 1975) 58
No. 3525 (XXX) (Dec. 1975) 483
No. 31/106A (16 Dec. 1976) 67, 476
No. 31/106B (16 Dec. 1976) 45
No. 32/5 (28 Oct. 1977) 52, 67
No. 32/20 (25 Nov. 1977) 50, 182
No. 32/91A (13 Dec. 1977) 465
No. 32/161 (19 Dec. 1977) 69
No. 33/15 (9 Nov. 1978) 32
No. 33/29 (7 Dec. 1978) 50
No. 33/113 (18 Dec. 1978) 184, 476
No. 34/37 (21 Nov. 1979) 32
No. 34/146 (17 Dec. 1979) 64
No. 35/19 (11 Nov. 1980) 32
No. 35/69A (15 Dec. 1980) 182
No. 35/122 (11 Dec. 1980) 190
No. 35/122A (11 Dec. 1980) 52, 244
No. 35/122B (11 Dec. 1980) 67
No. 35/169 (15 Dec. 1980) 186
No. 36/5 (21 Oct. 1981) 59
No. 36/120E (1981) 478
No. 36/150 (16 Dec. 1981) 69
No. 36/210E (10 Dec. 1981) 476
No. ES-9/1 (5 Feb. 1982) 190, 463, 479
No. ES-7/2 (19 Aug. 1982) 186, 463
No. ES-7/12 (19 Aug. 1982) 182
No. ES-7/16 (19 Aug. 1982) 182
No. 37/6 (18 Oct. 1982) 32
No. 37/123A (16 Dec. 1982) 465
No. 37/123A (16 Dec. 1982)
   Preamble 477
No. 37/123C (16 Dec. 1982) 476

Table of International Legislation, Treaties, and Conventions xxxiii

No. 37/253 (13 May 1983) 32
No. 37/88B (10 Dec. 1982) 184
No. 38/79 (1983) 483
No. 38/79B (15 Dec. 1983) 52
No. 38/79D (1983) 481
No. 38/140 (7 Dec. 1983) 59
No. 38/144 (19 Dec. 1983) 69
No. 38/180A (19 Dec. 1983) 479
No. 39/95C (14 Dec. 1984) 67
No. 39/101 (14 Dec. 1984) 69
No. 39/146A (1984) 478
No. 39/146C (14 Dec. 1984) 476
No. 40/7 (5 Nov. 1985) 32, 68
No. 40/61 (9 Dec. 1985) 64
No. S-41/1 (20 Sept. 1986) 32
No. 41/39 (20 Nov. 1986) 31
No. 41/63 (3 Dec. 1986) 50
No. 41/63A (3 Dec. 1986) 63
No. 41/63B (3 Dec. 1986) 52
No. 41/63C (3 Dec. 1986) 184
No. 41/63D (3 Dec. 1986) 69
No. 41/63E (3 Dec. 1986) 67
No. 41/162B (4 Dec. 1986) 192
No. 41/163B (4 Dec. 1986) 190
No. 43/19 (3 Nov. 1988) 59
No. 43/26 (17 Nov. 1988) 59
No. 43/33 (22 Nov. 1988) 59

SECURITY COUNCIL RESOLUTIONS
  No. 181 (II) (29 Nov. 1947) 4, 180
  No. 237 (14 June 1967) 52, 302
  No. 242 (22 Nov. 1967) 4, 5, 60, 140, 145, 180,
                                                                      182, 245, 477, 487
  No. 252 (1968) 476, 477
  No. 267 (1969) 476
  No. 284 (29 July 1970) 31
  No. 298 (1971) 476
  No. 301 (20 Oct. 1971) 31
  No. 330 (21 Mar. 1973) 426
  No. 338 (22 Oct. 1973) 5, 60, 140, 145
  No. 366 (17 Dec. 1974) 31
  No. 385 (30 Jan. 1976) 31
  No. 418 (1977) 463

No. 435 (1978) 473
No. 446 (22 Mar. 1979) 53, 465, 476
No. 465 (1 Mar. 1980) 68, 184, 190, 202, 465, 476
No. 469 (20 May 1980) 68
No. 476 (1980) 476–8
No. 478 (1980) 476–8
No. 497 260
No. 592 192
No. 601 (30 Oct. 1987) 31
No. 605 (22 Dec. 1987) 53
No. 607 (5 Jan. 1988) 53, 68
UN International Conference on the Question of Palestine
   (29 Aug.–7 Sept. 1983) PYIL 1 (1984) 66 61

Principal Abbreviations

Additional Protocol I	Protocol Additional to the Geneva Conventions of 12 August 1949, and Relating to the Protection of Victims of International Armed Conflicts, 1977
ADPIL	*Annual Digest of Public International Law*
AFDI	*Annuaire français de droit international*
AJIL	*American Journal of International Law*
Benvenisti, *1986 Report*	Meron Benvenisti, *1986 Report: Demographic, Economic, Legal, Social and Political Developments in the West Bank* (Jerusalem, 1986)
Benvenisti, *1987 Report*	Meron Benvenisti, *1987 Report: Demographic, Economic, Legal, Social and Political Developments in the West Bank* (Jerusalem, 1987)
British Manual	United Kingdom, War Office, *Manual of Military Law, Part III: The Law of War on Land*, 1958
BYIL	*British Yearbook of International Law*
EC	European Community
ECHR	European Commission of Human Rights
Final Record	Final Record of the Diplomatic Conference of Geneva of 1949, 3 vols.
Hague Regulations	The Regulations annexed to the 1907 Hague Convention IV Respecting the Laws and Customs of War on Land
HC	Decision of the Israeli High Court of Justice
HILJ	*Harvard International Law Journal*
ICJ	International Court of Justice
ICJ Reports	International Court of Justice Reports of Judgments, Advisory Opinions, and Orders
ICLQ	*International and Comparative Law Quarterly*
ICRC	International Committee of the Red Cross
ILC Yb	*International Law Commission Yearbook*
ILM	*International Legal Materials*
ILO	International Labour Organisation
ILR	*International Law Reports*
Int. Aff.	*International Affairs*
Int. Mil. Trib.	International Military Tribunal
IsLR	*Israel Law Review*
IYHR	*Israel Yearbook on Human Rights*

IDF	Israel Defence Forces
JPS	*Journal of Palestine Studies*
LSM	Law in the Service of Man, the West Bank affiliate of the International Commission of Jurists, now known as al-Haq
Mich. Law Rev.	*Michigan Law Review*
MO	Israeli Military Orders for the West Bank, published in 'Proclamations, Orders and Appointments of the IDF Forces in the West Bank Area'
NIS	New Shekel (Israeli currency)
NYIL	*The Netherlands Yearbook of International Law*
Official Records 1974–7	Official Records of the Diplomatic Conference on the Reaffirmation and Development of International Humanitarian Law Applicable in Armed Conflicts, Geneva 1974–7, 17 vols., 1978
Oppenheim, *International Law*	Lassa Oppenheim, *International Law: A Treatise*, i, *Peace*, 8th edn., ed. Hersch Lauterpacht (London, 1955); and ii, *Disputes, War and Neutrality*, 7th edn., ed. Lauterpacht (London, 1952). References are to these editions unless otherwise stated.
PCIJ	Permanent Court of International Justice
PD	Piskei Din (reports of the Israeli High Court of Justice)
Pictet, *Commentary*	Jean S. Pictet (ed.), *The Geneva Conventions of 12 August 1949: Commentary*, 4 vols. (Geneva, 1952–60). Reference is to vol. iv unless otherwise specified.
Proc. of the ASIL	*Proceedings of the American Society of International Law*
PYIL	*Palestine Yearbook of International Law*
RCADI	*Recueil des Cours: Collected courses of the Hague Academy of International Law*
Rev. Int. Studies	*Review of International Studies*
RGDIP	*Revue générale de droit international public*
RIAA	*Reports of International Arbitral Awards*
Schwarzenberger, *International Law*	Georg Schwarzenberger, *International Law as Applied by International Courts and Tribunals*, ii, *The Law of Armed Conflicts* (London, 1968)
Shamgar, *Military Government*	Meir Shamgar (ed.), *Military Government in the Territories Administered by Israel 1967–80, 1: The Legal Aspects* (Jerusalem, 1982)
Shehadeh, *Occupier's Law*	Raja Shehadeh, *Occupier's Law: Israel and the West Bank* (Washington, DC, 1985)

Texas Int. L. J.	*Texas International Law Journal*
Trans. Grotius Society	*Transactions of the Grotius Society*
Trans. Inst. British Geog.	*Transactions of the Institute of British Geographers*
UN	United Nations
UNGA	United Nations General Assembly
UNSC	United Nations Security Council
UNTS	*United Nations Treaty Series*
US Field Manual	United States, Department of the Army, *The Law of Land Warfare*, Field Manual FM 27–10, 18 July 1956
von Glahn, *Law Among Nations*	Gerhard von Glahn, *Law Among Nations: An Introduction to Public International Law*, 5th edn. (New York, 1986)
von Glahn, *Occupation*	Gerhard von Glahn, *The Occupation of Enemy Territory: A Commentary on the Law and Practice of Belligerent Occupation* (Minneapolis, 1957)
WBDP	The West Bank Data Base Project, directed by Meron Benvenisti
Yale L. J.	*Yale Law Journal*
Yb ECHR	*Yearbook of the European Commission for Human Rights*
YBUN	Yearbook of the United Nations

Note on Transliteration

Relatively few Arabic or Hebrew words are used in this text. Of those that *are*, many have long since acquired a familiar orthography in Latin script. For this reason, no attempt has been made to adopt a consistent system of transliteration.

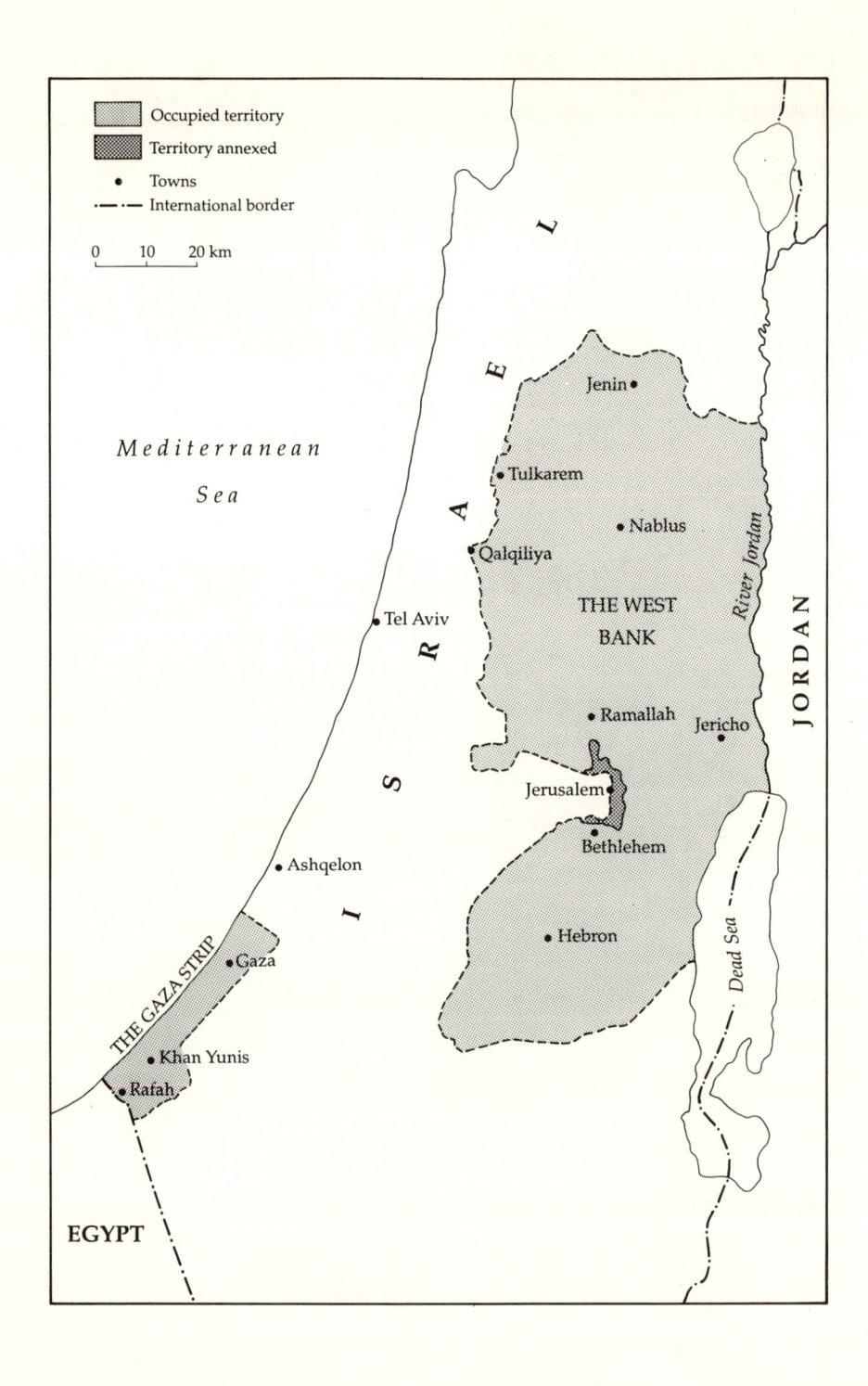

	Occupied territory
	Territory annexed
•	Towns
-·-·-	International border

0 10 20 km

Mediterranean Sea

ISRAEL

• Jenin
• Tulkarem
• Nablus
• Qalqiliya
THE WEST BANK
River Jordan
JORDAN
• Tel Aviv
• Ramallah
• Jericho
• Jerusalem
• Bethlehem
• Ashqelon
• Hebron
Dead Sea
THE GAZA STRIP
• Gaza
• Khan Yunis
• Rafah
EGYPT

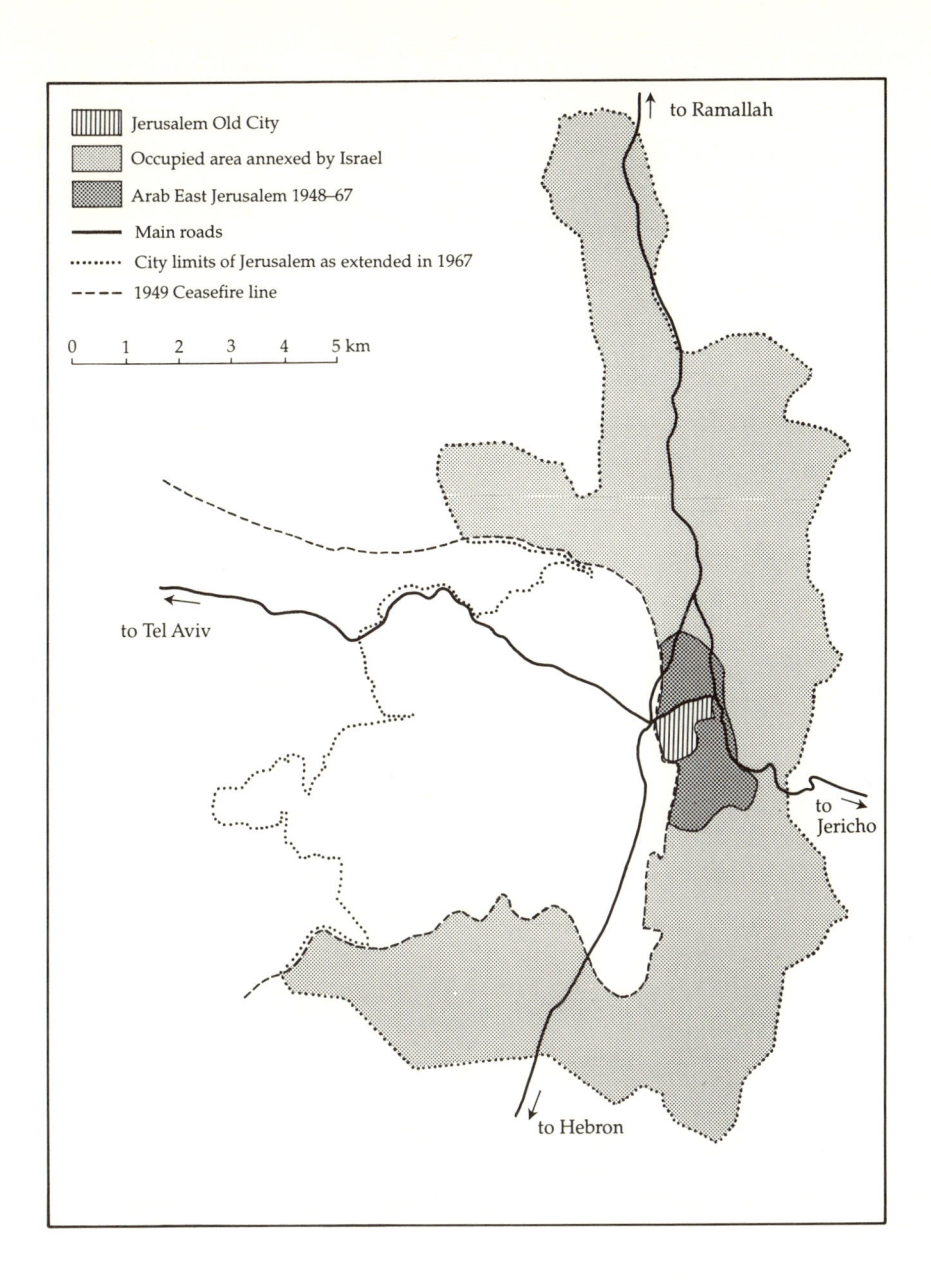

| Jerusalem Old City
| Occupied area annexed by Israel
| Arab East Jerusalem 1948–67
— Main roads
······ City limits of Jerusalem as extended in 1967
---- 1949 Ceasefire line

0 1 2 3 4 5 km

to Ramallah

to Tel Aviv

to Jericho

to Hebron

Introduction

EMMA PLAYFAIR

IN June 1987, the Israeli occupation of the West Bank and Gaza entered its third decade.[1] For twenty years, more than a generation, the Occupied Territories and a Palestinian population reaching over one and a half million[2] had been under the exclusive and alien rule of Israel. Neither a society nor a land can stand still for twenty years, yet how an occupier permits, prevents or forces change is all important for the fate and identity of those territories and their populations.

International law, which regards belligerent occupation as an inherently temporary state, contains rules designed not only to enable the occupier to ensure the safety of the occupying forces, but also to preserve the essential and distinct nature of the occupied territories. Israel, proud of its own image as a democratic state respecting the rule of law and human rights, has from the start consistently maintained that all actions in the territories are taken in accordance with the law. Citing provisions of local and international law, Israel has reassured observers that due consideration is taken of the restrictions and duties imposed on an occupier by international law, including the obligation to respect local law.

Yet Israel has also sought to differentiate its occupation—or administration, as it prefers to term it—from those anticipated by international law. Citing the length of the occupation and the previous uncertain status of its predecessors, Jordan and Egypt, as exceptional factors, Israel has developed new interpretations of the laws of war to

---

[1] The territory known as the West Bank, occupied by Israel in 1967, includes East Jerusalem, which was then annexed by Israel (see text at nn. 11 and 12 below). Israel's purported annexation of East Jerusalem is illegal, according to international law, and so has no effect on the status of East Jerusalem, which remains that of occupied territory. However, since Israel applies a different legal and administrative regime to East Jerusalem than to the rest of the West Bank, it is convenient to distinguish between the two areas. References to the West Bank should therefore be assumed to exclude East Jerusalem unless stated to the contrary.

[2] Statistics on population, and indeed on most matters in the Occupied Territories, are controversial and hard to verify. No census has been carried out since 1967, and estimates vary widely, especially on demographic issues. Israeli official sources exclude the population of annexed East Jerusalem from such data. For an excellent account of the difficulties of estimating the population of the Occupied Territories, and a clear exposition of the range of existing estimates, see A. Nixon, *The Status of Palestinian Children During the Uprising in the Occupied Territories*, i: *Child Death and Injury* (Jerusalem, 1990), 2, 313–17.

cover what it asserts is a situation *sui generis*. It has relied on these interpretations to justify extensive changes to the existing law, to the administrative structure, and even to the physical nature of the Occupied Territories. While some changes are undoubtedly necessitated by the passage of time, others cannot be so explained, most notably the extensive settlement of Israel's own civilian population in the Occupied Territories and the development of a separate infrastructure to serve that population.

Are the rules of international law applicable to an occupation of this length? If so, do their necessarily general provisions guide an occupier in the day-to-day administration of occupied territories? How has Israel in fact administered the occupation of the West Bank and the Gaza Strip? Have Israel's policies in administering the West Bank and Gaza Strip enabled those territories to maintain their distinct identity or hindered them from doing so? These were some of the questions posed by al-Haq, the Palestinian human rights organization and West Bank affiliate of the International Commission of Jurists, and addressed at a conference held in East Jerusalem in January 1988, from which this volume results. The conference brought together international experts in human rights and the laws of war with researchers from the Occupied Territories to explore some of the most problematic provisions of international law relating to the administration of occupied territories in the light of the Israeli occupation of the West Bank and Gaza.

This volume represents the first concerted attempt by non-Israelis to examine Israel's administration of the Occupied Territories in the light of international law. Its subject matter touches important issues of international law, human rights, and the Palestinian–Israeli conflict, which have so far been largely ignored. The laws regulating belligerent occupation have been rarely applied since World War II and the opportunity to review them in the light of Israel's contemporary occupation is challenging. From a human rights perspective, this book advances the discussion of the applicability of human rights standards and instruments in times of war and conflict, and addresses the intersection of humanitarian law and human rights, a complex area in which many issues remain unresolved. In all the literature on the Palestinian–Israeli conflict, the administration of the Occupied Territories has been little explored, and its importance underestimated in past years. While the papers in this collection do not exhaust these topics, al-Haq hopes that they will stimulate and promote further discussion and scholarship of these much neglected areas, vital to the fate of the Occupied Territories and their inhabitants.

In this Introduction, I will review briefly the historical and administrative background to the occupation of the West Bank and Gaza

Strip, and basic elements of the administrative and legal structure of the territories to place the discussion in context. I will then explain the aims and format of the project, outline the focus and scope of the papers in this volume and, finally, point to some of the main issues raised, both where there remains controversy and disagreement, and on which there is apparent unanimity.

I. Historical and Administrative Background

The Occupation of the West Bank and Gaza Strip

The Israeli occupation of the West Bank and the Gaza Strip resulted from the Arab–Israeli War of 1967. It is necessary, however, to look further back to understand the subsequent development and treatment of both territories.

After World War I, and following the fall of the Ottoman Empire, the whole of Palestine was placed under a Mandate entrusted to the British Government by the League of Nations.[3] The Mandatory authorities were to be:

> responsible for placing the country under such political, administrative, and economic conditions as will secure the establishment of the Jewish national home... and the development of self-governing institutions, and also for safeguarding the civil and religious rights of all the inhabitants of Palestine, irrespective of race and religion.[4]

Accordingly, Jewish immigration was facilitated under the Mandate. Between 1922 and 1939, as Nazi persecution increased in Europe, the Jewish population increased from 10 per cent to 30 per cent of the population in Palestine, to a population of some 450,000. This growth was accompanied by an effort to acquire land, spearheaded by Zionist organizations, with the result that Jewish landholdings also increased threefold between 1922 and 1939, though by 1948 they still represented only 6.6 per cent of the total land.[5]

Conflicting national aspirations and claims over land led to escalating communal strife and anti-British activities within Palestine. Having failed to make any progress towards a settlement acceptable to both parties, the British turned in 1947 to the infant United Nations to seek help in resolving the increasingly intractable 'Palestine Question'. On

---

[3] Transjordan, initially part of the same mandate, was placed under a separate mandate in 1922, and recognized as a sovereign state in 1946.

[4] The Mandate for Palestine, 24 July 1922 (Cmd. 1785, 1922).

[5] See F. J. Khoury, *The Arab–Israeli Dilemma* (Syracuse, 1985), 18; and A. Gresh and D. Vidal, *The Middle East: War Without End?* (London, 1988), 29.

29 November 1947, the UN General Assembly passed a resolution recommending the partition of Palestine into independent Arab and Jewish states, with an internationalized Jerusalem.[6] Since it provided some 55 per cent of the territory for the proposed Jewish state, including most of the best arable land which was already home to a substantial Arab population, this plan was entirely unacceptable to the Palestinian population and was rejected. Following the Partition resolution, with inter-communal strife and anti-British activities increasing to a level approaching civil war, the British authorities announced their intention to terminate the Mandate and hastily prepared to leave.

On 14 May 1948, the eve of the expiry of the Mandate, Jewish leaders declared the establishment of the State of Israel. War immediately broke out, involving not only the inhabitants of Palestine but also neighbouring Arab states. At the end of the war, Israel was in possession of all of Mandatory Palestine except those areas now known as the West Bank (including East Jerusalem) and the Gaza Strip. The Gaza Strip fell under Egyptian administration, while the West Bank was first administered, then in 1950 annexed, by Transjordan (now the Hashemite Kingdom of Jordan)[7] and thenceforth ruled as part of the Kingdom. An estimated three-quarters of a million Palestinians had fled from the new state of Israel by the end of the war, many of them to those parts of Palestine that remained under Arab control.[8]

In June 1967, simmering tension and hostilities between Israel and the neighbouring Arab states again broke out into war. At the end of a war lasting only six days, the Gaza Strip and the West Bank, including East Jerusalem, had fallen under Israeli occupation. The response of the United Nations, most notably its Security Council Resolution 242 of 22 November 1967, remains central to diplomatic and international efforts to resolve the conflict. Resolution 242 emphasizes 'the in-

---

[6] UN General Assembly Res. No. 181(II) of 29 Nov. 1947.

[7] As in many aspects of the history of Palestine, there is some controversy as to whether the West Bank was annexed by Jordan legally, at the legitimate request of the Palestinian inhabitants, or illegally, imposed by Jordan.

[8] The extent to which this flight was actively encouraged by forced eviction, as of the populations of Lid and Ramle in 1948, by terror of massacres, such as that carried out by Jewish fighters in the village of Deir Yassin in April 1948, and by rumours deliberately engendered that both may be repeated, is still to be fully understood. See D. K. Shipler, *Arab and Jew: Wounded Spirits in a Promised Land* (New York, 1986), 32–42, and B. Morris, *The Birth of the Palestine Refugee Problem, 1947–1949* (Cambridge, 1987).

There are many excellent accounts of the history of Palestine and the Arab–Israeli conflict though there remain differences of opinion on almost all aspects. Among the clearest accounts are W. Khalidi, *From Haven to Conquest: Readings on Zionism and the Palestinian Problem until 1948* (Beirnt, 1971), D. Hirst, *The Gun and the Olive Branch* (London, 1977), D. Gilmour, *Dispossessed: The Ordeal of the Palestinians* (London, 1982), I. abu Lughod, *The Transformation of Palestine* (Illinois, 1971), S. Flapan, *The Birth of Israel: Myths and Realities* (New York, 1987), E. Said, *The Question of Palestine* (New York, 1979), D. McDowall, *Palestine and Israel: The Uprising and Beyond* (London, 1989).

Introduction

admissibility of the acquisition of territory by war and the need to work for a just and lasting peace in which every State in the area can live in security', which must include the 'withdrawal of Israeli armed forces from territories occupied in the recent conflict'. This was later reinforced by Resolution 338 of 22 October 1973, which reaffirmed Resolution 242 and called for negotiation.

The Israeli view of its own occupation of the West Bank and Gaza Strip is somewhat ambivalent. Officially, Israel has steadfastly refused to concede that its presence in the territories is an occupation, on the grounds that to do so would be to recognize the sovereignty of the previous Jordanian and Egyptian governments respectively. Instead, it prefers to term its control over the land an 'administration'.

Israel has developed a correspondingly complex attitude towards the applicability of international law to its occupation of the West Bank and Gaza Strip. The rules of international law relating to situations of belligerent occupation form part of the laws of war generally characterized as 'humanitarian law'. The main instruments governing belligerent occupation are the Regulations annexed to the 1907 Hague Convention Respecting the Laws and Customs of War on Land ('the Hague Regulations'), generally considered declarative of customary law, and therefore binding on all nations, and the Fourth Geneva Convention Relative to the Protection of Civilian Persons in Time of War of 1949 ('the Fourth Geneva Convention').[9] As a result of the same desire to avoid recognizing the sovereignty of Egypt and Jordan, the Israeli Government has never accepted the applicability of the Fourth Geneva Convention to its occupation of the West Bank and Gaza; it does purport to abide voluntarily by the Convention's 'humanitarian' provisions, but has never specified which these are. Curiously, despite this stand, Israel has always accepted that it is bound by, and justifies its acts by reference to, the Hague Regulations. This apparently contradictory position, of critical importance to the determination of the rules government Israel's behaviour as an occupier, is examined in a number of the chapters in this volume.[10]

Land Control and Settlement

Within days of the occupation, the Israeli Government passed a law extending the boundaries of East Jerusalem to include outlying villages closer to Bethlehem and Ramallah than to the former boundaries of

---

[9] For citations of these instruments and also for details of other relevant instruments, see nn. 4 and 7 to Chapter 1.

[10] See particularly chapters by Roberts, Qupty, Falk and Weston, and Cassese.

Jerusalem.[11] It then applied Israeli law to this extended area. This effective annexation, condemned by the United Nations and almost all states as illegal, was confirmed in 1980, when the Israeli parliament, the *Knesset*, declared 'Jerusalem in its entirety' (i.e. West and East Jerusalem combined) to be the 'eternal capital' of Israel.[12]

Although the Israeli government may initially have expected its occupation to be of short duration, arguments for retention of part or all of the territories, whether for religious or military/strategic reasons, have been advanced from the start and pursued by all Israeli governments, Labour and Likud alike. Within weeks of the June war, Israeli Minister of Labour Yigal Allon presented a plan for Jewish settlement of the West Bank to the Knesset.[13] Although never approved, this plan, amended several times, guided official settlement policy until 1977. Following the 1973 'October War', the extremist ideological group, Gush Emunim,[14] became increasingly brazen in implementing its own settlement plan, more extensive than that of Allon. This was designed to settle all of 'Eretz Israel' ('the whole of the land of Israel'), by which is meant all of Israel and the Occupied Territories. It encountered little effective government opposition to its activities, even when these were not authorized by the government, and, with the advent of the Likud Government in 1977, the Gush Emunim's plan, in a form developed by the World Zionist Organization and known as the 'Drobless Plan',[15] was adopted as government policy. It provided for extensive settlement throughout the West Bank, designed to ensure, by sheer numbers and fragmentation of the Palestinian population centres, that Arab control could not be re-established in the region.[16]

The signing of the Camp David Accords in September 1978 by Prime Minister Menachem Begin of Israel and President Anwar Sadat of Egypt added new urgency to the activities of the settler movement. The accords had two constituent parts: the 'Framework for the Conclusion of a Peace Treaty between Egypt and Israel' and the 'Framework for Peace in the Middle East'. The latter, together with a supplementary exchange of letters between Begin and Sadat, contained provisions

---

[11] Municipalities Ordinance (Amendment No. 6) Law, 27 June 1967, *Laws of the State of Israel* 21 (1967), 75.

[12] Basic Law: Jerusalem Capital of Israel, 30 July 1980, *Laws of the State of Israel* 34 (1980), 209.

[13] See M. Benvenisti and S. Khayat, *The West Bank and Gaza Atlas* (Jerusalem, 1988), 63, 99.

[14] Gush Emunim, 'the Bloc of the Faithful', founded in 1974, was an offshoot of the Israel National Religious Party.

[15] See Benvenisti and Khayat, *The West Bank and Gaza Atlas*, 64, 102.

[16] On the pattern of settlement, see W. W. Harris, *Taking Root: Israeli Settlement in the West Bank, the Golan and Gaza–Sinai 1967–1980* (Chichester, 1980); G. Aronson, *Creating Facts: Israel, Palestinians and the West Bank* (Washington, 1987); and M. Benvenisti, *The West Bank Data Project: A Survey of Israel's Policies* (Washington, DC, 1984), 49–63.

supposed to lead to a comprehensive settlement of the Middle East conflict, including realization of the legitimate rights of the Palestinian people. It provided for the local election of an autonomous authority to preside over the territories for a five year transitional period during which the future status of the West Bank and Gaza was to be determined through negotiations based on UN Security Council Resolution 242.[17]

With the possibility of having to relinquish control over the territories looming, Israel, under a Likud Government, pursued settlement ever more aggressively. This policy, often described as 'creating facts', aimed for the establishment of such a substantial settler presence that full Israeli withdrawal would be impossible.[18] The number of settlements doubled between 1977 and 1980, some settlers motivated by ideological claims to the land, others attracted by considerable incentives of tax relief and subsidies offered to settlers by the Government.[19]

While the Egypt/Israel peace treaty was by and large implemented, no progress was made on the wider framework for peace, which indeed was strongly opposed by other Arab states, as well as by Palestinians. The settlement drive continued unabated throughout the 1980s. By 1985, an estimated 52 per cent of the land in the Occupied Territories had been brought under Israeli control.[20] By 1987, an estimated 65,000 Jewish settlers were living in the West Bank and 2,700 in the Gaza Strip, in 110 and 18 settlements respectively. This is in addition to a Jewish population of some 124,000 in East Jerusalem, not counted as settlers by the government, which considers East Jerusalem to be part of Israel.[21]

Although Likud's aim of achieving a settlement population of

---

[17] See M. Tessler, 'The Camp David Accords and the Palestinian Problem' in A. Lesch and M. Tessler (eds.), *Israel, Egypt, and the Palestinians: From Camp David to the Intifada* (Bloomington, Ind., 1989), 3–22.

[18] See Harris, *Taking Root, passim,* and Tessler, ibid., 13–14.

[19] Benvenisti, *The West Bank Data Project: A Survey of Israel's Policies,* 55–60.

[20] Of this land, 41 per cent is estimated to be under direct Israeli possession, and Palestinian use of the remaining 11 per cent is severely restricted (M. Benvenisti *et al., The West Bank Handbook: A Political Lexicon* (Jerusalem, 1986), 120). Land is brought under Israeli control by a variety of means: requisition for military or security reasons, closure for military purposes, expropriation for public purposes, declaration that land is 'state land', declaration that land is abandoned, and purchase, often using fraudulent means. R. Shehadeh, in *Occupier's Law: Israel and the West Bank* (Washington, DC, 1985), 15–59, describes these processes and documents how each, even the purchase of land for Jewish settlement, has been systematically facilitated by slight alterations, effected by military order, to the Ottoman laws governing land.

[21] These figures are approximate, based on information collated by the Jerusalem Media and Communication Centre, *Soviet Jewish Immigration and Israeli Settlement in the West Bank and Gaza Strip* (Jerusalem, 1990). See n. 2 above on the absence of reliable demographic statistics. There are no separate figures for Palestinians living in East Jerusalem, since Jerusalem is considered unified by the Israeli government. Figures for settlers are equally difficult to verify.

100,000 in the West Bank and Gaza by the end of the 1980s was not realized, 'facts' had indeed been created throughout the territories. The importance of settlement and the presence of settlers in determining Israeli policy in the Occupied Territories and their impact on the Palestinian population is evident in the papers in this volume.

Administrative and Legal Framework

International law does not specify the form of government that should prevail under conditions of belligerent occupation, but leaves this for the occupying power to determine, subject to established legal principles and guide-lines.[22] Since 1967, both the West Bank and the Gaza Strip have been subject to military government. Immediately after the occupation, Israeli military proclamations vested 'every governmental, legislative, appointative, and administrative power' in the military commander of each area.[23]

The structure of the military government has undergone several transformations over twenty years of occupation,[24] most notably with the establishment of a 'civilian administration' in each territory in 1979, following the Camp David Accords.[25] The Head of the Civilian Administration was given wide powers in relation to all civilian matters, while the military commander retained responsibility for security and military matters. The change was perhaps less radical than it may have sounded; in fact it formalized a division of responsibility already existent in the military government between civilian and military affairs. The Head of Civilian Administrations's powers are exercised in the name of the military commander and, having been delegated by him, can be revoked at any time. Overall command remains with the military, and both branches are answerable ultimately to the Minister of Defence, through a military chain of command. The change did however make more explicit the links, increasingly evident as the occupation became more entrenched, between government ministries in Israel itself and the administration of civilian affairs in the Occupied Territories, explained as follows:

Each branch [of the Civil Administration] is headed by an army officer who is responsible for the activity of the civilian offices functioning under him. The number and titles of the offices correspond basically to those of the Israeli

---

[22] See C. Greenwood's chapter in this book.
[23] IDF Military Proc. 2(3).
[24] See Rishmawi's chapter in this book.
[25] For detailed comment on this change, see J. Kuttab and R. Shehadeh, *Civilian Administration in the Occupied West Bank: Analysis of Israeli Military Government Order No. 947* (Ramallah, 1982), and J. Singer, 'The Establishment of a Civilian Administration in the Areas Administered by Israel', *IYHR* 12 (1982), 259–89. See also Rishmawi's chapter in this book.

Government Ministries. Each office is headed by a Staff Officer who is a civilian representative of the relevant Israeli ministry.[26]

As for the executive, the Jordanian system of national and local government remains only in severely truncated form. The severance of the West Bank from the Jordanian seat of government in Amman meant that the central government with all its branches became inaccessible. The annexation of East Jerusalem, the seat of the central of three regional governorates in the West Bank, created further havoc. The response of the Israeli authorities was to abolish entirely the middle level of administration: governorates, districts, and sub-districts. Only the municipalities continued to function. Elections were held in 1972 and 1976, but after the overwhelming success of PLO-supported candidates in the second election, they were not repeated, and many of those elected were later dismissed or deported and replaced by Israeli appointees. Sporadic efforts in recent years by the military authorities to establish local power structures by appointing either Israeli or Palestinian mayors have been consistently opposed by Palestinians, since those appointed without elections have no legitimacy.

The abrupt disbanding of several levels of government affected the judicial system also, crippling its legal guarantees of independence. In the West Bank, subject to the Jordanian legal system prior to 1967, the highest court of appeal, the Court of Cassation based in Amman, became inaccessible and was not replaced. The process of inspection of courts, vital for ensuring the smooth and just functioning of the judicial system and the independence of the courts, was inoperative except for a brief interlude in the mid-1980s.[27] Finally, the military authorities blocked the formation of a Bar Association which might have been able to address or compensate for some of these deficiencies and to regulate the legal profession.[28]

These developments are all the more serious in the light of the unparalleled complexity of the applicable law in the territories. The law in the West Bank prior to the occupation was already quite complex, containing elements of Ottoman, Islamic *Shari'a*, British Mandate, and Jordanian law.[29] From the first day of the occupation, the military

---

[26] Singer, 'Establishment of a Civilian Administration', 276.
[27] For description of the vital role of the Inspector of Courts, and of the changes to the court system and usurpation of the court's jurisdiction by the military, see Shehadeh, *Occupier's Law*, 76–84.
[28] The High Court's judgment in the case of HC 507/85 *Tamimi et al. v. The Minister of Defence et al.*, discussed below in Chs. 9 and 10, represented a step towards allowing such an association to be formed.
[29] At the time of the occupation of the West Bank, Jordanian law was in force. Governed by the Constitution of 1952, Jordanian law contains elements of Ottoman law, especially legislation regulating land issues and transactions, some regulations from the British Mandate period, and Islamic Shari'a law regulating personal status.

government began to pass military orders amending the law, totalling 1213 in the West Bank and 967 in the Gaza Strip by the end of 1987.[30] To add to the confusion, for more than ten years the military orders were neither regularly published nor reliably sequentially numbered. After repeated protests and expressions of international concern the orders were finally published. However, many regulations issued under powers delegated by military order, mostly relating to settlers and settlements, are still not made public.[31]

An unusual, probably unique, feature of Israel's occupation of the West Bank and Gaza is the availability of its own Supreme Court to the population of the Occupied Territories to challenge the legality of actions of the Israeli state and those acting under its authority, including officers of the military government. The court argues that its jurisdiction arises from its power to exercise judicial review over the legality of acts by those acting on behalf of the Israeli government. This jurisdiction, the court has argued, being exercised *in personam*, extends to such acts wherever they are committed, even beyond the territorial jurisdiction of the state. While the court's jurisdiction over actions which take place beyond the national territory, or the standing of West Bank and Gaza residents before the court may be questionable, successive attorney-generals have decided not to contest it.

The provision of this court to residents of the Occupied Territories is not a requirement of international law and Israel has rightly been congratulated for voluntarily instituting an element of review over the actions of the occupying authorities. It is important to note, however, that it does not act as a court of appeal. Moreover, while the Israeli High Court considers itself empowered to review the legality of acts by the military government or its officers, there are self-imposed limitations on its powers: most importantly, the court will only in exceptional circumstances enquire into any decision relating to security, and will not substitute its own considerations for those of the person responsible for security.[32] The role of the High Court, its effectiveness in protecting the rights of the occupied population, and its limitations are discussed in many of the contributions to this book.

---

[30] In the Gaza Strip, the legal system in force is derived from that applied by the British Mandatory Government. The Gaza Strip was never incorporated into Egypt and Egyptian law as such was not applied. The basic structure of the courts and the main civil and criminal ordinances issued before 1948 are therefore still in force. A number of laws and regulations have been amended by the legislative council that existed until 1967 and since then by the Gaza Area Commander in the form of military orders. Though details differ, essentially similar policies, neglect of the legal system, and interference with laws have led to a similar undermining and alteration of the judicial system and the law.

[31] R. Shehadeh and Kuttab, *The West Bank and the Rule of Law* (Geneva, 1980), 104.

[32] See discussion on security in Ch. 6.

II. Al-Haq and the Conference

Al-Haq and the Origins and Purpose of the Conference

Al-Haq, formerly known as Law in the Service of Man, was established by a group of Palestinian lawyers and activists in 1979 as the West Bank affiliate of the International Commission of Jurists. Al-Haq's mandate is to monitor and document human rights violations and to promote the rule of law and respect for human rights in the West Bank.[33] Relying on humanitarian law and international standards of human rights, and on its own scrupulous fieldwork, al-Haq studies and reports on the measures taken by the Israeli military authorities in the West Bank, challenges the legality of their actions, intervenes to stop illegal practices and to mitigate damage suffered, and seeks to promote respect for human rights and the rule of law within the Palestinian community.

Much of al-Haq's work involves addressing abuses of individual human rights by the Israeli occupying authorities, but it also attaches great importance to monitoring the treatment of the territories themselves and their infrastructure by the military authorities, since this is critical to the rights of the Palestinian people as a whole. The slow but possibly irreversible transformation and destruction of the infrastructure and distinct character of the territories—even the West Bank itself has been renamed 'Judea and Samaria', and the major town of Nablus, 'Shekhem'—may not be as dramatic as the daily violations of individual rights, yet they have profound implications for the ability of the Palestinian community to emerge from the occupation as an integral society capable of self-governance and of exercising the fundamental human right of self-determination.

Operating under the unusual conditions of a prolonged belligerent occupation, al-Haq works within the framework of the humanitarian law applicable to belligerent occupation, as well as international human rights standards binding on an occupying power. But the laws governing belligerent occupation are necessarily general in many respects, setting the principles and framework within which an occupier may act, without entering into detail. The scope this leaves for interpretation has tremendous implications for the treatment of the territories and their inhabitants. To give only one example, the Israeli High Court has adopted interpretations of certain provisions of humanitarian law which sanction both Israeli settlements and deportation of Palestinian

---

[33] Since 1989, in response to an unprecedented level of alleged violations of human rights in the Gaza Strip during the *intifada*, al-Haq has included the Gaza Strip within its mandate.

civilians. It continues to act on these interpretations, although the international community is overwhelmingly in agreement that these same provisions render both practices illegal. The challenge facing al-Haq, and all those concerned with the rule of law in the Israeli-occupied territories, is therefore to determine how these general provisions apply to the specific circumstances of this occupation.

As al-Haq sought clarification from legal authorities on such provisions, it was repeatedly frustrated by the dearth of legal scholarship on the laws governing belligerent occupation. On the more abstruse questions as to how occupied territories should be administered, there was almost no guidance to be found. With notable exceptions, there seemed little interest among academics in addressing the practical problems faced by a community living and operating under conditions of occupation. While there have been a number of situations of belligerent occupation since World War II, none have become institutionalized to the extent of Israel's occupation of the West Bank and Gaza. Consequently, many of the issues raised by this occupation have not been faced since the Fourth Geneva Convention came into force.

Israeli jurists, on the other hand, have naturally given priority to the subject. Faced with applying laws that were necessarily general, since they were designed to govern all forms of belligerent occupation, Israeli judges, scholars, and lawyers were called upon to interpret the laws in the light of Israel's own occupations, and many came to be considered authorities on the laws of war. Palestinians wishing to challenge the actions of the occupying power often found that the opinions most favoured by the court, and indeed those relied on in other fora to which they appealed, were those of jurists formerly or actually in the service of their adversary, the military government.

While there are rightly acknowledged experts in the field of military law amongst Israeli jurists, some of whom have repeatedly criticized the official Israeli position on the applicability of humanitarian law, al-Haq saw the need to involve other scholars, more distanced from the conflict, to address some of these issues and to apply their expertise to areas of conflicting interpretation. Al-Haq therefore initiated a research project, to culminate in an international conference, in which leading scholars of the laws of war and human rights, neither Arab nor Israeli, were invited to address aspects of humanitarian law relating to the administration of occupied territories. Simultaneously, al-Haq asked practitioners in the Occupied Territories to examine how the Israeli-occupied territories have in fact been administered. The project was not intended as a comprehensive review of Israeli practice, but rather as an attempt to elucidate the provisions of international law relating to the administration of occupied territories in the light of an actual occupation.

In inviting some of the most authoritative commentators on humanitarian law to participate in this project, al-Haq had in mind not only its own immediate needs as it sought advice on these issues, but also the weight which authoritative voices of scholars carry in the interpretation of law, in the absence of clear legal provisions. As Roberts and Guelff point out in the introduction to their collection of documents on the laws of war:

> The writings of distinguished specialists (often called 'publicists') on the subject of the laws of war have been cited frequently as evidence of where the law stands on particular issues . . . The general importance of such writings has not decreased despite the fact that formal codifications have increased. Indeed, the importance of such writings has perhaps increased owing to the evident need to clarify the greater number of codified provisions, to relate the provisions of the various codifications to each other and to other sources of law, and to consider other problems.[34]

With a few notable exceptions, such interpretation in relation to the West Bank and Gaza Strip has been left largely to the Israeli policy makers and their advisers, and to case law by the courts of the occupying power.[35] Al-Haq's aim was to elucidate and supplement commentary on and analysis of these issues with other authoritative opinions. A second, and ultimately more important, purpose was to stimulate interest among leading scholars in a subject which is often overlooked in favour of other more fashionable areas of the law of war, such as arms control.

The importance of authoritative opinion on such issues has also prompted me to allow some repetition in this volume, which might, for strictly editorial reasons, have been pared down. For instance, almost all the international contributors address the question of which international laws apply to the occupation of the West Bank and Gaza. For editorial purposes it might have been preferable to omit this discussion from some chapters. But to serve the fundamental purpose of adding to the scholarly writings on these critical issues, it is desirable for these opinions to be recorded.

The scope of this study is limited in several important respects, determined by the mandate and concerns of al-Haq. Firstly, as is apparent from the title, the subject of the book is the administration of occupied territories. Al-Haq and others have written extensively about

---

[34] A. Roberts and R. Guelff, *Documents on the Laws of War*, 2nd edn. (Oxford, 1989), 8.
[35] It is perhaps a measure of the need for this book that the only obstruction encountered by the editor was the refusal, by its editor, of copyright permission to use any material or extracts from the *Israel Yearbook on Human Rights*. The *Yearbook* is published by the Faculty of Law in Tel Aviv University, under the editorship of Professor Yoram Dinstein, and is the main English-language source for scholarly articles on law and human rights under Israeli rule and summaries of Israeli High Court case reports.

specific violations of human rights occurring under the Israeli occupation, including deportations, administrative detention, house demolition, enforced separation of families, and irregularities in military trials.[36] The intention here is not to revisit these issues but to focus specifically on detailed aspects of the administration of occupied territories, issues of immense importance in the long term, but which have been largely overlooked in the urgency of addressing immediate and flagrant violations of individual rights.

Secondly, the period covered in the book extends only to the date of the conference at the beginning of 1988 and shortly thereafter. There is deliberately no attempt to address the many developments of the sustained Palestinian uprising, commonly known as the *intifada*. Although the changes wrought by the *intifada*, in both the international arena and the Occupied Territories, are momentous, and the severity of the Israeli response means that the situation of those living in the Territories has deteriorated markedly in almost every respect, the fundamental nature of the problems described in this book remains unchanged. The issues dealt with here thus remain as relevant now as before, and indeed the need to address them is perhaps now only more urgent.

Thirdly, although the territories currently occupied by Israel include not only the West Bank and the Gaza Strip, but also East Jerusalem and the Golan Heights, both illegally annexed, and the so-called 'security zone' in Southern Lebanon, the primary focus of this work is on the West Bank and Gaza. Moreover, due to al-Haq's own focus and the comparative lack of documentation on the situation of Gaza, reference will often be to the West Bank alone. Similar issues urgently need addressing in relation to each of the other territories, but focusing mainly on the West Bank enables deeper discussion on each issue, much of which will also be relevant to the other territories.

Finally, it will be quickly apparent on reading this book that there are relatively few references to written sources on many aspects of the administration of the West Bank and Gaza. Much reference is made to original fieldwork, most notably in the chapters by Hiltermann, Jabr, Awartani, and Matar. These authors are exploring administrative and socio-economic matters on which published sources are few or non-existent. Access to information is not easy for Palestinian researchers, lacking the centralized government mechanisms for gathering and making available such data. Also obvious will be the very great reliance placed on the work of the West Bank Data Base Project, directed

---

[36] See for instance al-Haq's occasional papers on administrative detention, deportation, demolition of houses, planning, military courts, etc. and see also other reports by the National Lawyers' Guild, the Lawyers' Committee for Human Rights, Amnesty International, etc., listed in Ch. 3, n. 11.

by Meron Benvenisti. The West Bank Data Base Project did groundbreaking work in gathering data, often inaccessible to Palestinian researchers, on administrative and policy aspects of the occupation of the West Bank. That many of the contributors are much indebted to this work is acknowledged in copious footnote references.

Al-Haq's conference was held on 22–5 January 1988 in East Jerusalem. Unforeseen was the fact that it would take place only one month after the start of the Palestinian popular uprising, the *intifada*, which was to bring unprecedented and irreversible change to the face of the conflict. The *intifada* started in Gaza on 9 December 1987. By the date of the conference it had spread to all parts of the Occupied Territories. In the intervening weeks 41 Palestinians had already been killed, eighteen of them under the age of 18.

Initially participants at the conference expressed concern at discussing academic questions of law while conflict was escalating and lives lost outside. But it soon became apparent that the subject of discussion, though academic, was not abstract but related to the root cause of the struggle outside—the denial of a people's right to self-determination and the threatened absorption of occupied territories into the occupier's state. In fact the papers presented here mark the end of one era in the occupation, a long period of relatively quiet endurance of occupation. They portray the conditions which prevailed up to the end of 1987, and stand as the background against which years of pent-up frustration exploded into the *intifada*.

The Format and Organization of this Volume

Al-Haq's urgent need for clarification of the provisions of international law governing the administration of the West Bank under this lengthy occupation guided the design of the project. The topics are those which posed the organization problematic questions of international law. In relation to each topic, an international expert elucidates the relevant provisions of international law, and a local expert or practitioner reviews the practice in the Occupied Territories.

Ideally, the international and local experts would have worked in close conjunction on each topic so that the review of international law could address most directly the actual problems raised in the administration of the Israeli-occupied territories, but this was logistically impossible. Instead, al-Haq provided detailed outlines of the issues to be addressed in each paper, seeking to maintain coherence by ensuring that paired papers corresponded, while not insisting that each paper parallel exactly its counterpart. In some cases there is close complementarity, for instance between the papers of Christopher Greenwood and Mona Rishmawi, or those of Antonio Cassese and

Ibrahim Matar; in others, the authors saw more value in following different lines of argument and al-Haq did not attempt to restrict them over-much. Authors were invited to revise their papers in the light of the discussion at the conference, but readers will still find that certain aspects of the occupation described by local experts are not addressed in the legal papers, and vice versa. In some instances this reflects the unavailability of information about local practice, while in others it may reflect unrealistic expectations by laymen of international law's capacity to address detailed issues. We only hope that these papers will stimulate others to address some of these points.

The papers in this volume are organized into three broad sections. The first, comprising six papers, sets the framework of international law applicable to belligerent occupation in general and of the Israeli occupation of the West Bank in particular. The second examines in detail certain areas of administration of occupied territories: the administrative structure, popular organization within the territories, taxation and economy, land and natural resources. The last section, though short, focusses on the most important issue of all, the enforcement of international law. The provisions of international law and their application are of little worth, unless they can be enforced.

In the opening chapter, Adam Roberts presents a wide-ranging examination of the legal framework of occupation, and of prolonged occupation in particular. While repudiating the Israeli government's argument that such an occupation falls into a separate category not subject to the normal laws governing occupation, Roberts, like Antonio Cassese in a later chapter, considers that there are special considerations to be taken into account in an occupation that lasts as long as that of the West Bank and Gaza and examines what these are. Both point to the danger inherent in applying the law selectively, especially when it is the occupying power itself which determines which parts are applicable. Roberts also considers the extent to which human rights law is applicable to occupied territories, especially under a prolonged occupation, and stresses the importance of the role of the international community, pointing to the past shortcomings of some UN bodies and states, notably the United States, in this respect.

Next, Mazen Qupty explores the stance of Israel's High Court of Justice towards the application of humanitarian and human rights law in the Israeli-occupied territories, by reference to its judgments. This chapter elucidates the complex attitude of the government and the court to the status of the occupation. Qupty provides an insight into the attitudes of the court itself, enabling an assessment to be made of its strengths and weaknesses *vis-à-vis* the jurisdiction it exercises over the West Bank and Gaza.

Burns Weston and Richard Falk take a critical look at the relevance of international law to Israel's occupation of the West Bank and Gaza, an approach covering some of the same ground as, yet complementary to, Roberts' examination of its application. In arguing that international law has been largely ignored or overridden and that the international community has failed in its duty to protect those living under occupation, they look at some of the consequences of this, including the *intifada* itself. They go further to suggest that, as a result of Israel's failure to comply with international law, the occupation itself may be illegal and that, in the light of the demonstrably annexationist designs of the occupier, the Palestinian inhabitants may have the right to resist.

Taking the military orders issued by the military commander throughout the occupation as an indicator, Raja Shehadeh reviews the development of Israeli policy on the occupation of the West Bank. Dividing these orders for convenience into four stages, he charts the changing intentions and preoccupations of Israeli policy for the territories. He traces how the government, initially uncertain as to how to treat the territories, soon perceived the advantages of their retention, and developed extensive mechanisms of control over the land and the people. Anticipating international pressure to relinquish the territories, the government developed means to make more land available for settlement and to encourage Jewish settlers to establish a permanent presence there. Shehadeh explains how subtle amendments to the law had the effect of transforming the Jewish settlements into islands of Israeli sovereignty within the Occupied Territories. Meanwhile, other laws furthered the harnessing of the economy, infrastructure, and resources of the territories to those of Israel to the point of *de facto* annexation—annexation in all but name. Through this review of the military orders issued in the West Bank, Shehadeh shows how the limited legislative powers granted to an occupier have been used to establish a dual and discriminatory system of government for Palestinian inhabitants and Jewish settlers.

In the final pair of papers setting the framework of the occupation, Alain Pellet and I examine, respectively, the criteria which an occupier is required to apply to its treatment of occupied territories, and Israel's use of certain criteria in its treatment of the West Bank. Pellet reviews the underlying intention of the laws of war and the increasing stress laid by the international community on people's rights. Rejecting the traditional criteria of humanity and necessity as secondary, he concludes that the sole criterion to be used by the occupier is the sovereign rights of the occupied people.

In the following chapter, I take three principles frequently relied on by the Israeli authorities to justify measures taken in the Occupied Territories: the duty to restore and ensure public order, concern for the welfare of the population, and the occupier's right to ensure security.

Reviewing the use and interpretation of these criteria, each of which can be derived from international law, I argue that in each case the proper definition has been expanded to authorize much wider powers than those approved by international law and that the Israeli High Court has been willing to endorse these interpretations. Israel has thus been able to pursue its intended policies with little check, while appearing to comply with international law.

Part II examines in more depth particular aspects of the administration of occupied territories and of the West Bank. Christopher Greenwood seeks guidance in international law as to the form which an administration should take in occupied territories. While finding no precise forms prescribed by international law, leaving the occupier a fairly free hand in determining the form of administration imposed, he identifies certain restrictions that must be observed by an occupier, notably that the occupier cannot transform permanently the form of government of the occupied territory, and that the administration must be distinct from that of the occupier's own state.

Mona Rishmawi then describes the form of administration adopted in the West Bank by the Israeli occupying government. In tracing the development of the military government she argues that, while its initial aim was to preserve security, this purpose has increasingly been superseded by the political aim of creeping annexation. She maintains that, while nominally retaining the pre-existing administrative structure, drastic changes have robbed that structure of its content, and harnessed the administration closely to that of Israel.

The next two chapters in this section look at the right of association under occupation. A people's ability to organize is critical both to the preservation of the social and economic fabric of their society, and to their ability to reconstruct a viable and self-reliant society on the termination of the occupation. John Quigley examines the question of whether there is a right to organize trade unions in the laws of belligerent occupation, in customary law, and in human rights law. He finds that, as one of the earliest rights to be protected by international treaty, the right to organize is guaranteed under all these laws and reinforced by case law. He concludes that an occupant may restrict trade union rights in certain extreme circumstances—where there is a threat to national security and a declared public emergency—but only if this amounts to a threat to the existing order. Otherwise an occupier is bound to respect the right to organize.

Joost Hiltermann then reviews the history of popular organization under Israeli occupation, basing his paper largely on his own field research. Taking as examples trade unions and women's organizations, he shows how Israel, claiming that they are not *bona fide* organizations, has sought to obstruct the development of both. Hiltermann reviews the activities and achievements of these organizations, to establish that they are indeed *bona fide* in their aims to represent, protect the rights of, and educate workers and women respectively. He then examines the repressive measures the military government has taken to discourage trade union and women's organized activity, and reviews the attempts these organizations have made locally and internationally to enforce their right to organize.

Turning to more detailed aspects of the administration, Gerhard von Glahn examines the provisions of international law relating to taxation and customs duties. He finds that taxation receives very short shrift in the existing instruments, but draws on precedents and practices of states in earlier occupations to elucidate the applicable principles. He concludes that an occupier can collect taxes due to a central government and can increase the rates of these taxes, but that the power to introduce new taxes and collect existing local taxes is very restricted. After reviewing the practices of other states in earlier occupations, von Glahn turns to the Israeli occupation of the West Bank and Gaza Strip and considers the Israeli government's taxation policy. In particular, he reflects on the decision of the Israeli High Court in a landmark case on value added tax, in which his own expert evidence played an important part.

Hisham Jabr in his chapter reviews the financial administration of the West Bank under occupation and the structure of its budget, on both of which sources and information are badly lacking. Listing the various taxes imposed, Jabr finds that the tax burden compares unfavourably with that of Jordanians and Israelis, while benefits provided are lower. He further criticizes as random the collection of taxes.

Hisham Awartani then looks in more detail at the economy of the West Bank and its development under occupation. Examining first macro-economic indicators, then development planning and certain illustrative sectors, he shows the poor shape of the economy, and its dependence on its status as an extension and 'backyard' for Israel. Both these contributors argue that Israeli policies in the Occupied Territories have rendered their economies subservient to that of Israel, and demonstrate how this has been achieved by measures which link the economies of the Occupied Territories to that of Israel, creating dependency and discriminating against the territories.

Antonio Cassese's chapter addresses the powers and duties of an occupier in relation to land and natural resources, a key topic given the role of settlement in the occupation of the West Bank and Gaza. Viewing the laws of war in the contemporary world, Cassese argues that they should be construed in the light of the current circumstances— what he terms 'the evolutive effect'. While agreeing with the Israeli

High Court that present circumstances, including the length of an occupation, must be taken into consideration, he maintains that the prolongation of an occupation, far from releasing the occupier from the restrictions of the laws of belligerent occupation, actually requires such restrictions to be all the more strictly construed. Applying the evolutive principle, Cassese explains that the shift in emphasis by the international community during this century from an overriding respect for private property to a respect for public rights and the rights of people means that the restrictions on the way in which the occupier treats natural resources, such as land and water, are to be construed more rather than less strictly.

The counterpart to this chapter by Ibrahim Matar tells, mainly from his own field research, of the changes wrought to the land and water resources of the West Bank to provide for Jewish settlement and the impact this has had on the indigenous population. By example he shows how this has led to displacement, impoverishment, fragmentation of Palestinian communities, and limitation of economic growth, but he also recounts how the population has opposed this process, culminating in the *intifada*.

The final section addresses a question without which the discussion of international law would be to little purpose. How can these provisions of international humanitarian law and human rights be enforced under belligerent occupation? John Dugard, reviewing first a number of clear violations of international law by Israel in its occupation, focuses on methods by which international law might be enforced. He considers and rejects a direct enforcement model by states under the UN Charter or the Uniting for Peace resolution, since political factors render such an approach unrealistic. Turning instead to what he calls the indirect enforcement model, he advocates the mobilization of a wide range of opinion and action to apply economic coercion, or to bring complaints to various fora such as the ILO or even local domestic courts. Above all he urges that an advisory opinion be sought from the International Court of Justice on some of the issues in which international opinion is most clearly flouted by Israeli practice and interpretation, and suggests issues that might be addressed and the potential effect of such an opinion.

In the final chapter, Jonathan Kuttab presents the pragmatic view of one who has sought for years to rely on legal remedies to dispute Israeli violations of local and international law in the West Bank. He believes that, while legal strategies have validity and potential and should not be abandoned, the most effective forum for the defence of rights remains what he calls the 'court of public opinion'. By this he means the need to implicate the public, whether the international community, foreign governments, citizens of other states, international human rights organizations, or the Israeli public itself, by informing them of the facts and of their responsibilities and requiring them to take action. He stresses that this is not an easy task, necessitating unassailably accurate information, full documentation, objective and dispassionate presentation, and careful attention to the varying interests and abilities of different publics. Nevertheless, if all these points are assured, he believes that in time right will prevail.

Some Issues Arising

In designing the project, al-Haq did not seek unanimity among the legal scholars, but selected those it felt would bring a fresh look to the problems faced in the territories occupied by Israel. The complexity of these issues can be seen in the variety of responses to the different issues addressed in this book.

Certain points are nevertheless reinforced repeatedly throughout the volume, notably the applicability of the Fourth Geneva Convention to Israel's occupation of the West Bank and Gaza, a point which the Israeli government still denies. Another point much emphasized—although views differ on detail—is the applicability of human rights instruments to occupied territories, albeit with certain reservations. This has very important implications for the civilian populations of occupied territories since the human rights treaties reinforce in many specific issues the provisions of humanitarian law. The inherently temporary nature of belligerent occupation is also affirmed again and again, and the illegality of steps which seek to assert sovereignty or to pre-empt eventual withdrawal from occupied territories. Important too is the stress placed by a number of the contributors on the continuing applicability of humanitarian law to occupied territories no matter how long the occupation, and the assertion of some that the longer the occupation, the more important it is to interpret the provisions defining the occupier's powers restrictively.

On other points there is a difference of opinion. Thus Weston and Falk suggest that the occupation itself may be illegal, whereas Roberts considers that as yet international juridical opinion does not support this conclusion. Pellet and von Glahn differ over the weight an occupier may attach to military necessity, Pellet arguing that the importance traditionally afforded to this criterion is no longer valid in the modern world, while von Glahn argues that this remains an overriding and valid rationale. Weston and Falk argue for a right of resistance, and Pellet for the legality of a *levée en masse*, on the grounds that this is the expression of will of a sovereign people, but Roberts expresses doubts, saying that this is an area which does not yet admit of absolute answers. On more general points, views differ too on the extent to which the Fourth Geneva Convention constitutes customary law and to what degree the Geneva Protocol I is applicable to the West Bank and Gaza.

In the chapters addressing Israel's treatment of the Occupied Territories, common threads are apparent. Above all the intricate links established between Israel and the territories can be seen not only in the administrative structure but also in the economy, the law, communications, supply networks, planning, and governmental structure. Although primarily addressing abstract questions of international law, many of the international contributors also express their opinions on aspects of Israel's rule over the Occupied Territories. Most importantly, they overwhelmingly assert the illegality of Israeli civilian settlement in the territories occupied, and the annexation of any part of that territory. Finally, both local and international contributors subject the High Court to some criticism and find its performance, to varying degrees, disappointing.

The laws of war constitute the best effort of the international community to regulate the conduct of war in all its forms. Each occasion of war brings its own facts and new circumstances, and each poses new questions and challenges to international law. While change often comes too late for those affected by the war in question, it may result in increased protection for those involved in subsequent conflicts, and ultimately limit the human cost of war.

Since it seems that the world cannot yet look forward to a time when the laws of war will not be needed, the international community is bound to continue its efforts to increase the means of limiting the damage caused by such war, especially to innocent civilians. The laws of war evolve through the efforts of the international community to develop new means and instruments of protection, and through scholarship. We welcome the opportunity to contribute to this process, and hope in so doing to help not only Palestinians now living under belligerent occupation, but all others who may be similarly deprived of their sovereign rights now and in the future.

Part One

International Legal Framework

1

Prolonged Military Occupation: The Israeli-Occupied Territories 1967–1988

ADAM ROBERTS

To what extent are international legal rules formally applicable, and practically relevant, to a prolonged military occupation? The question has assumed prominence because of the exceptional duration of the occupation by Israel of various territories that came under its control in the war of 5–10 June 1967. The situation there has had two classic features of a military occupation: first, a formal system of external control by a force whose presence is not sanctioned by international agreement; and second, a conflict of nationality and interest between the inhabitants, on the one hand, and those exercising power over them, on the other. In highlighting these features, the Palestinian uprising, or *intifada*, which began in Gaza and the West Bank in December 1987, has added urgency to the question of the law applicable to prolonged occupations.

There is a simple answer, and a perfectly serious one, to the central question addressed here. Israel has given express commitments over the years to implement the terms of a large number of treaties, and is also, like all states, bound by international customary law. These are solemn obligations. There is no need to engage in the laborious business of seeking to prove that any or every commitment passes an artificial test of 'applicability' in a given situation. Rather, the burden of proof lies on an obligated state to show, if it can, that in the actual situation a given commitment does not apply. Hence, it can be asserted, simply but also persuasively, that the Israeli occupation of various territories has been, and continues to be, covered by a wide range of agreements, with which Israel must conform.

* This is a revised version of a paper presented at the conference organized by al-Haq in Jerusalem, 22–5 Jan. 1988, on the administration of occupied territories. A further revised and up-dated version appeared in *AJIL* 84 (Jan. 1990), No. 1.

This simple answer, though important as a starting point, is not the last word on the subject because of two main considerations, which form the *raison d'être* of this chapter. First, in a number of statements Israeli spokesmen and courts have suggested that certain international rules were never formally applicable to the Occupied Territories, or else that their application may be qualified in some ways owing to special circumstances, one being the long duration of the occupation. The validity of these Israeli statements needs to be examined. Second, even if it is accepted that the rules governing occupations should be applied (whether out of formal legal obligation or as a matter of policy), the question remains whether these rules are relevant to the practical problems that arise in a prolonged occupation—and, indeed, whether implementation of the rules is likely to serve their underlying purposes. In particular, are the rules a straitjacket that inhibits political, legislative, and economic change?

Although the present writer is a specialist in international relations rather than international law, the focus here is on legal issues. There are good reasons for this so far as the Israeli-occupied territories are concerned. First, the very concept of occupation, with its implicit assertion that external military control is temporary, is a triumph of legal thinking. Second, the appeal to general norms and standards has had great practical significance as regards the Israeli occupation: much of the international comment on it, especially within the framework of the United Nations, has emanated from legal as well as other considerations, or at least has been expressed in legal language.

Nevertheless, there are some hazards in discussing burning political issues in legal terms. Other methodologies—those of history and political science, even strategy and arms control—are necessary complements to law, and may be just as likely to assist understanding and to promote solutions. Moreover, while most international lawyers are, quite properly, cautious in their application of rules and principles to particular cases, sometimes law may get misused. The language of law can easily become a language of right and wrong, of moralistic reproach, of the clothing of interest in the garments of rectitude, of the concealment of factual changes with legal fictions, of refined scholasticism in the face of urgent practical problems, and of the facile application of general rules without a deep understanding of situations that are unique. Such approaches are hardly the highest expressions of law; nor are they necessarily the best way of addressing complex and multilayered international problems such as those encountered in the Occupied Territories.

Addressing as it does the single question of the rules applicable in a prolonged occupation, this chapter makes no attempt to assess the conduct of the Israeli occupation overall, or to cover the huge range of legal and practical issues to which it has given rise. For example, nothing is said here on such important and frequently raised matters as ill-treatment of detainees, since the basic pertinent rules are clear and are not affected by the duration of the occupation.

The chapter is divided into nine parts. The first three, which examine the law on occupations, are the most general; the rest deal centrally with the Israeli-occupied territories.

I. Purposes of the Law on Occupations

There is no single authoritative exegesis of the various purposes served by that part of the laws of war relating to military occupations—what is called here the 'law on occupations'. However, those purposes can be inferred from the principal conventions, from the events that gave rise to them, from their negotiating history, from military manuals, from court judgments, and from writings.

The law on occupations is both permissive (accepting that an occupant exercises certain powers) and prohibitory (putting limits on the actions of various parties, including occupying powers). Briefly summarized, it can have the following purposes:

1. Ensuring that those who are in the hands of an adversary are treated with humanity. (In this respect the rules on occupations serve a similar purpose to those on prisoners of war and internees.)
2. Harmonizing these humanitarian interests with the military needs of the occupant.
3. Preventing the imposition of disruptive changes in the occupied territory, and preserving the rights of the sovereign there. (Where the eventual disposition of territories awaits the outcome of peace negotiations, or the hold of the occupant might be reversed by the fortunes of war, there is a need for rules to inhibit any unilateral, drastic, and permanent changes in the political, economic, social, and legal orders.)
4. Preserving military discipline among the occupying forces. (Occupations typically present problems—such as uncontrolled exercise of power, numerous points of friction between occupants and inhabitants—that can easily lead to looting, general disorder, and a breakdown of military discipline. A modicum of rules is one safeguard against these dangers.)
5. Reducing the risk that relations between occupant and occupied will get out of hand and lead to renewed conflict.
6. Improving the chances that, if an occupant finds part of its own territory occupied, its population will in turn be treated with due

regard to international norms. (Sometimes military occupations in war are concurrent, with each side holding some of the other's territory; or they may be consecutive, with a country that had been an occupant having part of its territory occupied. Either circumstance can give an additional incentive for observing rules.)
7. Helping to maintain friendly relations between the occupying power and foreign states—whether allies, adversaries, or neutrals.
8. Facilitating the prospects for an eventual peace agreement.[1] (The prohibition of annexation of occupied territory, and the rules against transfers of populations into and from occupied territories, partly reflect this purpose.)

Whether the law has always succeeded in serving these purposes may be debated. Moreover, in any given situation determining the particular policies that will best reflect these purposes may well be a matter of delicate political judgement. However, the purposes themselves are enduring. They are not purely and simply humanitarian, but also practical—arising as they do from the interests and experiences of states over a long period.

As far as prolonged occupations are concerned, some or all of these purposes may remain important. Yet some may come to be seen as of less importance: to the extent that this is so, the detailed rules intended to reflect these purposes may be called into question.

II. Prolonged Occupations as a Distinct Category

An important, but implicit, assumption of much of the law on occupations is that military occupation is a provisional state of affairs, which may end as the fortunes of war change, or else will be transformed into some other status through negotiations conducted at or soon after the end of the war. However, many episodes during this century have called into question the assumption that occupations are of short duration. As Doris Appel Graber already noted in 1949:

Considering the complexity of modern occupations, such as those during World War I and II in which large areas were occupied for long periods of time, raising a multitude of legal questions about the rights and duties of occupants in particular situations and the legal effects of the occupant's actions after the war, the rules laid down in the landmark codes of the 1863–1914 period and expounded in the literature and in military manuals seem fragmentary indeed and inadequate to guide occupation policies.

---

[1] This can be inferred from, e.g., D. A. Graber, *The Development of the Law of Belligerent Occupation 1863–1914: A Historical Survey* (New York, 1949), 37–40.

But . . . they were developed in a relatively peaceful period in which no major wars occurred and in which belligerent occupations were generally of short duration so that occupants were not forced to assume the full governmental burdens which had rested on the displaced sovereign. Consequently, while general principles were evolved, few specific rules developed because of a lack of factual situations requiring application of specific rules often enough to permit their growth into law.[2]

In the period since World War II, there has been no shortage of cases of prolonged occupation, many of which have raised complex questions about the applicability and utility of international rules—rules that have of course developed significantly since Graber wrote. These occupations seem yet another proof of the paradox: 'Rien ne dure comme le provisoire.'

The precise definition of 'prolonged occupation' is likely to be a pointless quest. For the purpose of this chapter, it is taken to be an occupation that lasts more than five years and extends into a period when hostilities are sharply reduced—i.e. a period at least approximating peacetime.

A few examples from the post-1945 period are mentioned below. While by no means the only cases that might be viewed as prolonged occupations, they are sufficient to indicate how varied in character and purpose such occupations can be. Many of them have raised difficult questions: what body of international law applies in circumstances where the entire purpose of an occupation is (or ought to be) to bring about political change, rather than simply to preserve the status quo? And what rules apply when an occupation takes place (or continues) in peacetime?

The Allied Occupations of Germany and Japan

The Allied occupations of Germany and Japan after the Second World War lasted for 10 and 6 years, respectively.[3] They defied the neat legal categories on which the law on occupations often seems to be based. These were not cases of subjugation and annexation; hence, they were military occupations of a kind. However, the victors wished to exercise

---

[2] Ibid. 290–1.
[3] The US military occupation of Japan ended on 28 Apr. 1952, with the entry into force of the Peace Treaty between the two countries. The US occupation of the Ryukyu Islands, including Okinawa, lasted for 27 years, ending on 14 May 1972, in accord with the terms of the US–Japanese Okinawa treaty of 17 June 1971. The occupation by the three Western powers of West Germany ended on 5 May 1955. The Soviet occupation of East Germany can be said formally to have ended with the opening of diplomatic relations between the two countries on 20 Sept. 1955, following a Soviet government statement of 25 Mar. 1954.

their powers freely, and to make drastic political changes. They were not willing to be formally bound by the Hague Regulations.[4] One of the most cogent presentations of the argument for the Allied position suggested that the law of belligerent occupation had been designed to serve two purposes: (1) to protect the sovereign rights of the legitimate government of the occupied territory, and (2) to protect the inhabitants from being exploited for the prosecution of the occupant's war. Since neither of these purposes had much bearing on the situation the Allies faced, to have applied the law would have been 'a manifest anachronism'.[5] While this view of the applicability of the Hague Regulations was by no means uncontested, it did largely prevail. For those who found the Hague Regulations inapplicable, what rules of international law did apply to the Allied occupation of Germany after its unconsiditional surrender? Theodor Schweisfurth has said convincingly that this phase was subject to 'such rules of international law as limit the right of any Government to commit acts which constitute crimes against peace and crimes against humanity.'[6] Clearly, in these exceptional cases of prolonged occupation, any rules that could be interpreted as limiting the Allies' right to bring about significant political changes in the former Axis countries were deemed to be irrelevant.

Current and future military occupations, even post-surrender ones, cannot be governed by so few formal international rules as were these post-1945 cases. This is due to two legal developments. First, the Fourth Geneva Convention would appear to be applicable to a future post-surrender occupation by virtue of its common Article 2.[7] Second,

---

[4] Convention respecting the Laws and Customs of War on Land, with annexed Regulations, 18 Oct. 1907, 36 Stat. 2277, TS No. 539, 205 Parry's TS 277. See A. Roberts and R. Guelff, *Documents on the Laws of War*, 2nd edn. (Oxford, 1989), 43–59.
On the UK discussion of the legal status of defeated Germany, see especially F. S. V. Donnison, *Civil Affairs and Military Government: Central Organization and Planning* (London, 1966), 125–36.

[5] R. Y. Jennings, 'Government in Commission', BYIL 23 (1946) 112, 135–6.

[6] 'Germany, Occupation after World War II', in R. Bernhardt (ed.), *Encyclopaedia of Public International Law* 3 (Amsterdam, 1982), 191, 196–7.

[7] Convention Relative to the Protection of Civilian Persons in Time of War, 12 Aug. 1949, 6 UST 3516, TIAS No. 3365, 75 UNTS 287. See Roberts and Guelff, *Documents on the Laws of War*, 271–337. J. Pictet, *Commentary on Geneva Convention IV of 1949 Relative to the Protection of Civilian Persons in Time of War*, trans. R. Griffin and C. W. Dumbleton (Geneva, 1958), 22; G. von Glahn, *The Occupation of Enemy Territory* (Minneapolis, 1957), 281, 283; United Kingdom War Office, *Manual of Military Law*, iii: *The Law of War on Land* (1958), 140; and M. Greenspan, *The Modern Law of Land Warfare* (Berkeley, 1959), 216–17, 224–7.
There might thus seem to be at least a theoretical possibility that a future post-surrender occupation would be subject to the Geneva Convention but not to the Hague Regulations, inasmuch as the latter stress mainly the preservation of the *status quo* against the background of war, while the former puts somewhat more emphasis on the protection of the individual inhabitants. (Israeli courts have to some extent reversed this

the development of international human rights law since 1945 has greatly enlarged the scope of rules of international law that place limits on the right of any government to commit whatever actions it pleases against those under its control. (This point will be discussed in Section VI below).

South Africa's Occupation of Namibia

The presence of South Africa in Namibia after its international mandate there was terminated by the United Nations in 1966 was increasingly viewed as an occupation—especially after the advisory opinion of the International Court of Justice in 1971.[8] In this case, as in that of the Israeli-occupied territories, the international community made clear that it would like to see certain positive changes introduced, leading to the emergence of a new sovereign state.

This occupation raised the question of what bodies of international law should be applied. In its 1971 advisory opinion, the International Court of Justice said that some multilateral conventions 'such as those of a humanitarian character' may be viewed as binding as regards the occupation of Namibia.[9] For the purposes of the question it was addressing, it was not essential for the Court to specify which humanitarian conventions it had in mind: the important point is the endorsement of the applicability of international rules even though this occupation was seen as being marked by several exceptional features. In 1971 the UN General Assembly specifically urged South Africa to comply with the Third and Fourth 1949 Geneva Conventions in Namibia.[10]

---

formula, having relied more on the Hague than the Geneva rules.) However, most, if not all, future post-surrender occupations would be brought within the ambit of the Hague Regulations because of several factors, including (1) they are customary in character; and (2) in relations between powers bound by the 1899 or 1907 Hague Conventions, the Fourth Geneva Convention (Art. 154) states that it is 'supplementary' to the Hague Regulations.

[8] *Legal Consequences for States of the Continued Presence of South Africa in Namibia (South West Africa) notwithstanding Security Council Resolution 276 (1970), ICJ Reports* (1971), 16 (Advisory Opinion of 21 June).

Key UN resolutions on Namibia include the following. Before 1971: GA Res. 2145 (XXI) (27 Oct. 1966) (terminating South Africa's mandate); GA Res. 2372 (XXII) (12 June 1968) (referring several times to South Africa's 'occupation' of South West Africa and proclaiming that it 'shall henceforth be known as Namibia'); and SC Res. 284 (29 July 1970). After the Court's advisory opinion, a consistent stream of UN resolutions referred specifically to South Africa's 'illegal occupation' of Namibia. See, e.g., SC Res. 301 (20 Oct. 1971); SC Res. 366 (17 Dec. 1974); SC Res. 385 (30 Jan. 1976); GA Res. 2871 (XXVI) (20 Dec. 1971); GA Res. 41/39 (20 Nov. 1986); and SC Res. 601 (30 Oct. 1987).

[9] *ICJ Reports* (1971), 55.

[10] See, e.g., GA Res. 2871.

The occupation of Namibia also raised the question of the legitimacy of resistance movements. This old and difficult question in the laws of war received in this case a simple answer. The General Assembly consistently supported the legitimacy of the armed struggle of the South West Africa People's Organization.[11] So, notably, did Vice-President Ammoun in his separate opinion to the 1971 ICJ judgment on Namibia.[12]

Some Other Recent Cases of Prolonged Occupation

The presence of Turkish forces in northern Cyprus since the invasion of 20 July, 1974, has been viewed in some resolutions of the UN General Assembly as an occupation.[13]

The presence of Moroccan forces in Western Sahara since they intervened in December 1975 and January 1976 has similarly been viewed in some resolutions of the General Assembly as an occupation.[14]

The presence of Vietnamese forces in Kampuchea following the invasion of 27 December 1978, was also seen in some General Assembly resolutions as an occupation.[15]

Many other situations quite widely viewed as occupations could be cited. For example, the intervention of Soviet forces in Afghanistan from December 1979 was called an occupation by many governments.[16]

The idea that 'prolonged occupation' is a special category of occupation should be set in the proper context, namely, that there are many different types of occupation: the present writer has tentatively suggested seventeen types—a listing that is far from exhaustive. Neither the law as laid down in international conventions nor state practice justifies the restrictive approach of viewing the law on occupations as applying only to the classic case of belligerent occupation, in which one belligerent occupies the territory of another belligerent during an armed conflict. The law on occupations has in fact been applied to a wider range of cases than this: it is properly viewed as being formally applicable to, and capable of being applied in, many types of

---

[11] See, e.g., ibid.; GA Res. 2403 (XXIII) (16 Dec. 1968); and GA Res. S-14/1 (20 Sept. 1986).
[12] *ICJ Reports* (1971), 70.
[13] See GA Res. 33/15 (9 Nov. 1978); GA Res. 34/30 (20 Nov. 1979); and GA Res. 37/253 (13 May 1983). In subsequent years, the question of Cyprus has been deferred by the UNGA.
[14] GA Res. 34/37 (21 Nov. 1979); and GA Res. 35/19 (11 Nov. 1980). Subsequent resolutions do not use the term 'occupation' but do reaffirm the need for self-determination.
[15] GA Res. 37/6 (28 Oct. 1982); and GA Res. 40/7 (5 Nov. 1985).
[16] See, e.g., British statement of 13 July 1982, quoted in *BYIL* 53 (1982), 352.

occupation—and, indeed, many situations to which the opprobrious term 'occupation' is not actually attached. It contains some notable elements of flexibility.[17]

While the frequent occurrence of long occupations is beyond dispute, there are some grounds for doubt about the value of regarding them as constituting a special category. The danger in making such a suggestion is that it may seem to imply the further suggestion that those parts of the laws of war that deal with military occupations may not be fully applicable, and that departures from the law may be permissible. These conclusions would pose problems, especially if the applicability of major conventions were put in doubt, if the criteria for permitting departures from the law were vague and subjective, or if it were unclear what bodies have authority to suggest or make departures. However, it may be that departing from occupation law is not the only legal issue to be faced. There may also be some scope for variations within the framework established by existing international law. The laws of war treaties that govern occupations contain some scope for variations.

Further, in a prolonged occupation the applicability of other bodies of law—including the international law of human rights—assumes special importance.

While there may be some dangers in regarding 'prolonged occupation' as a special category, there are also very good reasons for doing so. At present, there is a distinct risk that the law on occupations, if not adapted to special problems arising in a prolonged occupation, could be used or abused in such a way as to contribute to leaving a society politically and economically undeveloped. During a long occupation, many practical problems may arise that do not admit of mere temporary solutions based on the idea of preserving the status quo ante: decisions may have to be taken about such matters as road construction, higher education, water use, electricity generation, and integration into changing international markets. Such decisions, although they involve radical and lasting change, cannot be postponed indefinitely. Nor can the setting up of political institutions be postponed indefinitely without creating the theoretical possibility (and in the West Bank and Gaza it is more than theoretical) that the law on occupations could be so used as to have the effect of leaving a whole

---

[17] Occupations that have differed in some respects from the classic case of a belligerent occupation include that of the Rhineland after 1918, the Franco-Belgian occupation of the Ruhr in 1923–5, the German occupation of Bohemia and Moravia from March 1939, and Namibia since 1971. In these cases, certain courts and tribunals have accepted the use of the term 'occupation' and the applicability of international rules, including, e.g., the Hague Regulations (A. Roberts, 'What is a Military Occupation?', BYIL 55 (1984) 249, 275, 278, 291–2).

population in legal and political limbo: neither entitled to citizenship of the occupying state, nor able to exercise any other political rights except of the most rudimentary character. If there is any risk at all that the law on occupations might provide, paradoxically, the basis for a kind of discrimination that might bear comparison with apartheid, the causes of that risk need to be identified, and possible solutions explored.

The category of prolonged occupation overlaps in certain respects with another category—peacetime occupation. Some writers have taken the view that in peacetime occupations the rights accruing to an occupant may be more limited than in the classic case of belligerent occupation. Thus, F. Llewellyn Jones wrote in 1924:

In the case of pacific occupation it is clear that the rights of the occupant are very much curtailed as compared with those of a belligerent occupant. In the latter case the occupant is an enemy, and has to protect himself against attack on the part of the forces of the occupied State, and he is justified in adopting measures which would justly be considered unwarranted in the case of pacific occupation... Belligerent military occupation is now largely regulated by the provisions of the Hague Convention, 1907, and obviously a pacific military occupant can have no powers more extensive than those laid down in the Articles of this Convention.[18]

Following this general approach, it could be argued that in a prolonged occupation, as in a pacific one, the rights of the occupants are vastly curtailed. This conclusion is very persuasive; and it conforms with the approach adopted in the Fourth Geneva Convention, discussed in the next part. However, this conclusion can hardly follow automatically in all cases, or on all issues. For example, if there is extensive and violent opposition to the occupation, or a general terrorist threat to the nationals of the occupying power, there may be a situation somewhat akin to war, in which the prolongation of certain emergency measures can be justified.

In a prolonged occupation there may be strong reasons for recognizing the powers of an occupant in certain specific respects—for example, because there is a need to make drastic and permanent changes in the economy or the system of government. At the same time, there may be strong reasons for limiting the occupant's powers in other respects. An examination of past occupations suggests that any variations in the rules may have a more complex and multifaceted character than simply the curtailment of the rights of one party or another.

---

[18] F. Llewllyn Jones, 'Military Occupation of Alien Territory in Time of Peace', *Trans. of the Grotius Society* 9 (1924) 149, 159–60. See also Roberts, 'What is a Military Occupation?', 273–9.

III. Prolonged Occupations in the Principal Conventions

The following are the main conventions that set out rules relating to the conduct of military occupations. All of them entered into force within 1–3 years of the date of signature.

The Fourth 1907 Hague Convention has 37 states parties.[19] Whether or not a state is a party to this Convention is of limited significance, because the annexed Hague Regulations have since at least 1946 been widely and authoritatively viewed as embodying customary international law.[20]

The Fourth 1949 Geneva Convention (like the other three 1949 Geneva Conventions) has 165 states parties.[21] This remarkably high number is one of several factors that have strengthened arguments that the Conventions are, in whole or in substantial part, declaratory of customary international law.[22]

The 1954 Hague Cultural Property Convention has 75 states parties: 63 of these are also bound by the 1954 Hague Protocol.[23] Various important powers—including China, Japan, the United Kingdom, and the United States—are not yet formally bound by this Convention.

The 1977 Geneva Protocol I has 76 states parties.[24] Several important powers—including France, India, Indonesia, Japan, the United Kingdom, and the United States—are not formally bound by this

---

[19] Also, 18 out of the 48 states parties formally bound by the very similar terms of the second 1899 Hague Convention did not become parties to the 1907 agreement (Convention with respect to the Laws and Customs of War on Land, 29 July 1899, 32 Stat. 1803, TS No. 403). Most of the provisions of the regulations annexed to these two Conventions are identical.

Information about states parties to the second 1899 Convention and the fourth 1907 Convention supplied by the depositary (the Netherlands Ministry of Foreign Affairs), and valid as of 1 July 1988. See Roberts and Guelff, *Documents on the Laws of War*, 44 and 58–9.

In addition, some states became bound by these two Hague Conventions through general declarations of succession to treaties (e.g. at the time of independence), even if they have not so notified the depositary.

[20] For the leading judgment to this effect, see *Trial of the Major War Criminals before the International Military Tribunal*, Nuremberg 22 (1948), 497.

[21] Information about states parties to the four 1949 Geneva Conventions supplied by the depositary (the Swiss Federal Department for Foreign Affairs), and valid as of 1 July 1988. See Roberts and Guelff, *Documents on the Laws of War*, 326–31.

[22] For an excellent discussion, see T. Meron, 'The Geneva Conventions as Customary Law', *AJIL* 81 (1987), 348.

[23] Convention and Protocol for the Protection of Cultural Property in the Event of Armed Conflict, 14 May 1954, 249 UNTS 240. Information about states parties supplied by the depositary (UNESCO), and valid as of 1 July 1988. See Roberts & Guelff, *Documents on the Laws of War*, 367–70.

[24] Protocol Additional to the Geneva Conventions of 12 Aug. 1949, and Relating to the Protection of Victims of International Armed Conflicts (Protocol I), opened for signature 12 Dec. 1977, 1125 UNTS 3. Information about states parties supplied by the depositary (the Swiss Federal Department for Foreign Affairs), and valid as of 1 July 1988. See Roberts & Guelff, *Documents on the Laws of War*, 459–62.

Protocol. However, some of its provisions are viewed as embodying customary law; and other provisions may be viewed, even by non-parties, as meriting inclusion in the rules governing their military operations.[25]

In none of the above agreements is any formal limit set on the duration of an occupation. Inasmuch as the subject of duration is addressed at all, it is more in writings and judgments than in conventions.[26] Meir Shamgar is correct in saying:

According to International Law the exercise of the right of military administration over the territory and its inhabitants had no time-limit, because it reflected a factual situation and pending an alternative political or military solution this system of government could, from the legal point of view, continue indefinitely. Military government does not derogate from the potential rights of either party but represents a minimum standard imposed by the Law of Nations and is co-extensive in time and space to the effective rule of the military.[27]

This is certainly a good starting point for considering the whole question of prolonged occupation. The proposition that the basic rules codified in the law on occupations must continue to be observed for as long as the occupation lasts is a useful compass-bearing to guide one through this difficult subject.

The 'One Year After' Provision of 1949

While the condition of military occupation (or, more euphemistically, 'military administration') may continue indefinitely, there is, or used to be, one formal provision for variation of the rules on the grounds of duration. This was Article 6, paragraph 3 of the Fourth 1949 Geneva Convention:

In the case of occupied territory, the application of the present Convention shall cease one year after the general close of military operations; however, the Occupying Power shall be bound, for the duration of the occupation, to the extent that such Power exercises the functions of government in such territory,

[25] See e.g. President Reagan's Letter of Transmittal of Protocol II to the US Senate, S. Treaty Doc. No. 2, 100th Cong., 1st Sess., at III (1987).

[26] Although a great deal of published writing has some bearing on the subject, very few papers or articles have been specifically devoted to prolonged occupation either in general or in the Arab–Israeli context. There have not been any such articles in some of the journals where they might have been expected, e.g., the *Israel Yearbook on Human Rights*, the *Revue Égyptienne de droit international* and the *Palestine Yearbook of International Law*.

[27] M. Shamgar, 'Legal Concepts and Problems of the Israeli Military Government—the Initial Stage', in Shamgar (ed.), *Military Government in the Territories Administered by Israel 1967–1980*, 1: *The Legal Aspects* (Jerusalem, 1982), 13, 43. For statements on the same issue in Supreme Court judgments, see text at nn. 154 and 155 below.

by the provisions of the following Articles of the present Convention: 1 to 12, 27, 29 to 34, 47, 49, 51, 52, 53, 59, 61 to 77, 143.

These provisions represent one attempt to address the issue of prolonged occupation. However, they are of little importance, for four main reasons.

First, Article 6, paragraph 3 has featured very little in legal analyses of prolonged occupations in the past 40 years; and the Israeli authorities have never invoked it as a means of reducing their obligations.[28]

Second, in particular cases, including the Israeli-occupied territories, there might be scope for debate about whether, or when, there was, in the words of Article 6, a 'general close of military operations'.[29] The renewed outbreak of international war in 1973 has been only one of several events that might have given rise to the argument that, even if military operations had earlier been viewed as closed, they had now reopened and, in consequence, the Fourth 1949 Geneva Convention was again applicable *in toto*.

Third, even if Article 6, paragraph 3 were invoked, many important provisions of the Convention would remain in force. The burden of the article is that from one year after the general close of military operations an occupying power is only obliged to observe 43 of the 159 articles of the Convention. However, these 43 do include no less than 23 of the 32 articles of that part of the Convention—section III—which deals most specifically with occupied territories. The 43 articles are important, covering as they do such matters as the humane treatment of protected persons.

In section III (Articles 47–78), the nine articles by which the occupying power would cease to be bound in a long occupation are 48 (dealing with foreign nationals in occupied territory), 50 (care and education of children), 54 (status of public officials and judges), 55 (food and medical supplies of the population), 56 (medical and hospital services), 57 (requisitioning of civilian hospitals), 58 (ministers of religion and articles for religious needs), 60 (relief consignments), and 78 (assigned residence and internment). The contents of these articles suggest that the framers of the 1949 Geneva Conventions may

---

[28] E. R. Cohen, *Human Rights in the Israeli-Occupied Territories 1967–1982* (Manchester, 1985), 51. Cohen also reports the opinion of Shabtai Rosenne, a legal adviser to the Israeli foreign ministry, given in a 1977 interview, that: '[T]he period of one year after the general cessation of hostilities set by the framers of Article 6 was arbitrary. While not admitting to the applicability of the Convention to the Israeli-occupied territories, he felt that all the humanitarian provisions of the Convention, and not just those provided in Article 6, should be applied *de facto*.' (Ibid. 62 n. 103.)

[29] For an analysis written in 1969 or 1970 claiming that there had been no 'general close of military operations' and that the Geneva Convention therefore remained fully applicable, see M. B. W. Hammad, 'The Culprit, the Targets and the Victims', in J. N. Moore (ed.), *The Arab–Israeli Conflict: Readings and Documents* (Princeton, 1974), 2, 366.

have optimistically assumed that, in the course of time, the rigours of occupation would gradually ease, and more and more responsibilities would be handed over to the institutions of the occupied territory.

The records of the 1949 Diplomatic Conference confirm this assumption. They show that the 'one year after' provision in Article 6 was the subject of much debate.[30] In his *Commentary*, Jean Pictet states that in drawing up this provision, 'the delegates naturally had in mind the cases of Germany and Japan'. He goes on to defend the provision on the grounds that 'if the Occupying Power is victorious, the occupation may last more than a year, but as hostilities have ceased, stringent measures against the civilian population will no longer be justified.'[31]

The final reason for doubting the importance of the provisions of Article 6, paragraph 3 of the Fourth Geneva Convention is that Article 3(b) of Additional Protocol I effectively abrogates the 'one year after' provision—at least so far as the parties to the Protocol are concerned. It states that 'the application of the Conventions and of this Protocol shall cease . . . in the case of occupied territories, on the termination of the occupation'. Bothe, Partsch, and Solf say of this abrogation:

Article 6(3) of the Fourth Convention . . . was a special *ad hoc* provision for certain actual cases, namely the occupation of Germany and Japan after World War II. There is no reason to continue to keep in force such provisions designed for specific historic cases. In 1972 the majority of government experts expressed a wish to abolish these time limits.[32]

The abrogation of the 'one year after' rule may reflect in part the proper desire of the international community to maintain the applicability of the law to occupations in general, and to areas occupied by Israel since 1967 in particular. However, the abandonment of Article 6, paragraph 3 has had little practical relevance to the Israeli-occupied territories. This was more because of the factor already mentioned (these provisions of Article 6 were not invoked by Israel anyway) than because of the more legalistic point that Israel has neither signed nor ratified Protocol I.

In general, the 'one year after' provision of 1949 must be viewed as a legal oddity. It may have correctly identified a problem—that the rules

---

[30] See, e.g., *Final Record of the Diplomatic Conference of Geneva of 1949*, 2A, 623–5.

[31] Pictet, *Commentary*, 62–3. In addition, Pictet suggests that where there has been no military resistance, no state of war, and no armed conflict, the Convention will remain fully applicable as long as the occupation lasts. However, it is far from clear (*a*) whether this was the intention of the negotiators; and (*b*) what the logic is in treating such occupations differently.

[32] M. Bothe, K. Partsch, and W. Solf, *New Rules for Victims of Armed Conflicts* (The Hague, 1982), 59, also 57. See also Y. Sandoz, C. Swinarski, and B. Zimmermann (eds.), *Commentary on the Additional Protocols of 8 June 1977 to the Geneva Conventions of 12 August 1949* (Geneva, 1987), 68.

designed for belligerent occupation during a war may require some modification in a prolonged occupation—but the solution it proposed was not equally appropriate to all occupations, and it has not commended itself greatly to military administrators, inhabitants of occupied territories, or international lawyers.

Other Possibilities of Variations

The main conventions relating to military occupations do not provide for any other variation in the rules specifically because of the length of an occupation. This omission does not mean that the conventions are inflexible or cumbersome on this matter. Rather, they contain a modest number of rules, intended primarily to prevent repetition of the worst excesses of previous occupation regimes. They do not govern all aspects of life, and their provisions leave substantial room for different policies, practices, and administrative systems. There are in fact many general possibilities for variations, and these could be germane in a prolonged occupation, as well as in other cases.

The scope for variation within the existing conventions is illustrated by the matter of the occupant's structure of authority, which can assume many different forms. The 1907 Hague Regulations refer variously to 'the hostile army', 'the occupant', 'a commander-in-chief', 'the commander in the locality occupied', 'an army of occupation', and 'the occupying State' as the bodies or individuals that exercise authority in occupied territory.[33] The Fourth Geneva Convention, which refers throughout to the 'Occupying Power' as the body with authority in occupied territory, says nothing about the precise administrative form of the occupation regime. Protocol I is identical in this regard. There is widespread agreement that the occupying power has substantial discretion as to whether it operates through a military or a civil administration, and whether through an imposed administrative system or indigenous authorities.[34]

---

[33] 1907 Hague Regulations, (see n. 4 above), Arts. 42, 43, 48, 49, 51, 52, 53, and 55.

[34] In *KNAC v. State of the Netherlands*, 16 Ann. Dig. 468 (Dist. Ct., The Hague, 1949), the Court said: 'Though the regime envisaged by the Hague Regulations for occupied territory comprised a military administration with civil departments subordinate to it, the setting up by the Occupant of a separate civil administration to control the existing civil administration left functioning, was not forbidden and must, on the contrary, be held to be a permissible complement of the maintenance of the latter administration in office.'

In HC 593/82, the *Ansar Prison* case, the Israeli Supreme Court said, apropos of Israel's occupation of parts of Lebanon: '[T]he application of the third chapter of the Hague Rules or of the parallel instructions in the Fourth [Geneva] Convention are not conditioned upon the establishment of a special organizational framework in the form of a Military Government.' For extracts and a short summary of this leading judgment, see *IYHR* 13 (1983), 360.

Some possibilities of variations are also evident in the rules on taxation. The Hague Regulations state in Article 48:

If, in the territory occupied, the occupant collects the taxes, dues, and tolls imposed for the benefit of the State, he shall do so, as far as is possible, in accordance with the rules of assessment and incidence in force, and shall in consequence be bound to defray the expenses of the administration of the occupied territory to the same extent as the legitimate Government was so bound.

Commenting on this article, Ernst Feilchenfeld says:

The provision would not seem to exclude, as has been asserted, taxation increases, particularly such changes as have been made desirable through war conditions or, in the case of an extended occupation, general changes in economic conditions . . .

[I]f the occupation lasts through several years the lawful sovereign would, in the normal course of events, have found it necessary to modify tax legislation. A complete disregard of these realities may well interfere with the welfare of the country and ultimately with 'public order and safety' as understood in Article 43.[35]

Special agreements between the high contracting parties are allowed for in the Fourth Geneva Convention. Such agreements can be about practically any matter, as long as the principle spelled out in Article 7, paragraph 1 is observed: 'No special agreements shall adversely affect the situation of protected persons, as defined by the present Convention, nor restrict the rights which it confers upon them.' In section III (on occupied territories), Article 47 further specifies that protected persons shall not be deprived of the benefits of the Convention 'by any agreement concluded between the authorities of the occupied territories and the Occupying Power'.

IV. The Israeli-Occupied Territories

In the wake of the June 1967 war, Israel was in control of the following territories:

The West Bank. This is the area, previously under Jordanian rule, that

---

On various possible forms of administrative structure under occupation, see *US Field Manual*, 10, 139, and 141; and *British Manual*, at 145. For an indication that there are limits to the constitutional changes an occupying power may bring about, see Pictet, *Commentary*, at 273.

On administration of occupied territories generally and of the West Bank in particular, see also Chs. 7 and 8 in this volume.

[35] E. H. Feilchenfeld, *The International Economic Law of Belligerent Occupation* (Washington, 1942). On taxation generally and in the Israeli-occupied territories see Chs. 11 and 12 in this volume.

lies between the River Jordan and Israel proper (i.e., Israel in its pre-1967 borders). On 17 December 1967, the Israeli military government issued an order stating that 'the term "the Judea and Samaria Region" shall be identical in meaning for all purposes . . . to the term "the West Bank Region".' This change in terminology, which has been followed in Israeli official statements since that time, reflected a historic attachment to these areas and rejection of a name that was seen as implying Jordanian sovereignty over them.[36] The 1978 Camp David accords, signed by Egypt and Israel, contained extensive provisions for a 'self-governing authority' in the West Bank and Gaza: these provisions—heavily criticized by Arab governments, by the leadership of the Palestine Liberation Organization (PLO), and by the residents of the territories—were never implemented.[37]

The Gaza Strip. This area was administered from 1948 to 1967 by Egypt, which did not claim sovereignty over it. Israeli official statements generally refer to it as 'the Gaza Region'. Gaza was mentioned both in the 1978 Camp David accords and in the 1979 Israel–Egypt Treaty of Peace (see below).

East Jerusalem. This area, previously part of the West Bank, came under Israeli law, with extended boundaries, on 28 June 1967, and was formally annexed on 30 July 1980.[38]

The Golan Heights. This area, part of Syria, has been under Israeli control since 1967. In the 1973 Middle East war, Israel gained additional Syrian territory in the area. Following the 1974 Israeli–Syrian disengagement agreement, Israel withdrew from all this additional territory, and also from some areas occupied in the 1967 war, including the devastated town of Quneitra.[39] Israeli law was extended to the Golan Heights on 14 December 1981.[40]

The Sinai Peninsula. This area, part of Egypt, came under Israeli control in 1967. For administrative purposes, the Israeli authorities divided it into two military government units: Northern Sinai (which was comparatively more inhabited), and Central and Southern Sinai

---

[36] A. Rubinstein, 'The Changing Status of the "Territories" (West Bank and Gaza): From Escrow to Legal Mongrel', *Tel Aviv University Law Review* 8 (1988), 61.

[37] Camp David Agreements, 17 Sept. 1978, Egypt–Israel–United States, *ILM* 17 (1978), 1466.

[38] The enabling legislation for the extension of Israeli law and of municipal boundaries was the Municipalities Ordinance (Amendment No. 6) Law, 27 June 1967, *Laws of the State of Israel* 21 (1967), 75. The act of annexation was the Basic Law: Jerusalem, Capital of Israel, 30 July 1980, *Id.* (1980), at 209. For a succinct Israeli exposition, see Y. Blum, *The Juridical Status of Jerusalem*, Jerusalem Papers on Peace Problems No. 2, Hebrew University (1974).

[39] Agreement on Disengagement between Israeli and Syrian Forces, 31 May and 5 June 1974, *ILM* 13 (1974), 880. The Israeli military withdrawal to the new lines was completed by 26 June 1974.

[40] Golan Heights Law, 14 Dec. 1981, *Laws of the State of Israel* 36 (1982), 7.

(containing only a sparse Bedouin population). Israel withdrew progressively from Sinai—initially under two partial disengagement agreements, concluded in 1974 and 1975;[41] and then under the 1979 Peace Treaty, which laid down a timetable for phased total Israeli withdrawal, completed on 25 April 1982.[42]

Although East Jerusalem and the Golan Heights have been brought directly under Israeli law, by acts that amount to annexation, both of these areas continue to be viewed by the international community as occupied, and their status as regards the applicability of international rules is in most respects identical to that of the West Bank and Gaza.[43]

In addition to the above territories, Israel briefly occupied parts of southern Lebanon during the Litani operation of March–June 1978. It occupied larger areas of Lebanon following the invasion of June 1982, and has maintained a security zone in the south since its withdrawal from the rest of the country in 1985. Although Israel has not established a formal military-administrative system in Lebanon along the same lines as in other areas, its position has been properly viewed as that of an occupant.[44]

For the most part, the Israeli occupation of territories since 1967 does belie the assumption that occupation is temporary. However, this brief listing shows that prolonged occupation does not necessarily mean permanent control: at least some areas, Sinai and part of the Golan, were returned (to Egypt and Syria, respectively) after long spells under Israeli control.

---

[41] Agreement on Disengagement of Forces in Pursuance of the Geneva Peace Conference, 18 Jan. 1974, Egypt–Israel, *ILM* 13 (1974), 23, which provided for the withdrawal of all Israeli forces from the areas they had held west of the Suez Canal since the cease-fire at the end of the 1973 war, and for an Israeli pullback east of the canal to the area covered by the Mitla and Giddi Passes; and Agreement on the Sinai and Suez Canal, Egypt–Israel, 4 Sept. 1975, and various associated agreements, *ILM* 14 (1975), 1450, which provided for an Israeli withdrawal from a further 2,500 square miles of occupied Egyptian territory in Sinai, including the oilfields at Ras Sudar and Abu Rudeis, in return for certain Egyptian political undertakings, and on the basis of major pledges and commitments by the United States. Full implementation of the latter agreement was completed on 22 Feb. 1976.

On the background, content and implementation of these agreements, and the role of the United States and United Nations, see *Keesing's Contemporary Archives*, 26,317, 27,429, and 28,381 (1974, 1975, and 1977).

[42] Treaty of Peace, 26 Mar. 1979, Egypt–Israel, *ILM* 18 (1979), 362. Article II stated: 'The permanent boundary between Egypt and Israel is the recognized international boundary between Egypt and the former mandated territory of Palestine... without prejudice to the issue of the status of the Gaza Strip.'

[43] See, e.g., UNGA and SC resolutions, nn. 71, 77–9 and 133 below. The Israeli laws on the status of East Jerusalem and the Golan Heights do not use the word 'annexation' and do not extend Israeli citizenship to the local population.

[44] It was so viewed by the Israeli Supreme Court in the *Ansar Prison* case (see n. 34), *IYHR* 13 (1983), 362–3. A question in the Knesset on 23 Mar. 1983 yielded the answer that the provisions of the Fourth Geneva Convention were applied in Lebanon 'on humanitarian grounds', implying that the Convention was not viewed as formally applicable (Rubinstein, 'The Changing Status of the "Territories"', 63).

A full political analysis of the reasons for the exceptional length of this occupation is beyond the scope of this chapter. The problems of ethnicity and nationhood in the Middle East, which are thrown into such sharp relief in the Occupied Territories, have deep historical roots. The outside powers involved in the area in the past, including Britain, did not resolve these problems and may have made them worse. Throughout this century, most attempts to achieve a negotiated settlement of Jewish–Arab tensions in the Middle East have failed. Since 1967, Israel has maintained its occupation for a mixture of reasons that have included understandable security concerns, religious-fundamentalist expansionism, and inertia. The situation was made more difficult to the extent (which is a matter of debate) that the PLO, Arab states, and/or Israel failed to come forward with credible proposals for the future of the Occupied Territories. Such proposals necessarily involve grasping many extremely painful nettles: acceptance of the existence of Israel; the creation of a Palestinian state that might be radical, or unstable, or both; and possible conflict within Arab states, or between them, if the Palestinian cause or the PLO leadership is alleged to have been 'betrayed' in a diplomatic compromise. Numerous other real or presumed obstacles to political settlement could be cited: various aspects of PLO, and Israeli, activities and pronouncements; and Israel's refusal to engage in direct talks with the PLO. At the superpower level, there has been a long history of disagreement between the United States and the USSR on the nature of the Middle East conflict and possible means of its amelioration. In this, as in some other cases of prolonged occupation, there can be no assumption that apportionment of blame for the length of the occupation will be a productive exercise, or will yield simple answers.

The Israeli occupation since 1967 has contained many special features quite apart from its unusual duration. These features, which inevitably inform the discussion in this article, include (1) the undecided previous legal status of the West Bank and Gaza; (2) the dispute over whether the Palestinians constitute an appropriate unit of self-determination; (3) the persistence of a threat to Israel itself, and of various types of violent incidents, all of which have tended to erode neat distinctions between 'war' and 'peace'; and (4) the existence among Israelis of expansionist and annexationist ideas of various kinds, which call into doubt the very idea of Israel as having only a provisional role in the Occupied Territories.

V. Applicability of the Law on Occupations to the Israeli Occupation

To consider how the law may be interpreted or varied to take account of the prolonged character of a particular occupation, it is first necessary to survey, at least briefly, some of the main viewpoints on what laws of war rules have been viewed as applicable to that occupation anyway.

The facts about states parties to treaties are straightforward: the states most directly involved (Israel, Egypt, Jordan, and Syria) are formally bound by the principal international agreements governing occupations as follows:[45]

The Fourth 1907 Hague Convention. None of the states involved has ever been a formal party. However, in view of the customary law status of the Regulations annexed to the Convention, all are bound.

The four 1949 Geneva Conventions. Israel and Jordan ratified these agreements in 1951, Egypt in 1952, and Syria in 1953.

The 1954 Hague Cultural Property Convention, and Protocol. Egypt ratified both in 1955, Jordan both in 1957, and Syria both in 1958; Israel ratified the Convention in 1957, and registered its accession to the Protocol in 1958.

The 1977 Geneva Protocol I. Israel has not made any indication of adherence; Egypt has signed but not ratified; Jordan ratified in 1979; and Syria acceded in 1983.[46]

The Official Israeli View

Israeli positions on the applicability of international legal norms in the Occupied Territories are complex and occasionally misunderstood. There have been some variations over time, and in different fora. They have to be seen against the background of changing political views about the significance or otherwise of the 'green line' separating Israel proper from the land held since 1967; and official use of such terms as 'administered territories', rather than the blunter 'occupied territories'. The seminal legal statement remains that by Shamgar in 1971, which

---

[45] See nn. 19-24 for the sources of depositary information about the states parties to these agreements, their customary law status, and details of declarations, reservations, etc.

[46] Syria, at accession in November 1983, made a declaration that its accession to Protocol I in no way amounts to recognition of Israel or the establishment of any relations with it regarding the application of the Protocol.

In a note to the depositary, Israel objected to this declaration: '[T]he Geneva Conventions and Protocols are not the proper place for making such hostile political pronouncements, which are, moreover, in flagrant contradiction to the principles, objects and purposes of the Conventions and the Protocols.' The Syrian declaration 'cannot in any way affect whatever obligations are binding ... under general international law or under particular conventions.' As for the substance of the matter, Israel would adopt towards Syria 'an attitude of complete reciprocity', Roberts and Guelff, *Documents on the Laws of War*, 466-7.

first advanced the argument that the terms of an agreement whose *de jure* applicability might be in doubt could nevertheless be applied on a *de facto* basis.[47]

This principle applies particularly to the Fourth 1949 Geneva Convention. Since the end of the June 1967 war, Israel has never stated that the Convention is formally applicable in the Occupied Territories on a *de jure* basis. However, it has indicated, along the lines advanced by Shamgar in 1971, that it is willing to observe the 'humanitarian provisions' of this Convention.[48] For some years, Israel's voting on UN General Assembly resolutions reflected the view that the applicability of the Convention was an open question; but since 1977, it has voted against *de jure* applicability.[49]

As to the 1907 Hague Regulations, whose provisions are briefer and more general, the present position is simpler. Their applicability, whether on a *de facto* or a *de jure* basis, is widely accepted.[50] Esther Cohen has gone so far as to say that 'no problem arises in regard to the Hague Regulations. . . . The official Israeli position is that these Regulations are applicable to the Israeli-occupied territories.' She has indicated that the only real question about the applicability of the Regulations concerns areas (East Jerusalem and the Golan Heights) that Israel has in effect sought to annex.[51] However, in the late 1970s, some authoritative statements cast doubt on the formal applicability of the Hague Regulations.[52] Some Supreme Court judgments before 1979

---

[47] M. Shamgar, 'The Observance of International Law in the Administered Territories', *IYHR* 1 (1971), 262–77. This very influential article was first presented at a symposium at Tel Aviv University in 1971, when the author was Attorney-General.

[48] Ibid. 266; and Rubinstein, 'The Changing Status of the "Territories"', 63. The latter refers to Order No. 3 as evidence that immediately after the 1967 war it seemed clear that the Convention would apply to the territories. However, that proclamation was in fact issued during the war; and, as he notes, the section mentioning the Convention was repealed soon after the war.

[49] Resolutions on the applicability of the Fourth Geneva Convention on which Israel abstained: GA Res. 3092A (XXVIII) (7 Dec. 1973); GA Res. 3240B (XXIX) (29 Nov. 1974); and GA Res. 31/106B (16 Dec. 1976). Since 1977, Israel has always voted against the applicability of the Convention: see n. 78.

[50] See Shamgar, 'The Observance of International Law'; see also Shamgar, 'Legal Concepts and Problems', 48; E. Nathan, 'The Power of Supervision of the High Court of Justice over Military Government', in Shamgar (ed.), *Military Government*, 109, 129, 131–2, and 163–6. On the Preamble to the Hague Convention Nathan says: 'This language would appear to express the intention of the parties . . . that insofar as the Regulations embody norms of international law, these are binding as minimum standards of international law, even in situations not directly covered by the Regulations. Ibid., 132.

[51] Cohen, *Human Rights in the Israeli-Occupied Territories 1967–1982*, 43, 51, and 58, nn. 49 and 50.

[52] For elements of such doubt about the Fourth Hague Convention, see the Israeli Ministry of Foreign Affairs, Memorandum of Law (1 Aug. 1977), *ILM* 17 (1978) 432, 432–3 and 442 (on offshore oil exploration in the Gulf of Suez). See also n. 142 below and accompanying text.

avoided expressing a view on whether the Hague Convention applied to the administered areas.[53] Since the 1979 decision of the Supreme Court in the *Beit El* case, a more positive view about the applicability and justiciability of the Hague Regulations has prevailed, based largely on acceptance that they are part of customary law.[54]

Israel deserves credit for acknowledging openly, albeit inadequately, the relevance of international legal standards. Its position contrasts with those of the many occupying powers in the past 40 years that have avoided expressing any view on the applicability of international legal agreements: such powers have included the Soviet Union in Hungary (1956), Czechoslovakia (1968) and Afghanistan (1979); and South Africa in Namibia. Israel also deserves credit for co-operating with the International Committee of the Red Cross, which has played an important role in the Occupied Territories by performing a wide range of tasks, including, in particular, monitoring conditions of detention.[55]

Nevertheless, Israel's position regarding the Fourth Geneva Convention is unsatisfactory in several respects, and merits closer scrutiny. The scope of application of the Convention is stated in common Article 2, whose first two paragraphs read as follows:

In addition to the provisions which shall be implemented in peacetime, the present Conventions shall apply to all cases of declared war or of any other armed conflict which may arise between two or more of the High Contracting Parties, even if the state of war is not recognized by one of them.

The Convention shall also apply to all cases of partial or total occupation of the territory of a High Contracting Party, even if the said occupation meets with no armed resistance.

The publicly stated grounds for Israel's scepticism about the applicability of the Convention relate to the pre-1967 status of the West Bank and Gaza. Before 1967, Israel did not accept that these territories were part of Jordan and Egypt, respectively. The territories therefore could not be viewed as 'the territory of a High Contracting Party' within the meaning of the second paragraph of common Article 2; rather, they had been under Jordanian and Egyptian occupation. Israel expressed concern that by accepting the automatic application of the Convention,

---

[53] See n. 152 and accompanying text.
[54] See text at nn. 147–56. Though see also Qupty's chapter in this book for a caution as to the Supreme Court's future application of the Regulations and for further discussion of relevant cases.
[55] See the ICRC statement on the twentieth anniversary of the occupation, *ICRC Bulletin*, No. 137, June 1987, 1, noting that the ICRC has had free access to all the Occupied Territories, but listing a number of 'persistent violations' of the Fourth Geneva Convention.

it might appear to accord Jordan and Egypt the status of an ousted sovereign with reversionary rights.[56]

This Israeli interpretation is open to several serious objections. Four principal ones are:

1. It has sometimes been based on what appears to be a technical error. To refer to the terms of the *second* paragraph of common Article 2 is of limited relevance, because it is in fact the *first* paragraph that applies when a belligerent occupation begins during a war. As shown above, this paragraph says nothing about 'the territory of a High Contracting Party', referring simply to 'all cases of declared war or of any other armed conflict' arising between two or more of the high contracting parties.[57]

2. The Israeli interpretation was never relevant to those occupied territories (Sinai and the Golan) whose pre-1967 status was not disputed by Israel, which were therefore clearly 'the territory of a High Contracting Party'.

3. It has not been advanced consistently: similar objections could be, but seldom have been, made about the applicability of the Hague Regulations, which contain a similar assumption; namely, that occupied territory is 'territory of the hostile state'.

4. The Israeli position ignores or understates the precedents for viewing the laws of war, including the law on occupations, as being formally applicable even in cases that differ in some respect from the conditions of application spelled out in the Hague Regulations and the Geneva Conventions.[58]

In fact, Israel has got into a little-noted logical muddle on the applicability of the Hague and Geneva Conventions. Distinguished Israeli lawyers have asserted that the status of belligerent occupation is

---

[56] The clearest expositions of this Israeli view are in Y. Blum, 'The Missing Reversioner: Reflections on the Status of Judea and Samaria', IsLR 3 (1968), 279; Shamgar, 'Legal Concepts and Problems', 13–60; and C. Farhi, 'On the Legal Status of the Gaza Strip', in Shamgar (ed.), *Military Government*, 61–83.

Crown Prince Hassan Bin Talal of Jordan has denied that Jordan's position in the West Bank up to 1967 was that of occupant. He does not specify the precise status Jordan did have there. He argues that even if Jordan was a belligerent occupant up to 1967, it would not follow that Israel was free of legal limitations after 1967—especially in light of the provisions of the Geneva Convention. H. Bin Talal, *Palestinian Self-Determination: A Study of the West Bank and Gaza Strip* (New York, 1981), 67–8.

[57] For an authoritative Israeli statement relying on the second paragraph of common Art. 2, see Shamgar, 'The Observance of International Law', 262–77. See also his revised presentation (responding to the argument that the relevant paragraph is the first, not the second) in Shamgar, 'Legal Concepts and Problems', 37–40.

For a commentary on Art. 2, see Pictet, *Commentary*, 21, which leaves little room for doubt that it is the first paragraph that is relevant to the territories occupied by Israel in the 1967 war.

[58] See n. 17.

dependent on the continued existence of a state of war between two countries. As Yoram Dinstein put it in 1978: 'Belligerent occupation continues as long as the occupant remains in the area and war goes on. That is to say, it is terminated if the occupant withdraws from the area or the war comes to a close (either with the occupant's victory or his defeat).'[59] Likewise, the Supreme Court indicated in a judgment on 15 March 1979, that the application of the law was linked to a state of belligerency.[60] However, since the Israeli–Egyptian Peace Treaty of 25 March 1979, there has been no state of belligerency between Israel and Egypt. Thus, the Gaza Strip has even more certainly than before not been 'territory of the hostile state'. Yet Israel has continued to justify its powers and actions there with reference to the law of belligerent occupation, including the Hague Regulations.[61] This is reasonable; but it shows that Israel itself, when it chooses, is prepared to depart from its own strict legal logic about the circumstances in which the relevant rules and conventions are applicable.

Several Israeli writers have argued that whether the Fourth Geneva Convention is formally applicable or not is academic because of Israel's stated willingness to observe the 'humanitarian provisions'.[62] However, formal applicability versus *de facto* application is not always a distinction without a difference, for three main reasons. First, although the term 'humanitarian provisions' is often interpreted to mean all of the provisions, Israel has never definitively clarified this point by specifying which provisions it regards as humanitarian. Second, the rejection of formal applicability has frequently been referred to in Israeli court proceedings, and has in the past been one of several factors making the courts reluctant to base their decisions fairly and squarely on the Fourth Geneva Convention.[63] Third, the hint of *ex gratia* about Israel's application of the Convention could be construed

---

[59] Y. Dinstein, 'The International Law of Belligerent Occupation and Human Rights', *IYHR* 8 (1978), 105.

[60] Justice Witkon, judgment in HC 606/78 and 610/78, the *Beit El* case, translated in Shamgar (ed.), *Military Government*, at 371, 374: 'Each of us obviously knows of recent political developments that have occurred in our region, of the peace negotiations... We deal with the rights of the parties according to the existing situation prevailing between Israel and the Arab countries. This situation is one of belligerency, and the status of the respondents in respect of the occupied territory is that of an occupying power.' On the *Beit El* case, see also text at nn. 147–50 below.

For international views on this issue, see also Chs. 5 and 11 in this book.

[61] See Y. Dinstein, 'The Israel Supreme Court and the Law of Belligerent Occupation: Reunification of Families', *IYHR* 18 (1988), 173–4.

[62] See, e.g., H. H. Cohn, Foreword to the Israel National Section of the International Commission of Jurists, *The Rule of Law in the Areas Administered by Israel* (Tel Aviv, 1981), vii–viii; M. Benvenisti, *A Survey of Israel's Policies* (Washington, DC, 1984), 37; and Shamgar, 'Legal Concepts and Problems', 32–3 and 42–3.

[63] On the Supreme Court's position in this regard, see text at nn. 146–51.

as carrying an implication that it might unilaterally interpret, or eventually abrogate, its terms.

Israel's refusal to accept the full *de jure* applicability of the Fourth Geneva Convention has not proved persuasive. It has been criticized by many legal writers, including some in Israel itself;[64] and, as mentioned below, it has been decisively rejected by virtually all the members of the international community—at least if their votes in the United Nations are a guide.[65]

PLO Views

There has never been a full and authoritative exposition of PLO views on the international legal status of the territories occupied by Israel since 1967. The PLO has been in something of a quandary, principally because of the Organization's commitment in the 1968 Palestinian National Covenant: 'Palestine, with the boundaries it had during the British mandate, is an indivisible territorial unit.'[66] Consequently, for a long time the PLO was reluctant to draw clear legal distinctions between the lands controlled by Israel before and after June 1967. The fact that until 1984 the PLO had no specialized agencies concerned with legal aspects of the Palestine question contributed to the confusion.[67]

The PLO has sometimes advanced the view that Israel is an aggressor or illegal occupant, and as such has no rights over the inhabitants under international law. The concept of 'illegal occupation', and the related proposition that an illegal occupant has no rights, have precedents, not least in the writings of some Soviet and Polish lawyers about the Nazi occupations in World War II.[68] In 1970 a PLO Research

---

[64] For a reasoned account and criticism by a leading Israeli international lawyer, see Dinstein, 'The International Law of Belligerent Occupation and Human Rights', especially 106–8. See also Cohen, *Human Rights in the Israeli-Occupied Territories 1967–1982*, 51–6; and Rubinstein, 'The Changing Status of the "Territories"', 63–7. For a critical view by a British academic, see J. R. Gainsborough, *The Arab–Israeli Conflict: A Politico-Legal Analysis* (Aldershot, 1986), 159.

[65] See nn. 77–9 and accompanying text.

[66] Art. 2, the Palestinian National Covenant, adopted by the PLO at its National Congress in Cairo in July 1968. The boundaries of Palestine during the British Mandate (which ended in 1947) encompassed all of the territory of Israel in its 1949–67 frontiers, plus the Gaza Strip and the West Bank; they had also encompassed Jordan until 1922. For the text and exposition of Art. 2, including discussion of whether it involves a claim to Jordan, see Y. Harkabi, *The Palestinian Covenant and its Meaning* (London, 1979), 33–9 and 113.

[67] *PYIL* 2 (1985), 191.

[68] See especially I. P. Trainin, 'Questions of Guerrilla Warfare in the Law of War', trans. from Russian and reprinted in *AJIL* 40 (1946), 534, 535.

Center Publication took this line.[69] Likewise, in 1981 a PLO document submitted to UNESCO about Military Order 854 of 6 July 1980 (which sought to bring higher education in the Occupied Territories under Israeli control), challenged the right of the Israeli authorities to justify it 'on the basis of statements "under international law" made by foreign authors in completely different contexts . . . because the existing occupation . . . has been illegalized by the Community of Nations which unanimously requested putting an end to it on various occasions and in many resolutions'.[70]

What these Palestinian writers appear to be suggesting is not that the law on occupations is not applicable at all, but rather that Israel cannot claim any rights under that law. This argument is questionable on several grounds. First, it is debatable whether Israel was an 'aggressor' in 1967, or acted out of a basically defensive intent. There is also reason to doubt whether the occupation itself (as distinct from some of the actions by the occupying power) has been definitively considered illegal by the international community.[71] But these points pale into insignificance beside the cardinal principle that the laws of war, including the law on occupations, are widely viewed as applying equally to all states, whether aggressors or victims of aggression. Moreover, it seems strange to insist that Israel or any other country could be expected to carry out all its obligations under the conventions, without at the same time having certain rights, or at least being 'suffered' by international law to take certain actions.

This Palestinian view has not commanded any significant international support, and by no means all Palestinian writers on these

---

[69] F. Yahia, *The Palestine Question and International Law* (Beirut: PLO Research Center, 1970), 184.

[70] UNESCO Doc. 22 C/18 (30 Aug. 1983).

[71] The term 'illegal occupation' has been used sparingly in UN resolutions. As regards the Israeli-occupied territories, GA Res. 32/20 (25 Nov. 1977) expressed concern 'that the Arab territories occupied since 1967 have continued, for more than ten years, to be under illegal Israeli occupation'. The term was also used in GA Res. 33/29 (7 Dec. 1978). These resolutions were the exception rather than the rule. The voting figures for each resolution, showing countries for and against and abstentions (102–4–29 and 100–4–33, respectively), contain substantially fewer votes in favour than most UNGA resolutions criticizing the Israeli occupation attracted in those years.

Some resolutions have implied the illegality of the occupation *per se*, without actually using the term 'illegal occupation'.

However, the great majority of the numerous resolutions of the UN General Assembly and the Security Council on the Israeli occupation have not stated that it is illegal *per se*. They have deplored Israel's conduct of the occupation, have condemned as illegal the purported annexation of parts of the Occupied Territories (including Jerusalem), and have called upon Israel to put an end to its occupation of Arab territories—but have not stated that the fact of the occupation is in itself illegal. See, e.g., GA Res. 41/63 (3 Dec. 1986). The omission of the term 'illegal occupation' from most UN resolutions on the Arab–Israeli conflict is in sharp contrast to its repeated use in those on Namibia. See n. 8 above.

matters have subscribed to it.[72] In statements in the last few years, the PLO has not reiterated the view, and indeed may have retreated from it in changing its policy in the direction of gradual acceptance of the existence of Israel. However, there does not appear to have been a clear PLO statement formally renouncing this view.

The Idea of 'Trustee Occupation'

International laws and institutions, including the United Nations, have long recognized the reality that certain territories and peoples are not self-governing, and that outside powers can exercise certain trustee-like functions in such territories.[73] Could Israel's occupation be viewed as at least an analogous case?

The idea that Israel's occupation of the West Bank might be of a special kind termed 'trustee occupation' was advanced by Allan Gerson in 1973 and 1978.[74] His reasoning in support of this proposition was, briefly, as follows: Since Israel's rights to sovereignty over the West Bank are not superior to those of either Jordan or the indigenous population, Israel's status is that of occupant, not lawful sovereign. Yet the law of belligerent occupation imposes heavy constraints on the alteration of the political *status quo ante*—constraints that may be contrary to the interests of the inhabitants of the West Bank, as any momentum towards self-determination may be stifled. This reasoning reflects real concerns and points to a central problem in applying the law on occupations in these territories.

Nevertheless, there is doubt about the extent to which 'trustee occupation' can usefully be viewed as a distinct legal category. Gerson himself leaves some doubt about what body of law would apply in such a case. In fact, as noted above, under its common Article 2, the Fourth Geneva Convention is applicable to a wide range of occupations and not just to 'belligerent occupation' narrowly defined. Moreover, some idea of 'trusteeship' is implicit in all occupation law anyway. Finally, the central question, which has become even more difficult since Gerson wrote, is whether Israel could be viewed, either

---

[72] Palestinian works that appear to accept that the Occupied Territories are subject to the normal rules relating to occupations include R. Shehadeh, *Occupier's Law: Israel and the West Bank* (Washington, DC, 1985); and A. Kassim, 'Legal Systems and Developments in Palestine', *PYIL* 1 (1984), 19, 29–32. However, neither of these studies contains a sustained and concentrated discussion of what parts of international law are applicable in the Occupied Territories.

[73] See, for example, the provisions regarding non-self-governing territories, and also regarding the trusteeship system, in the UN Charter, Arts. 73–85.

[74] A. Gerson, 'Trustee-Occupant: The Legal Status of Israel's Presence in the West Bank', *HILJ* 14 (1973), 1; Gerson, *Israel, the West Bank and International Law* (London, 1978), 78–82.

by Palestinians or by the international community, as an appropriate trustee for Palestinian interests. However, he does frankly accept that Israel has not in fact assumed the role of 'trustee occupant'.[75]

The View of the International Community

The view that the Fourth Geneva Convention is applicable, and should be applied, in all the territories occupied by Israel since 1967 has been very widely held internationally. Indeed, a remarkable degree of unanimity prevails on this matter. Countless international organizations, both intergovernmental and non-governmental, have taken this view.[76] Within the UN General Assembly, it has been upheld from the beginning of the occupation.[77] Since 1973, Israel has completely lacked positive support in the voting on General Assembly resolutions on this specific issue.[78] Since the beginning of the occupation, the Security Council has also consistently urged the applicability of the Convention.[79]

---

[75] Ibid., 82.

[76] The ICRC has done so consistently. See ICRC, *Annual Reports* for 1968 and subsequent years; and its statement (n. 55 above).

[77] The first such resolution, urging in general terms respect for the principles contained in the Third and Fourth 1949 Geneva Conventions, was GA Res. 2252 (ES-V) (4 July 1967) (116-0-2) (the figures in parentheses are votes for, votes against, and abstentions).

In 1968 came the first of a stream of resolutions making specific comments about the Occupied Territories, and calling on Israel to comply with the Fourth Geneva Convention, as well as with various other agreements, including the 1948 Universal Declaration of Human Rights. See GA Res. 2443 (XXIII) (19 Dec. 1968) (60-22-37). Similar resolutions in the first five years of the occupation included GA Res. 2727 (XXV) (15 Dec. 1970) (52-20-43); and GA Res. 3005 (XXVII) (15 Dec. 1972) (63-10-49). The resolutions in this period attracted less support than the 1967 resolution cited above, and less than those from 1973 onwards mentioned in n. 78. There are many possible reasons for this: one that should not be overlooked is that in these years the resolutions tended to combine statements about what law was applicable with other, more contentious statements.

[78] See, e.g., the following resolutions (in all cases of a negative vote, i.e. from 1977 onwards, it is Israel's):

GA Res. 3092A (XXVIII)	(7 Dec. 1973)	(120-0-5)
GA Res. 3240B (XXIX)	(29 Nov. 1974)	(121-0-7)
GA Res. 32/5	(28 Oct. 1977)	(131-1-7)
GA Res. 35/122A	(11 Dec. 1980)	(141-1-1)
GA Res. 38/79B	(15 Dec. 1983)	(146-1-1)
GA Res. 41/63B	(3 Dec. 1986)	(145-1-6)

The United States voted for these resolutions in some years (1973, 1974, and 1980), and abstained in the others. However, the United States continued to state that it viewed the Convention as applicable. 'The United States recognizes Israel as an occupying power in all of these territories and therefore considers Israeli administration to be subject to the Hague Regulations of 1907 and the 1949 Fourth Geneva Convention concerning the protection of civilian populations under military occupation.' US Dept. of State, *Country Reports on Human Rights Practices for 1987* (1988), 100th Cong., 2d Sess., 1189.

[79] For example, SC Res. 237 (14 June 1967), adopted unanimously (four days after the cease-fire came into effect), recommended to the governments concerned 'the scrupulous

None of the various attempts to argue that Israel's occupation of foreign territory is such a special case that some of the normal provisions of the law on occupations do not apply to it has proved persuasive: indeed, all these attempts have been based, in varying degrees, on dubious interpretations of the body of conventional and customary law relating to occupations. The better view is that both the Fourth 1949 Geneva Convention and the 1907 Hague Regulations are applicable. However, serious problems remain: not only of getting their applicability accepted, and seeing that their basic provisions are applied, but also of relating the law to particular problems of prolonged occupation.

VI. Applicability of Human Rights Law

This is not the place to examine all the arguments concerning the applicability of the international law of human rights to military occupations generally.[80] Suffice it to say that (*a*) this question is but a part of the larger one of the applicability of multilateral conventions in occupied territories;[81] (*b*) the main impetus for UN action after 1945 to develop human rights law was the near-universal reaction against Nazi oppression in Germany and in German-occupied territories in World War II;[82] (*c*) the scope-of-application provisions of human rights accords do not exclude their applicability in principle, even if they do, as noted below, permit certain derogations in time of emergency; (4) the idea of 'respect for human rights in armed conflicts' has been stressed in numerous UN and other resolutions since at least the late 1960s;[83] and (5) in some decisions, international courts and tribunals

---

respect of the humanitarian principles governing the treatment of prisoners of war and the protection of civilian persons in time of war contained in the Geneva Conventions of 12 August 1949'.

SC Res. 446 (22 Mar. 1979), adopted by 12 votes to none, with 3 abstentions (Norway, UK, and USA), reaffirmed the applicability of the Fourth Geneva Convention, as well as opposing the establishment of Israeli settlements in the Occupied Territories.

SC Res. 605 (22 Dec. 1987) was strongly critical of Israeli conduct and reaffirmed that the Convention 'is applicable to the Palestinian and other Arab territories occupied by Israel since 1967, including Jerusalem'. This resolution was adopted by 14 votes to none, with one abstention (the USA). Two weeks later, SC Res. 607 (5 Jan. 1988), adopted unanimously, reaffirmed the applicability of the Convention.

[80] See A. Roberts, 'The Applicability of Human Rights Law During Military Occupations', 13 *Rev. Int. Stud.* (1987), 39. See also Chs. 9 and 16 in this volume.

[81] See Meron, 'Applicability of Multilateral Conventions to Occupied Territories', *AJIL* 72 (1978), 542, reprinted (with slight alterations) in Shamgar (ed.), *Military Government*, 217.

[82] W. Bishop, Jr., *International Law: Cases and Materials*, 3rd edn. (Boston, 1971), 470.

[83] See, for example, GA Res. 2444 (XXIII) (19 Dec. 1968) (adopted unanimously), which is on respect for human rights in armed conflicts generally; and the numerous UNGA resolutions urging respect for human rights in specific armed conflicts and occupations, including those on the Israeli-occupied territories cited in n. 90 below.

have affirmed the applicability of human rights law in occupied territories either implicitly (Namibia)[84] or explicitly (northern Cyprus).[85]

The more specific question of the applicability of human rights law in the Israeli-occupied territories has been extensively discussed.[86] Cohen has suggested that in a prolonged occupation certain human rights accords may provide a useful guide for an occupying power, and should therefore be followed as a matter of policy:

[T]he concept of human rights was taken into account in drafting the Geneva Conventions, including the Fourth Geneva Convention.

Nevertheless, the Fourth Convention was designed to protect the civilian population under an essentially temporary occupation. While the Convention remains applicable to a large extent during the prolonged belligerent occupation phase, it is insufficient to ensure adequate protection for the needs of the civilian population during that phase. Further protection is called for. It is submitted that the Universal Declaration and the International Covenants on Human Rights may be used to guide the belligerent occupant in the administration of the territory occupied, just as civilian governments may be guided by these laws in the administration of their own territories.

Thus, in certain areas not covered by the Convention, such as economic rights, which involve a certain dynamism and initiative in order to avoid the stagnation which would result in their violation, the concept of human rights can serve to breathe new life into an otherwise stalemated situation.[87]

The Israeli government has frequently indicated a sceptical attitude towards the applicability of human rights instruments. One official publication has implied that human rights are totally dependent on the existence of peace: it has cited Article 4 of the 1966 International Covenant on Civil and Political Rights selectively, conveniently omit-

---

[84] In its advisory opinion on Namibia, the ICJ may have had human rights law in mind (as well as the laws of war, often called international humanitarian law) when it pointed to the applicability of 'certain general conventions such as those of a humanitarian character'. *ICJ Reports* (1971), 46, 55, and 57.

[85] The ECHR ruled applications by the government of Cyprus in respect of the Turkish occupation admissible in *Cyprus v. Turkey*. See 1975 *Yb ECHR*, 82 (Nos. 6780/74 and 6950/75, Decision of 26 May 1975); and 1978 ibid. 100 (No. 8007/77, Decision of 10 July 1978). The European Convention for the Protection of Human Rights and Fundamental Freedoms, 4 Nov. 1950, 213 UNTS 221, Art. 1, states that the High Contracting Parties shall secure certain rights and freedoms to everyone 'within their jurisdiction'. The Commission found: '[T]his term is not equivalent to or limited to "within the national territory" of the High Contracting Party concerned ... [T]he High Contracting Parties are bound to secure the said rights and freedoms to all persons under their actual authority and responsibility, not only when that authority is exercised within their own territory but also when it is exercised abroad.' 1978 *Yb ECHR*, 230.

[86] See particularly T. Meron, 'The International Convention on the Elimination of All Forms of Racial Discrimination and the Golan Heights', *IYHR* 8 (1978) 222; and Meron, 'West Bank and Gaza: Human Rights and Humanitarian Law in the Period of Transition', *IYHR* 9 (1979), 106; see also Meron, 'Applicability of Multilateral Conventions to Occupied Territories'.

[87] Cohen, *Human Rights in the Israeli-Occupied Territories 1967–1982*, 29.

ting all reference to those clauses of the Article which spell out that certain general obligations, and certain specific provisions of the Covenant, continue to apply even in time of public emergency.[88]

A particularly clear exposition of the Israeli view on the applicability of human rights accords is contained in a memorandum prepared by the Office of the Legal Adviser in the Israeli Foreign Ministry in 1984. Written in response to an inquiry about the applicability of seven human rights accords, the memorandum asserts that Israeli policy in the West Bank and Gaza was in accord with the provisions of the 1950 Agreement on the Importation of Educational, Scientific, and Cultural Materials; the 1960 Convention against Discrimination in Education; and the 1966 International Convention on the Elimination of All Forms of Racial Discrimination. However, in respect of some other agreements (the 1948 Universal Declaration of Human Rights and the two 1966 International Covenants), the memorandum says:

> The unique political circumstances, as well as the emotional realities present in the areas concerned, which came under Israeli administration during the armed conflict in 1967, render the situation *sui generis*, and as such, clearly not a classical situation in which the normal components of 'human rights law' may be applied, as are applied in any standard, democratic system in the relationship between the 'citizen' and his government. Hence the criteria applied in the areas administered by Israel, in view of the *sui generis* situation, are those of 'humanitarian law', which balances the needs of humanity with the requirements of international law to administer the area whilst maintaining public order, safety, and security.[89]

This passage contains a serious argument, namely, that much human rights law is about the relations between the citizen and his own government and is therefore not necessarily appropriate to the rather different circumstance of occupation. Nevertheless, it is doubtful whether human rights law only applies in 'a classical situation', and the memorandum itself does not view all human rights law in this rather limited way. Its insistence that the relevant criteria are those of 'humanitarian law' (i.e. the Hague Regulations and the Geneva Conventions) seems evasive in view of the elements of ambiguity in Israel's attitude towards the applicability of the Fourth Geneva Convention.

A very strong case can be made for asserting the general applicability

---

[88] Ministry of Defence, Co-ordinator of Government Operations in Judea-Samaria and the Gaza District, *A Sixteen-year Survey (1967–1983)* (1983), 60. For the International Covenant on Civil and Political Rights, 16 Dec. 1966, see 999 UNTS 171. See also Ch. 2 in this book for a review of Israeli Supreme Court decisions on this issue.

[89] Office of the Legal Adviser, memorandum (12 Sept. 1984), written for, and contained in, A. Roberts, B. Joergensen, and F. Newman, *Academic Freedom under Israeli Military Occupation* (London, 1984), 80, 81.

of human rights standards to military occupations, but this does not solve many problems. The relevance of the international law of human rights to the prolonged Israeli occupation needs to be assessed in individual cases, taking the following points into account.

1. There are different views on the exact legal status of some international agreements relating to human rights, including the 1948 Universal Declaration, whose applicability in the occupied areas has been urged in numerous UN General Assembly resolutions.[90]

2. Fewer states are parties to the international conventions on human rights than to the Geneva Conventions. For example, in 1988, the four Geneva Conventions had 165 states parties, including all the states in the area; whereas the two International Human Rights Covenants had 92 and 87 parties, respectively. Egypt, Jordan, and Syria are parties to both Covenants. Israel has signed both but has not ratified them.[91]

3. Many human rights conventions permit derogations from some of their provisions, for example, in time of public emergency. Israel is obviously inclined to view its military occupation, especially in the context of continuing armed conflict or internal revolt, as constituting such an emergency.

4. Over a wide range of issues, the laws of war rules regarding military occupations, as laid down in the Hague Regulations and the Geneva Conventions, may offer more extensive, detailed, and relevant guidance than can the general human rights conventions;[92] and their supervisory machinery may be more appropriate to the circumstances.

5. On a few specific issues, there may be an element of conflict between the law on occupations and human rights law. For example,

---

[90] See, e.g., GA Res. 2443 (XXIII) (19 Dec. 1968); GA Res. 2546 (XXIV) (11 Dec. 1969); GA Res. 2727 (15 Dec. 1970); and the subsequent annual resolutions entitled 'Report of the Special Committee to Investigate Israeli Practices Affecting the Human Rights of the Population in the Occupied Territories'. For the Universal Declaration of Human Rights, see GA Res. 217A (III), UN Doc. A/810, 71 (1948).

[91] See n. 21 and accompanying text. For the Covenant on Civil and Political Rights, and the Covenant on Economic, Social, and Cultural Rights, GA Res. 2200 (16 Dec. 1966), see *Multilateral Treaties Deposited with the Secretary-General: Status as at 31 Dec. 1988*, at 120, 130, UN Doc. ST/LEG/SER.E/7 (1989).

Syria, at accession to the Covenants in April 1969, made a declaration to the same effect as that of its declaration on Protocol I (n. 46 above). In a note to the depositary in July 1969, Israel objected to this declaration.

[92] Possible overlap between human rights law and the laws of armed conflict was raised in *Cyprus v. Turkey* where, because of the applicability of the third Geneva Convention on prisoners of war, the European Commission of Human Rights did not find it 'necessary to examine the question of a breach of Article 5 of the European Convention on Human Rights with regard to persons accorded the status of prisoners of war'. See T. Meron, *Human Rights Law-Making in the United Nations* (Oxford, 1986), 212 n. 229 (quoting ECHR, Report on Applications Nos. 6780/74 and 6950/75 (*Cyprus v. Turkey*) 109 (1976, declassified in 1979)). See also n. 85 above.

Article 13(1) of the Universal Declaration says: 'Everyone has the right to freedom of movement and residence within the borders of each state.' Article 78, paragraph 1 of the Fourth Geneva Convention says: 'If the Occupying Power considers it necessary, for imperative reasons of security, to take safety measures concerning protected persons, it may, at the most, subject them to assigned residence or to internment.'

6. There are some issues (such as discrimination in employment, discrimination in education, and the import of educational materials) that are addressed in considerable detail in certain human rights agreements, and are not so addressed in the law on occupations. In respect of such issues, the application of international human rights standards is highly desirable.

7. Some human rights accords contain procedures for dealing with an issue, for example, enabling individuals to raise a matter directly with some outside institution, of a kind lacking in laws-of-war rules.

8. In the event that there is a significant change in status of the territories, with Israel and other states viewing the occupation phase as ending, the role of the law on occupations would probably be attenuated, and human rights law might be the principal body of international law to remain applicable.

VII. Views of the International Community

The Israeli occupation since 1967 has attracted a vast amount of international attention: from writers, including many in Israel and the Occupied Territories;[93] from non-governmental organizations, especially those concerned with law and human rights; and from governments. Governmental interest has been evident at several levels: neighbouring states, inter-Arab organizations, the non-aligned movement, the members of the European Communities, the two superpowers, and the United Nations system.

This high degree of international interest has many causes. Politically, the occupation has been an appropriate target for the prevailing values and rhetoric of anti-colonialism. The importance of the Middle East in power politics, and the key role of its oil resources, especially after 1973, has meant that the occupation could not be ignored. In any case, it is proper that there should be international concern about the effects of a prolonged occupation, particularly where there is a plain conflict of interest between occupier and occupied. Further, in com-

---

[93] Critical work in English from the Occupied Territories includes many publications of the Palestinian affiliate of the International Commission of Jurists, al-Haq/LSM, Ramallah; and Shehadeh, *Occupier's Law*, which summarizes a range of complaints against Israeli practices.

mon Article 1 of the four 1949 Geneva Conventions the states parties 'undertake to respect and to ensure respect for the present Convention in all circumstances'. An additional basis for international interest in the territories is the large number of refugees there who are entitled to, and do, receive international assistance.

The preoccupation of the United Nations with the Occupied Territories has been especially noteworthy, and controversial. Many aspects of UN involvement have attracted considerable, and often justified, critical comment—especially the work of the Special Committee to Investigate Israeli Practices.[94] Dinstein has written that 'Israel is averse to proposals that the legality of the measures taken by its military government in the Occupied Territories will be subjected to scrutiny by international organizations (especially the United Nations, which it regards as totally dominated by hostile countries).'[95] Persistent attempts in the 1980s to deprive Israel of the right to participate in various UN bodies, although unsuccessful, have not enhanced Israeli respect for the Organization.[96] The General Assembly's attitude to Israel has often been strident and denunciatory—most notably in the 1975 resolution equating Zionism with 'racism and racial discrimination'.[97] Phraseology in some General Assembly resolutions suggests that in occupations, as in war, the laws of war can easily get used for political propaganda. Such resolutions have probably had little effect

---

[94] The work of the Special Committee to Investigate Israeli Practices Affecting the Human Rights of the Population in the Occupied Territories has illustrated the political hazards that can attend efforts to evaluate Israeli actions by reference to international legal standards. Since it was set up in 1968, the committee has submitted annual reports, published by the United Nations. See, e.g., its 15th report, UN Doc. A/38/13 (1983). In the eyes of many Israelis, the committee was biased from the beginning and its reports one-sided. For a critical Israeli review, see D. Shefi, 'The Reports of the UN Special Committees on Israeli Practices in the Territories', in Shamgar (ed.), *Military Government*, 285. The committee's work may have reinforced two already existing tendencies in Israel: distrust of international organizations and reliance on unilateral, rather than multilateral, approaches.

For another critical view of the committee's work, see R. Z. Alderson, J. W. Curtis, R. J. Sutcliffe, and P. J. Travers, 'Protection of Human Rights in Israeli-Occupied Territories', *HILJ* 15 (1974), 470. They suggest that the General Assembly, through the committee and through its resolutions concerning rights in the Occupied Territories, has had little discernible effect other than to antagonize Israel and add another element of contention to the disputes between Israel and its neighbours (ibid. 481). They conclude that parties to the Fourth Geneva Convention need to perfect and reaffirm the enforcement procedures prescribed in that agreement. They cannot rely exclusively upon UN action to ensure conformity with its provisions. A consistent theme in UN pronouncements on the enforcement of the Convention has been that it is only the parties themselves which are, in the last analysis, in a position to implement the procedures and exert the pressures which will make the Convention work (ibid. 482).

[95] Dinstein, 'The Israel Supreme Court and the Law of Belligerent Occupation', 174.

[96] See M. Tabory, 'Universality at the UN: The Attempt to Reject Israel's Credentials', *IYHR* 18 (1988), 189.

[97] GA Res. 3379 (XXX) (10 Nov. 1975).

other than to strengthen Israel's sense of isolation and defiance of international opinion. However, many UN resolutions have spelled out important positions on fundamental legal questions. These include the resolutions, already noted, on the applicability of international law to this occupation[98] and other resolutions, mentioned below, on additional key aspects of the legal framework of a prolonged occupation.

The Status of Territory and Self-Determination

When a prolonged occupation occurs because of ancient rivalries and deep-seated territorial-cum-political disputes, there may well not be a *status quo ante* to which states can easily revert as part of a diplomatic settlement. Moreover, during a prolonged occupation the aspirations of the inhabitants, and of the international community, may change. Thus, questions are raised about the extent to which the ousted sovereign, who had control before the occupation, continues to have rights with respect to the territory; and whether the inhabitants of the occupied territory have a right of self-determination and, if so, how any such right may be recognized and exercised. While there cannot be absolute answers to these questions, the case of the West Bank and Gaza suggests some partial answers and points to the emergence of procedures for addressing them.

The international community has favoured self-determination in respect of several recent and contemporary occupations—for example, in Kampuchea, Namibia, and Western Sahara.[99] However, the case for self-determination has not been pressed where the occupied territory is widely accepted as being part of an existing state, from which it has been forcefully separated and to which it may be expected eventually to revert. A case in point is northern Cyprus: any act of self-determination there might well be seen as a threat to the sovereignty and territorial integrity of Cyprus, and as a victory for the Turkish invasion and occupation.

The idea of Palestinian self-determination, which has been extensively advanced since 1967, is not new. There are strong grounds for doubt whether the West Bank and Gaza were, before 1967, simply integral parts of Jordan and Egypt, respectively.[100] There was also, even before 1967, some evidence of a tendency to view the inhabitants of Palestine as a people, and as candidates for self-determination—

---

[98] See nn. 77–9 and accompanying text.
[99] See, e.g., GA Res. 36/5 (21 Oct. 1981); and GA Res. 43/19 (3 Nov. 1988) (both on Kampuchea); GA Res. 2403 (XXIII) (16 Dec. 1968); and GA Res. 43/26 (17 Nov. 1988) (both on Namibia); and GA Res. 38/40 (7 Dec. 1983); and GA Res. 43/33 (22 Nov. 1988) (both on Western Sahara).
[100] See text at n. 56.

despite uncertainty and disagreement as to the geographical area in which it was to be exercised.[101]

In the period since June 1967, Palestinian nationalism has grown within the Occupied Territories.[102] Moreover, in many different ways the international community has come to accept the propositions that there is a Palestinian people; that it has a right of self-determination; and that this right is to be exercised in the West Bank and Gaza, rather than in the whole of former mandatory Palestine.[103] None of these propositions is self-evident, and in the nature of things their acceptance by the international community has been slow and uneven; for example, Palestinian self-determination was not mentioned in UN Security Council Resolutions 242 and 338.[104] Significant landmarks in the international acceptance of Palestinian aspirations have included General Assembly resolutions from 1969 onwards reaffirming 'the inalienable rights of the people of Palestine';[105] the September 1978 Camp David Agreements between President Sadat, Prime Minister Begin, and President Carter, with their proposals for a self-governing authority for the West Bank and Gaza for a transitional period of 5 years;[106] the June 1980 Venice declaration of the heads of government of the nine member states of the European Communities, calling for

---

[101] On the evolution within the international community of the idea of Palestinian self-determination, see especially S. V. Mallison and W. T. Mallison Jr., 'The Juridical Bases for Palestinian Self-Determination', *PYIL* 1 (1984), 36. On the emergence of nationalism among the Palestinian Arabs, see the important study by an Israeli scholar, Y. Porath, *The Emergence of the Palestinian–Arab National Movement 1918–1929* (London, 1974).

[102] On political developments in the West Bank, see particularly two fine studies by an Israeli and a Palestinian academic, respectively: M. Ma'oz, *Palestinian Leadership on the West Bank: The Changing Role of the Mayors under Jordan and Israel* (London, 1984); and E. Sahliyeh, *In Search of Leadership: West Bank Politics since 1967* (Washington, DC, 1988). In 1979–80 Ma'oz was an adviser on Arab affairs to the Israeli Defence Minister, and to the Co-ordinator for Activities in the Territories.

[103] See, for instance, Chs. 3 and 5 in this book; and also Ch. 16, where Dugard suggests that an advisory opinion of the ICJ be sought on this point.

[104] SC Res. 242 (22 Nov. 1967) provided for Israeli withdrawal from territories occupied in the 1967 war, coupled with a termination of all claims or states of belligerency. SC Res. 338 (22 Oct. 1973) reaffirmed Res. 242 and called for negotiations 'aimed at establishing a just and durable peace in the Middle East'. These resolutions, accepting as they did Israel's right to exist, and making no specific mention of Palestinian self-determination, were for many years viewed with deep suspicion by the PLO.

[105] The first such resolution was GA Res. 2535B (XXIV) (10 Dec. 1969). Another key resolution was GA Res. 2672C (XXV) (8 Dec. 1970), which recognized that 'the people of Palestine are entitled to equal rights and self-determination, in accordance with the Charter of the United Nations'. These early resolutions attracted only modest support: votes for and against and abstentions were, respectively, 48–22–47, and 47–22–50.

[106] Camp David Agreements (see n. 37 above). For a succinct account of the negotiation of these accords, referring to memoirs of participants, see S. Sofer, *Begin: An Anatomy of Leadership* (Oxford, 1988), 189–200. According to Sofer, as late as March 1978, 'Sadat was inclined to agree that a Palestinian state should not be established.' Ibid. 187.

recognition of two principles—the right to existence of all the states in the region and the legitimate rights of the Palestinian people;[107] the peace plan, adopted by the Arab summit at Fez in September 1982 and accepted by the PLO, calling for a settlement based on Israeli withdrawal from the territories occupied in 1967;[108] the September 1983 Geneva declaration on Palestine;[109] and the short-lived Jordan–PLO accord of February 1985.[110]

Apart from diplomatic moves, certain other developments, demographic and political, have weakened, if not undermined, extreme positions on both sides: by the late 1980s, neither the complete abolition of Israel nor complete Israeli settlement and domination of the Occupied Territories could be presented with the same conviction as in earlier periods.[111]

The effect of all these developments should not be exaggerated. They could not in themselves dissolve the encrusted bitterness of a long-standing and violent dispute, they could not alleviate deep fears on both sides about security, and they could not prevent the growth of religious fundamentalism among Arabs and Israelis. They have had, at best, a limited effect in persuading Israelis and Palestinians to work towards pragmatic compromise. The Israeli government remains obdurate; while on the Palestinian side, the belief that self-determination is an internationally recognized right still sometimes involves a corollary reluctance to think in terms of a transitional period before full independence, or to accept that there might be any obligation on Palestinians to demonstrate (to Arab states as much as to Israel) that a future Palestinian state would be a stable and responsible member of international society, accepting frontiers, regimes, and rules of co-existence.

Despite the many problems associated with them, the diplomatic and political moves since the occupation began together have reinforced the view of the West Bank and Gaza as territories that jointly are a candidate for self-determination, and have weakened alternative views. The idea that either of these territories might revert eventually to the state that previously controlled it is effectively dead. Thus, the

---

[107] *Keesing's Contemporary Archives* (London, 1980), 30,635.

[108] The Arab Peace Plan, adopted by the Twelfth Arab Summit Conference, held at Fez, 6–9 Sept. 1982, went some way towards accepting the existence of Israel. For details, including extracts from the Fez summit declaration, see *Keesing's Contemporary Archives* (1983), 32,037.

[109] This declaration was issued at the conclusion of the UN International Conference on the Question of Palestine, held at Geneva, 29 Aug.–7 Sept. 1983, reprinted in *PYIL* 1 (1984), 66.

[110] The text of the Jordanian–Palestinian Accord, 11 Feb. 1985, together with indications of the PLO Executive Committee's desired alternative wording, is reprinted in *PYIL* 2 (1985), 224.

[111] See e.g. Y. Harkabi, *Israel's Fateful Decisions* (London, 1988).

acts of the international community indicate that the implicit assumption of the law on occupations—that occupied territory is 'territory of a High Contracting Party'—need not be a straitjacket when it comes to consideration of the future status of a land and its people.

The emphasis placed by the international community on Palestinian self-determination has not meant a complete abandonment of Jordanian and Egyptian responsibility for the West Bank and Gaza, respectively. With Israeli consent, the ousted administering powers have maintained a modest degree of involvement in various spheres, including some educational matters. Until the Palestinians actually exercise self-determination, and decide on the form of a future Palestinian entity, the governments of Jordan and Egypt are likely to continue to have an important role in the territories—or at least in negotiations on their future.

The Legitimacy and Treatment of Resistance

In most cases of prolonged occupation, resistance emerges in some form, whether violent or non-violent. However, the main international conventions on occupations say little about its legitimacy or otherwise, and only slightly more about the treatment of those involved in it. The most detailed rules governing the treatment of resisters are in Articles 5, 49, and 68 of the Fourth Geneva Convention. There is also a much larger, but widely dispersed, body of case law, especially from the time of World War II.

The legitimacy of resistance in occupied areas, and of support from abroad for such resistance, has always been a difficult question for diplomatic conferences, courts, writers on the laws of war, and governments. It has been raised in sharp form by events in the 1980s in Afghanistan, Nicaragua, Namibia, and elsewhere. What is the status of combatants other than the members of the regular armed forces of a country? Is popular resistance (whether violent or non-violent) a breach of a notional contract between occupier and occupied?[112] Is active outside support of resistance in occupied areas justified? Is the recovery of lost territories, including those under prolonged occupation, a justification for war?[113] These questions, which are by no means new, do not admit of absolute answers: it is placing too heavy a

---

[112] A famous exploration of resistance is R. R. Baxter, 'The Duty of Obedience to the Belligerent Occupant', *BYIL* 27 (1950), 235.

[113] For a brief, sceptical discussion of this issue in relation to the 1973 war, which Egypt and Syria justified partly as a war for the recovery of territory under prolonged Israeli occupation, see W. O'Brien, *The Conduct of Just and Limited War* (New York, 1981), 286.

burden on international law to expect answers from it, but it can offer some criteria and guide-lines.

In the post-1945 period, following Allied support for resistance in Axis-occupied countries, and the ending of the European colonial empires, the international community has tended not only to support self-determination in principle, but also—and increasingly—to view resistance against outside domination as justifiable. The 1974 UN Definition of Aggression contained the statement:

Nothing in this Definition... could in any way prejudice the right to self-determination, freedom, and independence, as derived from the Charter, of peoples forcibly deprived of that right..., particularly peoples under colonial and racist régimes or other forms of alien domination; nor the right of these peoples to struggle to that end and to seek and receive support, in accordance with the principles of the Charter...[114]

As a corollary of this approach, a degree of recognition has been granted to certain liberation movements. Thus, on 13 November 1974 PLO Chairman Arafat addressed the UN General Assembly. On 22 November of that year, the Palestine Liberation Organization was one of several national liberation movements accorded observer status in the General Assembly and UN-sponsored conferences.[115]

In countless statements, UN bodies have criticized the actions taken by Israel in response to resistance of one kind or another. For example, a telegram dispatched by the UN Commission on Human Rights on 8 March 1968, called on Israel 'to desist forthwith from acts of destroying homes of the Arab civilian population in areas occupied by Israel'.[116] Eighteen years later, in 1986, a General Assembly resolution called on Israel 'to release all Arabs arbitrarily detained or imprisoned as a result of their struggle for self-determination and for the liberation of their territories'.[117]

Much Israeli policy and practice in dealing with resistance has deserved criticism—especially the policy of 'force, power, and beatings' enunciated by Minister of Defence Rabin on 20 January 1988. Yet the General Assembly's tendency to criticize almost all Israeli actions against resistance has resulted in failure to take note of those that have

---

[114] Definition of Aggression, Art. 7, Annexe to GA Res. 3314 (XXIX) (14 Dec. 1974). See also the similar formula in the Declaration on Principles of International Law concerning Friendly Relations and Co-operation among States in accordance with the Charter of the United Nations, Annexe to GA Res. 2625 (XXV) (24 Oct. 1970).

[115] GA Res. 3237 (XXIX) (22 Nov. 1974).

[116] Mentioned in GA Res. 2443 (XXIII) (19 Dec. 1968). House demolitions have been widely criticized as an extrajudicial measure of collective punishment.

[117] GA Res. 41/63A (3 Dec. 1986). In logic, one could question the claim that the Arabs have been detained 'arbitrarily', when the reason for their detention occupies the rest of the same sentence in the resolution. In reality, however, it does appear that many cases of detention and imprisonment have been arbitrary.

recognized legal standards in the treatment of resisters; and an equal failure to note that the dilemmas Israel faces are difficult and its rights under the law on occupations real. Consequently, General Assembly resolutions bearing on the treatment of Palestinian resistance have had diminished impact, having been easy for Israelis to dismiss.

In general, United Nations involvement in the subject of resistance has been highly controversial, and has contributed to criticism of the Organization. It has sought simultaneously to maintain the Charter prohibitions on the use of force and to offer an 'innovatory adumbration of the principles of the Just War'.[118] UN support for struggles of national liberation has often been expressed rhetorically, without addressing important issues. One finds little awareness of the Burkean distinction between the possible existence of a right (e.g., of resistance, or of recovery of territory through war) and the wisdom of actually exercising that right in a given situation. Further, one finds little serious discussion of choice of means of pursuing a given right; for example, UN resolutions have given no clue as to whether liberation struggles ought to be fought within limits derived from, or akin to, the laws of war. This omission has been especially serious since terrorist attacks against wholly innocent civilian targets were already alarmingly widespread in the early 1970s. The record of the United Nations in this respect has not been wholly negative: it has, of course, been involved in drawing up conventions and resolutions dealing with various aspects of terrorism, and it has been increasingly critical of this phenomenon.[119] The real criticism is that UN resolutions have lacked intellectual coherence, and (for a time at least) they lost sight of laws-of-war principles as a possible restraint not just on occupying powers, but also on liberation movements.

The issue of making legal restraints clearly applicable to liberation struggles is addressed in Geneva Protocol I, which includes within its scope of application 'armed conflicts in which peoples are fighting against colonial domination and alien occupation and against racist régimes in the exercise of their right of self-determination' (Article 1(4)). This formula, which is echoed in countless UN documents, clearly includes the peoples of southern Africa and Palestine.[120] If implemented, Protocol I would require any liberation movement to observe extensive restrictions as regards methods of operation, weaponry,

---

[118] M. Howard, 'The UN and International Security', in A. Roberts and B. Kingsbury (eds.), *United Nations, Divided World* (Oxford, 1988) 31, 37.

[119] For results of the UN consideration of terrorism, including the texts of conventions on the subject, see especially GA Res. 3166 (XXVIII) (14 Dec. 1973); GA Res. 34/146 (17 Dec. 1979); and GA Res. 40/61 (9 Dec. 1985).

[120] M. Bothe, K. Partsch, and W. Solf, *New Rules for Victims of Armed Conflicts*, 51–2. Since neither South Africa nor Israel has become party to the Protocol, its formal applicability to these territories is of course doubtful.

and targets. The provisions in respect of such movements, and, indeed, whether the Protocol encompasses such movements at all, have inspired considerable debate, especially in the United States.[121] Nevertheless, the Protocol does establish that there are rules that would apply to participants in liberation struggles as well as to other types of combatant—which is more than can be said of some UN resolutions.

Palestinian Deportations, Israeli Settlements

Over twenty years, no aspect of life can remain static. The changes in the demography of the Occupied Territories have been particularly significant. In September 1967, the Palestinian population of the West Bank and Gaza was just under one million. By the end of 1987, it reached an estimated 1,424,100 (860,000 in the West Bank and 564,100 in the Gaza Strip).[122] This growth is remarkable, considering that it has taken place against a background of substantial labour emigration, especially in the oil boom of the 1970s. Among Israelis, these figures have caused much concern because they suggest that within decades there might be an Arab majority in the overall area comprising Israel and the Occupied Territories.[123] For Palestinians, too, there are major causes for concern on demographic matters: deportations of Palestinians and Israeli settlements.

In accord with the view that occupation is a provisional state of affairs, the imposition of demographic changes within occupied territory has long been seen as undesirable. The Fourth Geneva Convention appears to be precise on the question, stating as it does in the first and sixth paragraphs of Article 49:

Individual or mass forcible transfers, as well as deportations of protected persons from occupied territory to the territory of the Occupying Power or to that of any other country, occupied or not, are prohibited, regardless of their motive . . .

The Occupying Power shall not deport or transfer parts of its own civilian population into the territory it occupies.

The individuals deported from the Occupied Territories fall into two broad categories: political leaders and those alleged to be involved

[121] The main positions are outlined in 'Agora: The US Decision Not to Ratify Protocol I to the Geneva Conventions on the Protection of War Victims', *AJIL* 81 (1987), 910; and its continuation, *AJIL* 82 (1988), 784.

[122] Central Bureau of Statistics, *Statistical Abstract of Israel 1988*, at 705. Note that these figures, since they are drawn from official Israeli sources, exclude the Arab population of annexed East Jerusalem, and see n. 2 to the Introduction on the difficulty of obtaining accurate demographic data on the Occupied Territories.

[123] Unofficial Israeli projections for mandatory Palestine as a whole (i.e. Israel, the West Bank, and Gaza) suggest that by the year 2010 there will be parity between the Jewish and Arab populations. See M. Benvenisti, *1987 Report* (Jerusalem, 1987), 5.

directly in hostile activities. The deportations began in 1967 in the first months of the occupation, have particularly affected the leadership, and have involved well over a thousand persons.[124] Some of the deportations have been defended, e.g. in Supreme Court decisions, on a variety of grounds, such as that these deportations were quite different in character and intent from those which took place in World War II; that the individuals concerned were not 'protected persons'; and/or that they were being deported, not to 'any other country', but to a country (e.g. Jordan) whose nationals they were.[125] Such arguments could not allay the deep fears among the Palestinian population that the deportations actually carried out by Israel were the thin end of the wedge, to be followed by larger expulsions.

The growth of Israeli settlements in the Occupied Territories, which has been most marked since 1977, has similarly fuelled fears of mass expulsions. At the end of 1976, after almost a decade of occupation, there were an estimated 3,176 Jewish settlers in the West Bank. By April 1987, there were approximately 65,000 Jews living in the West Bank, and 2,700 in the Gaza Strip.[126] As with deportations, so with settlements: there have been some claims that Israeli practices are compatible with international norms, including those of the Fourth Geneva Convention. A distinction has been drawn between the transfer of people—which is forbidden under Article 49—and the voluntary settlement of nationals on an individual basis; and it has been asserted that there is nothing wrong with settlements in the sense of army bases where soldiers are engaged in agriculture for part of the time.[127]

---

[124] Cohen, *Human Rights in the Israeli-Occupied Territories 1967–1982*, 106–7, reports figures indicating that over 1,100 people were deported from the West Bank and Gaza between 1967 and 1977. She quotes a senior military official as saying that only 68 of these were genuine deportations—that is, cases in which the individuals concerned were (*a*) recognized officially to be residents of the Occupied Territories, and (*b*) not transferred as part of an exchange with an Arab state. The deportations aroused opposition both internally and internationally; in 1980 they were discontinued, recommencing following a cabinet decision of 4 Aug. 1985.

A figure of 2,000 deportations for the whole period 1967–86, apparently from the West Bank alone, is given in M. Benvenisti, *The West Bank Handbook: A Political Lexicon* (Jerusalem, 1986), 87.

[125] For discussions of the legality of the deportations, see Dinstein, 'Refugees and the Law of Armed Conflict', *IYHR* 12 (1982), 94; Shefi, 'The Reports of the UN Special Committees', at 304–6; Cohen, *Human Rights in the Israeli-Occupied Territories 1967–1982*, 104–11. For a well-argued critique of the legality of deportations (mainly those of 1985–6), see J. Hiltermann, *Israel's Deportation Policy in the Occupied West Bank and Gaza* (Ramallah, 1986). See also Ch. 2 in this book, text at n. 95, for a discussion of Israeli Supreme Court judgments on deportation.

[126] Benvenisti, *1987 Report*, 51–5, and *The West Bank Handbook*, 66. The figures for settlers in the West Bank do not include the large number (80,000 in 1985, and still growing) in the extended municipal boundaries of Jerusalem.

[127] For an analysis suggesting that some Israeli settlements are compatible with the Fourth Geneva Convention, see Dinstein, 'The International Law of Belligerent Occupation and Human Rights', 124.

Civilian settlements have also been called necessary for the occupying power's security, and therefore essential if the occupying power is to preserve public order and safety.[128]

Such arguments are far from convincing. In particular, even if voluntary settlement of nationals on an individual basis were permissible under Article 49, the ambitious settlements programme of the 1980s, which was planned, encouraged, and financed at the governmental level, does not meet that description.[129] Moreover, it is doubtful whether the settlements programme was primarily intended to contribute to the occupying power's security and whether, in the event, it has contributed to that end; by causing friction with the Palestinian inhabitants of the territories, the programme may even have added to the work of the Israel Defence Forces (IDF).[130] The settlements programme is quite simply contrary to international law. However, it is now so far advanced, and so plainly in violation of the Geneva Convention, that it actually creates a powerful reason for Israel's continuing refusal to accept that the Convention is applicable in the Occupied Territories on a *de jure* basis.

The international community has taken a critical view of both deportations and settlements as being contrary to international law. General Assembly resolutions have condemned the deportations since 1969, and have done so by overwhelming majorities in recent years.[131] Likewise, they have consistently deplored the establishment of settlements, and have done so by overwhelming majorities throughout the period (since the end of 1976) of the rapid expansion in their numbers.[132] The Security Council has also been critical of deportations

[128] See, e.g., the material on various Supreme Court cases involving settlements in Shamgar (ed.), *Military Government*, at 152–3, 158, 313–19, 371–97, 404–41. See also text at nn. 147–51 below (referring to the *Beit El* and *Elon Moreh* cases), and see Ch. 6, text at n. 60 ff.

[129] See, e.g., Benvenisti, *1987 Report*, 51–65.

[130] On unauthorized violence by settlers, see the Ministry of Justice report: J. Karp et al., *Report of the Inquiry Team re Investigation of Suspicions against Israelis in Judea and Samaria* (1984), reprinted in *PYIL* 1 (1984), 185.

[131] The first was GA Res. 2546 (XXIV) (11 Dec. 1969). Subsequent resolutions condemning deportations received overwhelming majorities: GA Res. 41/63E (3 Dec. 1986) (131–1–21). The US abstained on these resolutions. However, the 'United States has stated that deportation is inconsistent with the Fourth Geneva Convention.' US Dept. of State, *Country Reports on Human Rights Practices for 1987*, 1193.

[132] See, e.g., the following examples, at 4-year intervals:

GA Res. 31/106A	(16 Dec. 1976)	(129–3–4)
GA Res. 35/122B	(11 Dec. 1980)	(140–1–3)
GA Res. 39/95C	(14 Dec. 1984)	(143–1–1)

The United States voted against the 1976 resolution above, and abstained on the others. When it abstained on GA Res. 32/5 (28 Oct. 1977) (131–1–7), the US representative said that the United States opposed the Israeli settlements, but that it had accepted a special responsibility as co-chairman of the Geneva Peace Conference on the Middle East, requiring it to remain impartial when the complex issues to be considered there were involved. 1977 *UNYB* 317–18.

and settlements;[133] and other bodies have viewed them as an obstacle to peace, and illegal under international law.[134]

Long-Term Economic Change

The idea that occupation is temporary, and that an occupying power has a role in some respects akin to that of a trustee, finds reflection in a number of rules on economic matters, particularly the 1907 Hague Regulations (Articles 48–56). Some of the foundations of the Hague rules now seem dated, especially the insistence (objectionable to Communist countries) that private property merits a higher degree of protection than state property. However, few in number and antique as they are, these rules do establish some important principles, such as on taxation.[135]

In the West Bank and Gaza since 1967, extensive economic changes have been brought about in such key areas as agriculture, land ownership, use of water resources, the road system, building construction, and taxation. Labour has become more mobile: large numbers work daily in Israel, and many have left on a longer-term basis to work abroad.[136] Not all these changes have been for the worse. For example, living standards rose, at least up to the mid-1970s. Nevertheless, some actual and planned economic measures have caused concern, on

---

For a clear statement of the US view that Israel's establishment of civilian settlements in the Occupied Territories is inconsistent with international law, see the letter of H. J. Hansell, Legal Adviser, Dept. of State, to House Committee on International Relations (21 Apr. 1978), *ILM* 17 (1978), 777.

The General Assembly has shown some consistency in criticizing other cases of demographic changes imposed by foreign occupation forces. See, for example, its expressions of concern 'about reported demographic changes being imposed in Kampuchea by foreign occupation forces', in GA Res. 40/7 (5 Nov. 1985).

[133] See, for example, SC Res. 469 (20 May 1980) (on deportations: quoting the Fourth Geneva Convention, Art. 49, and calling on Israel to rescind the expulsion of the mayors of Hebron and Halhoul, and the *Shari'a* Judge of Hebron); and SC Res. 465 (1 Mar. 1980) (calling settlements a 'flagrant violation of the Geneva Convention'). The latter resolution, which also criticized Israel's purported annexation of Jerusalem, was adopted unanimously, but the US Government subsequently stated that it was retracting its vote. For an account of 'the highly publicized snafu' over this vote, see Z. Brzezinski, *Power and Principle: Memoirs of the National Security Adviser, 1977–1981*, rev. edn. (New York, 1985), 441. Brzezinski presents much interesting material on the Carter administration's thinking on the settlements; see, e.g., ibid. 110, 258, 263 and 440–2. See also SC Res. 607 (5 Jan. 1988), adopted unanimously, calling on Israel to refrain from deporting any Palestinian civilians from occupied territory.

[134] See, e.g., the June 1980 Venice Declaration of the nine EEC countries (*Keesing's Contemporary Archives* (1980), 30,635 and accompanying text, which was blunt on the settlements issue.

[135] See, e.g., text at n. 154.

[136] On economic developments in the West Bank and Gaza, see S. Graham-Brown, 'The Economic Consequences of the Occupation', in N. Aruri (ed.), *Occupation: Israel over Palestine* (London, 1984), 167; also Benvenisti, publications cited in nn. 62, 123 and 124 above; and H. Awartani's chapter in this volume.

several grounds: discrimination against Palestinian economic activity, creation of an economy dependent on that of Israel, and use of certain resources in the territories for the benefit of Israelis rather than Palestinians.

The international community has made many pronouncements on economic aspects of the Israeli occupation. The numerous references in the annual reports of the UN Special Committee on Israeli Practices have been reflected in the annual General Assembly resolutions on the reports.[137] Other General Assembly resolutions have also addressed the legality of certain Israeli economic activities and plans. From 1973 to 1983, a series of resolutions on 'Permanent Sovereignty over National Resources in the Occupied Arab Territories' asserted that Israel, as an occupying power, had very limited economic rights, and condemned Israel for alleged exploitation of resources.[138] Resolutions in the period 1981–4 demanded 'that Israel cease forthwith the implementation of its project of a canal linking the Mediterranean Sea to the Dead Sea'.[139] All these resolutions reflect the underlying principle that an occupying power, even in a prolonged occupation, has particularly to avoid making drastic changes in the economy of the occupied territory— especially those which are of an exploitative character, or which would result in binding the occupied territory permanently to the occupying power. However, the international community has not been inflexible in its interpretation of this principle.[140]

---

[137] See, e.g., GA Res. 41/63D (3 Dec. 1986), which includes in its litany of complaints of Israeli policies and practices the following economic items:

... (c) Illegal imposition and levy of heavy and disproportionate taxes and dues; ...
(f) Confiscation and expropriation of private and public Arab property in the occupied territories and all other transactions for the acquisition of land involving the Israeli authorities, institutions or nationals on the one hand and the inhabitants or institutions of the occupied territories on the other; ...
(m) Interference with the system of education and with the social and economic and health development of the population in the Palestinian and other occupied Arab territories; ...
(o) Illegal exploitation of the natural wealth, resources and population of the occupied territories.

[138] The first was GA Res. 3175 (XXVIII) (17 Dec. 1973). It referred to the Fourth Geneva Convention. It was not until the fifth resolution on this subject, GA Res. 32/161 (19 Dec. 1977), that specific reference was made to the Hague Convention, which is more germane to the exploitation of natural resources. These resolutions received substantial, but not overwhelming, support. The voting on the last in this series, GA Res. 38/144 (19 Dec. 1983), was fairly typical: 120 for, 2 against, and 18 abstentions.

[139] If constructed, part of the canal would allegedly have gone through the Gaza Strip. The first GA resolution criticizing it was GA Res. 36/150 (16 Dec. 1981). The 1984 version, GA Res. 39/101 (14 Dec. 1984), stated that the canal, 'if constructed, is a violation of the rules and principles of international law, especially those relating to the fundamental rights and duties of States and to belligerent occupation of land'. This received 143 votes for, 2 against, and 1 abstention.

[140] One piece of evidence of discrimination by the international community is that there has been little, if any, international comment or censure regarding one apparent

Oil was a subject of some contention in Israel's relations with Egypt, and with the United States. The oilfields in the Sinai Peninsula, which were operated during the Israeli occupation and returned to Egypt in November 1975, were not the main problem. Difficulties principally arose over prospecting for additional oil in Sinai and the Gulf of Suez, raising questions about an occupant's right to make so significant a change in the economy of an area, and about its position regarding maritime matters. A Memorandum of Law by the US Department of State of 1 October 1976 concluded firmly: 'International law does not support the assertion of a right in the occupant to grant an oil development concession.'[141] An Israeli response dated 1 August 1977 included this statement bearing on prolonged occupation: '[I]f over a long period, such as in the case of the present occupation of Sinai, oil exploitation had been prevented, the development of the territory would have been delayed by that number of years.'[142] Although in the eyes of the international community there was considerable doubt about the legitimacy of Israel's oil exploitation policy, it does not appear in the end to have been an obstacle to peace with Egypt.[143]

VIII. Israeli Supreme Court Judgments on Prolonged Occupation

In a large number of cases, especially before the Supreme Court of Israel, questions of an inherently long-term character, or involving specific consideration of the prolonged nature of the occupation, have arisen. What follows is not in any sense a comprehensive survey of these cases, or even an account of the main issues raised in them, but rather a distillation intended to convey some of the main lines of the Supreme Court's thinking on a few such questions.[144]

An innovation was made in the territories occupied by Israel after

---

infringement by Israel of the law on occupations—the building of the main road from Jerusalem to Tel Aviv on a natural line that passes through what before 1967 was a demilitarized zone between the West Bank and Israel. Although this road in effect annexes a small portion of territory, Jordan and other states acquiesced in it.

[141] US Dept. of State, Memorandum of Law (1 Oct. 1976), ILM 16 (1977), 733, 752. This memo stated that concessions granted to AMOCO by Egypt were valid, 'whether granted prior to or post June 1967'.

[142] Israeli Ministry of Foreign Affairs, Memorandum of Law (1 Aug. 1977), ILM 17 434 (submitted to the US Dept. of State on 27 Oct. 1977). On 26 Mar. 1978, two wells in the Alma field in the Gulf of Suez began operation under a concession granted by Israel to the Neptune Oil Co., ibid. 432. All Sinai was returned to Egypt by 25 Apr. 1982.

[143] See further A. Gerson, 'Off-Shore Oil Exploration by a Belligerent Occupant: The Gulf of Suez Dispute', AJIL 71 (1977), 725; and B. M. Clagett and O. T. Johnson Jr., 'May Israel as a Belligerent Occupant Lawfully Exploit Previously Unexploited Oil Resources of the Gulf of Suez?', AJIL 72 (1978), 558.

[144] The facts and decisions in most of these cases are discussed more fully elsewhere in this volume, notably by Qupty.

the June 1967 war, namely, the establishment of a right to petition the Israeli Supreme Court against arbitrary or illegal acts by the occupant. The Court asserted its competence to review the legislation and acts of the military commander and other authorities in the West Bank and Gaza. The effectiveness of the Court in bringing rules of law, including those of international law, to bear on Israeli occupation policy has been much discussed.[145]

In reviewing acts by the occupant, the Supreme Court has had regard, *inter alia*, to the relevant rules of international law. However, it was not self-evident which rules of international law were to be applied by the Court or exactly how it was to apply them. The Court has had to take into account not only the Israeli government's position on the *de jure* applicability of the 1907 Hague and 1949 Geneva Conventions, but also complex questions of justiciability: do these agreements impose obligations and create rights directly enforceable under Israeli municipal law before an Israeli court? In addressing this issue, the Court has suggested that customary international law, including the Hague Convention, is justiciable; whereas conventional international law (in which category it has tended to include the Geneva Convention) is more problematical in this regard.[146]

Supreme Court Cases

The matter of Israeli settlements is central to any consideration of the long-term impact of the occupation. In the *Beit El* case,[147] Justice Landau supported the Israeli settlements against the obvious objection that there was an inconsistency between the temporary character of an

---

[145] E. Nathan, 'The Power of Supervision of the High Court of Justice over Military Government', in Shamgar (ed.), *Military Government*, 109, 133. For other Israeli assessments, see F. Domb, 'Judgments of the Supreme Court of Israel Relating to the Administered Territories', *IYHR* 11 (1981), 344; M. Negbi, 'The Israeli Supreme Court and the Occupied Territories', *Jerusalem Qtrly.* 27 (Spring 1983), 33; and Cohen, *Human Rights in the Israeli-Occupied Territories 1967–1982*, 80–92.

Many inhabitants of the Occupied Territories with whom I discussed the matter in Nov.–Dec. 1983 and Jan. 1988, welcomed this right of petition, and noted that it had fostered a few out-of-court settlements of certain issues, but argued that, overall, very few practical results had been achieved. These sources critical of the tendency of the Court (1) to accept 'security' as a justification for the acts of the occupant, and (2) to accept certain limits on the formal applicability or justiciability of the Fourth Geneva Convention. For a critical Palestinian view, see Shehadeh, *Occupier's Law*, 95–100, and see also Chs. 2 and 6 in this volume.

[146] These questions are examined in more depth by Qupty in Chapter 2. See also, e.g., Nathan, 'The Power of Supervision', 125–49; and Z. Hadar, 'The Military Courts', in Shamgar (ed.), *Military Government*, 171, 172–5; also the judgments in the *Beit El* and *Elon Moreh* cases, text at nn. 147–50 below.

[147] HC 606/78 and 610/78, the *Beit El* case, reprinted in Shamgar (ed.), *Military Government*, 371 ff. For a short report of this case, see *IYHR* 9 (1979), 337, and for the facts of the case see Ch. 6, text at n. 62.

occupation and the construction of permanent settlements.[148] Referring to the advocates for the petitioners and the respondents, he said:

Mr Khoury asks how a permanent settlement can be established on land requisitioned only for temporary use. This is a good question. But Mr Bach's answer, that the civilian settlement can only exist in that place as long as the IDF occupy the area by virtue of the Requisition Order, commends itself to me. This occupation can itself come to an end some day as a result of international negotiations . . .[149]

All the opinions in the *Beit El* case emphasized Israel's unique security problems as a basis for justifying the settlements.[150] The petition objecting to the requisition of land was dismissed.

It was on the basis of Article 52 of the Hague Regulations (which deals with requisitions) that the Supreme Court, in its famous judgment of 22 October 1979, in the *Elon Moreh* case, declared an Israeli civilian settlement near Nablus in the West Bank to be illegal.[151] Because the decision was based on this provision, it had little bearing on settlements that did not involve requisitions or were officially declared essential to Israeli security.

Numerous other Supreme Court judgments have tackled issues, including economic ones, directly related to the prolonged character of the occupation.

In *The Christian Society for the Holy Places v. Minister of Defence*, the Court considered whether an order by the Regional Commander of Judea and Samaria was *ultra vires* Article 43 of the Hague Regulations, which requires the occupant to respect, 'unless absolutely prevented, the laws in force in the country'. Justice Sussman observed that the occupant has a duty in respect of the population's welfare:

A prolonged military occupation brings in its wake social, economic, and commercial changes which oblige him to adapt the law to the changing needs of the population. The words 'absolutely prevented' in Article 43 should, therefore, be interpreted with reference to the duty imposed upon him *vis-à-vis* the civilian population, including the duty to regulate economic and social affairs. In this context, it is of special importance whether the motive for the

---

[148] Ibid. 387–90. See also Justice Witkon's statement that 'the provisions of the Geneva Convention regarding the transfer of population from or to occupied territory do not come under already existing law. They are intended to enlarge, and not merely clarify or elaborate the duties of the occupying power.' Ibid. 380.
[149] Ibid. 392.
[150] Ibid. 374–7, 392–3, 395–7.
[151] HC 390/79, the *Elon Moreh* case, reprinted in Shamgar (ed.), *Military Government*, 404, 419–26 and 437–8. For a short report, see *IYHR* 9 (1979), 345, and for the facts of the case see Ch. 6, text at n. 85.

change was the furtherance of the occupant's interests or concern for the welfare of the civilian population.[152]

In *Jerusalem District Electricity Company Inc. v. The Minister of Energy*, Justice Cahan said:

[G]enerally, in the absence of special circumstances, the Commander of the region should not introduce in an occupied area modifications which, even if they do not alter the existing law, would have a far-reaching and prolonged impact on it, far beyond the period when the military administration will be terminated one way or another, save for actions undertaken for the benefit of the inhabitants of the area.[153]

In the *Abu Aita* case, Justice Shamgar referred to the significance, so far as a prolonged belligerent occupation is concerned, of the above-mentioned judgment in the *Christian Society for the Holy Places* case. He stated that international law prescribes no limits to the duration of a belligerent occupation. He went on to endorse the criterion, advanced by Dinstein, that in most instances legislative steps taken by the occupant should be regarded as legitimate if the occupant takes equal legislative steps towards its own population; but he noted that this criterion is not exhaustive, and that situations may occur in an occupied territory that demand legislative steps not required in the home country.[154]

---

[152] HC 337/71 *The Christian Society for the Holy Places v. The Minister of Defence et al.*, as summarized in *IYHR* 2 (1972), 354, 355. Justice Cohn's dissenting opinion is at 355. For the facts of the case see Ch. 6 in this volume, text at n. 9. On the application of particular treaties the summary states that the Court refrained from considering two issues: first, whether the Hague Convention applied to the administered areas, and second, whether the two aforementioned Conventions (that is, the Fourth Hague Convention and the Fourth Geneva Convention) constitute law which could be invoked in an 'internal' dispute between a State and its citizens. The Court explained that it avoided these questions because Counsel for the State chose not to raise them, as he based the defence of the respondents on the argument that they observed the Conventions properly. Ibid. 356. See also the interesting discussion of this case, and the implications of prolonged occupation, in Dinstein, 'The International Law of Belligerent Occupation and Human Rights', 112–14.

[153] HC 351/80 *The Jerusalem District Electricity Company Inc. v. The Minister of Energy*, summarized in *IYHR* 11 (1981) 354, 357.

[154] HC 69/81 and 493/81, the *Abu Aita* case, translated in *Selected Judgments of the Supreme Court of Israel* 7 (1988), 6, 98–9. For a summary, see *IYHR* 13 (1983), 348. The article by Dinstein to which Shamgar referred was 'The Legislative Power Authority in Occupied Territories', *Tel Aviv Univ. Law Review* 2 (1972), 505 (in Hebrew). See also Dinstein, 'The International Law of Belligerent Occupation and Human Rights', 112–13, and G. von Glahn's chapter in this volume.

In a subsequent case, HC 118/84 *Atiyah v. IDF Commander in the Gaza Strip*, which concerned the treatment of mentally ill accused persons, the Supreme Court ruled that there was no obligation to make legislation in the Occupied Territories conform to Israeli legislation on similar matters; discretion for such conformity was vested in the commander of the region.

In *A Teachers' Housing Cooperative Society v. The Military Commander of the Judea and Samaria Region*, a central issue was whether the occupant had authority to initiate 'a civil project of long-range permanent implications lasting beyond the duration of the belligerent occupation'. Justice Barak said that, in defining the scope of the authority of a military administration, one must bear in mind the distinction between one of short duration and one that is prolonged. He cited Dinstein in noting that 'the needs of the civilian population become more valid and tangible when the occupation is drawn out'. Therefore, though the Hague Regulations had been codified against the background of a short occupation, 'nothing prevents the development—within their framework—of rules defining the scope of a military government's authority in cases of prolonged occupation'.[155] Barak concluded:

> The authority of a military administration applies to taking all measures necessary to ensure growth, change and development. Consequently, a military administration is entitled to develop industry, commerce, agriculture, education, health, welfare, and like matters which usually concern a regular government, and which are required to ensure the changing needs of a population in a territory under belligerent occupation.[156]

In *Mustafa Yusef v. Manager of the Judea and Samaria Central Prison*, the six petitioners, convicted of homicide by a court in Israel and sentenced to long prison terms, objected to their transfer from a prison in Israel to the newly opened Judea and Samaria Central Prison. Their petition was not successful. Justice Barak said in his judgment:

> The right to a 'civilized human life in prison' is granted to every 'criminal' or 'security' prisoner, both in Israel and in the Region. It is the duty of a military administration—in particular one of prolonged duration—to be concerned with the welfare of the inhabitants of the occupied territory, and this concern includes maintaining a minimal standard of prison conditions.[157]

Supreme Court Judgments: Some General Considerations

The judgments of the Israeli Supreme Court in cases arising from the occupation have been numerous, lengthy, erudite, and carefully argued. Many have reflected key aspects of international law, and have related them to the multitude of problems thrown up in this prolonged occupation. Even though the *de jure* applicability and justiciability of

---

[155] HC 393/82 *A Teachers' Housing Cooperative Society v. the Military Commander of the Judea and Samaria Region et al.*, summarized in *IYHR* 14 (1984), 301, 307–8 (referring to Y. Dinstein, *The Laws of War* (in Hebrew) (Tel Aviv, 1983), 216). For the facts of the case see Ch. 6 below, text at n. 40.

[156] *IYHR* 14 (1984), 309.

[157] HC 540–6/84 *Mustafa Yusef v. Manager of the Judea and Samaria Central Prison*, summarized in *IYHR* 17 (1987), 309, 312.

the Fourth Geneva Convention have been questioned, the Court has increasingly taken for granted the *de facto* applicability of its provisions. Nevertheless, problems remain.

1. Applicability *de jure* of the Fourth Geneva Convention to the Occupied Territories. Has the Court accepted too easily, without full scrutiny of all relevant issues, the position of the Israeli government?

2. Justiciability of the Fourth Geneva Convention. The Court has relied heavily on the assumption that the incorporation of provisions of international conventions into municipal law is a principal form of evidence that such provisions have the status of customary international law. Has it placed excessive reliance on this one form of evidence of customary law?

3. Interpretation of the Fourth Geneva Convention. The Court has often interpreted the Convention's provisions in a relative way that is not easily squared with their language or with the interpretations placed on them by other states.

4. Views of governments and international organizations. The Court's judgments contain very little reference to the opinions of governments and the resolutions of international organizations (e.g., the United Nations, UNESCO, the ICRC) on matters relating to the occupation. There is an argument for taking some account of such statements—at least in cases where they reveal a high degree of agreement among states or address issues on which there is a need to interpret existing legal provisions, for example, in the light of new circumstances.

5. Israeli settlements. The Court has sometimes appeared not just reluctantly to accept, but positively to espouse, the debatable argument that settlements contribute to Israel's security. Further, its view that their apparently permanent character is not inconsistent with the provisional character of the occupation, though justified by the example of the now-abandoned settlements in Sinai, invites scepticism.

6. The principle of equal legislative treatment. The judgment in the *Abu Aita* case relied on an interesting, but potentially problematical, criterion for judging new legislation: whether the occupying power takes equal legislative steps towards its own population. As the judgment itself implied, legislation that is suitable for one society (with its own laws and customs, ethnic and religious composition, and state of development) may not be at all suitable for another, very different society. Such an approach could also have the effect of integrating the occupied territory into that of the occupant, and separating it from other states with which the inhabitants may want association.

7. The changing needs of the population. The argument made in several judgments—that in a prolonged occupation, new (and

sometimes long-term) measures have to be taken in response to new problems—is powerful. However, it raises the question of exactly what individual or institution is able to assess and respond to the changing needs of the population, and by what means those needs or wishes should be determined.

Overall, the question arises whether the approach adopted by the Supreme Court—on the applicability, justiciability, and interpretation of international conventions—has not had the effect of reducing the Court's possibilities of intervention. Is there an extent to which the Court has served as a buffer to soften the apparent conflict between international legal provisions, on the one hand, and Israeli policy and practices, on the other?

IX. Issues and Conclusion

Prolonged Occupations Generally

1. Prolonged occupations, lasting more than five years, have not been uncommon in the post-1945 world. Although attaching the opprobrious label 'occupation' to a given situation is always controversial, many situations have been so identified by the international community, and some have not ended quickly. Condemnation of occupations, especially prolonged ones, is natural: but there is a need also to understand why they occur, and how the interests of the occupants and the inhabitants can be balanced.

2. Some or all of the underlying purposes of the law on occupations remain relevant in prolonged occupations. However, there may sometimes be tension among the various purposes; and difficult matters of political judgment are often involved in determining what particular policies flow from them.

3. The one diplomatic attempt to establish which rules apply to an occupation on the basis of its duration—namely, Article 6, paragraph 3 of the Fourth 1949 Geneva Convention—indicated that fewer rules would apply in a prolonged occupation. It was based on the assumption, confounded in the Israeli-occupied territories, that as time went by indigenous institutions would take over more and more responsibilities. The provision has never been formally implemented, was in effect rescinded by Protocol I, and must be regarded as a failure.

4. Any effort to get formal international agreement on a body of rules to apply specifically to all prolonged occupations is likely to fail, partly because prolonged occupations differ in their character and purpose, as recent and contemporary cases (including Kampuchea, Namibia, and northern Cyprus) demonstrate. Further, it has been hard

enough to get states to agree on the existing rules on occupations; to try to revise these rules, subdivide them or create special permutations of them would create acrimony and invite legalistic chaos. If prolonged occupations deserve a special body of rules, then why not occupations in which the indigenous government remains in post? Or occupations of territory whose status is in dispute? The most that could reasonably be expected is some broad guide-lines as to the principles that might inform any departure from or addition to the existing law—but even that would be difficult.

5. If a formal international agreement on the problems raised by prolonged occupations is unlikely, it may be more profitable to consider other means by which such problems might be tackled—especially the emergence of procedures, both national and international, for interpreting and implementing law in the light of changing conditions.

6. In an occupation, including a prolonged one, international organizations can have a number of important roles. They can remind all concerned of their obligations under international law; indicate which policies, or international legal provisions, remain not merely applicable but in urgent need of being applied; interpret legal provisions in the light of new circumstances; suggest appropriate action where there is a conflict between legal principles or provisions; engage in fact-finding or arbitration in respect of particular issues; and provide peace-keeping or observer forces to facilitate total or partial withdrawals by the occupant.

Whatever view is taken about the quantity, the quality, and the precise status in international law of the many UN resolutions on particular occupations (those relating to Israel are considered further below), their existence does suggest that the international community already has machinery for addressing certain questions that arise in such cases. Granted the reluctance of sovereign states to accept international scrutiny of how they use their armed force, this machinery will always need to be used with care.

7. Specific causes for concern about the relevance of the existing law on occupations to prolonged occupations include, but are not limited to:

(a) The law on occupations, especially as interpreted in some writings and military manuals, seems to allow, or suffer, the occupant to have a very large measure of authority, especially regarding the occupant's own security, the maintenance of public order, the keeping in force of already existing public order legislation, control of the media, and prohibitions on political activity. This degree of authority may be acceptable in a war, but can it be acceptable indefinitely? Statements by international bodies suggest that there is a widely held view that in a prolonged occupation, especially if it extends into something approximating peacetime, an occupant cannot exercise the draconian powers that may be permissible in a shorter occupation; the interests and wishes of the inhabitants must be accorded greater weight.

(b) The conventions sometimes seem to be based on assumptions about a territory—that its previous status as part of a sovereign state was clear, and its previous legal and political order was satisfactory—that are open to question in many recent and contemporary prolonged occupations.

(c) The conventions governing military occupations say little about certain issues that inevitably crop up in a prolonged occupation, including the safeguarding and promotion of the economic life of occupied territories.

(d) The conventions say little about the treatment of those involved in resistance activities of whatever kind (whether violent or nonviolent), apart from a few key references in the Fourth Geneva Convention (Articles 5, 49, and 68).

8. Causes for concern such as those listed above may be perfectly genuine, but they do not suggest that the relevant international agreements (especially the Hague Regulations and the Fourth Geneva Convention) should cease to be viewed as formally applicable. These agreements are not a rigid straitjacket, but a flexible framework. They leave room for special agreements between the parties if they are willing to conclude them; for interpretation by policy-makers in accord with their basic purposes and principles; for elucidation by various bodies; and for supplementation from other sources: from case law, writings, and other international agreements.

9. There are grounds for viewing international human rights law as applicable to occupations, including prolonged ones. Certain provisions of this body of law—for example, prohibitions of discrimination in education and of racial discrimination generally—usefully supplement the Hague and Geneva rules on occupations. In addition, some human rights conventions offer procedures of a kind lacking in laws-of-war conventions. However, the application of some provisions is not free from difficulties, especially in time of armed conflict or internal uprising.

10. The questions whether there is a right of resistance in territories under occupation (especially when prolonged), whether foreign states are justified in assisting such resistance, and whether states are justified in going to war to recover occupied territories, have cropped up in many recent conflicts. It is doubtful whether general answers in international law can be particularly helpful when the circumstances of

each case, including the purpose and character of the occupation, vary so greatly. Some statements on these matters made in UN General Assembly resolutions have been vulnerable to other criticisms as well. They have drawn attention neither to the key importance of the choice of means involved in pursuing any such rights, nor to the related issue of the application of laws of war limitations to the armed actions of liberation movements.

Israeli-Occupied Territories

11. Israel deserves credit for accepting the relevance in these territories of international legal norms, including those outlined in the Fourth Geneva Convention. However, its position that the latter is not necessarily applicable on a *de jure* basis is unconvincing.

12. During the long occupation, a continuous and, in the 1980s, increasingly strong litany of complaints has emerged about numerous aspects of Israel's rule: the annexation of East Jerusalem and the Golan Heights, the establishment of Israeli settlements, deportations of inhabitants, the treatment of institutions of higher education, the acquisition of land, the conduct of the judicial system, conditions of detention, and so on. Such complaints have often been expressed in legal form, as violations of particular international legal provisions or, indeed, of fundamental principles of humanitarian law. They are thus testimony to the continued salience, if not always to the efficacy, of international law in a prolonged occupation.

13. Both Israelis and Palestinians can point to ways that, in their view, the whole framework of the law on occupations has in some sense been abused by the adversary in this prolonged occupation:

(*a*) Israelis could argue that the law on occupations has provided a safety-net, enabling the Palestinians to escape the consequences of their leaders' folly, or that of some Arab governments, in not negotiating seriously about the future of the territories—a safety-net that it is not necessarily reasonable to maintain indefinitely. A related Israeli argument has been that the law is being used in a one-sided way if Palestinians claim legal rights at the same time as their leaders support 'terrorism' (itself a violation of the laws of war) or deny Israel's right to exist—a violation of even more fundamental norms.

(*b*) A concern widely shared by Palestinians is that the law on occupations has afforded Israel a cloak of legitimacy: while apparently respecting international law, Israel has actually interpreted it to suit its purposes. The Israelis are seen as claiming all the rights of belligerent occupants but shirking some of their legal obligations, and as introducing a system of permanent control under the legal cover that it is temporary. A further concern is that the law on occupations provides a basis for putting the inhabitants in a separate legal category and denying them normal political activity, keeping them in effect permanently under Israeli control, but as second-class citizens or worse. From this perspective, the longer the occupation lasts, the more akin to colonialism it seems.

Both these positions are serious. They point to the hazards of using the law on occupations selectively: the Palestinian tendency to take little account of the corrosive effects of terrorism is one example; so is the Israeli tendency to see in the law on occupations a justification for preventing or strictly controlling political activity indefinitely.

14. Consideration of the practical relevance of the two main instruments on occupations (the Hague Regulations and the Fourth Geneva Convention) to the situation in the territories is likely to yield the conclusions that both are of key importance in the various fields they address; that neither has lost its relevance because of passage of time; and that the Convention is germane to a wider range of currently critical problems, including treatment of detainees and the legality of deportations and settlements. The Convention has also been cited far more frequently in resolutions of international bodies.

15. The question whether, and if so to what extent, the Fourth Geneva Convention embodies customary law has become important in respect of the Israeli occupation and needs to be further considered. Some relevant facts to be taken into account include the large number of states parties, the time that has elapsed since 1949, resolutions of international bodies, incorporation into domestic legislation, state practice, and the opinions of writers. To the extent that its provisions are accepted as embodying customary law, the terms of the Convention might be taken into greater account by at least some Israeli decision-makers and courts.

16. Any consideration of how to get the law on occupations properly implemented has to start with the fact that the government of Israel has responsibility for these territories. (Indeed, there has always been some doubt whether other states would rush to pick up that responsibility if given the chance.) Israel does have a certain discretion in interpreting and applying the law on occupations—especially as that law, like much law, involves balancing different considerations. In these circumstances, criticisms of Israeli policy that are seen as ill-considered, intemperate, or unfair are obviously not likely to be heeded. Israel will pursue policies based on its view of its own interests, and up to a point it is right that it should do so. International law and

the national interest of states—even occupying powers—should not be seen as necessarily incompatible.

17. Some Israeli legal practices in this occupation have been notably innovative. One example is the abolition of capital punishment for murder, which shows that the duty in Article 43 of the Hague Regulations to respect, 'unless absolutely prevented, the laws in force in the country' need not be a bar to progressive legislation.

18. Another significant innovation is the right to petition the Israeli Supreme Court in respect of arbitrary or illegal acts by the occupant. Whatever the arguments about the effectiveness of this right in practice, and about the actual decisions reached by the Court, this innovation has potential as one additional means of bringing international law and occupation policy into some kind of relation with each other. (The other such means to have emerged in this occupation has been the United Nations, especially the General Assembly, discussed below. A difficulty is that the Supreme Court and the General Assembly have reached different conclusions on key matters and have largely ignored each other's positions.)

International Interest in the Israeli Occupation

19. The interest of the outside world in events in the Israeli-occupied territories is legitimate not only because an interest in human rights anywhere is legitimate, but also because the territories and those inhabitants who are refugees have a special status. There is no reason for this interest to decline, or to be viewed as less legitimate, on account of the great length of the occupation; rather the reverse.

20. The interest of the outside world has been manifested through mechanisms somewhat different from the formal system enunciated in the Fourth Geneva Convention. Some of the bodies that have exerted significant influence in the Occupied Territories are indeed mentioned in the Convention: the International Committee of the Red Cross, as well as individual governments, which have a responsibility under Article 1 to 'ensure respect for the Convention in all circumstances'. On the other hand, the formal system of protecting powers, mentioned extensively in the Convention, has not operated. Numerous UN bodies, not mentioned in the Convention, have had an important role.

21. The outside power with the greatest capacity to influence Israel on adhering to the law on occupations is the United States. Indeed, the United States played a central role in negotiations leading to Israeli withdrawals from Sinai and part of the Golan Heights. It may have been partly because of positions adopted by the United States that Israel has not annexed the West Bank and Gaza: against the objections of so important an ally, Israel could not throw the restraints of inter-

national law out the window, even if it wished to do so.[158] In the past, the United States has sometimes been diffident about restraining extreme Israeli policies, such as the extension of Israeli law to the Golan Heights in 1981, the invasion of Lebanon in 1982, and the building of settlements in the Golan Heights, the West Bank, and Gaza. The reasons for past US diffidence have included not just the much-vaunted Jewish lobby, but also a legitimate opposition to terrorism and to some of the PLO's aims; a genuine commitment to Israel's survival; a concern that extreme pressure could be counter-productive; a stated desire to maintain a degree of independence so as to sustain credibility in pursuit of a negotiated settlement; and perhaps a lack of confidence in the US government's own judgement (especially in view of Vietnam), combined with exaggerated respect for Israeli judgement. Further, in the early Reagan years, which were so fateful in the Middle East, the US administration went through a phase of, at best, lukewarm support for multilateral legal agreements and procedures. In 1988, US policy on a range of issues connected with the occupation began to change, partly due to the early effects of the *intifada* on US opinion.

22. The United Nations, and in particular the General Assembly, is sometimes seen as having done little but pass resolutions indiscriminately condemnatory of all aspects of Israeli policy. Although this is more a criticism of the member states than of the Organization as such, the United Nations is vulnerable to the charge of rebuking Israel endlessly, while maintaining a diplomatic silence in respect of certain brutalities committed by other governments, including some Arab governments. The Special Committee to Investigate Israeli Practices has been widely criticized. The potential of UN resolutions has been undermined by political partiality and intellectual inconsistency. The General Assembly's espousal in 1975 of the resolution equating Zionism with racism was the most spectacular, but not the only, example of a denunciatory and self-defeating approach. Too often, UN member states have seemed content to cast votes on the subject and leave it at that; painstaking fact-finding, authoritative argument, and diplomatic dialogue have sometimes been lacking. All this has conveyed the unfortunate impression that the law on occupations is a stick with which to beat occupants and a mechanism of political warfare, rather than a serious means of seeking to reconcile the conflicting interests of the parties. Elements in the approaches taken at the United Nations have made careful and sober consideration of some issues more difficult and may have reduced the Organization's chances

---

[158] A point argued impressively by A. Hertzberg, 'Israel and the West Bank: The Implications of Permanent Control', *Foreign Aff.* 61 (1983) 1064, 1072–5.

of exercising a useful role in mediation or negotiation. For the future, there is a case for reconsideration of the UN mechanisms both for the investigation of facts concerning prolonged occupations and for the articulation of opinion about them.

23. UN resolutions, though open to criticism, have had some consistency and utility. They have criticized other occupying powers and not just Israel. Many General Assembly and Security Council resolutions on the Israeli-occupied territories have usefully reaffirmed the value of key legal provisions and related these to changing factual situations. On basic matters, such as whether the West Bank and Gaza should eventually revert to the states that formerly controlled them or form a new state based on self-determination for the inhabitants, UN resolutions have been the principal means of expressing the changing views of the international community. On some issues, the United Nations has shown discrimination in its response to developments in the Occupied Territories: many extreme and one-sided resolutions have attracted fewer votes than more dispassionate ones.

24. During the Israeli occupation, international organizations not only have passed resolutions but have assumed other important roles. They have acted in mediatory, humanitarian, and peace-keeping capacities. From the beginning, the International Committee of the Red Cross has engaged in a wide range of activities, including observing prison conditions, arranging prisoner transfers, making private representations to the Israeli government, and issuing public statements about the international legal provisions applicable in the territories. The UN Relief and Works Agency for Palestine Refugees in the Near East (UNRWA) has continuously assisted those inhabitants of the West Bank and Gaza classified as refugees, and it has served as an important point of contact between the territories and the UN system. In schools in the Occupied Territories, the extremely sensitive problem of eliminating objectionable material in textbooks from Jordan and Egypt was eventually resolved through the good offices of UNESCO.[159] The United Nations has provided peace-keeping and observer forces in Sinai and the Golan Heights to facilitate Israeli withdrawals from occupied territory. As to the future, there have been several suggestions that UN peace-keeping or observer forces could have a role in monitoring elections in the West Bank and Gaza.

25. The International Court of Justice has not been asked to consider issues arising from the Israeli-occupied territories. Its important advisory opinion on Namibia of 1971 stands as a reminder that it can

---

[159] See Gerson, 'Trustee-Occupant: The Legal Status of Israel's Presence in the West Bank', 181–3; and the 1983 *Report of the Commissioner General of UNRWA*, 38 UN GAOR Supp. (No. 13) at 12, UN Doc. A/38/13 (1983).

play a role in clarifying certain legal questions in a prolonged occupation. It has sometimes been suggested that the General Assembly or the Security Council might refer certain legal matters to the Court, in accord with Article 96 of the UN Charter and Article 65 of the ICJ Statute. Theoretically, many questions might be put to the Court: for example, whether the Fourth Geneva Convention is applicable in the Occupied Territories on a *de jure* basis and in its entirety; whether the Convention embodies customary law, and if so to what extent; whether, in a prolonged occupation, there might in principle be some room for variations within, or even departures from, the law on occupations, and if so on what grounds; whether international human rights instruments are applicable in occupied territories; and whether settlements by nationals of the occupying power, or deportations of inhabitants, or major plans for new roads tying the territories to Israel proper accord with international law. Not all such questions are necessarily amenable to resolution by a legal body of this kind; and any such resolution would not of itself necessarily change political and military realities. The principal ground for considering the proposal at all is that, more than two decades after this occupation began, there is still basic disagreement about what parts of international law are formally applicable to the situation in the territories.[160]

The Ending of Prolonged Occupations

26. Consideration of prolonged occupations, against the background of more than twenty years of Israeli occupation, should encourage some reflection about how occupations end. One idea, widely accepted by lawyers and politicians, is of international negotiation leading to a formal treaty that terminates the occupation at a single point in time. However, the end of many occupations (and also colonial regimes) has included the gradual emergence (or re-emergence) of autonomous political institutions within the territory, which assume increasing responsibilities culminating in sovereignty and independence.[161] Past events there suggest that such a process would not be easy to initiate today in the West Bank and Gaza. However, some such process has been envisaged in several diplomatic proposals and should not be ruled out entirely on the all too familiar grounds of 'all or nothing'. Such a process could be especially important in view of the continuing need for Palestinians to show the rest of the world (including their Arab neighbours as well as Israel) that they can conduct their affairs

---

[160] See the proposal by John Dugard in this volume that an advisory opinion of the ICJ be sought, and Ch. 17 for an account of one unsuccessful attempt to do so.

[161] Examples include the ending of the occupations of Germany and Austria in the mid-1950s.

in a responsible and effective way. Since many occupations have only ended when the occupying power has made its own decision, in its own interest, that the time for termination has come, the value of steps that might provide a basis for an occupant to reach that decision is clear. The PLO still has a long way to go to get over encrusted suspicions, and to demonstrate clearly its acceptance of Israel, its opposition to terrorism, and its commitment to democracy.

27. Prolonged occupation may be a feature of the contemporary world, but it does not necessarily mean permanent occupation. However, the problem of the Israeli occupation remains outstandingly difficult to resolve: Israel has greater grounds than some other recent occupying powers to be concerned about threats to its security; the presence of settlers in the Occupied Territories makes withdrawal more difficult; the political strength in Israel of territorial claims is considerable; and drawing the borders of any future Palestinian state raises tangled problems, especially regarding Jerusalem.

28. The Israeli occupation, unlike some others, is therefore likely to be yet further prolonged. In these circumstances, the law on occupations cannot conceivably eliminate the fundamental conflict between the Israeli occupants and the Palestinian inhabitants. At most, it can mitigate some of the worst effects of that conflict. In particular, it can remind all concerned of the provisional status of the occupation and deter further drastic steps that would militate against an eventual settlement. If such modest functions are not to be wasted, the parties involved will need not just to use law, but to demonstrate statesmanship.

2

The Application of International Law in the Occupied Territories as Reflected in the Judgments of the High Court of Justice in Israel

MAZEN QUPTY

Introduction

DOES the Israeli Supreme Court sitting as the High Court of Justice apply international law to the activities of the military government and civilian administration in the Occupied Territories? Does it examine whether the activities of those authorities conflict with the provisions of international law that apply to an occupied territory?

Which international laws are applicable in an occupied territory? And which international laws are applicable in the territories occupied by Israel?

Is the officially declared policy of the State of Israel, whereby it applies customary international law—in particular the regulations annexed to the Hague Convention of 1907 as well as the humanitarian provisions of the Fourth Geneva Convention of 1949—to the activities of the military government in the Occupied Territories, limited to a declaration of policy, or is international law actually implemented in practice, serving as a guiding light for the military commander of the Occupied Territories in his administrative activities?

We will attempt to answer these questions and others in the following article by way of a detailed examination of Israeli High Court judgments in regard to the application of international law in the Occupied Territories, and by citing other opinions which conflict with Supreme Court practice, be they the minority opinions of the same court, or the opinions of Israeli scholars.

The following examination will reveal that, practically speaking, the dominant tendency in Israeli Supreme Court rulings is one of non-

* This paper was translated from the original Hebrew by Michael Jackson.

application of international law in the Occupied Territories, for considerations and reasons with which we will deal below. In cases in which the court is inclined or ready to agree to examine a given administrative action in light of the provisions of international law, we will show how the court interprets specific provisions to suit the requirements of the occupation authorities. Whether by a broad interpretation or a narrow one, the occupation authorities are thus able to reconcile their administrative activities with the provisions of international law.

We will devote the larger part of the following paper to the Fourth Geneva Convention of 1949 and the Hague Regulations of 1907, touching only briefly on the Universal Declaration of Human Rights of 1948. In accordance with the measure of application of each of the abovementioned conventions in the Occupied Territories, we will begin our discussion with the 1907 Hague Regulations, followed by the Fourth Geneva Convention, and end with the Universal Declaration of Human Rights.

I. The 1907 Hague Regulations Regarding the Laws and Customs of War on Land

The Applicability of the Regulations to the Occupied Territories

Seven years after Israel occupied the territories, the Supreme Court formulated its position in regard to the application of the Hague Regulations of 1907 in the well-known judgment of *Hilu v. The Government of Israel*.[1] Up to that time, the Supreme Court had been irresolute in its attitude to the Hague Regulations, as is apparent in the judgment of *The Christian Society for the Holy Places v. The Minister of Defence*,[2] in which the Supreme Court treated the Hague Regulations of 1907 (as well as the Fourth Geneva Convention) as 'undertakings between nations which are signatories to them and which oblige states to one another under international law'.[3]

The Supreme Court, in the words of Judge Sussman, had left open the question of whether the Convention also constituted legislation on the basis of which the Israeli Supreme Court could render judgment in 'internal' disputes between the state and its citizens. The state attorney had agreed to the Supreme Court examining the orders of the area commander on the assumption that the Hague Regulations did apply

---

[1] HC 302/72, HC 306/72, PD 27 [2] 169.
[2] HC 337/71, PD 26 [1] 574.
[3] Ibid. 580. Note, Israel is not among the signatories of the Fourth Hague Convention of 1907 and the Regulations annexed thereto.

to the Occupied Territories, or alternatively that, even if they did not, the provisions of Article 43 constituted a 'standard of legislative behaviour which the commanders of the Israeli Defence Forces had adopted as their own'.[4] The state attorney reiterated this same position in the later judgment in the case of the *Jerusalem District Electricity Company Inc. v. The Minister of Defence* ('the first *Jerusalem District Electricity Company* case',[5] in which the Supreme Court examined an action of the West Bank military commander in the light of international law solely on the basis of the state attorney's consent.

In the wake of these two rulings, Professor Yoram Dinstein, of the Department of International Law at Tel Aviv University, published two critical analyses of the manner in which the Supreme Court had treated the Hague Regulations and the Fourth Geneva Convention.[6] Dinstein tried to instil in the Supreme Court the idea that the Fourth Hague Convention and the annexed regulations form part of internal Israeli law and that the Supreme Court does not need the goodwill of the state attorney in order to examine the activities of the military government in the territories in light of international law. Dinstein wrote:

Once again the court has not attended to the declarative nature of the Hague Regulations, which reflect international law. This customary practice is obvious and is based on countless authorities, the principal one being the important ruling of the international military tribunal of Nazi war criminals in Nuremberg which clearly established that the Hague Regulations are recognized by all enlightened nations and are declarative in respect of the laws and conduct of war. Those who desire an Israeli authority can find one in the judgment of the Supreme Court (with five judges on the bench) in the Eichmann trial,[7] where it was stated that the Hague Convention of 1907 . . . only declared the rules of war as dictated by accepted humanitarian principles. This being the case, the Hague Regulations are automatically absorbed into internal Israeli law.[8]

So it was that in the *Hilu* case—on the basis of Dinstein's abovementioned remarks and a prior ruling of the Supreme Court—the Supreme Court judges consolidated the practice, still in force in Israel to this day, whereby customary international law, unless contradictory to another provision in internal law, is considered to have been ab-

---

[4] Ibid. 580, 586.
[5] HC 256/72, PD 27 [1] 124, at 136.
[6] Y. Dinstein, 'Legislative Authority in the Administered Territories' (in Hebrew), *Eyunai Mishpat (Tel Aviv University Law Review)* 2 (1972), 505; Dinstein, 'Judicial Review of the Actions of the Military Government in the Administered Territories' (in Hebrew), *Eyunai Mishpat* 3 (1974), 330, 332. Also see Dinstein's *International Law and the State* (Tel Aviv, 1971), 128 ff., esp. 143.
[7] *The Attorney-General v. Eichmann*, Criminal Appeal 3364/1961, PD 16, 2033, at 2054; *Butterworth's International Law Reports*, 36, 277 ff. See ch. 5, text at n. 60, and n. 64 below, for the relevant passage from this judgment.
[8] Dinstein, 'Judicial Review', 332.

sorbed into Israeli law without the need for any special legislation.[9] This position was further clarified in the Supreme Court ruling in the case of *Ayyoub v. Minister of Defence* ('the *Beit El* case').[10] In the words of Judge Witkon, the Hague Convention has come to give expression to law which is accepted as a matter of course by all enlightened nations and thus regarded as customary international law.[11] Judge Barak summed up the position of the Supreme Court in respect to the Fourth Hague Convention and the Regulations annexed thereto in the case of *A Teachers' Housing Cooperative Society v. The Military Commander of the Judea and Samaria Region*, in the following manner:

The rights of a resident of the area under military government vis-a-vis the military commander—rights subject to judicial review in a court of law of the occupying state—stem from the rules governing belligerent occupation in customary international law and contractual international law, insofar as they have been assimilated into the internal law of the occupying state by a valid internal act of legislation. In respect to Israel's belligerent occupation, and in the absence of legislation which internalizes the principle norms of the laws of war relating to belligerent occupation, [the rules in force] are those included in the [Hague] Regulations . . . Even though the Hague Regulations serve as an authority in this respect, the accepted attitude—which has also been accepted by this court—is that the Hague Regulations are declarative in nature and reflect customary international law, applicable in Israel without an act of Israeli legislation.[12]

Thus the official position of the State of Israel, as expressed by the representatives of the state attorney before the High Court of Justice and in the position taken by the Israeli Supreme Court, is that the Hague Regulations of 1907, being part of customary international law, are part of internal Israeli law. Hence, the Supreme Court has the authority to examine the actions of the military commander of the Occupied Territories on the basis of the provisions and regulations of the Hague Regulations—so long as the military commander in the Occupied Territories is an 'Israeli army officer who bears the appropriate constitutional responsibility'.[13] Moreover,

[S]ince officials in the military government are subordinate to the executive authority of the state, the court has the authority to review their activities under section 7(b)(2) of the Court Law 1957.[14]

---

[9] HC 302/72, HC 306/72, 180.
[10] HC 606/78, 610/78, PD 33 [2] 113.
[11] Ibid. 120.
[12] HC 393/82, PD 37 [4] 785, 793.
[13] Y. Dinstein, 'Judgment Regarding Pithat Rafiah', *Eyunai Mishpat* (*Tel Aviv University Law Review*) 3 (1974), 934, 936.
[14] HC 606/78, 610/78, the *Beit El* case, 126.

In light of this position of the Israeli Supreme Court, how does that court apply the Hague Regulations in practice *vis-à-vis* the actions and operations of the military commanders in the Occupied Territories? We will attempt to answer this question below.

Israel's Application of the Hague Regulations of 1907

In practically every discussion of a petition related to the Occupied Territories,[15] the argument is put forward that the actions of the military government contravene the Hague Regulations and should therefore be overturned. This holds in regard to the refusal to unify families;[16] to the authority of the military commander to alter existing laws in the territories;[17] to the expropriation of private land;[18] to the declaration of land as state land;[19] to labour conflicts;[20] to the supply of electricity;[21] to the imposition of value added tax;[22] to deportation from the territories;[23] and to the demolition of homes.[24]

The attitude of the Supreme Court has been consistent throughout its rulings. On the one hand, the court recognizes the Hague Regulations as part of internal Israeli law and examines the actions of the military authorities on the basis of the Regulations. However, when it comes to their practical application, the court interprets them in a narrow sense, in order to legalize the action in question from the standpoint of international law. This is true in relation to the majority

---

[15] Hundreds of petitions have been submitted to the Israeli Supreme Court by residents of the Occupied Territories. As of December 1987, 62 judgments had been published in the official publication of the judgments of the Israeli Supreme Court. In a research project carried out by Avishai Ehrlich, published in *Israeli Democracy*, May 1987, the researcher states that between July and December 1986, 59 petitions were submitted by residents of the Occupied Territories to the Supreme Court.

[16] HC 13/86, HC 58/86, *Shahin et al. v. The Military Commander of the Judea and Samaria Region*, PD 41 [1] 197.

[17] HC 393/82, the *Teachers' Housing Cooperative* case, 784; HC 256/72, the first *Jerusalem District Electricity Company* case, 124.

[18] HC 606/78, the *Beit El* case, 113; HC 390/79 *Dweikat v. The State of Israel et al.* ('the *Elon Moreh* case'), PD 34 [1] 1.

[19] HC 277/84, *A'aryab v. The Appeal Committee*, under an order regarding state property, PD 40 [2] 57; HC 285/81, *Al-Nazir v. The Military Commander of the Judea and Samaria Region*, PD 36 [1] 701.

[20] HC 337/71, the *Christian Society for the Holy Places* case, 574.

[21] HC 256/72; and HC 351/80, HC 764/80, *The Jerusalem District Electricity Company Inc. v. The Minister of Energy and Planning et al.* ('the second *Jerusalem District Electricity Company case*'), PD 35 [2] 673.

[22] HC 69/81, *Abu Aita et al. v. The Military Commander of the Judea and Samaria Region*, PD 37 [2] 197.

[23] HC 97/79, *Abu Awad v. The Military Commander of the Judea and Samaria Region*, PD 33 [3] 309.

[24] HC 897/86, *Jaber v. The Central Area Commander*, PD 41 [2] 522.

of published judgments of the Supreme Court that deal with the Occupied Territories.[25]

The interpretation of Article 43 of the Hague Regulations gives a telling illustration of the application of the Regulations by the Supreme Court. At the beginning of the occupation, the court's interpretation of the article was not unreasonable, while, in this author's view, that given in the minority opinion of Judge Haim Cohn was accurate.[26] As the occupation continued, the court was drawn into making very broad interpretations, allowing its decisions to sanction the actions of the military governor. In certain instances, Article 43, as interpreted by the court, was used to legalize actions of the military governor which were clearly prohibited by other provisions of the Hague Regulations.

The case of *The Christian Society for the Holy Places* was the first petition in which the interpretation of Article 43 was discussed in the Supreme Court. The court was split between Judge Sussman and Judge Y. Cohen, and Judge H. Cohn, who was in the minority.[27] In this judgment, the Supreme Court attempted to amplify the authority of the Israeli military governor on the basis of the argument that his authority under Article 43 in a prolonged occupation is broader than it would be under a brief occupation. The majority opinion held that:

In an area where military occupation lasts for a prolonged period until peace is achieved, the occupant's duty *vis-à-vis* the civilian population even obliges it to alter the law, for the needs of the society change with time and the law must meet those changing requirements.[28]

In contrast to the opinion of Judge Sussman, Judge H. Cohn, in a minority opinion, defined Article 43 narrowly. According to him:

The first thing which comes to light is that authority is granted in order to restore (*rétablir*) public order and civil life, and they are not to be restored to anything other than what they were... Only if 'absolutely prevented' from

---

[25] Among all the judgements published by the Supreme Court to the end of 1987, the time of writing, the court accepted three petitions: (1) HC 802/79, *Samra et al. v. The Commander of the Judea and Samaria Region*, PD 34 [4] 1, in which the judgment does not deal at all with the question of the application of the Hague Regulations of 1907; (2) HC 351/80, the second *Jerusalem District Electricity Company* case, in which the Supreme Court cancelled the decision of the West Bank Area Commander to annul the Jerusalem Electricity Company's concession on the supply of electricity to the area of the West Bank, on the grounds that such a decision contravenes customary international law, especially Art. 43; and (3) HC 390/79, the *Elon Moreh* case, wherein the Supreme Court cancelled the decision of the West Bank Area Commander to expropriate private land, on the grounds that the expropriation was to be carried out for the purpose of establishing a civilian settlement without there being any military reason that demanded the expropriation of land, which was in contravention of Art. 52 of the Hague Regulations.
[26] HC 337/71, the *Christian Society for the Holy Places* case, 588.
[27] Ibid. 582.
[28] Ibid.

restoring the order without changing these laws can they be altered, and then only to the extent absolutely necessary...

The authority granted under Article 43 is not simply 'for restoring' but also 'for ensuring' public order and civil life. In the view of the respondent, ensuring public order and civil life may necessitate different or additional means than those thought necessary by the previous administration...

Firstly, it seems to me that these two objectives 'to restore and to ensure' should be considered as one. Hence, it is the responsibility and the obligation of the occupying administration to restore public order and civil life and to ensure their existence in the future; it is not enough to restore them, they must also be upheld... Secondly, it is possible that public order and civil life under a military government will, in many ways and by the nature of things, be different from the public order and civil life under the previous administration... And thirdly, it is possible that the public order and civil life which existed under the previous administration will not be considered by the military administration to constitute either public order or civil life... in that case, there is nothing to 'restore' but there is something to 'ensure'.[29]

The judge summed up his position by saying:

The authority given to the respondent in accordance with Article 43 is not to set the world aright and establish an ideal order and life in the territories, or even a form of public order and civil life which appears to him to be the most desirable; the authority is to restore the same public order and civil life that existed previously and to ensure their existence in the future.[30]

In the wake of this ruling, Dinstein published his reflections in an article,[31] in which he attacked both minority and majority opinions of the Supreme Court. He argued that the judges' interpretation of Article 43 is so narrow that it 'fetters the occupied population' and that the Court's 'interpretations are not underpinned by any authority'. In Dinstein's opinion:

Since, according to the conclusion of Article 43 of the Hague Regulations, the legislative authority of the occupier is contingent on the existence of [his being] 'absolutely prevented', the question arises what this term means. First of all, it is generally agreed that the adjective 'absolutely' is not as absolute as it may sound and does not really add or detract anything. The proper and accepted interpretation is that 'absolutely prevented' is to be understood in terms of necessity...[32]

Laws of war generally make for a delicate balance between two magnetic poles: on the one hand, military necessity, and on the other hand, humanitarian considerations. However, with respect to this issue, absolute prevention—i.e.

---

[29] Ibid. 586–7.
[30] Ibid. 588.
[31] Dinstein, 'Legislative Authority in the Administered Territories', 505 ff.
[32] These words of Dinstein's were adopted in HC 69/81, the *Abu Aita* case, 310.

necessity—can arise either from the legitimate interests of the occupier or from concern for the occupied population. It can be truthfully stated that the legitimate requirements of the occupier are more comprehensible in this context than concern (which is not always real) for the occupied population . . .

In actual fact, occupation and the requirements of the occupier do not negate the needs of the local population, and the legislative authority granted to the occupier is broad enough to take these needs into account.

The needs of the local population, as correctly stressed in the majority opinion, are more valid and more meaningful when the occupation is of long duration: the economic and social situation changes and it is inconceivable that the legislation in force should be frozen without taking the changing times into account.[33]

A few months after the ruling in the *Christian Society for the Holy Places* case was given, the Supreme Court returned to deliberate over the validity of the legislative acts of the Military Governor of the West Bank in light of Article 43 of the Hague Regulations. In the first *Jerusalem District Electricity Company* case, the question arose whether the supply of electricity to meet the needs of the local population was the responsibility of the military government, as part and parcel of its duty to ensure the public welfare of the population.

The court, in answering the question in the affirmative and in establishing that Article 43 of the Hague Regulations had not been violated in practice, established that the responsibility of the military governor is not only to tend to the economic welfare of the population of the region (that is, the native inhabitants of the occupied territory), but also to tend to the needs of the residents of the Jewish settlement of Kiryat Arba. These residents are citizens of the occupying state living in the occupied territory, but 'to this end, the residents of Kiryat Arba should be viewed as persons added to the local population who are likewise eligible to receive a regular supply of electricity'.[34]

On the basis of the authority vested in the military government in Article 43, as interpreted by the Supreme Court, the court validated a number of administrative actions, including the prohibition on the circulation of the East Jerusalem *Al-Talia* weekly newspaper.[35] In the *Al-Talia Weekly Magazine v. The Minister of Defence et al.* judgment, Judge Shamgar stated:

Since the establishment of the military government, it has been obliged and permitted to adopt measures which could allow the new administration to fulfil its obligations in accordance with Article 43 and to ensure the safety of our military forces, including the military government. This is so even if these measures are not based upon laws that were in force in the area on the eve of

---

[33] Dinstein, 'Legislative Authority in the Administered Territories', 509–11.
[34] HC 256/72, 138.
[35] HC 619/78 PD 33 [3] 505.

the establishment of the military government, or if their imposition required that changes be made to the existing law ... The obligation to preserve security and public order and to ensure the safety of the residents of the area provides the military administration with, *inter alia*, the authority to prohibit political activity and to limit and even ban political publications.[36]

In other instances the court not only established that it was the obligation of the military administration to preserve security and ensure the safety of the residents of the area on the basis of Article 43; it also established that this regulation served as the basis for the rejection of the argument that another provision of the Hague Regulations prohibits certain actions.

In the *Beit El* case,[37] Article 43 served as a conduit for squeezing the concept of 'ensuring public order and safety' (arising from Article 43) into Article 52 of the Hague Regulations, which prohibits the seizure of private land unless carried out for the 'needs of the army of occupation'. The court further established that the settlement of civilian residents of the occupying power in the occupied territory is in fact required by the occupying army in accordance with Article 52, as it ensures the public order and safety which the regional governor is charged with preserving under Article 43.

In the words of Judge Landau:

The principal role imposed on the army in the administered territory is to 'ensure public order and safety', as stated in Article 43 of the Hague Regulations. *What is required to achieve these objectives is by definition required for the administering army, as implied in Article 52.* The preservation of security in Judea and Samaria imposes on the army special tasks and it is obliged from time to time to undertake military operations even in times of comparative peace, to forestall the danger of terrorist acts originating outside the administered territory or within. (emphasis added)[38]

In another case, Article 43 of the Hague Regulations served as one of the bases for the rejection of the argument that the deportation of a West Bank resident violates Article 49 of the Fourth Geneva Convention. In the opinion of the Supreme Court:

[The Fourth Geneva Convention] does not diminish the obligation of the administering power to tend to the preservation of public order in the administered area, in keeping with Article 43 of the Hague Convention of 1907, nor from its right to employ measures necessary for its own security.[39]

---

[36] Dinstein, 'Legislative Authority in the Administered Territories', 510.
[37] HC 606/78, 113.
[38] Ibid. 130–1. A similar attempt occurred in the *Hilu* case, HC 302/72, 178. In that judgment, the Supreme Court employed Art. 43 in order to validate the actions of the governor, which violated Arts. 46 and 23(g) of the Hague Regulations.
[39] HC 97/79, the *Abu Awad* case, at 316.

Finally, we will consider three important judgments in which the Supreme Court dealt with Article 43 or parts thereof, interpreting the regulation in so broad a manner that at present the military governor is practically unrestricted in his ability to legislate any law he wishes, or to implement actions which violate other provisions of the Hague Regulations.

First, we will cite the case contesting the imposition of value added tax, the *Abu Aita* case.[40] In this case the petitioners argued that, on the basis of Article 43 of the Hague Regulations, the military commander is obliged to respect the existing law, save if absolutely prevented from doing so. Such circumstances did not exist, they claimed, in the imposition of value added tax.

The Supreme Court determined that, in regard to this specific case, absolute prevention did actually exist, and that the military commander was authorized to legislate for a value added tax, under the interpretation of the term 'restoration and maintenance of public order'. Speaking on behalf of the court, Judge Shamgar adopted the interpretation which he himself had used in an article he had written.[41] He said:

The expression 'restoration and maintenance of public order' (*la vie publique*) is, it would seem, a paraphrase of the words 'normalization and rule of law'. 'Rule of law', in its turn, is based on the defined norms of a given legal system.[42]

The Supreme Court also raised the question of the obligations of the occupying power when the resources at its disposal through the collection of taxes cannot cover the costs of administering the territory. Does such a situation oblige the military government, in light of Article 43, to make up the difference by drawing on its own resources in order to fulfil its obligation 'to restore and ensure, as far as possible, public order and safety'?[43]

In other words, while the petitioners argued that the military commander is barred by force of Article 43 from legislating a military order whereby a new tax will be imposed in the area, the Supreme Court examined the question of whether the military commander is not obliged, under Article 43, to legislate precisely such a law.

The Supreme Court did not answer the question, making do with raising it for debate, as 'such an argument was not put forward by any of the parties'.[44] On the other hand, the court did adopt the viewpoint

---

[40] HC 69/81, PD 37 [2] 197. See further discussion of this case in ch. 11.
[41] M. Shamgar, 'The Observance of International Law in the Administered Territories', *IYHR* 1 (1971), 262, 266.
[42] HC 69/81, 229.
[43] Ibid. 261.
[44] Ibid.

that the authority vested in the occupying administration to impose a new tax falls under its general legislative authority. An action carried out in accordance with Article 43 of the Hague Regulations and interpretations of that article,[45] in the opinion of the court, cannot conflict with the provisions of Article 48 of the Hague Regulations, which is solely intended to regulate the specific issue of existing tax collection and does not bar the implementation, in so far as it is necessary, of the stated provisions of Article 43 for the purpose of corrective or new fiscal legislation.[46] In fact Articles 48 and 49, according to the Court, are subordinate to the general provision of Article 43 which is not encroached on by them.[47]

The second ruling was in the case of *Tabib et al. v. The Minister of Defence*.[48] In this case, the legality of expropriating the private land of the petitioners in order to build a road linking the various settlements in the occupied West Bank was discussed by the court. The petitioners argued that the expropriation of land for the purpose of building a road contravened international law applicable to occupied territory. In dealing with Article 43, from which the military government derives its authority, the court interpreted the term 'ensuring public life'

to mean the provision of an administration which protects the rights of citizens and tends to the maximum welfare of the population. If the realization of this objective demands deviation from existing laws, it is permissible and even obligatory to deviate from them.

In the opinion of the court,

[T]oday, 14 years after the [beginning of the] occupation, one can no longer speak about 'the restoration of order and public life'—they were restored long ago. Hence, one must speak about 'ensuring' them, i.e., operating an orderly administration and all its departments, as is customary in an enlightened country, including security, health, education, welfare, and also, *inter alia*, quality of life and transportation.[49]

The final ruling concerns the *Teachers' Housing Cooperative* case.[50] This petition dealt with the authority of the military commander to expropriate the petitioner's land for the purpose of building roads in the West Bank which, in the future, would link towns in the West Bank with Israel.

In this case, the Supreme Court reiterated the practice established in

---

[45] Ibid. 293, 308; see also 324.
[46] Ibid. 294.
[47] See Y. Dinstein's article on this judgment: 'Value Added Tax in the Administered Territories' (in Hebrew), *Eyunai Mishpat* (*Tel Aviv University Law Review*) 10 (1985), 159.
[48] HC 202/81, PD 36 [2] 622.
[49] Ibid. 629.
[50] HC 393/82.

two preceding cases—the *Abu Aita* case and the *Tabib* case—placing special emphasis on the effect of the lengthy occupation on the authority vested in the military commander by dint of Article 43, and further stating that actually, this authority was broader in scope than Article 43 itself provided for, owing to the fact that it had considered solely occupations of short duration. In the words of the court:

> In establishing the scope of the authority of the military government in accordance with the formula 'the regulation of public life', it would appear to be obvious that a distinction must be drawn between a military government of short duration and a military government of long duration... This distinction between a military government of short duration and a military government of long duration has great ramifications for the manner in which 'public life and order' is to be ensured... [I]t is only natural that under a short-term military occupation, military and security requirements are paramount. In contrast, under a long-term military occupation, the requirements of the local population are given greater validity. Hence, legislative practices which would be inappropriate under a short-term military government may become appropriate under a long-term military government.[51]

The conclusion the court drew from this was as follows:

> This distinction between types of military government, made on the basis of duration, may constitute a proper political consideration in regard to all those instances in which there is room to develop such a policy within the context of the Regulations themselves. A clear example of this is Article 43. Public life and order require consideration of the time element and the fact that all the Regulations were formulated for short-term military governments should not prevent practical developments from taking place in regard to the scope of authority of a long-term military government, within the broad and flexible framework which Article 43 of the Hague Regulations engendered.[52]

Hence:

> [T]he authority of a military administration applies to taking all measures necessary to ensure growth, change, and development.[53]

Will the Hague Regulations Continue to be Applied in the Occupied Territories?

Although we have examined the practices of the Supreme Court in regard to the application of the Hague Regulations of 1907 and their practical implementation in various judgments rendered on the issue, there remains the question of whether the Supreme Court, after so long a period of occupation, and in the wake of dozens, possibly

---
[51] Ibid. 800–1.
[52] Ibid. 802.
[53] Ibid. 804. See ch. 1, text at n. 156 in this volume for the rest of this passage.

hundreds of judgments on the issue, will establish that there is no longer any reason to impose the Hague Regulations on the territories occupied by Israel, particularly in the West Bank and the Gaza Strip.

While the likelihood of such a development may be slight, it is my opinion that existing tendencies among some of the Supreme Court judges should not be ignored. There are indeed some judges who have said that the Hague Regulations should be treated in the same manner as the Fourth Geneva Convention of 1949, that is to say, that these regulations should not be applied to occupied territory which was not under sovereign rule prior to the occupation. They argue that, as Israel claims that the West Bank and the Gaza Strip were not under Jordanian or Egyptian sovereignty prior to the Israeli occupation, the Hague Regulations and the Fourth Geneva Convention should not be applied to them. To apply them, it is argued, would be tantamount to *de facto* recognition of the sovereignty of these two states over the territories in question, something which Israel opposes.

The claim that the territories of the West Bank and Gaza Strip were not under sovereign rule prior to their occupation by Israel has been argued a number of times before the Supreme Court. The court chose not to render a ruling on the issue as the petitions submitted did not require its resolution.[54] So it remained until the judgment in *Elyakim Ha'etzni v. The State of Israel*[55] in which, for the first time, the court expressed a clear position in favour of this claim. The court, in the words of Judge Landau, stated:

The fact that Jordan was never the legal sovereign in the areas of Judea and Samaria is correct, but this should not lead one to think that the regional commander could not declare the laws that existed in the region prior to the entry of the IDF to be valid.[56]

This leads to the question of whether the Supreme Court may actually decide that the Hague Regulations are not applicable in the Occupied Territories—particularly in the West Bank—as the territories were not under sovereign rule when occupied.

The likelihood of such a development begins to prove worrisome when there appear hints in Supreme Court judgments according to which the Hague Regulations should not be applied if they conflict with either local Israeli law or the local law of the occupied territory. In the event of a conflict between local law and the Hague Regulations, this argument runs, the provisions of local law should be preferred and not vice versa.

---

[54] See HC 390/79, the *Elon Moreh* case, 13; see also HC 302/72, the *Hilu* case, 179; and HC 606/78, the *Beit El* case, 129.
[55] HC 61/80, PD 34 [3] 595
[56] Ibid. 597; see also HC 69/81, the *Abu Aita* case, 229.

It is our opinion that, up to now, the Supreme Court has sought and found a variety of ways to justify the practical non-application of the Hague Regulations of 1907. Likewise, it would not come as a surprise if one day it were to employ the arguments used to justify the non-application of the Fourth Geneva Convention, to be discussed more fully below, against the application of the Regulations. The President of the Supreme Court, for one, has expressed support for this argument in his private capacity.[57]

This impression is buttressed by a judgment rendered in May 1987 and published in December 1987 regarding the case of *Ramzi Hana Jaber v. OC Central Command*,[58] which will be discussed more fully in the following section. This petition dealt with the authority of the central region army commander to order the demolition of a room on the roof of the petitioner's house by dint of the authority vested in him under Article 119 of the Defence (Emergency) Regulations of 1945.

The petitioner argued that the exercise of the authority granted to the military commander under the above-mentioned Article 119 is in contravention of the provisions of the Hague Regulations of 1907 and the Fourth Geneva Convention.[59] In rejecting the petitioner's arguments, the Supreme Court established for the first time that the authority vested in the regional commander under the internal law of the occupied territory cannot be challenged by the provisions of international law, and that the authority of the commander cannot be subject to review by force of international law.[60]

So long as this position of the Supreme Court continues to be upheld, the Israeli position, whereby the Hague Regulations apply to the Occupied Territories, is stripped of all meaning. The Defence (Emergency) Regulations of 1945, which include the above-mentioned Article 119, provide the military governor with extremely broad authority. If these regulations are underpinned by law against challenges made on the basis of the Hague Regulations, the day is not far off when the Hague Regulations may become no more than a 'legal catchword' rather than a means for the efficient legal supervision of the activities of the military government.

---

[57] M. Shamgar, 'Legal Concepts and Problems of the Israeli Military Government: the Initial Stage', in Shamgar (ed.) *Military Government in the Territories Administered by Israel 1967–1980*, i: *The Legal Aspects* (Jerusalem, 1982), 38 n. 48.

[58] HC 897/86, PD 41 [2] 522.

[59] Ibid. 524.

[60] Ibid. 525–6. Note that this position totally conflicts with the remarks of Judge H. Cohn in the minority judgment in HC 698/80, *Qawassmeh et al. v. The Minister of Defence et al.*, PD 35 [1] 617, 645. There, Judge Cohn says that since Art. 112 of the Defence Regulations, which authorizes the military commander to deport a resident of the Occupied Territories, conflicts with the rules of international law, in this case with Art. 49 of the Geneva Convention, Art. 112 is overruled by Art. 49.

II. The Fourth Geneva Convention of 1949 Relative to the Protection of Civilians in Times of War

The Israeli position and the position of the Supreme Court in regard to the Hague Regulations of 1907 was that these Regulations were to be applied to the Occupied Territories. However, with the passage of time, there has been a marked tendency—which has become more pronounced over the years, particularly in the decisions of the Supreme Court—whereby the scope of the practical application of the Regulations has been made extremely narrow, as shown in the first section of this paper. In respect to the Fourth Geneva Convention, the Israeli attitude has always been clear-cut. Since the beginning of the occupation, Israel has maintained that the Fourth Geneva Convention cannot be applied to the territories occupied by Israel for reasons which shall be explained below. Any legal attempt to apply this Convention is doomed to failure.

In the following, we will present the position of the Israeli government on the issue and the legal explanations given by the Supreme Court for the non-application of the Convention—which we will deal with at length. Next, we will turn to the interpretations given to Article 49 of the Geneva Convention by the Supreme Court both to justify the deportation of residents of the territories and to show that such acts are in keeping with the provisions of the Geneva Convention. In this section we will examine the position of the Supreme Court in regard to the provisions of the Convention in the wake of the state attorney's agreement to allow the court to deliberate on the issue. And finally, we will review some of the arguments put forward by Israeli scholars who believe that both the State of Israel and the Supreme Court are mistaken in their refusal to apply the Fourth Geneva Convention in the Occupied Territories. We will examine the question of whether such views are likely to influence the Supreme Court to apply the Convention in the territories and the manner in which the Convention could be applied.

The Official Israeli Position Regarding the Non-Application of the Fourth Geneva Convention in the Occupied Territories

The official Israeli position regarding the non-application of the Fourth Geneva Convention in the Occupied Territories can be summed up by a few principles according to which: (*a*) Article 2 of the Geneva Convention stipulates that the Convention is to be applied to occupied territories captured from states which held sovereignty over those territories; (*b*) the territories of the West Bank and the Gaza Strip were never under Jordanian or Egyptian sovereignty—Jordan's status in the

West Bank was one of an occupying state replete with a military government, while the Gaza Strip was, at most, under Egyptian administration; (c) if Israel were to agree to the application of the Fourth Geneva Convention it would be tantamount to Israeli recognition of Jordanian and Egyptian sovereignty over these territories.[61]

The President of the Supreme Court, Judge M. Shamgar, wrote an article in which he gave a detailed explanation of the Israeli position.[62] He explained that:

Israel's position was that as a signatory of the Fourth Convention it was generally bound by the Convention; but in relation to every convention... a second question always arises as a corollary, namely whether the convention... actually applies to the specific set of circumstances under consideration. In order to decide this issue one has to refer to the provisions relating to the application of the Convention...

According to the Israeli position, the question that should be posed is:

(W)hether the actual words and context of the Convention involve its applicability to each and every factual situation of military occupation or only to the occupation of territory which was under the sovereignty of another High Contracting Party prior to its occupation.[63]

Judge Shamgar goes on to examine the text of Article 2 of the Fourth Geneva Convention[64] and attempts to provide a legal foundation for the Israeli position that, on the basis of this Article, the Convention is not applicable to the Occupied Territories, as they were not under sovereign rule. While the first paragraph of the Article, which deals with peacetime and situations of armed conflict, refers to all cases of war or armed conflict between High Contracting Parties, the second paragraph, dealing with occupation, refers only to occupation of the

---

[61] Regarding the legal status of the West Bank, much has been written. See E. Lauterpacht, *Jerusalem and the Holy Places* (London, 1968), 46–7; J. Stone, *The Middle East Under Ceasefire: Notes on the Legal Position Before the Security Council in October 1967* (Sydney, 1967), 12, and *No Peace—No War in the Middle East: Legal Problems of the First Year* (Sydney, 1969), 17; S. M. Schwebel, 'What Weight to Conquest?', *AJIL* 64 (1970), 344; S. Boyd, 'The Applicability of International Law to the Occupied Territories', *IYHR* 1 (1971), 258; A. Gerson, 'Trustee-Occupant: The Legal Status of Israel's Presence in the West Bank', *HILJ* 14 (1973), 1, and *Israel, the West Bank and International Law* (London, 1978), 78; T. S. Kuttner, 'Israel and the West Bank—Aspects of the Law of Belligerent Occupation', *IYHR* 7 (1977), 175; Y. Dinstein, 'Zion to be Ransomed by International Law' (in Hebrew), *Hapraklet* 27 (1971), 5, and 'And the Ransom has not been Redeemed, or Not Demonstrations but Action' (in Hebrew), *Hapraklet* 27 (1971), 519; Y. Blum, 'East Jerusalem is not Occupied Territory' (in Hebrew), *Hapraklet* 28 (1972), 182, and 'Zion Ransomed by International Law' (in Hebrew), *Hapraklet* 27 (1971), 315.
[62] Shamgar, 'Legal Concepts and Problems', 13–59.
[63] Ibid. 32–4.
[64] For text of Art. 2, see ch. 1, text at n. 56.

territory of a High Contracting Party. The question Shamgar poses is as to whether these paragraphs are to be read conjunctively or independently. He concludes that:

If the paragraphs are independent and not of a cumulative effect, and only the second paragraph defines the extent of the application to occupied territory, the one and only conclusion arising is that the Convention applies merely to the occupation of *the territory of a High Contracting Party* and not generally to territories held under military occupation.[65]

This position has never been deliberated upon in the Supreme Court since the state attorney has never subjected it to the judicial review of the Supreme Court.[66] In the *Ha'etzni* judgment, however, the Supreme Court expressed its support of this position even though it did not examine it.[67]

Israel's official position has been subjected to harsh criticism which has also come from inside Israel. In the opinion of Professor Dinstein, this position of the government of Israel

is based on shaky legal foundations; but it is especially difficult to understand on account of the fact that the Fourth Geneva Convention is not contingent on recognition of property rights.

In his opinion:

There is not a state in the world which is ready to accept this strange position and the entire issue of the application of the Fourth Geneva Convention in the Occupied Territories has become a whip which Israel consistently flogs.[68]

As mentioned earlier, this position has never served as the legal basis for the non-application of the Fourth Geneva Convention to the Occupied Territories by the Supreme Court. For this reason we shall not delve into the above position, but have presented it in the context of a comprehensive review of the issue.

The Application of the Humanitarian Provisions of the Fourth Geneva Convention

In order to deflect harsh international criticism of Israel's refusal to apply the Fourth Geneva Convention to the Occupied Territories for the reasons stated above, the Attorney-General of Israel declared on behalf of the Government in the course of a symposium held at Tel

---

[65] Shamgar, 'Legal Concepts and Problems', 37–8. Emphasis in the original.
[66] See HC 390/79, the *Elon Moreh* case, and HC 606/78, the *Beit El* case, 127.
[67] HC 61/80, 597.
[68] Dinstein, 'Judgment regarding Pithat Rafiah', 938. See also B. Rubin, 'The Adoption of International Conventions by Israel in Israeli Courts' (in Hebrew), *Meshpatiem* 13 (1983), 210, 231; also see Y. Dinstein, *The Laws of War* (in Hebrew) (Tel Aviv, 1983), 212.

Aviv University that Israel had decided that in practice it would act in accordance with the humanitarian provisions of the Fourth Geneva Convention.[69]

What are the humanitarian provisions of the Fourth Geneva Convention? In the opinion of the Israeli Attorney-General at that time, 'Humanitarian law concerns itself essentially with human beings in distress and victims of war, not states or their special interests.'[70] But does this position have any legal meaning?

The Israeli position does not allow one to conclude that the Supreme Court is authorized to examine on its own accord whether the activities of the military government are in keeping with the Fourth Geneva Convention. Only if the state attorney agrees to such a judicial review can the Supreme Court examine the actions of the governor in light of the provisions of the Convention.[71]

In the opinion of the court in the *Hilu* case, the state attorney customarily allows the examination of the actions of the military government in light of the Fourth Geneva Convention. Such agreement is occasionally granted in regard to defined issues and without any obligation that it will be given in every petition, something which 'makes our deliberations into a kind of arbitration which is contingent on the agreement of the respondent'.[72]

In the *Elon Moreh* case as well, the state representative requested that the Supreme Court 'confirm that in respect to the Fourth Geneva Convention, no reproach could be lodged against the authorities for transferring land to settlers for their settlement'. The state attorney argued that the action did not contravene the humanitarian provisions of the Convention which are accepted by the government of Israel. The court, in rejecting the request, established that the 'humanitarian' provisions in the Convention do not simply apply to the 'protection of human life, health, liberty or dignity', but also to the protection of property.[73]

As stated above, the assertion that 'the humanitarian provisions' of the Geneva Convention are applied has no real legal meaning since they are not applied automatically. They are applied only if and when the State of Israel agrees to their application, and only in cases in which the state attorney is convinced that the interpretation given by the Supreme Court to a specific provision covers the action against

---

[69] See also Shamgar, 'The Observance of International Law', 261, 263, 266; and Shamgar, 'Legal Concepts and Problems', 42.
[70] Shamgar, 'The Observance of International Law', 263.
[71] Dinstein, 'Judgment of Pithat Rafiah', 939; HC 369/79, *Ben Zion v. The Military Commander of the Judea and Samaria Region*, PD 34 [1] 145, 150.
[72] HC 302/72, the *Hilu* case, 181.
[73] HC 390/79, 29.

which the High Court of Justice has been petitioned. This will be discussed more fully below.

The Geneva Convention as Part of Contractual International Law

It took the Supreme Court a not inconsiderable time to formulate the position whereby the Fourth Geneva Convention is not considered part of internal Israeli law, being contractual rather than customary international law. It was the case of the *Beit El* settlement which prompted Judge Witkon to distinguish between the Hague Regulations of 1907 and the Fourth Geneva Convention, in the following manner:

> [T]he first question which we must answer is: do the petitioners, as protected persons, have the right to demand, on their own behalf, their rights in accordance with these conventions—and to do so in a 'municipal' (internal) court of the occupying state. Or are only the states which are parties to these conventions authorized to demand the rights of protected persons, and to do so, of course, solely in an international context.
>
> The answer to this question is contingent on another question, namely: has this same provision in an international convention which we are being requested to enforce, become part of the municipal law of the state whose court is being petitioned in regard to the matter; or has this provision remained an agreement among states and only states and not been assimilated into internal municipal law?
>
> In the first instance we are speaking about 'customary' international law recognized in municipal courts so long as there does not exist a provision of municipal law which conflicts with it; while in the second instance we are speaking about 'contractual' international law which, as previously stated, solely obliges states to one another.[74]

Since the *Beit El* case, until the present time, the Supreme Court has reiterated this position whenever it has been argued in court that the provisions of the Geneva Convention apply to the matter under discussion. This position has taken root in Supreme Court judgments to the point where it is difficult to believe that the Supreme Court will alter it, even though other views have been put forward by Israeli scholars.[75]

The practice which has crystallized in dozens of judgments was summed up by Judge Barak in the *Teachers' Housing Cooperative Society* case. After confirming that the Hague Regulations are indeed part of customary law applicable in Israel,[76] he continued as follows:

---

[74] HC 606/78, PD 33 [2] 119–20.
[75] Rubin, 'The Adoption of International Conventions', 241; see also T. Meron, 'West Bank and Gaza: Human Rights and Humanitarian Law in the Period of Transition', *IYHR* 9 (1979), 111–12.
[76] See text at n. 52.

The same does not apply to the [Fourth] Geneva Convention . . . which, even if applicable to Israel's belligerent occupation of Judea and Samaria—a question which is extremely controversial and which we will not address—constitutes above all else a constitutive convention which does not adopt existing international customs, but generates new norms whose application in Israel demands an act of legislation.[77]

As mentioned earlier, the position of the Supreme Court is clear-cut. It is opposed to the application of the Fourth Geneva Convention to the actions of the military government in the Occupied Territories. However, in spite of this, do there exist ways whereby it is possible to circumvent the practice of the Supreme Court and convince it to examine the acts of the government in light of the Geneva Convention?

One of the ways this can be done is through acquiring the agreement of the state attorney to examine the actions of the military government, turning the court into a kind of arbitrator between the parties. Another way is to attempt to prove to the Supreme Court that the Fourth Geneva Convention has, to all intents and purposes, become part of customary international law, or that specific provisions (such as Article 49, which prohibits deportation) have become part of customary international law; thus such provisions reflect international declarative law and, in keeping with the practice of the court, should be applied. A third way is to show that the practice of the Supreme Court, according to which the Geneva Convention cannot be applied in Israel because it is a contractual international convention, is incorrect. It can be argued that, while international conventions of a contractual nature do not automatically apply to internal Israeli law, this does not affect the application of conventions which are legislative in nature, such as the Geneva Convention. Another way is to ascertain whether the provisions of the Fourth Geneva Convention can already be considered part of internal Israeli law, under the orders of the General Staff, in particular General Staff Order No. 33.0133. Finally, the question of whether the Geneva Convention is part of the internal law of the Occupied Territories should be considered, whether by means of military legislation or by legislation existing prior to 1967 on the basis of Jordan's becoming a party to the Fourth Geneva Convention in 1958.

Before examining these methods we wish to discuss another obstacle encountered recently to any attempt to apply the Geneva Convention to the actions of the military governor, or at least to those actions carried out under the Defence (Emergency) Regulations of 1945, issued during the British Mandate.

---

[77] HC 393/82, 793. Note also the opinion of Judge Witkon in the *Elon Moreh* case: 'It is a mistake to think that the Geneva Convention does not apply to Judea and Samaria. It does apply, even though . . . it is not within the jurisdiction of this court', HC 390/79, 29; see also the similar view of Dinstein in *Laws of War*, 213.

In the *Jaber* case,[78] the O.C. Central Command issued an order under the authority vested in him by Article 119 of the Defence Regulations, to demolish a room on the roof of Jaber's house and seal up the second floor. The petitioner argued that the military commander's order contravened the provisions of the Hague Regulations of 1907 and the Fourth Geneva Convention. In rejecting this argument the court established that:

Article 119 is part of the law that applied to Judea and Samaria on the eve of the establishment of IDF rule. In accordance with the principles of public international law, which also found expression in the Proclamation Regarding the Regulation of Administration and Law (Judea and Samaria) (No. 2) of 1967..., local law was preserved, save for certain restrictions which do not concern the issue now before us. Hence, the authority vested under the above-mentioned Article 119 is within the bounds of the local law which exists and is applied in Judea and Samaria, since during the previous administration or that of the military government [the Defence Regulations] were not rescinded, and we have not been presented with legal arguments for considering them to have been rescinded now.[79]

According to this position of the Supreme Court, so long as there exists an internal law in the territories, the internal law outweighs the provisions of the Geneva Convention and the Hague Regulations as well, and in such instances there is no need to examine the activities of the military government in accordance with the standards established by international law.

This position of the Supreme Court actually conflicts with the practice established in the *Qawassmeh* case.[80] In this judgment the court ruled that it was doubtful whether the Defence Regulations of 1945 were still in force in the West Bank on the eve of the IDF's entry into the area in light of Article 9(1) of the Jordanian Constitution of 1952.[81]

In the opinion of the court, the Defence Regulations were in force in the area of the West Bank owing to the area commander's legislation of February 1968, at which time he issued the Order Regarding Interpretations (Additional Provisions) (No. 5) (Judea and Samaria) (No. 224) 1968, which established in Article 2 that 'emergency legislation, as understood in accordance with Article 3 of the 1945 Regulations, is annulled only by legislation which clearly establishes, by direct reference, that it is annulled'. When the legislation of the area commander carried out under the authority vested in him under Articles 112 and 119 of the Defence Regulations comes up against a rule of customary international law, it is accepted that the rule laid down

---

[78] HC 897/86, 522.
[79] Ibid. 525–6.
[80] HC 698/80 (n. 60 above).
[81] Ibid. 625.

by customary international law overrules the legislation of the area commander.[82]

If in the end the position put forward by Judge Shamgar in the *Jaber* case is accepted—that is, that the Defence Regulations are part of internal law rather than imposed by legislation of a military commander—this additional obstacle may come to constitute an immovable impediment to any attempt to apply the Geneva Convention to the actions of the military commander in the Occupied Territories. The powers given under the Defence Regulations encompass so many administrative actions—including demolition of houses, deportation, closure of areas, administrative detention, etc.—and are so widely invoked by the military commander that, in view of the ruling of the Supreme Court that in the case of a conflict between international law and local law, the local law should be preferred, there may be no case in which the Convention could override local law. In the meantime, until there are new developments in regard to Supreme Court judgments, we will amplify the discussion of the possible ways in which the Geneva Convention can be applied in the Supreme Court.

The Application of the Convention Following the Agreement of the State Attorney

The very first time a petition was submitted to the High Court of Justice about an issue related to the Occupied Territories, the question of the application of the Geneva Convention arose. Did the Convention have the status of a law according to which the court could rule in internal controversies between a citizen and the state? Even at that time, the state representative chose not to put these questions before the court. Instead, he agreed to examine the actions of the area commander in light of the Geneva Convention, arguing that the commander had acted in accordance with the Convention.[83]

State representatives have agreed to do this in every case in which the specific provisions of the Geneva Convention, as interpreted by the State of Israel, did not, in the eyes of the state, conflict with the action taken by the military government[84]. However, no assurance was ever given that this would always be the case.

In the opinion of the Supreme Court, this agreement—granted from time to time in regard to defined issues and without any obligation to grant it for each and every petition—turned the role of the court into

---

[82] Ibid. 645.
[83] HC 337/71, the *Christian Society for the Holy Places* case, 580.
[84] For a case in which the state representative did not consent to the examination of the military government's actions in the light of the Geneva Convention, see HC 698/80, the *Qawassmeh* case (n. 60 above).

one of arbitration, contingent on the agreement of the state.[85] In the *Beit El* case, the court refused to examine the actions of the military government in light of the Geneva Convention on the following grounds:

[I]f I was convinced that the Conventions have not been made part of municipal law, it would not be right, nor would it be fitting, for us to discuss them, even if the parties were agreed that we should do so. In my opinion, it is not our role to wrap ourselves in the cloak of an arbitrator or of a professor of law expressing his expert opinion about an issue which is essentially academic.[86]

When the state representative agrees to apply the provisions of the Geneva Convention, it can lead to the cancellation of the act of the military commander; such was the case in the deportations of Mayors Mohammed Milhem and Fahd Qawassmeh. However, in this case the state attorney did not agree to the Supreme Court examining the act of deportation in light of Article 49 of the Geneva Convention.[87]

In the judgment, Judge Landau, the president of the court, presented a variety of arguments regarding the legality of the act of deportation, but avoided ruling on the question, since the Geneva Convention

does not constitute a part of customary international law and therefore was not contravened as the deportation orders were issued under the internal law of the State of Israel and the Judea and Samaria area, in accordance with which this court renders judgment.[88]

Even when the state attorney agreed to the actions of the military government being judged in light of the Geneva Convention, the court interpreted it in a manner which validated the actions of the military government,[89] as is readily apparent in the attitude of the court to the

---

[85] HC 302/72, the *Hilu* case (n. 1 above), 181.

[86] Remarks of Judge Witkon in HC 606/78, the *Beit El* case, 120. Recently, the State Attorney has expressed his willingness to examine the right of residents of the territories to family reunification in light of the provisions of the Fourth Geneva Convention. See HC 13/86, 58/86, the *Shahin* case (n. 16 above), 197.

[87] HC 698/80, 636. In this judgment, Judge H. Cohn gave a minority opinion that the deportation should be cancelled on account of the provisions of Art. 49 of the Geneva Convention, which is part of customary international law. Also see Rubin, 'The Adoption of International Conventions', 236; and see HC 606/78, the *Beit El* case, 113; and Y. Dinstein, 'Settlements and Deportation in the Administered Territories' (in Hebrew), *Eyunai Mishpat (Tel Aviv University Law Review)* 7 (1979), 188, 190.

[88] HC 698/80, 627.

[89] In respect to internal Israeli law, the scope of intervention permitted to the High Court of Justice against the deportation orders issued by a military commander is very narrow. The Supreme Court, in hearing the petition of a person against whom a deportation order has been issued, 'does not know and should not know what security factors require the deportation of the petitioner from the country . . . In regard to everything that concerns the security justifications of deportation orders, for the court the case is closed.' (HC 17/71, *Morrar v. the Minister of Defence*, PD 25 [1] 141, 142–3). Likewise, the court does not review the effectiveness and the wisdom of the decision taken, on the

110   *Qupty*

provisions of Articles 49(1) and 49(6) of the Geneva Convention, prohibiting deportations of protected persons and transfer of the occupier's own civilian population into the occupied territory respectively.[90]

Article 49(6) of the Convention was discussed in the *Beit El* case and the *Elon Moreh* case. While in the *Elon Moreh* case, the court refused to discuss the issue of the application and interpretation of Article 49(6) of the Convention,[91] in the *Beit El* case, though ruling that the actions of the military government should not be examined in light of the Geneva Convention, the court tended to accept the interpretation of Article 49(6) according to which this article is not applicable to the voluntary transfer of citizens of the occupying power to the occupied territory.[92]

The Supreme Court has had many opportunities to discuss Article 49(1) of the Geneva Convention. Each time, the argument that an action of the military government is in contravention of the provisions of the article has been rejected. In the *Abu Awad* case,[93] the court established that Article 49(1) was intended to prevent atrocities like those perpetrated by the Germans in World War II. The Germans deported millions of people from their homes for a variety of reasons. Generally they were brought to Germany to serve as forced labourers for the enemy, and Jews and others were deported to concentration camps to be tortured and exterminated.[94] Thus, it is argued, the provisions of the article do not apply to the deportation of a lone individual. In the *Qawassmeh* case, it was established that the deportation of a West Bank resident who is a citizen of Jordan to Jordan itself does not contravene Article 49(1).[95] This position was reiterated in the

---

basis that this deviates from the bounds of judicial review and belongs within the bounds of political decision-making (HC 698/80, the *Qawassmeh* case, 634–5). And if the considerations of the military commander have passed the review of the Advisory Board, the court will not intervene in these considerations (HC 97/79, the *Abu Awad* case, 317); only if the court is convinced that the area commander did not take substantive account of the considerations given in Art. 108 of the mandatory Defence (Emergency) Regulations of 1945, will the court be prepared to intervene in the commander's judgement, no matter what the recommendations of the Advisory Board are (HC 698/80, the *Qawassmeh* case, 635).

[90] See ch. 1, text at n. 124.
[91] HC 390/79, 14.
[92] HC 606, 610/78, 128. In Dinstein's opinion, this interpretation of Art. 49(6) is mistaken: '[W]hen a clearly civilian settlement is located in Samaria, in accordance with the direct decision of the Israeli government and in the wake of the expropriation of private land, it is difficult not to consider this to be a violation of the Geneva agreement.' See Dinstein, 'Settlements and Deportation in the Administered Territories', 189.
[93] HC 97/79, 309.
[94] Ibid. at 316.
[95] HC 698/80, 649. This opinion later gained the approval of Dinstein, who said that, had the military governor sent the petitioners in the *Qawassmeh* case to the Kingdom of Jordan, there would be no grounds for speaking about a violation of Art. 49(1) of the Geneva Convention. In Dinstein's opinion, this article prohibits the deportation of protected persons from the occupied territory to the territory of the occupying power or to that of another state. However, the word 'another' should be defined as a state which

Nazal case and in the *Kasrawi* case.[96] In the latter, the court said that Article 49

does not relate, in any of the legal versions known to us, to the deportation of a person from a territory which he consciously entered illegally following the establishment of military rule in the territory. In accordance with its accepted interpretation, it cannot relate to someone who infiltrated the line which divides two sides at war with each other[97]

An equally surprising position was taken by the Supreme Court in the *Abu Awad* case when it ruled that deportation in this instance was intended to protect public order and safety, and that this was a legitimate reason to deport a person. In the opinion of the court, the Geneva Convention

does not reduce the obligation of the occupying power to tend to the preservation of public order in the administered territory as dictated by Article 43 of the Hague Convention of 1907, nor does it [reduce] its right to employ measures necessary to preserve its own security.[98]

The Geneva Convention as Part of Customary International Law

We have already reviewed the practice of the Supreme Court according to which an Israeli court must apply customary international law, and only customary international law, as part of internal Israeli law. Customary international law expresses the international rules of conduct that exist, and which are accepted by the nations of the world, whereas constitutive contractual law is intended to legislate new international rules of conduct and does not constitute part of internal Israeli law, unless it has been adopted by special Israeli legislation, in the view of the Supreme Court.

The Supreme Court also ruled that the Fourth Geneva Convention, in contrast to the Hague Regulations of 1907, is part of constitutive contractual international law and not part of declarative customary law. As such, the Geneva Convention does not constitute part of internal Israeli law. Hence, a petitioner cannot base his argument on it when coming before the High Court of Justice. The circumvention of this court practice can occur if the court becomes convinced that the Fourth

---

is not the state of citizenship of the deportee. (Dinstein, 'The Deportation of the Mayors from Judea' (in Hebrew), *Eyunai Mishpat (Tel Aviv University Law Review)* 8 (1981), 158 and 170).

[96] HC 256/85, 513, 514/85, *Nazal et al. v. The Military Commander of the Judea and Samaria Region*, PD 39 [3] 645, 654, and HC 454, 456/85 *Kasrawi et al. v. The Minister of Defence*, PD 39 [3] 401, 410.
[97] HC 454/85, 410.
[98] HC 97/79, 316. Dinstein criticized this position in 'Settlements and Deportation in the Administered Territories' 188 and 193.

Geneva Convention is part of declarative customary international law, or that, between its legislation and the present time, the Convention has become part of customary international law, or that specific provisions of the Convention have become generally accepted as being among the rules of customary international law which also bind Israeli courts.

A number of international legal scholars have already expressed their view in favour of the position whereby the Geneva Convention is considered to be part of customary law. For instance, Jean Pictet:

> The Convention does not, strictly speaking, introduce any innovation in this sphere of international law. It does not put forward any new ideas. But it reaffirms and ensures, by a series of detailed provisions, the general acceptance of the principle of respect for the human person in the very midst of war—a principle on which too many cases of unfair treatment during the Second World War appeared to have cast doubt.[99]

Two other scholars, Yingling and Ginnane, reached an identical conclusion:

> The new civilian convention is an extension and codification of earlier rules and practices governing the treatment of alien enemies in a belligerent country and in the treatment of the inhabitants of territory under military occupation.[100]

Other scholars state that, if not all the provisions of the Convention are part of customary international law, at least some specific provisions of the Convention do actually constitute norms of customary international law of which the Geneva Convention was declaratory.

According to Georg Schwarzenberger:

> The question of whether the Geneva Red Cross Convention IV is declaratory or constitutive is not settled conclusively in the Convention. It is merely stated that the Convention is 'supplementary' to the corresponding sections of the Regulations of 1899 and 1907. Some of its provisions are no more than attempts to clarify existing rules of international customary law ... To the extent, however, to which existing legal duties of occupying powers are not merely elaborated, but enlarged, the Convention must be treated as constitutive and applied only between the parties.[101]

Likewise, the American Jewish legal scholar Theodor Meron argues that the Geneva Convention should not be considered a constitutive convention. In his opinion:

---

[99] J. Pictet, *Commentary on Geneva Convention IV of 1949*, trans. R. Griffin and C. W. Dumbleton (Geneva, 1958), 9.

[100] R. T. Yingling and R. W. Ginnane, 'The Geneva Conventions of 1949', *AJIL* 46 (3) (1952), 393, 411.

[101] G. Schwarzenberger, *International Law as Applied by International Courts and Tribunals*, 2: *The Law of Armed Conflict* (London, 1968), 165. This passage was cited in HC 606/78, the *Beit El* case, 121.

As regards the Geneva Convention, I would not question the opinion which regards it as conventional rather than customary. However, account must be taken of the fact that some provisions of the Geneva Convention are indeed declaratory of customary international law ... Rather than view all the provisions of the Geneva Convention as reflecting conventional international law and therefore as non-invocable in domestic courts, it is suggested that the High Court of Justice should, in the future, examine each relevant provision of that convention in order to determine whether it is declaratory of customary international law or not.[102]

The Supreme Court was ready to accept the above suggestion and did actually examine—in the minority opinion of Judge Haim Cohn—whether the beginning of Article 49 prohibiting deportation constitutes part of customary international law. He concluded that 'in the beginning of Article 49 of the Geneva Convention there exist the seeds of customary international law which has always been followed throughout the world'.[103]

In the opinion of this author, Judge H. Cohn's ruling, in spite of his being in the minority, constitutes at present the only possible means for deportees to try to prevent their deportation, especially if they are neither West Bank residents nor being deported to Jordan.[104]

Another possibility, which we believe to be less practical, is to try to show that a certain provision of the Geneva Convention, or the Convention as a whole, has over the time that has passed since 1949 until now, become part of customary international law.

Customary international law is defined in Article 38 of the constitution of the International Court of Justice to be 'international custom, as evidence of general practice applied by law'. That is to say, so long as the international standard of behaviour upheld by states is considered to have the status of an obligation, or is considered legally just, the general rule that arises from this behaviour is usually considered to be a rule of the customary law of nations.[105] In the opinion of Professor Dinstein, which appears to be correct:

---

[102] Meron, 'West Bank and Gaza: Human Rights and Humanitarian Law', 111–12.

[103] In HC 698/80, the *Qawassmeh* case, 636. Dinstein, agreeing with the judge's approach, notes that, '[I]n theory this approach is correct and we do not wish to dispute it. However, in practice, there are not many effects of this approach.' Dinstein, 'The Deportation of the Mayors', 167n.

[104] The President of the Supreme Court avoided discussion of the argument that Art. 49 is part of customary law in the *Nazal* deportation case (n. 96 above). He did so on the grounds that, in his opinion, the deportation of a West Bank resident to Jordan is not prohibited by a literal reading of Art. 49 of the Geneva Convention. HC 256/85, 654.

[105] See L. Oppenheim, *International Law*, i, 8th edn. (London, 1955), 27. Also see HC 256/85, the *Nazal* case, 638, and the *Shahin* case (HC 13/86, 209–10) in which Judge Shamgar examines the question of whether there is a generally accepted legal practice obliging an occupying state to allow entry and residence in occupied territory to a resident of an enemy country. In the opinion of the judge: 'In no case have general

The State of Israel is the first to be asked (as a party) to implement the Geneva Convention in law and practice. Granted, hopefully and perhaps likely, the Convention will indeed be implemented in the future, perhaps when an international custom is established. However, in the meantime, this is no more than a wish or an expectation.

In Dinstein's opinion,

It is not impossible that some of the provisions scattered through the Convention already were of a declaratory nature, without relation to the constitutive status of the entire document. However, this must be proven by state practice. And I am not referring to practice in time of peace, but to practice during times of war.[106]

The Geneva Convention as a Legislative Convention rather than a Contractual Convention

Binyamin Rubin, an employee of the Ministry of Justice in Israel, published an illuminating article in 1983 in which he argues that there is no practice in Israel according to which only customary international law constitutes part of internal law.[107] This would be in keeping with English practice, which Rubin considers to be correct, but to have been misinterpreted in Israel.

In Rubin's opinion, the distinction made by the Israeli court between the Geneva Convention and the Hague Regulations—both laws relating to war, one pertaining to contractual international law and the other to customary international law—whereby the latter constitutes part of the law of the country and the former does not, is an incorrect distinction. In Rubin's opinion:

In England itself, from where this distinction between contractual law and customary law ostensibly stemmed, laws of war are the exception to this distinction. English laws of war are part of the country's laws, whether they fall under customary law or contractual law. This is only one of the reasons why the Geneva Convention, more than other legislative conventions, should be viewed as being part of the law of the land.[108]

According to Rubin,

Beginning with the claim that waging a war is part of the 'royal prerogative', in England they arrived at the conclusion that the crown is entitled to bind its own hands in the conduct of war, and the conventions to which it is a

principles crystallized creating an obligatory customary norm which is generally to be applied to the area under belligerent occupation. Nor have there been any precedents in this area which could serve as a kind of evidence of generally accepted practice in law.'
[106] Dinstein, 'The Deportation of the Mayors', 168.
[107] Rubin, 'The Adoption of International Conventions', 211.
[108] Ibid. 211.

signatory become a part of internal law without the need of legislation for this purpose.[109]

In dealing with the Israeli practice established in judgments in the two cases of *The Custodian of Absentee Property v. Samara*[110] and *KLM v. The Minister of Transportation*,[111] Rubin attempts to show that actually these two judgments dealt with an international convention of a contractual nature which therefore did not constitute part of internal Israeli law, in contrast to legislative conventions which are part of general international law.

In Rubin's opinion:

When discussing legislative conventions, there is no point whatsoever in making a distinction between them and customary international law. Now that it has been established that the rules of customary international law which bind Israel are part of the laws of the land, it would appear that the same must now be established in respect to the rules in legislative conventions to which Israel is party.[112]

Rubin concludes by saying:

In order for part of a convention to be considered law in this country, it is not enough for it to be of a legislative nature. It must also be a 'self-executing treaty', that is, one whose provisions can be implemented as they are without requiring other measures arising from the convention.[113]

On the basis of the above reasoning and the argument that follows, Rubin arrives at the conclusion that no distinction should be drawn between the Geneva Convention and customary international law and that, for all intents and purposes, the Fourth Geneva Convention should be considered to be part of internal Israeli law and that the Supreme Court must rule in accordance with it. In Rubin's opinion, this conclusion follows from, *inter alia*, the fact that the role of the military commander in occupied territory was established by international law, particularly by the laws of war. Laws of war place the area commander under certain obligations, as these laws both establish the role he is required to fulfil and the limits of his power and his obligations.

This feature of the role of an area commander makes it obligatory for his actions to be examined in accordance with the laws of war which he is required

---

[109] Ibid. 214. Also see n. 14 on same page, in which Rubin turns to A. D. McNair, *The Law of Treaties* (Oxford, 1961), 89–91, and F. A. Mann, 'The Enforcement of Treaties by English Courts', *Trans. of the Grotius Society* 44 (1958–9), 29, 37–9.
[110] HC 25/55, PD 10 [3] 1825.
[111] HC 380/81, *KLM v. The Minister of Transportation* (unreported). See Rubin's treatment of this judgment, 'The Adoption of International Conventions', 224.
[112] Ibid. 226.
[113] Ibid. 227.

to uphold, and in this respect there is no difference between customary law and contractual law.[114]

In order to pressure the Israeli Supreme Court into adopting the Fourth Geneva Convention as part of internal Israeli law, any means available should be employed, including the path proposed by Rubin. However, in our opinion, the likelihood of Rubin's arguments being accepted is slight, not least because the practice of applying only customary international law as part of Israeli law has become so rooted that it is realistically impossible to believe that it will ever be changed.

The Application of the Geneva Convention as Part of the Orders of the General Staff

The inception of the idea that the Geneva Convention was within the context of Israeli law, on account of being included among the orders issued by the general staff, actually came from a remark made by Judge Barak in the judgment in the *Teachers' Housing Cooperative* case. Judge Barak said:

> There is a question here as to whether the humanitarian sections of the Fourth Geneva Convention, in accordance with which the government of Israel has decided to act, do not on their own account constitute obligatory norms, and not only in part, by dint of their being part of the internal guidelines of the government to military commanders and by dint of their being independent guidelines of the general staff itself.[115]

The above idea serves to introduce an article written by Hillel Sommer,[116] who advocates the application of the Geneva Convention provisions under Israeli law, by reason, he argues, of a general staff order instructing IDF soldiers, including the military commander of the administered territory, to behave in accordance with those provisions.

General Staff Order No. 33.0133 of 20 July 1982 states the following:

Discipline—behaviour in accordance with the conventions to which Israel is a party.

The Geneva Convention
(1) From 12 August 1949, Israel has been party to the four Geneva Conventions for the protection of the victims of war . . .

(2) These Conventions have been published in official gazettes, under Convention Records No. 30, on 30 September 1951, and also in the 'Library of Military Law—17–24'.

---

[114] Ibid. 237.
[115] HC 393/82, 793–4.
[116] H. Sommer, 'In Spite of This, the Provisions [Should] be Applied', *Eyunai Mishpat (Tel Aviv University Law Review)* 11 (1986), 263.

(3) All IDF soldiers are required to act in accordance with the provisions included in the above Conventions....[117]

The Conventions themselves form Appendix 61 to the order of the general staff and the army sees them as an integral part of the orders issued to the army. Such is the official opinion of the chief military advocate of the IDF: 'The Geneva Convention is one of the orders of the army and its provisions have been adopted in the wording given in Appendix 61 of the general staff orders.'[118] The question is, however, whether the orders of the general staff, among which can be found the Geneva Conventions, constitute part of internal Israeli law.

The definition given to 'law' in Article 3 of the Law of Interpretation of 1981 includes 'legislation'; legislation is defined in the same article as a 'law or regulation', 'regulation' being defined as an instruction issued by force of law enacted by legislation. In regard to the second characteristic—'enacted by legislation'—the orders of the general staff clearly fall into this category as they meet the criteria established by the Supreme Court.[119]

Hence, we must pose the question of whether military orders are issued by force of law. Article 5 of The Basic Law: Army stipulates: 'The authority to issue instructions and orders in the army will be established by law or by force of law'. In 1978, the Military Jurisdiction Law 1955 was amended (Amendment No. 12) by Article 2A, which states:

2A(a) The orders of the Supreme Command are the general orders issued by the Chief of Staff with the approval of the Defence Minister, and they will lay down principles related to the organization of the army, administration, and discipline, for safeguarding its well-ordered operation.

(b) The orders issued by the general staff are general orders and they will establish the details of the issues mentioned in subsection(a).

(c) Under the instructions of the supreme command, other types of general orders can be issued by those authorized to do so which are binding on the army...

2B In respect to the instructions and orders mentioned in Article 2A, they do not require official publication and will be brought to the attention of the concerned parties as the chief of staff sees fit to order.

In light of the above, it is clear that these orders of the general staff constitute part of Israeli law and that, therefore, the Geneva Convention is actually part of obligatory Israeli law. However, this conclusion must contend with the provision of Article 3(a) of the Military Jurisdic-

---

[117] Ibid. 268.
[118] Ibid. 268. See also n. 31 on the same page.
[119] Ibid. 271.

tion Law, according to which: 'In respect to this law, military orders and other general orders are to be considered law'. This provision was important prior to the amendment and the addition of subsection A to Article 2, which to all intents and purposes strips it of all meaning, since Article 2A actually establishes that the orders of the general staff constitute part of the law. However, practically all the substance is removed from this idea by the interpretation of the above-mentioned Article 3(a) in an incidental observation given by Judge S. Levine in the judgment of *Hiram v. Minister of Defence*:

> Legally speaking, the respondents argued that the provisions of the Supreme Command under discussion have the status of law, yet this claim is doubtful, as by dint of Article 3(a) of the Military Jurisdiction Law 1955, the orders of the Supreme Command are to be seen as law only in regard to this specific law and not to other matters.[120]

And indeed, if the position of Judge Levine is correct, the orders issued by the general staff, including Order No. 33.0133, constitute law solely under the Military Jurisdiction Law, but not for any other purpose, including the obligation of the Supreme Court to examine the actions of military commanders in accordance with these orders.

In Sommer's opinion, Judge Levine's interpretation should be rejected. If not, the amendment of 1979 is meaningless and such an interpretation would actually conflict with Article 133 of the Military Jurisdiction Law and Article 12 of the Penal Code 1977.[121] So it is that he reaches the conclusion that:

> [I]n so far as the Geneva Convention constitutes part of the orders of the army, and in so far as these orders are part of the law applied to IDF soldiers (including those who hold positions in the Israeli military government in the administered territories), the military government is obliged to abide by its provisions, and a deviation from them may bring about the annulment of their decisions.[122]

The path proposed by Sommer does not appear to be realistic, for two reasons. One, it demands a further ruling of the Supreme Court about everything concerned with Article 3(a) of the Military Jurisdiction Law,[123] and not in the framework of a discussion about the application of the Geneva Convention. In our opinion, if such a hearing takes place before the court has established its position in regard to Article

---

[120] HC 69/80, PD 35 [4] 505, 511.
[121] Sommer, 'In Spite of This', 275–8.
[122] Ibid. 279.
[123] In HC 69/85, *Frumer v. The Military Appeals Court*, PD 40 [2] 617, 623, Judge Levine reiterated his position in the *Hiram* case, saying that 'By dint of Article 3 of the law, the orders of the general staff are considered to be legislation under the law.' Judge Helima also supported this position.

3(a), it would seem likely that the Supreme Court would reject the idea proposed above on the grounds that the orders of the general staff constitute 'law' only for the sake of the Military Jurisdiction Law itself. The second reason for our reservations is that Sommer proposes to apply the Geneva Convention solely by dint of the orders of the general staff. But these orders can be changed very easily and it is not even necessary that the changes are published, as stated in Article 2(b) of the Military Jurisdiction Law.[124]

The Geneva Convention as Part of Internal Law in the Occupied Territories

If local law grants a certain kind of authority, and the military commander wishing to exercise it deviates from it, in keeping with what we understand by this term in our judgments, neither in respect to the exercise of his legislative authority nor in the implementation [of a decision], but rather erroneously or maliciously employing local law, or not acting in accordance with the standards incumbent on him in exercising his authority under local law, it is possible that his action will be declared to be null and void solely in light of the essence of the provisions of local law.

This is the law in respect to security legislation; a deviation by a military authority from the bounds set by the commander of IDF forces in the area can also provide grounds for the intervention of this court, even if the matter is not related to an action which contravenes the laws of war but rather to an action which contravenes local law, in force under Proclamation No. 2, i.e. the law in force on the eve of the establishment of IDF rule or the legislation passed by the commander of IDF forces in the area.[125]

Judge Shamgar's remarks in the *Abu Aita* case provoke the question of whether the local law in force on the eve of the military occupation of the territories in 1967, or the security legislation enacted in its wake, include any provisions for applying the Geneva Convention.

The answer to this question is affirmative. At the beginning of the occupation of the West Bank an order was published in regard to defence provisions which included, under Article 35, the following:

Observance of the Geneva Convention—35. The military court and the administrators of the military court must apply the provisions of the [Fourth] Geneva Convention... with respect to judicial procedures. In case of a conflict between this Order and the said Convention, the Convention shall be preferred.[126]

---

[124] Sommer, 'In Spite of This', 279.
[125] HC 493/81, 69/81, PD 37 [2] 197, 232.
[126] *Booklet No. 1* (1967), 5, at 12. It would appear that the order was published in the month of June 1967 in a proclamation regarding orders and appointments issued by the IDF headquarters in the West Bank area.

If anyone was surprised by the existence of this article, the surprise did not last longer than a few months. In October 1967, the above-mentioned Article 35 was changed in an enigmatic manner by Amendment No. 9 to the Security Provisions Order No. 144,[127] which replaced Article 35 with an entirely different article on calculation of prison sentences, having nothing whatsoever to do with the Geneva Convention.

Once again, did the Fourth Geneva Convention constitute a part of local law in the West Bank prior to 1967? We will attempt to answer this question in part.[128]

Jordan acceded to the Geneva Conventions of 1949 on 29 May 1951. Article 33 of the Jordanian Constitution, which deals with the signature and authorization of international agreements, states:

(1) The King declares war, makes peace, and authorizes treaties.

(2) Peace treaties, alliances, commerce, shipping, and other conventions which involve alterations in the territory of the kingdom or the reduction of the right of sovereignty to it, or which involve expenditures by the Treasury, or a violation of Jordanian rights—whether they be public or private—will not be valid unless they have been approved by the national council. It is strictly forbidden for the specific conditions of any contract to be in conflict with the standing conditions.

Article 33(b) has been interpreted by the Supreme Council of Jordan, whose role as defined in Article 57 of the Jordanian Constitution includes interpretation of the articles of the Constitution. The Council's Decision No. 2, published in the official Jordanian Gazette No. 1224 on 16 April 1955, states:

It is clear that this formulation amending the constitution divides agreements into two categories in this section: (1) peace treaties, and trade and shipping agreements; and (2) other agreements which involve changes in regard to state land, sovereign rights, Treasury expenditure, or which involve violations of Jordanian rights, public or private. Agreements of the first type will not be valid under any condition save if they have been authorized by the parliament, without consideration of their essence or the obligations they impose. Agreements of this type by nature touch on the basic rights of the state, its sovereignty and its rule over land, sea and air. The execution of other agreements do not require the authorization of parliament, save if they involve a change in regard to state land, or its sovereignty, etc. In so far as this is not the case, these agreements will be valid after they have been reviewed and signed by the

---

[127] *Booklet No. 8* (1967), 303.

[128] As the author of this article is a Palestinian citizen of Israel, he has been unable to examine the relevant documents regarding Jordanian law, nor is there any possibility of his travelling to Jordan to do so. Thus, an answer to the above-mentioned question has only been posed in general terms and the author invites others to develop this idea and examine its validity.

executive authority without any need for parliamentary approval in view of the unimportance of the obligations entailed therein.[129]

Evidently, the Fourth Geneva Convention does not fall under the first category of agreements as delineated above. The question is whether the Convention falls under that part of the second category of agreements that also requires parliamentary approval, or does it constitute part of Jordanian law following the authorization or affirmation of the Jordanian government, without the need for special parliamentary approval?

It is clear that Jordan's accession to the Geneva Conventions and the approval, if given, by the executive authority, that is the government, do not involve any amendment in regard to the territory of the state of Jordan or its sovereign rights. In the event of Jordan conquering territory, the Treasury would not be involved, as according to international law the occupier can finance the expenses of its armed forces deployed in the occupied territory by taxes and levies on the residents of the occupied territory itself.

In our opinion, the most likely possibility is that the Fourth Geneva Convention falls under the category of agreements which do not require the approval of the Jordanian parliament, and, as such, it has constituted part of internal Jordanian law since Jordan became a party to the Convention. Hence, this Convention was actually part of the internal law which was in force on the eve of the occupation and the government of the occupying army is obliged, in accordance with Article 43 of the Hague Regulations of 1907, to respect the existing law and to operate in accordance with it.[130]

On the other hand, it can also be argued that, as in England, since the declaration and conduct of war fall under the prerogative of the crown according to Article 33(1) of the Jordanian Constitution, the King has the authority to bind his hands in the conduct of a war by the conventions to which he is signatory, which thus become part of internal law without the need for legislation or ratification.[131]

Is There any Possibility of Applying the Fourth Geneva Convention to the Occupied Territories?

In the opinion of this author, the Supreme Court will employ any legal means available for obstructing the application of the Fourth Geneva

---

[129] *Official Jordanian Gazette*, No. 1224, 16 April 1955, 42.
[130] The author tried to ascertain whether the Jordanian Parliament had ratified the Convention, or whether the Government had affirmed the Convention, but without success. If at any time prior to 7 June 1967 the Jordanian Parliament did ratify the Geneva Conventions, the argument made here would receive considerable reinforcement.
[131] Rubin, 'The Adoption of International Conventions', 214; also see Mann, 'The Enforcement of Treaties by English Courts', and McNair, *The Law of Treaties*.

Convention to the Occupied Territories. The latest method employed by the court was established in the judgment on the *Jaber* case. It may, in time, actually suppress any attempt to apply the Fourth Geneva Convention in the Occupied Territories.

In spite of this, we retain hope and continue to seek ways and means to persuade the Supreme Court to apply the Convention and examine the actions of the occupying military authorities in accordance with the standards set by this Convention. The ideas put forward in this paper, and in other papers, may assist toward the achievement of this goal. And perhaps, in the end, they will prove effective.[132]

III. The Universal Declaration of Human Rights of 1948

We will deal only briefly with the Universal Declaration of Human Rights, on account of the fact that the Supreme Court has never really delved into the matter in any depth.

While the major problem in regard to the Hague Regulations and the Fourth Geneva Convention was whether they apply to the territories occupied by Israel—without there being any controversy over their being part of the laws of war which should be applied to occupied territory—the major problem in regard to the Universal Declaration of Human Rights of 1948 is whether this Declaration forms part of the laws of war.

It would appear that there is some agreement that this Declaration

---

[132] Prof. A. Rubinstein, the leading authority on constitutional law in Israel, has raised another view about the application of the Geneva Convention. While this idea has yet to be developed by Rubinstein, the gist of it can be garnered from the following:

> In respect to parliamentary regimes of a type similar to that of England and Israel, only the legislator can alter the internal law of the state; however, when we come to deal with a convention which, by its very nature, is not at all intended to be applied within the jurisdiction of the state and thus is not intended to influence the essentials of internal law within it and which deals in its entirety with territories and relations which are outside the territory under jurisdiction, a doubt arises in regard to the need for this process of 'absorption' into internal law. One can argue that, in such cases, the need for such absorption vanishes, destroying the logical foundation which justifies it: no alteration of internal law is required by the adoption of the convention and there is no need to bring the matter before the Knesset. In the network of international obligations of the state, the approval of the convention suffices by itself. It would be hard to comprehend how the Knesset could, even if it so desired, legislate a convention, as the Knesset employs its authority, by virtue of its nature, in regard to persons and territories under its rule. To the best of my knowledge, this is the reason why the Geneva Convention was not 'legislated' into the municipal legal systems of the states which are party to it.

See A. Rubinstein, 'The Changing Status of the Occupied Territories' (in Hebrew), *Eyunai Mishpat* (*Tel Aviv University Law Review*) 11 (1986), 439, 446.

constitutes part of customary international law.[133] This has been established by a number of Supreme Court judgments, in some instances by a minority opinion. In the case concerning the *Beit El Mission* in Haifa, Judge Haim Cohn ruled that the Universal Declaration expresses customary international law, as it was formulated by legal experts from around the globe and approved by the United Nations General Assembly, to which the great majority of nations in the world belong.[134]

Likewise, in the *Qawassmeh* case, Judge H. Cohn began with the premise that the Universal Declaration actually constitutes part of customary international law.[135] However, in the later judgments of the Supreme Court, the court refused to rule on whether the Universal Declaration does constitute part of customary international law, and the question of whether it applies to the Occupied Territories was answered in the negative.[136] In the opinion of the court:

> The Universal Declaration of Human Rights is not intended for dealing with factual circumstances such as those before us, i.e. in a territory under military government which is being administered as such in the wake of a war, and so long as the situation of war continues.[137]

Perhaps we can end this section with a quotation from the work of Professor Meron, which reveals the problems involved in the application of the Universal Declaration of Human Rights in the territories occupied by Israel:

> What about other provisions of customary international law of human rights which have not been expressly designed to apply, in whole or in part, to occupied territories? Take for instance the Universal Declaration of Human Rights, which many legal scholars tend to regard as having acquired, since its adoption in 1948, the characteristics of customary international law . . .
>
> A principle which appears in the preamble and in Article 2 of the Declaration states that no distinction shall be made on the basis of the political jurisdiction or international status of the country or territory to which a person belongs, whether it be independent, trust, non-self-governing or under any other limitation of sovereignty.[138]

---

[133] On the applicability of international human rights law in occupied territories, see chapters by Roberts, Quigley, and Dugard in this volume.

[134] HC 103/67, *The American European Beit El Mission v. the Minister of Welfare*, PD 21 [2] 325, 333.

[135] HC 698/80, 644–5. In Dinstein's opinion, the Universal Declaration is today accepted as, by and large, reflecting customary international law ('The Deportation of the Mayors', 159).

[136] HC 13/86, the *Shahin* case, 210.

[137] HC 629/82, *Mustafa et al. v. The Military Commander of the Judea and Samaria Region*, PD 37 [1] 158, 161; this position of the court was hinted at in former Supreme Court President Judge Landau's judgment in the *Qawassmeh* case, HC 698/80, 630.

[138] Meron, 'West Bank and Gaza: Human Rights and Humanitarian Law', 112.

Conclusion

This paper attempts to examine the degree of application of international laws of warfare as reflected by the judgments of the Israeli Supreme Court related to the examination of the activities of the military government in the territories occupied by Israel. Unfortunately, in the great majority of cases one must reach the conclusion that the Supreme Court does not apply the laws of war to the Occupied Territories, and that when it does so, it interprets international law to condone the actions of the military government.

We also attempted to present and amplify a number of arguments whose acceptance by the Supreme Court would make the application of the Fourth Geneva Convention to the activities of the military government obligatory. Although in our hearts we have few hopes that these ideas will succeed in changing the position of the Supreme Court, we believe hopelessness is the worst enemy, and therefore urge the employment of these arguments in an effort to convince the Supreme Court to change its position on the issue.

3

The Relevance of International Law to Israeli and Palestinian Rights in the West Bank and Gaza

RICHARD A. FALK and BURNS H. WESTON

I

WHEN demonstrations against Israel's occupation of the West Bank and Gaza erupted in Gaza in December 1987 and shortly thereafter spread to the West Bank, few perceived that what was in the making was a resistance quite unlike the sporadic 'riots' that had aggravated Israeli-Palestinian relations since the Six Day War and the beginning of the occupation in 1967. By late February 1988, however, even the Israeli General Staff had adopted the Arabic word *intifada*,[1] the term preferred by the Palestinians themselves to define what was happening.[2] As Middle East expert Don Peretz has written, 'December 1987 may have been a Palestinian version of the 1916 "Easter Rising", a revolt which opened a struggle that lasted years before its goals were approached.'[3]

Why is this 'uprising', this new variant of mass civil resistance,

---

* © 1988 Richard A. Falk and Burns H. Weston
An revised and updated version of this paper, which was first presented at al-Haq's conference, was published in *HILJ* 32(1) (Winter 1991).

[1] From the Arabic verb 'to shake loose'.
[2] Persons sympathetic to the 'uprising' see it as the functional equivalent of a civil war relative to the whole of Palestine (Israel, the West Bank, and Gaza) or, alternatively, a war of national liberation against a colonial oppressor, leading to the birth of a new Palestinian state. Critics see it as the outward manifestation of an unseen, generation-long battle between the PLO and King Hussein of Jordan for control of the Palestine Arab nation.
[3] D. Peretz, 'Intifadeh: The Palestinian Uprising', *For. Aff.* 66 (1988), 964, 980. The 'Easter Rising' of 1916 crushed the last English illusion that Ireland could be pacified as a colony, yet the eventual grant of a sovereign state to the Irish people has not ended the struggle over the eventual status of the six northern counties, so-called Northern Ireland.

without precedent in the long history of the Israeli–Palestinian conflict, happening at this time? What explains its pervasiveness and, so far, its durability? What has led the Palestinians to so high a degree of unity and intensity?

There are some obvious candidates for explanation: (i) cramped cities and towns as well as refugee camps made worse by high birth-rates and restrictions upon Arab urban and rural expansion; (ii) squalid social and economic conditions exacerbated by declining employment opportunities (among the Palestinian youth especially), by confiscated natural and financial resources, and by a consequent dependency upon an increasingly colonizing Israeli economy; (iii) draconian governmental practices that have resulted in stifled cultural/political expression and in swollen detention centres and jails; and (iv) a lethal mixture of humiliation, frustration, and anger from years of foreign rule (Ottoman, British, Egyptian, and Jordanian as well as Israeli), abetted by a profound disillusionment about the will and capability of the outside world—including, perhaps most importantly, the outside Arab world—to provide a solution. Few of the total Palestinian population of the Occupied Territories have known anything other than these crabbed conditions. Almost none of the youth have known anything else.[4]

Perhaps less apparent, but no less an answer, because it fuels the *intifada* with that same sense of righteousness of which successful revolutions often are made, is a conviction of profound legal as well as moral wrongdoing on Israel's part, a wrongdoing established not merely by Arab accusations but by the minimum standards of an entire world community that slowly but steadily struggles to temper the conduct of war and otherwise limit human suffering. Civil resistance by almost the entire Palestinian population is seen to be justified—indeed mandated—by the long duration and especially the harshness of the Israeli occupation, an occupation that has included and continues to include large-scale, severe, and persistent violations of the law of belligerent occupation and systematic deprivations of fundamental human rights, perhaps most importantly the right of self-determination.

II

The perception of extensive Israeli violation is, we believe, a correct one. Numerous informed individuals, organizations, and govern-

---

[4] For a vivid, depressing account of the realities and perceptions of various residents of the West Bank (including Jewish settlers), see D. Grossman, *The Yellow Wind* (New York, 1988).

mental agencies—including, for example, the United Nations Special Committee to Investigate Israeli Practices Affecting the Human Rights of the Populations of the Occupied Territories,[5] the United States Department of State, Amnesty International, al-Haq,[6] the International Commission of Jurists, the International Committee of the Red Cross, The National Lawyers' Guild, the Palestinian Human Rights Information Center,[7] the Physicians for Human Rights, the Swiss League for Human Rights, and the West Bank Data Base Project[8]—have abundantly and persuasively documented Israel's violation of the limited rights that the law of war assures an occupied people; and they have done the same, too, regarding Israel's failure to uphold the international human rights of the Palestinian people in general.[9] The settlement of more than 55,000 of Israel's Jewish citizens in the West Bank and Gaza (plus nearly 100,000 in East Jerusalem) and the establishment of approximately 120 settlements there; the refusal to repatriate thousands of Palestinians displaced during the 1967 fighting; the summary deportation of prominent Palestinian citizens from many walks of life (including lawyers); systematic arbitrary arrests and detentions and the denial of procedural rights in respect of alleged security violations; the imposition of collective punishment, especially

---

[5] Candour compels acknowledging that the work of the Special Committee has been highly controversial. According to many Israelis, the Committee was biased against Israel from the time of its founding and its investigative reports have been one-sided. See, for example, D. Shefi, 'The Reports of the UN Special Committees on Israeli Practices in the Territories' in M. Shamgar (ed.), *Military Government in the Territories Administered by Israel 1967–1980*, 1: *The Legal Aspects* (Jerusalem, 1982), 285. See also Alderson, Curtis, Sutcliffe, and Travers, 'Protection of Human Rights in Israeli-Occupied Territories', *HILJ* 15 (1974), 470, 481–2. Y. Dinstein has written that 'Israel is averse to proposals that the legality of the measures taken by its military government in the occupied territories [should] be subjected to scrutiny by international organizations (especially the United Nations, which it regards as totally dominated by hostile countries).' Y. Dinstein, 'The Israeli Supreme Court and the Law of Belligerent Occupation: Reunification of Families', *IYHR* 18 (1988), 173, 174.

[7] Formerly the Database Project on Palestinian Human Rights.

[8] The West Bank Data Base Project is a privately funded, Jerusalem-based organization founded in 1982 by Meron Benvenisti, an Israeli former Vice-Mayor of Jerusalem, to collect and catalogue data relative to Israeli policy in the West Bank. The publications of the Project have become a standard reference for persons concerned about human rights conditions in the West Bank.

[9] See, e.g., al-Haq/LSM, *Briefing Papers on Twenty Years of Israeli Occupation of the West Bank and Gaza* (Ramallah, 1987); M. Benvenisti, *1987 Report*; Physicians for Human Rights, *The Casualties of Conflict: Medical Care and Human Rights in the West Bank and Gaza Strip* (1988); *Report of the National Lawyers Guild 1977 Middle East Delegation: Treatment of Palestinians in Israeli-Occupied West Bank and Gaza* (Washington, DC, 1978). See also J. Hiltermann, *Israel's Deportation Policy in the Occupied West Bank and Gaza* (Ramallah: al-Haq, 1986); E. Playfair, *Administrative Detention in the Occupied West Bank* (Ramallah: al-Haq, 1986); J. Quigley, *Palestine and Israel: A Challenge to Justice* (1990); R. Shehadeh and J. Kuttab, *The West Bank and the Rule of Law* (Geneva, 1980); H. Kochler (ed.), *The Legal Aspects of the Palestine Problem* (Vienna, 1981). See also the authorities cited in n. 11 below and several of the chapters in this volume, especially that by Professor John Dugard.

in the form of the destruction of family residences; and the mistreatment (including torture) of detainees—all these and other abusive policies and practices directed at the Palestinian population as a whole are a matter of record.[10] And so too are the beatings and maimings and killings resulting from Israel's 'Iron Fist' policy, applied almost without relief since August 1985 and conspicuous since the beginning of the *intifada* in December 1987 thanks to the unrelenting television camera and the testimony of such organizations as al-Haq, Amnesty International, and the National Lawyers' Guild,[11] not to mention the provocative justifications of cruel and repressive violence by Israeli leaders such as Prime Minister Yitzhak Shamir and Defence Minister Yitzhak Rabin.[12] An objective application of the 1907 Hague Convention (No. IV) Respecting the Laws and Customs of War on Land ('Hague IV') and annexed Regulations ('Hague Regulations')[13] and the 1949 Geneva Convention IV Relative to the Protection of Civilian Persons in Time of War ('the Fourth Geneva Convention'),[14] the primary embodiment of the law that is applicable to this situation,[15] attests to these findings; and so also does an objective application of

[10] See, for example, the authorities cited in nn. 9 and 11. It may be noted, in addition, that the UN Security Council, on 5 Jan. 1988, about one month after the commencement of the *intifada*, voted *unanimously* to condemn as a violation of international law Israel's deportation of nine Palestinians from the West Bank and Gaza, described by Israel as 'leading activists and organizers involved in incitement and subversive activities on behalf of [the PLO]'. Significantly, the US voted *for* the resolution, the first time it had voted to condemn Israeli policy since the annexation of the Golan Heights in 1981. For convenient reference, see *Keesing's Contemporary Archives* 34 (Apr. 1988), 35,858. For related comment, see n. 20 below. Similarly, on 8 Feb. 1988, the EC Council of (Foreign) Ministers, the only institution of the EC which directly represents the member governments, approved unanimously a resolution calling for an end to 'repressive' measures by Israel and 'deeply deplored the violation of human rights.' Ibid. 35,860.

[11] See, for instance, al-Haq, *Punishing a Nation: Human Rights Violations during the Palestinian Uprising, December 1987–December 1988*, (Ramallah, 1988); Amnesty International, *Israel and the Occupied Territories—The Misuse of Tear Gas by Israeli Army Personnel in the Israeli Occupied Territories* (AI Index: MDE/15/26/88) (June 1988); and *Israel and the Occupied Territories—Excessive Force: Beatings to Maintain Law and Order* (AI Index: MDE/15/32/88) (Aug. 1988); Lawyers Committee for Human Rights, *An Examination of the Detention of Human Rights Workers and Lawyers from the West Bank and Gaza and Conditions of Detention at Ketziot* (New York, 1988); *1988 Report of the National Lawyers' Guild: International Human Rights Law and Israel's Efforts to Suppress the Palestinian Uprising* (Washington, DC, 1989).

[12] See, e.g., *Keesing's Contemporary Archives* 34 (April 1988), 35,859.

[13] For full citations and references to these instruments, see Ch. 1 in this volume, nn. 4, 7.

[14] Other pertinent agreements, some provisions of which are viewed as embodying customary international law, are the Protocols I and II Additional to the Geneva Conventions of 12 Aug. 1949 (see Ch. 1, n. 24). See also the Hague Convention and Protocol for the Protection of Cultural Property in the Event of Armed Conflict, 14 May 1954 (see Ch. 1, n. 23).

[16] 'A Framework for Peace in the Middle East Agreed at Camp David, 17 Sept. 1978, Egypt–Israel–United States', *State Dept. Bull.* 78 (Oct. 1978), 7, reprinted in *ILM* 17 (1978), 1463. The Camp David Accords contain many provisions for a 'self-governing

the Camp David Accords,[16] the United Nations Charter,[17] and the widely accepted customs and conventions comprising international human rights law generally.[18] Israeli policies and practices over the last twenty-one years cannot reasonably be reconciled with these rules and standards of international law.[19] Indeed, by its severity and cumulative impact the pattern of Israeli transgression appears to violate, with historic irony, even the principles laid down at Nuremberg

authority' in the West Bank and Gaza. At the time of their adoption at Camp David, however, they were strongly criticized by other Arab governments, the PLO, and the residents of the West Bank and Gaza, and accordingly were never implemented.

[17] Agreed in San Francisco, 26 June 1945, 1976 *YBUN*, 1043. See especially Arts. 1(2) and (3), 55, and 56.

[18] The Israeli government has frequently voiced scepticism about the applicability of international human rights instruments in the Occupied Territories. See, for example, the memorandum of 12 Sept. 1984 prepared by the Office of the Legal Adviser in the Israeli Foreign Ministry for, and contained in A. Roberts, B. Joergensen, and F. Newman, *Academic Freedom under Israeli Military Occupation* (London, 1984), wherein the Office of the Legal Adviser contended that the so-called International Bill of Human Rights—i.e. the Universal Declaration of Human Rights, the International Covenant on Economic, Social, and Cultural Rights, and the International Covenant on Civil and Political Rights—does not apply to the Israeli-occupied territories because the 'classical situation' of human rights law, concerning 'the relationship between the "citizen" and his (*sic*) government' does not obtain in the circumstances of foreign occupation. This position is at least implicitly undermined, however, by the Israeli assertion, in the same memorandum, that Israeli policy in the West Bank and Gaza was in accord with several other important international human rights instruments (including, questionably, the International Convention on the Elimination of all Forms of Racial Discrimination, 7 Mar. 1966), thereby conceding that human rights law need not be thus restricted. Additionally, international tribunals, on at least two occasions, have affirmed the applicability of international human rights customs and conventions in occupied territories. In its advisory opinion in *The Legal Consequences for States of the Continued Presence of South Africa in Namibia (South West Africa) notwithstanding Security Council Resolution 276*, 1971 *ICJ Reports* 16, at 46, 55, 57, the ICJ did so implicitly; and in *Cyprus v. Turkey*, 1975 Yb. ECHR 82 (Nos. 6780/74 and 6950/75, Decision of 26 May 1975) and ibid. at 100 (No. 8007/77, decision of 10 July 1978), the ECHR did so explicitly. True, it might be argued that human rights standards do not apply to military occupations. But as E. Cohen usefully observes, in *Human Rights in the Israeli-Occupied Territories 1967–82* (Manchester, 1985), 29, '[t]he concept of human rights was taken into account in drafting the [1949] Geneva Conventions' and that therefore, 'in certain areas not covered by [the Fourth Geneva Convention], such as economic rights . . . , the concept of human rights can serve to breathe new life into an otherwise stalemated situation', providing for an occupying power a helpful policy guide. For extensive treatment of the question of the applicability of human rights law in the Israeli-occupied territories, see T. Meron, 'The International Convention on the Elimination of All Forms of Racial Discrimination and the Golan Heights', *IYHR* 8 (1978), 222; and 'West Bank and Gaza: Human Rights and Humanitarian Law in the Period of Transition', *IYHR* 9 (1979), 106. See also Meron, 'Applicability of Multilateral Conventions to Occupied Territories', *AJIL* 72 (1978), 542; A. Roberts, 'The Applicability of Human Rights Law During Military Occupation', *Rev. Int. Studies* 13 (1987), 39.

[19] By far the most detailed analytical account is to be found in R. Shehadeh, *Occupier's Law: Israel and the West Bank*, rev. edn. (Washington, DC, 1988). For helpful overview, see A. Roberts, 'Decline of Illusions: The Status of Israeli Occupied Territories Over 21 Years', *Int. Aff.* 64(3) (1988), 345. Cf. also Roberts, 'The Palestinians, the Uprising and International Law', *Journal of Refugee Studies* 2 (1988), 26–39, and his chapter in this volume.

in 1945 to establish a framework binding upon all governmental leadership.[20]

Of course, the Israeli government and international lawyers sympathetic to Israel argue against such allegations, usually at high levels of abstraction and often with artful ingenuity. Their arguments fall into two main clusters of contention: first, that the international law of war as embodied in the Fourth Geneva Convention does not apply to Israel's presence in the West Bank and Gaza because that presence is not properly regarded as an instance of belligerent occupation (although Israel has shifted its ground on the status of its occupation when, on several occasions, it has announced its intention to adhere *voluntarily* to international humanitarian legal standards in so far as those standards, as expressed in the Hague Regulations, pertain to the Occupied Territories[21]); and, second, that Israel is, in any event, authorized to pursue its present policies and practices in the West Bank and Gaza for reasons of 'security', as construed according to the dictates of military necessity, which by legal tradition confer considerable discretion upon an occupying belligerent government.[22]

The Alleged Inapplicability of the Fourth Geneva Convention

Regarding the claimed inapplicability of the Fourth Geneva Convention, the Israeli Government appears to have relied upon and

---

[20] The common Israeli practice of deportation, for example, which is absolutely prohibited by Article 49 of the Fourth Geneva Convention, is defined in Article 6(c) of the Nuremberg Charter as a 'crime against humanity'. See Agreement for the Prosecution and Punishment of the Major War Criminals ('The London Agreement'), 8 Aug. 1945, 82 *UNTS* 279. For convenient text, see A. Roberts and R. Guelff, *Documents on the Laws of War* (Oxford, 1982; 2nd edn. 1989) 155; D. Schindler and J. Toman (eds.), *The Laws of Armed Conflicts* (Alphen, 1982), 913, 914. For related comment, see n. 10 above and n. 50 below and accompanying texts. See also Hiltermann, *Israel's Deportation Policy in the Occupied West Bank and Gaza*.

[21] The basic official Israeli position, involving a stated willingness to observe the Hague Regulations and, *de facto* but not *de jure*, the 'humanitarian provisions' of the Fourth Geneva Convention, was first expressed at a 1971 symposium at Tel Aviv University by then Israeli Attorney-General Meir Shamgar, and published in 'The Observance of International Law in the Administered Territories', *IYHR* 1 (1971), 262. See also Shamgar, 'Legal Concepts and Problems of the Israeli Military Government: the Initial Stage', in Shamgar (ed.), *Military Government*, 48. Cohen, *Human Rights in the Israeli-Occupied Territories*, 43, asserts that 'no problem arises in regard to the Hague Regulations' because '[t]he official Israeli position is that these Regulations are applicable to the Israeli-occupied territories [of the West bank and Gaza]', a position that is confirmed by the Israeli High Court of Justice in at least one case, HC 390/79, the *Elon Moreh* case: '[T]he Hague rules, which bind the military administration in Judea and Samaria, being part of customary international law . . .'. Problems do arise, however, relative to the applicability of the Hague Regulations in East Jerusalem and the Golan Heights which Israel has claimed to annex. See Cohen, *Human Rights in the Israeli-Occupied Territories*, 51 and 58.

[22] For pertinent discussion, see ibid. 72–6; see also Ch. 6 in this volume.

adopted the argument of the 'missing reversioner' advanced in 1968 by Professor Yehuda Z. Blum, then a Lecturer in International Law at the Hebrew University of Jerusalem, later Israel's Permanent Representative to the United Nations during the period of the government of Menachem Begin.[23] The crux of this argument is that the law of belligerent occupation in general, and the Fourth Geneva Convention in particular, presupposes that the belligerent occupant shall have displaced a 'legitimate sovereign' (to whom the territory in question shall revert following the cessation of hostilities); that neither Jordan in the West Bank nor Egypt in Gaza were legitimate sovereigns (or 'reversioners') in 1967 because of their acts of alleged unlawful aggression during Israel's 'War of Independence' in 1948–9; and that the Government of Israel is therefore released from the constraints of the law of belligerent occupation in general and the Fourth Geneva Convention in particular. According to this argument, thus, Israel's presence in the West Bank and Gaza is not an 'occupation' that displaces a sovereign power, but an 'administration' in the absence of a sovereign, unaccountable to the Fourth Geneva Convention and the law of belligerent occupation generally—although the argument is sometimes made, too, that Israel is present in the West Bank and Gaza as a result of a 'defensive conquest' that confers legal title in the absence of a prior sovereign. Since 1977, when the Likud was first elected to power, Israel has insisted that the Occupied Territories fall within Israel's exclusive sovereign domain, that they form an integral part of 'Greater Israel,' constituting ancient Judea and Samaria, in respect of which the humanitarian laws of war are inapplicable.[24]

Somewhat analogously, albeit less to escape the constraints of the humanitarian law of war in general than to ensure the legitimacy of Israeli settlements in the West Bank and Gaza in particular, Professor Eugene V. Rostow, Professor Emeritus of the Yale Law School, now at the National Defense University in Washington, DC, takes the view that the failure so far of the international community to achieve any final resolution of the underlying territorial status of the West Bank and Gaza results in a continuing lease on life for the Palestine Mandate which, according to Rostow, authorizes Jews to settle throughout the

---

[23] See Y. Blum, 'The Missing Reversioner: Reflections on the Status of Judea and Samaria', IsLR 3 (1968), 279. For indication that the Govt. of Israel has adopted Prof. Blum's thesis, see Shamgar, 'The Observance of International Law'.

[24] For a helpful summary of the evolving Israeli approach to the Occupied Territories, see Shehadeh, *The West Bank and the Rule of Law*, vii–xvii. A more general treatment of Israel's international law status is found in W. T. Mallison and S. V. Mallison, *The Palestine Problem: International Law and World Order* (Harlow, 1986), 240–75. See also Quigley, *Palestine and Israel: A Challenge to Justice*.

mandate territory, which includes the West Bank.[25] Relying upon analogies drawn from the Namibia advisory opinions of the International Court of Justice, including the *Advisory Opinion on the International Status of South-West Africa*,[26] Professor Rostow thus contends that the 1917 Balfour Declaration,[27] as repeated in the 1922 League of Nations Mandate for Palestine,[28] is the law applicable in the Occupied Territories, not the Fourth Geneva Convention or the law of belligerent occupation generally.

Finally, there is Professor Allan Gerson's argument that the special, prolonged (now twenty-two years) character of Israel's occupation makes Israel 'a trustee-occupant' rather than 'a belligerent-occupant' of the West Bank and Gaza.[29] Professor Gerson acknowledges that the Palestinian inhabitants possess a legal entitlement to some reasonable form of autonomy (to be shaped by an eventual, overall negotiated settlement of the Israeli–Palestinian dispute); but the effect of his argument, terminating the status of belligerent occupation, is to give Israel greater discretion during the period of Israel's continuing occupation than is conferred by the Fourth Geneva Convention. Israel becomes the *de facto* sovereign power according to this line of thinking.

These and similar arguments, we submit, are strained and artificial in character, and have commanded little to no respect among 'highly qualified publicists' or within the organized international community. Professor Blum's 'missing reversioner' thesis, in addition to requiring a method of treaty interpretation that is unknown to international law (that is, a disregard of the expressed purposes and cognate negotiating history of the Fourth Geneva Convention[30]), is premised on a wrong provision of the Fourth Geneva Convention,[31] and, in any event, is

---

[25] See E. V. Rostow, 'Palestinian Self-Determination: Possible Futures for the Unallocated Territories of the Palestine Mandate', *Yale Studies in World Public Order* 5 (1979), 147.

[26] *ICJ Reports* (1950), 128.

[27] For convenient text, see J. N. Moore (ed.), *The Arab–Israeli Conflict: Readings and Documents* (Princeton, 1974), 484–5; also Mallison, *The Palestine Problem*, 427–9.

[28] See 2 *Report to the General Assembly of the United Nations Special Committee on Palestine—Annexes, Appendix and Maps*, UN Doc. A/364 Add. 1 (9 Sept. 1947), 18–22. For convenient text, see Moore, *The Arab–Israeli Conflict*, 891–901.

[29] See A. Gerson, 'Trustee-Occupant: The Legal Status of Israel's Presence in the West Bank', *HILJ* 14(1) (1973).

[30] Blum disregards the fact that the Fourth Geneva Convention is concerned with protecting an occupied people from the abuses of the occupying power at least as much as it is concerned with protecting the ousted sovereign's reversionary interest. Cf. Cohen, *Human Rights in the Israeli-Occupied Territories*, 53. G. von Glahn writes that protection of the reversionary interest of the ousted sovereign is only of secondary importance, behind military necessity for security and the protection of the occupied population. See von Glahn, *The Occupation of Enemy Territory* (Minneapolis, 1957), 43.

[31] Blum relied erroneously on the *second* para. of Art. 2 of the Fourth Geneva Convention, which addresses an occupation that 'meets with no armed resistance', a circumstance quite unlike that which greeted the commencement of Israel's occupation of

unsupported by authority or practice.[32] Professor Rostow's 'continuing mandate' argument makes light of both the terminating acts of Great Britain as mandatory power and the unanimous authoritative decision of the United Nations mandate, which itself provides one of the firmest legal grounds for Israel's own legal status as a sovereign state.[33] And Professor Gerson's 'trustee-occupant' theory rests essentially on the personal authority of Professor Gerson himself, having no support in the relevant legal literature or the appraisals of territorial status made by competent international institutions and being, moreover, unpersuasive as a matter of policy inclusively conceived. For all the ingenuity these lines of argument display, they are not juridically credible and have not been influential either with the wider community of international law specialists, including scholars more or less sympathetic to Israel,[34] or with diplomats.

To be sure, the character of belligerent occupation always has been somewhat problematic. It has been complicated in the present instance by the confused and overlapping claims to sovereign identity that have attached to the West Bank and Gaza both prior to and since the 1967 Six Day War.[35]

Nevertheless, in its essence, the institution of belligerent occupation represents an acknowledgement by governments (relatively recent, historically speaking) that territorial changes may not normally be effected by force of arms; it represents a step away from rights to territory acquired by conquest and reinforces and complements the contemporary legal notion that war, regardless of circumstance, no longer provides a legal foundation for territorial claims.[36] Of course,

---

the West Bank and Gaza, which began during the 1967 Six Day War. Blum should have relied instead on the *first* para. of Art. 2, which addresses an occupation that begins in 'cases of declared war or of any other armed conflict...'. For authoritative commentary on Art. 2, see Pictet, *Commentary*, 21, which leaves little doubt that it is the first paragraph that is relevant to the territories occupied by Israel during the Six Day War.

[32] Most leading scholars, including some leading Israeli scholars, dispute Israel's 'missing reversioner' claim that the Fourth Geneva Convention is inapplicable to the Israeli-occupied territories. See, e.g., Cohen, *Human Rights in the Israeli-Occupied Territories*, at 51–6; J. Gainsborough, *The Arab–Israeli Conflict: A Politico-Legal Analysis* (Aldershot, 1986), 159; Dinstein, 'The International Law of Belligerent Occupation and Human Rights', *IYHR* 8 (1978), 105, 106–8; A. Rubinstein, 'The Changing Status of the "Territories": From Escrow to Legal Mongrel', *Tel Aviv Univ. Studies in Law* 8 (1988), 61, 63–7. In addition, if votes in the UN may be relied upon as a guide, so also do most of the State members of the international community.

[33] For additional criticism, see text following n. 43 below.

[34] See, e.g., Cohen, *Human Rights in the Israeli-Occupied Territories*, 51–6.

[35] Since this statement's writing, King Hussein's decision to break Jordan's legal and administrative ties to the West Bank added a further layer of confusion even as it simplified, for the moment, the number of political actors asserting sovereign rights in the territories.

[36] Among the most useful treatments in this connection are M. McDougal and F. Feliciano, *Law and Minimum World Public Order* (New Haven, 1961), 82–6, 732–832, and

prior aggression by the occupant is not a prerequisite for the condition of belligerent occupation. Belligerent occupation connotes only a temporary, provisional circumstance and an implicit duty to withdraw once hostilities have been brought to an end.

Thus, while a belligerent occupant clearly has certain rights—for example, to assert some practical claims against the indigenous population and to protect its own security interests, as acknowledged in the Hague Regulations—the conventional and customary law of war requires the belligerent occupant to defer to the pre-belligerency political identity of the occupied territory and to act as if the territory's former status had not been superceded or even suspended for the duration of hostilities.[37] This conception of belligerent occupation obliges the occupant to sustain the pre-occupation character of all facets of civilian life as much as possible, respecting the dignity and well-being of the occupied people and making exceptions only to the extent *reasonably* required for the security of its occupation—and even then, doing so in a manner that places minimum burdens on the occupied population.[38] The ultimate purpose of the law of belligerent occupation, it may be said, is to facilitate the prospects for an eventual peace agreement.[39]

In sum, the forcible occupation of territory beyond existing boundaries is treated by the modern law of war, *including the customary law of war that applies in the current era*, as a temporary, provisional, reversible incident of ongoing hostilities.[40] And it is on the basis of this normative judgment that an overwhelming majority of the world community, including on several occasions the United States Government, endorses the view that Israel's maximum legal claim on the West Bank and in Gaza is based on its temporary supervisory control of these territories pursuant to the law of belligerent occupation, which entails a duty to comply with the Hague Regulations and, more significantly, the Fourth Geneva Convention. It is not merely the Arab countries or the Islamic

---

R. Baxter, 'The Duty of Obedience to the Belligerent Occupant', BYIL 27 (1950), 235. For extended treatments of the law of belligerent occupation, see, e.g., D. A. Graber, *The Development of the Law of Belligerent Occupation 1863–1914: A Historical Survey* (New York, 1949); and von Glahn, *Occupation*.

[37] See, e.g., Art. 44 of the Hague Regulations, which declares that '[a] belligerent is forbidden to force the inhabitants of territory occupied by it to furnish information about the arm of the other belligerent, or about its means of defence. To similar effect, Art. 45 states that '[i]t is forbidden to compel the inhabitants of occupied territory to swear allegiance to the hostile Power', and Art. 46 states that '[f]amily honour and rights, the lives of persons, and private property, as well as religious convictions and practice, must be respected,' adding that '[p]rivate property cannot be confiscated'.

[38] See, e.g., the entire set of legal standards in Section III of the Fourth Geneva Convention, entitled 'Occupied Territory'.

[39] Cf., e.g., Graber, *The Development of the Law of Belligerent Occupation*, 37–40.

[40] See, e.g., the authorities cited in n. 36 above.

world or even the Third World generally, but the entire membership of the United Nations—excepting Israel—that resists Israel's arguments to the contrary.

It is, thus, only a diversion to argue, as Professors Blum and Rostow do, that the disputed sovereignty of the Occupied Territories releases Israel's occupation of the West Bank and Gaza from assessment according to the standards imposed by the international law of belligerent occupation in general, and the Fourth Geneva Convention in particular. And, we would add, it is only perverse to contend, as Professor Rostow does, that the Namibia litigation before the World Court, sustaining the survival of South Africa's mandate in South-West Africa (Namibia) so as to avoid the extension of South Africa's apartheid system,[41] supports also the survival of the Palestine Mandate, in this instance to avoid the humanitarian safeguards of the Fourth Geneva Convention. Indeed, if one is to accept the survival of the Palestine Mandate, as some scholars do on the grounds that the UN General Assembly never terminated the Mandate for failure to implement the UN Partition Resolution of 1947,[42] an objective reading of the Namibia decision would lead one to affirm, as Professor Boyle contends, the General Assembly's legal competence to supervise the West Bank and Gaza and the applicability of the Fourth Geneva Convention along the road to independent Palestinian self-governance.[43] In any event, more pertinent is Judge Ammoun's endorsement, in his separate opinion in the *Namibia* case, of the legitimacy of armed resistance in an occupied territory[44] and the action taken by the political organs of the United Nations to revoke South Africa's authority as mandatory power and to replace it with the authority of the organized international community (as embodied in the United Nations), invoking the widely accepted reasoning that there was no other way to carry out 'the sacred trust of civilization' to the primary issue of the well-being of the inhabitants of Namibia.[45]

In sum, Israel cannot credibly claim exemption from—indeed, is unequivocally bound by—the requirements of the Fourth Geneva Convention and other obligations comprising the modern-day law of belligerent occupation. It has flagrantly and defiantly contravened both the letter and spirit of these requirements and obligations by way of

---

[41] See 1971 *ICJ Reports*, 16.
[42] See F. Boyle, 'Create the State of Palestine!', *American–Arab Aff.* 25 (Summer 1988), 85. For historical details regarding the UN Partition resolution, see W. Laqueur, *A History of Zionism* (London, 1972), ch. 11; Quigley, *Palestine and Israel*, ch. 4.
[43] See n. 42 above.
[44] See n. 41, 70.
[45] For pertinent discussion, see, e.g., R. Falk, *Reviving the World Court* (Charlottesville, 1986), ch. 4.

the harsh character of its administration in the West Bank and Gaza over the last twenty-one years; and it has but aggravated its failed responsibility toward the Palestinian people by the length of its occupation, by its establishment of Jewish settlements, by its refusal to commit itself to eventual withdrawal, and, not least, by its opposition to negotiating within the normative framework deemed reasonable by an overwhelming majority of the international community. Such a record not only warrants severe criticism but casts doubt on whether Israel has even retained its status as legitimate belligerent occupant.

The Cogency of the Plea of Security Concerns (or Military Necessity)

Traditionally, the law of war has sought to delineate the legal limits of belligerent conduct by a balancing of the customary principle of military necessity, on the one hand, against the customary principles of humanity and chivalry, on the other. In our modern era of mechanized and automated warfare, the principle of chivalry, 'a somewhat romantic inheritance from the Medieval Ages'[46] that 'denounces and forbids resort to dishonourable means, expedients, or conduct in the course of armed hostility,'[47] is said to have diminished in its distinctiveness relative to the principle of humanity;[48] and in the tension ever present between the remaining two principles, manifested in the customary principles of discrimination and proportionality, the line of compromise, again because the conduct of war has become more and more impersonal, 'has . . . tended to be located closer to the polar terminus of necessity than that of humanity'.[49] Nevertheless, except insofar as it imposes a duty of some obedience on the part of the inhabitants of a militarily occupied territory *vis-à-vis* the commands of the occupying authorities,[50] the law of war insists absolutely upon the principle of humanity over that of military necessity in the administration of a belligerent occupation, emphasizing the principles of non-discrimination and proportionality. While '[t]he administration of the occupant is in no wise to be compared with ordinary administration, for it is distinctly and precisely military administration,'[51] the protection and humane treatment of the inhabitants of a militarily occupied territory remain fundamental to the international law of belligerent occupation,[52] and a long list of the rights guaranteed such inhabitants is carefully spelled

---

[46] McDougal and Feliciano, *Law and Minimum World Public Order*, 522.
[47] Roberts and Guelff, *Documents on the Laws of War*, 5.
[48] See McDougal and Feliciano, *Law and Minimum World Public Order*, 522.
[49] Ibid. 523.
[50] See generally von Glahn, *Occupation*, ch. 5.
[51] Oppenheim, *International Law*, ii, 437.
[52] See, e.g., the authorities cited in nn. 36–48 above.

out in the Hague Regulations and the Fourth Geneva Convention principally,[53] and in the 1977 Protocol I Additional to the 1949 Geneva Conventions.[54]

In both word and deed, however, the Government of Israel, though declaring in veiled form its willingness to observe the humanitarian provisions of the Fourth Geneva Convention *ex gratia*,[55] denies virtually all legal responsibility for the suffering caused to the Palestinians of the West Bank and Gaza. Routinely, the Israeli authorities cite 'security concerns' (presumably as the functional equivalent of the venerable defence of military necessity) for many of the actions they take,[56] and on this basis justify a number of the fundamental features of their occupation, including: land confiscation and the establishment of settlements; the introduction of Jewish civilian settlers; radical changes in the administrative structure of the Occupied Territories; and punitive measures against the Palestinian population such as restrictions upon freedom of movement, arbitrary arrest and detention, the demolition and sealing of houses of families of individuals suspected of resistance activity, and other acts of collective punishment. Because Israel contests the applicability of international humanitarian law to its occupation, Israeli authorities have strained to avoid arguing that the occupied Palestinians are under a legal duty to obey their military orders. Ordinarily a belligerent occupant relies heavily on such a duty to justify actions against any signs of defiance by the local population.[57]

The question therefore arises: may Israel properly invoke security concerns (or military necessity) to release itself from tortious and/or criminal responsibility that under international humanitarian law would result from its treatment of the Palestinian population subject to its military control? In keeping with our foregoing discussion, the question presupposes, naturally, the applicability of the law of belligerent occupation, in general, and the Hague Regulations and the Fourth Geneva Convention, in particular.

It is of course true that Israel has substantial security concerns. Ever since its birth in 1948, it has been beset by hostile, typically violent,

---

[53] See Arts. 42–56 of Hague Regulations, and Arts. 47–78 of the Fourth Geneva Convention.
[54] See Arts. 48–79 of Geneva Protocol I.
[55] See n. 21 above and accompanying text.
[56] The Government of Israel has been consistently vague about specifying these security concerns. They also do not rely upon the language of 'military necessity', probably because they do not wish to present themselves in any way beholden to international law. For Israeli practice, see R. Shehadeh, *Occupier's Law*; for background and effects, G. Aronson, *Creating Facts: Israel, Palestinians and the West Bank* (Washington, DC, 1987); and see also Chs. 2 and 6 in this volume.
[57] See, e.g., von Glahn, *Occupation*, 45–56.

acts at the hands of Palestinians and other Arabs throughout the Middle East, against not only its people and territory (however defined) but, as well, its very claim to lawful existence. The controversial history of this challenge, stemming from the persisting debate about the attack by the Arab armies in 1948 and the related expulsion of Palestinians from pre-1967 Israel,[58] is so well known that it needs no elaboration here.

Until recently, however, aside from the periodic wars in the region, most of the violence directed against Israel has been planned and perpetrated not by the actual subjects of the Israeli occupation but by exiled liberation forces outside Israel-controlled territory. There have been a variety of splits and shifts of position among the various Palestinian factions on the issue of appropriate tactics and resistance. Before the *intifada*, however, the Palestinian population of the Occupied Territories rarely challenged Israeli occupation policy by direct action.

On the other hand, even if the inhabitants of the West Bank and Gaza were principally responsible for the anti-Israeli violence that has taken place in the past, the doctrine of military necessity, while helping to clarify permissible acts of repression and deprivation, has never been internationally recognized as an unqualified licence to disregard the well-being of an occupied people or as a pretext to undermine their underlying sovereign rights. Indeed, it is precisely to guard against such excesses that the Fourth Geneva Convention (as well as the other three 1949 Geneva Conventions and the two 1977 Protocols Additional) was negotiated and made law. The purpose was to ensure a measure of discrimination and proportionality in the administration of belligerent occupation and, in so doing, to overcome the discredited *kriegsraison* theory of military necessity that had been championed by German publicists before World I and practised by the German General Staff thereafter through World War II.[59]

Yet many of the legally dubious policies and practices pursued by

---

[58] For documentary narrative through 1967, see R. H. Magnus (ed.) *Documents on the Middle East* (Washington, DC, 1969). See also Moore, *The Arab–Israeli Conflict*. For historical discussion that is critical of Israel, see Mallison and Mallison, *The Palestine Problem*, 18–239 especially; Quigley, *Palestine and Israel*, passim. See also the sensitive treatment given to the 1948 Arab attack by the late Simha Flapan, National Secretary of Israel's Mapam Party from 1954 to 1981, in Flapan, *The Birth of Israel—Myths and Realities* (New York, 1987), 119–152. Flapan summarizes: 'My research indicates that the Arab states aimed not at liquidating the new state [of Israel], but rather at preventing the implementation of the agreement between the Jewish provisional government and [the pro-British Hashemite Emir of Transjordan] Abdallah for his Greater Syria scheme.' Ibid. 9.

[59] It is true that, generally speaking, the principle of military necessity 'is of the proximate military order of *raison de guerre* rather than of the final political order of *raison d'état*'. (W. V. O'Brien, 'Legitimate Military Necessity in Nuclear War, *World Polity* 2 (1960), 35, 51.) At all times, however, but especially when delineation between these two

Israel exceed the legitimate reach of military necessity and therefore may be associated more with suppressing Palestinian resistance to Israeli annexationist programmes (e.g. the establishment of settlements populated by Israeli Jews) than with safeguarding Israeli society. Illustrative in this regard are individual and group deportations; collective punishment in the form of, for example, the extra-judicial demolition and sealing of suspect houses; indiscriminate administrative detention of individuals without charge or trial for renewable periods of six months; intensive interrogations by prison personnel coupled with serious beatings and other forms of maltreatment and humiliation; the prevention of the reunification of families; the confiscation of land; the destruction of crops (mainly olive orchards) and the diversion of scarce water resources; and so forth. Even granting Israel the benefit of the doubt that its continued occupation is itself legal, its suppression of Palestinian resistance to Israeli annexationist policies and practices and of Palestinian activity associated with Palestinian concerns to sustain Palestinian cultural and political identity is in no way excused by appeals to security concerns or military necessity. To be sure, it is difficult to identify precisely and differentiate among the various claims of the Palestinian population (just as it is difficult to identify precisely and differentiate among the various claims of the Israeli population). But interference with legally protected rights imposes a heavy burden upon an occupying power to connect its use of force and other suppressive policies with the requirements of occupation *per se*. Having remained in the Occupied Territories for more than twenty years, refusing to confirm Palestinian sovereignty rights (as recognized in, for example, United Nations General Assembly Resolution 181 of 29 November 1947[60]), and undertaking such practices as the appropriation of land and water and the transfer to the West Bank and Gaza of Israeli Jews with promises of permanent settlement, virtually invalidate any Israeli claim to use force for any reason other than the discriminating and proportionate requirement of direct defence against attack. The whole point of the framework of belligerent occupation is to remove this status from the more wide-ranging tolerance of force associated with belligerent operations in general—and the more this is true, the more the occupation is prolonged. Whatever security concerns Israel may raise in defence of its policies and practices, they must bend to this fundamental precept.

---

orders proves difficult or impossible, it is shaped by what all agree, after Aristotle, is the proper object of war, namely, the bringing about of those conditions that are needed to establish a just and lasting peace.

[60] GA Res. 181 (II) (Concerning the Future Government of Palestine), 2 UN GAOR, Resolutions 16 Sept.–29 Nov. 1947, 131–2, UN Doc. A/519 (8 Jan. 1948). For convenient text, see Moore, *The Arab–Israeli Conflict*, 907.

However, it is not simply the test of proportionality that informs the principle of military necessity (or security) and against which Israeli policies and practices in the West Bank and Gaza must be measured. Israel's prerogatives as belligerent occupant are conditioned, we submit, by its good faith willingness to acknowledge and implement its international legal duty to respect the rights of the indigenous Palestinian population and to remain no longer than the occasion of hostilities reasonably mandates. Also qualifying, in other words, is a test of fairness or justness which presupposes that the policies and practices carried out by a belligerent in the name of military necessity (or security) are not themselves, however proportionate to their immediate provocation, an expression of unreasonable or illegitimate purpose. Whether rooted in the modern-day version of the just war doctrine (which seeks to distinguish between legal and illegal war[61]) or in some general principle of estoppel recognized by civilized nations that insists upon 'clean hands' in the assertion of justificatory claims, this test precludes a belligerent from bootstrapping the defence of military necessity to exonerate acts meant to advance improper or illegal objectives. A plea of military necessity (or security) is imperfectly assessed, in other words, stripped of its originating context.

In this regard, then, it is important to note that, from the time of its birth in 1948 and especially since the Six Day War in 1967, Israel, in defiance of UN General Assembly Resolution 181[62] and Security Council Resolutions 242 and 338,[63] has consistently pursued the Zionist dream of a Jewish State essentially co-extensive with the boundaries of the British Palestine Mandate,[64] and, to this end, has denied the Palestinian inhabitants of the West Bank and Gaza (as well as Palestinians deported or otherwise involuntarily abroad) their international right to self-determination. Contrary to the popular mythology, which poses Israel from its beginnings as an innocent victim of Arab

---

[61] Because of the extreme subjectivities it set into motion, the classical 'just war' doctrine was virtually abandoned during the eighteenth century. Its modern-day version, however, distinguishing between legal and illegal wars, is manifest in the Covenant of the League of Nations and thereafter in the Kellogg–Briand Pact, the Nuremberg Charter, the UN Charter, and the Resolution on the Definition of Aggression. The main documentation may be conveniently found in R. Falk, G. Kolko, and R. Lifton (eds.), *Crimes of War* (New York, 1971), 31–176.

[62] See Falk, *Reviving the World Court*, ch. 4.

[63] SC Res. 242 (Concerning Principles for a Just and Lasting Peace in the Middle East), UN Doc. S/INF/22/Rev. 2 (1967), 8; SC Res 338 (Concerning the October War), UN Doc. S/INF/29 (1973), 10. For convenient text, see Moore, *The Arab–Israeli Conflict*, 1083–4, 1188–9.

[64] It may be noted that in 1919, two years after Great Britain issued the Balfour Declaration (see n. 27), the World Zionist Organization proposed a 'homeland' to the Paris Peace Conference with borders extending not only over the whole of Palestine, but also over territories exceeding even those of today's 'Greater Israel' (i.e. the 1948 State of Israel plus the West Bank, the Gaza Strip, the Golan Heights, and East Jerusalem).

intransigence, recalcitrance, and revenge, Israel has been engaged in a long-term and large-scale effort at territorial expansion and annexation, dating back to the land acquisitions begun even before its birth in Basel under the auspices of the World Zionist Organization at the end of the nineteenth century. Influenced by a mixture of powerful religious and geopolitical convictions and—never to be forgotten—by a notorious history of persecution, Israel's objective has been to unite the Land of Israel to the extent possible, avoiding thereby the inconvenience and uncertainties that would arise from a territorial compromise with the Palestinian Arabs.[65]

To be sure, Zionism speaks with many voices on the crucial question of the rightful extent of Israeli territory. The Likud Party is far more dogmatic than the Labour Party, for example, essentially associating Israel with the full reach of the British Mandate in Palestine, whereas Labour has tended to be more pragmatic, regarding the boundaries of Israel as flexible, conditioned by opportunities and related to security needs. Yet Labour as well as the Likud has endorsed annexationist occupation policies. While maintaining a formal willingness to trade 'territory for peace', it has not challenged the appropriation of land and water resources, the establishment of settlements, or the continued longevity of the occupation. From the perspective of international law, the Israeli government, despite some variations in diplomatic stance, has maintained a unified position relative to the West Bank and Gaza.

Not to be overlooked either, not least because it has abetted the world-wide public confusion regarding Israel's posture toward the West Bank and Gaza, is the actuality and many voices of Palestinian and other Arab opposition to the very idea of a Jewish homeland, much less to the idea of a distinct state. This opposition, which dated back to the period of the British Mandate, manifestly contributed to the armed hostilities with the Israeli entity that took place in 1948 when the United Nations partition plan was sought to be put into effect, and thereafter to the long-term maintenance of a state of belligerency and continued withholding of explicit diplomatic recognition to the State of Israel. Factors such as these, however much debated, make it exceedingly difficult, obviously, to perceive clearly the essential thrust of Israel's intentions, much less to bring about the conditions that are needed to establish a just and lasting peace.

But reconstructing the history of the Israeli–Palestinian conflict is bound to be inconclusive, except for the fact that neither side can

---

[65] Some of this controversial revisionist history, drawn from recently declassified Israeli materials, is found in Flapan, *The Birth of Israel*. See also Quigley, *Palestine and Israel*; I. Lustick, *For The Land and the Lord: Jewish Fundamentalism in Israel* (New York, 1988); N. Chomsky, *The Fateful Triangle: The United States, Israel and the Palestinians* (Boston, 1983); E. Said, *The Question of Palestine* (New York, 1979).

plausibly contend that its sovereign domain is on legally firm ground while that of its adversary is not. To avoid weighing this fact and its associated history in the balance of relevant legal considerations, controversial though this fact and history surely are, is fundamentally to misunderstand, we believe, the comprehensive basis upon which Israel's plea of military necessity must be judged. If it can be empirically substantiated, as indeed it can be, that Israel's ethnocentric and frequently unlawful policies and practices *vis-à-vis* the West Bank and Gaza are themselves the cause of the violence against which Israel retaliates on grounds of military necessity (or security), then clearly Israel's efforts at legal and moral justification ring exceedingly hollow. Israel is estopped from pleading a defence in respect of acts that, for the most part, its own illegality has provoked, and for which it has ultimately itself to blame.

III

This assessment of Israel's legal position relative to the West Bank and Gaza is reinforced by the character of its coercive policies towards the *intifada* itself, inflicting casualties in a one-sided manner, using combat tactics rather than methods of riot control, abusing Palestinian civilians held in detention for long periods, challenging symbolic expressions of Palestinian patriotism such as song and flags, interfering continuously and contemptuously with the educational and religious life of the Palestinian people, deporting especially Palestinians who appear to represent the popular will of the community (including prominent advocates of Palestinian non-violence), and so forth. Such a record does not, in our view, suggest a programme associated with the maintenance of security solely for the purpose of a temporary administration incident to hostilities, particularly in the absence of any careful attempt on the part of the Israeli authorities to demonstrate a need for the specific policies upon which they rely to respond to the security threat they perceive in the Occupied Territories. Rather, it reinforces an impression of Israeli design to subjugate the Palestinian inhabitants of the West Bank and Gaza altogether.

There are, of course, some extremely complicating aspects to the overall situation that need to be taken into account, here as elsewhere. External Palestinian forces have resorted to terrorist tactics at various times, and mass resistance by the Palestinian inhabitants of the West Bank and Gaza has confronted the Israeli authorities with a daunting, and to a large extent unparalleled, challenge during the period of the *intifada*. But even after acknowledging these complexities we are not inclined to alter our firm conclusions about the illegal nature of Israel's practices and the overall character of its occupation, and notwithstanding that belligerent occupants traditionally enjoy a wide measure of discretion in defining and responding to security threats. The threats of Palestinian terrorism, even if planned and perpetrated entirely within the Occupied Territories, do not warrant violence or retaliation against the occupied Palestinian population as such, although they surely do justify greater precaution. The Palestinian resistance, it seems obvious, is directed as much against Israel's evident intention to exceed its rights as belligerent occupant and the consequent erosion of Palestinian sovereignty rights as it is against the Israeli occupation *per se*. The excessiveness of Israel's suppressive tactics, and their cruelty, appear incompatible with the contention that Israel is acting within the margin of appreciation or discretion authorized an occupying power, a conclusion that is only reinforced by Israel's having long ago repudiated the duties associated with such status under international law in favour of a claim to sovereign or quasi-sovereign control of the Occupied Territories. This claim, as shown earlier, rests on legally unacceptable lines of argument and has been rejected by the vast majority of the international community, including even the United States.

It is, in any event, this backdrop of prolonged and oppressive Israeli occupation of the West Bank and Gaza, marked by serious, systematic, and repeated breaches of Israel's duties as a belligerent occupant and member of the international human rights community, that accounts for the pervasiveness and durability as well as the fact of the *intifada* as it has unfolded so far. Also, because Israel has failed to be responsive over the years to complaints made on behalf of Palestinian rights, often validated by formal actions by various organs of the United Nations, it provides an underlying legal justification for a right of resistance against the Israeli authorities who have, in essence, abandoned their status as belligerent occupant and simultaneously abused the populations of the West Bank and Gaza in severe and systematic ways.

As established earlier, it is widely accepted that the West Bank and Gaza constitute occupied territory within the compass of the Hague Regulations and the Fourth Geneva Convention and that these treaty instruments constitute legal undertakings that are, in any event, declaratory of customary international law (especially relative to the general tenor of deference to the pre-belligerency status of the occupied territory and the unchanged underlying allegiance of the civilian population). It is widely accepted, too, to the point of virtual unanimity, that Israel's rights are circumscribed by two elements: (*a*) the upper limits of legal right being fixed by Israel's status as belligerent occupant; and (*b*) the locus of sovereignty for the territories residing in the Palestinian people. Even the Israeli Government has partially acknowledged this framework, albeit in an ambiguous (and unacceptable) manner, by its vague acceptance of the Camp David framework that included an autonomy plan for the Occupied Territories, however vague, as an integral element. Of course, the autonomy plan envisaged, and autonomy as a status, can be viewed as more consistent with Israeli than Palestinian formal sovereignty; it is too often overlooked, but must be appreciated, that the representatives of the Palestinian people never participated in the Camp David process, that all of their principal Arab allies (including even Jordan) boycotted and rejected the process, and that the main objective of the negotiations concerned the Egyptian–Israeli bargain over Sinai and the diplomatic normalization of relations between those two States and those two States alone. Nevertheless, by accepting an autonomy plan in a solemn international instrument the Government of Israel, at the very least, acknowledged conclusively the Palestinian character of the territories and confirmed its own fundamental duty to refrain from incorporating them into Israel, including indirectly by eroding their Palestinian character through population transfers in the form of either Palestinian deportations or Israeli settlements.

Thus, what remains unresolved legally is an authoritative process of implementation of Palestinian self-determination. The question is not whether there is a legal basis for Palestinian self-determination, even to the extent of full statehood, but how to terminate the Israeli occupation and provide an appropriate format for the exercise of Palestinian sovereign rights. Given the history of relations in the Middle East, it is reasonable and desirable to bring security considerations into any negotiations to shape an Israeli–Palestinian solution, but it is essential to do so mutually. Israel, to be sure, has ample reason to protect against renewals of Arab militarism; but Palestine, too, has ample grounds for fearing Israeli military intervention. Possibly only a combination of superpower, United Nations, and regional security guarantees regarding the inviolability of both political entities can address the valid security requirements of both sides.

As of this writing, the prospect of terminating Israeli occupation and establishing Palestinian rights by voluntary agreement seems remote, perhaps even impossible. The remoteness arises from the refusal of either of the main political parties in Israel to accept the PLO as the legitimate representative of the Palestinian people or to agree to the establishment of a Palestinian state as a vehicle for the realization of Palestinian rights. It arises, as well, from the Arab/PLO refusal, so far, to recognize the legitimacy of Israel's existence altogether unambiguously.[66] The main barrier to a negotiated solution results

---

[66] Since the time of this essay's writing, on 15 Nov. 1988 in Algiers, the Palestine National Council (PNC), upon proclaiming an independent State of Palestine, implicitly accepted the existence of Israel and a two-State solution to the Israeli-Palestinian problem

from persistent patterns of Israeli conduct that, in deed if not always in word, reject not only the law of belligerent occupation, in general, and the Fourth Geneva Convention in particular, but even a minimalist acceptance of the conditions needed to implement Palestinian autonomy rights as provided for in the Camp David Accords (as noted, heavily criticized by the Palestinians and by Arab governments). Conspicuous examples include the establishment of more than 118 Israeli settlements inhabited by over 150,000 Jewish settlers in the West Bank, Gaza, and East Jerusalem, and the appropriation of large portions of the land and its dedication to purposes implying a permanent Israeli presence.[67] Theoretically, of course, Israeli settlements and investments are reversible, even compatible with the fulfilment of Palestinian claims; but not practically. As a practical matter, the combination of an Israeli political consensus that rejects minimal Palestinian demands and a set of operative policies evolved over a period of more than twenty years that looks toward the permanency of Israeli occupation make it evident that a negotiated settlement along lines that might be acceptable to representative Palestinian leaders is implausible in the foreseeable future. Such an assurance is reinforced by the refusal of Israel to accept the authority of the United Nations and by the failure of the United States government, as Israel's principal benefactor, to exert sufficient pressure on Israel either to withdraw from the West Bank and Gaza or to negotiate in good faith within the parameters of the United Nations consensus, to wit, with the PLO as the legitimate representative of the Palestinian people and a Palestinian state as the eventual embodiment of self-determination.

It is against this backdrop that we must address the situation of the Palestinians, particularly those who are resident in the West Bank and Gaza. They are victims of a policy of occupation by Israel that violates both fundamental norms of the law of war and basic human rights; and, in addition, they are confronted by an occupation that seems conclusively opposed to the exercise of the right of self-determination. At the same time, positive international law is more or less silent on these matters. There is no legal analysis offered in the Hague Regulations or the Fourth Geneva Convention (or even in the Geneva Protocols of 1977) to address the situation of a belligerent occupant which is a serious violator or which converts the condition of tempor-

---

by proposing an international conference on the Middle East on the basis of UN Security Council Resolutions 242 (Concerning Principles for a Just and Lasting Peace in the Middle East), UN Doc S/INF/22/Rev. 2, 8 (1967), and 338 (Concerning the October War), each of which accepted Israel's right to exist (and for this reason were viewed with great suspicion by the PLO for many years).

[67] For authoritative confirmation, see the studies of The West Bank Data Base Project. The most recent of these is M. Benvenisti, *1987 Report*.

ary presence into one of indefinite duration under claims of at least quasi-sovereign right.

Under these circumstances, it should come as no surprise that the efforts of the *intifada* are not restricted to demonstrations and the throwing of stones, but involve, rather, since January 1988 (about a month after the uprising began), the coalescence of the Unified National Leadership of the Uprising, an underground command comprising respresentatives from each of the main PLO factions committed to the development of an 'internal front' and the nurturing of Palestinian statehood.[68] And it should come as no surprise, either, that, in light of the evidence of a widely shared Palestinian commitment to engage in struggle on behalf of their rights, including above all their pursuit of self-determination, there exists now the moral and legal foundation for a positive endorsement of their struggle. If political theory is generally supportive of 'a right of revolution' to oppose tyranny and domestic oppression, then surely such a right exists in relation to *alien* forms of oppression.[69]

It remains to consider the legal implications. The late Richard R. Baxter, among the most authoritative interpreters of the law of war in our time, and an adherent to a rather strict variant of positivist thinking, offered some guidance in a path-breaking article on belligerent occupation. 'The fundamental question of the relationship existing between the inhabitant and the occupying Power,' he wrote, 'remains for the most part a problem of the common law of war and is illuminated only fitfully by explicit provisions of the new Geneva Convention.'[70] In Baxter's view, in other words, the content of the law of war, in general, and the law of belligerent occupation, in particular, is to be derived largely from past practice and a general ethical directive despite the existence of comprehensive treaties, an orientation that is strengthened by a further observation by Baxter that '[t]he protection of the civilian population of occupied areas against oppression by the occupant has consistently been a guiding principle of the law of belligerent occupation.'[71] This latter imperative is qualified to some extent by the confirmed rights of the occupier to uphold its security. But in the instant case, the occupier is confronted by threats to its

---

[68] The main factions of the PLO consist of Yasser Arafat's *Fatah*, the largest; George Habash's *Popular Front for the Liberation of Palestine*; Nayef Hawatmeh's *Democratic Front for the Liberation of Palestine*; the *Palestine Communist Party*; and the *Islamic Jihad*.

[69] A much respected exploration of the right of resistance in instances of belligerent occupation is Baxter, 'The Duty of Obedience to the Belligerent Occupant', BYIL 27 (1950).

[70] Ibid. 235. These duties are elaborated more fully in Geneva Additional Protocol I, but the legal regime is nowhere extended to circumstances of prolonged occupation in sustained violation of both conduct norms and respect for underlying sovereign rights of the inhabitants.

[71] Baxter, 'The Duty of Obedience', 235.

security that arise, as noted earlier,[72] primarily, and especially in the most recent period, from a pronounced and sustained failure to restrict the character and terminate its occupation so as to restore the sovereign rights of the inhabitants. Israeli occupation, by its substantial violation of Palestinian rights, has itself operated as an inflaming agent that threatens the security of its administration of the territory, inducing reliance on more and more brutal practices to restore stability which in turn provokes the Palestinians even more. In effect, the illegality of the Israeli occupation regime itself set off an escalatory spiral of resistance and repression, and under these conditions all considerations of morality and reason establish a right of resistance inherent in the population. This right of resistance is an implicit legal corollary of the fundamental legal rights associated with the primacy of sovereign identity and assuring the humane protection of the inhabitants.[73]

Of course, it might be useful to have such a legal right of resistance embodied in the form of a declaration of principles issued by, say, the International Law Commission or, even better, in a widely endorsed convention, draft or otherwise, on the legal consequences of gross abuses of the status of belligerent occupation.[74] In the meanwhile, however, the legal relations of the parties in the West Bank and Gaza support the claims and tactics of the *intifada*, especially the reliance on mass recourse by the Palestinian population to non-violent forms of resistance, and including recourse to the limits established by the laws of war safeguarding especially the sanctity of civilian life. Resistance to the activities of Israeli military forces under these circumstances is, in our judgement, a legitimate exercise of Palestinian rights of self-determination. Israel's continuing actions in defiance of the rights of civilians involves more than violations of the law of war and of human rights. The cumulative effect of Israel's inhumanity toward the Palestinian inhabitants of the territory, aggravated by the absence of a security rationale that is wholly persuasive and legitimate, amounts to patterns of continuing crimes against humanity in the Nuremberg sense, and makes Israeli civilian leaders and military commanders personally liable for patterns of conduct that are violative of governing rules and standards of international law.[75]

---

[72] See text accompanying nn. 40–4 above.
[73] For clarification of issues bearing on this point, see J. J. Paust, 'The Human Right to Participate in Armed Revolution and Related Forms of Social Violence: Testing the Limits of Permissibility', *Emory Law Journal* 32 (1983), 545. See also Baxter, 'The Duty of Obedience'.
[74] This argument draws upon and is more fully elaborated in R. Falk, 'Some Legal Reflections on Prolonged Israeli Occupation of Gaza and the West Bank', *Journal of Refugee Studies* 2 (1989), 40–51.
[75] Our point here is not to equate the Israeli subjugation of the Palestinian people with the Nazi persecution of Jews during the Holocaust. It is, rather, to observe that one

IV

International law is challenged by the character of the prolonged Israeli occupation of the West Bank and Gaza. The literal situation, it is true, has not been adequately anticipated in the treaty framework set forth in the modern law of war, even though it can be persuasively assessed from a perspective that relies upon relevant international law principles, doctrines, and rules. However, insofar as conventional international law is concerned, the Government of Israel has pursued policies and practices that challenge severely the humanitarian provisions of the Hague Regulations and the Fourth Geneva Convention, the human rights provisions of the United Nations Charter as authoritatively interpreted by the competent organs of the United Nations,[76] and the increasingly authoritative 'International Bill of Human Rights', comprising the Universal Declaration of Human Rights,[77] the International Covenant on Economic, Social, and Cultural Rights,[78] and the International Covenant on Civil and Political Rights,[79] each of which assures humane treatment and the self-determination of peoples. As far as customary international law is concerned, the Israeli authorities have violated traditional human rights policies to a degree that in the past has served to justify 'humanitarian intervention'[80] and that today, as we have argued, justifies a Palestinian right of resistance. And as far as 'general principles of law recognized by civilized nations' is concerned, the Israelis have violated the principle of good faith by failing to make effective the assurances they have given the international community at various times for the just treatment of the Palestinian inhabitants of the Occupied Territories. Each of these established 'sources' of international law thus provides authoritative guidance for the judgement rendered here, and the status of this guidance is underwritten by an overwhelming consensus of governments, manifest in a stream of formal pronouncements from diverse organs of international authority and control, especially the United Nations, as well as by the weight of impartial expert commentary.

cannot—must not—allow a notorious history of persecution to obscure deeds that shock the conscience and violate the fundamental norms of modern civilization.

[76] See the Preamble and Arts. 1(2) and (3), 13(1)(b), 55, and 56 of the UN Charter (see n. 12).

[77] 10 Dec. 1948, UNGA Res 217A (III), UN Doc. A/810, (1948), at 71.

[78] Opened for signature, 19 Dec. 1966; entered into force, 3 Jan. 1976. UNGA Res. 2200 (XXI), 21 UN GAOR, Supp. (No. 16) 49, UN Doc. A/6316 (1967). See, in particular, Articles 1 and 2.

[79] Opened for signature, 19 Dec. 1966; entered into force, 23 Mar. 1976. UNGA Res. 2200 (XXI), 21 UN GAOR, Supp. (No. 16) 52, UN Doc. A/6316 (1967). See, in particular, Arts. 1 and 2.

[80] For a range of views about humanitarian intervention, see R. Lillich (ed.), *Humanitarian Intervention and the United Nations* (Charlottesville, 1973).

In such circumstances, there is no acceptable excuse for invoking a condition of legal indeterminacy, or—worse—deferring to the *de facto* circumstances imposed by Israeli annexationist designs. As with the international campaign against apartheid, the clarity of the legal situation suggests the appropriateness of mobilizing as much international pressure as possible to end the circumstance of illegal and criminal occupation and to encourage the proper fulfilment of Palestinian claims of self-determination, a process that is fully compatible with Israel's own legitimate rights of statehood and security.[81] Ending Israel's occupation of the West Bank and Gaza comports not only with the requirements of international law and justice but also with the future peace and stability of the Middle East and the world.

---

[81] This position is further strengthened by the now constant reassurances of the most authoritative Palestinian leaders, including Yasser Arafat, that legitimate Israeli sovereign and security rights will be protected in the course of establishing a Palestinian State.

4

The Legislative Stages of the Israeli Military Occupation

RAJA SHEHADEH

THE 1,200 military orders that are reviewed here provide a good source for the study of Israel's changing policies in the occupied West Bank. These military enactments, referred to as 'proclamations' in the first days of the occupation and then as 'military orders', were passed by the Area Commander of the Israeli army, who acquired, according to Proclamation No. 2, issued the day the Israeli army entered the West Bank, 'all legislative powers'. To this day, this absolute power to legislate has not been circumscribed. The one-man parliament continues to produce amendments and additions to the Jordanian law in force when the Israeli army conquered the West Bank, without any process of consultation at any level with the local Palestinian inhabitants.

Until 1982, this significant body of law remained unavailable both to the general public and to practising lawyers. There was a general belief prevalent amongst those following events in the Occupied Territories that, by and large, Israel complied with international law in the conduct of its occupation. Few bothered to study the military orders to assess the truth of this general impression.

In the preface to *The West Bank and the Rule of Law*, one of the earliest publications to review the military orders passed before 1980[1], Niall MacDermot, Secretary-General of the International Commission of Jurists, wrote:

There have been isolated cases, as in Chile, where one or two decrees of a military government have been treated as secret documents and not published. However, this is the first case to come to the attention of the International Commission of Jurists where the entire legislation of a territory is not published in an official gazette available to the general public.[2]

In 1982, fifteen years after the beginning of the Israeli occupation, the military orders were finally published in their totality. Many of the

---

[1] R. Shehadeh and J. Kuttab, *The West Bank and the Rule of Law* (Geneva, 1980).
[2] Ibid. 7.

secondary regulations as well as a number of orders made by virtue of the published orders, still remain unavailable. However, enough is available to enable the jurist to attempt to trace the changing policies that the Israeli government has sought to enforce in the territories it has occupied since 1967.

What is attempted in this paper is a general survey of the 1,213 military orders issued up to 3 December 1987, the time of writing. In topic and thrust, these orders illustrate four legislative stages. The more significant legal changes that occurred in each stage are identified and described. No attempt is made here to examine the consistency of these orders with international law, and only the orders applicable to the West Bank (excluding East Jerusalem) are reviewed here.

I. The First Legislative Stage

The first legislative stage, from 1967 to 1971, is perhaps the most significant. The roughly 400 military orders issued during these four and a half years laid the foundation for the occupation. The orders were not published and were not available even to lawyers.

Perhaps the single most empowering order issued by the area commander, by which the commander assumed all legislative, executive, and judicial powers, is Proclamation No. 2. This order was issued on the first day that the Israeli army occupied the West Bank. Having assumed the power to legislate without consultation in any form with the people to whom the legislation would apply, the Israeli commander became very prolific. Over forty orders of major importance had already been issued before the end of the first month of occupation.

The orders issued during the first legislative stage extended military jurisdiction over diverse facets of life in the territories. The military government was given full control of all transactions in immovable property (MO 25), the use of water and other natural resources (MOs 58, 59, and 92), the power to expropriate land (MOs 108 and 321), and the authority to operate banks (MOs 9, 45, and 255). In addition, the orders made illegal the import and export of agricultural products to and from the West Bank without military permission (MOs 47 and 49). Drivers' licences (MO 215), travel permits, and licences to practise a variety of professions (MOs 260, 324, and 437) also came to require the approval of the military authorities. Moreover, during this period the system of control through identity cards was initiated (MO 297) as was control over the municipal councils (MO 194) and over the village councils (MO 191). The system of military rule thus seems designed to give Israel full control of the Palestinians in the Occupied Territories.

True, it can be argued that an occupier may be entitled to issue certain orders dealing with the security of the occupier's troops. But even these often exceeded reasonable limits in safeguarding the Israeli army. The most important order issued during this period concerning what the military called security was Proclamation No. 3 (later replaced by MO 378). This order established the military courts and the 'security' offences which only the newly established military courts had jurisdiction to try. This, together with other orders issued during this first stage, legalized far-reaching restrictions on the basic rights of Palestinians living under Israeli rule. MO 101 made the 'congregation of ten people or more in a place where a speech is heard on a political subject . . . or who are gathered for the purpose of deliberating on such a subject' punishable by 10 years in prison. It also, along with MO 50, imposed a complete ban on printed material unless special permission is obtained from the military to print, import, or distribute. Proclamation No. 3 authorized arrests without warrant and detention for as many as 18 days, renewable, without charge or trial. The order also empowered Israeli soldiers to conduct searches of homes without search warrants.

The restructuring of the judicial system contributed significantly to enabling the military authority to assume full and unchallenged control over all aspects of Palestinian life inside the Occupied Territories, including those matters which did not pertain to security such as industry, agriculture, and development.

The following are some of the ways in which this was achieved:

1. Cancelling the Court of Cassation which, under the Jordanian system, is the highest court of appeal.
2. Removing the independence of the judiciary by giving the military the power to appoint, dismiss, and promote all judges and prosecutors in the civilian courts (MO 129).
3. Removing from the jurisdiction of the civilian courts many of the matters over which they previously had jurisdiction, such as appeals against tax assessments, land expropriation, and refusal of permits for certain economic enterprises.
4. Giving jurisdiction to the newly established military courts over all criminal matters, concurrently with the civilian courts. The decision as to whether a criminal case is to be heard by the civilian or the military courts is made by the area commander.
5. Conferring immunity upon civil servants working in the military and/or civilian government of the Occupied Territories.

The Jordanian law in force provided the citizen with the right to appeal administrative decisions to the High Court of Justice. This right was seriously circumscribed by MO 164, issued on 3 November 1967, which declared that no local court could hear any case against any of the employees or agents of the State of Israel, the Israeli army, or any authorities established by them, unless special permission was obtained from the military authority.

Although it has often been said by Israeli apologists that the Israeli High Court of Justice has been made available to hear appeals against decisions of Israeli officials, it is evident from the record of the court that the Israeli court has only on very rare and exceptional occasions been willing to overturn a decision made by the military authority or any of its employees and has in any case not accepted to substitute its own opinion on the wide range of matters described as security matters over the opinion of the security apparatus.[3] Its effectiveness as an administrative court for the Occupied Territories has not therefore been apparent.

In addition to restructuring the judicial system, thereby reducing the ability of the courts to review the actions of the executive, the military administration also relieved itself of the duty to be accountable to the tax-payers regarding taxes collected. According to the Jordanian Constitution, the government must publish the budget, which then becomes a public document. However, despite its legal obligation to do so, the Israeli military government has failed to comply.

As the occupation continued, public funds were being created for which the government levied new taxes. Some of these were established by military orders issued during the period under consideration, such as MO 103. The fund created by virtue of this order was to be used to develop the economy of the area. At least three other funds were created after 1971. These were:

1. 'The Fund for the Development of the Area', established by MO 974.
2. 'The Fund for Agricultural Products', established by MO 1051 to compensate farmers, *inter alia*, for providing agricultural products for industry.
3. 'The Deduction Fund', in which the Israeli government claims to deposit the money deducted from the salaries of workers working in Israel for benefits they do not enjoy.[4] The military government never accounted to the Palestinians as to how the money deposited into these funds was spent.

Relations between the West Bank (excluding East Jerusalem) and Israel were also legislated for during this period. A review of the orders pertaining to this issue reveals that Israel was not following a clearly defined policy. While, on the one hand, the orders which its military

---

[3] See Chs. 2 and 6.
[4] On the Deduction Fund, see also Chs. 12 and 13.

government issued treated the West Bank as a separate juridical area, other orders resulted in a *de facto* annexation of the area to Israel. These two sets of orders, all issued during the period under consideration, are reviewed below.

Military Orders Rendering the Territories a Separate Juridical Area

Proclamation No. 2, issued on 7 June 1967, describes the area to which the order applies in both the Arabic and Hebrew versions as 'the West Bank' and declares, in Article 2, that the laws which were in force up to 7 June 1967 shall remain in force to the extent that they do not contravene Proclamation No. 2 or any other order issued by the military, or any changes that are brought about as a consequence of the introduction of military rule in the area.

There is in this order a clear recognition by the occupier of the occupation of an area which has separate legal status and therefore different laws to those which apply within the State of Israel. These laws were to apply until and unless amended by military legislation. Israeli law came to apply outright only in the area which was officially annexed, namely East Jerusalem and its environs.

Many of the military orders that followed this early order are also based on a recognition of the distinctness of the Occupied Territories as a separate juridical area. Thus, MO 39 (later replaced by MO 412), for example, began the restructuring of a judicial system separate from both Jordan and Israel and under the control of the military administration, as will be described below. MO 384 dealt with the conflict of law problem in the execution of judgments between two separate juridical areas, namely Israel and the Occupied Territories, and stated how judgments made in the courts of each can be executed in the other area.

MO 47, as amended, regarding transport of agricultural products, prohibited the transport into or out of the West Bank of any plant or animal products (except for canned goods) without a permit from the military authority.

MOs 397 and 398 created separate West Bank Companies and Trademarks Registration Departments. The orders also declared that all registrations that had taken place before 7 June 1967 will only be recognized if re-registered. The recognition of the separateness of the area from both Jordan and Israel is again very clear here.

Shortly after the beginning of the occupation, the newly acquired areas were made accessible to Israelis and tourists visiting Israel. However following the policy of treating the areas as separate from Israel, despite their accessibility, MO 65 was issued which, in effect, required a work-permit for non-residents of the Occupied Territories (including Israelis) intending to take employment there.

Perhaps the most graphic indicator that the occupied areas were to be treated as a separate unit from Israel was MO 5 (later replaced by MO 34) which declared the whole of the West Bank a closed military area, exit and entry to be according to orders and conditions stipulated by the military. The later orders restricting imports and exports into and out of the area are based on this order.

The above are only a few examples of military orders that illustrate the legal separateness of the areas conquered in 1967 from Israel itself; many more could be mentioned. The orders cited above are among the fundamental orders that dealt with the establishment of the basic structures of Israeli rule over the Occupied Territories.

Military Orders Rendering the Territories de facto *Annexed to Israel*

A number of military orders that have contributed to this process were issued during the period under consideration. Many more were issued after 1971. I shall describe here some of the earlier orders.

1. The preamble of MO 103 issued on 27 August 1967 reads as follows:

Whereas there is a need to take measures to ensure regular trade in the area [of the West Bank] and to facilitate for the inhabitants the marketing of their products through free trade in order to improve their economy in general and in particular to establish a fund for developing the economy of the area, and whereas this order is necessary in order to ensure export, vital services, and regular rule in the area, I order as follows . . .

Article 1 of the order imposes customs duties on goods brought into the area of the West Bank from all other areas except Israel. The determination of these duties is left to 'the person responsible' who is appointed by the area commander. To the extent that goods brought into the West Bank from Israel were not considered as brought in from a foreign country, the two juridical areas were treated as one.

2. MO 31 vested all powers arising from the Jordanian laws and regulations relating to customs duties, fees and taxes, and all powers of delegation and appointment given by them, in the Israeli officer appointed for this purpose by the area commander. Seven orders were issued by the person appointed under MO 31 between July and September of 1967. The most important of these declared the imposition of fees on locally produced goods which are listed in the appendix to the first order. The order also required all producers to submit to the officer responsible a form showing all relevant details about their place of work and the goods produced there. Except for this

requirement to submit information, the continuation of the work was not made conditional upon obtaining any other approval of the military officer appointed under MO 31. This of course was later changed. At this early stage, the Israeli administration was more concerned with getting 'normal' life to continue and to defeat the Palestinian boycott which had started as a form of protest against the occupation.

3. MO 59 vested all government immovable properties in the hands of what the order called 'the Custodian of Public Property'. Later on (by MO 364) the definition of public property was expanded to include any property of which the owner fails to convince a military committee (according to the rules of evidence they determine) that it is private property. By virtue of this order, over 30 per cent of the land in the Occupied Territories was eventually registered in the Israeli Lands Authority as Israeli public land.[5]

4. MO 92 vested the powers defined in all Jordanian laws dealing with water in the hands of an Israeli officer appointed by the area commander. Using these powers, the officer assumed full control over water resources and connected the West Bank with the Israeli water grid. Thus 'public' land and water were considered as belonging to Israel, thereby denying the separateness of the two areas. After 1979, responsibility over water resources was transferred from the military government to the national water company, Mekorot.

It has already been mentioned that the first legislative stage was the most significant period, when the foundations of the occupation were laid. But it was also the period when Israeli policy towards the newly conquered territories was still in flux. Perhaps the best indicator of this is the clear admission of the applicability of the Fourth Geneva Convention of 1949 to the Occupied Territories which was made in Article 35 of Proclamation No. 3. This article stated that the military court and its officers 'must apply the provisions of the Geneva Convention of 13 August 1949 Regarding the Protection of Civilians in Time of War as to all which pertains to legal proceedings'.[6]

Military Proclamation No. 3 was issued on 7 June 1967. Four months later, on 22 October, the same military commander issued MO 144 which repealed Article 35. Since then Israel has refused to accept that it is bound to apply the provisions of the Fourth Geneva Convention to the territories it conquered in 1967.

Although the policy of settling Jews in the conquered areas began during the first legislative stage, it was still not so extensive as to require the changes in the land law that characterized the second

---

[5] On the legality of this step and those pertaining to water, see Ch. 14.
[6] For full text of this article, see Ch. 2, text at n. 126.

legislative stage, when large areas of land began to be expropriated. These changes will be described below.

II. The Second Legislative Stage

The second legislative stage, from 1971 to 1979, placed particular emphasis on facilitating Jewish settlement in the West Bank. We have already seen how, during the first stage, several orders were issued which enabled the military authorities to take possession of land through expropriation and through seizure of the land as absentee and state property.

This process continued during the second stage. More amendments were made to the land law to enable the acquisition of land by non-Jordanians through means other than expropriation and seizure. MO 419, for example, enabled the area commander to give special dispensation to certain foreign bodies, on a list that he draws up, to purchase immovable property even if they do not fulfil the requirements of the Jordanian law concerning the acquisition of land by foreign bodies. MO 569 created 'a department for special transactions in land' for the registration of land for Jewish settlement. MOs 811 and 846 extended the validity of irrevocable powers of attorney from 5 to 15 years, thus validating purchases made to Jews outside the area. The Area Commander thus showed himself willing to amend by military orders any Jordanian law that had restricted sale of land to non-Jordanians. He was also willing to make those amendments in the law that would enable, as well as facilitate, the clandestine sale of Palestinian land to Jews.[7]

Large areas of land were being acquired using the means provided through the changes in the land law made during the first and second stages. What was needed now was the power to determine the use of land acquired for Jewish settlement without Palestinian interference and to restrict the Palestinians from using the land that was left. MO 418 was issued on 23 March 1971 to fulfil these twin objectives.

Consisting only of 9 articles, the effect this order had on the Jordanian Planning Law of 1966 was devastating. The Jordanian law contains procedures for the participation in its operation of various local institutions, such as the Engineers' Union. It imposes a hierarchical structure of local, district, and national planning committees. MO 418 abolished all local participation in the planning operations outside of municipal boundaries. Within municipal boundaries, the order restricted the

---

[7] R. Shehadeh, *Occupier's Law: Israel and the West Bank*, rev. edn. (Washington, DC, 1988), 39–41.

licensing powers of municipalities. All planning powers were vested in the Higher Planning Committee composed of Israeli officers only and appointed by the Area Commander. The powers of the District Committee as well as the Local Committee were transferred to the Higher Planning Council which was also empowered to appoint what the order calls 'Special Planning Committees' and to determine their powers. Article 7 of the order also gave wide-ranging powers to the Higher Planning Council which included the power to:

1. Cancel or amend or suspend for any period the effect of any regulation or permit
2. Assume any of the powers of the other planning councils
3. Issue any licence which the other planning councils are empowered to issue or to amend or cancel
4. Exempt any person from the duty of obtaining any licence which is required by the law.[8]

With the land made available to Jews in the West Bank and zoning plans completed for some settlements, the number of settlers began to increase. But if their settlements were to prosper they could not be made subject to the same restrictive laws concerning local government. Jewish settlements could never be made subject to the extensively amended Jordanian law applicable to Village Councils or Municipal Councils and be expected to prosper. They had to have a status separate from that available to their Palestinian neighbours, so that those restrictions placed on the local government units of the Palestinians would not be applicable to them.

The first order relating to the administration of Jewish settlements pertained to Kiryat Arba, one of the earliest settlements, established in 1968 near the Palestinian town of Hebron. This order declared that the settlement was to be administered 'in accordance with administrative principles which the Military Commander shall declare by internal regulations'.

Then, on 25 March 1979, MO 783 was issued. This order declared the establishment of four Jewish regional councils. The jurisdiction of these councils covered the whole of the land under Israeli ownership or control, not merely the built-up area of the settlements. The order announced that the administration of these regional councils shall be in whatever way the area commander shall declare in 'regulations'. The date of this order was significant. It was issued only a few days before the signing of the Camp David Agreement. Although the principle that Jewish councils would not be administered in accordance with the law

---

[8] For a more detailed examination of the effects of military orders on the planning process, see Ch. 8.

in force in the area was established, it was only during the next legislative stage that the 'regulations' according to which the settlements were to be administered were issued.

III. The Third Legislative Stage

The third legislative stage extended from the signing of the Egyptian–Israeli peace treaty in 1979 to 1981. It was characterized by a greater influx of Israeli citizens into the West Bank than in any previous stage. The military orders issued during this period served the following objectives:

1. Organizing the administration of Jewish settlements to make it consistent with the local government in Israel; i.e. extending Israeli regulations regarding regional and local councils to the settlements of the West Bank. MO 892 established local councils for the administration of particular settlements. The powers and responsibilities of the local councils are identical with those of Israeli municipalities. Thus, through the guise of a military order, the Israeli Municipalities Law was extended to the Occupied Territories and made to apply only to the Jewish settlements. The Palestinian municipalities continued to be subject to the amended Jordanian Municipalities Law.

2. Tightening the links between Israeli citizens living in the Occupied Territories and Israel by extending Israeli law to the Jewish settlers and excluding them from the jurisdiction of the West Bank courts.

Under the Israeli Law and Administration Ordinance of 1948, the Prime Minister or any other Minister has the power to make emergency regulations 'as may be expedient in the interests of the defence of the state, public security and the maintenance of supplies and essential services',[9] following a public declaration that a state of emergency exists.

Immediately following the 1967 war, the Minister of Justice introduced regulations entitled Emergency Regulations (Areas held by the Defence Army of Israel—Criminal Jurisdiction and Legal Assistance) 1967. The validity of these Regulations has been extended annually and later bi-annually by the Israeli Knesset. These regulations enable a court in Israel to try any person for any act or omission which occurred in any region (defined in Regulation 1 as 'any of the areas held by the Defence Army of Israel') and which would constitute an offence under Israeli law if it were committed in Israel.[10]

---

[9] Section 9(a).
[10] On the relevant provisions of international law, see Ch. 7.

This has meant that Israeli courts acquired jurisdiction to try Israelis residing in the Occupied Territories for criminal offences committed within Israeli settlements or elsewhere in the Occupied Territories. This is in addition to the competence of special military courts established in the Occupied Territories to try Israeli settlers for such offences.

In civil matters, Israeli courts have ruled that they have jurisdiction if any bond to Israel can be found. As to service of documents, regulations made in 1969 provided that service of documents in the Occupied Territories is effected in the same manner as in Israel, i.e. either by mail or by hand.[11]

An amendment to the Israeli Income Tax ordinance in 1980 provided that any income of settlers produced or received in the West Bank was to be treated as though its source were Israel. Through an 'administrative order', it was possible to extend the applicability of Israeli laws to Israelis living in the West Bank by amending the definition of 'Israeli resident' to include 'any person whose place of residence is in the region and who is an Israeli citizen or entitled to acquire Israeli citizenship pursuant to the Law of Return 1950'.

This process of extending Israeli laws to Israeli citizens living outside the state continued beyond the period under consideration here as will be shown below.

3. Reorganizing the military government in the West Bank and giving some of its functions to the newly established Civilian Administration.

This was achieved mainly through MO 947 which declared the establishment of a 'civilian administration', to be headed by a person whose nationality is not specified, who holds the title 'Head of the Civilian Administration', and who is appointed by the Area Commander.

MO 947 had two main and closely related effects. The first was to institutionalize the already existing separation of the civilian from the military functions in the military government of the West Bank by formally establishing a new structure of civilian government which is empowered to function within the limits determined by the order. The second is to make it possible to elevate the status of a large number of military legislative enactments promulgated by the area commander from the status of temporary security enactments to the level of permanent laws. MO 947 was the most significant military order issued during this third legislative stage.[12]

---

[11] See 'Service of Documents to the Administered Territories Regulations', amending the Civil Procedure Regulations of 1963. For a more complete discussion of the judiciary and the Israeli settlements, see M. Drori, 'The Israeli Settlements in Judea and Samaria: Legal Aspects', in D. J. Elazar (ed.), *Judea, Samaria and Gaza: Views on the Present and Future* (Washington DC: AEI, 1982), 70–9.

[12] See Ch. 8 for further discussion of MO 947.

IV. The Fourth Legislative Stage

The fourth legislative stage extends from 1981 to the time of writing, December 1987. Some 260 military orders were issued during this period (from MO 950 to MO 1213).

The military orders issued during these six years have expedited the *de facto* annexation of the West Bank to Israel, the extension of Israeli law to the Jewish settlements, and the legal and administrative separation of Jews and Palestinians in the occupied areas.

Large areas of land continued to be acquired at a faster pace than ever before, through declaring the land as 'state land'. Those lands which could not be acquired by one or other of the methods used during the previous thirteen years were subjected to severe restrictions on use.

Perhaps the most important means of restricting land use which has increased during the fourth legislative stage relates to zoning measures, or, more precisely, the withholding of building permits in Arab areas. Although Palestinian villages and small towns (those without municipal councils) have officially been encouraged to make town plans, none of these plans has been approved since 1985 on the grounds that no final statutory plan of the area has yet been made. In the absence of approved planning documents, all individual building licences outside municipal boundaries (small towns and villages by definition lie outside municipal boundaries) must be approved by the military planning authorities. From January 1987 to the time of writing, no building licence in these areas was granted for Palestinian residents of the West Bank. While Palestinian projects were at a standstill, 274 statutory plans for areas of Jewish settlement had been processed as of mid-1987. Of these, at the time of writing, December 1987, 86 had been approved, 110 had been disputed, and 78 were still awaiting approval.

Another means of restricting land use has been the increase in the number of approvals needed from different departments before any development of the land is permitted. MO 1167, for example, made it necessary to obtain the approval of the Antiquities Department before the Planning Department could consider applications submitted to it for building-licences. Jurisdiction over violations of the Jordanian Antiquities Law was transferred from the local Palestinian courts to the military courts.

Even the use of Palestinian land through cultivation was subjected to more restrictions. The Jordanian Nursery Law Number 20 of 1958 was amended by MOs 1002 and 1248 to increase the powers of the military authorities regarding the licensing and regulation of plant nurseries. MO 1015 made it necessary to obtain permission from the military authorities to plant fruit trees or to change the kind of existing fruit trees through grafting. Similar restrictions were placed on the planting of vegetables by MO 1039. The restriction according to the order was on the planting of tomatoes and eggplants, but other vegetables could be added by amending the appendix of the order.

Separate offices were created during this stage, one to administer and oversee the affairs of Jewish 'local and regional authorities', and the other to oversee Palestinian 'village and municipal authorities'. Similarly, there are now two separate departments for land planning, one dealing with the Palestinian sector and the other with the Jewish sector. Israeli Jews head both departments.

The processes which began in the previous stage of expanding the powers of the Jewish local councils continued, as did the tightening of links between Israeli citizens living in the Occupied Territories and Israel. MO 892 established municipal courts in the settlements, and MO 898 amended an earlier order (MO 432) concerning the guarding of settlements, by empowering the guards to carry weapons and giving them added powers of arrest and interrogation of suspects. Also, under Emergency Regulations 6B of 1984, a list of nine Israeli laws were made applicable to settlers by extending the meaning of 'Israeli resident' as described above. These laws are:

1. Entry into Israel Law 1952
2. Defence Services Law 1959
3. Chamber of Advocates Law 1961
4. Income Tax Ordinance
5. Population Register Law 1965
6. Emergency Labour Services Law 1967
7. National Insurance Law (Consolidated Version) 1968
8. Psychologists Law 1968
9. Emergency Regulations Extension (Registration of Equipment) Law 1981

Other military orders passed during this stage concern the appointment by the military of Israelis (and sometimes Palestinians) to replace Israeli officers acting as mayors in place of the elected Palestinian mayors deposed in 1982. Similarly, for the Chambers of Commerce, new military orders provided for the appointment of Palestinians to replace the elected Palestinians deposed by the military government. One example is an amendment to MO 697 declaring on 30 April 1987 that new members of the Hebron Chamber of Commerce would be appointed.

On the level of increasing the control of the military authority over the daily activities of Palestinians, a number of military orders were passed during this period. These made it necessary to obtain the approval of the military over activities which did not previously require such approval. MO 1149, for example, requires anyone who wishes to trade spare parts or assemble any type of road vehicle to obtain permission from the military. MO 1140 requires all newspapers distributed in the West Bank to publish without payment any notices submitted by the military authorities. Failure to do so could provoke the withdrawal of the newspaper's licence. MO 1141 prohibits Jewish settlements from employing any Palestinian from the Occupied Territories except through the government public employment office. Palestinian workers from the West Bank working in the West Bank are thus now subject to the same bureaucratic requirements and restrictions that would apply if they were working in Israel.

MO 1208 (amending MO 297 concerning identity cards) adds a new provision to Article 11 of the original order whereby a child born to resident parents can be registered in the occupied area if he or she is under 16. A child born outside the area to resident parents can be registered only if he or she is not over 5 years old.

Special attention was paid during this period to stemming the flow of money into the West Bank from organizations Israel considered hostile. MO 952, issued on 20 January 1982, ordered that permission from the military was necessary before any of the following could be carried out:

1. Transactions in a foreign currency to which a resident of the territories is a party, whether the transaction was carried out in the area or outside;
2. Exporting of money from the area to the outside;
3. Bringing in of Israeli money to the area, whether by remittance or otherwise;
4. Any transaction involving property in the area if a resident of a foreign country was a party thereto, and any transaction involving property outside the area if a resident of the area was a party thereto;
5. Possession of foreign currency by a resident of the area.

'Transaction' is defined by the order to include sales, purchases, transfer of ownership, loans, trusts, credit, lease, issuance of cheques, grants, releases, pensions, admissions and exonerations from debts, or any transaction which will create rights over property or alter or transfer or cancel them whether conditionally or unconditionally, and whether the person carries it out for himself or for another and whether he is acting in his personal capacity or through an attorney.

Regulations have been issued from time to time giving general or specific permits allowing some of the proscribed activities under this order. These have varied according to the policies being pursued by the government.

The other major legislation concerning financial activities is MO 973, dated 9 June 1982, concerning the importation of money into the area. This order prohibits (unless there is a specific or general order to the contrary) the importation of money into the area. Money, as defined by the order, includes local and foreign currency and gold. It should be noted here that the receipt of a permit under this order does not exonerate the recipient of the permit from obtaining the permits required under MO 952. Violation of this order subjects the violator to large fines or to imprisonment of up to five years, or to both punishments.

While attempting to restrict the flow of money reaching Palestinian institutions and individuals, the military has tried to increase its own revenues by introducing new taxes (such as the Value Added Tax) and amending tax laws in existence when the occupation began. The Jordanian Income Tax Law has been amended thirty-two times since the occupation began, most recently by MO 1206 of 13 September 1987, with the result that income taxes paid by Palestinians have increased dramatically through changes in tax brackets and reductions in exemptions.[13]

Two positive changes occurred as a result of military orders passed during this stage. MO 1133 increased an employee's entitlement under the Jordanian Labour Law to include sick-leave payments. MO 1180, amending the Jordanian Banks Law, made it possible to reopen the West Bank branches of the Cairo-Amman Bank, closed since 1967 by the military authorities.

A review of the orders issued during this stage makes it clear that, after the first thirteen years of the occupation, the military authority became more clear and deliberate than at any time in the past in the policies it pursues in the territories conquered in 1967 and the objectives it aims to achieve. It could perhaps be argued that the processes described above had already been formulated and pursued before 1981. While this may be true, it is clear that at no other stage do the military orders reflect what the occupation was intended to serve with such clarity and deliberation as in this fourth stage. The fact that after 1981 a high proportion of Israelis working at the military and civilian governments were residents of Jewish settlements in the West Bank contributed to the self-confidence and singularity of purpose reflected in the military orders issued during the fourth stage.

MO 1213, dated 3 December 1987, and the last to have been published at the time of writing, declared the Jewish settlers living in the West Bank to be local residents for the purposes of MO 65, which prohibits

---

[13] On the introduction of VAT, and levying of taxes in the Occupied Territories generally, see Chs. 11 and 12.

non-residents from working in the West Bank without permission. MO 1213 as an instrument of law merely confirmed long-standing practice: the Jewish settlers were considered part of the local population when it was convenient to do so, but retained their special status with regard to the Israeli civil rights denied to the Palestinians. The practice of treating citizen-settlers of the occupying power as if they were local residents of the occupied territory stands international law on its head, since it implies that they are part of the 'protected population' whose interests, as distinct from those of the occupier, international law sets out to protect.

It should come as no surprise that MO 1213, with its grave violation of international law, should have been issued. With the settlers now intimately involved in the administration of the Occupied Territories, what best serves the interest of their settlements is no longer a theoretical matter but a straightforward question of self-interest.

Along with the clarity of purpose came a marked sloppiness both in the form of the military orders and in the lack of concern to offer even a formal justification of the orders according to international norms. New military orders continue to be informally produced, even though they are official documents. In the four-page Arabic version of MO 1180, amending the Jordanian Banks Law, for example, there are some forty handwritten insertions, including entire lines added after the order was typed.

Serially numbered military orders have been published since 1982, but at best three months after being issued. Much 'legislation' in the West Bank, however—unnumbered military orders that are subsidiary legislation made by virtue of the numbered orders—is either never published or only long afterwards. There are also oral orders and directives of which an individual learns only in encounters with the bureaucracy or the authorities. An example is the prohibition on sending packages over a certain weight through West Bank post offices. No regulation was ever published or announced on the subject, but the prohibition is strictly enforced.

It has already been pointed out that the one-man parliament producing the military orders discussed above is neither accountable to, nor consults with the local population which is subject to these new laws and to changes in the existing law. Perhaps, in view of this, neither the content of the orders nor their sloppy production should come as a surprise.

V. Conclusion

The legislative stages reflect the gradual changes in Israel's presentation of its occupation. At first, Israel acknowledged its status as an occupying force and stated that the occupation would continue pending a final settlement, under which land would be exchanged for peace. Then Israel announced that, since the occupied areas were of strategic importance to its defence, land for settlements serving a security interest would be expropriated. Nonetheless, it continued to maintain that land would be exchanged for peace. With the advent of the Likud Government in 1977, the territories were held to belong to Israel by right, indeed by divine right: there could be no question of expropriating or occupying what was rightfully Israel's. As of that time, land designated by Israel as public, i.e. 'state land', was taken over and given to the only public Israel recognized—the Jewish settlers. The term 'West Bank' fell into disuse and 'Judea' and 'Samaria', the only officially recognized designations, began to be used by the public as neutral terms.[14] The word 'occupation' was also definitively dropped. The territories were now 'administered', as were the 1.5 million Palestinian inhabitants.

The Israeli occupation of Palestinian lands has been a legalistic occupation, whereby every new change was accompanied by a military order. This makes the military orders a good source from which the changing thinking of Israeli policy-makers can be studied.

When the time for negotiations between the parties to this long-lasting conflict comes, the legality of these military orders issued by Israel to amend and add to the law that was in force when the occupation began will have to be studied. The majority of these unilateral actions issued by the area commander without consulting the local inhabitants will be found to be in violation of international treaties. What Israel seems to count on, however, is not that a neutral international arbiter will rule that these orders are consistent with international law, but that, by the time the pressure mounts on Israel to enter into negotiations with their adversaries, the legal changes will have brought about irreversible transformations that will become facts on the ground that cannot be ignored, whatever the state of the law.

[14] See Ch. 1.

5

The Destruction of Troy will not Take Place

ALAIN PELLET

> There is but one criterion applicable in the law of belligerent occupation: respect for the sovereign rights of the occupied people.

Introduction

THE very idea of law of war can only be envisaged when two conditions are met: the fact—or, in any case, the possibility—of armed conflict (law is called upon to provide a framework to human activities, not fantasies) and the will to limit barbarism (in the absence of which arms alone would be left to speak). It is a matter then of reconciling the cold realism of Creon and the Lament of Antigone.

Speaking, then, in abstract and general terms, one can say that the law of war is born of the dialectic of two principles: that of necessity and that of humanity.

It is, today, an underlying assumption—though not for that a false one—that 'the great truism' of the law of war 'is the balancing of the military needs against the humanitarian values'.[1] Whether one considers the law of military operations or humanitarian law, whether one takes one's perspective from 'the law of the Hague' or from 'the law of Geneva', the finding is always the same: the law of war arises from a balance between military exigencies—which are a matter of

---

* This chapter tries to identify the operative criterion or criteria of the law of belligerent occupation in accordance with general international law; it is not intended, at any rate as a priority, to determine whether Israel, in the territories it occupies, is complying with such criterion or criteria.

The English translation from the original French is by Alexandra Campbell. After its presentation at al-Haq's conference, the paper was published in French in *Palestine Yearbook of International Law* 4 (1987/8), 44–84.

[1] G. I. A. D. Draper, 'The Geneva Conventions of 1949', RCADI 114 (1965–I), 77.

fact—and those of the protection of the human person—which are the products of conscience.[2]

These obvious points call, none the less, for clarification on two fronts.

On the one hand, certain rules may appear to relate to one or other of the two main principles. But, very often, *both* are found to inspire the same rule; the compromise is realized not by the opposition of two distinct norms, but *through* and at the heart of the norm. A typical example of the close fusion of the principles of necessity and humanity is found in the noteworthy Article 22 of the Regulations of 1907: 'The right of belligerents to adopt means of injuring the enemy is not unlimited.'

Belligerents may destroy the enemy—this is clear, indeed necessarily implied in the wording of this rule—and it is an expression of the principle of necessity; but this right to destroy is not unlimited—and here the principle of humanity emerges. A hundred similar examples could be cited.[3] This equilibrium is the very *raison d'être* of the law of war: men fight each other—this is a fact; they seek to moderate the suffering that results—this is a moral necessity. Law is born of these contradictory elements.

On the other hand, the compromise that is the essence of the law of war is not inflexible: military techniques evolve; the demands of conscience also. The contrary has sometimes been asserted: for some authors, the principle of necessity is undoubtedly contingent, while that of humanity has an immanent character.[4] Here we have a point of debate: the means of destroying the enemy progress, certainly; but so does the human conscience; and both evolve as one. It is probably *because* humanity has endowed itself with the possibility of destroying all traces of life on earth that it has, at the same time, grown concerned to prevent this eventuality.

These general considerations are wholly relevant to the law of occupation—at any rate to the law of belligerent occupation.[5] There is no practical doubt that the latter constitutes a branch of the general law of war, at the heart of which it is gradually emerging as a distinct chapter. With the emergence of the nation as an actor in history—an

---

[2] See, in relation to the law of war *stricto sensu*, P. Fauchille, *Traité de droit international public* (Paris, 1921), 2, 214; on the subject of humanitarian law, J. Pictet, *Humanitarian Law and the Protection of War Victims* (Leiden, 1975), 28, or M. Torrelli, *Le Droit international humanitaire* (Paris, 1985), 12.

[3] See, for example, Arts. 23(g) of 1907 Hague Regulations, 27 and 64 of 1949 IV Geneva Convention, 35 and 48 of 1977 Additional Protocol I, etc.

[4] See above all K. Obradovic, 'La Protection de la population civile dans les conflits armés internationaux' in A. Cassese (ed.), *The New Humanitarian Law of Armed Conflict* (Naples, 1980), 135–6.

[5] On the distinction between the different forms of occupation, see A. Roberts, 'What is Military Occupation?', BYIL 55 (1984), 249–305.

emergence given a decisive forward impulse by the principles of the French Revolution—the contours of occupation begin to appear, distinct from those of invasion and annexation. Conscious of having its word to say in the determination of its destiny, the population of the conquered state ceases passively to accept a change of master according to the dictates of arms. The concept of occupation is the logical and necessary consequence of this emergence.[6] But, as shown by a study of events, occupation, far from being an end to war, is a continuation of it in another form: the conqueror finds himself in enemy territory and, precisely because the population of this territory is hostile to him, he is obliged to devote *military* means, often considerable, to retaining his ground.

For the rest, the codification of the law of occupation cannot be dissociated from that of the law of war as a whole and, materially speaking, the important texts governing the law of war include the rules applicable to occupation. The rules are contained principally in Section III of the Regulations appended to the Hague Conventions II and IV of 1899 and 1907, relating to laws and practices of war on land, in Section III of Part III of the Fourth Geneva Convention of 1949, relating to the protection of civilians in times of war, and in Section III of Part IV of Protocol I of 1977 relating to the protection of victims of armed international conflicts.

The natural thought-process of the jurist, then, is to try to relate the criteria of the rights of the occupier (and those of the 'occupied'— the one being the counterpart of the other) to the main guiding principles of the law of war: the principle of necessity and the principle of humanity. But could these two principles be considered as 'criteria' of belligerent occupation?

Legal vocabulary converges with everyday language: a criterion is an instrument of discrimination, an element used, in a given circumstance, to determine what enters into and what forms no part of a certain category; and, since in the first instance the practice of law consists in distinguishing that which is lawful from that which is not, the juridical function of a criterion will be to exercise this process of distinction in each actual case.

If one accepts these premises, it becomes apparent that in themselves the principles of necessity and humanity cannot constitute the 'criteria' of the rights of the occupier, even though they pervade the law of war as a whole and the law of occupation in particular. It is precisely because they form the very substance of the applicable rules that they can offer no help as criteria.

---

[6] Cf. L. Oppenheim, *International Law: A Treatise*, 6th edn. by H. Lauterpacht (London, 1944), 337–8; C. Rousseau, *Le Droit des conflits armés* (Paris, 1983), 135; or G. von Glahn, *The Occupation of Enemy Territory* (Minneapolis, 1957), 7.

The question can be formulated thus: How, in the face of an act or specific behaviour of the occupier, can one determine if this action or behaviour is lawful? It is, obviously, impossible to resolve the problem by reference to the principles of humanity and necessity precisely because, in any given circumstance, the issue is to know whether one or the other should take priority; or, perhaps, more exactly, to establish whether a certain rule should, in the context to which it will be applied, be interpreted in its 'humanitarian' or in its 'realistic' variant since, generally speaking, the two approaches are justified by the wording of the rule.

Let us take the example, to which we will return later (see II: 'Humanity and Necessity' below) of Article 43 of the Regulations of 1907. Its provisions, of fundamental importance, are worded thus:

The authority of the legitimate power having in fact passed into the hands of the occupant, the latter shall take all the measures in his power to restore, and ensure, as far as possible, public order and safety, while respecting, unless absolutely prevented, the laws in force in the country.

This text confirms, in the clearest terms, that the principles of humanity and necessity are weighed in the balance at the heart of virtually each rule of the law of occupation. However, when one asks oneself, for example, whether Israel is complying with these requirements in ordering the banishment from the Occupied Territories of Palestinian 'agitators', the answer will probably be affirmative if one refers to the principle of necessity, and negative if one appeals to the principle of humanity. In reality, one will have answered the question with another question without making any progress towards a solution. In itself, the wording of the rule justifies the two answers, and it is clear that a *criterion* of application must be sought elsewhere.

Probably having in mind the rules applicable to the law of armed reprisals,[7] certain writers have sought to find the criterion of the rights of the occupier in the principle of proportionality. Thus, for example, M. Pictet considers that 'The principle of humanitarian law... is a relationship of proportionality'.[8] For their part, Professors M. S. McDougal and F. P. Feliciano take the view that 'the principles of military necessity and of humanity may be synthesized and generalized on a concept of a minimum unnecessary destruction'[9] and assert

---

[7] See award of 31 July 1928, *Réclamations portugaises contre l'Allemagne* (Naulilaa incident), RIAA II (1949), 1025; on the law of armed reprisals see F. Kalshoven, *Belligerent Reprisals* (Leiden, 1971); or D. W. Bowett, 'Reprisals Involving Recourse to Armed Force', *AJIL* 66(1) (1972), 581–96.

[8] Pictet, *Humanitarian Law and the Protection of War Victims*, 31.

[9] M. S. McDougal and F. P. Feliciano, *Law and Minimum World Public Order: The Legal Regulation of International Coercion* (New Haven, 1961), 530.

that it is possible to rely on two concepts in applying this important principle: relevancy and proportionality.[10]

It would surely be excessively legalistic to deny the pertinence of the concept of proportionality in the application of the rules of the law of war and, more specifically, of those relating to occupation. There is a fundamental rule of moderation to be found in all contemporary legal systems when it comes to inflicting unpleasantness (sanctions, punishment, counter-measures) on any legal subject.[11] However, in the first analysis, the very omnipresence of a principle leads to doubt as to whether it is truly of use in the determination of the rights of the occupier. Furthermore, and above all, proportionality seems more a general directive than a criterion in the proper sense of the word; its appraisal rests on the subjective judgement of those involved and, for this reason, it is ill-suited to serve as a means of distinguishing that which is lawful from that which is not, a process which is the *raison d'être* of a criterion.[12]

In fact it is probably to the intrinsic character of *the legal institution* of belligerent occupation that one can best turn. It seems legitimate to take as one's starting point the definition of occupation, as this appears to be the subject of general agreement among writers; they are able indeed to base themselves on a rule well-established in law: occupation is a practical power which confers territorial jurisdiction on the occupier but does not transfer sovereignty. Consequently, respect for the sovereign rights of the occupied people constitutes the criterion of the law of occupation and, at the same time, of the rights of the occupier, since this essential consideration determines the field of application of the guiding principles of humanity and necessity.

I. Respect for the Sovereign Rights of the Occupied People Constitutes the Criterion of the Rights of the Occupant

The dialogue of the occupying power and the occupied territory is not that of Creon and Antigone; it is that of two people at war, enemies, equal sovereigns; that of Ulysses and Hector,[13] but in a devastated Troy.

The great difference between the wars of the past and those of the

---

[10] Ibid. particularly at 524.
[11] See E. Zoller, *Peacetime Unilateral Remedies: An Analysis of Countermeasures* (New York, 1984), 131–7, and *Enforcing International Law through US Legislation* (New York, 1985), 147–54.
[12] In this sense, see R. R. Baxter, 'Criteria of Prohibition on Weapons in International Law', in *Festschrift für Ulrich Scheuner Zum zu Gebürstag* (Berlin, 1973), 46; or A. Cassese, 'A Tentative Appraisal of the Old and the New Humanitarian Law of Armed Conflict' in Cassese (ed.), *The New Humanitarian Law of Armed Conflict*, 478.
[13] Cf. J. Giraudoux, *La Guerre de Troie n'aura pas lieu*, Act 2, Scene 13.

twentieth century is, in effect, that the former were combats between leaders, not peoples. The populations were victims twice over: cannon fodder, men waged war; and their fate was determined by arms. In this sense wars were more 'total' than those of today. While the twentieth century has indeed witnessed a terrifying development of means of destruction, it has also enshrined the juridical existence and, in a certain sense, the 'eminent dignity' of peoples. Conquered, they do not cease to exist; occupied, they retain their rights.

Occupied people continue in fact to have an existence of their own, in the absence of which the legal institution of belligerent occupation would cease to have any degree of autonomy: it becomes indeed inconceivable if the occupier gains sovereignty of the occupied territory. This definition holds true in all circumstances and allows one to distinguish the criterion of the rights of the occupier, which find their absolute limits in the respect of the sovereign rights of the people whose territory is occupied. The definition thus applies in the context of the Israeli occupations, in particular in that of the West Bank, despite the special situation of the Palestinian people.

Occupation, Annexation, and Sovereignty

1. *Occupation does not transfer sovereignty* The law of occupation is the object of much doctrinal controversy. Its application by national and, to a lesser extent, international jurisdictions has given rise to contrasting and heterogeneous case law, the solutions reached by certain judges often being totally irreconcilable with those adopted by others.[14] None the less, apart from these divergences, there is one point on which writers and judges agree: occupation does not transfer sovereignty. As a consequence of occupation, power changes hands, not sovereignty.

Implicitly established by the Permanent Court of International Justice in the *Franco-Hellenic lighthouse case*,[15] the principle according to which the occupier does not acquire sovereignty in occupied territory has been spelt out most clearly by Eugène Borel in 1925 in the affair of the *Ottoman Debt Arbitration*:

Quels que soient les effets de l'occupation d'un territoire par l'adversaire avant le rétablissement de la paix, il est certain qu'à elle seule cette occupation ne pouvait opérer juridiquement le transfert de souveraineté.[16]

---

[14] For methodical analyses of law, see G. Schwarzenberger, *International Law as Applied by International Courts and Tribunals*, 2: *The Law of Armed Conflicts* (London, 1968), 163–358; and J. H. W. Verzijl, *International Law in Historical Perspective*, IX-A: *The Laws of War* (Alhen, 1978), 167–290.

[15] PCIJ judgment, 17 Mar. 1934, ser. A/B, no. 62, especially at 19 and 25.

[16] *RIAA* I (1948), 555. For internal law, see decisions cited by Verzijl, *International Law in Historical Perspective*, 171 and 209–27; Cass. Crim., 20 Dec. 1919, *Naoum et al.*, GP 1920 1 62

The international military tribunal of Nuremberg was founded on the same idea (see below), which doctrine has echoed.

While it would be neither possible nor useful to make an exhaustive catalogue of all opinions on this issue, it is none the less interesting to observe that all specialists start from the same observation: occupation constitutes a temporary situation neither operating nor implying any devolution of sovereignty.[17]

It is not irrelevant to observe that the best Israeli authors share this point of view. In particular, Yoram Dinstein considers that:

The most basic tenet of the law of belligerent occupation is that occupation as such does not transfer title to the territory.[18]

De jure sovereignty remains vested in the occupied State, though *de facto* authority passes into the hands of the occupant.[19]

These views are confirmed by the standard definitions of occupation. Articles 42 and 43 of the Hague Regulations above all emphasize the *facts* that constitute occupation:

Territory is considered occupied when it is *actually placed* under the authority of the hostile army.

The occupation extends *only* to the territory where such authority *has been established* and *can be exercised*. (Article 42)

The authority of the legitimate power *having in fact* passed into the hands of the occupant ... (Article 43)[20]

---

[17] We have, for example, the clear statements of Oppenheim: 'There is not an atom of sovereignty in the authority of the occupant', in 'The Legal Relations between an Occupying Power and the Inhabitants', *Law Quarterly Review* (1917), 364; and in *International Law*, 6th edn., 338 ff.; of McDougal and Feliciano in *Law and Minimum World Public Order*, see particularly at 752; and of Schwarzenberger: 'In the abstract, the territorial sovereignty remains entitled to dispose of the occupied territory', in *International Law*, 179; see also A. Gerson, 'War, Conquered Territory, and Military Occupation in the Contemporary International Legal System', *HILJ* 18(3) (1977), 535; and C. Rousseau: 'On peut ramener l'effet juridique essentiel de l'occupation de guerre (ou *occupatio bellica*) aux deux idées suivantes: 1) cette occupation n'est pas translative de souveraineté; 2) mais elle entraîne une répartition particulière des compétences dans les rapports de l'État occupant et de l'État occupé', in *Le Droit des conflits armés*, 136; and Nguyen Quoc Dinh, P. Daillier, and A. Pellet, *Droit international public* (Paris, 1987), 435 and 842. The same idea is also found in the monographs that Professor Gerhard von Glahn and Mme Odile Debbasch have devoted to belligerent occupation. For the former: 'It appears established that the rights and the sovereignty of the legitimate government remain in existence in the case of enemy occupation; they are only suspended when they come into collision with the stronger power of the occupant during the period of actual occupation' (*Occupation*, 33). Mme Debbasch, echoing this theme in *L'Occupation militaire—Pouvoirs reconnus aux forces armées hors de leur territoire national* (Paris, 1962), 10, bases her entire thesis on the following premise: 'Porté à étendre ses compétences, l'occupant se voit imposer par le droit international une limite essentielle qu'il ne pourra jamais franchir. Il pourra participer au pouvoir souverain. Il ne pourra jamais l'acquérir.'

[18] Y. Dinstein, 'The International Law of Belligerent Occupation and Human Rights', *IYHR* 8 (1978), 105.

[19] Ibid. 106.

[20] Italics added.

None the less, it is clear, on the one hand, that this situation is temporary and, on the other, that for so long as it continues, the occupied State does not cease to exist in law. Articles 2, 6, and 47 of the Fourth Geneva Convention tend, albeit indirectly, in the same direction; and, in laying down that 'Neither the occupation of a territory nor the application of the Convention and this Protocol shall affect the legal status *of the territory in question*',[21] Article 4 of Protocol I of 1977 shows, with absolute clarity, that occupation involves no transfer of sovereignty.

Thus, the principle according to which the sovereignty of the occupied territory rests in the hands of the conquered is not a simple consequence of occupation, but constitutes an essential element of its definition: occupation appears as an actual situation, a temporary one, which justifies the exercise by the occupier of territorial control extending over the occupied territory, but which involves no transfer of sovereignty in its favour. These two elements, the one positive—an actual situation justifying the exercise of territorial control, the other negative—the non-transfer of sovereignty, are inseparable and both are necessary conditions for occupation to exist. In the absence of effective control of the territory by an enemy army, the legal regime does not apply, any more than if sovereignty changes hands and passes from occupied to occupier. This is the very essence of the legal institution constituting occupation.

2. *Occupation Excludes Annexation* It is therefore immediately apparent that occupation is incompatible with annexation in the sense that the two legal regimes cannot coexist and are mutually exclusive: if the conqueror annexes the occupied territory, this signifies that he intends to subject it to his sovereignty and so put an end to the occupation. Israel made no mistake in this: at the same time as she moved to 'annex' East Jerusalem, on 27 June 1967, and the Golan Heights, on 14 December 1981, she also put an end to the regime of occupation.

This incompatibility is an objective fact, a simple matter of common sense, following from the legal definition of the two concepts. The situation envisaged here has no connection with a condominium; in the case of the latter institution, the two states concerned—not having established a joint exercise of sovereignty—agree to exercise territorial jurisdiction together;[22] in the case of occupation/annexation, on the contrary, the states involved each claim total sovereignty. There is no place for the simultaneous exercise of two competing sovereignties over the same territory. Either sovereignty belongs to the conquered

---

[21] Italics added.
[22] See Nguyen Quoc, Daillier, and Pellet, *Droit international public*, 437–8; or Charles Rousseau, *Droit international public*, III: *Les compétences* (Paris 1977), 22–30.

state and one has a situation of occupation, or it rests with the conqueror, and one has annexation. It is, then, the concept of sovereignty itself which imposes the alternatives: neither plenitude nor exclusivity, which are the marks of territorial sovereignty, can be conceived of as shared.

It is, moreover, significant that the incompatibility of annexation with belligerent occupation has been recognized ever since the latter emerged as an autonomous legal institution[23] and that a new juridical rule—not the unavoidable logical consequence, but an extension—rapidly came into being: the prohibition of annexation for so long as the war has not come to a formal end. Professor Georg Schwarzenberger thus describes the development of this norm:

> Since the nineteenth century, a growing determination is noticeable in State practice, strongly supported by an increasing number of writers on international law, to treat wartime annexation as premature and, therefore, not to recognise it unless completed by cession in one form or another. This has been the decisive factor in shaping the law on wartime annexation. It has produced a rule of international customary law which prohibits the unilateral annexation of territories under belligerent occupation. Purported annexation constitutes, therefore, an illegal act of an Occupying Power in relation to the enemy State concerned. The same would be true of the recognition of such an annexation by a third State.[24]

It is worth observing at this stage that the reasoning is wholly independent of the lawfulness of recourse to force: whether or not it complies with international law, victory can lead to occupation, but is not enough to permit annexation. This was very clearly recalled by the International Military Tribunal at Nuremberg:

> A further submission was made that Germany was no longer bound by the rules of land warfare in many of the territories occupied during the war, because Germany had completely subjugated those countries and incorporated them into the German Reich, a fact which gave Germany authority to deal with the occupied countries as though they were part of Germany. In the view of the Tribunal, it is unnecessary in this case to decide whether this doctrine of subjugation, dependent as it is upon military conquest, has any application where the subjugation is the result of the crime of aggressive war. The doctrine was never considered to be applicable so long as there was an army in the field attempting to restore the occupied countries to their true owners, and in this case, therefore, the doctrine could not apply to any territories occupied after the 1st September 1939.[25]

---

[23] Cf. Cass. Req., 1 Feb. 1837, *Magill*, S.1837.1.457, and various examples cited by Rousseau, *Le Droit des conflits armés*, 136–8.
[24] Schwarzenberger, *International Law*, 166–7.
[25] Int. Mil. Trib. of Nuremberg, Judgment of 1 Oct. 1946, *ADPIL* (1946), 220; italics added.

In other words, independent of all considerations linked to *jus ad bellum*, the distinction between annexation and occupation is grounded in logical necessity, which derives from the very definition of the two concepts, and the prohibition of annexation of occupied territory in time of war arises from the traditional *jus in bello*.

It does not follow, however, that today the prohibition of recourse to force in international relations has no relevance in these circumstances. It is certainly impossible to draw the conclusion derived by certain Palestinian writers from the prohibition of war of aggression, according to which Israel would be deprived of the recognized rights of an occupying power.[26] Apart from the question of whether it is possible to define Israel as aggressor, one would be thrown back on the very *raison d'être* of the law of war (*jus in bello*), which is precisely to limit the horrors of armed conflict independently of the origin of the conflict and the validity of the claims made by the belligerents.[27] Furthermore, this would not be compatible either with the jurisprudence following World War II, which condemned the war of aggression waged by the Axis Powers, while at the same time considering that they were bound by the law applicable to occupation, nor with the fundamental principle according to which *jus in bello* should be brought into operation in all circumstances (see II: 'The Powers of the Occupier' below).

Less radically, some writers seem to consider that the ends pursued by the parties should be the yardstick used to measure their rights. This view is very evident in the work of Professors McDougal and Feliciano:

In the principle of minimum order, newly resurrected in the Charter of the United Nations and other authoritative formulations distinguishing between permissible and impermissible resort to coercion, may, it is believed, be found new limits to give new specificity to the principle of military necessity.[28]

In other words, the legitimacy of the objectives pursued by the occupier is to be the criterion, or, at least, one of the criteria, of his rights. This theory is open to numerous objections and is hardly distinguishable from the extreme 'Palestinian' thesis. For one, the two parties run into a considerable practical difficulty: each proclaims the legitimacy of its cause loud and clear and experience shows that it is virtually

---

[26] See for example M. Yahia, *The Palestine Question and International Law* (Beirut: PLO Research Centre, 1970), 184.
[27] See also Ch. 1 above, text at nn. 68–71.
[28] McDougal and Feliciano, *Law and Minimum World Public Order*, 527. See also certain affirmations of von Glahn, *Occupation*, 6, and, with more subtlety, 23—but this writer draws little in the way of practical inference from his presuppositions.

impossible to decide between them in law, the procedures laid down by the Charter of the United Nations being almost inevitably blocked before a resolution can be reached. For another, the encroachment of *jus in bello* by *jus ad bellum* is not compatible with the principle of equality of the parties, an equality that can hardly be assured except by the 'neutrality' of the first in relation to the second. The two writers acknowledge this, after a fashion, when asserting with conviction that the parties to the conflict are *equally* bound by the principles of necessity and humanity; furthermore, they are wary of drawing any specific inferences from their initial assumption,[29] to which, moreover, they do not return in relation to occupation itself.[30] If there is a criterion here, it is scarcely practicable.

Furthermore, it is not at this level that the principle of prohibition of recourse to force makes itself felt, but, rather, in reinforcing the traditional rule. Thus we find that, as long as the law of war (*jus in bello*) is applicable, annexation is impossible. Furthermore, because of the prohibition in Article 2, paragraph 4 of the Charter, annexation can never, under any circumstances (see II: 'The Powers of the Occupier' below), be a means of putting an end to occupation. One can moreover reflect that, far from favouring one or other of the parties, the rule can be objected to as much by one as by the other: annexation as the outcome of a war of legitimate defence is no more admissible than if it follows a war of aggression, at all events when effected by a unilateral decision of the conquering State. At the very most, one could allow that, within the scope of the powers it derives from Article 51 of the Charter, the Security Council could decide that a partial transfer of territory is required as a 'measure necessary to maintain international peace and security', but, for the rest, contemporary international law is that of territorial *status quo*, in which connection Article 2, paragraph 4, lays a firm embargo on recourse to force.

The exclusion of all annexation following recourse to force constitutes, today, a principle too well established to require further emphasis. It suffices to mention that, in terms of the Declaration of 24 October 1970 relating to the Principles of International Law concerning Friendly Relations between States, 'No territorial acquisition resulting from the threat or use of force shall be recognised as legal,'[31] and that this principle was strongly recalled in the precise context of

---

[29] McDougal and Feliciano, *Law and Minimum World Public Order*, 528 ff.
[30] Ibid. 740 ff.
[31] Res. 2625 (XXV). This fundamental text makes no distinction between the different hypotheses concerning use of force. It thus confirms that Art. 5, para. 3 of Res. 3314 (XXIX) relating to the definition of aggression, according to which 'no territorial acquisition . . . resulting from aggression . . .' is lawful, should not be interpreted *a contrario*— see in this context the note attached to this disposition.

the Israeli–Palestinian conflict and, moreover, by the well-known Resolution 242 of the Security Council on 22 November 1967.

Thus the prohibition of annexation rests today both on grounds derived from the law of war *stricto sensu* (*jus in bello*), and on a factor which is outside it: the prohibition of recourse to force, which is part of *jus ad bellum*. The fundamental principle according to which sovereignty is not transferred on the sole basis of occupation is even more clearly reinforced by the fact that the prohibition of recourse to force derives without any doubt from *jus cogens*, that is to say from an imperative norm accepted as such by the international community of States in its entirety.

'Annexation' is 'transparent'[32] if one adheres to *jus in bello*; it is a non-existent act if one relates it to *jus ad bellum*. In all cases, it can have no bearing on the rights of the occupier, who does not acquire, as a result of his act, any supplementary power. In terms of international law, the sovereignty which the conqueror claims to appropriate does not change hands.

Occupation and the Right of Peoples to Self-Determination

1. The Legal Existence of the Palestinian People It is true that the Palestinian question is also a question of sovereignty. To retain the West Bank, Israel plays on the doubts arising in the wake of a particularly complex history in relation to the devolution of sovereignty on this territory in order to deny the existence of the sovereign rights of the Palestinian people and to seek to evade the obligations that international law imposes on the occupying power (see II: 'The Powers of the Occupier' below).

The history of the problem is well known: an Ottoman possession, Palestine was placed under British mandate by the League of Nations in 1920. A supplementary clause added to the mandate in 1922 having authorized the United Kingdom to administer Transjordan separately, the latter acceded to independence in March 1946. The plan for the partition of Palestine itself, adopted by the General Assembly on 29 November 1947 (Resolution 181 (II)), was never put into effect, Israel instead appropriating the territories which it had not been granted, while the 'independent Arab State' never saw the light of day. Putting an end to the hopes of the Arab High Commission of Palestine and the Grand Mufti El Husseini, King Abdallah of Transjordan annexed the West Bank in January 1949, followed on 24 April 1950 by the passing

---

[32] V. Coussirat-Coustère, 'Israël et le Golan—Problèmes juridiques résultant de la loi du 14 décembre 1981', *AFDI* (1981), 197.

of the Unification Act of the 'Hashemite Kingdom of Jordan' by the Jordanian Parliament.[33] The situation thus effectively created has, however, never been accepted either by Israel or by the other Arab States. The problem of the future of the West Bank has been periodically raised as a result with the League of Arab States which has constantly endeavoured to avoid prejudging the future legal status of the Palestinian people.[34] Moreover, despite the Unification Act of 1950, Jordan itself has never completely denied Palestinian identity and, specifically, Jordanian legislation has never been comprehensively introduced in the West Bank. In compliance with the law of 16 September 1950:

> Even though the two Banks of the Hashemite Kingdom of Jordan were united, the laws and regulations that are in force in each of them shall remain in effect until new unified and universal laws for both Banks are issued...[35]

Whatever happens, two new elements have fundamentally altered the nature of the problem: first, the acceptance of the formation of the Palestine Liberation Organization by the Palestinian National Congress on 28 May 1964; next, the recognition of the PLO as 'sole and legitimate representative' of the Palestinian people by the eighth Arab Summit at Rabat in October 1974, with the agreement of Jordan.

It is true that, in its initial drafting, the Palestinian National Charter specified that the PLO 'shall not exercise any territorial sovereignty over the West Bank (Region), in the Hashemite Kingdom of Jordan, the Gaza Strip, or the Himmah area'.[36] However, on the one hand, the amendments made to the Palestinian Charter in July 1968[37] very clearly assert the sovereign rights of the Palestinian people; on the other, the question of the sovereignty of the PLO is one thing, that of the Palestinian people another.

It is from this point of view that the Israeli thesis denying the sovereign rights of the Palestinian people is untenable: whatever may have been the vicissitudes of history, this people exists. Moreover, it is contradictory to deny the rights of Jordan on the West Bank of the Jordan River (see II: 'The Powers of the Occupier' below) and, at the same time, not to recognize the existence of the Palestinian entity. Taking into account the points briefly stated above, the first proposition seems justified: Jordan seems, at best, the administrative power

---

[33] See L. Gaspar, *Histoire de la Palestine* (Paris, 1968), 149, or A. F. Kassim, 'Legal Systems and Developments in Palestine', *PYIL* 1 (1984), 19–35.

[34] See particularly J.-P. Colin and G. Petit, 'L'Organisation de Libération de la Palestine', Annuaire du Tiers Monde (1975), 115 ff.

[35] Cited by Kassim, 'Legal Systems and Developments in Palestine', 28.

[36] Art. 24. Reproduced in J. N. Moore (ed.), *The Arab–Israeli Conflict*, III: *Documents* (Princeton, 1974) 699, 704.

[37] Ibid. 706. Palestine National Council, Cairo, 10–17 July 1968.

of the territory it has 'represented' between 1950 and 1974. On the other hand, the legal identity of the Palestinian people in relation to international law cannot be denied.

If one feels a certain reluctance to infer the legal existence of a people from its martyrology, it remains no less true that the Palestinian people has, by the steadfastness of its struggle, borne ample witness to its reality.[38] After all, a more formal analysis does not lead to a different conclusion.

Recognized by the League of Nations, as evidenced by its mandate, the legal existence of the Palestinian people—distinct from that of Transjordan since 1922—has been confirmed in unambiguous terms by the General Assembly in the partition plan of 1947. And it did not require the closure of the Jordanian parenthesis in 1974 for the United Nations to take cognizance of this existence.

After the Six Day War of 1967, the first resolutions adopted by organs of the UN undoubtedly demonstrated an ambiguity in requiring, as does Resolution 242 of the Security Council, 'a just settlement of the refugee problem'.[39] But, very rapidly, the General Assembly restored the question to its proper context. From 1969, indeed, the Assembly '[r]e*affirms* the inalienable rights of the people of Palestine',[40] and, two years later, '[r]e*cognises* that the people of Palestine are entitled to equal rights and self-determination, in accordance with the Charter of the United Nations'.[41]

This is henceforth to be its constant standpoint.[42] The recognition of the PLO as 'representative of the Palestinian people'[43] completes this legal picture but, without underestimating its extreme political importance, does not add a great deal to the legal existence of the Palestinian *people* itself; for the latter, this last step is the difference between recognition of a government and recognition of a State.

2. *The Sovereign Rights of the Palestinian People* Since it exists legally, the Palestinian people can lay claim to equality of rights with other

---

[38] Cf. C. Chaumont, 'Le droit des peuples à témoigner d'eux-mêmes', *Annuaire du Tiers Monde* (1976), 15–31.

[39] Italics added. On the recognition of the Palestinian people as a legal entity, see particularly Colin and Petit, *L'OLP*, 112–13 and 130–4; A. F. Kassim, 'The PLO's Claim to Status—A Juridical Analysis under International Law', *Denver Yb. of Int. Law & Pol.* 9 (1980), 1 ff.; or S. V. Mallison and W. T. Mallison Jr, 'The Juridical Bases for Palestinian Self-Determination', *PYIL* 1 (1984), 36–67.

[40] Res. 2535 B (XXIX), 10 Dec. 1969.

[41] Res. 2672 C (XXV), 8 Dec. 1970.

[42] See particularly Res. 2792 D (XXVI), 6 Dec. 1971; 2763 E (XXVII), 13 Dec. 1972; 3089 D (XXVIII), 7 Dec. 1973; 3236 (XXIX), 22 Nov. 1974; 35/69 A, 15 Dec. 1980; ES-7/6, 19 Aug. 1982; etc.

[43] Res. 3210 (XXIX), 14 Oct. 1974. See also e.g. Res. 32/20, 25 Nov. 1977; Es-7/12, 19 Aug. 1982; etc.

people and to its right to self-determination in accordance with Articles 1, 2, and 55 of the Charter of the United Nations.

While it is not necessary, or possible, to summarize all the consequences of these principles,[44] it is appropriate none the less to make three series of comments.

(i) Although all peoples have rights, it is none the less true that as a general rule these rights are exercised by States. Only peoples deprived by force of the ability to exercise their right of self-determination are brought to recognize the possibility of direct or immediate action. Such is the case of colonial peoples, for whom Resolution 1514 (XV) of 14 December 1960 was drafted, and in whose favour a very full and operational legal statute has been drawn up, principally within the United Nations. Very quickly this statute was extended to two other categories of peoples subjected to other forms of foreign domination: those who are victims of a regime of racial discrimination—this envisages the peoples of South Africa—and those whose territory is occupied—which concerns the Palestinian people.

Anticipated by the very general formulation of the Declaration of 1960—which refers to peoples undergoing 'subjugation, domination and foreign exploitation'—the assimilation of occupied peoples to colonial peoples appears very clearly in numerous subsequent resolutions which, moreover, aim to provide in one sole formula for 'peoples subject to colonial and foreign domination', which shows it to be a matter of ideas that are distinct in their origins but have a common purpose in their legal consequences. Thus, for example, in Resolution 2649 (XXV) of 30 November 1970, the General Assembly

> affirms the legitimacy of the struggle of peoples under colonial and alien domination... and condemns those Governments that deny the right to self-determination... of the peoples of Southern Africa and Palestine.

In consequence, there is no doubt that the Palestinian people can claim the benefits of a very comprehensive legal regime applicable to colonial peoples and that, in compliance with the formulations

---

[44] Among the very prolific literature devoted to the right of peoples to self-determination are: V. A. Rigo-Sureda, *The Evolution of the Right of Self-Determination* (Leiden, 1973), 398; J.-F. Guilhaudis, *Le Droit des peuples à disposer d'eux-mêmes* (Grenoble, 1976), 226; 3ème Rencontre de Reims, 'La notion de peuple en droit international' in *Realités du droit international contemporain* (Reims, 1976), 117–278; A. Cristescu and H. Gros Espiell, *Le Droit à l'autodétermination*, UN (1979) E/CN.4/Sub.2/Rev.1 and 405/Rev. 1; M. Pomerance, *Self-Determination in Law and Practice: The New Doctrine in the United Nations* (The Hague, 1982), 154; A. Pellet, 'Qui a peur du droit des peuples à disposer d'eux-mêmes?', *Critique socialiste* (1984), 89–103; A. Cassese, 'Commentaire de l'article 1, 2', in J. P. Cot and Alain Pellet (eds.), *La Charte des Nations Unies* (Paris, 1985), 39–55; E. Jouve, *Le Droit des peuples* (Paris 1986), 128; and see also Chs. 1 and 3 in this volume, and that of John Dugard proposing an advisory opinion from the ICJ on this issue.

of the Charter, one can use the general designation 'right of self-determination'.

(ii) This right of self-determination constitutes a principle of *jus cogens* which cannot be waived and must be universally respected in all circumstances. It appears moreover in the list of examples of mandatory rules laid down by the International Law Commission in its report of 1966 on the Law of Treaties.[45] Article 19 of the Commission's draft articles on the responsibility of States views 'the serious breach of an international obligation of essential importance for safeguarding the right of self-determination of peoples' as an example of an international crime.[46] Further, the members of the Commission seem to be in agreement as to the inserting of the 'maintenance by force of colonial domination'—this latter expression to be taken in a broad sense—among the crimes against humanity in the projected Code now being prepared.[47]

(iii) The term 'right to self-determination' should not be abused: it is not simply a matter of allowing the peoples in question freely to choose their destiny and, specifically, if they so wish, to constitute a sovereign State, however obviously important this aspect of the law of peoples may be. Two further aspects are of particular importance in determining the rights of the occupier.

The law of peoples signifies in the first place that the collectivity that constitutes a people has a right to preservation of its integrity which means in particular that its territorial integrity be guaranteed, that its demographic composition should not be shattered, that its own character be respected, and that its sovereignty over its wealth be protected in the context of its right to development. Since 1972,[48] the General Assembly has readily expressed this idea and the Security Council took it up in its Resolution 465 of 1 March 1980, determining that:

all measures taken by Israel to change the physical character, demographic composition, institutional structure, or status of the Palestinian and other Arab territories occupied since 1967, including Jerusalem, or any part thereof, have no legal validity.

In the second place, clearly as a result of its inclusion in the first article of each of the two international covenants of 1966, the 'right to self-determination' is also a right of the individual human being[49]

---

[45] *ILC Yb* (1966), II, 270.
[46] See *ILC Yb* (1976), II, pt. 2, 89–113.
[47] See particularly the ILC's *Report* at the 39th session of the UNGA, A/39/10, 27.
[48] Res. 2949 (XXVII), 8 Dec. 1972. See also, for example 3092 B (XXVIII), 7 Dec. 1973; 33/113, 18 Dec. 1978; 37/88 B, 10 Dec. 1982; 41/63 C, 3 Dec. 1986; etc.
[49] On the simultaneously individual and collective character of the right to self-determination, see Gros-Espiell, *Le Droit à l'autodétermination*, 10, and, particularly on the

which relates to the respect of basic human rights. In other words, the right of the Palestinian people to self-determination is also a right for each man and each woman to see his or her membership of this collectivity recognized and to be protected in his or her physical and intellectual integrity and dignity.

One might question the utility of the initiative of the United Nations in assimilating the law of occupied peoples to that of colonial peoples: the rights of the former, first of all to existence, independent of all considerations linked to the right of peoples of self-determination as lately interpreted (see I: 'Occupation, Annexation, and Sovereignty' above), result in fact from the traditional law of war. In a certain sense, occupied peoples can be considered to be the first category of peoples whose personal rights have been recognized in international law.

The assimilation effected by the United Nations is none the less of great practical importance, for two reasons. In the first place, it permits an indispensable process of 'updating' to be carried out. The old legal institution that is belligerent occupation cannot be interpreted today as it was in the nineteenth century; the prohibition of recourse to force, the principle of respect for the territorial integrity of all countries, the emergence of individuals and of peoples in the sphere of international law, require a reinterpretation of the rules. As has been said by the International Court of Justice, the interpretation of the classic principles of international law

cannot remain unaffected by the subsequent development of law, through the Charter of the United Nations and by way of customary law. Moreover, an international instrument has to be interpreted and applied within the framework of the entire legal system prevailing at the time of the interpretation.[50]

It must also be noted in this connection that Protocol I Additional to the Conventions of 1949, adopted on 12 December 1977, formally effects the integration of legal principles which have crystallized since 1949. Moreover, these must need apply to Israel, as to any other State, quite independently of the stance taken on the controversial question of the legal nature of each provision of the Protocol (see II: 'The Powers of the Occupier' below) which, in any case, in the general terms employed, only reinforce their legal weight.

In the second place, the developments in law since 1945, far from jeopardizing the traditional principle by which an occupied people retains the sovereign rights that belong to it, give it a content that is

right to development, see A. Pellet, 'Note sur quelques aspects juridiques de la notion de droit au développement' in M. Flory (ed.), *La Formation des normes en droit international du développement* (Paris, 1984), 78–80.

[50] ICJ Advisory Opinion, 21 June 1971, *Legal Consequences for States of the Continued Presence of South Africa in Namibia, ICJ Reports* (1971), 31.

infinitely clearer and more precise. In the classic law of war, the non-acquisition of sovereignty by the occupier constitutes the criterion of occupation, but the very general character of this directive does not provide a very workable guide to determining the respective rights of the occupier or the occupied. However, thanks to the 'subsequent development of law through the Charter of the United Nations and by way of customary law',[51] the respect of the sovereign rights of the occupied people has become the effective criterion not only of occupation itself, but also of the rights of the occupier.

II. The Respect for the Sovereign Rights of the Occupied People Constitutes the Criterion of the Rights of the Occupant

The United Nations are undoubtedly right to affirm that the fundamental consequences of the Palestinian people's right to self-determination are

(a) the right to self-determination without external interference, and to national independence and sovereignty;

(b) the right to establish its own independent sovereign State.[52]

But it does not follow that, for so long as the exercise of these rights is refused, the occupation to which the people are subject is beyond the reach of the law. Even if the deprivation of its right to self-determination infringes an imperative norm of international law, occupation remains a legal institution, governed by the rules of law, the respect for which imposes itself on all and in all circumstances, failing which *jus in bello* would cease to exist (see I: 'Occupation, Annexation, and Sovereignty' above); and, to the international crime of maintenance by force of foreign domination would be added another crime involving a grave violation of the laws and customs of war.

In this respect, the situation is on every score comparable to colonialism: the maintenance by force of colonial domination is contrary to a principle of *jus cogens*, but contemporary international law none the less accepts that the administering power can exercise territorial jurisdiction over the colonial territory, although not endowed with any degree of sovereignty since 'The territory of a colony or other non-self-governing territory has, under the Charter, a status separate and distinct from the territory of the State administering it.'[53] However, the exercise of

---

[51] Ibid.
[52] Res. ES-7/2, 19 Aug. 1982; see also, for example, Res. 35/169, 15 Dec. 1980, and others cited in n. 42 above.
[53] Res. 2625 (XXV), 24 Oct. 1970.

its powers is doubly limited: firstly, the administering power must respect the general directives given in Chapter XI of the Charter, as subsequently developed and codified by the United Nations; secondly, it must submit to outside control, principally by the various bodies of the UN.

The same applies in the case of belligerent occupation. Notwithstanding the incompatibility of occupation with the principles of peoples' right to self-determination and prohibition of recourse to force in international relations, the occupying power does have rights; but their exercise is circumscribed and controlled by the rules of international law, which operate a balance between the demands of humanity and the necessities of war, the principle of respect for the sovereign right of the occupied people constituting the criterion of the rights of the parties in both respects.

The Powers of the Occupier are Limited by International Law

Occupation is most certainly a fact. But it is a juridical fact (see I: 'Occupation, Annexation, and Sovereignty' above), that is to say an objective situation giving rise *ipso facto*, by sole reason of its existence, to certain legal consequences. These consequences are determined by traditional *jus in bello*, to be applied and interpreted in the light of the traditional rules developed by modern international law.

It would not be necessary to linger on this point—which lies 'upstream' of the question of the criterion of the rights of the occupier—if Israel did not entertain a very great uncertainty as to its position in this respect. Undoubtedly, the occupying power seems to adopt 'the position that its activities in the West Bank are governed by international law, and are consistent with it.'[54] But it seems to have doubts as to the standing of the rules applicable to the case in point.

These doubts apparently derive from three series of considerations:

1. The Palestinian people not constituting a State, the interstate rules governing belligerent occupation are not transposable to the case in point;
2. Hostilities having ceased, there is no occasion to apply principles drawn up for times of war;
3. The occupation of the West Bank having lasted now for over twenty years, the powers of the occupier are not to be limited by the norms established with a provisional and temporary situation in mind.

If these objections were justified, the very standing of the applicable law, in its entirety, would be thrown into jeopardy and the criterion

---

[54] R. Shehadeh, *Occupier's Law: Israel and the West Bank* (Washington, DC, 1985), 3.

of the rights of the occupier would apply in a context *sui generis* by which the equilibrium between the rights of the occupied people and those of the occupier would be profoundly modified. It is necessary therefore to investigate the merits of the case.

It is fair to remark that in none of these three points is the Israeli position wholly unambiguous; rather, it varies according to circumstances and the vagaries of internal political and international relations. Thus, touching on the applicability of the principle of the international instruments regulating *jus in bello*, the attitude of the occupying power has fluctuated considerably over the years and the jurisprudence of the Israeli tribunals is far from being 'all of a piece'.[55]

It is particularly interesting to remark in this respect that Proclamation No. 3, issued by the occupation authorities on 7 June 1967, anticipated the pre-eminence of the provisions of the Fourth Geneva Convention over the rules imposed by the occupier:

The Military Court ... must apply the provisions of the Geneva Convention dated 12 August 1949, Relative to the Protection of Civilians in Time of War, with respect to judicial procedures. In case of conflict between this Order and the said Convention, the Convention shall prevail.[56]

Even though this disposition was revoked by Military Order 144 on the following 22 October, it can be asked whether there is not here a unilateral declaration giving birth to rights on the part of the Palestinian people which Israel cannot revoke at will (*estoppel by conduct*).[57]

Be that as it may, doubt is almost unanimously cast—even by some of the firmest supporters of Israeli politics, though with, it is true, a few nuances of opinion—on the merits of the theses of the occupying power relating to the inapplicability of the rules of the law of occupation.[58] It suffices therefore to list only briefly the principal elements that lead one to cast aside the views of the Israeli authorities. Summary as this examination may be, it is necessary nonetheless to identify the different instruments which, from 1907 to 1977, have presided over the codification of the law of belligerent occupation.

---

[55] See particularly T. Meron, 'West Bank and Gaza—Human Rights and Humanitarian Law in the Period of Transition', *IYHR* 9 (1979), 107 ff.

[56] For full text of this article see Ch. 2, text at n. 126. The wording of Proc. No. 1 follows closely the terms of Art. 43 of the 1907 Convention.

[57] Cf. ICJ Judgment, 20 Dec. 1974, *Nuclear Tests Case, ICJ Reports* (1974), 270.

[58] Cf. T. S. Kuttner, 'Israel and the West Bank—Aspects of the Law of Belligerant Occupation', *IYHR* 7 (1977), 169 ff.; B. M. Clagett and O. T. Johnson Jr., 'May Israel as a Belligerent Occupant Lawfully Exploit Previously Unexploited Oil Resources of the Gulf of Suez?', *AJIL* 72(3) (1978), 560; Dinstein, 'The International Law of Belligerent Occupation and Human Rights', 107; Meron, 'West Bank and Gaza', 108 ff.; Roberts, 'What is Military Occupation?', 281 ff. *Contra*, see M. Shamgar, 'The Observance of International Law in the Administered Territories', *IYHR* 1 (1971), 262–6, whose opinion is not however categorical.

There is no room for doubt in relation to the Hague Regulations of 1907 whose dispositions have acquired a customary value which renders them applicable to every State, whether party to them or not. In the words of the International Military Tribunal of Nuremberg, they are 'recognized by all civilized nations' and are 'regarded as being declaratory of the laws and customs of war'.[59] The Supreme Court of Israel has endorsed this position, stating notably in the *Eichmann* case:

> war crimes are deemed to constitute in essence *international* crimes; they involve the violation of the provisions of customary international law which obtained before the Hague Conventions of 1907, the latter merely 'declaring' the rules of warfare as dictated by recognized humanitarian principles.[60]

Binding on every State, the rules of 1907 apply independently of the ratification of the Hague Regulations by the parties to the conflict. The same reasoning holds true in relation to the Geneva Conventions of 1949 and, in particular, to the Fourth Convention. One can perhaps legitimately argue that, at the time of their completion, they, on the one hand, codified existing law while, on the other, they brought about progressive development.[61] But after forty years, the division of the rules of the law of Geneva into two legal categories is no longer appropriate: the near universal adoption of the four Conventions[62] scarcely leaves room for doubt that today it is their provisions as a whole which derive from customary law.[63]

In addition, Israel is party to the Geneva Conventions and cannot legitimately free itself from the obligation to apply them on the pretext that the Palestinian people, which is 'the principal party to the question of Palestine',[64] is not a party to them. For one, in the terms of paragraph 3 of Article 2 of the Fourth Convention of 1949, a power not bound by this text can benefit from it if it 'accepts and applies the provisions thereof'; moreover, the PLO—which, not being a State, can probably not become party to the above provisions—has constantly called for their application and even formally requested adherence to them on 21 January 1975; in addition, as is stressed by the most authoritative commentary, the acceptance of the party that is not bound can be tacit, and the aforementioned disposition should be

---

[59] International Military Tribunal of Nuremberg, 1 Oct. 1946, *ADPIL* (1946), 253–4.
[60] *Attorney-General of the Govt. of Israel v. Eichmann*, 29 May 1962, *ILR* Vol. 36, 293.
[61] See Schwarzenberger, *International Law*, 165–6; or Meron, 'West Bank and Gaza', 112.
[62] On 1 Jan. 1987, the Fourth Geneva Convention had been ratified by 165 states, including Israel and all the Arab States involved in the conflict, the latter not having put forward their customary reservation concerning non-recognition by Israel.
[63] Cf. ICJ Judgment, 20 Feb. 1969, *North-Sea Continental Shelf Cases*, *ICJ Reports* (1969), 41 ff.
[64] Res. 3210 (XXIX) of the UNGA, 14 Oct. 1974.

open to broad interpretation.[65] Further, and above all, the provisions of the Fourth Convention relating to occupation can in no way be defined as a bilateral contract: their exclusive concern is the protection of persons and lays no kind of obligation on any party to the conflict except the occupying power; even supposing that the reasoning of the Israeli courts in refusing the benefits of the Third Geneva Convention to Palestinian combatants was based on the pretext that they do not respect the rules relating to the conduct of operations,[66] this argument is certainly not transposable to the case of belligerent occupation (see below). Moreover, Article 4 of Protocol I of 1977 clearly lays down:

The application of the Conventions and of this Protocol, as well as the conclusion of the agreements provided for therein, shall not affect the legal status of the Parties to the conflict. Neither the occupation of a territory nor the application of the Conventions and this Protocol shall affect the legal status of the territory in question.

This interpretation is incontestable and holds for all States, whether party to the Convention or otherwise.

It is, then, impossible not to agree with the United Nations in considering

that the implementation of the Geneva Convention of 12 August 1949 cannot and should not be left open in a situation involving foreign military occupation and the rights of the civilian population of those territories.[67]

In any event, even if the detailed provisions of the Fourth Convention were not strictly applicable in the West Bank, Israel would be no less bound to respect the spirit of the Convention. Its conduct should be evaluated in the context of the general principles which form the basis of the Convention,[68] and in keeping also with the spirit of the well-known *Martens clause* which has inspired the whole of *jus in bello* since 1899.

These latter considerations hold equally true, moreover, in relation to the Additional Protocol I of 12 December 1977, which Israel has neither passed, signed, nor ratified. Despite certain opinions to the contrary,[69] it would be unreasonable to claim that the provisions of

---

[65] J. Pictet, *Commentary on Geneva Convention IV of 1949*, trans. R. Griffin and C. W. Dumbleton (Geneva, 1958), 22–5.

[66] See, for example, the Ramallah Military Tribunal, case 4/69, 13 Apr. 1969, *The Military Prosecutor v. Omar Mahmoud Kassem et al.*, cited by J. Rideau, 'Le Problème du respect des droits de l'homme dans les territoires occupés par Israel', *AFDI* (1970), 223–4.

[67] Res. 3240 (XXIX) A of 29 Nov. 1974; see also e.g. Res. 2252 ES–V, 4 July 1967; 2851 (XXVI), 20 Dec. 1971; 35/122, 11 Dec. 1980; ES–9/1, 5 Feb. 1982; 41/163 B, 4 Dec. 1986; the Programme of Action of Geneva for the Achievement of Palestinian Rights, 7 Sept. 1983, Ch. 1, 4; or Res. 465 of the UNSC of 1 Mar. 1980.

[68] Cf. ICJ Judgment, 27 June 1986, *Case concerning Military and Paramilitary Activities in and against Nicaragua, ICJ Reports* (1986), 113–14.

[69] See e.g. S. E. Nahlik, 'Droit dit "de Genève" et droit dit "de la Haye": unicité ou dualité?', *AFDI* 24 (1978), 1–27.

the Protocol must apply as they are to Israel which, throughout the whole Diplomatic Conference on the Reaffirmation and Development of International Humanitarian Law, has clearly manifested its opposition to a number of those provisions.[70] All the same, even if the occupying authorities cannot be held to the detail of the rules, they will not be able to rely on their opposition in order to 'freeze' the humanitarian law of war as it was in 1949. To the extent that Protocol I 'harmonise le droit humanitaire avec le droit international contemporain',[71] and concentrates on making the adjustments necessitated by the evolution of the modern law of nations, these trends apply to Israel and this is especially the case in relation to the right of peoples to self-determination (see I: 'Occupation and the Right of Peoples to Self-Determination' above).

The second Israeli objection to the applicability of the traditional rules of the law of belligerent occupation scarcely calls for comment: the cessation of hostilities assuredly does not suspend the rules. An almost unanimous doctrine recognizes that the end of the fighting is in no way equivalent to the end of the state of war and, in consequence, the law of occupation continues to be wholly applicable,[72] as is confirmed by jurisprudence. Thus, for example, an American tribunal has judged that the United States were bound by the Hague Regulations in the case of their occupation of the Japanese island of Okinawa, 'until the terms of peace have been finally settled by treaty, proclamation, or otherwise'.[73] This corresponds both to legal requirements and to logical necessity.

It follows from the very definition of occupation that its existence is a question of fact, independent of the existence of current military activities (see I: 'Occupation, Annexation, and Sovereignty' above), and even of past ones.[74] Further, a number of provisions of the Fourth Geneva Convention stress the fact that the Convention applies 'in

---

[70] See Philippe Bretton, 'L'Incidence des guerres contemporaines sur la réaffirmation et le développement du droit international humanitaire applicable dans les conflits armés internationaux et non internationaux', *JDI* 105(2) (1978), 208–71, *passim*, particularly 216 ff.

[71] G. Abi-Saab, 'Les Guerres de libération nationale et la Conférence diplomatique sur le droit humanitaire', *Annales d'Etudes Internationales* 8 (1977), 71. See also G. Cahin and D. Carkaci, 'Les Guerres de libération internationale et le droit internationale', *Annuaire du Tiers Monde* 2 (1976), 32–56; and J. J. A. Salmon, 'La Conférence diplomatique sur la réaffirmation et le développement du droit international humanitaire et les guerres de libération nationale', *Revue Belge de Droit International* (1977), 27–52.

[72] Gerson, 'War, Conquered Territory, and Military Occupation', 530; Clagett and Johnson, 'May Israel as a Belligerent Occupant', 561; Dinstein, 'The International Law of Belligerent Occupation and Human Rights', 142; Roberts, 'What is Military Occupation?', 271 ff.; etc.

[73] *Cobb v. US*, 191 F. 2d. 604 (9th Cir. 1951), cited by Clagett and Johnson, 'May Israel as a Belligerent Occupant', 561.

[74] See Art. 2, para. 2, common to the four Geneva Conventions of 1949.

all circumstances'[75] or 'in any case or in any manner whatsoever'.[76] Certain recent resolutions of the United Nations have insisted on this point. Thus, in its Resolution 41/162B of 4 December 1986, the General Assembly reaffirmed—in reference to the Golan Heights, but the same holds equally true of the West Bank:

> that all relevant provisions of the Regulations annexed to the Hague Convention IV of 1907, and the Geneva Convention relative to the Protection of Civilian Persons in Time of War, of 12 August 1949, continue to apply . . . and calls upon the parties thereto to respect and ensure respect for their obligations under these instruments *in all circumstances*.[77]

It could not be otherwise: in the absence of the application of the law of belligerent occupation after the end of hostilities, the parties would find themselves confronted by a legal void. In particular, no limit would be set on the power of the occupier, which would in practice allow the latter to proceed to annex the occupied territory. This cannot be the law (see I: 'Occupation, Annexation, and Sovereignty' above). Moreover, as the most authoritative commentator has observed, 'it is . . . when a country is defeated that the need for international protection is most felt'.[78]

The same arguments also dispose, at least in part, of the third objection raised by Israel to the applicability of the traditional law of occupation. As emerged clearly in the aforementioned texts, the passage of time is not a circumstance allowing the occupier to exempt himself from the application of the rules of *jus in bello*. The expression 'in any circumstances' undoubtedly excludes any interpretation which would allow the occupier insidiously to achieve the annexation forbidden by the imperative norms of international law.[79]

It is true that development of the law of belligerent occupation occurred in the context of temporary situations, and, at the beginning of the century, no one imagined that such situations might endure for decades. When such is the case, numerous legal and practical problems can arise which the traditional rules, designed for times of war, may prove ill-adapted to resolve.[80] It is this predicament that paragraph 3 of Article 6 of the Fourth Geneva Convention seeks to

---

[75] Art. 1, common to the four Conventions; see also, e.g. Art. 27, para. 1 and the Preamble to Art. 1, para. 1 of Protocol I of 1977.
[76] Art. 47.
[77] See also SC Res. 592.
[78] Pictet, *Commentary*, 22. See Ch. 11 in this volume for further support for this view; see also Adam Roberts' comment in Ch. 1 on the Israeli government's logical muddle on this point *vis-à-vis* the Gaza Strip after the cessation of hostilities with Egypt.
[79] Although he generally supports moderate theses, Dinstein appears not entirely to exclude the possibility of an acquisitive prescription—'The International Law of Belligerent Occupation and Human Rights', 106.
[80] Cf. Roberts, 'What is Military Occupation?', 271 and 273.

remedy in limiting its field of application after one year: from this date, the occupying power is bound only by 43 of the 149 articles constituting the 'core' of the Convention.[81]

To understand the spirit in which this article was formulated, one can usefully and at length cite the *Commentary* to the Fourth Convention drawn up under the direction of Jean Pictet:

> One year after the close of hostilities, the authorities of the Occupied State will almost always have regained their freedom of action to some extent; communications with the outside world having been re-established, world public opinion will, moreover, have some effect. Furthermore, two cases of an occupation being prolonged after the cessation of hostilities can be envisaged. When the Occupied Power is victorious, the territory will obviously be freed before one year has passed; on the other hand, if the occupying Power is victorious, the occupation may last more than a year, but, as hostilities have ceased, stringent measures against the civilian population will no longer be justified.
>
> The Diplomatic Conference drew up a list of Articles which the Occupying Power must observe after the period of one year has elapsed, so long as the occupation lasts, in so far as that Power exercises governmental functions. They include, first and foremost, the general Articles (1 to 12); this is most important, especially in view of the activities of the Protecting Powers provided for in Article 9: they also include Article 27, which prescribes the humane treatment of protected persons, and Articles 29 to 34, which lay down a certain number of fundamental rules for the treatment of persons in the hands of a Power of which they are not nationals. On the other hand, the provisions which concern situations connected with military operations—in particular Articles 48, 50, and 54 to 58—will no longer apply. The same applies to the clauses relating to internment, with the exception of Article 143 dealing with supervision by the Protecting Power, which will remain in force.[82]

These authoritative explanations lead clearly to the following conclusions: Article 6 of the Fourth Convention seeks to lessen the 'stringent measures' that can be taken against the population of the occupied territory and in no way to strengthen the powers of the occupier on whom external control, one presumes, should more easily be exercised.[83] This conclusion is strongly reinforced by the contemporary prohibition of recourse to force and its corollary, the illegality of all

---

[81] 'In the case of occupied territory, the application of the present Convention shall cease one year after the general close of military operations; however, the Occupying Power shall be bound, for the duration of the occupation, to the extent that such Power exercises the functions of government in such territory, by the provisions of the following Articles of the present Convention: 1 to 12, 27, 29 to 34, 47, 49, 51, 52, 53, 59, 61 to 77, 143'.

[82] Pictet, *Commentary*, 63.

[83] See, however, the argument made by Adam Roberts in Ch. 1 that Art. 6 may no longer be applicable, and generally for discussion of prolonged occupation.

annexation following armed conflict, and by the emergence of the rights of peoples in the forefront of the legal scene.

La prolongation de l'occupation, autrefois favorable à un renforcement des pouvoirs de l'occupant, n'est plus une justification de pouvoirs accrus dès lors qu'est affirmée *l'inadmissibilité de l'annexion par l'occupation*: bien au contraire, cette situation incite à passer d'un régime réglementé, dont le respect doit être recherché par les procédures classiques de la responsabilité internationale, à un régime contrôlé, en particulier par les Nations Unies.[84]

Humanity and Necessity: Application of the Criterion

1. The Guiding Principles of Humanity and Necessity   It is by now beyond question that Israel, the occupying power, is bound to apply the laws of belligerent occupation. Indeed, Professor Adam Roberts finds, quite reasonably, that the occupation of the Palestinian territories of the West Bank and of Gaza very closely approximates to the 'standard case' envisaged by the 1907 Regulations as well as by the 1949 Convention in relation to the protection of civilians.[85]

In any case, if these two instruments deal with the same situation, they do so from slightly differing perspectives and, in particular, the closely associated pair 'humanity/necessity' (see 'Introduction' above) figures in an original way in each case. In both cases, it remains the pivot round which the whole fabric of the law of belligerent occupation is formulated. But in the Hague text military necessity predominates: the interests of persons are not taken into account except inasmuch as is allowed by the constraints of the conduct of hostilities, held to be intangible. Despite the ambiguity of its wording, it is probably thus that one should understand the well-known passage from the preamble to the Regulations of 1907:

According to the views of the high contracting Parties, these provisions, the wording of which has been inspired by the desire to diminish the evils of war, *as far as military requirements permit*, are intended to serve as a general rule of conduct for the belligerents in their mutual relations and in their relations with the inhabitants.

In 1949, on the contrary, the means of destruction having become almost limitless, no protection of the human person could be envisaged if one meant to let arms speak first; it is thus:

[A]u contraire l'intérêt de l'individu qu'on s'efforce de protéger et c'est au nom des exigences humanitaires que l'on rend la guerre plus difficile à mener.[86]

---

[84] Nguyen Quoc, Daillier, and Pellet, *Droit international public*, 436—emphasis in original.
[85] Roberts, 'What is Military Occupation?', 304.
[86] Obradovic, 'La Protection de la population civile', 147. See also McDougal and Feliciano, *Law and Minimum World Public Order*, 523.

This evolution encompasses the law of occupation. As M. Obradovic has excellently put it:

[T]andis que le Règlement de la Haye précise les droits et les devoirs de la puissance occupante, et, par répercussion seulement, les droits de l'individu, dans la Convention [de 1949] le procédé est tout à fait inverse. En outre, comme à l'époque du Règlement, l'individu était... protégé par la nature même de la guerre, le Règlement se soucie davantage de protéger sa propriété que lui-même...[87]

and Protocol I of 1977 further accentuates this tendency.[88]

Thus, while in 1907 the principle of humanity came to moderate that of necessity which formed the substance of the law, it is the reverse that applies in our day: the considerations of humanity constitute an absolute directive which military necessities, themselves subject to strict interpretation, temper. It is extremely significant in this respect that, as a general rule, the 1907 Convention proceeds by prohibitions laid on the occupying power: 'A belligerent is forbidden...' (Art. 44); 'It is forbidden...' (Art. 45); 'No contribution shall be collected...' (Art. 51), etc. In contrast, numerous provisions of the 1949 Convention confer rights on persons: 'Protected persons are entitled...' (Art. 2); 'Protected persons... may avail themselves...' (Art. 48); 'A convicted person shall have the right...' (Art. 73), etc. This approach is moreover in keeping with the new legal climate and, specifically, with the principle of prohibition of recourse to force and the new concern with the international protection of human rights.

Furthermore, as Judge Ago wrote, while special rapporteur to the International Law Commission, on the responsibility of States:

Where the exception is not expressly mentioned, there is no justification for presuming it. Secondly, when one thinks it over, the mere idea of generalizing the exception... would have been completely at variance with the purpose of the instruments that were drawn up. The rules of humanitarian law relating to the conduct of military operations were adopted in full awareness of the fact that 'military necessity' was the very criterion of that conduct. The representatives of States who formulated those rules intended, by so doing, to impose certain limits on States, to provide for some restrictions on the almost total freedom of action which belligerents claimed in their reciprocal relations, by virtue of that criterion. And they surely did not intend to allow necessity of war to destroy retrospectively what they had so arduously achieved... It would be absurd to invoke the idea of military necessity or necessity of war in order to evade the duty to comply with obligations designed precisely to prevent the necessities of war from causing suffering which it was desired to proscribe once and for all.[89]

---

[87] Obradovic, 'La Protection de la population civile', 150.
[88] Ibid. 159; and Cassese, 'A Tentative Appraisal', 181.
[89] ILC, Supplement to 8th Report on the Responsibility of States, *ILC Yb* (1980), II, 1, para. 53.

What has been possible to maintain in relation to the Hague Regulations[90] is not in any doubt today: the exception of necessity cannot be invoked in the absence of a specific rule and, when it figures expressly in a text, it is subject to strict interpretation.

It must be remembered that 'military necessities' should be interpreted in a strict sense and not merely as a convenient rationalization. In integrating the notion of military necessities with the law itself, in domesticating it, the law of armed conflicts thus succeeds in combining that notion with the humanitarian principle. The compromise between the two principles is made when the rule itself is being created.[91]

Article 1, common to the four Geneva Conventions, is moreover perfectly clear on this point: 'in all circumstances'; the expression leaves no place for any military necessity which is not expressly provided for in the Convention.[92] Necessity cannot figure either *contra*, nor *praeter legem*; it is taken into account only if the law makes express provision,[93] while, on the contrary, the principle of humanity, which infuses all the law of occupation, is to be a guide to interpretation.

This, to speak the truth, is very far from solving all the problems that can arise because, though restricted, military necessities are not in any way removed from the law of belligerent occupation. It is legitimate to strive to limit their effects, but it would be absurd to deny their existence—that would be to deny war itself, or occupation, which are facts.

Furthermore, as is emphasized above ('Introduction'), not only is the dialectic of humanity and necessity at the origin of the law of occupation and the law of war as a whole, but the two principles are, very often, found intermingling at the heart of a norm, each being the counterpart of the other.

Often, military necessities justify the exceptions to the humanitarian measures that are imposed on the occupying power. Thus, Article 27 declares the general rights of protected peoples, but its last paragraph stipulates: 'However, the Parties to the conflict may take such measures of control and security in regard to protected persons as may be necessary as a result of the war'. In other, rarer, cases, humanitarian reasons or military necessities constitute alternative motives which can

---

[90] Von Glahn, *Occupation*, 224.

[91] D. Bindschedler-Robert, 'A Reconsideration of the Law of Armed Conflicts', in Carnegie Endowment for International Peace, *The Law of Armed Conflicts* (New York, 1971), 15–16.

[92] See J. Pictet, *Développement et principes du droit international humanitaire* (Paris 1983), 106–7, or Draper, 'The Geneva Conventions of 1949', 73 and 129.

[93] In accordance with Art. 33, para. 2b, of the draft articles of the ILC relating to the responsibility of states, a 'state of necessity' cannot be invoked by the occupant as a 'ground for procluding wrongfulness', such a possibility being implicitly excluded by IV Geneva Convention of 1949.

justify certain forms of behaviour on the part of the occupier. For example, the second paragraph of Article 49 authorizes the occupying power to proceed to partial or total evacuation, 'if the security of the population or imperative military reasons so demand'. In still other hypotheses, the two concepts under consideration are inextricably entangled. The aforementioned Article 43 (see 'Introduction' above) of the 1907 Convention probably constitutes the best example.

In the words of this provision, the occupying power should 'restore, and ensure, *as far as possible, public order and safety*, while respecting, *unless absolutely prevented*, the laws in force in the country' (emphasis added). Each of the expressions underlined poses a problem, because each refers back, vaguely, to the principle of humanity as well as to the principle of necessity.[94] In particular, as has often been remarked, the obligation to guarantee public order is explained as much by reasons of security as by humanitarian motives; the idea can be invoked both in the interests of the occupier and in those of the occupied; it forms the basis of the rights of the authorities in occupation at the same time as it limits them.[95]

In addition, each of the two principles of humanity and necessity is, in itself, extremely ambiguous. Like all 'functional' notions, they are susceptible to very varied and highly subjective interpretations. My perception of necessity is not yours, any more than is my feeling of humanity, while both are subject to considerable variations according to time and circumstances. Hence the absolute necessity for a criterion whose function will be, at the same time, to allow the realization of a balance between the two guiding principles and to specify the contents of each of them. Respect for the sovereign rights of the occupied people constitutes the criterion because it is suited to fulfil both these functions.

Even if the distinction is extremely artificial, one can verify it by saying a few words about the use of the criterion in relation to the application of the principle of necessity on the one hand, and the principle of humanity on the other.

2. *The Guiding Principles in the Light of the Criterion* The concept of necessity itself has always baffled jurists who, with varying degrees of success, have endeavoured to break it down into different categories according to the objectives in view.[96] Dealing with military necessity,

---

[94] Art. 64 of the 1949 IV Geneva Convention poses problems of the same kind.
[95] See McDougal and Feliciano, *Law and Minimum World Public Order*, 793, or Debbasch, *L'Occupation militaire*, 233.
[96] See M. Huber, 'Die Kriegsrechtlichen Verträge und die Kriegsraison', *Zeitschrift für Volkerrecht* (Geneva, 1913), 352–5; C. de Visscher, 'Les lois de la guerre et la théorie de la nécessité', *RGDIP* (1917), 87 ff.; von Glahn, *Occupation*, 225; see also the remarkable

it is certain that the notion is more difficult to define in relation to the conduct of the occupier than to military operations in the strict sense. In the latter, the justification rests in the action itself; but, in relation to occupation, the action is remote, in spatial terms always, in time sometimes—and this is the case in the Israeli–Arab conflict from 1967 to 1973 on the one hand, and since 1973 on the other.

In such circumstances, the military necessities, however they may be defined, are less pressing.[97] They cannot be linked to current military operations: these have ceased. They may be related to military operations to come; but, with the passage of time, one can consider that the occupier will have taken all the precautions required, and that little more will be justified in the way of exceptional measures. Occupation becomes, then, an end in itself. Military necessities cannot, logically, relate to anything other than the security of the forces of occupation. In certain cases, the nature, the quality, and the extent of the 'necessities' that the occupant can invoke in support of the measures taken are articulated with reasonable precision by the relevant conventional provisions. Thus, for example, Article 68 defines, with an abundance of detail, the conditions that govern the pronouncement of sentences of deprivation of liberty or the death penalty. Similarly, Article 57 restricts the requisition of civilian hospitals in the occupied territory to 'cases of urgent necessity' and only 'for the care of military wounded and sick'.

In other cases, the exceptional measures that the occupier can take are very strictly tied to military operations *stricto sensu*. Thus, Article 53 of the Fourth Convention of 1949 forbids all destruction of public or private property, 'except where such destruction is rendered absolutely necessary by *military operations*'. Likewise, the second paragraph of Article 49 authorizes, exceptionally, the evacuation of the population, 'if the security of the population or imperative military reasons so demand'. But the last sentence in this provision requires the reinstallation of the evacuated persons 'as soon as *hostilities in the area* in question have ceased' (emphasis added). This is clearly to say that the 'imperative military reasons' are inseparable from the actual hostilities in progress.

However, such precision is by no means always to be found in the relevant text. For example, Articles 55 and 143 limit the rights of control of the protecting power if this is rendered necessary 'by imperative military requirements' or 'necessity'. This, undoubtedly,

---

analysis of the concept of necessity by Ago in the Supplement to the 8th Report to the ILC on the Responsibility of States, 1–81.

[97] See particularly von Glahn, *Occupation*, 226; McDougal and Feliciano, *Law and Minimum World Public Order*, 740; Schwarzenberger, *International Law*, 178.

determines the exceptional character of any suspension in relation to the rights of control, but it hardly elucidates the circumstances in which such suspension is lawful.[98] A great many other formulae are also just as nebulous. Thus, Article 27 authorizes 'such measures of control and security in regard to protected persons as may be necessary as a result of the war', but does not define 'result of the war', any more than Articles 62, 63, or 78 indicate what is to be understood by 'imperative' or 'urgent reasons of security', or Article 64 by 'a threat to [the occupying power's] security'.

Precise definitions would have been particularly useful since, if 'the concept of military needs may be greatly extended',[99] that of security is even more extensible. As demonstrated by Admiral Sanguinetti, the concept of security is infinitely more nebulous, more indefinable, than that of defence;[100] it can be invoked almost without limit; it contains nothing precise.

The words 'unless absolutely prevented' in Article 43 of the 1907 Convention (see II: 'Humanity and Necessity' above) give rise to the same type of questions. Nor is the relatively prolific jurisprudence on this point following the two world wars of great help, the tribunals having adopted viewpoints which are, at the very least, open to interpretation.[101] It is then difficult to invalidate or to confirm the views that this expression should be interpreted 'functionally'.[102] In accordance to what 'function' should the occupier act?

It is here that a criterion seems absolutely necessary and that vigilance over the respect for the sovereign rights of the occupied people is most urgently required.

It is this principle which finally marks the extreme limit of the occupier's powers. Israel cannot, in the name of security, either threaten the very existence of the occupied population—this goes without saying—nor alter its demographic composition, nor jeopardize its means of livelihood. Moreover, the law of peoples being inseparable from the fundamental rights of the human person (see I: 'Occupation and the Right of Peoples to Self-Determination' above), military or 'security' exigencies cease the moment the essential rights of the

---

[98] Pictet's *Commentary* for the ICRC, 576 ff., emphasizes the exceptional character of such a suspension but gives no indication of the circumstances in which it can occur.

[99] Bindschedler-Robert, 'A Reconsideration of the Law of Armed Conflicts', 15.

[100] Antoine Sanguinetti, 'Rapports entre la notion de sécurité et les atteintes aux droits des hommes et des peuples', in Georges Fischer and Eugene Schaeffer (eds.), *Armement—Développement—Droits de l'homme—Désarmement* (Brussels, 1985), 495–500. On the exceptionally extensive conception of the notion of 'necessity' in Israeli jurisprudence, see Shehadeh, *Occupier's Law*, 109 ff.

[101] Cf. Verzijl, *International Law in Historical Perspective*, 175–7, and 227–33.

[102] See Kuttner, 'Israel and the West Bank', 186, and Dinstein, 'The International Law of Belligerent Occupation and Human Rights', 112.

Palestinians, taken either individually or in groups, are threatened.[103]

Prima facie, the criterion of respect for the sovereign rights of the occupied people, presented thus, seems to relate to the principle of humanity. This is not at all the case if one takes into consideration the whole complexity of this concept: certainly, to all appearances, it is protective of the rights of the inhabitants of the occupied territory, but it is interesting to question the manner in which it operates in practice, what one can call its *modus operandi*.

In reality, in many hypotheses, many of the occupier's powers derive from the principle of humanity because it is the occupier who must put the principle into effect. It is the occupier who has the duty to 'restore and ensure... public order and safety' *(l'ordre et la vie publics)* (Art. 43 of 1907 Convention); who determines 'the requirements of the civil population', so as to supply provisions and medical goods in compliance with Article 55 of the Fourth Convention of 1949; and again, who decides on the reasons bearing on the security of the population which can justify its temporary evacuation (Art. 49), etc.

Using its powers with bias, the occupier can drain the legal institution of belligerent occupation of its substance. In the name of the interest of the population, 'for its own good', the occupying power can come to behave like a veritable sovereign although exercising only a temporary and practical power, imposed by force, and remaining the enemy. Inevitably, the measures it imposes, in the name of lofty sentiments, are infused by ethnocentrism and there is a serious temptation to consider that what is for its own good is also good for the occupied population. But then it is towards annexation that it will inch its way and this is not compatible with the idea of occupation itself.

This leads one to distrust humanitarian considerations in their pure and unadulterated state. It seems difficult to affirm, for example, as does Professor Migliazza, that

> le droit international reconnaît désormais à l'occupant tout pouvoir, en lui imposant même le devoir, de modifier les institutions et l'administration du territoire occupé si cêlà est nécessaire pour la sauvegarde des droits de l'homme.[104]

One hesitates, naturally, to dispute such a generous idea. But here too, and subject to the fundamental rights of the human person, which derive from *jus cogens*, the conception of human rights can be very different from one people to another and, short of accepting that the occupier can impose his ideas on the occupied, the very concept of

---

[103] See A. Migliazza, 'L'évolution de la règlementation de la guerre à la lumière de la sauvegarde des droits de l'homme', *RCADI* (1972–III), Vol. 137, 141–241, particularly 224.

[104] Ibid. 224.

belligerent occupation is incompatible with such a thesis, compelling as it may be at first sight.[105]

The same ethnocentrism characterizes the proposition put forward by Yoram Dinstein. Pointing out that 'there is no objective criterion in practice for drawing a distinction between sincere and insincere concern for the civilian population', he none the less adds:

> But, to my mind, in most instances, the criterion may be simple enough, namely, whether or not the occupant is equally concerned about its own population.[106]

This suggestion lays itself open to a serious objection: the occupier is not the territorial sovereign. He cannot legislate for the occupied people as he does within his own frontiers. It would correspond more to the concept of occupation for the Israeli authorities to refer to the PLO—which is perhaps too much to ask—or to Jordan to decide what is in the interests of the inhabitants of the West Bank. Doubtless Dinstein is right to point out 'that the occupant does not have to respect laws enacted by the authorities of the occupied State subsequent to the occupation';[107] but there is nothing to stop him taking into consideration the legislative and statutory evolution of the country whose territory is occupied and considering this evolution as worthy of note, it being understood that he is free to take it into account or not. A solution of this type would have the advantage of countering the risks of opposition to progress entailed in an occupation which is excessively prolonged while not falling into the disadvantages of ethnocentrist subjectivity.

It should be made clear that the problem does not lie with the occupier's intentions. This is, in general, the ground seized on by Palestinian writers. Thus Raja Shehadeh writes:

> In assessing Israel's claim that certain changes are justified as being for the benefit of the Palestinian population, Israel's declared aim of eventually annexing the occupied territories must be kept in mind. This ultimate illegal objective violates the presumption that certain actions are done for the benefit of the population.[108]

Undoubtedly Israeli intentions are an aggressive factor; but the real question in law does not lie here. The lawfulness of the occupier's conduct does not relate to the objectives he pursues; it can, and should, be judged in relation to a far more objective element, the

---

[105] See on this subject the subtly expressed theses of Kuttner, 'Israel and the West Bank', 187 ff.
[106] Dinstein, 'The International Law of Belligerent Occupation and Human Rights', 113.
[107] Ibid.
[108] Shehadeh, *Occupier's Law*, 13.

criterion of the sovereign rights of the people whose territory is occupied.

To the extent that the 'humanitarian' measures taken by the occupation authorities do not threaten these rights, they are lawful. They cease to be so, even if inspired by apparently commendable intentions, the moment that they 'change the physical character, demographic composition, institutional structure, or status of the Palestinian and other Arab territories'.[109] Without being systematic, the Fourth Geneva Convention of 1949 includes a number of specific dispositions which relate to this fundamental principle. This is the case in Article 27 whose first paragraph requires the occupying power to respect, for instance, the 'manners and customs' of the protected persons; in Article 58 relating to freedom of worship; in Article 47 which 'neutralizes' 'any change introduced, as the result of the occupation of a territory, into the institutions or government of the said territory'; or, even more so, in Article 56 whose fourth paragraph declares:

In adopting measures of health and hygiene and in their implementation, the Occupying Power shall take into consideration the moral and ethical susceptibilities of the population of the occupied territory.

From the very definition of the criterion which is imposed on the occupying power, it is clear that the people whose sovereign rights must be taken into consideration is the people, the enemy, against whom the occupier is fighting or has fought. This point would be wholly superfluous if certain decisions of the Israeli tribunals had not extrapolated some singular views in this respect, considering 'the interests of the population' of the Occupied Territories to be, primarily, those of the Israeli settlers.[110] The answer to this is given in the most formal terms in Article 4 of the Fourth Convention of 1949:

Persons protected by the Convention are those who, at a given moment and in any manner whatsoever, find themselves, in case of conflict or occupation, in the hands of a Party to the conflict or Occupying Power *of which they are not nationals* (emphasis added).

Paraphrasing the District Court of Utah in the *Aboitiz v. Price* (1951) affair, one can say that an enemy conqueror is not a very likely person in whom to repose the trust of ensuring the respect of the sovereign rights of occupied people. 'He is on the ground, however, and has the

---

[109] UNSC Res. 465 of 1 Mar. 1980.
[110] See particularly HC 256/72 *The Jerusalem District Electricity Co. v. Minister of Defence et al.*, and HC 393/82 *A Teachers' Housing Cooperative Society v. the Military Commander of Judea and Samaria*—cited by Shehadeh, *Occupier's Law*, 110–11; and see also Ch. 6 in this volume.

power to enforce his commands.'[111] His power is not, for all this, unlimited: he derives it from his military strength, but he can exercise it only within the limits clearly drawn by law.

Without any doubt, for as long as the occupation continues, the occupying power is, in practice, the principal judge of the application of these rules. It will tend to interpret in particularly strict terms the criterion which, in all circumstances, sets limits on the lawfulness of its conduct, and which derives as much from the law of belligerent occupation itself as from the imperative requirements of contemporary international law: the respect for the sovereign rights of the people whose territory is occupied.

It remains nonetheless true that the occupier has accounts to render. It has often been said that 'it is in connection with the laws of war that the impossibility of enforcing the law is most striking'.[112] This is only partially true in the case of the law of belligerent occupation.

On the one hand, being disapproved of by international law—because it necessarily results from recourse to force, which is prohibited in principle—occupation is the object of international control. The impact of this control, though it can only properly be evaluated by specialists in the field of political science, is probably not negligible and is due as much to public opinion as to international institutions, and above all to the United Nations. Furthermore, the Palestinians are far from having exhausted the means at their disposal and one may regret, in particular, that they have not, up to the present moment, sought an opinion from the International Court of Justice on the respective rights and duties of Israel and the Palestinian people or its representatives.[113] Further still, the conquered people is occupied, it is true; it is not—and cannot be—wiped out or enslaved; its resistance, active[114] or passive, can and does constitute an effective counterweight to the power of the occupier.

On the other hand, when the occupation comes to an end, the territorial sovereign, its rights restored, will distinguish between the lawful and unlawful acts of the occupier and there will be full scope

---

[111] Cf. *Aboitiz v. Price*, 99 F. Supp. 602 (D. Utah 1951); cited by Gerson, 'War, Conquered Territory, and Military Occupation', 542.

[112] B. V. A. Roeling, 'Aspects of the Criminal Responsibility for Violations of the Laws of War', in Cassese (ed.), *The New Humanitarian Law of Armed Conflict*, 199; on the question in general, see G. Abi-Saab, 'The Implementation of Humanitarian Law' in Cassese, ibid., 310–45.

[113] But see Ch. 17 for reference to an unsuccessful attempt by Palestinians to seek such an opinion. See also Ch. 16 on the advisability of seeking an advisory opinion from the ICJ.

[114] The question of the lawfulness of the *levée en masse* of the population of an occupied territory remains controversial. It is, however, the expression of the will of a sovereign people and its lawfulness should be recognized as such.

for the application of the criterion.[115] In the international field, the responsibility of the occupying State

est engagée par tout acte contraire au droit des gens, ordonné, ou toléré, par les autorités militaires ou civiles en territoire occupé.[116]

This is the revenge of history, because Troy, today, cannot be destroyed.

---

[115] See particularly F. Morgenstern, 'Validity of the Acts of the Belligerent Occupant', *BYIL* 28 (1951), 291–322.

[116] Arbitration decision of 30 June 1930, *Responsabilité de l'Allemagne à raison des actes commis postérieurement au 31 juillet 1914 et avant que le Portugal ne participât à la guerre* (Affaire du Lysné), *RIAA* II, 1040.

6

Playing on Principle? Israel's Justification for its Administrative Acts in the Occupied West Bank

EMMA PLAYFAIR

Introduction

ISRAEL'S occupation of the West Bank and the Gaza Strip is a legalistic one. The military government invariably seeks to defend its actions in the Occupied Territories with reference to legal provisions or principles, whether of international or local law. Emphasizing its claim to respect the standards and principles of international law, the military authorities informed an academic delegation to the Occupied Territories that:

[T]he criteria applied in the areas administered by Israel ... are those of 'humanitarian law', which balances the needs of humanity with the requirements of international law to administer the area whilst maintaining public order, safety and security.[1]

The Israeli government's equivocal position as to which provisions of 'humanitarian law' apply to its occupation of the West Bank and Gaza is examined in many of the chapters in this volume[2] and will not be further discussed here. The purpose of this paper is rather to examine Israel's application of certain principles derived from international law, summed up in the statement above: the maintenance of 'public order and safety', concern for the welfare of the local population, and the ensurance of security.

---

[1] See A. Roberts, B. Joergenssen, and F. Newman, *Academic Freedom under Israeli Military Occupation* (London, 1984), 80.

[2] Israel accepts that the Hague Regulations of 1907, being customary law, apply to its occupation of the West Bank and Gaza Strip, but contests the *de jure* applicability of the Fourth Geneva Convention of 1949. It claims nevertheless to respect voluntarily 'the humanitarian provisions' of the Fourth Geneva Convention, but has never defined this term or specified which of the convention's provisions it considers to fall within this category. In this way it is able to ignore certain provisions, such as Article 49 prohibiting deportation, while claiming credit for respecting others. For further discussion, see chapters by Roberts, Qupty, Pellet, Cassese, and others in this volume.

Guidelines on how occupied territories should be administered are said to have been laid down in the Israeli army military manual before the occupation of the West Bank and Gaza Strip in 1967.[3] These apparently stressed the concomitant rights and duties of an occupying power, and the military government's duty to ensure, as far as possible, public order and safety and to restore the life of the population to normal. In accordance with these directives, the Israeli army announced its assumption of control over the West Bank in Proclamation No. 1, issued on 7 June 1967, stating that: 'The Israel Defence Forces have today entered this area and assumed responsibility for security and maintenance of public order.'

That this responsibility entails both rights and duties has been reiterated throughout the occupation by the Israeli government and High Court alike. In an early judgment relating to the West Bank, *The Christian Society for the Holy Places v. The Minister of Defence*, the Israeli High Court stressed:

Alongside an occupier's right to do all that is necessary in the occupied territory for military purposes and for the safety of its forces, is a duty imposed by international law to be concerned with the welfare of the population.[4]

Nearly twenty years later, in February 1987, the Permanent Representative of Israel to the UN reaffirmed that

La politique d'Israel dans ces régions est basée sur la securité et l'ordre public, le combat contre la terrorisme à tous ses niveaux et dans un même temps l'amélioration de la qualité de la vie de la population dans son ensemble.[5]

How Israel interprets, balances, and uses the three principles mentioned above is the subject of this paper. Each of these issues will be considered in turn, examining not only the military government's use of these principles to explain its actions in the Occupied Territories, but the decisions of Israel's High Court of Justice, which has the power to review these actions. The decisions of the court provide valuable source material, since the court is the only public forum in which the military government is obliged to explain—albeit only to a limited extent, as will be seen—the grounds for its actions. It is also important to examine the role of the High Court, since its rulings add weight and authority to those practices which it endorses, and Israeli officials often

---

[3] S. Teveth, *The Cursed Blessing: The Story of Israel's Occupation of the West Bank* (London, 1970) 10–11, 32, cited by S. M. Boyd in 'The Applicability of International Law to the Occupied Territories, *IYHR* 1 (1971), 259.

[4] HC 337/71 *The Christian Society for the Holy Places v. The Minister of Defence et al.*

[5] In a letter dated 4 Feb. 1987, addressed to the President of the United Nations Commission for Human Rights by the Permanent Representative of Israel to the United Nations in Geneva. UN Doc. E/CN.4/1987/43.

cite the existence of the court as the best guarantee for the rule of law in the Occupied Territories.[6]

Although this chapter will address primarily the situation in the West Bank, most of the discussion is equally applicable to the Gaza Strip as well, since the principles and criteria relied on by the Israeli military authorities in both territories are essentially identical.

I. The Duty to Restore and Ensure Public Order and Safety

In justifying its actions based on public order, Israel claims to act in accordance with Article 43 of the Hague Regulations. In the English version of the official French text, this reads:

> The authority of the state having passed *de facto* into the hands of the occupant, the latter shall do all in his power to restore and ensure, as far as possible, public order and safety, respecting at the same time, unless absolutely prevented, the laws in force in the country.[7]

This article contains firstly a general duty to restore and maintain 'public order and civil life' (a more accurate translation of the official French text), and secondly a restriction on the extent to which, in carrying out this duty, the occupying authority may alter existing legislation.

The interpretation of this provision is all important since it serves as the main guidance on the responsibilities and duties of an occupant. How it is construed may determine the extent to which the occupied territories are able to retain their distinct nature and character. Yet, as so often in the laws of war, this provision sets more of a guideline than a clear rule. In the first part of the Article at least, much is left to interpretation; in particular, the nature of the order and life that is to be restored is not detailed. The second part of the Article seems clearer, but it too leaves room for interpretation.

Under the authority of Article 43, the military authorities have taken measures transforming the infrastructure, law, and the administration in the Occupied Territories. Military orders issued in the name of

---

[6] The Israel National Section of the International Commission of Jurists, *The Rule of Law in the Areas Administered by Israel* (Tel Aviv, 1981), xi, 42.

[7] For citation of the regulations, see Ch. 1, n. 4. The English text, which is not official, is an inaccurate translation of the official French text. In the French, the phrase translated above as 'public order and safety' reads 'l'ordre et la vie publics'. There is no consensus as to the proper translation into English, but it is evident that the word 'safety' is an unsatisfactory translation of the French. A preferable translation may be that adopted by E. H. Schwenk: 'public order and civil life' (in 'Legislative Power of the Military Occupant Under Article 43, Hague Regulations', *Yale L. J.* 54 (1945), 393), which will be used here. For further discussion, see Chs. 7, 11, and 14 below.

public order have influenced all aspects of civilian life, effecting radical changes in taxation, land use, financial systems, trading practices, municipal structures, local court systems, and innumerable other areas. The extent of the military's power under Article 43 has been challenged many times before the Israeli Supreme Court. The Court's decisions, overwhelmingly endorsing the authorities' actions, have been extensively reviewed elsewhere.[8] Here, I will trace only the pattern of interpretation of two important phrases in Article 43—'to restore and ensure public order and safety' and 'respecting ... unless absolutely prevented, the laws in force in the country'—to illustrate the breadth of the use of these provisions and to examine the effectiveness of the High Court in supervising the military government's exercise of its powers under this provision.

'To Restore and Ensure Public Order and Safety'

The first part of Article 43 requires the occupier both 'to restore' and 'to ensure' public order and safety, or civil life. The interpretation of this phrase was to determine whether the military authorities were basically restricted to restoring the order and life which existed under Jordanian rule (or Egyptian in the case of Gaza), or were permitted to introduce change so as to establish a different form of civil life.

Early in the occupation, in the *Christian Society for the Holy Places* case of 1971,[9] the petitioners claimed that a military order issued by the Staff Officer for Labour Affairs was *ultra vires*, since it introduced an innovation into the arbitration process established by Jordanian law. That law required certain employers' and workers' organizations, which at the time of the occupation had not yet been established, to participate in the arbitration process. The respondents claimed that, since there were no such organizations to restore, and the law was ineffective without them, the military government was obliged to establish a new arbitration body to enable the Jordanian law to take effect.

The court had to determine whether 'restore' and 'ensure' should be read together, or as independent duties. If the former, the occupier would be required to restore the situation to that which pertained before the occupation, and ensure its maintenance in that state. If so interpreted, the provision would strictly limit any innovative action by the occupier in the administration of occupied territory. If, on the other hand, 'restore' and 'ensure' are to be read separately, it can be argued that once the former state of affairs has been restored, the military

---

[8] See particularly Ch. 2.
[9] HC 337/71 *The Christian Society for the Holy Places v. The Minister of Defence et al.*

government is free to take additional steps to ensure what it considers to be public order and civil life.

The majority decision supported the latter view, and so agreed with the respondent that, since the arbitration body defined by the law had not been constituted before the occupation and therefore could not be restored, the law could only be implemented if a new arbitration body was established. Judge Haim Cohn, dissenting, argued that the commander's powers were restricted, except where there was no pre-existing law or order, to restoring and ensuring the state of affairs previously existing. The commander should not seek, as in this case, to fill gaps left by the previous legislator, even if it appears to him that this would be good or even ideal.[10] This was a minority view, however. The prevailing view was later reaffirmed by Judge Barak in the *Teachers' Housing Cooperative Society* case, where he stated that:

[T]he authority of the military government extends not only to restoring public order and life, but also to ensuring them. Indeed restoring and ensuring are not synonymous. Along with the authority to restore the public order and life that were disrupted, the authority exists to ensure public order and life even if these were not disrupted, or if public order and life have already been restored to normal.[11]

Having ruled that the duty to ensure public order and civil life is not restricted to restoring and maintaining the *status quo ante*, the Court then had to determine what nature of change is permissible to ensure public order and civil life under that provision. In judgments in subsequent cases, the court authorized a progressively looser definition of 'public order and civil life', allowing the occupying authorities ever greater freedom of action.

In the *Christian Society for the Holy Places* case of 1971, Judge Sussman, already viewing the occupation as prolonged, held that the duty to restore public order and civil life 'includes the duty to regulate economic and social affairs of the occupied population'.[12] Judge Shamgar, in the *Kandil* case of 1981, approvig Feilchenfeld's view that 'disregard of ... realities may well interfere with the welfare of the country and ultimately with "public order and safety" as understood in Article 43 ...',[13] held that the duty 'should be fulfilled according to changing reality in all fields of life: security, the economy, health, transport, and others'. Judge Shilo expanded on this in the *Tabib* case of 1981, ruling

---

[10] HC 337/71.
[11] HC 393/82 *A Teachers' Housing Cooperative Society v. The Military Commander of the Judea and Samaria Region et al.*
[12] HC 337/71.
[13] HC 69/81 *Abu Aita et al. v. The Military Commander of the Judea and Samaria Region*, and 493/91 *Kandil et al. v. The Military Commander of the Gaza Strip Region*, hereafter referred to together as 'the *Kandil* case'.

that the occupant is obliged 'to maintain an orderly administration, including all branches existing nowadays in an enlightened society, such as security, health, education, welfare, as well as quality of life and of transportation', and suggested that the 'ensurance of public life' be explained as 'the establishment of a regime which protects civil rights and concerns itself with the welfare of most of the population'.[14]

At this stage the distinction between the duties of an occupying government and a sovereign one already seems blurred. The court did however acknowledge that any action taken is restricted by the inherent temporariness of the occupation. Thus, in the *Elon Moreh* case, Judge Landau stated:

[T]he decision to establish a permanent settlement intended from the outset to remain in its place forever—even beyond the duration of the military government which was established in Judea and Samaria—encounters a legal obstacle which is insurmountable, because the military government cannot create in its area facts which are designed *ab initio* to exist even after the end of the military rule in the area.[15]

In the second *Jerusalem District Electricity Company* case, the court qualified this stand. It ruled that, since any military administration is temporary by nature, its main task is to ensure public order and civil life, and it should not introduce far-reaching modifications in the area, likely to have an impact beyond the end of the occupation, 'save for action undertaken for the benefit of the inhabitants of the area'.[16]

Far wider powers of the military government were approved in the judgment in the *Teachers' Housing Cooperative Society* case the following year, in which the court seemed to endorse a much more interventionist role for the military government, holding that:

[T]he authority of the military government extends to taking all the necessary means to ensure *growth, change, and development*. Hence the conclusion that the military government may develop industry, commerce, education, agriculture, health and welfare, and so forth, relating to orderly administration and required to ensure the changing needs of the population in an area under belligerent occupation . . . [T]he life of a population, like the life of an individual, is not static but is in constant motion consisting of development, growth, and change. A military government cannot ignore this. It may not freeze life.[17]

Such an interpretation effectively frees the military government from the primary obligation to maintain the *status quo* in any of the spheres mentioned, which cover most aspects of life. Relying on the above-

---

[14] HC 202/81 *Tabib et al. v. The Minister of Defence et al.*
[15] HC 390/79 *Mustafa Dweikat et al. v. The State of Israel et al.* ('the Elon Moreh case').
[16] HC 351/80, HC 764/80 *Jerusalem District Electricity Company Inc. v. The Minister of Energy and Planning et al.*
[17] HC 337/71, emphasis added.

mentioned ruling in the second *Jerusalem District Electricity Company* case, that changes can occur if for the good of the population, the court held that:

> [L]ong-term basic investments, which could bring about permanent changes that may persist even after the termination of the military government, are permissible if they are required for the good of the local population, provided that they do not bring about any substantive change in the region's basic institutions.[18]

The court concluded that the planning of such basic investments with outside elements, even if this means collaboration between the military government and the occupying power's government, is legitimate, provided that it is also for the benefit of the local population.

Through the years, the court has approved indisputably permanent changes, including the construction of settlements which have developed into towns in the Occupied Territories, and the linking up of electricity, telephone, water, and road systems to those of Israel. As to the prohibition on substantial changes in the region's 'basic institutions', this seems to have little meaning in practice, since changes have in fact been implemented and approved by the court in all manner of local institutions, including public utilities, universities, courts, and municipalities.

The restrictive provisions of the first part of Article 43 of the Hague Regulations, regarding the duty to restore and ensure public order and civil life, have therefore been more and more loosely interpreted to the point where they permit the military government almost unrestricted authority to alter all aspects of the infrastructure of the Occupied Territories. For from restricting intervention and keeping change by the occupying authorities to a minimum, the provision has been interpreted so as to endorse sweeping changes almost indistinguishable from those of a sovereign power. There remains the restraint that these changes must be for the benefit of the local population, but, as will be seen below, this control is of little value if the local population whose interest is considered is the Jewish settlers in addition to or even rather than the Palestinian population.

'Respect for the Existing Law'

The second part of Article 43 of the Hague Regulations places specific limits on the power of the occupier to legislate. It states that the existing law must be respected *'sauf empêchement absolu'*—except when absolutely prevented.

[18] HC 393/82.

The existing law when the West Bank was occupied was that of Jordan, while in the Gaza Strip it was the law in force under Egyptian administration. Since the beginning of the occupation, the military commander has issued over 1,200 military orders in the West Bank, and in Gaza over 900 military orders, each altering the pre-existing law. In their book *The West Bank and the Rule of Law*, Raja Shehadeh and Jonathan Kuttab describe how:

> Initially the military authorities exercised their wide-ranging legislative powers cautiously. The Area Commander generally prefaced military orders with some justification explaining his rationale as to why he believed the order to be necessary for security reasons. Later on however this ceased to be the case and the military freely and confidently legislated in the most sweeping manner.[19]

This was written in 1980, when 854 military orders had been issued. Eight years later, a review of all the military orders published revealed that 65 per cent of the orders bore no justification at all, supporting Shehadeh and Kuttab's proposition. 25 per cent of the orders cite security and public order and 10 per cent cite the benefit of the local population.[20] By far the majority of such acts are therefore unaccompanied by any explanation of either the legal justification or the factual reason for the decision. Amongst the orders which give no rationale are almost all those dealing with land transactions and with matters relating to Jewish settlers and settlements.

By and large, the military commander has been able to exercise his legislative powers without interference, but on a few occasions residents of the Occupied Territories have challenged military orders in the High Court. The phrase '*sauf empêchement absolu*', which does not on the face of it seem to admit much interpretative leeway, was first considered in 1971 in the *Christian Society for the Holy Places* case. In this case, mentioned above,[21] the Jordanian law governing settlement of labour disputes could not be implemented, since the arbitration body envisaged by the law had never been established. The military authorities therefore prepared a new arbitration body to which the petitioners objected, saying that there was nothing which absolutely prevented the occupier from respecting Jordanian labour law. Judge Sussman held that the words 'absolutely prevented' should be interpreted with reference to the duty imposed on the occupier *vis-à-vis* the civilian population, including the duty to regulate economic and social affairs. He held that, under the special circumstances of a prolonged military occupation, this duty obliged an occupier to adapt the law according to the

---

[19] R. Shehadeh and J. Kuttab, *The West Bank and the Rule of Law* (Geneva, 1980), 101.
[20] Unpublished research by R. Shuqeir carried out for al-Haq in 1988.
[21] See text at n. 9 above.

changing needs of the population over a period of time, due to social, economic, and commercial factors. He concluded that:

> [A]s long as the laws in force in the occupied territories do not enable the military ruler to fulfil the duty imposed on it towards the citizens of the territory, this constitutes an absolute impediment, which authorizes it to amend the same laws.[22]

The restrictive nature of the provision was acknowledged by Judge Shamgar in the *Kandil* case, regarding the introduction of value-added tax (VAT) in the West Bank,[23] in which he held that 'absolute prevention' implies necessity and that 'necessity to modify existing laws may be derived from military needs of the occupant, or from humanitarian consideration for the welfare of the population'. However, he then endorsed the view of Israeli scholar Yoram Dinstein, that legislation is permissible in occupied territories when an occupier introduces the same legislation into its own state,[24] although this proposed parity appears unrelated to the necessity he had just identified as the only legitimate reason to change laws.

In the *Tabib* case, Judge Shilo considered the same matter. He reviewed various authorities, notably an article by Edmund H. Schwenk, whose opinion broadly was that necessity based on the social or economic needs of the civilian population could constitute an 'absolute prevention' in respect of the existing law. Having quoted, with approval, Schwenk's conclusion that:

> It seems that Article 43 allows [the occupier] to alter civil and criminal laws where the alteration is justified by *necessity* of public good or the military interests [of the occupier].[25]

Judge Shilo went on to conclude, somewhat surprisingly, that:

> [A]ctually, 'the prevention' mentioned at the end of Article 43 is not absolute at all... The question [whether an absolute prevention exists] is one of the *preferable and convenient means* for achieving the purpose as stated in the beginning of Article 43, namely 'ensuring public order'—a term which I propose to interpret as meaning the existence of an administration safeguarding civil rights and concerned about the maximal welfare of the population. If the achievement of this purpose requires a deviation from the existing laws, there is not only a right but, indeed, a duty to deviate from them.[26]

---

[22] HC 337/71.
[23] HC 69/81, emphasis added.
[24] Y. Dinstein, 'Legislative Authority in the Administered Territories', *Eyunai Mishpat* 2 (1972), 505, 511.
[25] HC 202/81, emphasis added.
[26] Ibid.

He thus replaced Schwenk's concept of necessity with one of preference and convenience, which seems far from the interpretation intended by Schwenk.[27]

Judge Shilo's interpretation may at first sight seem not unreasonable, but he went on to apply this argument to the case then at hand, which concerned expropriation of Palestinian land. Jordanian law requires a landowner whose land is to be expropriated to be served with notice of the requisition in person. This had not occurred in this case. According to Judge Shilo, such procedural steps are of secondary importance and can be disregarded if another method is used which seems to the authorities more 'practical and efficient' under the circumstances of belligerent occupation. Following this argument, the judge saw no objection to an alternation in the law allowing the military authorities to inform not the landowners but the local *mukhtar*, or village leader, of the decision to requisition land. Relying on this interpretation of international law, he annulled, for reasons of convenience, a major element of protection for Palestinian landowners against arbitrary expropriation of their property.[28]

Through a series of judgments, the High Court thus made the transition from a fairly literal interpretation of the words of Article 43 themselves, which are clearly intended to be restrictive of the powers of the occupier, to a view that the natural development of the population in a long occupation will require some changes. Developing this argument as the occupation lengthened, the court first authorized changes required by the changing needs of the occupied population, and then those which the government considered preferable and convenient. The court has finally reached a position which effectively allows the military government to legislate and administer the territories as though it was indeed the legitimate sovereign, taking Jordanian law only as a starting point, not as the basis which the occupier should strive to maintain.

While it is evident that society does not stand still over a period of years, and that some changes may be necessitated by population growth or deterioration of facilities, these cases illustrate the danger inherent in depleting the strict limitations on an occupier's actions. The clear aim of Article 43 is to preserve the independent nature and character of the occupied territories, protecting them from exploitation and integraton or the loss of their own identity. In the case of an occupation lasting many years, the protection afforded by a restrictive interpretation of Article 43 may come at some cost to the territories'

---

[27] See also Dinstein's reflections on the meaning of 'absolute prevention' in 'Legislative Authority in the Administered Territories', *Eyunai Mishpat* 2, 509, quoted in translation in Ch. 2, text an nn. 31–3 in this volume.

[28] HC 202/81.

development, but international law holds this preferable to the exercise of sovereign powers over the territory by an alien occupier.

II. The Welfare of the Local Population

In the last section we saw how considerations of the welfare or benefit of the inhabitants of occupied territories were deemed to permit departure from a general rule. The duty to observe the welfare of the population has been held by the Supreme Court to be a key consideration in determining whether or not the military government can introduce changes into the administration or law of the Occupied Territories.[29] The duty to ensure the welfare of the population is the other side of the powers the military is entitled to exercise to ensure public order and its own security. As explained by the authors—mainly military lawyers—of *The Rule of Law in the Areas Administered by Israel*,

The fact that the occupant is given the competence to administer the territory in place of the former administration is intended to prevent a vacuum in the efficient administration of everyday life and the maintenance of public order. Thus rather than being a right of the occupying state, it is a duty owed by it to administer the territory for the benefit and welfare of the local population.[30]

The importance of this consideration was stressed by General Shlomo Gazit, former co-ordinator of activities in the Occupied Territories:

It is the responsibility of the state of Israel to provide a decent life for the people in the territories. The fact that the military administration is the only ruler of the area makes it responsible for the welfare of the population.[31]

It was further endorsed by the Israeli High Court in the *Christian Society for the Holy Places* decision, when it ruled that:

Alongside an occupier's right to do all that is necessary in the occupied territory for military purposes and the safety of its forces, is a duty imposed by international law to be concerned with the welfare of the population in the territory.[32]

While the integrity of the concept is evident, its practical implementation is problematic. An occupier is at best alien and at worst may be exploitative or expansionist. In the best of cases, an occupier, whose society, culture, and values may differ markedly from those of the

---

[29] See text at n. 4 above.
[30] The Israel National Section of the International Commission of Jurists, 2.
[31] D. Bavly, *An Experiment in Coexistence* (London, 1971), 14.
[32] HC 337/71.

occupied population, cannot satisfactorily stand in the shoes of the occupied population to determine what is in their best interests. At worst, an occupier may seek to evade the strict controls of humanitarian law by representing actions taken with other motives as serving the welfare of the local population. Unless the procedures or criteria for its use are clearly established or controlled, the opportunity for abuse is clear.

The military government has cited the welfare or benefit of the local population as the rationale for military orders affecting matters such as insurance, health, agricultural produce, appliances, local courts, price fixing, etc. Under this rubric, the government has also sought to justify substantial changes to the law or infrastructure, has expropriated land for public use, and has undertaken major works including road construction and the merging of water and electricity networks with those of Israel.

Two main concerns arise in reviewing actions taken by the Israeli military authorities purportedly for the benefit of the local population. The first is that, while some of these actions may have enhanced the immediate quality of life of the Palestinian inhabitants, they may be detrimental to the long-term interests of the population as a whole by increasing dependence on Israel. Secondly, in some cases it appears that the population to benefit from such actions is not the local Palestinian population but the Jewish settlers. These questions are examined further below.

Determination of the Best Interests of the Population

The determination as to what best promotes the welfare of the population of occupied territories over a period of twenty years is inevitably complex. Some of the measures taken by the Israeli military authorities may be fairly universally considered to be for the benefit of the local Palestinian population. Such measures include, for instance, the abolition of a mandatory death penalty for certain offences, the introduction of 'no-fault' compensation for traffic accident injuries, and the extension of sick leave in labour law. More often, however, this rationale is given for measures which may satisfy short-term material interests of the Palestinian population, improving the immediate quality of life, but which may prejudice longer-term interests.

The supply of basic utilities to the West Bank illustrates the tension between the satisfaction of the immediate material benefit of the occupied population and giving priority to their long-term interest. The Israeli government maintains that by linking up the Occupied Territories to Israeli supplies, a more efficient service may be provided than by sustaining the territories' own independent services. Palestinians argue that this in fact serves the Israeli government's interest in integrating the Occupied Territories and Israel and rendering the territories dependent on Israel, thus placing further obstacles in the way of the territories' eventual independence.

Pursuing this policy, the Israeli government has granted the major water-supplying rights for the West Bank to the Israeli water company, Mekorot.[33] The mail and telephone system of the West Bank have been almost entirely integrated with that of Israel.[34] Only with regard to electricity have Palestinians managed to retain some control, due in part to a rare ruling of the Supreme Court in favour of Palestinian petitioners.

The struggle waged over many years between the Palestinian-owned Jerusalem District Electricity Company and the Israeli Electricity Corporation for control over supply to the West Bank still continues. The military government has relied on the local population's evident need for a reliable electricity supply to order that successive segments of the West Bank be connected up to the Israeli Electricity Corporation's network, in preference to the Palestinian-owned Jerusalem network. The military authorities argue, possibly correctly, that the Israeli corporation is technically better able to supply the needs of the population. That the collective and long-term interests of the West Bank population may be better served by the maintenance and development of an indigenous power supply, even at the cost of a less reliable system, was seemingly not considered.

The Israeli High Court has been called on several times to rule on the legality of this process. The first occasion, in 1972, concerned the supply of electricity to the Hebron area, including the settlement of Kiryat Arba. The court approved the decision of the military commander to hand over the supply of electricity to the Israeli Electricity Corporation, on the basis that, since the Corporation was superior to the appellant Jerusalem Company in everything pertaining to technical and economic competence, the local population would be better served by the Corporation.[35] The desirability of a large West Bank town being dependent on the occupying state for the supply of a major amenity seems not to have been taken into consideration.

However, in 1980, in one of less than a handful of cases in which the High Court has overturned an order of the Military Commander in favour of the local population, the High Court refused to approve the wholesale linkage of the West Bank electricity system with that of Israel. On this occasion, it accepted that this was a far-reaching modi-

---

[33] M. Benvenisti et al., *The West Bank Handbook: A Political Lexicon* (Jerusalem, 1986), 225.
[34] Ibid. 172.
[35] HC 256/72 *The Jerusalem District Electricity Company Ltd v. The Minister of Defence et al.*

fication which was not, as claimed, 'necessitated' by electricity requirements, since the local company was indeed capable of meeting the demand.[36]

Despite this ruling, the Israeli government, which as occupier inherited the contract with the Jerusalem Electricity Company from the Jordanian government, continues efforts to transfer the entire concession to the Israeli corporation. Most recently, in 1987 the Israeli government refused to renew the concession, agreeing only to grant a limited twelve-year concession over part of the area previously covered. While the dispute continued, the government first threatened to grant the entire concession to the Israeli Corporation, then unilaterally disconnected all settlements and West Bank areas served from the Jerusalem Company and reconnected them to the Israeli Corporation.[37]

The West Bank road system has fared little better, radical changes to the Palestinian network having been implemented by the military government and approved by the High Court. At the time of occupation, the West Bank road system ran on a north-south axis, consistent with the demography and geography of the area. In the late 1970s and 1980s a new road-plan was drawn up, covering the West Bank and parts of Israel, in co-operation with the Israeli planning authorities. The planned road system was to alter radically the existing north-south road grid; instead, the emphasis, according to the new plan, would be the development of roads running east-west, linking the West Bank with Israel, and the construction and upgrading of roads linking and providing access to Israeli settlements, while avoiding Palestinian population centres. Quite apart from its questionable benefit in terms of use to the Palestinian population, the plan necessitated the expropriation of vast tracts of land and restrictions on the use of much more. The plan envisaged six-lane highways in some parts, including service roads, large junctions, and restrictions on building within a 100-metre margin on each side.[38]

This plan came before the Supreme Court on two occasions, the petitioners in each case contesting requisition of land. In the first case, the *Tabib* case,[39] the authorities justified the road-plan as being required for security reasons. Since, as will be seen in the next section, the High Court's practice is not to intervene when issues of security are involved, it authorized the road. The legitimacy of the same road-plan was later challenged again, in the *Teachers' Housing Cooperative Society*

---

[36] HC 351/80.
[37] See Benvenisti, *West Bank Handbook*, 75–6; *Al-Fajr*, 12 July and 6 Sept. 1987; and *Jerusalem Post*, 10 Aug., 29 Oct., 6 Dec., 11 Dec., and 31 Dec. 1987.
[38] A. Shehadeh, F. Shehadeh, and R. Shehadeh, *Israeli Proposed Road Plan for the West Bank: A Question for the International Court of Justice?* (Ramallah, 1984).
[39] HC 202/81.

case,[40] in which the petitioners contested the refusal of permission to build on land on or near the site of a proposed major junction. In this case, the military authorities did not justify the plan on security grounds, as in the *Tabib* case, but claimed that it served the benefit of the local population. The military authorities argued that the road-plan would serve daily commuters into Israel from the territories. These commuters include both Israeli settlers and Palestinians from the Occupied Territories who travel to work in Israel every day. The Palestinian petitioners presented evidence to the effect that the existing road system, which already included access roads to Israel, was adequate for local Palestinian needs and, should it become outdated due to a growth in traffic, the existing roads could be improved to serve the increasing need.

The judges did acknowledge puzzlement over the fact that, whereas the plan had been justified to them in the earlier case of *Tabib*[41] as being necessary for security purposes, the very same plan was now justified as serving the welfare of the population. This did not, however, cause them to doubt the good faith of the expert evidence provided by the military government and they approved the plan on the basis that it would benefit the local population.

Since occupation is by definition temporary, it seems improbable that the total restructuring of the territory's road system with the express aim of linking the occupier's land with the occupied territory, as opposed to maintenance and upgrading of the existing system, which already contains roads linking Israel and the West Bank, can really be considered in the best interests of the occupied population. Similarly, in a temporary occupation it is unlikely that the effective elimination of a local service, even an inefficient one, is in the long-term interest of the indigenous local population. Unless eventual annexation, or at least future dependence on Israel is assumed, the integration and dependence of the local Palestinian population on Israel for their supplies and vital amenities surely cannot be in their interest.

The High Court has approved two guidelines to help it determine whether the military government has legitimately acted in the interest of the local population. In the *Christian Society for the Holy Places* case, in which the Court held that innovatory measures were permissible under Article 43, it affirmed that, in deciding whether a particular action was permitted under this article,

the legislator's motive is of great importance. Did he pass the law in order to further his own interests, or out of a desire to look after the welfare of the civilian population, *la vie publique* mentioned in Article 43?[42]

[40] HC 393/82. [41] HC 202/81. [42] HC 337/71.

This must be correct, but it does not follow from the integrity of the legislator's motivation that his opinion on what is to the benefit of the population can be relied upon. It merely rules out *misuse* of the power for improper motives.

Much later, when reviewing the imposition of VAT in the Occupied Territories in the *Kandil* case, the Court accepted that a measure taken for the benefit of the population can be considered legitimate if the same measure is applied in the occupier's own country. This view seems to fly in the face of the body of humanitarian law, whose aim is precisely to see that occupied territories maintain their own identity and do not become an extension of the occupier's own territory. True, the situation is somewhat obscured when occupied and occupier's territories are adjacent, and there may be cases in which an action benefiting one may benefit also the other, but this cannot be a justificatory factor in itself. Neither of these tests provide much guidance and both fail to address the problematic issue of how a foreign occupier can determine what is in the interests of the occupied population without a mechanism for consultation with that population.

An even more fundamental point in determining whether the Israeli military authorities are acting in accordance with international law when relying on the welfare of the population, is how the military authorities define 'local population'.

Who is the Local Population?

As is well known, the Israeli-occupied territories are now inhabited by two distinct populations: Palestinians, who are the population protected by the Fourth Geneva Convention, and Jewish settlers, who have moved into the Occupied Territories, with the approval of the Israeli state, during the occupation.[43] In affirming the duty of the occupying power to consider the welfare of the local population, is Israel referring only to the protected Palestinian population, or does it also include in this definition the Jewish settler population? There are many indications that it is the latter.

Over the years, military orders have made substantial changes to the local law, establishing a separate administrative structure for the Jewish settlements. In effect, the settlers are largely empowered to run their own affairs, and are rendered subject to Israeli law and adminis-

---

[43] See also Pellet's chapter above at n. 112 on the definition of protected population. The UN and almost all states have condemned the introduction of Israeli settlers and the establishment of Israeli civilian settlements in the Occupied Territories as illegal, being in violation of Article 49 of the Fourth Geneva Convention. Nevertheless, all Israeli governments, Labour and Likud alike, have steadfastly maintained a policy of promoting settlement.

tration, rather than to military government and the local courts in the Occupied Territories.[44] Since a dual system of administration, and the consequent effective immunity of settlers from prosecution under local law, is clearly contrary to the interests of the local Palestinian population, the only interest served by such legislation is that of the Jewish settlers.

The planning process offers another instance where both legislation and practice is changed contrary to the interests of the local Palestinian population, but to the benefit of the settler population and without legitimate justification. Whereas Jordanian planning procedures provided for local consultation at several stages in the planning process, military orders have transformed the planning procedure, collapsing various steps together, abolishing all local consultation, and staffing all committees with military officers. Settlers habitually hold influential positions on these committees. The result is a procedure from which the local population is virtually excluded, and which has enabled the needs of settlers to take priority over those of the local Palestinian population.[45] This process was best summed up by Meron Benvenisti:

The preamble of Order 418 (which vested all planning powers in the Higher Planning Committee) reads: 'Whereas I consider it necessary for the orderly management of development and construction operations in the Area and for securing proper planning and licensing procedures, I order...'. From the perspective of 30,000 Israeli settlers, 'proper planning and licensing procedures' seem to have been carried out smoothly. From the perspective of 750,000 West Bank Palestinians, the preamble reads like a macabre joke.[46]

In other instances, it is the application of a principle which makes it clear which population's interests are served. For instance, water use for both domestic and agricultural purposes is very strictly controlled by quotas and permits. Only a handful of permits for artesian wells have been granted throughout the occupation. The reason given is to conserve the limited water supply for the general benefit of the population. This appears reasonable, until a comparison is made between the allocation of water for use by Palestinian population centres and that allowed to settlements. Estimates forecast that by 1990, 60 million cubic metres of water will be available to some thirty Israeli agricultural settlements; this is equivalent to one-third of the amount available to

---

[44] For a detailed account see Shehadeh, *Occupier's Law* (Washington, 1985), *passim*.
[45] See M. Rishmawi, *Planning: In Whose Interest?* (Ramallah, 1987), and her chapter in this book, and see a forthcoming study by Anthony Coon on planning in the Occupied Territories, commissioned by al-Haq. See also discussion of the *Teachers' Housing Cooperative Society* case above. On the granting of building licences, see Shehadeh's chapter in this book.
[46] M. Benvenisti, *The West Bank Data Project: A Survey of Israel's Policies* (Washington, DC, 1984), 28.

400 Palestinian villages.[47] Not only are the regulations and the supply discriminatory, but settlers also receive heavy subsidies for the cost of the water.[48]

Similarly Military Order (MO) 1015 imposes restrictions on the planting of grape-vines and plum trees, allegedly for the benefit of the local population, again to protect the water supply. Yet many of the major settlements in the heart of the West Bank, such as Kiryat Arba which is next to the Palestinian town of Hebron, are lush with water-consuming decorative plants, making a nonsense of restrictions on neighbouring farmers' means of survival. In the light of discriminatory applications, it is hard to credit that these orders are intended to benefit primarily the local Palestinian population.[49]

The High Court, far from opposing the inclusion of Jewish civilians in the term 'local population', has endorsed it more than once. As early as 1971, in the first *Jerusalem District Electricity Company* case, the court held that the Jewish settlers of Kiryat Arba 'should be viewed as persons added to the local population' whose needs were to be taken into account.[50] Much more recently, in the *Teachers' Housing Cooperative Society* case, mentioned above, the Court endorsed the military government's decision to construct a network of roads, described as benefiting the local population, even though the declared aim of the plan was to benefit the settlers as much as, if not more than the Palestinian population.[51]

Jewish settlement in the Occupied Territories having been approved by the military authorities, the Israeli government, and the High Court, it seems that the settlers themselves are now to be considered as part of the local population. As such, the authorities appear to consider their needs on a par with, or even give them precedence over, those of the supposedly protected Palestinian population.

Application of the principle of the welfare of the population is therefore problematic. Israel has used these powers to justify extensive changes. Yet when the reasons given for such actions are closely examined, we see that while they may improve the immediate quality of life, they are often highly prejudicial to the long-term sovereign interests of the Palestinian population. Furthermore, in some cases the population in question is not, or not only, the Palestinian population but the Jewish population, illegally settled in the territories. Moreover, many of these actions serve the purpose of strengthening the links between the Occupied Territories and Israel and improving services

---

[47] Benvenisti, *West Bank Handbook*, 223–5.
[48] Ibid. 224.
[49] These remarks are based on the author's own observations.
[50] HC 256/72, and see also Mazen Qupty's paper, text at n. 43.
[51] HC 393/82.

and living conditions for settlers. These acts appear designed rather to serve the political aim of obstructing the return of the territories, than to benefit the Palestinian population.

If the occupier is serious about wishing to serve the welfare of the occupied population, mechanisms can be established for consultation with the population, even without instituting full elections. Yet Israel has made no attempt to establish any independent means for assessing what is in the local population's interests; indeed, in the planning process, where the law did provide for such consultation, it was abolished.

The difficulties inherent in an occupier assessing what is in the interests of the population of the territories it occupies, and the opportunities a loose interpretation offers for abuse, emphasize again the wisdom of the conservative nature of Article 43 of the Hague Regulations. Only in cases of absolute necessity will the occupying power have to exercise its own judgement. In most such cases it is submitted that mechanisms for consultation with the local population can easily be developed. Without such consultation the determination of what is in the best interests of the population is, at best, guess-work.[52]

III. Security

The Israeli military authorities rely on security grounds to justify a wide range of administrative and legislative actions in the Occupied Territories.[53] They argue, correctly, that an occupying power has the right to carry out many actions, including some which would otherwise be in violation of international law, if necessary to protect its own security. However, the actions so explained embrace every aspect of the lives of the Palestinian population. They range from the most fundamental, the occupation itself, to deportation of individuals, expropriation of land, establishment of Jewish civilian settlements, arming of the settlers, censorship of newpapers and books, denial of building permits, prohibition of traffic lights, refusal of permission for driving licences, and even the banning of clothes and carrier bags combining the colours of the Palestinian flag. The military authorities, when required to justify these actions, refer to local[54] or international

---

[52] In this respect, see also Ch. 14.

[53] A revised and expanded version of this section was published in *Arab Studies Quarterly* 10 (4) (1988), 406.

[54] Wide-ranging powers to ensure security were contained in military orders issued early in the occupation and repeatedly amended since then. Most notable are MO 378, the Order on Security Provisions, and MO 101, the Order Concerning the Prohibition of Incitement and Adverse Propaganda. In addition, Israel also relies heavily on the pro-

law, but in most cases those affected are told simply that it is 'for security reasons'.[55]

According to international law, requirements of security can justify on the one hand quite stringent measures of control and punishment against the occupied population, and on the other hand can authorize fundamental changes in the law and infrastructure which, if not necessary for security, would not be legitimate. However, although considerable leeway is allowed to an occupier to take measures to ensure its own security, there are limits. According to Jean Pictet, in his *Commentary* on the Geneva Conventions,

What is essential is that the measures of constraint [the occupier] adopt[s] should not affect the fundamental rights of those concerned.[56]

And later,

It will be seen that the powers which the Occupying Power is recognized to have are very extensive and complex, but these varied measures must not under any circumstances serve as a means of oppressing the population.[57]

---

visions of the British Mandatory Defence (Emergency) Regulations of 1945, which permit a range of harsh restriction orders if the Military Commander believes these to be 'necessary or expedient . . . for securing the public safety, the defence of Palestine, the maintenance of public order, or the suppression of mutiny, rebellion, or riot' (Article 108). These powers are extensively used on a daily basis to impose travel restrictions, place curfews on camps, declare areas temporarily or permanently closed, prevent distribution of newspapers, and also to order deportations, administrative detention, and demolition of houses.

The legality of the use of these regulations has been strongly contested by Palestinian lawyers, who maintain that they were revoked by the British just before the end of the Mandate and thus did not, as Israel claims, form part of the local law in 1967. See M. Moffett, *Perpetual Emergency* (Ramallah, 1989).

[55] The concept of 'security' is not precisely defined in international law, but it appears in many guises. In addition to the customary rules that allow an occupier to take measures necessary to ensure the safety of the occupying forces, enshrined in the general terms of Art. 43 of the Hague Regulations cited above, Art. 64 of the Fourth Geneva Convention allows the occupier to enact new penal provisions if these are 'essential . . . to ensure the security of the Occupying Power, of the members and property of the occupying forces or administration, and likewise of the establishments and lines of communication used by them'; Art. 78 permits internment or assigned residence 'if necessary for imperative reasons of security'; Art. 41 provides that the maximum measure of constraint that can be placed on someone who is considered a threat to security is internment; and Art. 27, after making general observations regarding the need to respect the occupied population, provides that '[T]he Parties to the conflict may take such measures of control and security in regard to protected persons as may be necessary as a result of the war.' Other provisions, such as Article 52 of the Hague Regulations which allows requisitions if needed for the occupation army, make no specific reference to security, but may depend on the establishment of security needs for their applicability. See also more detailed discussion in Chs. 1, 3, 5, and 11 in this volume.

[56] J. Pictet, *Commentary on Geneva Convention IV of 1949*, trans. R. Griffin and C. W. Dumbleton (Geneva, 1958), 207.

[57] Ibid. 337.

While there is no authoritative definition of either 'fundamental rights' or of 'oppressing the population', these do provide some guidance to the restraints on an occupier's actions.

This section will examine where Israel draws the limits in its reliance on security grounds to justify actions in the West Bank and Gaza Strip. Has it justified on this basis only those actions necessary for security or also those which merely serve security interests? Is it only the security of the occupying forces that is to be taken into consideration, or that of the occupier's own population, wherever they may choose to live, or of the occupying state as a whole? If it is the state as a whole, is it restricted to consideration of its immediate security needs while the occupation continues, or is it entitled to make permanent transformations to serve its long-term security needs, beyond the end of the occupation? What supervision is exercised over the military authorities' application of this principle and what guarantees are there against abuse of power? Israel's responses to these questions are examined below.

The Expanding Scope of 'Security Needs'

Some of the most stringent measures against individuals and communities are taken in the name of security. The military government invokes the British Mandatory Defence (Emergency) Regulations of 1945[58] and military orders derived from them to order deportations, house demolitions, closure of institutions, curfews, administrative detention, etc. The Regulations give the military commander power to impose any of these measures if he believes that they are necessary or expedient for security.[59] Similarly, blanket travel restrictions are frequently imposed on a whole area, for instance the Tulkarem area, preventing anyone from that area from crossing into Jordan. Other such measures include closures of trade union offices, closures of universities, prohibition of exports from a given area, disconnection of electricity, water, fuel or communications. In such cases, the duration of the measure, the remoteness of those affected from any act threatening security, the absence of security measures by the military such as search or cordonment, often suggest that collective or individual punishment is the purpose of the measure rather than security as stated.

Curfews for instance are frequently imposed on camps, villages, and towns for days or sometimes weeks. Such restrictions used immediately after an incident, to contain an offender or to carry out an intensive

[58] HC 337/71.
[59] Regs. 108–19, and MO 378.

search, may be legitimate security measures. Often, however, a curfew or travel restriction continues well beyond this initial period, and there is no serious attempt at search or containment. In this case it seems that the security measure is being abused and an extrajudicial, punitive measure is masquerading as a security measure.[60]

A series of cases regarding the requisitioning of land for security reasons illustrates the military government's use and definition of security in circumstances where punishment is not the intention, and also the High Court's interpretation and supervision of these powers. Until 1980, almost all land for Jewish settlement was requisitioned in reliance on Article 52 of the Hague Regulations, which allows land to be requisitioned temporarily if needed for the occupation army. The military authorities argued in each of the cases below that the land was needed by the army for security reasons. Those claiming title to the land requisitioned challenged the action on the ground, *inter alia*, that the real motive for the requisition was the political one of increased settlement. Several of these cases came under closer review when the landowners appealed to the Israeli High Court.

In the first case in which the court considered this issue, the *Hilu* case, members of a Bedouin tribe contested their expulsion from their lands, which the military authorities had proclaimed a closed area. The authorities claimed that the area

> served for a long period as a centre for hostile terrorist activity and a way-station for the perpetration of terrorist acts outside of the area, such as mining roads and passes, shooting at Israeli cars, murdering local inhabitants, destroying buildings and installations . . . , as a place of storage and a way-station for the transit of arms and ammunition to terrorists operating in the Gaza Strip and the State of Israel, and as a way-station, refuge, and hide-out for Egyptian intelligence agents . . .[61]

They produced detailed allegations of attacks in the area, of arrests made and of arms caches discovered. It was well known, however, that a settlement was to be built on these lands, and the Bedouin argued that the requisition was made not for genuine reasons of military necessity but for undisclosed political reasons. To the petitioners' claim that the security considerations were no more than a ploy to prepare the area for settlement, the military authorities responded that the requisitioning of the land was genuinely prompted by security considerations, and that the intention to construct a settlement, whether or not it served security needs, did not negate the security purpose. Moreover they claimed that the presence of the settlements

---

[60] See, for instance, al-Haq's *Newsletter* 7; also Shehadeh, *Occupier's Law*, 133–41 on prolonged curfews, and *passim* on other measures mentioned.
[61] HC 302/72.

itself served security needs. The High Court approved the action of the military authorities.

Several years later, similar claims were raised in the *Beit El* case.[62] The military authorities initially requisitioned privately-owned land on the basis that it was necessary 'for essential and urgent military needs', but a civilian settlement was later constructed on this land. Since Article 52 authorizes requisition of lands only temporarily while actually needed for military purposes, the land must be returned to its owners unless a continued need can be shown. The court had to decide whether present usage indeed justified the continued possession of the land. Although the settlement was initiated and planned by civilian agencies of the Government of Israel, the military government claimed that the retention of the land was legitimate since it 'serve(d) military need'. The military government's expert on security, Major-General Avraham Orly deposed in his affidavit submitted to the court that:

[T]he establishment of the settlement in the area of Beit El camp *is not only not inconsistent with, but actually serves military need*, as part of the Government's concept of security, which bases the security system *inter alia* on Jewish settlements ... In times of peace and tranquillity these settlements mainly serve the need for 'presence' and control in vital areas, for maintaining observation and the like. Their importance increases particularly in wartime, when regular military forces are generally moved from their bases for operational needs, and the said settlements form the principal element of 'presence' and security control in the areas in which they are located.[63]

It is notable that, in justifying the settlement, Orly does not claim that it is essential for security purposes, but only that it *serves* those purposes. The nature of the 'security needs' cited are also very different from those cited in the *Hilu* case. There the authorities claimed that their actions were intended to forestall actual military actions, while in this case they relate to strategy, not in response to any immediate threat, past or present, but as one convenient element in a future defence system. The lack of essentiality in the matter is echoed in the comment of Judge Witkon, in accepting Orly's argument and ruling against the landowners, that:

[T]he two areas in which the petitioners' land was requisitioned are in sensitive strategic locations ... It is difficult to assume that an occupying power would leave control of such areas in the hands of elements likely to be hostile.[64]

There was though no suggestion that those from whom land was taken were themselves engaged in hostile activities. Inhabitants of bel-

---

[62] HC 606/78, 610/78 *Ayyoub et al. v. The Minister of Defence* ('The Beit El case').
[63] HC 606/78, 610/78, emphasis added.
[64] HC 606/78, 610/78.

ligerently occupied lands can generally be assumed to be hostile towards the occupying power, but this cannot mean that each member of the population poses an actual security threat. If the rationale for requisitioning land for military needs is to be this casual, there would be little to prevent any land in occupied territories from being requisitioned.

The process of acquiring land for settlement on the grounds that settlement served security purposes continued unchecked until a political dispute over the Elon Moreh settlement revealed the tenuousness of this claim. In this case, again contesting the establishment of a settlement on privately-owned land, fierce political and strategic disagreements inside both the army and the government came out into the open. Evidence by the Chief of Staff that the settlement would serve military needs was forcefully opposed by other high-ranking Israeli military experts. Authoritative figures in the army stated their views that not only did the settlements serve no security function at all, but that indeed they would be a burden in time of war since troops would have to be deployed to protect civilians there. The settlers too, seeking endorsement of the religious basis for settlement, disputed the security argument and proclaimed that the main reason for the settlement was to reclaim the whole land of Israel; to the extent that settlement also served security needs, this was secondary and entirely incidental. In the face of this evidence, the court had to conclude that security was not the determining factor and so ruled that the settlement was not authorized.[65] Only the overwhelmingly strong evidence in this case that security was not the primary purpose of the requisitioning forced the High Court to re-examine its former blanket approval of such requisitions.

These cases show how an ever looser definition of security 'need' has been endorsed by the High Court, which has enabled the military authorities to rely on provisions of international law to secure land for settlement. After the *Elon Moreh* case undermined this rationale, other means were used to acquire land for settlement,[66] but the damage was already done. By the time the court was forced to question the military authorities' claim that civilian settlements served security, the presence of permanent settlements in the West Bank and in the Gaza Strip had been achieved under the guise of security. By 1980, there were over 100 such settlements, mostly established on land expropriated by this

---

[65] HC 390/79. For further discussion of the court's ruling see below, text at n. 85.

[66] See Shehadeh, *Occupier's Law*, 22–41, for description of other methods used to acquire land for settlement. After the *Elon Moreh* case, land was still requisitioned citing security reasons, bringing more land under Israeli control, but not when it was to be used for settlement. For instance, several thousand dunums of registered land in Ramallah were seized in 1983, restricting the growth of the town and its industrial area. The military claimed that the land was needed for the use of an army camp, but the camp is at some distance from the land claimed.

method.[67] These were not temporary settlements to be removed and the land returned to the owners when the need had passed, but permanent civilian settlements and towns, with foundations, roads, and infrastructure. Both the settlements and the settlers living in them had become 'facts' to be taken account of, and, as will be seen, the 'security' needs of the settlers created the justification for further restrictive measures in the Occupied Territories.

Whose Security?

The land cases referred to above illustrate the scope of the definition of security, but these cases raise also another question: whose security is to be assured? There is no doubt that international law permits an occupier to ensure the security of its own forces. In some cases, however, the aim seems to be more long-term, to serve the defence of the State of Israel itself.

In the *Beit El* case[68], Major-General Orly argued that the settlements were needed to build up a future defence system, not only for times of war, but as a 'presence' in peacetime as well. Petitioners in the *Amira* case[69] sought to recover land initially requisitioned to serve military needs, but which was used two years later for a civilian settlement. The land in question is in a part of the West Bank overlooking the Israeli littoral, where Israel's Ben Gurion airport is located. The respondents deposed in their affidavit that the settlement would form part of a defensive line, based on three civilian settlements, to protect Ben Gurion, Israel's main international airport. The military expert stated that the existence of the settlement would enable the army to deploy observers and military forces there in case of an attack on the airport. The land seized also formed the site of a junction for roads that could be used during times of unrest in the West Bank. Although this strategy clearly related more to the security of Israel than to that of the occupying forces, the court accepted this argument, as it had accepted that in the *Beit El* case.

Similarly, having purportedly introduced settlers to serve security purposes, the provision of security for the settlers themselves provides the justification for a whole range of additional measures. For their protection in hostile territory, settlers are allowed to carry arms, creating a further distinction between them and the Palestinians living in the same area, and lending a higher risk factor to any confrontation. The settlers pass towns and refugee camps on their way through the

---

[67] See J. Metzger, M. Orth, and C. Sterzing, *The Land is our Land* (London, 1983), 19, and Benvenisti, *A Survey of Israel's Policies*, 49.
[68] HC 606/78, 610/78.
[69] HC 258/79 *Amira et al. v. Minister of Defence et al.*

Occupied Territories to their settlements, so high wire fences have been erected in front of many refugee camps, to satisfy their concerns about safety. In the longer term, as has been seen, new roads are planned to provide access for the settlers and to bypass Palestinian population centres, for the settlers' security, necessitating acquisition of more land. Where a settlement is in a particularly provocative site, as is that built on Tel Rumeida in the town of Hebron, extra forces must be drafted in to guard the settlement, thus provoking increased confrontation with the Palestinian population.

This process is exemplified by the settlement of Beit Hadassa in the centre of the Palestinian town of Hebron or al-Khalil. Established in defiance of government orders, the settlement was set up in a building in a crowded market area of the town. The proximity of Palestinians and settlers inevitably led to daily tensions, as was clearly predictable. Security needs might have prompted the authorities to prohibit the settlers from occupying the building. Instead, the government took a number of measures to protect them, initially providing guards, then erecting a fence in front of a row of neighbouring shops. Access to these shops has since been available only by walking behind the wire fence after being subjected to an army search. The cause for this measure, economically disastrous for the shopkeepers and humiliating for their customers, is the need to protect the Beit Hadassa settlers. When the Mayor of Hebron submitted a complaint regarding the harassment of neighbouring shops by the settlers, the court found that, in contrast to the protection granted to the settlers, complaints brought by the townspeople had been dealt with very inadequately. The court ordered the re-examination of the complaints, but, since the government had in the meantime confirmed that the settlement met with its 'consent and approval', declined to order the removal of the settlers.[70]

Palestinian security, however, seems rarely to be taken into consideration. As seen above, Jewish settlers, who have been responsible for much violence against Palestinians[71] have been granted effective immunity from local courts. Nor do the local police force provide protection to Palestinians. Attempts by Palestinians even to submit complaints meet with obstruction, and follow-up is minimal.[72] While curfews are routinely imposed on Palestinian population centres following any kind of disturbance, it is unknown for an Israeli settlement to be placed under curfew. For example, on the night of 6 June 1987 a group of some 200 armed settlers from Kiryat Arba invaded Deheisheh Refugee Camp, shooting and causing extensive damage until eventually

---

[70] HC 175/81 *Al-Natshe et al. v. Minister of Defence et al.*
[71] See the Karp Report, reprinted in *PYIL* 1 (1984), 185; see also Shehadeh, *Occupier's Law*, 184–200.
[72] See the *Karp Report*, and also Ch. 17 in this book.

forced out by the army. It was however the refugee camp and not Kiryat Arba which was then placed under curfew, although it was the settlers who threatened security and who could have been contained by a curfew.[73]

Thus the military government uses its powers to serve the security interests not only of the occupying forces, but also those of the settlers and of the state itself, but rarely those of the Palestinians.

Supervision of Powers

As the jurists McNair and Watts point out, 'That the power of the occupant affords unique opportunities for the abuse of law is obvious.'[74] One of the most obvious opportunities is that afforded by the vagueness of the definition of 'security', by reference to which an occupier can justify actions which would otherwise be considered illegal.

Despite the exceptional nature of acts based on security and the great impact such actions have on the population of the Occupied Territories, there is virtually no supervision of these powers, or review of decisions purportedly taken on the basis of security. Israel's history of past insecurity and its population's continuing sense of vulnerability has led to a mystification of the concept of security. The consequent reliance on those responsible for maintaining security means that few are willing to doubt, far less challenge, decisions made by security experts. This attitude stretches beyond the general public to the government, the Knesset, and even the courts. Yehuda Ben-Meir, a former deputy Foreign Minister for Israel, explains how:

[N]ational security issues in Israel are invariably and inextricably related to and associated with military considerations, causing deliberations on these issues to remain secret. This approach to secrecy is supported by *social norms* as well as legal sanctions, and has been maintained over a long period of time.[75]

Responsibility for security in each of the Israeli-occupied territories is in the hands of one individual, the Israeli area military commander, who holds all executive, legislative, and judicial powers. His decisions as to security needs are based largely on advice and information provided by the Israeli army ('the IDF') and, above all, by Israel's domestic Intelligence Service ('the *Shin Bet*').[76]

The Shin Bet plays an overwhelmingly important part in the lives of

---

[73] See *al-Haq Newsletter* No. 20 (July/Aug. 1987), 5.
[74] A. D. NcNair and A. D. Watts, *The Legal Effects of War*, 4th edn. (Cambridge, 1966), 371.
[75] Y. Ben-Meir, *National Security Decision-Making: The Israeli Case* (Tel Aviv, 1985), 5 (emphasis added).
[76] On the Shin Bet, see also Ch. 8 below.

residents of the Occupied Territories. Firstly, it is in reliance on intelligence information from Shin Bet operatives that the Military Commander will issue such drastic orders as deportation, administrative detention, or town arrest orders. At the next level, the Shin Bet also carries out most of the investigation and interrogation in relation to all but minor offences in the Occupied Territories and Israel. Finally, 'security clearance' from the Shin Bet has to be sought each time a Palestinian requests any of a wide range of permits and licences, including permits to travel, for family reunion, to learn to drive, and even to have a telephone. Any of these will be refused unless the Shin Bet gives its approval.

In these circumstances, the integrity of the Shin Bet and its close supervision and accountability are obviously imperative. However, the Shin Bet is answerable directly and only to the Prime Minister. Two enquiries in the past few years, exposing some of the excesses of the Shin Bet, have shown how inadequate that supervision is. The first enquiry related to the hijacking of an Israeli bus by Palestinians from Gaza in 1984. It revealed that two of the hijackers, said to have died in the operation to free the bus, had in fact been arrested without injury but were then summarily executed by the Shin Bet. Furthermore, in subsequent investigations the Shin Bet itself then effected a cover-up, involving the highest levels of government. The second enquiry, by the Landau Commission in 1987, followed the discovery that the confession on the basis of which Itzhak Nafsu, a Circassian officer, had been convicted of treason, had been extracted from him under torture by the Shin Bet. This enquiry revealed not only the Shin Bet's extensive use of torture but also that the Shin Bet had systematically lied in their evidence to court throughout the past sixteen years.

The Landau Commission's report claimed that the disclosures and findings of the enquiry, in particular the perjury of the Shin Bet, came as a surprise to the judges to whom the Shin Bet had lied. To the Palestinian population they came as no surprise. Innumerable Palestinians have challenged the evidence of the Shin Bet, most often as to the circumstances under which their confessions were taken, but also as to the facts alleged against them, but have found that the evidence of the prosecution witnesses was almost invariably believed over their own.

Despite its findings, the Landau Commission recommended that no criminal charges be made in relation to past instances of perjury or use of illegal methods of interrogation, and in fact no prosecutions have resulted. Any hope there may have been that the Commission would lead to better control of the Shin Bet's activities was dashed by these results, which demonstrate clearly that the government has no intention of penalizing abuse of power by the Shin Bet. The Shin Bet it seems is justified in its assumption that it can operate outside the law with impunity, if it only exercises a modicum of discretion.

As for the Israeli High Court, it shares the general reluctance to look behind a claim of security holding that:

The court is not the proper place to decide whether a military-security operation . . . —if grounded in law and undertaken for reasons of security—was indeed warranted by the security situation or whether the security problem could have been resolved by different means . . . (I)ssues related to the army and defence, similar to issues of foreign affairs, are not among the subjects fit for judicial review.[77]

The court has repeatedly stated that it will not question the judgement of the military commander on issues of security, since he alone is responsible for maintaining public order and civil life in the Occupied Territories, and must know better than anyone else what steps are required to ensure that security.

The Court will intervene therefore only if it is convinced that the military commander's discretion is exercised in an arbitrary way or not in good faith.[78] Yet should the petitioner try to bring his own security expert to counter the evidence of the government security expert, he faces a more or less insurmountable difficulty before the court. Judge Landau considered such evidence in the *Amira* case and concluded that:

In a dispute such as this, involving questions of a military-professional character in which the Court does not have its own founded knowledge, it will presume that the professional arguments . . . of those actually responsible for security in the occupied areas and within the Green Line are valid. This presumption may only be rebutted by very convincing evidence to the contrary.[79]

As will be seen below,[80] the only evidence which the court has found to be 'very convincing' to date has been evidence by other members of the military establishment of similar or higher rank to those giving evidence for the government. Under normal circumstances, such evidence is very unlikely to be available to ordinary plaintiffs, and so the burden is effectively insuperable.

In the series of cases concerning land requisition referred to above, this attitude of the Court enabled it to accept the military authorities' assertion that civilian settlement served security purposes, not questioning the sworn evidence of government security experts that this was the case.[81] In the *Hilu* case the court ruled that:

[77] HC 302/72 *Sheikh Suleiman Hussein Odeh Abu Hilu et al. v. The Govt. of Israel et al.*
[78] HC 369/79 *Ben Zion v. Military Commander of the Judea and Samaria Region et al.*
[79] HC 258/79.
[80] See text at n. 85.
[81] HC 302/72, HC 606/78 and 610/78, HC 258/79.

We shall most definitely not intervene in the judgement of the military commanders who are convinced that the establishment of a buffer zone was necessary to ensure calm in the Gaza Strip and beyond and to prevent the infiltration of terrorists.[82]

The court did not rule in that case on whether or not the settlements served security needs, but contented itself with saying that:

It is clear that the fact that these same plots—whether all or part—are earmarked for Jewish settlement, does not strip the action as a whole of its defensive character.[83]

Despite the High Court's repeated insistence that it is not qualified to assess security matters, Judge Witkon felt able to *endorse* the Commander's view on security needs in the *Beit El* case, stating that:

[A]s regards the pure security aspect, it cannot be doubted that the presence in occupied territory of settlements—even 'civilian' settlements—of citizens of the occupying power contributes appreciably to security in that territory and makes it easier for the army to carry out its task . . .

He concluded firmly that: 'Jewish settlement in occupied territory serves actual security purposes.'[84]

Only in the *Elon Moreh* case was the court forced to examine the security claim, and it did not stand up to close scrutiny.[85] As seen above, the petitioners were extraordinarily lucky in the evidence available to them. These circumstances are highly unlikely ever to recur. The court was only willing to question the view of the respondent's military security witness because it was faced by conflicting evidence from the highest-ranking Israeli military experts. Even in this case, the court did not investigate the security issues, but based its ruling against acquisition of the land on its finding that security was not the determining factor in the decision to establish the settlement. The Court distinguished between this case and the *Beit El* case by stating that it was the primary purpose which should be taken into account. In most cases such evidence is not available to the petitioners, and the court maintains its attitude of strict credence in the evidence of the military authorities as to security matters.

Similar impediments face those appealing orders of administrative punishment based on the broad security grounds contained in the British Mandate Defence (Emergency) Regulations of 1945.[86] Orders imposing administrative punishment typically refer in very general terms to activities in a hostile organization, to continuing activity with-

---

[82] HC 302/72.
[83] Ibid.
[84] HC 606/78 and 610/78.
[85] HC 390/79.
[86] See above, n. 54.

in that organization, and to previous imprisonment if any, and conclude that the person therefore represents a threat to security, public order, etc. The burden of proof then lies on the appellant to show that he or she is *not* a security risk, a task that is all but impossible on the basis of such vague allegations, exacerbated by the authorities' general refusal to reveal the evidence relied on, and often even any detail of the accusation.

Those affected by an administrative order of this kind can appeal to the High Court, and in some cases also to a military committee. They are likely however to encounter one of the most disturbing aspects of security-related measures, dubbed 'the Sphinx strategy' by Ian Lustick, whereby explanation of the security reasons for a particular action is itself deemed impossible 'for security reasons'.[87] That is to say that when someone seeks to challenge a decision based on security, for instance a decision to deport, he or she is told that no further details of the security charge can be given, since to reveal them would itself endanger security. The military authorities invariably refuse to disclose all, and often any of the information on the basis of which the person is considered a security risk, nor is the person given a chance to question the operative who provided the information. The reason usually given for this is that to reveal the evidence would also be to reveal the informant, and would destroy the effectiveness of the *modus operandi* of the security services by endangering their sources. This further diminishes the petitioner's chances of providing the incontrovertible evidence that the High Court requires before it will question the evidence of those responsible for security, who thus continue to act more or less unfettered by any effective review.

Some steps have been taken in an attempt to improve this situation. For instance, in appeals against deportation one of the High Court judges can now examine the evidence and decide how much of it (if any) can be revealed. In practice, however, not enough is revealed to enable a proper defence to be submitted, so it is doubtful if there is any real improvement. The deportation of Akram Haniye provides just one example. Haniye was served with a deportation order on 3 November 1986. He challenged this order first before a military committee and then in the High Court of Justice, but at neither level was his lawyer permitted to see the evidence. Unable to challenge the allegations in any meaningful sense, Haniye withdrew his appeal, considering that he had no chance of a fair hearing, and was deported on 28 December 1986.

---

[87] I. Lustick, 'Israel and the West Bank after Elon Moreh', *Middle East Journal* 35 (Autumn 1981), 564.

A review of the military authorities' reliance on security needs to justify actions in the Occupied Territories has shown how such needs are invoked with great frequency to explain all manner of actions. These include those intended to provide for the security of the Israeli nation as a whole, for its future defence, and for the security of the settlers. In some cases it is used to cloak other purposes, such as the creation of settlements, or extrajudicial punishment. Since it can rarely be challenged and those responsible for its imposition cannot be questioned, its use is essentially beyond control. The High Court is most ineffective precisely where there is most scope for abuse of power by the military commander, in relation to the issue of security.

Members of the Israeli public and even of the judiciary have expressed concern about excessive use of power under the rubric of 'security'. Judge Haim Cohn, a senior member of the judiciary, owned that:

> I myself am far from happy and complacent about certain aspects of the military administration ... Not everybody in Israel subscribes to the prevailing military concept of security requirements.

but like others he concludes:

> ... so long as the Army has the responsibility for maintaining security, and so long as the administered areas are exposed both from within and from without to terrorist influence and attacks, these concepts must prevail.[88]

These concepts have prevailed now for over twenty years. The potential for abuse of any powers that are exercised without effective review over this period of time is very great indeed.

Conclusion

Three legal justifications often relied on by Israel to justify its administrative and legislative actions taken in the Occupied Territories have been briefly examined above. In each case it has been argued that these terms have been stretched to, and eventually beyond, their limits, to justify an ever wider range of actions.

The duty to ensure public order and civil life came to be interpreted in such a way as to enable the occupier effectively to exercise the powers of a sovereign. The accompanying restriction that existing legislation must be respected unless absolutely prevented was found to allow changes in legislation if, in the view of the military commander, this is a convenient and preferable means of providing for the welfare of the population. Similarly, actions justified as being for the

---

[88] The Israel National Section of the International Commission of Jurists, *The Rule of Law*, xi.

benefit of the local population were found to encompass those benefiting the Jewish settlers in the Occupied Territory. Security, the factor most often heard by Palestinians, embraces not only those actions needed for the occupying forces' security, but also those which serve or are convenient for security, those which serve the security of the Jewish settlers in the Occupied Territories, and those of Israel's own long-term defence interests.

Three elements stand out in each of these interpretations:

1. The continuing expansion of the interpretation of the legal provisions to allow the authorities most freedom of action, often stretching the definition beyond its natural interpretation and beyond that endorsed by international legal opinion
2. The inclusion of the Jewish settler population, allowed and encouraged to settle in the Occupied Territories by the Israeli government, as part of the local population whose interest is to be served and protected in addition to, and often in preference to, that of the Palestinian population
3. The integration of the Occupied Territories with Israel itself and the colonization of those territories through these measures.

More seriously still, in a number of instances there is strong reason to doubt whether the justification given publicly and to the court is in fact the real purpose behind the action. For instance although the sequence of land acquisitions for settlement on the basis of security stopped abruptly after the failure of the *Elon Moreh* case, acquisition of land for settlements continued thereafter at the same rate, only using different justifications.[89] Meron Benvenisti concludes, in his *Survey of Israel's Policies*:

> The actions of the military administration have been aimed, under Likud, at making Israel's control permanent. To be sure, security and other purposes compatible with international law have been cited, and the facade of military administration has been maintained. But... [i]t seems that 'ensuring public order'..., interpreted by legal experts as ensuring to the greatest possible extent 'the good of the native population', has been interpreted by the Israeli authorities as referring to the minuscule 'Israeli settler public' and not to the Palestinian public, the original 'protected population'.[90]

Regrettably, the Israeli Supreme Court has done little to restrict the military government's actions to those authorized under the restrictive terms of the laws of war. Instead, it has legitimized actions that clearly go beyond the intention of the international community, expressed in humanitarian law: to ensure the security of the occupier's forces while

---

[89] See n. 66 above.
[90] Benvenisti, *A Survey of Israel's Policies*, 38–9.

protecting the rights of the civilian population living under occupation and preserving the identity of the occupied territories in preparation for the end of an occupation that is, by definition, temporary.

In the absence of a Protecting Power, the lives of those living in the West Bank and Gaza under Israeli occupation are entirely in the hands of the Israeli military government. A second generation is now growing up having experienced no other life. In a situation where power is so imbalanced, and conflict of interest is clear, treatment of the occupied population and territories must be based on well-defined and fair principles endorsed by international law for the peculiar circumstances of occupation of one land by an alien power.

Some of the provisions of international law governing belligerent occupation guiding an occupier's conduct do lack precision, being designed to cover a variety of situations. Yet this author believes that the breadth of the interpretation of these provisions by both the Israeli authorities and by Israel's High Court exceeds the natural meaning of these provisions and cannot be explained only by the lack of clarity in the law. In the absence of any representation in local or international fora, the population of the Israeli-occupied territories must look to the international community to provide greater protection to Palestinians living under occupation. In the longer term, the international community can take this opportunity to clarify and develop international law and to establish better mechanisms for supervising an occupier's administration of occupied territories, to ensure greater protection in the future to civilian populations subjected to occupation.

Part Two

Administration of Occupied Territories

7

The Administration of Occupied Territory in International Law

CHRISTOPHER GREENWOOD

Introduction

THE purpose of this paper is to examine the principles of international law applicable to the administration of occupied territory.[1] In the course of this inquiry, an attempt will be made to answer the following questions:

1. Does international law specify the administrative structure which must prevail in occupied territory?
2. To what extent is the occupying power free to depart from the administrative structure which existed in the territory prior to the occupation? In particular, may the occupying power create different geographical units of administration?
3. How far is it lawful for the occupying power to integrate the administration of the occupied territory with the administration of its own State?

A strong case has been made for the view that at least some of the rules of international law regarding occupied territories apply to a range of situations falling outside the scope of belligerent occupation,

---

[1] See G. von Glahn, *The Occupation of Enemy Territory* (Minneapolis, 1957), chs. 3, 8, 9, 10, and 20; M. Greenspan, *The Modern Law of Land Warfare* (Berkeley, 1959), 209–77; M. S. McDougal and F. P. Feliciano, *Law and Minimum World Public Order* (New Haven, Conn., 1961), ch. 7; A. D. McNair and A. D. Watts, *The Legal Effects of War*, 4th edn. (Cambridge, 1966), ch. 17; L. Oppenheim, *International Law: A Treatise*, ii: *Disputes, War and Neutrality*, ed. Lauterpacht, 6th edn. (London, 1944), ch. 12; J. Pictet, *Commentary on Geneva Convention IV of 1949*, trans. R. Griffin and C. W. Dumbleton (Geneva, 1958); J. Stone, *Legal Controls of International Conflict*, rev. edn. (New York, 1959), ch. 26; *Manual of Military Law*, iii: *The Law of War on Land* (UK War Office, 1958), ch. 12; Field Manual FM 27–10, *The Law of Land Warfare* (US Dept. of the Army, 1956), ch. 6; US Dept. of the Army, *International Law*, ii, 27–161–2 (1962), ch. 6; M. Whiteman, *Digest of International Law*, i (Washington DC, 1963), 946–96, and x (Washington, DC, 1968), 540–98; R. R. Baxter, 'The Duty of Obedience to the Belligerent Occupant', *BYIL* 27 (1950), 235; Y. Dinstein, 'The International Law of Belligerent Occupation and Human Rights', *IYHR* 8 (1978), 104, and F. Morgenstern, 'Validity of the Acts of the Belligerent Occupant', *BYIL* 28 (1951), 291.

in the normal sense of that term.[2] The applicability of the law in such cases, however, is seldom free of controversy and raises questions which fall outside the scope of the present discussion. This paper will therefore be concerned solely with the law applicable to what one may describe as the classic cases of belligerent occupation—that is to say, cases in which a State engaged in an international armed conflict gains control of territory which, prior to the conflict, was under the control of one of its adversaries.[3]

Israel's occupation of the territories captured in the 1967 war is the most important, as well as the most long-lived, instance of belligerent occupation since World War II.[4] Not surprisingly, therefore, it raises all the questions set out above. Reference will accordingly be made to various aspects of the Israeli occupation. Nevertheless, it is not the intention to embark upon a detailed analysis of the administration of the Israeli-occupied territories. That task has been undertaken elsewhere.[5] The focus of the present paper will be upon the law relating to the administration of occupied territory in general.

The principal treaties concerning the law of belligerent occupation say very little about the administration of occupied territory. Before addressing the questions outlined above, therefore, it will be necessary to consider the general principles of international law which constitute the legal framework of belligerent occupation. This task is attempted in Part I. Part II then seeks to draw some conclusions about the juridical nature of belligerent occupation. Parts III, IV, and V address the three questions set out in the opening paragraph. The study then concludes with discussions of the administration of justice in occupied territory and the special problems inherent in a prolonged occupation.

I. The Legal Framework of Belligerent Occupation

The basic principles of the law respecting the administration of occupied territory are to be found in the Regulations annexed to Hague Conven-

[2] See A. Roberts, 'What is Military Occupation?', *BYIL* 55 (1984), 249.

[3] Similarly, the case of post-surrender occupation, in which a State occupies the territory of an adversary which has surrendered unconditionally, will not be considered here. In 1945, the Allies took the view that they were not bound by the provisions of the Hague Regulations in their occupation of Germany after the German surrender.

[4] On the Israeli-occupied territories, see E. R. Cohen, *Human Rights in the Israeli-Occupied Territories 1967–1982* (Manchester, 1985); M. Shamgar, *Military Government in the Territories Administered by Israel (1967–1980)*, i: *The Legal Aspects* (Jerusalem, 1982), chs. 1, 4, 5, and 7; R. Shehadeh, *Occupier's Law* (Washington, DC, 1985); Israel National Section of the International Commission of Jurists, *The Rule of Law in the Areas Administered by Israel* (Tel Aviv, 1981); J. Kuttab and R. Shehadeh, *Civilian Administration in the West Bank* (Ramallah, 1982); and M. Benvenisti, *West Bank Data Base Project 1987 Report* (Jerusalem, 1987).

[5] See ch. 8.

tion No. IV Respecting the Laws and Customs of War on Land, 1907 ('the Hague Regulations'), and Geneva Convention No. IV Relative to the Protection of Civilian Persons in Time of War, 1949 ('the Fourth Geneva Convention'), supplemented in some respects by Protocol I, 1977.[6] It is these instruments which create the international legal framework within which an occupying power must operate. An occupying power may also be required to observe the provisions of various human rights agreements in occupied territory[7] but such agreements do not, in general, affect the basic framework for the administration of the territory but rather impose certain specific constraints on what that administration may do.

The principles set forth in the Hague Regulations and the Fourth Geneva Convention apply to any belligerent occupation, irrespective of whether it results from unlawful aggression or the legitimate use of force in self-defence. Although it has occasionally been suggested that a State which invaded territory in violation of international law did not acquire the rights of a belligerent occupant under international law,[8] this view was emphatically rejected in *United States v. List*, one of the leading war crimes trials held after World War II, in which the United States Military Tribunal pointed out that

> International Law makes no distinction between a lawful and an unlawful occupant in dealing with the respective duties of occupant and population in occupied territory... Whether the invasion was lawful or criminal is not an important factor in the consideration of this subject.[9]

This statement, which is no more than an application of the fundamental principle that the law of armed conflict applies with equal force to both sides in a conflict, has generally been followed even after the adoption of the United Nations Charter.[10]

The principles contained in the Hague Regulations and the Fourth Geneva Convention are not concerned with the status of the territory prior to its occupation, so that their application by an occupant is without prejudice to any underlying dispute concerning sovereignty over the territory. Thus, the law of belligerent occupation is applicable whenever one State occupies, in the course of an armed conflict, territory which was previously under the control of a hostile party to that conflict, irrespective of whether the displaced power was the

---

[6] For full details of these instruments, see Ch. 1; for texts see A. Roberts and R. Guelff, *Documents on the Laws of War*, 2nd edn. (Oxford, 1989), 43, 271, and 387 respectively.

[7] See the decision of the European Commission on Human Rights in *Cyprus v. Turkey* (Appln. No. 8007/77) 62 ILR 4 at 74 and 86. See also Chs. 1, 9, and 16 in this volume.

[8] See, e.g., the statements made by the PLO, quoted in Ch. 1, text at no. 70.

[9] 15 Ann. Dig. 632 at 637; XI *Trials of War Criminals* 1230 at 1247.

[10] See C. Greenwood, 'The Relationship between *Ius ad Bellum* and *Ius in Bello*', *Rev. Int'l. Studies* 9(4) (1983), 221.

lawful sovereign in that territory. This principle finds a measure of expression in Article 4 of Protocol I and is widely accepted in theory, though not always in practice. Israel has declined to accept the *de jure* applicability of the Fourth Geneva Convention to its occupation of the West Bank and the Gaza Strip, because of the doubtful status of those territories prior to 1967, although it has undertaken to apply the humanitarian provisions of the Convention and acknowledges that it is, in any event, bound by the principles set forth in the Hague Regulations.[11] The International Committee of the Red Cross,[12] and the international community as a whole,[13] have taken the position that the Convention is applicable *de jure* and that position is shared by the present writer. It should, however, be pointed out that other States have declined to apply any of the provisions of the Hague Regulations or the Fourth Geneva Convention in cases where they have occupied territory over which they claimed sovereignty.[14]

The starting point for any discussion must inevitably be Article 43 of the Hague Regulations, which provides:

> The authority of the legitimate power having in fact passed into the hands of the occupant, the latter shall take all the measures in his power to restore and ensure, as far as possible, public order and safety, while respecting, unless absolutely prevented, the laws in force in the country.

From this text may be deduced the four principles which lay down the international legal framework for the government of occupied territory.

1. The occupant acquires temporary authority, not sovereignty, over the occupied territory.

The emphasis in Article 43 on the *de facto* nature of the occupant's authority and the requirement of respect for the law already in force in the occupied territory reflect the principle, already clearly established by the time the Hague Regulations were adopted, that the military occupation of territory during a war did not confer sovereignty upon the occupying power.[15] Occupation was seen as a temporary state of affairs and any change in the status of the territory had to wait until the conclusion of a treaty of peace or the complete subjugation of the

---

[11] For a discussion of Israel's position, see Shamgar, *Military Government*, 31–43. More critical discussion may be found in Cohen, *Human Rights in the Israeli-Occupied Territories*, 43–56; Dinstein, 'The International Law of Belligerent Occupation and Human Rights', 104; and Roberts, 'What is Military Occupation?', 249; and in other chapters in this volume.

[12] See the statements to this effect in successive issues of the *Annual Report of the ICRC*.

[13] See, e.g., UNGA Res. 35/122A, 11 Dec. 1980.

[14] See text at n. 55 in Adam Roberts' chapter in this volume for reference to several such instances.

[15] Oppenheim, *International Law*, 432–4; *British Manual*, para. 510; *US Field Manual*, para. 358.

State which had formerly exercised sovereignty in the territory. Several consequences flow from this principle.

First, even in the days when conquest could confer a valid title to territory in international law,[16] the annexation of occupied territory before the end of the conflict was prohibited. At Nuremberg the International Military Tribunal held that even where the State whose territory was occupied had been completely overwhelmed, annexation remained unlawful and did not transfer title so long as the occupying power remained at war with the allies of the State concerned.[17]

Secondly, a purported annexation of occupied territory by the occupying power is ineffective to alter the status of the territory or its inhabitants, who remain subject to the law on belligerent occupation. This principle, which was also asserted by the International Military Tribunal, was reaffirmed in Article 47 of the Fourth Geneva Convention, which makes clear that a purported annexation by the occupying power has no effect upon the rights conferred by the Convention on the inhabitants of the territory.

Thirdly, the fact that a belligerent occupant does not acquire sovereignty and has a duty under Article 43 of the Hague Regulations to respect the laws in force in the occupied territory makes any change introduced by the occupant in the constitution or institutions of the occupied territory of doubtful legality. Certainly, no such changes can relieve the occupying power of its obligations under the Hague Regulations or the Fourth Geneva Convention. Quite apart from that, however, an attempt by an occupying power to effect permanent changes in the constitution of occupied territory may, in itself, involve a violation of the Hague Regulations. Article 43, it has been suggested, 'protects the separate existence of the State, its institutions, and its laws'.[18] An occupant is entitled to suspend the operation of certain constitutional guarantees and the functioning of the political organs of the constitution (at least at the level of central government) for the duration of the occupation. Permanent changes in the constitution of the occupied territory, on the other hand, are probably lawful only if they are necessary to enable the full implementation of the Hague Regulations and the Fourth Geneva Convention or other rules of international law.[19]

---

[16] Since 1945, the use of force does not give title to territory; see UNSC Res. 242 and the Declaration on Principles of International Law Concerning Friendly Relations and Cooperation among States 1970.
[17] Cmd. 6964, 65. See also discussion in Ch. 5.
[18] Pictet, *Commentary*, 273.
[19] Thus, the allied powers maintained, when they occupied parts of Germany towards the end of World War II, that they were not required to respect the racially discriminatory laws and institutions created by the Nazis. See Oppenheim, *International Law*, 446–7.

2. The occupying power is permitted and required to administer the occupied territory.
International law undoubtedly permits a State which captures territory from an enemy in the course of an armed conflict to administer that territory and thus accepts that the occupant has the powers necessary to provide for the government of the territory. Discussion of belligerent occupation tends to concentrate upon whether an occupant has exceeded those powers in its administration of the territory. It is important, however, not to overlook the fact that international law actually imposes upon an occupant a duty to provide for the government of the occupied territory. Article 43 of the Hague Regulations requires the occupant to 'take all the measures in his power to restore, and ensure, as far as possible, public order and safety'. As the United States Military Tribunal put it in *United States v. List*:

> The status of an occupant of the territory of the enemy having been achieved, international law places the responsibility upon the commanding general of preserving order, punishing crime, and protecting lives and property within the occupied territory. His power in accomplishing these ends is as great as his responsibility. But he is definitely limited by recognized rules of international law . . . [20]

The English text of Article 43 suggests that this duty is limited to the restoration of a minimum level of law and order. However, the phrase 'public order and safety' is an inadequate translation of *'l'ordre et la vie publics'*, the term used in the French text, which is the only authentic text of the Hague Regulations. A duty to restore *'l'ordre et la vie publics'* reaches far beyond the mere restoration of public order and extends to the conduct of 'the whole social, commercial and economic life of the country'.[21] The occupant is thus under a duty to prevent economic collapse as well as a breakdown of law and order. This duty probably extends to requiring the occupant to ensure that there is a functioning currency in the occupied territory and that essential services are maintained.

The Fourth Geneva Convention imposes a number of specific obligations upon the occupying power. Thus, the occupation administration has a responsibility for:

(a) the provision of education (Article 50);
(b) the supply of foodstuffs and medical supplies to the civilian population (Article 55);
(c) the maintenance of medical and hospital facilities (Article 56);

---

[20] XI *Trials of War Criminals* 1230 at 1244–5.
[21] *Grahame v. Director of Prosecutions* 14 Ann. Dig. 228 at 232. See also the decision of the Supreme Court of Israel in HC 393/82 *A Teachers' Housing Cooperative Society v. The Military Commander of the Judea and Samaria Region*, noted in *IYHR* 14 (1984), 301.

(d) the distribution of books and articles required for religious needs (Article 58(2)); and

(e) the facilitation of relief efforts where necessary (Articles 59–62).

Other duties are implicit in the provisions of the Fourth Geneva Convention.

In addition to these duties, the occupying power is free to take such measures as are necessary for the protection of its armed forces and administration and the preservation of its military position, subject to the safeguards contained in the Hague Regulations and the Fourth Geneva Convention. In addition to the security measures which may obviously be introduced, such as prohibiting the possession of firearms or other weapons by the civilian population, the occupant may impose restrictions upon, or take control of, the media, means of communication and transport facilities.[22]

3. The occupant has the duty, unless absolutely prevented, to respect the existing law.

Article 43 of the Hague Regulations requires the occupying power to respect the laws in force in the occupied territory unless he is 'absolutely prevented' from doing so. Similarly, Article 64(1) of the Fourth Geneva Convention provides that

> The penal laws of the occupied territory shall remain in force, with the exception that they may be repealed or suspended by the Occupying Power in cases where they constitute a threat to its security or an obstacle to the application of the present Convention.

These two provisions show that international law does not recognize a general legislative competence in the belligerent occupant. Changes in the law of the territory will be contrary to international law unless they are required for the legitimate needs of the occupation.

Nevertheless, the exceptions to the general duty of respect for the existing law are extensive. The occupying power is entitled to suspend or repeal existing laws or to introduce new laws where this is necessary for the security of its armed forces and administration.[23] It may also make changes in order to discharge its duties under the Fourth Geneva Convention and Article 43 of the Hague Regulations. Since, as we have seen, these duties are extensive, the corresponding legislative powers are also far-reaching.

In addition, the British Manual of Military Law and the United States Field Manual both envisage that laws relating to normal political life, such as those concerned with freedom of the press, free association, etc., are suspended for the duration of the occupation, since belligerent

---

[22] *British Manual*, paras. 532–4; *US Field Manual*, paras. 377–8.
[23] *British Manual*, para. 523; *US Field Manual*, paras. 369–71.

occupation is a military, rather than a normal political, regime.[24] Insofar as a belligerent occupant is bound to observe the provisions of a human rights agreement in the occupied territory, such agreements generally include provision for derogation in times of war or national emergency which will enable the occupying power to suspend the operation of the normal political process during the occupation.[25]

A further limitation is that the members of the occupant's armed forces and occupation administration, together with other nationals of the occupant who accompany the occupying forces, are not normally subject to the jurisdiction of the local courts. In criminal matters they will be subject to the military law of the occupying power, while in civil matters which affect them alone, such as a contract dispute between members of the occupying forces, they will generally be subject to the law in force in the occupying power's own territory.[26] Ordinary civilian nationals of the occupying power, not connected with the armed forces or the occupation administration, who visit the occupied territory, however, are subject to the local law as lawfully modified by the occupying power.[27]

The duty of respect for the law already in force in the occupied territory does not extend to laws enacted by the displaced power after the occupation has begun. Thus, if a State which has been displaced from part of its territory during an armed conflict adopts changes in its legal system, those changes are not applicable in the occupied territory. Although the displaced sovereign retains sovereignty over the occupied territory, he cannot exercise that sovereignty within the occupied territory for the duration of the occupation. Nevertheless, it is widely assumed that the occupying power is free, if it wishes, to choose to give effect to changes enacted by the displaced power. This was the approach taken in the Schio massacre incident, in which some Italian nationals were convicted of murdering fascist prisoners held in a part of Italy which was under military occupation by the allies during World War II. Under the law in force in the occupied parts of Italy, the defendants were liable to the death penalty. After the commencement of the occupation, however, the Italian Government had abolished the death penalty. The occupation authorities commuted the defendants' sentences to life imprisonment on the ground that, although the aboli-

---

[24] *British Manual*, para. 519; *US Field Manual*, para. 371. A similar view is expressed by von Glahn, *Occupation*, 98, and Greenspan, *The Modern Law of Land Warfare*, 223.

[25] See, e.g., the International Covenant on Civil and Political Rights of 1966, Art. 4, and the European Convention on Human Rights of 1951, Art. 15. Those provisions of human rights treaties from which no derogation is permitted protect basic humanitarian standards rather than rights such as freedom of speech or assembly.

[26] *British Manual*, para. 522; *US Field Manual*, para. 374.

[27] Dinstein, 'The International Law of Belligerent Occupation and Human Rights', 115–16. See also Ch. 4 in this volume, for Israel's practice in this regard.

tion of the death penalty was effective only in the unoccupied parts of Italy, it was appropriate to take note of it in the present case.[28]

Finally, it must be remembered that the duty of respect for the existing law does not mean that an occupying power is required to take advantage of the full range of powers which might be available to the government under the law in force prior to the occupation. An occupying power cannot rely upon the fact that national law already in force in the occupied territory permits the imposition of a particular sanction in order to justify taking action which is contrary to a provision of the Hague Regulations or the Fourth Geneva Convention. For example, if the law in force in the West Bank prior to 1967 permitted the deportation of residents of the West Bank for activities detrimental to State security, that would not justify Israel, as the occupying power, in deporting a protected person contrary to Article 49 of the Fourth Geneva Convention.[29] Even where the conduct in question would not involve a violation of one of the specific provisions of international law, the duty of respect for the existing law does not make it mandatory for the occupying power to impose a penalty, or exercise a power, which was discretionary under the local law, so that Israel's decision not to impose the death penalty for offences committed in the West Bank, even where the local law and international law permitted its imposition, is entirely lawful.

4. The powers of the occupant are constrained by the specific duties and prohibitions imposed by international law.

It has already been shown that international law requires a belligerent occupant to establish an administration which discharges at least some of the functions of government. It must also be noted that the Fourth Geneva Convention and, to a lesser extent, the Hague Regulations impose a number of specific limitations upon the occupant, the principal purpose of which is to provide a minimum level of humanitarian protection for the population of the occupied territory. It would be beyond the purpose of this paper to discuss in detail these provisions, since they tend to relate to the way in which an occupying power's administration behaves, rather than the structure of the administration itself.

---

[28] Whiteman, *Digest of International Law*, i, 966; E. Stein, 'Application of the Law of the Absent Sovereign in Territory under Belligerent Occupation: The Schio Massacre', *Mich. Law Rev.* 46(3) (1948), 341.

[29] For discussion of the legality of deportation in the territories occupied by Israel, see Cohen, *Human Rights in the Israeli-Occupied Territories*, 104–11; see also Ch. 1 in this volume. Israel has argued that Art. 49 does not prohibit the expulsion of troublesome individuals under the power existing under pre-1967 Jordanian law and this argument was apparently accepted by the Supreme Court of Israel in HC 97/79 *Abu Awad v. Commander of the Judea and Samaria Region*, *IYHR* 9 (1979), 343. It is difficult, however, to reconcile that conclusion with the express wording of Art. 49(1), cited in ch. 1 above.

Neither the Fourth Geneva Convention nor the Hague Regulations seeks to ensure anything approaching the level of human rights protection which treaties such as the International Covenant on Civil and Political Rights require. The emphasis is rather upon the preservation of minimum humanitarian standards, through the prohibition of reprisals and collective punishments against the civilian population of the occupied territory, hostage-taking, torture, inhuman and degrading treatment, deportation, slave labour, wholesale seizure of property, and compulsion to perform work of military value. Both the Hague Regulations and the Fourth Geneva Convention also forbid the exploitation of the economy of the occupied territory for the benefit of the occupant's own economy. In exercising its power to determine such matters as exchange rates, the amount of money in circulation in the occupied territory, and the terms and conditions of trade, the occupying power must seek to provide for the good economic government of the occupied territory and not merely feather its own nest.[30]

III. The Juridical Nature of Belligerent Occupation

The principles discussed in the preceding section enable us to draw a number of conclusions about the juridical nature of belligerent occupation. The first such conclusion is that occupation, like war itself, is a fact recognized and regulated by international law, not an institution created by it.[31] Unlike the administering authority in a mandated or trust territory, the belligerent occupant derives its authority not from international law but from the successful exercise of military power. International law imposes certain limitations upon the occupying power's exercise of that authority and requires certain positive acts on the part of the occupying power. In doing so, however, it is seeking to impose a degree of regulation upon a situation which in many cases will have been created in violation of international law and which, in any event, falls short of the ideal to which the international legal system aspires.

The occupying power does not, therefore, administer occupied territory as a trustee, either for the population or for the displaced power. International law makes various demands of the occupant for the benefit of the population and the displaced power. These demands

---

[30] See the judgment of the Int. Mil. Trib., Cmd. 6964 at 53–5, and the judgment of the US Mil. Trib. in *In re Krupp*, 15 Ann. Dig. 620. The Supreme Court of Israel has also accepted the principle that an occupant may not use its administration in occupied territory to promote the economic or social interests of its own State (see the *Teachers' Housing Cooperative* case, n. 21 above). For a review of Israel's practice in the West Bank, see Chs. 12 and 13 in this volume.

[31] Oppenheim, *International Law*, 202.

may mean that an occupant is sometimes required to perform certain functions akin to those of a trustee. For example, in exercising its power to control the economic life of the territory, the occupant must act in the interests of the territory. While it may take account of the needs of the occupation, it may not exploit the economy of the territory in order to benefit the economy of its own State.[32] To see the occupation as a whole as a form of trusteeship, however, is to overlook the fundamental fact that the basis of the occupant's position in the occupied territory is the successful use of force, whereas trusteeship is an institution founded upon law. Moreover, the duties imposed by the law of belligerent occupation are far more rudimentary than those of any concept of trusteeship. The law on belligerent occupation endeavors to strike a balance between the military interests of the occupant, the humanitarian protection of the population, and the preservation, pending a final settlement, of certain interests of the displaced power, rather than requiring the occupant to act as a disinterested administrator for the benefit of others.

The vexed question of whether international law imposes upon the population of occupied territory a duty to obey the lawful orders of the occupant needs to be considered in this light.[33] Although international law does not prohibit a belligerent occupant from imposing its will, subject to the limitations which we have discussed, upon the population of occupied territory, that is not the same thing as saying that international law authorizes the imposition of that will. The occupant's power to command obedience is derived not from law but from its own superior force and it is thus force, not law, which is the basis of the relationship between the occupying power and the population of the occupied territory. In jurisprudential terms, the occupant has a liberty to impose certain measures upon the occupied territory and the exercise of that liberty entails no violation of international law. But the occupant does not have a claim, correlative to a duty of obedience on the part of the population, to take measures for the enhancement of its position in the territory. Only where the occupant performs acts which international law actually requires it to perform, such as the distribution of foodstuffs to the population, is it arguable that there is a duty of obedience derived from international law.

It is true that both the British Manual of Military Law and the United States Field Manual speak of a duty of obedience owed to the occupying power.[34] Both publications are, however, over thirty years old and

---

[32] See the discussion in the *Teachers' Housing Cooperative* case, HC 393/82, noted in *IYHR* 14 (1984), 301.

[33] See Baxter, 'The Duty of Obedience to the Belligerent Occupant', 235, and Stone, *Legal Controls of International Conflict*, 723 ff.

[34] *British Manual*, para. 544; *US Field Manual*, para. 432. Note that the British Manual is couched in more ambiguous terms on this point than is its US counterpart.

it is doubtful whether either State would include such a statement in a contemporary publication. It is suggested that the relationship between the population and the occupying power is more accurately summed up in De Mulinen's *Handbook on the Law of War for Armed Forces*, published by the International Committee of the Red Cross, which states that

> The law of war requires a minimum cooperation between the Occupying Power and the inhabitants of the occupied territory.[35]

That degree of co-operation, however, is a factual necessity if the law is to work effectively; it is not rooted in an international law duty of obedience to the occupant.

The fact that the relationship between the population and the occupant has its roots in military power rather than international law, even though international law seeks to regulate certain aspects of that relationship, also helps to explain the limited objectives of international law in this context. Since there is no normal relationship of government and governed in occupied territory, the law of armed conflict does not function here in the way that the law of human rights functions in imposing duties upon States with regard to their own citizens in times of peace. In particular, there is no requirement that the occupant further the creation of a political process, let alone a democratic society, in the occupied territory. In its regulation of belligerent occupation, international law concentrates on the preservation of certain basic humanitarian values. Its aim is not to create a liberal democracy in occupied territory but to ensure that an inevitably authoritarian regime at least respects the most elementary humanitarian imperatives. In addition, since belligerent occupation is conceived as a temporary state of affairs, the law seeks to preclude the imposition of measures which will pre-empt the final disposition of the territory at the conclusion of the conflict.

It is in the light of these features of the framework and juridical nature of belligerent occupation that we can now turn to consider some of the specific questions about the administration of occupied territory which were raised in the opening section.

III. Does International Law Specify the Administrative Structure which must Prevail in Occupied Territories?

International law does not specify the administrative structure which must prevail in occupied territory in the sense of containing a 'blue-

---

[35] F. De Mulinen, *Handbook on the Law of War for Armed Forces* (Geneva, 1987), para. 806.

print' for occupation government. The treaties on the law of armed conflict contain no express provisions regarding the structure of the administration. It is clear, therefore, that an occupying power enjoys a considerable freedom to choose the administrative structure which it will adopt. Any limitations upon that freedom are to be found not in express treaty provisions but in the general principles considered in the two previous sections, from which it is possible to make certain deductions about the form which an occupation administration must take.

It appears that whatever the occupying power chooses to call its administration, it will be a military government in all essential respects. In the words of the United States Field Manual,

It is immaterial whether the government over an enemy's territory consists in a military or civil or mixed administration. Its character is the same and the source of its authority the same. It is a government imposed by force, and the legality of its acts is determined by the law of war.[36]

A number of statements made by Israeli spokesmen on the establishment of the civil administration in the West Bank and Gaza in 1981 make the same point.[37] Similarly, it makes no difference that civilian personnel are brought in to staff the government or that nationals of the occupied territory are recruited to work in the administration.

The term 'military government' is not a term of art and reveals little about the administrative structure which an occupant may adopt, other than that it is inevitably part of the military command structure in the occupied territories. It is suggested, however, that the administrative structure which is adopted must comply with certain general principles laid down in international law.

1. The administrative structure adopted must be compatible with the principle that a belligerent occupant acquires only temporary authority over occupied territory and is not permitted to annex that territory. This requirement is examined in more detail in Part V.

2. The occupying power must adopt an administrative structure which enables it effectively to discharge its responsibility under Article 43 of the Hague Regulations to provide government for the territory, as well as its specific duties under the Fourth Geneva Convention. Thus, the duty to provide for the education of children imposed by Article 50 of the Fourth Geneva Convention requires that some part of the administration be allocated the responsibility for education.

3. The administration must not take a form which is likely to entail

---

[36] *US Field Manual*, para. 368. See also *British Manual*, para. 518 and Dinstein, 'The International Law of Belligerent Occupation and Human Rights', 109.

[37] See, e.g., J. Singer, 'The Establishment of a Civil Administration in the Areas Administered by Israel', *IYHR* 12 (1982), 259.

the violation of any of the specific requirements of international law regarding occupations, including the duty to respect the existing law.[38]

In other respects the occupying power remains free to choose the administrative structure which best suits its needs and is entitled to take into account its own military and administrative convenience in determining the shape of that administration. As Professor Mossner has put it:

> The occupying power has the right to choose the organizational structure which seems best to fit its needs. According to international law both military and civilian governments in occupied territories derive their rights and duties from the occupying power, which in turn is based on the military authority within the relevant territory. For that reason military government is sometimes defined as the exercise of supreme power in an occupied territory by the occupying power irrespective of whether *in concreto* it is exercised through military or civilian persons.[39]

In particular, there is no general requirement in international law that the administrative structure adopted by an occupant should include provision for any kind of democratic participation. An occupying power may have sound political or military reasons for wishing to consult the local population and by doing so may make it easier to defend changes in the law as being for the benefit of the population. Moreover, as will be seen in Part IV, where there was a democratic structure already in existence in the territory, the occupant may be under an obligation to retain part of it, as long as it does not attempt to undermine the occupant's position. There is, however, no general principle that an occupation administration must operate in a democratic way and the general assumption appears to be that it will not do so.

IV. To what extent is the occupying power free to depart from the administrative structure which existed in the territory prior to the occupation?

Since international law does not lay down a blueprint for the administration of occupied territory, the next question which must be asked concerns the relationship between the occupation administration and the administrative structure which existed in the occupied territory prior to the occupation. To what extent is the occupying power free to

---

[38] See Part IV.
[39] J. M. Mossner, 'Military Government' in R. Bernhardt (ed.) *Encyclopaedia of International Law* (Amsterdam, 1982), iii, 270.

depart from the existing administrative structure? In particular, may the occupying power create new geographical units of administration or is it required to follow the boundaries of the existing administrative units?

The answer to these questions turns to a large extent upon the scope of the duty of respect for the existing law under Article 43 of the Hague Regulations. Does this duty extend to requiring the occupant to retain the existing administrative and legislative institutions? Unfortunately, the textbooks and military manuals give no clear answer. On the one hand, several authoritative textbooks suggest that the occupying power must administer the territory in accordance with 'the existing rules of administration'[40] and that 'the minimum alteration should be made to the existing administration'.[41] On the other hand, the *British Manual of Military Law* and the *United States Field Manual* appear to assume that the existing administration goes into abeyance unless the occupant chooses to make use of it.[42]

Although there is undoubtedly some uncertainty about the relationship between the occupying power and the existing administrative structure, the law is in fact somewhat clearer than these apparently contradictory statements may suggest. The commencement of occupation means that legislative and executive power in the occupied territory becomes vested *de facto* in the occupant. The existing legislative and administrative institutions cannot, therefore, function independently of the occupying power. According to the *British Manual of Military Law*:

The legislative, executive, and administrative functions of the national government, whether of a general, provincial, or local character, cease when military occupation commences.[43]

That does not mean that the existing institutions will necessarily cease to function at all. Although legislative power, at least at the level of primary legislation, will probably be retained by the military commander of the occupying forces or someone appointed by him, the occupant will probably wish to make use of the existing administrative institutions in order to govern the territory. Nevertheless, if the existing administrative institutions are retained, they will derive their authority from the occupant.

In addition, the occupying power is not obliged to retain the existing officials. Article 54(2) of the Fourth Geneva Convention expressly rec-

---

[40] Oppenheim, *International Law*, 437.
[41] G. I. A. D. Draper, *The Red Cross Conventions* (London, 1958), 39; McNair and Watts, *The Legal Effects of War*, 369.
[42] *British Manual*, para. 516; *US Field Manual*, para. 367.
[43] *British Manual*, para. 516.

ognizes the right of the occupant to remove public officials from their posts, a right which the official ICRC Commentary on the Convention describes as 'a right of very long standing which the occupation authorities may exercise in regard to any official or judge for reasons of their own'.[44] The occupying power may choose to retain the existing officials and, at least in the case of the lower administrative officials, will probably do so, but it is not obliged to retain them. Conversely, the existing officials are not obliged to work for the occupying power. Article 54(1) of the Convention prohibits the imposition of sanctions against officials who decline to continue in office. The only partial exception to this rule is that the occupant may, in certain circumstances, requisition the services of essential officials under Article 51. If the occupant chooses to retain existing officials, it is forbidden to alter their status in any way.

The question remains, however, whether the occupant is required to work through the existing administrative structure, even though it may replace the members of the administration with its own nominees if it wishes, or whether, in contrast, it is entitled to adopt an entirely new administrative structure. The answer, it is suggested, will depend on the facts of each case. The extent of which there is an existing administrative structure capable of being used will vary enormously from one occupation to the next. Two questions appear to be of cardinal importance: (1) Is there an administrative structure in the territory which is capable of being used by the occupying power? (2) If so, is that structure sufficient to enable the occupant to discharge its duty to provide government for the territory and to meet the legitimate needs of its armed forces?

Where there is no functioning administrative structure or that structure is not capable of providing an adequate government in the unusual circumstances of belligerent occupation, the occupant is entitled to create such new administrative bodies as are necessary. Where, however, the occupant finds a functioning administrative structure already in place, there is a presumption that that structure will be retained even if some or all of the officials are removed from their posts. Departures from the existing structure will be justified only where they are necessary to enable the occupant to meet the needs of its armed forces or to discharge its governmental duties under the Hague Regulations and the Fourth Geneva Convention.[45]

Although the factual situation will vary greatly from one occupation to another, it is likely that the need to supersede the existing administration will diminish the further down the administrative hierarchy one

---

[44] Pictet, *Commentary*, 308; Oppenheim, *International Law*, 445.
[45] See *Kemeny v. Yugoslav State*, 4 Ann. Dig. 549.

progresses. Thus, local government bodies, such as municipal and village councils, are both more likely to have remained in place and less likely to operate in a way which undermines the position of the occupant or makes it necessary for the occupant to intervene in the name of good government. For that reason, the presumption in favour of retaining the existing administrative structure is particularly strong with regard to the smaller units of local administration.

For the same reasons, it has sometimes been suggested that the occupant's power to suspend elections and political activity in occupied territory[46] does not automatically extend to elections for municipal and other local authorities. Thus, von Glahn has argued that local elected authorities should be allowed to continue to operate and elections should continue to be held unless they threaten the occupant's security by becoming a focal point for opposition to its rule.[47] This approach appears to have been adopted by the Israeli Supreme Court in *'Amar et al. v. Minister of Defence*, in which the Court held that 'the Occupying State is prevented from denying the right of the indigenous population to vote for its local authorities so long as the latter perform purely municipal functions'.[48] The Court upheld orders suspending elections and dissolving a municipal council not on the basis of a general and automatic right on the part of the occupant but on the ground that the Court accepted that there was good reason to believe that elections would be used to undermine the occupant's position.

The principles outlined in the preceding paragraphs allow the occupant considerable discretion to vary the existing administrative structure. It must, however, be borne in mind that the temporary nature of the occupant's authority in the occupied territory means that it will not be lawful for an occupant to attempt to make permanent changes in the government of occupied territory. Existing administrative and legislative structures and the political process may be suspended for the duration of the occupation but an occupant will exceed its powers if it attempts, for example, to create a new State, to change a monarchy into a republic or a federal into a unitary government. An occupant may, therefore, suspend or bypass the existing administrative structure where there is a legitimate necessity of the kind discussed in the preceding paragraph but any attempt at effecting permanent reform or change in that structure will be unlawful.[49]

The same principles apply to the question of how far the occupying

---

[46] As to which, see *British Manual*, para. 519; *US Field Manual*, para. 371; Greenspan, *The Modern Law of Land Warfare*, 223.
[47] *Occupation*, 98.
[48] HC 774/83; noted in *IYHR* 15 (1985), 274.
[49] Oppenheim, *International Law*, 437; von Glahn, *Occupation*, 96; Stone, *Legal Controls of International Conflict*, 698.

power may depart from the geographical units of administration already existing in occupied territory. An occupying power is not invariably bound to follow the administrative and political sub-divisions already in existence. In the first place, those boundaries may not coincide with the boundaries of the occupied territory. Secondly, military considerations such as proximity of areas to a combat zone, troop concentrations and the like, as well as the displacement of refugees from an area of danger, may mean that the existing administrative units lose much of their meaning as population and the need for government services become concentrated in different areas. While these considerations are more likely to be relevant to occupation during active hostilities, a prolonged occupation, such as that in the Middle East, may raise similar problems. Population shift over a period of years may mean that the previous administrative boundaries become a positive hindrance to the proper administration of the occupied territory.

The occupant is therefore entitled to depart from the existing administrative units where military needs require, for example by dividing the territory into combat and rear zones the boundaries of which would be dictated by the military position rather than the administrative boundaries previously in operation. In addition, the occupying power's responsibility for the government of the territory may justify departures from the existing administrative boundaries, where, for example, a shift of population to a city has led to large-scale urban growth outside the pre-occupation limits of the city. On the other hand, there appears to be agreement that a new division of the territory for purely *political* purposes is contrary to Article 43 of the Hague Regulations.[50]

The point may be illustrated by a comparison between the German division of occupied Belgium into two separate provinces in 1917 and the British division of occupied Libya in 1942. Belgium was divided into two provinces largely along linguistic lines, one province being predominantly Flemish and the other Walloon. This measure seems to have been adopted in the hope of dividing the Flemish population from the rest of the country and, perhaps, of setting up a pro-German satellite regime in the Flemish province. There was no suggestion that the administrative or military considerations required the introduction of such a change.[51] By contrast, the division of Libya into two districts, Cyrenaica and Tripolitania, was based upon the legitimate consideration that the existing Italian administration had remained more or less in place in Tripolitania whereas in Cyrenaica the Italian authorities had

---

[50] Oppenheim, *International Law*, 437; von Glahn, *Occupation*, 96.
[51] J. W. Garner, *International Law and the World War* (London, 1920), II, 78 ff.

fled in the face of the allied advance leaving 'a complete administrative void'.[52]

These principles are, however, easier to state than they are to apply. The German division of Belgium was defended by the German authorities as a measure which was needed to deal with unrest amongst the Flemish population.[53] The British measures in Libya were also explained in part on the ground that 'there is no love lost between the Arab of Tripolitania and the Arab of Cyrenaica'.[54] The extension of a municipality's administration to take in new suburbs which have grown up around the town is seldom uncontroversial even in a democratic State, since it may well have tax implications for residents and affect the political balance in the municipality. If an occupying power decides to go ahead with elections at any level, the retention, especially in a prolonged occupation, of the existing ward or constituency boundaries may produce grossly unrepresentative results. Yet the redefinition of boundaries has tended to be one of the most controversial issues in any democracy. How much more controversial would it be if carried out by an occupying power? Above all, since occupants are understandably reticent about their military needs and are likely to run administrations which are not noticeable for an attachment to 'open government', it may be extremely difficult to determine whether changes in the administrative structure are justified.[55]

Nevertheless, the fact that the principles we have considered are difficult to apply does not remove their validity. They continue to show that a belligerent occupant does not enjoy an unlimited freedom in international law to alter the administrative structure of occupied territory.

V. How Far is it Lawful for the Occupying Power to Integrate the Administration of the Occupied Territory with the Administration of its own State?

It has already been seen that one of the cardinal principles on which the law of belligerent occupation is based is that the occupant does not

---

[52] G. T. Watts, 'The British Military Administration of Cyrenaica, 1942–1949', *Trans. of the Grotius Soc.* 37 (1951), 69.
[53] Oppenheim, *International Law*, 437.
[54] Watts, 'The British Military Administration of Cyrenaica', 72.
[55] For a decision of the Israeli Supreme Court that a proposed change in the administration of public utilities in the West Bank was unnecessary, see HC 351/80 *Jerusalem District Electricity Company v. Minister of Energy and Planning et al.*, noted in *IYHR* 11 (1981), 354.

acquire sovereignty over the occupied territory and is forbidden to annex it during the armed conflict. It follows from this prohibition of annexation and the essentially temporary nature of the occupant's authority that the occupying power may not extend its own administration to the occupied territory, for to administer the occupied territory as part of the occupant's own State is annexation in all but name.[56] The 1981 Israeli law extending 'the law, jurisdiction and administration' of the State of Israel to the Golan Heights was therefore a violation of Israel's duties as the occupying power and was condemned as such by the United Nations Security Council in Resolution 497.[57] The occupying power is required to administer the occupied territory as a separate entity, distinct from its own territory.[58]

More problematic is the case in which the administration of the occupied territory remains separate but is closely modelled upon the administrative structure existing in the occupant's own State. On the one hand, if it is necessary for the occupant to create a new administrative structure in the occupied territory in order to discharge its duties to provide government, there is obvious sense in the occupant taking its own home administration as the model. That is the administrative structure with which the occupying power and those of its nationals who will staff the higher ranks of the administration are most familiar. This factor is of particular importance where civilians are employed in the administration, since they are likely to be seconded from the occupant's civil service. Moreover, the administrative structure which is employed in the occupying power's own territory is presumably the structure which that power considers to be best suited to efficient government, since it is the structure which it employs to ensure '*l'ordre et la vie publics*' in its own territory.

On the other hand, there is inevitable scope for abuse in cases where the administration of the occupied territory is modelled upon the administration of the occupant's own State. A close identity between the two may lead to 'creeping annexation', with officials in the various departments of the occupation administration reporting to and taking instructions from the corresponding departments in the home administration, rather than regarding themselves as answerable to the commander of the occupying forces or an administrator appointed by him. In those circumstances, the danger is that an official in the occupation administration responsible for, for example, economic matters will act

---

[56] McNair and Watts, *The Legal Effects of War*, 369.
[57] For the text of the Knesset Law, see *ILM* 21 (1982), 163; the text of UNSC Res. 497 appears at 214.
[58] The judgment of the Israeli Supreme Court in the *Teachers' Housing Cooperative* case, HC 393/82, noted in *IYHR* 14 (1984), 301, takes this point for granted. The case concerned the administration of the West Bank.

in the interests of the economy of the occupying power, whereas his duty is actually to the economy of the occupied territory.

There is no reason why an occupying power should not apply to the administration of occupied territory the lessons learnt in the administration of its own State. Moreover, co-operation between the departments of the two administrations is both inevitable and desirable, particularly when (as is the case in the Middle East) the occupied territory is adjacent to the territory of the occupying power. It is difficult to see, for example, how the officials in the West Bank occupation administration could discharge their responsibility for the provision of transport without close co-operation with their counterparts in the Government of Israel. The test of legality, however, must be whether the administration of the occupied territory remains genuinely distinct from the administration of the occupant's own State and whether the occupation administration fulfils its responsibility to provide government for the territory rather than administering the territory's economy solely in the interests of the occupying power.[59]

VI. The Administration of Justice in Occupied Territory[60]

Since the Fourth Geneva Convention is rather more explicit about the operation of the courts in occupied territory, it is appropriate to deal with the administration of justice in a separate section, although most of the general principles which have already been discussed are also relevant here.

The law in force in occupied territory will comprise international law, the local law in force prior to the occupation and the occupation laws enacted by the occupying power. In principle, the occupying power must allow the local courts to continue to function with regard to the application of the local law and the occupant must not alter the status of the judges.[61] However, Article 64(1) of the Fourth Geneva Convention makes the requirement that the local courts be allowed to function subject to 'the necessity for ensuring the effective administration of justice'. In addition, the occupant is entitled to remove the judges from office in the same way as it may remove officials. The result is that the occupant may (and, if no functioning local courts remain, must) appoint judges from the ranks of local lawyers or bring in judges of its own nationality. In the latter case, the occupant is entitled to create a

---

[59] See the *Teachers' Housing Cooperative* case, at 304.
[60] See Stone, *Legal Controls of International Conflict*, 699–702, and von Glahn, *Occupation*, ch. 9.
[61] IV Geneva Convn., Arts. 64 and 54(1).

new court structure if that is necessary for the effective administration of justice.[62] Nevertheless, even if the court structure is modelled upon that in the occupant's own State and staffed by judges of the occupant's nationality, it remains a system of local courts administering local law, as amended by the legislation of the occupying power.

Alongside this structure of local courts, the occupant may set up its own courts to try breaches of the criminal provisions which it enacts. These courts must be 'properly constituted, non-political military courts'[63] and are required to observe certain procedural standards designed to ensure a fair trial. The trial courts must sit in the occupied territory and appeals from them should preferably be heard in the occupied territory.[64]

Finally, breaches of internal discipline by the members of the occupying armed forces and accompanying civilians are generally excluded from the jurisdiction of the local courts and will be tried by military tribunals under the military code of the occupying power.[65]

In general, the courts of the occupant's own State have no part to play, although they may have jurisdiction in respect of civil disputes arising between members of the occupying forces and administration.[66] Nevertheless, it is likely that the courts of many States would follow the example of the Supreme Court of Israel and hold that the actions of the occupation administration were subject to judicial review,[67] for example to determine whether they infringed the requirements of the occupant's constitution. So long as this remedy is additional to and involves no derogation from the remedies required by international law and provided that compliance with constitutional requirements will not involve violations of international law, such an innovation is to be welcomed.

VII. The Special Problems of Prolonged Occupations

As we have seen, one of the pillars on which the law of belligerent occupation rests is the principle that an occupying power has only a temporary authority. In dealing with belligerent occupation, international law seeks to perform a holding operation pending the

---

[62] Dinstein, 'The International Law of Belligerent Occupation and Human Rights', 114–15.
[63] IV Geneva Convn., Art. 66.
[64] Ibid.
[65] *British Manual*, para. 522; *US Field Manual*, para. 374.
[66] Dinstein, 'The International Law of Belligerent Occupation and Human Rights', 115–16.
[67] E. Nathan, 'The Power of Supervision of the High Court of Justice over Military Government', in Shamgar, *Military Government*, 109.

termination of the conflict. A prolonged occupation, such as that in the West Bank, Gaza, and the Golan Heights, thus creates special problems and places the law under considerable strain. As Greenspan put it, 'human existence demands organic growth, and it is impossible to mark time indefinitely'.[68] The subject of prolonged occupation is discussed in a number of other chapters.[69] Nevertheless, its effect upon the law relating to the administration of occupied territory requires some consideration here.

Although it is obviously difficult to apply the law of belligerent occupation in a prolonged occupation, that law is not thereby rendered inapplicable. Prolonged occupation raises many questions to which the Hague Regulations and the Fourth Geneva Convention provide no express answers. In particular, there is a need for change on a far greater scale during a prolonged occupation simply because of the way in which circumstances change over time. Nevertheless, there is no indication that international law permits an occupying power to disregard provisions of the Regulations or the Convention merely because it has been in occupation for a long period, not least because there is no body of law which might plausibly take their place and no indication that the international community is willing to trust the occupant with *carte blanche*. Any changes, it is suggested, must take place within the framework of the Hague Regulations and the Fourth Geneva Convention, the principles of which are flexible enough to accommodate at least some of the needs of a prolonged occupation.[70]

In relation to the administration of occupied territory, a prolonged occupation will make it necessary for the occupant to make greater changes in the existing administration. Officials will die or retire and have to be replaced. New needs will arise requiring a governmental response. Demographic changes will frequently force a re-examination of existing administrative boundaries and the units of administration. Yet, as has been shown, the principles of international law regarding the administration of occupied territory are couched in very broad terms. There is, for example, no rigid requirement of adherence to existing administrative boundaries and the occupant is free to introduce changes in the administration where its military needs or the good government of the occupied territory require. The longer the occupation lasts, the greater the degree of change which is likely to be required but changes should still be made only in accordance with the broad principles outlined in the preceding sections.

One problem, however, requires special attention: to what extent, if

[68] Greenspan, *The Modern Law of Land Warfare*, 225.
[69] See especially Ch. 1, and also Chs. 11 and 14.
[70] See the consideration of this question in the *Teachers' Housing Cooperative* case, HC 393/82, noted in *IYHR* 14 (1984), 301.

at all, does a prolonged occupation lead to a requirement that the occupant introduce an element of democracy into the administration? It has already been suggested that there is no general requirement of democratic involvement in the government of occupied territory and that an occupant may, and probably will, suspend elections and the political process except perhaps at local level. In a protracted occupation the occupying power may wish to involve the local population at least in a consultative capacity. Moreover, where the occupant considers making changes in the local law in order to promote *'l'ordre et la vie publics'*, the approval of the local population through elected representatives can only strengthen the case for maintaining that such a change is justified. It is suggested that the presence or absence of such approval represents a more reliable criterion for determining whether a change is in the interests of the occupied territory than the *'bonus paterfamilias'* test of whether the occupant has introduced similar legislation in its own territory.[71]

Nevertheless, it must be recognized that there are serious problems inherent in any attempt to create a democratic structure in occupied territory. If no democratic structure existed in the territory prior to occupation, or if that structure did not operate after the occupation commenced, an occupant which created a new structure of elected bodies with real powers would be altering the existing form of government in the territory in a way which it might be impossible to undo after the occupation ends. The creation of a democratically governed unit in the occupied territory smacks of a permanent change which the occupant has no authority to make. It must also be remembered that occupying powers wishing to establish satellite States have often cloaked their occupation administrations with a fig-leaf of democratic pretence. Although the Fourth Geneva Convention makes clear that changes in the institutions of the occupied territory, such as the creation of a supposedly local government, do not affect the applicability of the Convention,[72] in practice local puppet governments, especially if they have an element of popular support, have generally ignored international law altogether.

Even if the occupant merely permits an existing democratic process to continue, problems arise. Since ultimate legislative power will reside with the occupant, the scope for conflict with elected bodies is immense. Changes in electoral boundaries or the franchise, always controversial,[73] are likely to be even more contentious when effected by an

---

[71] Compare the views of Dinstein, 'The International Law of Belligerent Occupation and Human Rights', 113, with those expressed by Pellet in Ch. 5, text at nn. 106–7.

[72] IV Geneva Convn. Art. 47.

[73] See, e.g., the dispute over the most recent report of the Boundary Commission for England and Wales; *R. v. Boundary Commission for England and Wales, ex parte Foot* [1983] QB 600.

alien occupying power, even if that power acts in good faith. Above all, a system of government which rests upon military power, restrained in some respects by international law, is unlikely to coexist satisfactorily with any kind of democratic process.

Consequently, it is suggested that, even during a prolonged occupation, there is no general requirement that the occupant provide for democratic participation in the government of occupied territory. While it is desirable that some mechanism for consultation and involvement of the local population be established, anything which smacks of a permanent constitutional change will be unlawful and other democratic involvement will be workable only in the event that there is a basic willingness to co-operate on both sides. Perhaps the most that can be said is that in a prolonged occupation there is a stronger presumption in favour of permitting existing democratic bodies, especially at local level, to continue to operate (or to resume operating if they were suspended during the initial phase of the occupation).

VIII. Conclusions

International law contains few express provisions about the administrative structure in occupied territory. The emphasis is upon the actions, rather than the form, of the occupant's administration. Nevertheless, the occupant does not have a completely free hand in shaping the administration of occupied territory. The general principles on which the law of belligerent occupation is based and the specific duties which that law imposes upon an occupying power have implications for the administrative structure which the occupant may adopt. The following principles are particularly important:

1. The occupant has a duty to establish an effective administration in occupied territory.
2. That administration will inevitably work closely with the administration of the occupant's own State but must be separate from it. Occupied territory must be governed as a separate unit.
3. Since the occupant has only a temporary authority, it has no power to make permanent changes in the constitution or form of government of the occupied territory.
4. Where there is an existing administrative structure capable of functioning, the occupying power should make only such changes as are necessary to meet its legitimate military objectives and to provide for the government of the territory, although it may replace the officials who staff the administration if it wishes.
5. The same principle applies to the alteration of the boundaries of administrative units. The occupant may alter the geographical units

of administration where this is necessary for military or administrative reasons but may not make such changes for purely political reasons.
6. There is no general requirement that an occupant make provision for democratic involvement, although there is a presumption (especially in prolonged occupations) that elected local bodies should be allowed to continue to function, with regular elections being held, unless those bodies undermine the position of the occupant or impede its administration of the territory.
7. The scope and need for change will be greater in a prolonged occupation but must still take place within the framework of these principles.

These principles leave the occupant considerable latitude to change the structure and the personnel of the administration to suit its military needs and to provide for the government of the territory. It is not required to maintain every feature of the existing administrative structure and may suspend the political process within the territory. Above all, an occupying power is not required to establish a form of democracy in occupied territory, although it may permit some form of electoral process to continue or establish mechanisms for consulting the population of the territory if it wishes. It is accepted that this conclusion is controversial but it is important to realize the limitations of international law in its attempts to regulate occupations. If the conclusions of this paper are considered unsatisfactory, it is because alien military rule for a prolonged period is inherently unsatisfactory. The answer lies in a development of the machinery for bringing about an end to the conflict which produced the occupation, not in trying to turn a body of law designed to ensure that a military regime observes basic standards of humanity into a device for establishing a liberal democracy or other long-term solution.

8

The Administration of the West Bank under Israeli Rule

MONA RISHMAWI

Introduction

DURING its twenty-year occupation of the West Bank and Gaza, Israel has attempted to integrate the administration of the Occupied Territories into its own central system of government. This chapter attempts to show that, while the military government may be the most visible administrative body in the Occupied Territories and has at times been described as being autonomous, decisions concerning the administration of the West Bank are in fact in the hands of Israeli cabinet ministers and government sub-committees. The alternating years of Likud and Labour Party administrations have brought only changes in tactics in their treatment of the Occupied Territories and not changes in their aims or goals. Both parties support a policy of *de facto* annexation of the West Bank and Gaza.

In order to fulfil its annexionist aims in the West Bank, Israel has also gone beyond the absorption of the West Bank administration into the Israeli government, by changing significantly the pre-1967 administrative structure of the West Bank. In its alterations of the Jordanian-implemented administration, Israel has effectively denied the Palestinian population any participation at the decision-making level while simultaneously allowing interested Jewish parties to participate in the governing of the West Bank.

To justify its actions in changing the administrative structure of the West Bank, Israel claims that it was faced with a technical problem when it occupied the area. The West Bank had a local administration, but was without a central government, since the central government was located in the Jordanian capital of Amman. Israel submits that it had to fill this structural gap, and thus had to change the administrative structure in place at the time of occupation. This argument is challenged, however, by the fact that the Israelis followed much the

---

* The author expresses her gratitude to Susan Rockwell for her editorial assistance.

same procedures in Gaza, despite the existence there of a pre-1967 special administrative unit. This unit, although subject to some intervention by the Egyptian government, had its own independent legislative, executive, and judicial functions and responsibilities.

This paper describes the Israeli administration of the West Bank in order to show that the policies behind the system aim at replacing the central government of Amman with that of Jerusalem in order to serve Israeli colonial interests. For lack of space, the paper discusses only the Israeli administration of the West Bank, not that of Gaza.

While the Jordanian laws, which were in force in the West Bank before the Israeli occupation, identified clearly the structure of the Jordanian government by specifying the jurisdiction, powers, obligations, and goals of each governmental department, the Israeli military orders introduced into the West Bank since 1967 are vague. Consequently it is impossible to describe fully the structure of the Israeli administration through a review of the military orders since, as in the case of Military Order ('MO') 418 governing planning, the functions of the bodies which that order allows to be created are not even identified. The exception to this trend is MO 947, which in 1981 established the 'civilian administration'.

Although the Jordanian law which sanctions the structure of the administration of the West Bank is still in force technically, it has become a mockery of its former self. Principal decision-making is now in the hands of the central political authorities within Israel itself. With the exception of some alterations brought about by the 1981 introduction of the 'civilian government' in the Occupied Territories, the following bodies have been responsible for the administration of the West Bank:

1. The principal policy-making body is a ministerial committee chaired by the Prime Minister. Within this committee the Minister of Defence is directly responsible for the Occupied Territories.

2. The implementation of policies made by the ministerial committee is in the hands of two sub-committees:

(*a*) the Co-ordination Committee which deals with security and political affairs.

(*b*) the Committee of Directors-General for Economic Affairs, which deals with all civil and economic matters.

3. The decisions of the above bodies or committees are channelled through the Department for Co-ordinating Operations in the Ministry of Defence.

4. The implementation of the orders is carried out by the military government in the Occupied Territories.[1]

[1] A. Gerson, *Israel, the West Bank and International Law* (London, 1978), 112–13.

As the Israeli researcher Meron Benvenisti puts it:

> The key to all legislation in the Occupied Territories is the formulation: 'Anyone empowered to act in Israel according to Israeli law may so act in the territories'. The Defence Ministry, through the Civil Administration, is, in effect, military governor of the 'local' population, its jurisdiction being defined not as territorial, but ethnic. The Ministry of Housing decides how many flats will be built in Ariel and Kiryat Arba [Jewish colonies in the West Bank], in the same way as it decides how many apartments will be built in Petah Tikva [an Israeli town near Tel Aviv].[2]

It is important to note that a key player in the decision-making apparatus in the Occupied Territories is omitted from this paper. The Israeli Secret Service, or Shin Bet, as it is known, is a highly secretive unit which reports directly to the Prime Minister. While the Shin Bet has no powers of enforcement, its recommendations are heeded. The actions of this unit range from recommending the arrest of Palestinians to interrogating them, from recommending individual administrative detention and deportation orders, to preparing secret evidence to be presented before the various governmental review committees, and include also the power to agree to or deny the issuance of, *inter alia*, import and export licences, driving licences, telephone permits, and travel permits.[3]

The Shin Bet officers are not accountable to the IDF commanders or even to the Minister of Defence; they are solely responsible to the Prime Minister. This has allowed its agents to operate relatively free from effective control. Despite the unveiling of the Shin Bet by the 1987 Israeli Landau Commission report,[4] the report failed to find any individual accountable or to rectify the method of accountability of the agency. Since the structure of the *Shin Bet* is not known, it cannot be further addressed here.

The body of this chapter is divided into five main sections. The first describes the administrative structure of the West Bank under Jordanian rule, the second is an introduction to the military government, the third addresses the establishment of the civilian administration, the

---

[2] M. Benvenisti, *West Bank Data Base Project 1987 Report* (Jerusalem, 1987), 70.

[3] For further discussion of the Shin Bet, see Ch. 6.

[4] On 31 May 1987, the government of Israel established a Commission of Enquiry, chaired by High Court Justice Moshe Landau, to investigate the GSS (Shin Bet)'s 'methods of interrogation in regard to hostile terrorist activities' and court testimony regarding interrogations. The Commission was established against the background of two cases—the 'Nafsu' case and 'Bus 300' affair—which prompted extensive Israeli and international criticism about the operational methods of the GSS. The Commission published a report on 30 October 1987, which became known as 'the Landau Report'. The Commission found that, since 1971, the GSS had systematically given false testimony under oath with the aim of concealing their methods of interrogation and facilitating the conviction of accused persons.

fourth describes local administration under Israeli rule, and the fifth presents a case-study of one function of local administration, physical planning under the occupation.

Four charts are provided: the first outlines the structure of the Jordanian government; the second is a skeletal description of the Israeli decision-making apparatus in the Occupied Territories; the third outlines the structure of the Israeli civilian administration; and the fourth outlines the decision-making processes for official settlement projects.

I. The Administration of the West Bank under Jordanian Rule 1948–1967

On 15 May 1948, following the establishment of the State of Israel in Palestine, the West Bank fell under the political, legal, and administrative control of the Jordanian Kingdom. West Bank Palestinians were given Jordanian citizenship.

On 1 January 1952, the Jordanian Constitution ('the constitution') was enacted in the Kingdom. It is instructive to look at the constitutional sanctions of the governmental structure in order to understand the structure of government during the Jordanian period and to compare it with the Israeli administration of the West Bank. It is also important to examine the Jordanian Constitution because it forms part of the local law which—at least in theory—is currently applied in the Israeli-occupied West Bank.

According to the constitution, Jordan is a kingdom ruled by a central government which sits in the capital of Amman.

1. *The Legislative Power*. The constitution grants the King of Jordan and the Jordanian Parliament—the National Council—legislative power. The National Council consists of two houses: the House of Representatives, elected by Jordanian citizens, including those from the West Bank, and the House of Senators, appointed by the King. The King may, and does, appoint West Bank Palestinians to the Senate.

2. *The Executive Power*. The constitution grants the King executive power which he exercises through his ministers. West Bank Palestinians have been included in the Jordanian ministerial cabinet, or council.

Although the Ministerial Council alone is entitled to govern all internal and external state affairs, Article 120 of the constitution does give the Ministerial Council the right to issue regulations concerning local administrative subdivisions in the Kingdom. In order to facilitate the work of the ministry of the interior, Jordan and the West Bank were divided into districts, governments, and sub-governments. The heads of these divisions were given responsibilities connected primarily to their role as intermediaries between the central government and local administrations.

Each municipal council constitutes a legal body which elects its head. Only in exceptional cases may the elected municipal council and/or its head be dismissed by and replaced by a committee appointed by the Minister of the Interior.

Jordanian law stipulates that the municipalities are responsible for such subjects as local land-use planning, the granting of building permits and business licences, fire-fighting, public health, and other such local affairs. These municipalities are not autonomous; their work is co-ordinated and supervised by the central government.

3. *The Judiciary.* The Jordanian constitution emphasizes the independence of the judiciary. It recognizes three types of courts: regular, religious, and special tribunals. The regular courts are granted jurisdiction over all civil and criminal matters, including suits brought by or against the government itself. The religious courts deal with all issues of personal status. The special tribunals were established to deal with special issues, such as land and water disputes.

The Law on the Constitution of Regular Courts was enacted to address the question of the jurisdiction and function of the various levels of the courts. This law also called for the establishment of a High Court of Justice which has the jurisdiction to annul any act which it considers unconstitutional.

Figure 8.1 provides a skeletal description of the Jordanian governmental apparatus, prepared according to the Jordanian law in force in the area up to 6 June 1967.

II. The Introduction of the Military Government

When the Israeli forces occupied the West Bank on 6 June 1967, a military government was established immediately under the high-ranking officer, General Haim Herzog. General Herzog started to issue military proclamations in the name of the Area Commander (the IDF Commander of the central command), who was in fact lower in rank than General Herzog himself.[5]

Article 3(a) of the second proclamation that was issued on 7 June 1967 stated that:

All powers of government, legislation, appointment, and administration in relation to the area or its inhabitants shall henceforth be vested in me [The

---

[5] M. Shamgar (ed.), *Military Government in the Territories Administered by Israel (1967–80)*, i: *The Legal Aspects* (Jerusalem, 1982), 27.

FIGURE 8.1. *Jordanian governmental structure (skeletal description)*

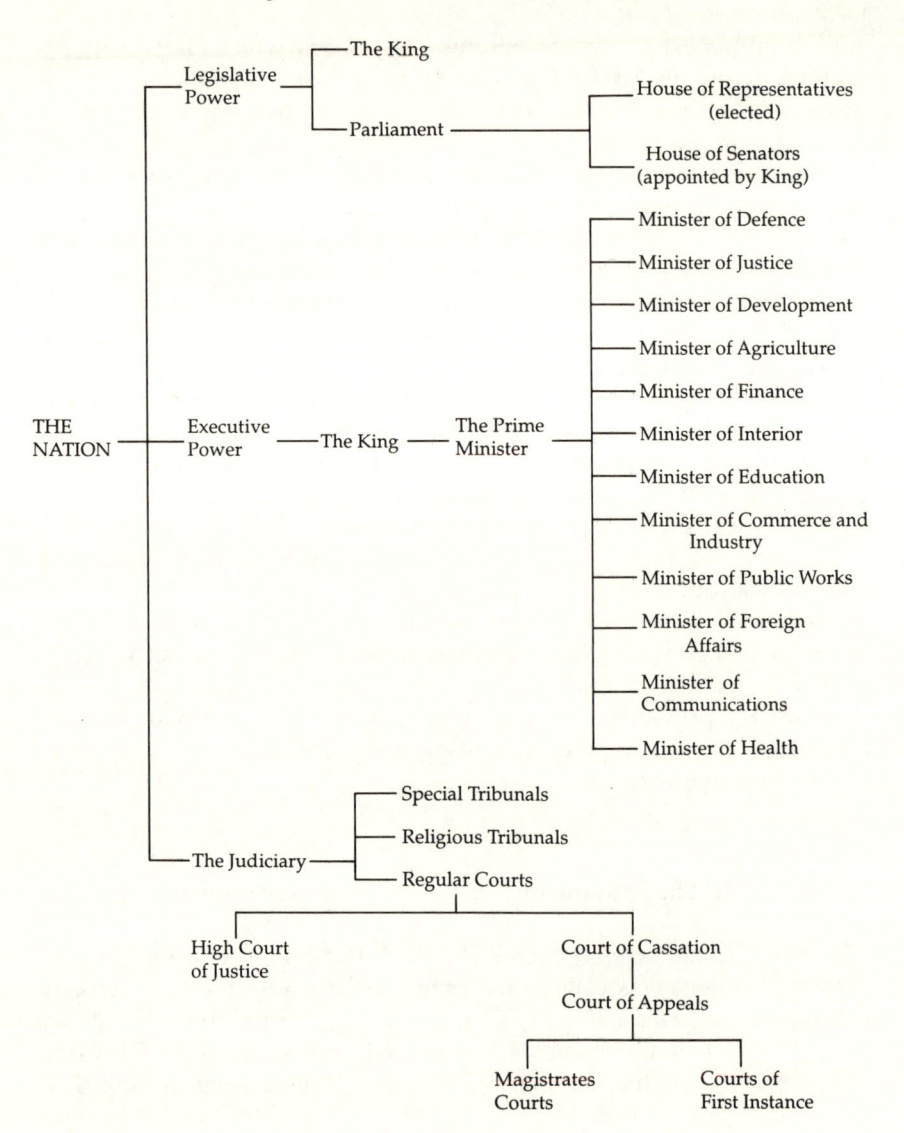

```
                                   ┌── The King
                   ┌── Legislative ─┤
                   │   Power        │              ┌── House of Representatives
                   │                └── Parliament ─┤    (elected)
                   │                                └── House of Senators
                   │                                     (appointed by King)
                   │                                 ┌── Minister of Defence
                   │                                 ├── Minister of Justice
                   │                                 ├── Minister of Development
                   │                                 ├── Minister of Agriculture
                   │                                 ├── Minister of Finance
THE ───────────────┤── Executive ── The King ── The Prime ── Minister of Interior
NATION             │   Power                    Minister   ├── Minister of Education
                   │                                 ├── Minister of Commerce and
                   │                                 │    Industry
                   │                                 ├── Minister of Public Works
                   │                                 ├── Minister of Foreign
                   │                                 │    Affairs
                   │                                 ├── Minister of
                   │                                 │    Communications
                   │                                 └── Minister of Health
                   │                  ┌── Special Tribunals
                   │                  ├── Religious Tribunals
                   └── The Judiciary ─┤
                                      └── Regular Courts
                                                │
                             ┌──────────────────┴──────────────────┐
                       High Court                            Court of Cassation
                       of Justice                                   │
                                                            Court of Appeals
                                                                    │
                                                    ┌───────────────┴────────────┐
                                               Magistrates                  Courts of
                                               Courts                       First Instance
```

(Figure prepared by al-Haq in accordance with the Jordanian Constitution and Laws collected in the Jordanian Legislative Encyclopaedia, Vol. 21).

West Bank Area Commander] alone and shall only be exercised by me or by persons appointed by me for that purpose or acting on my behalf.

Consequently, the military government in the West Bank has been exercising complete legislative and administrative powers, as well as the power to appoint and supervise the function of the judiciary. This mandate has continued over the past twenty years despite several internal changes within the structure of the military government, the most significant being the November 1981 introduction of the 'civilian administration'.

The first structure of the military government in the Israeli-occupied West Bank lasted for only ten days, and therefore will not be dwelt upon in this paper. It will suffice to say that the first administration of the Occupied Territories was purely a military one: all affairs and decisions passed through a hierarchy of four tiers of military ranks. Civilian matters were not addressed. However, according to Joel Singer, head of the International Law Branch in the Military Advocate-General's office:

> After ten days it was realised that this structure was awkward and therefore the second tier of the military government (i.e. the HQ of the Commander of the IDF in the Area) was rearranged: The military arm was dissolved and the civilian arm was integrated into the central command HQ as a separate and additional branch under the direct control of the Commander of the central command, who assumed the office of the Commander of the IDF in the Area. Thenceforth, the orders issued by the Commander were signed under the title 'Commander of the central command and Commander of the IDF in the Area'.[6]

The most important point of this first restructuring of the administrative body was the dissolution of the military arm of the military headquarters and the integration of the civilian arm into the central command. Because of this shift and other restructurings which switched administrative emphasis to civilian affairs, more attention was consequently paid to the conduct of daily life in the West Bank. It may be argued that after the first ten days of occupation Israel's intention to keep the territories for a longer period of time became clearer and, accordingly, it began to rearrange the structure of the administration of the territories. This structure will be elaborated on in the section on physical planning, below.

Before the end of 1967, further changes in the administrative structure of the military government took place.[7] In December 1967, the military government was separated from the central command HQ and a new title, 'Commander of the Area', was created for its head. The commander of the central command continued, however, to be responsible for external and internal security. Internal security was enforced by brigade commanders deployed in the area.

In 1976, responsibility for internal security shifted from the central command to the military government.[8] These various shifts of responsi-

---

[6] J. Singer, 'The Establishment of a Civilian Administration in the Areas Administered by Israel', *IYHR* 12 (1982), 270–1.
[7] Ibid. 271–2.
[8] Ibid. 272.

bility to and from the central command reflect in part the structural changes made within the Ministry of Defence itself during the respective Likud and Labour Party administrations. It also appears that, as the occupation continued, the Israeli government amended the structure of the military government in order to give less authority to professional military personnel as strategic concerns of maintaining control over the territories dwindled. More power and infrastructural support was given to government ministers and interested parties, with the intention that they could implement Israeli aims of incorporating the West Bank into the Israeli system of administration.

The following principles, based on the governmental committee resolution of 11 October 1968 and adopted by the Israeli government on 27 November 1970, display the early interdependence between the various branches of the military government and the government of Israel itself:

1. The Supreme authority in an area administered by Israel is vested in the Commander of the IDF in the Area (hereinafter: the Area Commander).
2. The Area Commander is the exclusive formal authority within the area; he legislates when necessary, he is the executive, he appoints local officials including local judges, when necessary. The Area Commander is the sole address for the local inhabitants.
3. The Area Commander is subordinate to the Defence Minister through the IDF channels of command.
4. The various civil activities in the area will be conducted by the appropriate governmental offices, each office within its authority and budgetary responsibility. The representatives of the ministries shall co-ordinate their activities with the Area Commander. The representatives of the ministries will be—as has been the case till now—Staff Officers of the Area Commander.
5. A representative of a ministry will act according to directives given by his minister and the directorate of his office within the framework of the authorized budget. Such activities are subject to co-ordination with and approval of the Area Commander.[9]

The basis of this structure continues to apply to the West Bank, despite the inclusion of several amendments at the time of the 1981 establishment of the civilian administration. Those amendments, discussed later in this paper, focus on the introduction of the post of the 'head of the civilian administration'.

As noted earlier, the policies through which the Occupied Territories

---

[9] Procedures adopted by the Committee of Directors-General on Civil Affairs in the Occupied Territories during its meeting on 27 November 1970, cited in Singer, ibid., 275.

are administered are determined by a ministerial committee chaired by the Prime Minister. Within this committee, the Minister of Defence is responsible for the Occupied Territories.

In exercising his powers in the West Bank, the Minister of Defence is assisted by a co-ordinator of activities. Until 1981 the chief of the military government department in the Israeli Forces general staff also participated in co-ordination. According to Joel Singer:

> Coordination between the military government and the Israeli ministries is maintained through two channels: (a) between the ministry and the Staff Officer representing it in the Civil Administration; and (b) between the ministry and the Coordinator.[10]

As noted above, the military government of the West Bank was, until 7 November 1981, divided into two sections: the military section which dealt with political and security matters, and the civil section which dealt with the civilian affairs in the region. The period from 1967 to 1981 was characterized by absolute centralization. The 'civil arm' and the 'military arm' were not permitted to decide separately on military or civil matters. In general, it may be said that during that period the difference between the two arms had no practical significance because they were fused together at the top and bottom levels.[11]

III. The Establishment of the Civilian Administration

MO 947, which established the 'civilian administration', was issued on 8 November 1981, in preparation for the implementation of Israel's interpretation of the autonomy plans under the Camp David accords. In Israel's view, the 1979 agreement calls only for the 'withdrawal' of the military government and not its 'abolition'. Accordingly the military command continues to be directly responsible for any 'self-governing administrative council'. In fact, according to an official announcement made by the spokesperson of the Ministry of Defence on 29 September 1981—about one month before the issuance of the official order—the civilian administration was to be under the direct control of the Defence Minister. The announcement implied that the administration would gradually be taken over by civilians and that local Palestinians would assume the administrative tasks.[12]

MO 947 established a new position entitled 'the Head of the Civilian Administration'. The head, whose nationality and civilian/military

---
[10] Ibid. 277.
[11] M. Benvenisti, *Israeli Rule in the West Bank: Legal and Administrative Aspects* (Jerusalem: WBDP, 1983), 24–5.
[12] Singer, 'The Establishment of a Civilian Administration', 278.

status were not specified in the military order, is appointed by the area commander. Since the nationality of the designate was not specified, this position is technically open to a Palestinian. MO 947 and its explanatory memorandum is exceptional because it not only creates this office, but also specifies the powers which accompany it. This is the only military order to which the authorities attached an explanatory memorandum. The military order states, in part, that the tasks of the civilian administration are 'to see to the civilian affairs of the local residents, this while paying heed to consideration of public order'.[13]

Professor Menachem Milson, the first head of this civilian administration and previously an Israeli 'arabist' at the Hebrew University, elaborated on the above points in an interview with the *Jerusalem Post* by saying:

The Civil Administration is part of the separation of the civilian functions from the military functions of the defence minister's executive organs in the area. The Israeli government has not changed the legal status of our operations in the area . . .

Civil Administration does not mean that this is an administration operated by civilians but an administration dealing with the affairs of civilians. It reflects the understanding that the separation of executive functions between military and civilian affairs would better suit the needs of the population and the policy aims of the government.

But of course we hope and believe that the atmosphere in the area will be such that moderate people, pragmatic people, will be encouraged to join the peace process, and in that respect we may be in a sense preparing a political atmosphere which may be conducive to the full implementation of the Camp David accord.[14]

The Palestinians rejected this formula categorically. In their analysis of the order, al-Haq researchers went as far as to term it 'a unilateral declaration of a constitutional change'.[15] They pointed out that MO 947 had two principal and closely related effects: the first was to institutionalize the already existing separation of the military and civilian functions in the military government by formally establishing a new structure of civilian government; the second was to make it possible to elevate a large number of military orders and other legislative enactments promulgated by the area commander from the status of temporary security enactments to that of permanent laws.[16] These were

---

[13] Art. 2 of MO 947.
[14] *The Jerusalem Post*, 19 Feb. 1982.
[15] J. Kuttab and R. Shehadeh, *Civilian Administration in the Occupied West Bank: Analysis of Israeli Military Government Order No. 947* (Ramallah, 1982), 8.
[16] Ibid. 14 and R. Shehadeh, *Occupier's Law: Israel and the West Bank*, rev. edn. (Washington DC, 1988), 69–70.

to remain in effect after the abolition of the military government in accordance with the Camp David autonomy plan.

Article 4 of the explanatory memorandum prepared by Baruch Hollander, then legal adviser to the military government, to interpret Article 3 of MO 947, defines the powers given to the head of the civilian administration as:

(a) All the powers set forth in the local law, except for the military powers set forth in a number of local laws that are set forth in the first schedule to the order.

(b) All the civilian powers that are set forth in the security legislation and which are detailed in the second schedule to the order. This schedule sets forth all the orders in which powers have been accorded to staff officers, heads of branches, the Area Commander, the Deputy Commander of the Region, and the other officials in the civilian spheres.[17]

The first schedule of the order referred to in (a) above includes only four Jordanian enactments: the Law for the Defence of East Jordan of 1935 and the orders and regulations passed by virtue thereof, the Defence (Emergency) Regulations of 1945, the Prisons Law of 1953, and the Village Guards Law of 1925. The application of these laws and their amendments remained in the hands of the area commander.

As for the head of the civilian administration, who, according to the order, has no power to alter or amend the structure but merely to administer it,[18] the second schedule of MO 947 lists 162 military orders that the head of the civilian administration is charged with administering. Eight more military orders were later added to the list.

The military orders enable the civilian administration to regulate and control economic life in the West Bank. Some orders regulate imports, exports, prices, finances, and banks; others regulate taxes, customs, and duties. Some orders regulate control over land, water, and electricity; others regulate postal communication and other services. The licensing of professionals and the regulation of civil service appointments are subject to military orders. The orders also concern themselves with the supervision of plays, films, publications, and textbooks. Military orders exist which establish objections committees and delegate judicial powers. The subject of Jewish settlements also appears in this schedule since various military orders which regulate the establishment of regional councils are included.

The second schedule of MO 947 also includes some military orders with quasi-police functions like regulation of the use of explosives, the

---

[17] Translation given in Kuttab and Shehadeh, *Civilian Administration in the Occupied West Bank*, 24.
[18] Ibid. 16.

regulation of identity cards, the guarding of holy places, and the forcing of shops and businesses to remain open.[19]

As for the delegation of powers in the civilian administration, Article 5 of MO 947 authorizes the head of the civilian administration to: (*a*) make appointments in the civilian administration; (*b*) delegate to such appointees the authorities given to him by virtue of the law or security regulations; and (*c*) delegate to others the authority to create secondary legislation (rules and regulations) based on the law and military orders he is charged with administering.

An attempt to give some power to the 'village leagues'—armed militias within Palestinian communities created and encouraged by the military government as an anti-PLO and pro-Camp David alternative to local leadership—was unsuccessful. This was due first to the low standing of the leagues' members within their own communities, and secondly to their terrorizing of the Palestinian community through, among other acts, murder and vandalism.[20]

Civilian administration officials instructed villagers and townsfolk to go to the village leagues in order to acquire recommendations without which building licences, travel permits, and family reunion requests, among others, were denied. Village league recommendations also helped to curtail prison terms and to remove persons from the blacklist.[21]

These leagues were perceived by the majority of Palestinians as traitorous and were subsequently boycotted. Thus, the post-1981 civilian administration attempt to delegate some power to local sources failed. In practice, and during the last six years, the only powers which were vested in Palestinians were routine and low-level administrative ones. In contrast, a number of senior positions in this administration are occupied by Jewish settlers. For example, the chief military prosecutor from 1985–8 was a settler.

In the last few years it appears that the ability of the civilian administration to implement the autonomy plan has diminished seriously, in part because the Camp David accords themselves have lost their impact. The civilian administration now functions as an arm of the military government which deals with civil affairs in the West Bank.

Figure 8.2 provides a skeletal description of the present Israeli

---

[19] For the summary of these military orders, see ibid. 29–58.

[20] Al-Haq has collected many affidavits about the acts of the village leagues, some of which were published in *In Their Own Words: Human Rights Violations in the West Bank* (Geneva, 1983).

[21] This 'blacklist' is an unpublished list kept by the military government of people whom they consider activists. Such individuals are usually not allowed to leave the Occupied Territories, and are also denied other services from the military government such as obtaining a permit to learn how to drive, a telephone line, and various other services. Individuals usually learn that their names are blacklisted when their applications for permits are denied.

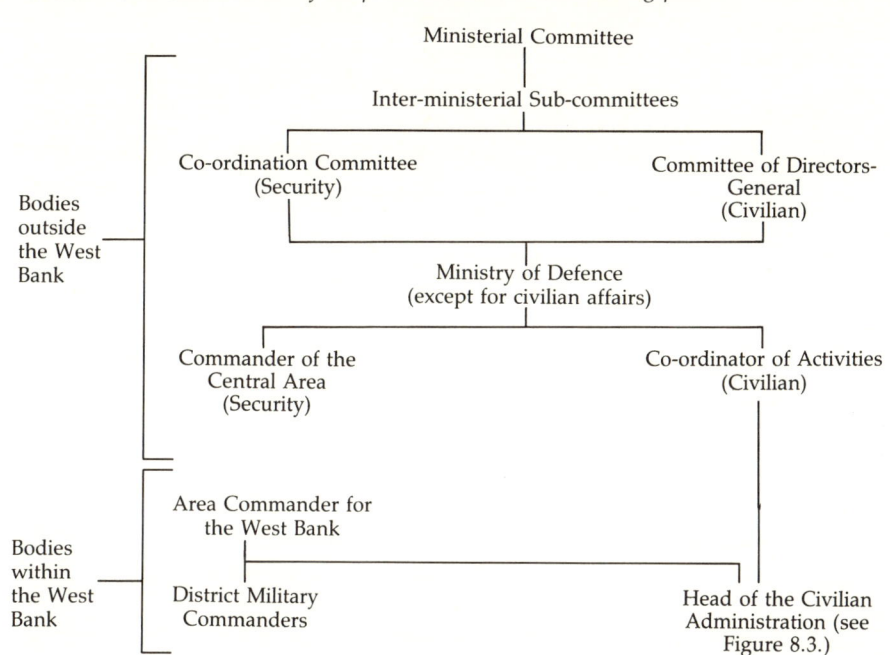

FIGURE 8.2. *Skeletal chart of the present Israeli decision-making process*

```
                          Ministerial Committee
                                  |
                       Inter-ministerial Sub-committees
                                  |
              ┌───────────────────┴───────────────────┐
              Co-ordination Committee          Committee of Directors-
Bodies        (Security)                       General
outside                                        (Civilian)
the West      └───────────────────┬───────────────────┘
Bank                              |
                          Ministry of Defence
                       (except for civilian affairs)
                                  |
              ┌───────────────────┴───────────────────┐
              Commander of the                 Co-ordinator of Activities
              Central Area                     (Civilian)
              (Security)

              Area Commander for
              the West Bank
Bodies                |
within        ┌───────┴───────────────────────────────┐
the West      District Military                Head of the Civilian
Bank          Commanders                       Administration (see
                                               Figure 8.3.)
```

(prepared by the author)

decision-making apparatus regarding the Occupied Territories. The structure of the civilian administration is shown in Figure 8.3.

The internal administrative structure within the military government itself was also affected by the introduction of the civilian administration. Some other new posts, such as deputies and liaison officers, were introduced. The former jurisdiction of the district commanders to deal with military affairs was given to the brigade commanders. The district commanders now deal with civil matters under the supervision of the head of the civilian administration, while the brigade commanders were reinstated as military commanders responsible to the commander of the IDF in the area. The work of the co-ordinator of activities was also changed, his powers being split in two:

(a) the co-ordination of military activity of the commanders of the Israeli forces is now carried out by the military government department of the general staff of the Ministry of Defence.
(b) the co-ordination of the work of the civilian administrations in both the West Bank and the Gaza Strip is now carried out by the co-ordinator of activities.[22]

---
[22] Singer, 'The Establishment of a Civilian Administration', 287.

FIGURE 8.3. *The structure of the Civilian Administration*

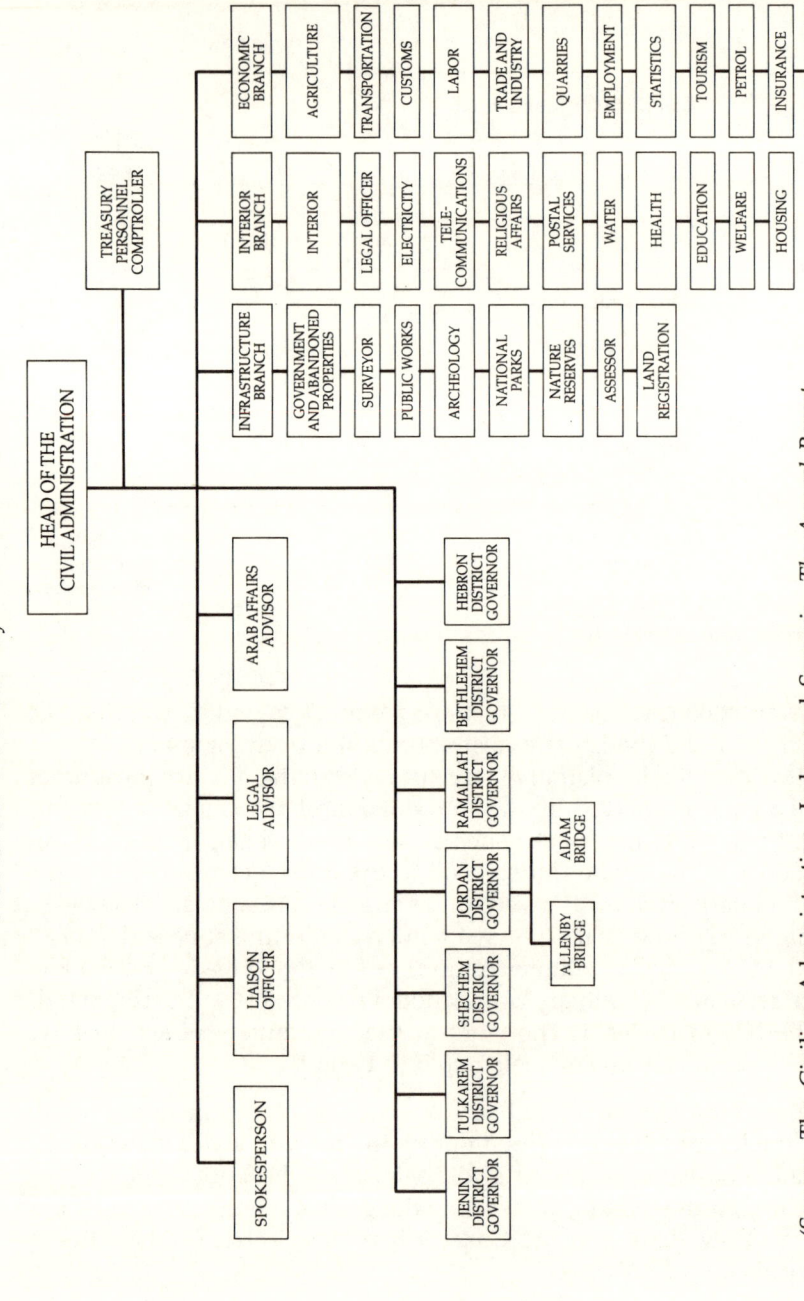

(Source: The Civilian Administration, Judea and Samaria, *The Annual Report: 19th Year of Administration, April 1, 1985–March 31, 1986* (Jerusalem, 1985), 51.)

According to Joel Singer, close liaison is maintained between the unit of the co-ordinator and the department of military government in the general staff.[23]

IV. Local Authorities under Occupation

At the time of the Israeli occupation of the West Bank, the existing Jordanian law on local government provided for only two types of local administrative units: the municipality and the village. The regional and the local councils which had existed at the time of the British Mandate were abolished by the Jordanian Municipal Law of 1955.[24]

According to Jordanian law, a group of people in a village can petition the district commissioner to declare their village a municipality. This function has since been assumed by the person appointed by the Israeli area commander. All the municipalities functioning today in the West Bank existed before the Israeli occupation.

The municipalities function according to the Jordanian Municipal Law which was amended by several Israeli military orders. Municipality business includes planning and building, to be elaborated on below, business-licensing, fire-fighting, public health, sewage, cleanliness, and other related matters.

Since the beginning of the Israeli occupation, several military orders have been enacted which interfere with the affairs of the Palestinian municipal function. Prominent amongst them are a number of military orders which deal with municipal elections.[25]

In August 1967, a few months after the occupation began, municipal elections were due in the West Bank in accordance with the municipal law. These elections were postponed, however, by virtue of MO 80, and held only in 1972.

Four years later, in 1976, elections were again held. But when the municipal elections were due again in 1980, they were postponed and the function of the existing municipal councils was extended. The Israeli justification behind this move was that, if elections were held, pro-PLO elements would be elected.

In 1982, after the establishment of the civilian administration, the municipal councils decided to boycott this administration in accordance

---

[23] Ibid.
[24] Art. 105(a) declared all municipalities and local councils repealed. These councils were considered municipal councils under the 1955 law.
[25] See Ch. 7, text at n. 46 on provisions of international law regarding local elections; but see also Adam Roberts' view in Ch. 1 of this volume ('Some Other Cases of Prolonged Occupation'), that the establishment of political institutions cannot be delayed indefinitely.

with the Palestinian rejection of the Camp David accords. In retaliation, the head of the first civilian administration dismissed most of the Palestinian elected councils and mayors, appointing Israeli officials to replace them. Israelis continued to head most municipalities of the West Bank until 1986.

In 1986, following the freezing of the Hussein–Arafat agreement, Jordan decided to reactivate its role in the region in an attempt to retain influence over the West Bank in the case of some kind of territorial compromise. The Israeli government was at this time headed by the Labour Prime Minister Shimon Peres, who purportedly also sought a 'territorial compromise'. This Labour administration welcomed a 'functional partition' between Israel and Jordan.[26] Israel therefore agreed to replace the Israeli mayors with appointed pro-Jordanian elements who would push for the Jordanian option in the West Bank. During the Palestinian popular uprising which started on 9 December 1987, the Israeli-appointed mayors were asked by the underground Unified National Leadership to resign. Some handed in their resignation. A call for municipal elections was amongst the demands of the Uprising, as articulated by Leaflet No. 2 of the Unified Leadership. At the time of writing, no elections have taken place.

When Israel wanted to establish local authorities for its Jewish colonies in the West Bank, it did not use the Jordanian law. Two military orders and their accompanying regulations were enacted, authorizing the establishment of regional and local councils for the Israeli settlements. The councils are similar to those in Israel.

On 25 March 1979, one day before the signing of the peace treaty between Israel and Egypt, the military authorities in the West Bank issued MO 783. MO 783 established regional councils in the West Bank, without defining them, and declared all settlements listed in the order's appendix to be considered regional councils. The appendix named four such councils.

In March 1981, MO 892 was issued in the West Bank establishing five local councils. By virtue of Article 2(a) of the order, regulations were passed outlining rules for the administration of these councils. The powers and functions of these regional and local councils differ considerably from those of the above-mentioned Jordanian municipal councils.[27] They are, however, identical to those of the local and regional councils within Israel.[28]

---

[26] For more on the Jordanian plan, see Benvenisti, *1987 Report*, 24 and 46.

[27] For the comparison between the military orders dealing with the Jewish colonies and the Jordanian law, see R. Shehadeh, 'Legal System of Israeli Settlements', International Commission of Jurists', *Review* 27 (Dec. 1981), 59–74.

[28] According to Benvenisti, 'The regulations governing the regional councils' powers and functions, defined in MO 783 as amended, are identical to the Israeli Legislation

The Administration of the West Bank 283

As of April 1987, 118 Jewish colonies exist in the West Bank, excluding Jerusalem.[29] The West Bank is now divided into three regional councils which are themselves divided into ten local councils.[30]

These colonies, inhabited exclusively by Jews, though not necessarily Israeli subjects[31], operate as islands where Israeli law, system of administration, and government replace that of Jordan. The jurisdiction of several Israeli laws was extended to apply extra-territorially to any person whose place of residence is in the region and who is an Israeli citizen or entitled to acquire Israeli citizenship pursuant to the Law of Return of 1950, in order to ensure the integration of the Jewish settlements with the Israeli system. These laws include Entry into Israel Law of 1952, Income Tax Ordinance Law of 1961, Defence Service Law of 1959, Chamber of Advocates Law of 1961, National Insurance Law of 1968, and others.[32]

The Israeli ministries use the Jewish councils to provide state services to the settlements. The budgetary allocations for such services are incorporated into the general budget of the Israeli civilian ministries. In education, welfare, and religious services, the services allocated to the Jewish councils are even more generous than those within Israel itself. 'The priority given to the West Bank settlements', writes Benvenisti, 'is clearly manifested by comparing the incentives granted to settlers and entrepreneurs in the area, relative to development towns in Israel proper.'[33]

Benvenisti continues:

Less than 38 per cent of development towns are granted highest incentive status (A+) for industrial development, ... whereas all settlement industrial parks are entitled to that status. Nineteen out of 29 development towns in the northern part of Israel (45 per cent) and 3 out of 14 towns (22 per cent) in the south are classified as 'A+ towns'. All 18 industrial settlements enjoy that status. Subsidy for housing (families lacking housing) in development towns, all in depressed areas, is NIS 26,000 (for families with up to 3 children) and NIS 38,900 in the West Bank. Families with 4–5 children receive 40,400 and 43,200 respectively; singles get 13,000 in development towns and NIS 19,500 in the

---

(Local Councils Regional Councils Order 1958).' Benvenisti notes that the powers of the local councils established by virtue of MO 982 'are identical to the powers and responsibilities of ordinary Israeli municipalities, since the Order is a copy of the Israeli Municipal Ordinances (with some alterations)'. Benvenisti, *Israeli Rule in the West Bank: Legal and Administrative Aspects* (Jerusalem, 1983), 9.

[29] Benvenisti, *1987 Report*, 55.
[30] Ibid. 37.
[31] The reference here and elsewhere to 'Jewish', as opposed to 'Israeli' settlements and settlers, is accurate. Many of those moving to settlements are not Israeli citizens, though they have the right to become so under the Law of Return.
[32] Shehadeh, *Occupier's Law*, 66, and see chapter by same author in this collection; see also Ch. 7, text at n. 26 for provisions of international law on this point.
[33] Shehadeh, *Occupier's Law*, 61.

West Bank. Settlers joining the 'Build Your Own Home' scheme, pay for a state owned lot 16 per cent of its assessed value in 'A+' development towns (in Israel proper), 40 per cent in 'A' towns and 60 per cent of its value in 'B' towns. In all West Bank settlements one pays only 5 per cent of the land value. Income tax reduction in development towns (only 18 of 35 towns are eligible) ranges between 3–10 per cent. All West Bank settlements are eligible for 7 per cent income tax relaxation.[34]

All the above is in accordance with the Israeli law which is applied in Israel proper and extended to the West Bank Jewish colonies. Needless to say, the Palestinian sector in the West Bank enjoys none of these privileges.

Not only are the Jewish colonies in the West Bank in a very privileged position, they also participate in all high level decision-making bodies regarding the Occupied Territories. They are represented in the Inter-ministerial Committees, and in the Higher Planning Council which determines all land-use planning in the West Bank (to be discussed in the next section). This participation in high-level committees allows them to push for policies and measures in the West Bank which will serve their exclusive interests. The Palestinians, on the other hand, are denied any form of participation in the policy-making process in the Occupied Territories.

In contrast with the interference in Palestinian council elections, the leadership of the Jewish councils continue to be elected regularly in accordance with the provisions of MO 783 and 892 and regulations issued by virtue of these orders.

The major source for public funding for the Jewish settlements is the Ministry of the Interior. This ministry is responsible for channelling government funds in order to cover the many services which local authorities usually provide. The West Bank Jewish councils are considered an integral part of the local government system. Meron Benvenisti states:

Total government grants to [Jewish] local councils in the West Bank was US$14.7 million in 1984, US$13.2 million in 1986 and US$16.5 million in 1987. Other government ministries (Religion, Defence, Health) provide an additional US$15 million and the World Zionist Organization maintains absorption centers and Hebrew schools in settlements. The total regular (maintenance), state-provided, budget is therefore estimated at US$45–50 million, and total public expenditure, at US$75–85 million.[35]

The public financing of settlements from all sources is concentrated in the hands of the regional council bureaucracies. As noted above, the budgets of the Jewish colonies in the West Bank are not included in the

[34] Ibid.
[35] Ibid. 62.

budget of the military government. This institutional independence from the military government allows the councils of the Jewish colonies to wield considerable influence when dealing with the military government apparatus in the Occupied Territories.

In contrast, the Palestinian Councils receive their funds primarily from the military government. They are not allowed to borrow money or to collect contributions without the approval of the military government. Even some of the taxes which are payable technically to the municipalities, among them the property tax and customs duties, are collected by the military government. The Palestinian municipalities are not allowed to borrow money or to collect contributions without the approval of the person responsible to the Israeli area commander. During the period when elected councils ran the affairs of the Palestinian municipalities (see below), the Israeli authorities frequently refused or delayed requests for budget allocations. At the same time, several military orders were enacted to prevent any individual or public body in the West Bank from receiving money from outside the region.[36]

The elected councils therefore suffered serious deficits in their budgets. According to Meron Benvenisti, between 1985 and 1987, the loans and grants to Palestinian local authorities almost doubled and 21 per cent of the total development budgets in the years 1984–7 was spent on these local authorities. To place this in context, it is important to mention that the total capital investment in US millions of dollars for the years 1983–7 was $24, $21, $38, $56, and $31.2 respectively. The total expenditure of the Jewish settlements in 1987 reached about US$75–85 million.[37] In other words, the budget which is allocated for 65,000 Israelis is more than double that which is allocated for 813,000 Palestinians.[38]

According to Meron Benvenisti, in addition to their financial independence from the military government and their participation in the highest level decision-making apparatus, the Jewish settlers also 'belong to the security forces, being an integral part of the Israeli army (Territorial Defence Units)'. Benvenisti estimates that these settlers possess no less than 10,000 firearms of all types, as well as other military equipment such as wireless sets and vehicles.[39]

A recent incident when the head of the Binyamin Regional Council shot to death a Palestinian youth on 11 January 1988 after he alleged that stones were thrown at his car, is only one example of the settlers'

---

[36] MOs 952, 973, 974, and 998.
[37] Benvenisti, *1987 Report*, 29.
[38] For further details of budget allocations for Palestinians and Jewish settlers in the Occupied Territories, see Ch. 12 in this volume.
[39] Benvenisti, *1987 Report*, 41.

use of their weapons.[40] When al-Haq wrote to the military commander of the central area after a raid by armed settlers on the Deheisheh Refugee Camp on 6 June 1987, in order to inquire about the precautions that the authorities take, if any, to ensure that settlers will not misuse their weapons, al-Haq's question was ignored by the authorities.[41]

V. The Effects of the Israeli System of Administration on the Life of the Indigenous Population

The above description shows that the administrative apparatus of the West Bank is not run autonomously. At the policy-making level and in the routine of daily life, close co-ordination exists between the West Bank administrative apparatus, the central government in Israel itself, and interested Israeli individuals and groups.

In establishing these links, Israel has altered the administrative structure of the West Bank from that provided in the Jordanian law. Departments which existed under the Jordanian law were omitted while others were added.[42]

Under this altered structure, Israel has changed the Jordanian law in force in the West Bank in order to deny the indigenous Palestinian population any involvement at the policy-making level. In addition, in contrast to the Jordanian law which details the different administrative departments, their formation, hierarchy, and functions, the military orders enacted in the West Bank by the area commander provide only vague descriptions of the administrative system.

The following section describes the administrative structure of land-use planning and its alteration during the Israeli occupation. The example of land-use planning was chosen since land-use planning has very little to do with the security of the occupying forces. An examination of other administrative areas, such as the legal system, would show very similar changes.

Physical Planning under Occupation

On 26 July 1967, six weeks after the war, the Israeli Cabinet met to discuss the first version of a scheme submitted by the Minister of Labour, Yigal Allon, regarding the recently occupied territories.[43] The

---

[40] *The Jerusalem Post*, 1 Dec. 1988.
[41] Al-Haq's letter to the military commander for the Central Area, 7 Aug. 1987.
[42] See the example of land-use planning given below; and see Ch. 7 in this volume for a discussion of the legality of such changes.
[43] W. W. Harris, 'War and Settlement Change: The Golan Heights and Jordan Rift 1967–1977' in *Trans. Inst. British Geog.*, NS, III, 3 (1978), 411–12.

plan, later referred to as the Allon Plan, was based on the notion that Israel must retain direct rule over the areas of the Occupied Territories which conferred clear strategic advantages. The proposal further recommended that Israel go beyond establishing military sites in the Occupied Territories and implement immediately a comprehensive policy of Jewish colonization.

This plan had great significance for, as researcher William Harris notes correctly,

> without ever being formally accepted, it gradually became the territorial and ideological base for large scale official settlement programs in the Occupied Territories.[44]

Allon's proposal represented a central position between the divergent ministerial viewpoints of the early Labour government and also provided a convenient informal framework for early 'fact creation'.[45] While intent on establishing strategic settlements, Labour at this time did profess a willingness to consider future territorial compromise.

In 1977, when the Likud Party came to power, this attitude changed. The Likud Party holds the view that the West Bank is not 'occupied' at all and that 'Eretz Israel' ('Greater Israel', which includes all of Mandatory Palestine) is the Jewish people's rightful historic inheritance. According to the Likud Party, the Arabs of 'Eretz Israel' should at most be given 'autonomy' under Israel's sovereign rule, an idea later put forth by Israel in the Camp David accords.

During its terms in power, the Likud Party intensified general land acquisition, using various methods whose legality is seriously disputed.[46] This land has been used to build new settlements or to expand old ones in order to prevent any kind of territorial compromise in 'Eretz Israel'.

Decisions concerning the establishment of settlements are in the hands of various ministerial bodies within the Israeli central government. As was mentioned in the previous section, the most important body is the Ministerial Committee for the Territories. As early as 1970, however, this committee was swamped by settlement-related work and so a sub-committee entitled the Settlement Committee was founded. This committee has served as the primary cabinet institution for dealing with colonization proposals. It is chaired by a senior government figure and attended by representatives of various ministries and settlers' organizations.[47] Proposals for settlements are made either by the

---

[44] W. W. Harris, *Taking Root: Israeli Settlement in the West Bank, the Golan and Gaza–Sinai 1967–1980* (Chichester, 1980), 36.
[45] Ibid. 36.
[46] For the methods of land acquisition, see Shehadeh, *Occupier's Law*, part 1.
[47] Harris, *Taking Root*, 48.

government itself, by interested groups like the World Zionist Organization (WZO), or by settlers' organizations like Amanah (the settler wing of Gush Emunim, set up in Kiryat Arba, Ofra, and many other West Bank settlements). All steps involved in the settlement planning process then occur within the overall land-use planning for the West Bank based, to a large extent, on the WZO's master settlement-plan.

Settlement planning in rural areas is channelled to the Inter-ministerial Settlement Committee via the Settlement Department in the Jewish Agency, while settlement planning in urban areas is directed to the same committee through the Ministry of Housing. If the Ministerial Committee disputes the proposal, it then requires, under the Labour government, a full cabinet decision, or, under the Likud government, discussion behind closed doors of the Cabinet Security Committee. After the proposal is approved, it is submitted to the Agriculture Planning Board which includes representatives from the Settlement Department, the Ministry of Agriculture, and the Ministry of Housing. It is then passed on to the Location Committee which consists of settlement representatives and experts from both the Ministry of Justice and the Israel Land Authority, the latter serving as the custodian of absentee and state land in the West Bank. Finally, the Location Committee informs the settlement department in the Ministry of Housing of its decision.[48] Figure 8.4 describes the decision-making process of establishing Jewish colonies in the Occupied Territories.

In contrast to the lengthy and involved participation of Israeli national planning and building authorities in the establishment of Israeli settlements, building-planning within the Palestinian sector of the West Bank has occurred in a haphazard fashion.

The basic land-use law in force in the West Bank remains the Jordanian Planning Law of 1966. The law is based on a hierarchy, with the jurisdiction and power of each level clearly defined. The law was amended, however, by several Israeli military orders in 1971 and 1975, which manipulated the fundamental structure and logic of the law by cancelling the middle planning levels and replacing them with 'special' committees whose roles and members were not identified.

Under the Jordanian Planning Law, the participation of indigenous individuals and institutions was assured at every level of a very detailed and strict planning process. The Israeli military orders altered this structure in order to deny local individual or institutional participation at all at the highest levels and in any significant capacity at the lowest levels.

The Israeli government has, for example, revived old planning schemes like the Region Jerusalem 5 Plan, commonly known as the RJ5

---

[48] Ibid. 48–50.

The Administration of the West Bank 289

FIGURE 8.4. *Israeli decision-making process for official settlement projects in the Occupied Territories*

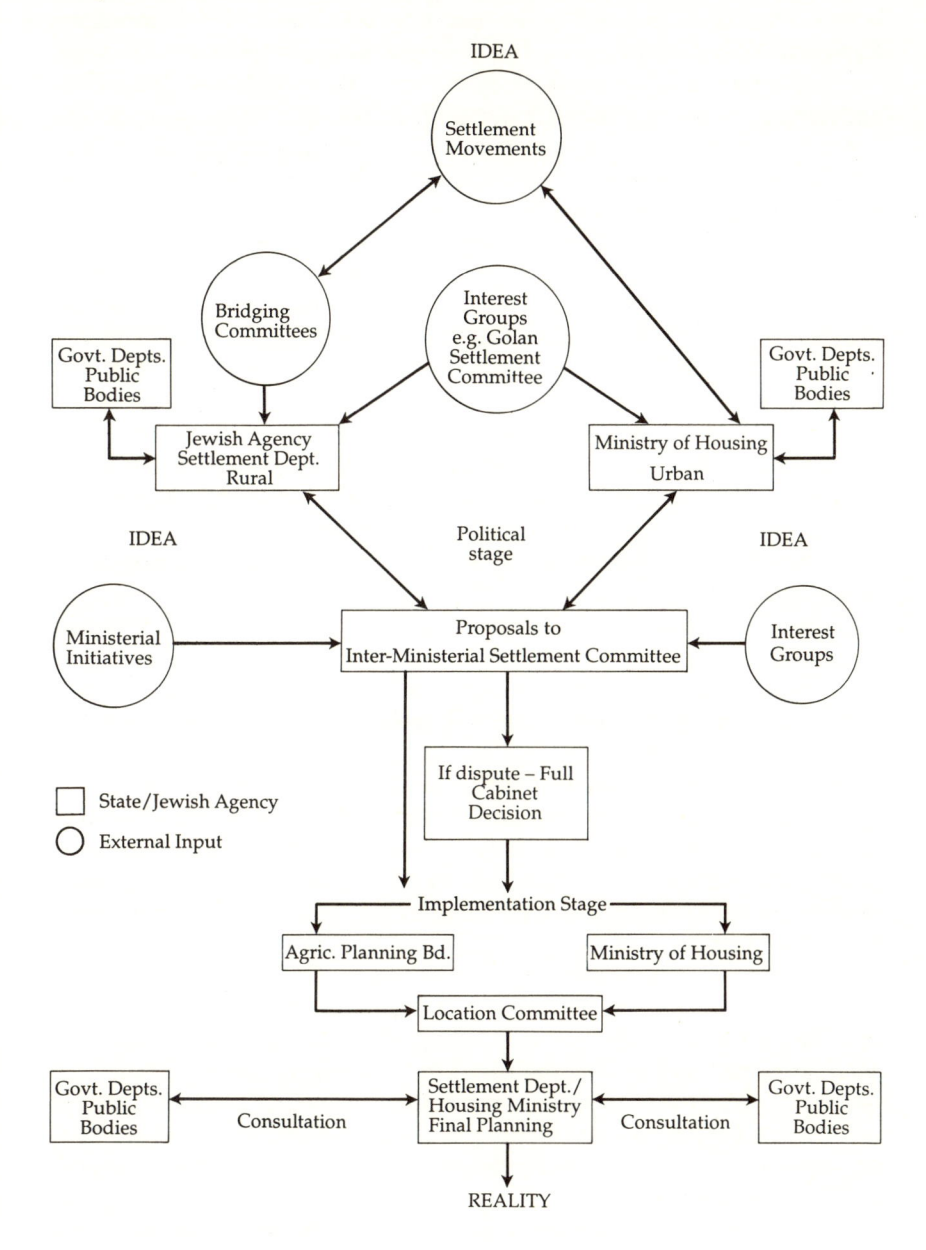

(Source: William Wilson Harris, *Taking Root: Israeli Settlement in the West Bank, the Golan and Gaza–Sinai, 1967–1977* (Chichester, 1980), 49, fig. 11.)

plan. This plan was passed for publication on 11 September 1941 and was approved on 16 April 1942. Although prepared at the end of the British Mandate, the RJ5 plan was never implemented during the subsequent Jordanian period for both practical and technical reasons: the map which accompanied the plan's regulations was lost. The Israeli authorities, however, revived the plan in the late 1970s, despite the absence of the map, and began implementing it without taking into consideration the natural growth of the Palestinian population in the intervening thirty-odd years.[49]

In order to illustrate Israeli changes enacted through military orders to the Jordanian planning law, a brief outline of the original planning structure and the changes made to each element is presented below. All references to 'the law' are to the Jordanian Planning Law of 1966.

1. *The Minister of the Interior*   According to the law, the Minister of the Interior is the head of the planning system and the chairperson of the Higher Planning Council (see below). His responsibilities include co-ordinating the use of the land under his authority according to the public interest, and seeing to it that the planning schemes conform with the overall development plans and economic and social objectives of the government.

Under MO 418 of 1972 concerning Town, Village, and Building Planning, these tasks and responsibilities were transferred to a position filled by a person appointed by the military commander of the area. Until 1985, this appointee was the Israeli officer in charge of interior affairs, who assumed the powers of the Jordanian Minister of the Interior. Since the summer of 1985, this position has been filled by an appointee from the 'infrastructure branch' of the civilian administration in the West Bank. This branch is also responsible for confiscation of land.[50] Palestinian land which has been confiscated so far has been largely used for the establishment and expansion of Jewish settlements in the West Bank.

2. *The Central Planning Department*   The law established a Central Planning Department under the jurisdiction of the Ministry of the Interior. This office has now also come under the 'infrastructure branch' of the Israeli civilian administration, as described above. This department is responsible for preparing regional and outline schemes for towns where these plans do not exist, and, among other tasks, serving as a consultant for planning committees.

In July 1986, several Israeli and Palestinian officials responsible for

---

[49] For more on this plan, see M. Rishmawi, 'Planning in Whose Interest? Land Use Planning as a Strategy for Judaization', al-Haq Occasional Paper No. 4 (Ramallah, 1986), 13–18.

[50] Benvenisti, *1986 Report*, 34.

planning and licensing in the Palestinian sector were accused of corruption. As a result, the department was closed to the public for more than six months with no consideration given to the effect of the closure on development within the area. No building licences were granted to Palestinian residents during that period.

3. *The Higher Planning Council* The law names the Higher Planning Council as the main planning body and states that the responsibilities of the Council include designating specific areas as planning zones, approving planning schemes for the West Bank, and amending or cancelling illegal or unauthorized building licences which may have been granted by the lower planning levels. The Council also serves as an appeal committee for decisions taken by district committees.

According to the Jordanian law, the Council must include the head of the engineers' union, the Attorney-General, the head of the Housing Institute, and various other individuals who represent the interests of the local population. MO 418 gives the IDF commander of the area authority to appoint this Council, but the order does not specify the Council's composition.[51] In fact, the Council is now comprised solely of Israelis. The local population and indigenous institutions which could safeguard the public interest have effectively been excluded from the planning process which affects Palestinian daily life.[52]

The Council was also given the authority to amend, cancel, or suspend a licence for an undefined period of time. MO 418 further gave the Council the right to appoint subcommittees and to define the authority and the jurisdiction of these committees. Neither the number of these committees nor their authority and jurisdiction were specified in the Order or in any other legislation of which this writer is aware.

MO 418 also grants the Council the authority to assume jurisdiction over other committees. In one particular case in which this writer was involved professionally,[53] the Council cancelled the building licence of one Mr Abed al-Jabbar Siyouri of Hebron which the local committee (described below) had granted to him. The Council claimed that the licence was for an area which had previously been declared a closed area. Significantly, Mr Siyouri's land is situated near Kiryat Arba, a large Jewish settlement near Hebron.

4. *The District Planning Committees* MO 418 cancelled completely this level of planning by abolishing the district planning committees and transferring their jurisdiction to the Higher Planning Council.

[51] Benvenisti, *1987 Report*, 34.
[52] See Ch. 14, penultimate section, for comments on the exclusion of local input on matters affecting the local population's interests.
[53] Case 1351/83, *The Municipality of Hebron v. Abdel Jabber Siyouri*, Hebron Magistrates' Court, 1983.

The committees that were abolished had guaranteed that the local population played a crucial role in the planning process. The law stated that these committees were to be established in each of the districts established during Jordanian rule. The responsibilities of these committees included: (a) approving the detailed plans in their area; (b) serving as an appeals committee to look into objections submitted against the regional, outline, and detailed plans in the area of their jurisdiction, and making recommendations to the Higher Council; and (c) serving as a local committee in the area of their jurisdiction, in those villages and zones where no local committee existed.

In place of these committees, the military commander, through MO 604 of 1975 concerning Town, Village, and Building Planning, which amends MO 418, appointed special committees in the areas which fall outside municipal boundaries or the jurisdiction of the village councils. In practice this means that those committees were formed to serve Jewish settlements.

5. *The Local Planning Committees* The law also established local committees in areas that had been designated as planning zones. Most of the West Bank towns enjoyed the status of planning zone, as did some villages. The municipal councils in the towns and villages played the role of planning committees.

The responsibilities of a local committee, according to the law, include the duty to prepare outline and detailed planning schemes, to organize construction, and to issue building licences and violation notices in cases where construction was proceeding contrary to the licence issued in the area of its jurisdiction.

Most of the elected municipal councils in the West Bank were dismissed in 1982 and replaced by Israeli-appointed officials. While the decision to dismiss these councils was apparently made for political reasons, it also served Israel's planning interests in the West Bank. Raja Shehadeh, in his book *Occupier's Law*, states:

In Hebron, for example, where a Jewish settlement has been established, the existence of an Israeli mayor is a great asset to the development of the settlement. Before his dismissal, the Palestinian mayor, Mustafa Natshe, had taken proceedings before the High Court of Justice to challenge the expansionist activities of the Jewish settlement inside his town. When the Israeli mayor took over, he promptly withdrew the case from the Court. On 21 May 1984, the boundaries of the town were changed to allow more areas to be given to the nearby settlement of Kiryat Arba. The Israeli mayor has also been granting licences for the settlers inside the town to proceed with the enlargement of their settlement and, in some cases, has withdrawn licences that had been granted to Arab residents by the previous mayor. In one case he even took criminal proceedings against a Palestinian who had built a house on the basis of a licence given to him by the previous mayor... On 5 May 1983, the Israeli mayor moved the bus station and transferred the old site to the Jewish settlers. In the other West Bank towns, town plans are being designed by Israeli planners while the Palestinian planning boards are presided over by Israeli officials. The Jewish Council's planning committee members are elected by the settlers.[54]

By changing the structure of the planning hierarchy in the West Bank through the amendment of Jordanian laws, Israel has denied the local Palestinian population the right to participate in the planning process, while at the same time granting the settlers representation. Thus Israel has been able to plan for the West Bank in a way that serves its own exclusive interest.

Conclusion

Israel has designed a system of governance for the West Bank and Gaza to serve an annexationist aim. This chapter has argued that the purpose of the Israeli-introduced administrative structure in the West Bank is to integrate the administration of the Occupied Territories into Israel's own central governmental system.

The chapter examined the West Bank system of government on both central and local level. It also attempted to show the different systems designed for Palestinians and Jewish settlers. While Palestinians are denied any participation in the decision-making apparatus and fall under the direct control of the military government, the Jewish settlers participate in decision-making and are served directly by the Israeli ministries in Israel proper. To show the effects of these changes on the daily life of the Palestinian population, a case-study of one function, land-use planning, has been presented.

In other words, Israel's annexationist aims have been revealed by the manner in which it has chosen to administer the territories it occupied in 1967.

[54] Shehadeh, *Occupier's Law*, 55–6.

9

The Right to Form Trade Unions under Military Occupation

JOHN QUIGLEY

STATES occupying territory in belligerent occupation are typically hostile to organizations formed by the occupied population. Such organizations, from the standpoint of the occupant, hold the danger that they will foment opposition to the occupation. The law of military occupation requires a belligerent, however, to protect freedom of association, and specifically trade union organizing. A right to organize trade unions is deemed by human rights law to be necessary for the economic and social well-being of workers.

This article analyses the duty of a military occupant to permit trade union organizing. It argues: (*a*) that a military occupant bears a customary law obligation to permit trade union organizing in territory under its occupation; (*b*) that a military occupant bears an obligation towards the occupied population to apply any treaties that specify a right to trade union organizing; (*c*) that with respect to either customary or treaty obligations to permit trade union organizing, a military occupant may restrict this right only in circumstances threatening its vital interests as occupant.

I. Customary Law Obligation to Permit Trade Union Organizing during Military Occupation

A military occupant is obliged by customary law to permit trade union organizing. This is so because (*a*) customary human rights law includes a right to trade union organizing and (*b*) the customary law of human rights is binding on a military occupant in relation to the occupied population.

---

* A revised version of this paper, which was written for al-Haq's conference, was published under the title 'Trade Unions and War: The Right to Organize under Belligerent Occupation' in *Hastings International and Comparative Law Review* 13(2) (1990).

Customary law recognizes a right to trade union organizing

The right to trade union organizing is fundamental in the modern world. '[F]reedom of association for trade union purposes is a major postulate of democratic government in an industrial society', writes Jenks, a leading commentator on labour rights.[1] One of the first areas of human rights to receive international protection was labour rights. Following World War I the international community founded the International Labour Organisation (ILO), in part out of a recognition that industrial harmony was a prerequisite for international peace, and in part because of the importance to workers of the right to organize.[2]

Since that time, the ILO has developed a prodigious body of labour standards. Perhaps the most important of these is the right of labour to organize trade unions. This right is necessary in an industrial context if workers are to have meaningful participation in setting the conditions of their labour.[3] It is also necessary in order to prevent unfair exploitation by employers, particularly in a period of scarcity of work, when market forces permit an employer to offer only minimal compensation for work performed.

The question of whether freedom of association is a customary law right has been explored but little, primarily because so many states adhere to treaties carrying an obligation to recognize freedom of association. It is accepted by the ILO, however, that the right has entered customary law as a result of widespread recognition of it:

> The principle of freedom of association is particularly important in the ILO, where it is looked upon as a kind of customary rule which has become part of the common heritage of man in the twentieth century independently of the provisions of international labour conventions.[4]

The ILO's Fact-Finding and Conciliation Commission on Freedom of Association has stated that 'freedom of association has become a customary rule above the [ILO] Conventions'.[5]

A freedom to form trade union organizations is established in customary law by widespread adherence by states to relevant international instruments and by state practice in actually permitting trade unions to function.

State Practice Reflected in International Instruments Jenks finds a customary law obligation in the Universal Declaration of Human Rights.

---

[1] C. W. Jenks, *Human Rights and International Labour Standards* (London, 1960), 50.
[2] Constitution of the ILO, 9 Oct. 1946 (amended text), Preamble, *UNTS* vol. 15, 35.
[3] N. Valticos, *International Labour Law* (Deventer, 1979), 79.
[4] G. Caire, *Freedom of Association and Economic Development* (Geneva, 1977), 29.
[5] ILO, *The Trade Union Situation in Chile: Report of the Fact-Finding and Conciliation Commission on Freedom of Association* (Geneva, 1975), 108, para. 466.

The Declaration provides: 'Everyone has the right to form and to join trade unions for the protection of his interests.'[6] It is forcefully argued by many commentators that all norms in the Universal Declaration have entered customary law as a result of state practice: 'This constant and widespread recognition of the principles of the Universal Declaration clothes it, in my opinion, in the character of customary law.'[7]

With respect to a right to trade union organizing, recognition of the right does not rest on the Universal Declaration alone, however. It is strongly supported by the practice of states in permitting trade unions to function. Nearly all states permit trade union organizing, though regulation varies widely.

Every major human rights treaty of general scope has included a right to trade union organizing. This uniform recognition constitutes formidable state practice indicating that states view such a right as part of customary law.

The two major human rights treaties at the universal level both recognize a right to form trade unions. The International Covenant on Civil and Political Rights provides: 'Everyone shall have the right to freedom of association with others, including the right to form and join trade unions for the protection of his interests.'[8] The International Covenant on Economic, Social and Cultural Rights provides a 'right of everyone to form trade unions and join the trade union of his choice, subject only to the rules of the organisation concerned, for the promotion and protection of his economic and social interests'.[9]

The regional human rights treaties uniformly provide for a right to trade union organizing. The Convention for the Protection of Human Rights and Fundamental Freedoms (Europe) provides: 'Everyone has the right to freedom of peaceful assembly and to freedom of association with others, including the right to form and to join trade unions for the protection of his interests.'[10] The European Social Charter provides: 'With a view to ensuring or promoting the freedom of workers and employers to form local, national, or international organizations for the protection of their economic and social interests and to join those organizations, the Contracting Parties undertake that national law shall

---

[6] Jenks, *Human Rights and International Labour Standards*, 50. UDHR Art. 23(4). UNGA Res. 217, 10 Dec. 1948.

[7] H. Waldock, 'Human Rights in Contemporary International Law and the Significance of the European Convention', *ICLQ* 14, Supp. Pub. No. 11 (1965), 14. To the same effect, see J. Humphrey, 'The Universal Declaration of Human Rights: Its History, Impact and Juridical Character', in B. G. Ramcharan (ed.), *Human Rights: Thirty Years after the Universal Declaration* (The Hague, 1979), 33; M. G. Kaladharan Nayar, 'Human Rights: The United Nations and United States Foreign Policy', *HILJ* 19 (1978), 816.

[8] Art. 22(1); 16 Dec. 1966, entered into force 23 Mar. 1976; *UNTS* 999, 171; *ILM* 6 (1967), 368.

[9] Art. 8(1)(a); entered into force 3 Jan. 1976; *UNTS* 993, 3; *ILM* 6 (1967), 360.

[10] Art. 11(1); 4 Nov. 1950; *UNTS* 213, 222.

not be such as to impair, nor shall it be so applied as to impair, this freedom.'[11] The American Convention on Human Rights provides: 'Everyone has the right to associate freely for ideological, religious, political, economic, labor, social, cultural, sports, or other purposes.'[12] The African Charter on Human and Peoples' Rights states: 'Every individual shall have the right to free association provided that he abides by the law.'[13]

Thus, the major universal and regional human rights treaties protect trade union organizing. In addition, a treaty specifically on the right to trade union organizing has been ratified by over ninety states. The Freedom of Association and Protection of the Right to Organise Convention of 1948 provides:

Workers and employers, without distinction whatsoever, shall have the right to establish and, subject only to the rules of the organisation concerned, to join organisations of their own choosing without previous authorisation.[14]

Beyond the indicated treaties, all states belonging to the International Labour Organisation, of which there are approximately 150, recognize a right to association. The ILO bases its structure on the premise that governments, management, and organized labour each have a role in industrial relations. The ILO Governing Body is composed of representatives of workers, employers, and governments.[15] The Annex to the ILO Constitution proclaims as an aim of the ILO that 'freedom of expression and of association are essential to sustained progress'.[16] Thus, a failure to recognize a right of labour to organize is inconsistent with membership in the ILO. Under ILO procedures, complaints alleging violation of the right of freedom of association may be brought against even those member states that have not ratified the Freedom of Association and Protection of the Right to Organize Convention.[17]

The International Labour Organisation has developed a substantial

---

[11] Art. 5; 18 Oct. 1961, entered into force 26 Feb. 1965; *Treaty Series* No. 38 (1965), Cmd. 2643.

[12] Art. 16; 22 Nov. 1969, entered into force June 1978; Org. of American States, *Official Records* OEA/SER.K/XVI/1.1, Doc. 65, Rev. 1, Corr. 1, 7 Jan. 1970; *ILM* 9 (1970), 673.

[13] Art. 10(1); 27 June 1981, entered into force 21 Oct. 1986, *ILM* 21 (1982), 58; *Human Rights Law Journal*, 7 (1986), 403.

[14] Art. 2; 9 July 1948, ILO No. 87, *UNTS* 68, 17.

[15] Constitution of the ILO, 9 Oct. 1946 (amended text), Art. 7(1) *UNTS* 15.

[16] Declaration concerning the Aims and Purposes of the ILO, Annex to ILO Constitution, 104.

[17] Valticos, *International Labour Law*, 248. For an example, see ILO, *The Trade Situation in Chile*, 108, para. 466, where the Freedom of Association Commission stated that, though Chile had not ratified the Freedom of Association and Protection of the Right to Organize Convention (No. 87), '[B]y its membership of the International Labour Organisation, Chile is bound to respect a certain number of general rules which have been established for the common good of the peoples of the twentieth century.' The Commission found freedom of association included among those general rules.

body of practice in implementation of the right of trade union organizing. The Freedom of Association Committee of the ILO's Governing Body adjudicates complaints alleging violation of the freedom of association.[18] The European Human Rights Commission has enforced the European treaty's provision on association, finding that the state may not interfere with trade union activity. The Commission has ruled that the provision 'requires that trade unions should be able to pursue their tasks, including in particular the protection of the interests of their members without interference by State authorities'.[19]

State Practice has Created a Customary Norm Protecting Freedom of Association Standards for finding that a state practice has become a customary norm of international law are not without ambiguity. However, the consistent state practice in recognizing a right to trade union organizing, plus the cited international resolutions, treaties, and practice, suffices to establish a right to trade union organizing as a customary norm.

A United States court faced with the issue of whether torture is prohibited by a customary norm concluded that it was so prohibited. In reaching that conclusion, the court cited evidence similar to that cited here, referring to the Universal Declaration of Human Rights, and universal and regional human rights treaties.[20] Moreover, the state practice in recognizing a right to organize trade unions is more consistent than the state practice in refraining from torture. The US court found torture to be prohibited by customary law even though torture is widely practised by states.

With the right to trade union organizing, one finds a concurrence of a virtually uniform practice of states in permitting trade unions to exist, and a virtually uniform recognition by states in international instruments that they are obliged to permit trade unions to exist. Thus, both the state practice and *opinio juris* required for formation of a customary norm are present.[21]

Content of the Customary Norm on Freedom of Association A difficulty in determining the content of the customary right to freedom of association is that most practice has taken place through the ILO, which typically applies treaties, since so many states adhere to labour protec-

[18] ILO, *Freedom of Association. Digest of Decisions and Principles of the Freedom of Association Committee of the Governing Body of the ILO*, 3rd edn. (Geneva, 1985), paras. 208–83.
[19] X. v. United Kingdom, Applcn. No. 7990/77, Decision of 11 May 1981, para. 7, in Council of Europe, ECHR, *Decisions and Reports*, 24 (1981), 57.
[20] *Filartiga v. Pena-Irala*, US Ct. of App., 2nd Jud. Circ., *Federal Reporter* 630 (1980), 2d ser., 876.
[21] The *North Sea Continental Shelf* cases (FRG v. Denmark, FRG v. Netherlands (1980)), in *ICJ Reports* (1969), paras. 37, 71.

tion treaties. This fact is not, however, an insurmountable obstacle to determining the content of the customary norm on freedom of association.

The International Court of Justice was faced with a similar problem in *Nicaragua v. United States of America*. In that case Nicaragua alleged that the United States was committing aggression against it. The Court found that for reasons relating to limitations in the United States' acceptance of the Court's jurisdiction it must decide Nicaragua's allegations not on the basis of the United Nations Charter but on the basis of customary law. Confronted with the fact that most state practice had turned on the Charter, it concluded, with little discussion, that customary law did not differ from the Charter law as to use of force.[22]

The same may be concluded regarding the content of the customary right to freedom of association. ILO practice implementing treaties on freedom of association may serve as a guide to the content of the customary norm. To provide a comprehensive enumeration of protected rights exceeds the scope of this analysis, but one can conclude that, at a minimum, the customary norm includes a right to form trade unions,[23] a prohibition against governmental exclusion of a worker from a trade union because of the worker's political opinion,[24] a prohibition against governmental interference in election of trade union officers, such as a procedure whereby candidates must be approved by the government,[25] a prohibition against dismissal from their posts by the government of trade union officials, in any situation, but including removal because of a trade union official's political activity,[26] and a prohibition against government closure of a trade union.[27] The ILO Freedom of Association Committee has found all these concepts within the right to freedom of association. The customary norm also prohibits detention as punishment for trade union activity.[28]

Customary Human Rights Law is Binding on a Military Occupant

Customary human rights norms, including that on freedom of association, must be applied by a state exercising belligerent occupation of

---

[22] *Nicaragua v. USA, ICJ Reports* (1986), paras. 187–201.
[23] ILO, *Freedom of Association*, para. 208.
[24] Ibid. para. 212.
[25] Ibid. paras. 455–61. *Accord: Case of Arab Lawyers Union*, High Court of Israel, Ruling of 16 Sept. 1987, invalidating an administrative order permitting government officials to appoint executive board of a lawyers union. *Al-Fajr*, 18 Oct. 1987, 8.
[26] ILO, *Freedom of Association*, paras. 476–9.
[27] Ibid. paras. 487–8.
[28] See, e.g., two decisions of the Human Rights Committee that implements the ICCPR: (1) *Case of Ismael Weinberger*, Communication No. R. 7/28, finding a violation of Art. 19(2) (freedom of expression) 'because he was detained for having disseminated information relating to trade-union activities', *Report of the Human Rights Committee*, 36

territory not its own. It has been correctly concluded, for example, that the population of the territory occupied by Israel in 1967 should have the right to invoke customary human rights norms in Israel's courts.[29]

This conclusion that customary human rights norms are binding on a military occupant is reflected both in United Nations practice and in the practice of the European Commission of Human Rights.[30]

1. State Practice in the United Nations United Nations reports, resolutions, and decisions on military occupation reflect state practice for the position that customary human rights law applies in military occupation.

The United Nations General Assembly affirmed in a near-unanimous resolution the applicability of human rights law to armed conflict: 'Fundamental human rights, as accepted in international law and laid down in international instruments, continue to apply fully in situations of armed conflict.'[31]

The Assembly has referred to the Universal Declaration of Human Rights as providing law applicable in military occupation. In establishing a committee to monitor human rights in territories occupied by Israel in 1967, the Assembly stated that it was 'guided by... the Universal Declaration of Human Rights'.[32] In a resolution calling on Israel to accept recommendations made by that monitoring committee, the Assembly asked Israel 'to comply with its obligations under... the Universal Declaration of Human Rights'.[33]

After conducting a study mandated by the General Assembly, the Secretary-General too found human rights law to apply in wartime:

[T]he human rights provisions of the [UN] Charter, the Universal Declaration of Human Rights and the International Covenants on Human Rights apply both in times of peace and in times of war and armed conflicts.[34]

He found, referring to the United Nations Charter, that

UN GAOR Supp. (No. 40) at 119, UN Doc. A/36/40 (1981); (2) *Case of Rosario Pietraroia* (an official of the Uruguay metal-workers union), Communication No. R.10/44, finding a violation of Art. 19(2) 'because he was arrested, detained and tried for his political and trade-union activities', ibid. at 159.

[29] T. Meron, 'West Bank and Gaza: Human Rights and Humanitarian Law in the Period of Transition', *IYHR* 9 (1979), 113.

[30] For a more detailed discussion, see J. Quigley, 'The Relation between Human Rights Law and the Law of Belligerent Occupation: Does an Occupied Population Have a Right to Freedom of Assembly and Expression?', 12 *Boston College Int. Comp. Law Rev.* (1989), 1. See also chs. 1 and 16 in this volume.

[31] UNGA Res. 2675, 25th sess., 1922nd plen. mtg., 9 Dec. 1970, para. 1. The vote was 109 to 0, with 8 abstentions.

[32] UNGA Res. 2443, 23rd sess., 1748th plen. mtg., 19 Dec. 1968, preambular para. 1.

[33] UNGA Res. 2727, 225th sess., 1931st plen. mtg., 15 Dec. 1970, para. 2.

[34] UNGA, *Official Records*, 25th sess., *Respect for Human Rights in Armed Conflicts: Report of the Secretary-General*, 18 Sept. 1970, UN Doc. A/8052, Annex I: 'General Norms Concerning Respect for Human Rights in their Applicability to Armed Conflicts', 87, para. 3.

[t]he phraseology of the Charter would . . . encompass persons living under the jurisdiction of their own national authorities and persons living in territories under belligerent occupation.[35]

The Secretary-General considered as reflective of state practice Security Council Resolution 237, adopted following the 1967 Arab–Israeli conflict, which contemplated the applicability of human rights norms in wartime:

The principle that human rights shall be protected not only in peacetime but also under conditions of armed conflict was significantly repeated more recently by the Security Council when, in its resolution 237 (1967) of 14 June 1967, it stated that 'essential and inalienable human rights should be respected even during the vicissitudes of war'.[36]

The Human Rights Commission of the United Nations, like the General Assembly, has relied upon the Universal Declaration of Human Rights in calling upon Israel to refrain from certain actions in territory it occupied in 1967.[37] The Commission stated that,

in accordance with the provisions of the Charter of the United Nations and those of the Universal Declaration of Human Rights, Member States bear a special responsibility to ensure the protection of human rights and to reaffirm faith in fundamental human rights and in the dignity and worth of the human person.[38]

The reference to the Charter is evidently to its provisions on human rights—Articles 1, 55, and 56. The Commission has also referred to the International Covenant on Civil and Political Rights as a document by which it is 'guided' in assessing the situation in the Arab territory occupied by Israel in 1967.[39]

That United Nations bodies should consider human rights law applicable in occupied territory is consistent with the history of the development of human rights law by the United Nations. The United Nations promoted human rights law in part because of the atrocities committed in occupied territory during World War II:

The prominence given to human rights in the Charter was the consequence of the appalling atrocities and degradations inflicted by the Nazi regime on the Jews of Europe and on peoples of the *occupied territories*. The motive behind its provisions was the desire to prevent any recurrence of such outrages upon

---

[35] UNGA, *Official Records*, 24th sess., *Respect for Human Rights in Armed Conflict: Report of the Secretary-General*, 20 Nov. 1969, UN Doc. A/7720, 12, para. 23.
[36] Ibid. 15, para. 31.
[37] Human Rights Commission Res., 23 Mar. 1972, preambular paras. 1 and 2.
[38] Ibid. preambular para. 4.
[39] 'Question of the Violation of Human Rights in the Occupied Arab Territories, Including Palestine', UNGA Res., 9 Feb. 1987, preambular para. 2, UN Doc. E/CN.4/1987.L.4.

humanity by making the preservation of the fundamental rights and freedoms of the individual everywhere a matter of international concern to every State.[40]

2. European Commission Rulings An extensive body of adjudicatory law has been developed under the European Convention for the Protection of Human Rights and Fundamental Freedoms by the Commission on Human Rights and Court of Human Rights established under that Convention. While the Court of Human Rights has not considered the applicability of customary human rights in military occupation, the Commission on Human Rights has twice addressed this question. In both cases, the Commission has decided that human rights law applies during military occupation.

In *Cyprus v. Turkey*, filed after Turkey occupied a portion of Cyprus in 1974, Cyprus alleged human rights violations by Turkey in that territory. Turkey denied that it was in military occupation, on the ground that a new government had been established in the portion of Cyprus in question, and that Turkey did not exercise control there.

In finding Cyprus' application admissible, the Commission decided that Turkey did exercise control as a military occupant. Turkish forces, it said, had

> entered the island of Cyprus, operating solely under the direction of the Turkish Government and under established rules governing the structure and command of these armed forces including the establishment of military courts.[41]

The Commission cited Article 1 of the European Convention, which renders states parties responsible for human rights 'to everyone within their jurisdiction'. It stated that this Article means

> that the High Contracting Parties are bound to secure the said rights and freedoms to all persons under their actual authority and responsibility, not only when that authority is exercised within their own territory but also when it is exercised abroad.[42]

The Commission's decision in *Cyprus v. Turkey* has been characterized as 'a significant recognition in principle of the applicability of international human rights law to occupied territories'.[43] The Commission's rationale is that a state party is responsible in any territory over which

---

[40] Waldock, *Human Rights in Contemporary International Law*, 1 (emphasis added).
[41] *Cyprus v. Turkey*, Decision on Admissibility, 10 July 1978, Appln. No. 8007/77, ECHR, *ILR* vol. 62 (1982), 75, para. 21.
[42] Ibid. 74, para. 19.
[43] Adam Roberts, 'What Is Military Occupation?', *BYIL* 55 (1985), 287. For agreement with the statement in text that the Commission ruled that the Convention was applicable to a state party exercising belligerent occupation, see T. Buergenthal, 'To Respect and to Ensure: State Obligations and Permissible Derogations', in L. Henkin (ed.) *The International Bill of Rights: The Covenant on Civil and Political Rights* (New York, 1981), 76–7.

it exercises jurisdiction. Thus, a state coming into control of territory is responsible even if it has not established a military government.[44]

The Commission had reached the same conclusion in a previous case. Rudolf Hess was incarcerated in Spandau Prison, Berlin, on conviction for World War II crimes against peace. His wife petitioned for his release. The United Kingdom was one of four states in joint military occupation of Berlin. The Commission dismissed the complaint. It decided that the United Kingdom was not responsible for Hess's incarceration under Article 1 of the European Convention, but only because of the quadripartite character of the occupation:

> The commission is of the opinion that the joint authority cannot be divided into four separate jurisdictions and that therefore the United Kingdom's participation in the exercise of the joint authority and consequently in the administration and supervision of Spandau Prison is not a matter 'within the jurisdiction' of the United Kingdom, within the meaning of Article 1 of the Convention.[45]

The Commission said 'that there is in principle, from a legal point of view, no reason why acts of the British authorities in Berlin should not entail the liability of the United Kingdom under the Convention.'[46] Thus, though it found that the quadripartite character of the occupation relieved the United Kingdom of responsibility, the Commission considered the European Convention to cover the United Kingdom's actions while in military occupation of foreign territory.

3. State Practice in Exercise of Military Occupation The practice of states exercising belligerent occupation has typically followed that of states in other situations, namely, to permit trade unions to be formed. The World War I Allies occupying the German Rhineland, from 1918 to 1923, permitted trade unions to form and function, though they imposed limitations on their activity.[47] The World War II Allies occupying Germany permitted trade unions with fewer limitations than in the Rhineland occupation.[48] Israel, in occupation of the West Bank since 1967, has permitted trade unions to exist while imposing limitations on their activity;[49] in its occupation of the Gaza Strip, also since 1967, it

---

[44] Ibid. Buergenthal, 76–7.

[45] *Ilse Hess v. United Kingdom*, Decision on Admissibility, 28 May 1975, ECHR, *Decisions and Reports* 2 (1975), 72, at 74.

[46] Ibid. 73.

[47] E. Fraenkel, *Military Occupation and the Rule of Law: Occupation Government in the Rhineland, 1918–1923* (London, 1944), 41–2.

[48] E. H. Litchfield, *Governing Postwar Germany* (New York, 1953), 364–5. See, e.g., 'Directive of the US Joint Chiefs of Staff to the Commander-in-Chief of the US Forces of Occupation Regarding the Military Government of Germany' (JCS 1067), April 1945, para. 23, in B. R. von Oppen (ed.), *Documents on Germany under Occupation 1945–1954* (London, 1955), 23.

[49] R. Shehadeh and J. Kuttab, *The West Bank and the Rule of Law* (Geneva, 1980), 119–20; Israel National Section, International Commission of Jurists, *The Rule of Law in the Areas Administered by Israel* (Tel Aviv, 1981), 79.

banned trade unions until 1979, permitting them to function thereafter but forbidding the holding of elections for union officers.[50]

With respect to a group of lawyers seeking the right to form a union in the West Bank, the Israeli military governor issued an order retaining for himself the right to appoint the members of the executive committee of the union, and prohibiting independent financing of the union. The Supreme Court of Israel, ruling on an appeal filed by the lawyers, stated that the lawyers had a right to elect their own executive committee and to fund the union themselves.[51] The Court based its finding not on human rights law, but on Article 43 of the 1907 Hague Regulations, which requires an occupier to restore 'public life'.[52] The Court held that the 'public life' that an occupant is required to restore is that of a democratic late twentieth-century state.[53] The Court thus found a requirement to follow democratic practices, which it said included a right for this particular union to elect its own officers, subject, it said, to the power of the military governor to dismiss union officers who might have a connection with a 'hostile organization'.[54] It found freedom of trade union activity to be protected in democratic society.[55] The Court thus found certain basic trade union rights protected under humanitarian law.

II. A Military Occupant must Apply Treaties that Protect Trade Union Organizing

A state exercising belligerent occupation is obliged to apply towards the occupied population applicable treaties that protect the right to trade union organizing. It must apply its own treaties as well as those in force for the displaced sovereign.

Treaties of the Displaced Sovereign

A state exercising belligerent occupancy is obliged to apply the law in force at commencement of its occupation. Any treaties relating to labour standards form part of that law and must therefore be applied by the occupant.

1. Obligation to Apply Law in Force at Commencement of Occupation A military occupant is required by the customary law of military occupa-

---

[50] J. R. Hiltermann, 'Palestinian Unions: Force for Change in the West Bank', *Nation*, 3 Oct. 1987, 340.
[51] HC 507/85 *Bahij Tamimi et al. v. Minister of Defence et al.*, ruling of 16 Sept. 1987.
[52] For citations and details of Hague Regs., see Ch. 1, text at n. 4.
[53] HC 507/85, *Bahij Tamini et al. v. Minister of Defence et al.*, para. 2.
[54] Ibid. para. 10.
[55] Ibid. para. 1.

tion to retain in force the law in effect in territory it occupies. The 1907 Hague Regulations impose on an occupant an obligation to 'respect ..., unless absolutely prevented, the laws in force in the country'.[56] This norm is considered to have entered customary law.[57]

2. Prior Labour Conventions as Part of the Law in Force Labour conventions adhered to by the displaced sovereign prior to commencement of the occupation and in force for it at commencement of the occupation constitute part of the law in force in the occupied territory. They therefore are part of the law that a military occupant is obliged to enforce.

Not all treaties adhered to by the displaced sovereign need be enforced by the military occupant. A treaty of military alliance, for example, would not be part of the law in force since it would not create rights and duties for persons inhabiting the territory that came under occupation. However, a labour convention creates rights and duties for persons and therefore is part of the law in force.

This is true of any treaty considered by the displaced sovereign to have been part of the law in force. That sovereign might have legislated the treaty into domestic law, or it might by other legislation or by practice have considered it to be part of the law in force without legislative incorporation of the particular treaty.

The view of Meron on this point is:

> If, prior to the commencement of the occupation of a territory, the territorial sovereign had ratified an international labour convention and adopted the necessary implementing legislation, the occupant must respect the relevant labour standards as part of the local legislation in force.[58]

This view is correct, except, as noted, that the treaty may have entered into domestic law other than by enactment of implementing legislation for the specific treaty.

The ILO Governing Body concurs with this view with respect to the Freedom of Association Convention,[59] finding that the Convention is applicable in territory under military occupation if the sovereign displaced by the occupation was a party to it at the commencement of the occupation.[60]

---

[56] Art. 43.

[57] M. Shamgar, 'Legal Concepts and Problems of the Israeli Military Government: The Initial Stage', in Shamgar (ed.), *Military Government in the Territories Administered* by Israel *1967–1980*, i: *The Legal Aspects* (Jerusalem, 1982), 28.

[58] T. Meron, 'Applicability of Multilateral Conventions to Occupied Territories', in Shamgar (ed.), *Military Government*, 228.

[59] Art. 2; 9 July 1948, ILO No. 87, *UNTS* 68, 17.

[60] Such may be inferred from the Governing Body's statement, in the course of deciding whether the Convention is binding on Israel with respect to the West Bank: 'It

Treaties of the Occupant

A state exercising belligerent occupation is also obliged to apply labour rights treaties to which it adheres, if by their terms they are applicable in a situation of military occupation. The Convention on the Protection of Human Rights and Fundamental Freedoms (Europe) obliges states parties to 'secure to everyone within their jurisdiction' the rights enumerated in the Convention.[61] The Commission on Human Rights, applying that provision, found the Convention applicable to military occupation in the *Hess* and the *Cyprus v. Turkey* cases.[62] The American Convention on Human Rights uses similar phrasing, obliging states parties to protect 'all persons subject to their jurisdiction'.[63] The International Covenant on Civil and Political Rights requires a state party to protect 'all individuals within its territory and subject to its jurisdiction'.[64]

The Convention Concerning Freedom of Association and Protection of the Right to Organize contains no language specifying the territory in which the Convention is to apply. A provision of the Convention does indicate that it is to apply in 'colonies, protectorates, and possessions which are not fully self-governing'.[65] It is thus clear that the Convention applies outside the metropolitan territory of a state party.

Human rights treaties are construed expansively to provide maximum protection of rights. It was to achieve maximum applicability that the International Court of Justice decided in 1951 to permit reservations to the Genocide Convention. At a time when reservations were not generally admitted in multilateral treaties, the Court found that they should be permitted in the case of the Genocide Convention because of its humanitarian purpose.[66]

Neither the universal and regional human rights treaties nor the Convention Concerning Freedom of Association mention the situation of military occupation. They should be construed to apply wherever a

---

may be noted that Convention No. 87, which has not been ratified by Jordan, was not applicable to the West Bank at the time of the occupation.' Governing Body, International Labour Office, *Report of the Director-General: Sixth Supplementary Report: Second Report of the Officers of the Governing Body: Representation submitted by the Union of Building and Construction Workers of Nablus and thirteen other trade unions under Art. 24 of the Constitution of the ILO alleging non-observance by Israel of the Freedom of Association and Protection of the Right to Organise Convention, 1948 (No. 87)*, para. 6, 23 June 1986, 233rd sess., ILO Doc. No. GB.233/16/30 (1986).

[61] Art. 1.
[62] See nn. 41–6 above.
[63] Art. 1.
[64] Art. 2(1).
[65] Art. 12 (referring to Art. 35 of the ILO Constitution, which uses the quoted language).
[66] The *Genocide* case. Reservations to the Convention on the Prevention and Punishment of the Crime of Genocide, Advisory Opinion of 28 May 1951 *ICJ Reports* (1951), 23.

state party exercises jurisdiction, whether *de jure* or *de facto*. Reports have been filed with the ILO by Israel regarding its compliance with ILO conventions in the West Bank, over which it exercises belligerent occupation.[67]

The only conceivable objection to applying such treaties in military occupation is the possible affront to the sovereignty of the displaced sovereign.[68] This consideration has been raised in ILO proceedings. However, application of a human rights treaty does not imply sovereign rights for the occupant. The humanitarian purpose of human rights law makes it particularly important that such treaties be applied. As indicated by the International Court of Justice in the *Genocide* case:

In such a convention the contracting States do not have any interests of their own; they merely have, one and all, a common interest, namely, the accomplishment of those high purposes which are the *raison d'être* of the convention. Consequently, in a convention of this type one cannot speak of individual advantages or disadvantages to States, or of the maintenance of a perfect contractual balance between rights and duties. The high ideals which inspired the Convention provide, by virtue of the common will of the parties, the foundation and measure of all its provisions.[69]

The ILO has decided this matter in keeping with this view. It has determined, in accord with the fact that all states members of the ILO are obliged to allow freedom of trade union association,[70] that a state member is bound by this obligation with respect to territory it holds under military occupation.[71] It has, however, determined that member states are not bound to submit to the jurisdiction of the ILO Governing Body, which also investigates freedom of association violations, as regards territory they hold in military occupation.[72] It so decided by construing the Director-General's Standing Orders, which authorize the Governing Body to hear complaints regarding matters arising 'within' a member state's 'jurisdiction'.[73]

This decision is inconsistent with the European Commission's finding that reference to actions 'within' a state's 'jurisdiction' applies to actions in territory held in military occupation by a state.[74] The Commission's interpretation is more in keeping with the humanitarian character of human rights law.

---

[67] Meron, 'Applicability of Multilateral Conventions to Occupied Territories', 222.
[68] Ibid. 223. See also John Dugard's proposal in this volume that this question be put to the ICJ for an advisory opinion.
[69] The *Genocide* case, 23.
[70] See notes 15–17 above.
[71] *Report of the Director-General* (n. 60 above), para 10.
[72] Ibid. para 7.
[73] Standing Orders, Art. 2, para. 2(f), quoted in *Report of the Director-General* (n. 60 above), para. 4.
[74] See nn. 41–6 above.

III. A Military Occupant may Restrict Trade Union Organizing only in Extreme Situations

Under either treaty or customary law, a military occupant may restrict the right to trade union organizing in two situations. These situations are: (*a*) threat to national security or public order; (*b*) a declared public emergency.

Threat to National Security or Public Order

The human rights instruments quoted above typically permit a state to limit those rights to protect national security and public order. The Universal Declaration of Human Rights permits a state to restrict any of the rights enumerated in the Declaration:

> In the exercise of his rights and freedoms, everyone shall be subject only to such limitations as are determined by law solely for the purpose of securing due recognition and respect for the rights and freedoms of others and of meeting the just requirements of morality, public order, and the general welfare in a democratic society.[75]

The International Covenant on Economic, Social, and Cultural Rights permits restrictions on the right to form and join trade unions only as follows:

> No restrictions may be placed on the exercise of this right other than those prescribed by law and which are necessary in a democratic society in the interests of national security or public order or for the protection of the rights and freedoms of others.

Similarly, the right of trade unions to 'function freely' may be 'subject to no limitations other than those prescribed by law and which are necessary in a democratic society in the interests of national security or public order or for the protection of the rights and freedoms of others.'[76]

The International Covenant on Civil and Political Rights, providing a right to freedom to form and join trade unions, states:

> No restrictions may be placed on the exercise of this right other than those which are prescribed by law and which are necessary in a democratic society in the interests of national security or public safety, public order (*ordre public*), the protection of public health or morals, or the protection of the rights and freedoms of others.[77]

---

[75] Art. 29(2).
[76] Art. 8(1).
[77] Art. 22(2).

The European Convention permits limitations on the right to form and join trade unions as follows:

No restrictions shall be placed on the exercise of these rights other than such as are prescribed by law and which are necessary in a democratic society in the interests of national security or public safety, for the prevention of disorder or crime, for the protection of health or morals, or for the protection of the rights and freedoms of others.[78]

The European Social Charter permits limits on any of its enumerated rights if the limits 'are prescribed by law and are necessary in a democratic society for the protection of the rights and freedoms of others or for the protection of public interest, national security, public health, or morals.'[79]

The American Convention on Human Rights protects trade union organizing 'subject only to such restrictions established by law as may be necessary in a democratic society, in the interest of national security, public safety or public order, or to protect public health or morals or the rights and freedoms of others.'[80] In addition, the American Convention limits all the rights it enumerates as follows: 'The rights of each person are limited by the rights of others, by the security of all, and by the just demands of the general welfare, in a democratic society.'[81]

The African Charter on Human and Peoples' Rights provides that, with respect to all enumerated rights, 'The rights and freedoms of each individual shall be exercised with due regard to the rights of others, collective security, morality, and common interest.'[82]

In ILO practice, these limiting circumstances have been little used.[83] They may not be invoked to prohibit normal trade union activity. In particular, political opinion or activities of a trade union, its officials or members, may not serve as a reason for limiting trade union rights.[84]

Public Emergency

Human rights instruments also typically permit derogation during wartime or other public emergency to the extent necessitated by the emergency. The International Covenant on Civil and Political Rights permits a state party to declare a 'public emergency' in a situation that 'threatens the life of the nation'.[85] It lists certain provisions from which

---

[78] Art. 11(2).
[79] Art. 31(1).
[80] Art. 16(2).
[81] Art. 32(2).
[82] Art. 27(2).
[83] Valticos, *International Labour Law*, 233.
[84] See notes 23–7 above.
[85] Art. 4(1).

no derogation is permitted even during an emergency.[86] The protection of the right of trade union association is not non-derogable.[87]

The European Convention provides that 'in time of war or other public emergency threatening the life of the nation' derogation is permitted 'to the extent strictly required by the exigencies of the situation'.[88] The European Social Charter, similarly, provides:

> In time of war or other public emergency threatening the life of the nation any Contracting Party may take measures derogating from its obligations under this Charter to the extent strictly required by the exigencies of the situation, provided that such measures are not inconsistent with its other obligations under international law.[89]

The American Convention allows derogation 'in time of war, public danger, or other emergency that threatens the independence or security of a State Party ... to the extent and for the period of time strictly required by the exigencies of the situation.'[90]

A public emergency must be found to exist on objective criteria. A state declaring an emergency is entitled to a 'margin of appreciation' in assessing the threat,[91] but it bears a burden of proving conditions that justify the declaration.[92]

The European Court of Human Rights found a 'public emergency' to exist in the Republic of Ireland in 1956–7. The government had taken extraordinary measures after declaring an emergency. The Court found that 'a secret army engaged in unconstitutional activities and using violence to attain its purposes' was operating in Ireland. It found a 'steady and alarming increase in terrorist activities from the autumn of 1956 and throughout the first half of 1957'.[93] The Court defined a 'public emergency' as 'an exceptional situation of crisis or emergency which affects the whole population and constitutes a threat to the organised life of the community of which the State is composed'.[94]

The European Commission on Human Rights found no 'public emergency', however, in Greece in 1967, after the governing military

---

[86] Art. 4(2).
[87] Ibid.
[88] Art. 15(1).
[89] Art. 31(1).
[90] Art. 27(1).
[91] The *Greek* Case, Report of the ECHR, 18 Nov. 1969, *Yb ECHR* (1972) 12, part 2, 72, para. 154; E. Schwelb, 'Some Aspects of the International Covenants on Human Rights of December 1966', in A. Eide and A. Schou (eds.), *International Protection of Human Rights: Proceedings of the Seventh Nobel Symposium 1967* (New York, 1968), 116; R. Higgins, 'Derogations under Human Rights Treaties', *BYIL* 48 (1976–7), 297–301.
[92] The *Greek* Case, Report of the ECHR, 18 Nov. 1969, *Yb ECHR* (1972) 12, part 2, 72, para. 154.
[93] The *Lawless* Case, Judgment of 1 July 1961, European Court of Human Rights, *Series A: Judgments and Decisions* (1961), 56, para 28.
[94] Ibid.

junta had declared a state of siege. The junta asserted that a government takeover by insurgents was imminent, but the Commission found no evidence to substantiate that claim. The junta cited street demonstrations and labour strikes, but the Commission did not find their scope extraordinary. It found no 'public emergency' though it conceded that Greece had experienced 'political instability and tension ... an expansion of the activities of the Communists and their allies, and ... some public disorder'.[95] The Commission said that for a 'public emergency' there must be an imminent threat to the existing order, not merely the possibility that the current situation might lead to such a threat.

As for war as 'public emergency', the ILO has taken the position that war does not free a state of its obligations to comply with international labour standards, though belligerents may agree to suspend such obligations as between them during a war.[96]

As indicated above, military occupation does not constitute a 'public emergency'. States have recognized an obligation to permit trade union organizing under military occupation.[97] The ILO has found wartime restrictions applicable only during actual hostilities.[98]

IV. Conclusion

A right to trade union organizing exists under military occupation. Such a right is found in customary law. It may also exist as a result of treaty obligations assumed by the displaced sovereign or by the occupant. This right may be restricted only in extraordinary circumstances.

This state of the law reflects the importance of the right of trade union organizing. Under international law such a right is deemed fundamental to the ability of individuals to earn a livelihood. For that reason, strong protection of the right is found in international law even in a situation of military occupation.

---

[95] The *Greek* Case, Report of the ECHR, 18 Nov. 1969, *Yb ECHR* (1972) 12, part 2, 73–5, paras. 155–61.
[96] Valticos, *International Labour Law*, 233.
[97] See notes 47–55 above.
[98] ILO, *Freedom of Association*, para. 422.

10

Mass-Based Organizations in the West Bank and Gaza: Offering Services Because of and Despite the Military Occupation

JOOST R. HILTERMANN

Introduction

PALESTINIANS in the twentieth century have lived under a succession of foreign rulers. The continued absence of a national authority of their own regulating the life of their society has meant that those basic services needed in any society that were not provided by the foreign ruler had to be furnished by Palestinians themselves. Consequently, in Palestinian society the types of organizations like trade unions, which in western democracies serve a complementary role to that played by the state and constitute a counterweight to the state's transgressions, have instead played a substituting role under Israeli military occupation, filling the gaps created by the occupying power which had no compelling interest in satisfying the basic needs of the Palestinian population. These organizations, which in the 1980s include trade unions, voluntary work committees, women's committees, medical and agricultural relief committees, and others, have gone further: they have built an autonomous Palestinian economic, social, and political infrastructure in the Occupied Territories in the absence of an independent state.

The Israeli authorities see Palestinian popular organizations and institutions not as an alternative to the Palestinian state, but *as the basis* for a future Palestinian state, and therefore view these organizations as a threat to Israel's own long-term political interests in the area. Israel is on record as opposing the establishment of a Palestinian state in the West Bank and Gaza Strip, and has pursued a policy of *de facto* annexation of the Occupied Territories since 1967. The military authorities have therefore tried to inhibit the growth of an indigenous Palestinian institutional infrastructure, claiming that popular organizations are not involved in *bona fide* service-oriented activities but are acting instead as fronts for the Palestinian Liberation Organisation (PLO) in the Territories.

The purpose of this essay is (*a*) to show the *bona fide* nature of popular organizations in the West Bank and Gaza Strip through a historical analysis of their development and work; and (*b*) to show how the Israeli military authorities have interdicted the work of such organizations, effectively denying Palestinians the right to association and development. Due to restrictions on space, this essay is limited to an analysis of the labour and women's movements, with special emphasis on the work of trade unions, which have suffered most from army repression. This essay was extracted from the author's doctoral dissertation[1], research for which was conducted in the Occupied Territories in 1985–7. Since few, if any, other sources on this subject are currently in existence, most information used here is based on interviews with Palestinian trade union and women's movement activists, and on magazines, leaflets, and other materials provided by the trade unions and women's committees.

I. Emergence and Growth of Mass-Based Organizations in the West Bank and Gaza

Early Organizing Efforts

Palestinian trade unions were first established during the British Mandate (1917–48), and developed despite the destruction of Palestinian society in 1948, operating throughout Jordanian rule over the West Bank (1948–67). In addition, a generation of charitable organizations emerged during Jordanian rule; they played an important role in providing emergency care to the Palestinian population after the defeat of the Arab armies in the 1967 war.

During the first years of the Israeli military occupation there was little organizational activity in the West Bank and Gaza. This was so for the following reasons:

1. the existing trade unions in Gaza were outlawed, and those in the West Bank were systematically harassed (with their leaders arrested and some deported) by the military authorities.
2. Palestinians needed time to rearrange their lives, learn to cope with displacement, readjust their hopes and expectations following the shattering experience of defeat.

---

[1] Since published as J. R. Hiltermann, *Behind the Intifada: Labor and Women's Movements in the Occupied Territories* (Princeton, 1991).

3. The prevailing perception among Palestinians during the early years of the occupation was that the occupation would be of short duration. Those who held this opinion were strengthened in their belief by official Israeli statements suggesting that there might be a willingness on the Israeli side to 'trade land for peace'.

In the early 1970s this began to change. In Gaza, effective armed resistance to the occupation was smashed by the Israeli military, and so too were the hopes nurtured by many Palestinians of bringing about a speedy reversal of the military defeat of 1967. At the same time, it became clear that Israel was digging in to stay for an extended period in the Territories, dimming the likelihood, if it ever existed, of a 'land-for-peace' arrangement. Consequently, Palestinian perceptions about the length of the occupation began to change. They were reinforced by the energetic Likud drive after 1977 to establish new settlements in the Territories.

From the beginning of the occupation it was apparent that Israel was not simply negligent in terms of providing basic services to the population, but actively disrupted Palestinian efforts in this field. In the words of Rita Giacaman, a lecturer at Birzeit University:

The first ten years of occupation or so everybody worked very hard to inhibit the breakdown of the infrastructure—the economic, social, health, educational, and political infrastructures in the West Bank. It was clear to Palestinians that this attempt on the part of the Israeli military to break down the social and economic infrastructures really meant a fight for survival. That infrastructure, we all knew, was crucial for the reconstruction of Palestinian society in the future. We knew that much. We knew that the Israeli military was out to possess the land without us people. We knew that, too. What we didn't know was how to mobilize under occupation, when it was becoming practically impossible to move and do anything at the political or other levels without being subjugated to arrests or attacks from the Israeli military.[2]

It is in this context that we must see the efforts in the early 1970s, primarily of schoolchildren and college students in West Bank towns like Ramallah and Nablus, to clean streets and pave roads there as well as in the nearby villages and refugee camps. From street-cleaning the teenagers moved on to mobilize volunteers' energies to address the problems caused by the atrophying social infrastructure in general.[3] The popular euphoria in the Territories that was sparked by the psychological victory of the Arab forces in the October War in 1973, by the Rabat Conference in 1974 which recognized the PLO as the sole

---
[2] 'An Interview with Rita Giacaman: Women, Resistance, and the Popular Movement', *Palestine Focus* 24 (July–Aug. 1987), 3.
[3] M. J. Fasheh, *Education as a Praxis for Liberation: Birzeit University and the Community Work Program*, Ph.D. thesis (Harvard, 1987), 161–74.

legitimate representative of the Palestinians, and by Yasser Arafat's speech in the United Nations in 1974 added fuel to the fire, generating new energies and new ideas among Palestinian activists, especially the young. The ascendancy of pro-PLO mayors in the 1976 municipal elections and the subsequent Israeli cutting of funds to these municipalities served as the catalyst for the mobilization of large segments of the population in local socially-oriented organizations in a spirit of reinforcing Palestinian national identity. Popular committees sprang up in the various localities, eventually evolving into the so-called 'voluntary work committees' that operate throughout the Territories and are co-ordinated centrally, usually in Jerusalem or Ramallah or Nablus.

The Labour Movement

During the 1970s the economic structure of the Occupied Territories experienced a dramatic transformation. In the wake of massive land expropriation by the Israeli state and its agents, and the marginalization of Palestinian agriculture by the loss of land and by restrictions imposed by the military authorities on the cultivation and marketing of certain crops, a growing number of Palestinian peasant farmers were pushed into the labour force. They either found employment in the Territories or became itinerant workers journeying daily across the 'Green Line' into Israel.

In 1985, the Occupied Territories had an active labour force of 251,200 out of a total population of 1,338,900, according to official Israeli statistics.[4] Of these, 89,400 were said to be employed across the Green Line.[5] This last figure is in all likelihood far too low. It does not include a large number of undocumented workers who find work through the informal labour markets and who are therefore not counted by the official labour exchanges, nor does it include women and children working irregularly in agriculture, who are easily skipped in household surveys. Residents of East Jerusalem are also excluded from West Bank statistics since East Jerusalem has been annexed by Israel. Palestinian estimates, including estimates made by trade unionists, indicate that a daily average of approximately 120,000 workers from the Territories have been employed in Israel in the last decade; this number fluctuates seasonally, reaching possible peaks of 150,000 during the summer and fall harvests. In Israel half of the workers from the Territories are employed in construction. The remainder are evenly divided over agriculture, industry, and the hotel and restaurant business.[6] Their average wage is approximately $6.40 per day.[7]

---

[4] *Statistical Abstract of Israel 1986* (No. 37) (Jerusalem, 1986), 700. [5] Ibid. 706.
[6] Ibid. [7] Ibid. 707.

During the second decade of occupation, the Territories were progressively transformed into a reservoir of cheap labour for the Israeli economy, as well as a market for Israeli products. With the creeping *de facto* annexation of the Territories, an artificial 'common market' arrangement came about, whereby the Israelis have taken advantage of the occupation 'without borders'. In this arrangement, Palestinians in the West Bank and Gaza have carried most of the burdens and enjoyed few of the benefits. Whereas a social welfare system is thriving in Israel itself, basic services like a centrally-organized health insurance programme, social security, and welfare remain wanting in the West Bank and Gaza. Documented workers employed in Israel have the same percentage deducted from their pay-slips by the official labour exchanges as do Israeli citizens employed in the same job (a measure taken by the authorities ostensibly to ensure that the cost of an Israeli worker is equivalent to that of a worker from the Territories), but they are entitled to fewer benefits. The sums deriving from these deductions remain in Israeli government hands; their use is not known.[8]

In addition, the rights of Palestinian workers employed in the West Bank are protected under a now antiquated law, the Jordanian Labour Law of 1960 which, although amended in Jordan in 1972 and in later years, is still in force unamended in the West Bank. Important provisions concerning severance pay, sick leave, paid vacations, and minimum wages that have been included in the amended Jordanian law still do not apply to West Bank workers. A small number of Israeli military orders have brought improvements in this area, for example concerning paid sick-leave, but similar provisions in the amended Jordanian Labour Law encompass more and are more progressive.

Facing such conditions, Palestinians revived the labour movement around the time that others started to be involved in voluntary work committees and student and women's organizations. Existing unions were reactivated, and new unions set up in branches where none existed. In addition, labour organizers for the first time began targeting West Bankers who worked across the Green Line in Israel. A large proportion of the new recruits since the mid-1970s have been young workers, usually between the ages of 18 and 25, the majority of whom are employed in Israel.

West Bank trade unions are formed according to the Jordanian Labour Law of 1960. Any twenty or more workers in the same occupational sector or in the same workplace can decide to set up a trade union. According to the law, they must apply for a licence from the author-

---

[8] International Center for Peace in the Middle East, *Research on Human Rights in the Occupied Territories 1979–1983* (Tel Aviv, 1985), 75–7. On the Deduction Fund, see also Chs. 12 and 13 in this volume.

ities, who will issue one if the union satisfies the conditions stipulated in the law. Unions, in turn, may establish labour federations, which can affiliate with international union organizations.[9]

Trade unions were established first in the towns and only later—and to a more limited extent—in the villages. Workers from refugee camps usually join a union in the nearest town. Most West Bank unions are small, not exceeding 250 members. This is partly due to the size of Palestinian enterprises: there are no major industries in the Territories. Two-thirds of all industrial and commercial establishments in the West Bank and Gaza employ only three workers or less; only 55 establishments in the West Bank and 17 in Gaza employed more than twenty workers in 1985.[10]

By the end of 1987, there were close to a hundred active trade unions in the West Bank. Unions are organized per trade and per geographic location. Thus each major town has at least a construction workers' union, a sewing industry union, and a carpentry workers' union, to mention the main branches of Palestinian economic activity. The largest unions are the so-called 'general institutions' workers' unions, catch-all unions aimed at recruiting the average itinerant West Bank labourer who may be working on a construction site in Israel today, is unemployed tomorrow, and loads and unloads trucks at the local vegetable market the next day. The general institutions workers' unions are especially meant for West Bankers employed in Israel because of the irregularity of work in any one particular trade there. Such unions are often the first to exist in a village, drawing in workers employed in all trades. Because the West Bank labour force is divided over a large number of small workshops or worksites and is irregularly employed, unions established solely in a particular workplace are rare. They can be found only in the largest companies and institutions like, for example, the Jerusalem Electric Company, al-Makassed Hospital, and Birzeit University.

West Bank unions have formal structures, in keeping with the provisions of Jordanian labour law. A card-carrying union member has the right to sit in the union's General Assembly. This body routinely elects an administrative (or executive) committee which governs the union for a specified period of time, usually no more than one or two years.[11] The union sends a number of its administrative committee members to the General Assembly of the General Federation of Trade Unions in the West Bank (the GFTU), the number depending on the size of the

---

[9] Arts. 68–89, Provisional Labour Law of the Hashemite Kingdom of Jordan: Law No. 21 of 1960, *Official Gazette*, No. 1491 (21 May 1960).
[10] *Statistical Abstract 1986*, 718–9.
[11] Parts 7, 8, and 9, *By-Laws of the Construction and General Institutions Workers' Union in Ramallah/al-Bireh*, 1983.

union.¹² The GFTU's Federation Council, which is drawn from the General Assembly representing all affiliated West Bank unions, elects the GFTU's executive committee every two years, which in turn elects from among its members the GFTU General Secretary and other officials.¹³ The GFTU represents, defends, and directs the labour movement in the West Bank, and governs relations between and within individual unions.¹⁴

In addition to these formal structures, most workers identify with a particular workers' bloc, which is an informal organization that is characterized mainly by its political orientation within the Palestinian national movement. At present there are four such blocs that compete with each other for the same pool of workers: the Progressive Workers' Bloc (PWB), the Workers' Unity Bloc (WUB), the Workers' Youth Movement (WYM), and the Progressive Unionist Action Front (PUAF). Since formal splits in the union movement and the GFTU in 1981 and 1985, three of these blocs (the PWB, WUB, and WYM) have created their own general federations, all based in Nablus. Not all union members are affiliated with a certain bloc. Those who are pay annual dues and elect their bloc's leadership in regular elections. The blocs direct their members' struggle inside the individual unions throughout the West Bank.

Continuing military occupation has provoked unions to articulate nationalist positions, because workers experience the occupation in all aspects of their everyday lives, and because unions see themselves as representative organs of the workers and seek to act accordingly. The WUB, for example, explains:

> The Occupied Territories became annexed [*de facto*] to the Israeli economy because it supplied cheap labour and constituted a consumer market for Israeli products preventing Arab commodities produced under severe competitive conditions from being sold. Consequently, the effects of the Israeli economic crisis (inflation and high prices) were reflected in the Occupied Territories, leading to an intensive exploitation and oppression of the working class, particularly those working in Israeli enterprises. So the working class suffered the most from occupation policy. Hence it badly needs and fights for the end of occupation; it started to use its important role and influence amongst the ranks of the Palestinian people in the battle of liberation and national independence.¹⁵

The paramount presence of the military occupation and the impact it has on everyday life has led to a *de facto* alliance between trade unions and Palestinian employers in the Territories. In the words of the head of one of the three federations, Adel Ghanem:

---

¹² Art. 22, *By-Laws of the General Federation of Trade Unions in the West Bank*.
¹³ Ibid. Arts 5 and 6.
¹⁴ Ibid. Art. 5.
¹⁵ *Workers' Unity Bloc in the West Bank and Gaza Strip* (WUB, April 1985), 4.

This is a unique occupation. It wants to remove us from our land, whereas the British [during the Mandate] only wanted to exploit us. So we have to strike a kind of balance between the national and the class struggle and help the local, national industries, because this way we would also protect the workers.[16]

In Gaza, union activity was virtually non-existent during the first two decades of occupation. The six unions that existed before 1967 were closed down by the Israeli military authorities when they took control of the Gaza Strip. After pressures from the International Labour Organisation (ILO), the authorities did allow the unions to reopen, in 1979, but prohibited them from holding elections or recruiting new members. Only in 1987 did labour organizers succeed in reviving the unions by defying the authorities' ban on union elections. In February of that year, the Carpenters' and Building Workers' Union elected a new administrative committee, and in April the Commercial and General Services Workers' Union did the same, but in the face of heavy repression.[17]

Estimates of the size of union membership in the West Bank range from 12 to 35 per cent of the active labour force; the lower figure is the more likely one. Unionists have made major efforts to attract West Bank workers employed inside the Green Line. The rights of these workers are more difficult to protect than those of workers employed in the Territories themselves, because West Bank unions have no jurisdiction in Israel. Yet unions have recruited a large number of the workers employed in Israel through their programmes which are aimed at addressing the specific problems these workers face, especially discrimination in net wages, the withholding of certain benefits despite deductions, and summary dismissals. Unions have provided health insurance schemes for their members and their families, and procured the services of lawyers to take cases to Israeli courts.

In the West Bank itself, unions are involved in two types of activities: negotiating with employers on behalf of workers, and providing a number of specific services to workers. Regular union demands include fixed working hours, tying wages to the cost of living, paying wages in Jordanian dinars rather than in Israeli shekels, paid holidays, special days like May Day, Women's Day and Palestinian national days off, workmen's compensation, sick leave, collective contracts, work safety, etc. In attracting workers to a union, different strategies have been applied. The most common one is the one followed by, for example, the Printing Press Workers' Union in Jerusalem:

---

[16] Interview with Adel Ghanem, general secretary of the PWB and of the PWB's GFTU, Nablus, 14 Dec. 1985.

[17] 'Gaza Carpenters Defy the Israelis: A Union Votes', *The New York Times*, 22 Feb. 1987. See also J. R. Hiltermann, 'Palestinian Unions: Force for Change in the West Bank', *The Nation*, 3 Oct. 1987.

The first thing we did was to organize all the workers in the Arab sector [i.e. East Jerusalem]. We visited them in their workplaces and encouraged them to join. The main benefit for them was that the union would represent them and their demands. Our second activity was to organize cultural events, meetings and lectures on workers' rights, labour law, and the benefits for a worker of having a union. Our third activity was to improve working conditions and obtain benefits such as holidays, and to try to get work agreements between workers and employers. We succeeded in two or three workplaces in this. Our fourth activity was to organize a monthly goods cooperative for workers in our union building, where we sell food, clothes, etc. at lower prices than store prices for the same products. Finally, we set up a cooperative society for printing workers in [the Jerusalem suburb of] Shuʿfat. We have bought machines and other equipment, and have set up our own presses so that unemployed workers can find work there. The profits from the printing press will go to our health insurance fund.[18]

A normal first step for unions in their relations with employers is to negotiate a collective contract for workers doing a specific activity in a specific workplace. Strikes are rare in the Territories, and are carried out only as a last resort when negotiations with an employer have clearly failed. One typical, small strike took place at a pharmaceutical company in Nablus in 1985 when workers demanded higher wages and a better work structure. The strike was resolved in two stages following mediation by the Municipality and General Institutions Workers' Union, as well as by the Israeli labour inspector.[19]

The Women's Movement

The women's committees were established on the crest of the general efforts to organize the masses in the Territories in the 1970s, and at the same time in reaction to the perceived limitations of the existing trade unions and charitable societies. The latter provided care for a sector of the population, especially women, but they did not provide these women with the tools that might enable them to involve themselves actively in the operations of Palestinian society and to effect social change. The trade unions, on the other hand, might have offered this opportunity to women workers. However, social restrictions against women joining organizations that were seen as men's institutions and a perceived lack of a receptive interest on the part of the unions' male leadership in the problems encountered by women in the workplace proved initially prohibitive to the recruitment of women in trade unions.[20]

---

[18] Interview with WUB unionist in Jerusalem, 20 May 1985.
[19] Interview with WYM unionist in Nablus, 21 Dec. 1985.
[20] Interview with PWB unionist in Nablus, 26 Jan. 1986, and with UWWC activist in al-Bireh, 22 Nov. 1985.

In 1978 activist women in the Ramallah/Jerusalem area set up the Union of Women's Work Committees (the UWWC). The UWWC defines itself as

> a framework of democratic and fighting women that forms an inseparable part of the Palestinian women's movement, including in its ranks women from all national classes, and which works to unite the struggle of all women in the defence of all national rights: the right of return, the right to self-determination, and the right to establish an independent national state, and which also works in the interest of women's causes, the improvement of women's social, economic and cultural situation, and the defence of women's right to work, be educated, acquire experience, develop their personality and involve themselves in the development of society.[21]

Reflecting tensions in the Palestinian national movement, a number of women split away from the UWWC after 1978, and set up three other committees: the Union of Palestinian Working Women's Committees (the PWWC), the Union of Palestinian Women's Committees (the PWC), and the Women's Committee for Social Work (the WCSW). Divided along political lines, the four committees share none the less a common programme where it concerns the position of women in Palestinian society. They are agreed on the need to free women from their household chores and involve them in social and economic activities outside their homes and the family sphere. To this end they have striven both to enhance women's consciousness of their position as women, particularly as Palestinian women, and to provide certain facilities to smooth the transition from home to wage-labour or to make the dual tasks of wage-labour and continuing household responsibilities, including child-raising, possible. In the words of one commentator: 'Encouraging women to break away from a dependent life is possible only by providing alternatives; thus the women's committees try to complement one activity by another: child-care frees women to leave the home to attend self-improvement classes; sewing classes can give women a basic skill for outside jobs; and health information helps self-reliance.'[22] The committees have been most successful in setting up child-care facilities and organizing literacy and skill-training programmes throughout the Occupied Territories.

The UWWC, like the other committees, has aimed to reach women from all layers of society: 'The ideal committees are those which include a majority of housewives, some employees, and working women, and they must also include a good number of women from the age group 30–50, and what we could call 'ladies', [women] who usually

---

[21] *Amended Program of the Federation of Palestinian Women's Work Committees in the Occupied Territories*, an undated UWWC pamphlet.
[22] 'Woman Power in Palestine', *al-Fajr Jerusalem Palestinian Weekly*, 7 Mar. 1984.

have influence and social status in the area.'[23] The UWWC encourages the students and wage-workers among its members to join student committees and trade unions, respectively: working women must 'move toward ... becoming members in the ... unions. In addition to that, they [may] organize within the framework of the UWWC and take part in its activities and social programmes, especially those which directly concern them.'[24]

One of the main foci of the women's committees has been on working women. Several women's committees started in the offices of local unions. The PWWC branch in Hebron, for example, operated from the local sewing industry union until criticism from male workers and denunciations in the mosque drove them out.[25] Likewise, the Nablus branch of the PWWC began in the sewing industry union in Nablus, but moved out following a conflict between the women members and the union's male leadership. The committee now offers advice to women who face problems at work, but sends them to the union if they need union support.[26] The UWWC contributed to the setting up of new trade unions in economic sectors dominated by women, like sewing, when they discovered that the unions existing in those fields resisted the entrance of women. The UWWC was, for example, instrumental in the establishment of the sewing industry union in Ramallah/al-Bireh, which today has a predominantly female membership.[27]

The women's committees are financed mainly by contributions from their own members, who pay an admission fee and an annual membership fee (usually 1 dinar), by donations, and by revenues from periodical sales. Increasingly, the committees are also attracting the attention of western development organizations, who have funded individual projects like kindergartens.

Other Organizations

In the 1980s, other mass-based organizations emerged: medical relief committees, agricultural relief committees, cultural committees, professional associations, and others. The Union of Palestinian Medical Relief Committees deserves special mention. Founded in 1979, the Union has set the following objectives:

1. Participation in elevating the low standards of health in the West Bank, particularly due to the absence of a national government willing to perform and interested in such a task.

[23] 'All Efforts Toward Organizing Housewives and Women in Villages and Camps', *Women's Struggle* (*Nidal al-Mar'a*), a one-time publication of the UWWC (1985), 27.
[24] Ibid. 28.
[25] Interview with PWWC activist in Hebron, 9 Dec. 1985.
[26] Interview with PWB unionist in Nablus, 26 Jan. 1986.
[27] Interview with UWWC activist in al-Bireh, 22 Nov. 1985.

2. Provision of basic medical services to villages and inaccessible areas including refugee camps that are in need of such services.
3. Raising the consciousness of the population to the problems of health, and organization of campaigns against the spread of epidemic, infectious, and communicable diseases.
4. Investigation of the health situation in the area, including the identification of the most common diseases in the various districts, their causes, and methods of control and prevention. Data collected is used for planning and recommendation of action.[28]

In 1983, the Union reported that it had over 150 health professionals active in the field on a voluntary basis, most of them originating from villages and camps. During the last few years, the Union mobilized a veritable grassroots movement devoted to improving the health situation in the West Bank and Gaza, providing services which are otherwise not available.[29]

The aim of the new generation of Palestinian popular organizations in the Occupied Territories has been to educate and provide basic services and protection to a population living in a situation of lawlessness and deprivation, in addition to keeping the Palestinian national heritage alive. Because of the overwhelming impact of the military occupation on Palestinian society, however, few of these organizations have hesitated to articulate or endorse nationalist positions, usually reflecting one of the four main trends in the Palestinian national movement headed by the PLO.

II. Israeli Repression of Mass-Based Organizations and the Lack of Recourse

In the twenty years of military occupation, any expression of nationalist sentiment by Palestinians has been anathema to the Israeli authorities, and has provoked repressive measures. These measures have not been limited to those who have engaged in or advocated armed struggle, but have extended to any organized, non-violent activity, including trade union activity. The trade union movement has in fact been a prime target for repression during the last decade. Other organizations, like the women's, medical relief, and voluntary work committees, have all suffered from interference in their work, but not to the same extent as the trade unions, which perhaps are seen by the authorities as more powerful and more explicitly nationalist in their

---
[28] Union of Medical Relief Committees, *Statement of Purpose and Activities* (Jerusalem, 1983).
[29] Ibid.

programmes. Below, the emphasis will therefore be mainly on the repression of the labour movement.

Repression of Mass-Based Organizations

The military authorities' treatment of popular organizations ranges from non-recognition, indirect pressures, and intimidation to outright repression. The severity of punitive measures is usually contingent either on the political climate prevailing at any particular time or on the perceived militancy of the organization, or a combination of these two.

The first encounter between trade unionists and the military authorities is when twenty or more workers submit an application for a union to be officially registered. Until the late 1970s, when the union movement was not perceived as a major threat by the military authorities, new unions could still be registered with relative ease, but there were few applications at the time; about five official unions were added to the twenty-six existing ones during this period. With the revival of the labour movement in the late 1970s, the authorities began rejecting or ignoring workers' applications to set up new unions. According to the ILO, no new union has received a licence since 1979.[30] At least eighty unlicensed unions have come into existence in the West Bank in the 1980s. In 1986 alone, some thirty-one applications for registration were submitted to the authorities; according to the ILO, none were accepted.[31]

In Gaza, the authorities did not allow the six unions that had existed before 1967 to operate until 1979, and then recognized only the pre-1967 leadership and members. Any unionist activity beyond that structure was considered illegal and was suppressed.[32] In 1987, two unions notified the Gaza military authorities of their intention to hold elections despite the ban. In the case of the Commercial and General Services Workers' Union, the authorities prohibited the elections for technical reasons, stating that the union had not provided the authorities with its annual budget.[33] The union defied the authorities, however, and the elections took place, not in the union office (which had been closed by the authorities for the occasion) but at a hastily arranged alternative site.[34] The union sent a complaint to the ILO's Committee on Freedom

---

[30] ILO, *Report on the Situation of Workers of the Occupied Arab Territories* (Geneva, 1987), 34.
[31] Ibid.
[32] Ibid. 33.
[33] The Gaza Building Workers' and Carpenters' Union and the Gaza Commercial and Public Services Workers' Union, 'Violations against the Right to Organize by Israeli Authorities in the Occupied Gaza Strip', complaint submitted to the ILO, 2 June 1987.
[34] I personally observed the elections of the Commercial and General Services Workers' Union in Gaza City on 4 Apr. 1987.

of Association in June 1987 to protest the ban on the elections and the subsequent repression.[35]

In East Jerusalem, which was annexed by Israel in 1967 and consequently falls under Israeli law, Palestinian unions were declared illegal from the beginning of the occupation. Palestinian workers were told that if they wished to unionize, they could join the Israeli trade union federation, the Histadrut. Palestinians do not recognize the annexation of East Jerusalem, however, and the majority of workers from East Jerusalem have therefore refused to join the Histadrut. Palestinian activists revived unions in East Jerusalem in the mid-1970s despite the prohibition.

Unable to contain the growing union movement, the authorities were forced to resort to other repressive measures, sometimes operating through their agents in the Palestinian community. Some unions report having been denied link-up to basic services like electricity in those municipalities controlled by a mayor who collaborates with the military authorities. The head of a union office in Jenin reported, for example, that the mayor of Jenin had refused to provide the office with water and electricity until the unionists would produce their union's operating licence. But, said the union organizer, 'We requested a permit from the Israeli labour office a long time ago, and we never got an answer.'[36]

In a direct attempt to control union activity in the West Bank, the military authorities amended provisions in the Jordanian labour law concerning union elections. In 1980, the authorities issued Military Order No. 825, which amends Article 83 of the Jordanian Labour Law of 1960. Article 83 concerns elections to the executive committee of a trade union. The unamended version reads:

(a) No persons other than workers or those employed full-time by a trade union can be elected to its executive committee.

(b) No person convicted of a felony punishable by more than three years' imprisonment or of offences involving public disgrace can be a member of the executive committee of the union.[37]

MO 825 changed Article 83 (b) as follows:

(b) In addition to clause (a), none of the persons mentioned below shall be allowed to be members of the Union's Administrative Committee:
   i. any person convicted in a competent court in the Area or in Israel of committing a crime punishable by five years or more;

---

[35] Gaza Building Workers et al., 'Violations against the Right to Organize' (complaint submitted to ILO, 2 June 1987).
[36] Interview with WUB unionist in Jenin, 31 Jan. 1986.
[37] Art. 83, Jordanian Labour Law, *Official Gazette*, 1491 (21 May 1960).

ii. any person convicted in a competent court in the Area or in Israel of committing a crime against honour.

MO 825 also added clauses to the original law, including:

(c) The Union shall present to the person responsible at least thirty days before the election a list of candidates for membership of the Administrative Committee. The person responsible may strike out from the said list the name of any candidate proved to the responsible person's satisfaction not to fulfil the rules of clauses (a)–(b) above.

By changing 'felony' into 'crime', and therefore leaving room to include 'security' offences, the military authorities sharply reduced the potential membership of a union's administrative committee. Many Palestinians have served prison terms for 'security' offences, and the existing military orders allow for high maximum penalties in case of such offences. For example, MO 101 (1967), the 'Order Regarding Prohibition of Acts of Incitement and Hostile Propaganda', which covers offences like possession and distribution of illegal materials, raising the Palestinian flag, and membership of an illegal organization, allows for a maximum penalty of ten years in prison. MO 378 (1970), the 'Order Concerning Security Regulations', which covers more serious offences like possession of firearms and attacks on members of the Israeli armed forces, allows for a maximum penalty of life imprisonment. By thus changing the existing law, and by taking power to eliminate any candidates for administrative posts, the authorities tried to block the unions' development. They have failed so far in doing so only because the unions collectively ignored the new legislation.

Even without an official permit and without water and electricity, and despite military orders designed to restrict union elections, a trade union can function relatively normally as a trade union. There are many ways in which such restrictions can be circumvented. But one essential ingredient unions cannot do without is a steady membership of workers. One of the tactics deployed by the military authorities against the unions has therefore been to intimidate the unions' actual and potential membership. One common practice involves harassing, and sometimes beating, workers inside a union building or at the outer door for no apparent reason. On 28 October 1985, for example, soldiers were posted outside the entrance of the Construction and General Institutions Workers' Union in Ramallah/al-Bireh, and photographed anyone entering the building.[38] Several unions report that members have been summoned to military headquarters where they were interrogated about their activities and discouraged strongly from continuing with their union work.

---

[38] Interview with PWB unionist in Ramallah/al-Bireh, 2 Nov. 1985.

In addition, regular break-ins by soldiers of union offices have a deterrent effect on members, especially when those present in the office are detained, usually for a period of between a few hours to a couple of days, and threatened with worse trouble if they are seen near the union office again. Break-ins of union offices abound. No search warrant is needed under military regulations, and no prior warning is given. Soldiers will enter a union office, line up those they find inside, arrest all or a few of them, and confiscate union materials. For example, a union office in Jenin was raided by the army in December 1984 and again in April 1985. All materials present in the office were confiscated on both occasions. The second time, seventeen workers were detained for a few hours and questioned about their activities. The head of the office at that time, Walid Nazal, was placed under town arrest, and eventually deported to Jordan in October 1985.[39] According to the present head, 'The Israelis used the files they confiscated during the break-in to call in union members individually and to intimidate them. The father of one of our members drives a taxi to the bridge [at the border with Jordan]. The authorities revoked his permit and asked him questions about his son.'[40] The office was again raided on 12 February 1987. According to al-Haq, which intervened in the case:

Soldiers and police carrying out the raid assaulted one union official, threatened union leaders with detention, destroyed several displays in the office, and confiscated office supplies, publications, and documents, including the union's membership lists and pamphlets prepared by al-Haq on workers' rights.[41]

The effect of such measures, in the words of one unionist, is to

create fear. When workers come who have not been active or who are new to the union and they see these attacks, they won't come back. They are afraid. They don't want trouble.[42].

On more than one occasion, unionists have been brought to trial for 'possession of prohibited publications' confiscated during a raid. Such publications often include union calendars, pamphlets from an international labour federation, or the union's by-laws. According to Military Order No. 101 (1967), no publications can be brought in, sold, printed, or kept in someone's possession in the West Bank unless a permit has been obtained for them. Since it is impossible, for purely practical reasons, to obtain a permit for every single book, magazine, pamphlet, or other printed material that is brought into or printed in

[39] See Ch. 2, text at n. 96 for the High Court decision supporting Nazal's deportation.
[40] Interview with WUB unionist in Jenin, 31 Jan. 1986.
[41] Al-Haq/LSM, 'Raid on Jenin Trade Unions', in *Newsletter No. 18* (March/April 1987), 9.
[42] Interview by an American researcher with a PUAF unionist in Jerusalem, 8 Feb. 1986.

the West Bank, few Palestinians have permits for the publications they hold in their possession. It is equally impossible for the military authorities to enforce MO 101. The problem, however, is one of selective enforcement.[43] There is no easier pretext for bringing a unionist to trial than his possession of illegal publications confiscated during a raid. In fact, the conviction justifies the raid, which itself serves to deter the union from being too active.

For example, on 10 July 1987, the military authorities informed Qalqiliya unionist Feisal Hindi verbally that he would be charged with having published materials without a permit. The materials included information on labour laws, workers' rights to certain benefits, and other information, mostly provided by the Histadrut and the Israeli government. Hindi's crime, it appears, was not publishing without a permit materials which were anyway freely available anywhere in Israel, but carrying out his role as a unionist *effectively*.[44]

Short arrests without charges are very frequent. A Ramallah unionist reported that three members of the executive committee of the local Construction and General Institutions Workers' Union had been called in by the military authorities for questioning on separate occasions during the spring of 1986. A fourth member was detained for eighteen days (the maximum amount of time a person can be detained without having to be brought before a military judge), and then released.[45] One union activist reported having been detained eleven times over a period of several years, each time for eighteen days. He was never charged or brought to court.[46] At other times, unionists have been convicted of 'membership of an illegal organization', which usually means a faction of the PLO. Research of 1983 military court records shows that Palestinians accused of membership of a banned organization received stiffer sentences if it turned out that they were also active in the labour movement.[47]

Individual union leaders have been barred from entering their union office or from engaging in unionist activity for certain periods. Following elections in the Commercial and General Services Workers' Union in Gaza in April 1987, for example, which were declared illegal by the military authorities, several unionists were ordered to stay away from the union building, and in May 1987 eight unionists were barred from any activity for their union at the risk of legal reprisal.[48]

[43] V. Falloon, *Excessive Secrecy, Lack of Guidelines: A Report on Military Censorship in the West Bank* (Ramallah, 1986).
[44] 'Censorship in the West Bank', *International Labour Reports*, 24 (Nov./Dec. 1987), 14.
[45] Interview with PWB unionist in Ramallah/al-Bireh, 28 June 1986.
[46] Interview with PWB unionist in Hebron, 2 Dec. 1985.
[47] Research of military court records, commissioned by al-Haq/LSM, Ramallah.
[48] Gaza Building Workers *et al.*, 'Violations against the Right to Organize' (complaint submitted to ILO, 2 June 1987).

In another example, in November 1987, fifteen unionists of the WUB-controlled Construction and General Institutions Workers' Union in the village of Deir al-Ghussoun in the West Bank were forced by the military authorities to sign statements agreeing not to engage in any unionist activity for a period of six months. The union office was closed down for a similar period. The unionists were verbally informed that they could not educate workers about their rights, that they could not help workers find lawyers in case of labour disputes, and that they could not solicit blood for workers injured at work, as they had been doing. They were also told that they would face administrative punishments like deportation and administrative detention if they broke the ban. The apparent pretext for the ban was a poster in the union office protesting a recent house demolition in the village and denouncing the 'Zionist occupation'.[49]

Another measure taken against individual unionists involves travel restrictions. For example, Adnan Dagher, general secretary of the Construction and General Institutions Workers' Union in Ramallah/al-Bireh, was refused an Israeli travel document (*laissez-passer*) in 1987.[50] Many unionists report similar problems, including Shaher Sa'ad, the general secretary of the general federation of the WYM, who was barred from attending a labour conference in Great Britain in November 1987 to which he had been invited by a British trade union.[51]

One final measure against union activity in general is the closure of meeting halls to prevent union gatherings from taking place. For example, on 4 July 1985 the military authorities closed down al-Hakawati Theatre in East Jerusalem for twenty-four hours to prevent the general conference of the WUB, scheduled for 5 July. A sit-in staged by unionists and supporters outside the theatre on 5 July was violently broken up by Israeli border guards. Three Palestinians were reportedly beaten and arrested.[52] On 1 May 1987, the authorities closed down Cinema al-Hamra in East Jerusalem for twelve hours to prevent WUB members from holding May Day celebrations. The High Court overturned the order later that day, but most union members had already gone home by that time.[53] The next day, the authorities closed al-Hakawati for a similar period to prevent the PUAF's celebration of Workers' Day.[54]

Other popular organizations have suffered from similar repression. Women's and voluntary work committees have complained of inter-

---

[49] Affidavits obtained by al-Haq/LSM, Ramallah.
[50] Interview with PWB unionist in Ramallah/al-Bireh, 28 June 1986.
[51] Files of al-Haq/LSM.
[52] *Al-Fajr Jerusalem Palestinian Weekly*, 12 July 1985.
[53] Files of al-Haq/LSM.
[54] *Jerusalem Post*, 3 May 1987.

ference in their activities and arrests of their members. The Union of Palestinian Medical Relief Committees' branch in Gaza protested harassment and intimidation at the hands of the military authorities in July 1986. Doctors carrying out voluntary work in Jabaliya Refugee Camp were arrested and accused of having violated the law governing charitable societies by providing services to the population without written permission from the authorities.[55] A kindergarten of the UWWC in Ya'abad in the West Bank was threatened with closure in 1985 because the authorities claimed that it lacked a permit and that the kindergarten run by the local charitable society was sufficient to fill the need.[56] Women's committees' exhibits of national products, folklore, and handicrafts are frequently raided, materials confiscated, and members arrested, for example in the case of the WCSW's exhibition in Tulkarem in 1983.[57] Al-Hakawati Theatre in Jerusalem was closed down for three days in July 1985, according to the *Jerusalem Post*, to 'prevent a meeting that security officials claimed was backed by the PLO', involving two women's organizations 'allegedly associated with Nayef Hawatmeh's Democratic Front for the Liberation of Palestine'.[58] A UWWC organizer in Gaza, Na'ima Hilu, was charged in 1986 with 'possession of illegal publications' following a raid on her house in Jabaliya Refugee Camp. The materials included UWWC pamphlets and a number of books which are freely available in bookshops in Israel and the Occupied Territories.[59] Ten women activists from various women's committees were barred from leaving the Territories in July 1985, preventing them from attending the International Women's Conference in Nairobi that month.[60]

Repression against Palestinian individuals and organizations in the Territories escalated with the launching of the 'Iron Fist' policy by the Israeli authorities in August 1985. On 4 August 1985, Defence Minister Yitzhak Rabin officially announced a new policy of deportations, administrative detentions, and house demolitions. On 5 August, the *Jerusalem Post* intimated that the policy's chief targets would be 'West Bank Arabs in student, professional and municipal groups, ranging from trade unionists to lawyers to members of student-union executives'.[61]

In the autumn of 1985, two unionists, including the general secretary of the WUB, Ali Abu Hilal, were deported to Jordan. Scores of trade

---

[55] 'Gaza Medical Relief Committee Under Fire', and 'Renewed Repression of Gaza Medical Relief Committee', press releases issued by the Union of Palestinian Medical Relief Committees in Gaza on 23 July 1986 and 31 July 1986, respectively.
[56] Interview with a UWWC activist in Ya'abad, 8 Nov. 1985.
[57] Interview with WCSW activist in Nablus, 15 Dec. 1985.
[58] *Jerusalem Post*, 28 July 1985.
[59] 'Women's Literature "Illegal" in Gaza', UWWC *Newsletter*, 5 (August 1986), 4.
[60] *Al-Fajr Jerusalem Palestinian Weekly*, 19 July 1985.
[61] *Jerusalem Post*, 5 Aug. 1985.

unionists were placed in administrative detention or given town arrest orders. A number of activists in voluntary work committees and women's committees were also issued restriction orders. For example, Muharram Barghouti, the head of the Higher Committee for Voluntary Work, was placed under town arrest in al-Bireh for six months in May 1987; the order was renewed in November 1987. Zahira Kamal, head of the UWWC, was under town arrest in Jerusalem intermittently between 1980 and 1987, i.e. for seven years, without trial. Several other women activists of the UWWC and WCSW in the Jerusalem, Ramallah, and Nablus area were serving town arrest orders in 1987.[62] In its annual report of 1987, Amnesty International noted that it had 'received the names of 66 people, mostly students and trade unionists, who during 1986 were restricted to their home towns or villages'.[63]

One increasingly frequent method of union repression in 1986 and 1987 was the army-ordered closure of union offices. For example, two union offices in Nablus were closed at the beginning of March 1986 for a period of six months. The order was renewed for six months for one of the unions, and for a year for the other on 23 September 1986. The headquarters of the federation of the WYM in Nablus were shut down for one month on 24 August 1986. The headquarters of another federation in Nablus were ordered closed for a year on 20 October 1986. The Construction and General Institutions Workers' Union in Ya'abad was shut for a year on 9 October 1986.[64] A co-operative printing press run by the Jerusalem Printing Press Workers' Union in Shu'fat was shut down for six months in July 1987.[65] The office of the Construction and General Institutions Workers' Union in Deir al-Ghussoun was shut down for six months in November 1987.[66]

Together, these practices by the Israeli authorities amount to a clearly deliberate attempt to block the development of an autonomous Palestinian institutional infrastructure in the Occupied Territories. The net result is a serious impairment of the provision of needed services to relatively deprived sectors of the population.

Palestinians' Recourse Against the Army's Repression

The Israeli authorities have on occasion proclaimed that they are not opposed to trade union activity in the Territories that is, in their words, 'legitimate' or *bona fide* trade union activity, but to trade union activity that is 'hostile' to the authorities. In a letter dated 8 December 1986,

---

[62] Files of al-Haq/LSM, Ramallah.
[63] Amnesty International, *Amnesty International Report 1987* (London, 1987), 351–2.
[64] Files of al-Haq/LSM, Ramallah.
[65] Files of al-Haq/LSM, Ramallah. See also: 'Statement by the Printers' Cooperative Association and the Printers' Union in Jerusalem', 31 July 1987.
[66] Affidavits obtained by al-Haq/LSM.

David Yahav, the legal adviser to the military government in the West Bank, explained in response to a query by al-Haq:

The Commander of the Israel Defence Forces in the area and the authorities under his command do not consider organized activities within the framework of legal unions, whose objectives are to improve the welfare of the workers of the area in particular and of the population in general, to be illegal as long as these activities fall within the unions' objectives.

When enough evidence is available to the commander of the area or to any authority empowered by law or by security legislation that there are hostile activities in a professional union or a labour federation that could endanger the security of the area, the safety of the Israel Defence Forces, the general order, or proper administration, this commander or authority should take the necessary preventive and administrative measures, such as restriction orders, administrative detention orders, or closure orders, to stop such activities.[67]

In a case concerning the establishment of a Palestinian bar association in the West Bank, sought by a number of Palestinian lawyers, the Israeli High Court of Justice ruled in May 1987 that the military commander should be guided in his decisions by two paramount considerations. The first one—and here the court quoted an earlier High Court decision—was that 'freedom of association is one of the guiding principles of democracy and one of the fundamental rights of the citizen', even under military occupation, because the occupying power has a duty to ensure the interests of the local population. The second one was the need to protect the occupying power's security interests in the area. However, the court left it to the discretion of the military commander to define 'security interests' and to weigh these interests against the population's right of association since, according to the ruling, the Court was in no position to evaluate the security situation in the Territories.[68]

The stated policy of the authorities to protect the right of association and to allow 'legitimate' trade unions is, however, belied both by measures they have taken against unionists who were clearly engaged in unionist activity (for example, confiscation of materials on workers' rights, interference in union elections, and barring unionists from performing explicitly unionist activities), and by their general repression of the union movement which makes any form of unionizing extremely difficult.

The standard justification used by the army for repressive measures taken against Palestinian trade unions is that they are allegedly fronts

---

[67] Files of al-Haq/LSM. See also al-Haq/LSM, 'Closure of the Nablus Trade Union Federation', *Newsletter* 17 (Jan./Feb. 1987), 6–7.
[68] *HC 507/85 Bahij Tamimi et al. v. The Minister of Defence et al.*, judgment given on 25 May 1987.

for factions in the PLO. The PLO is a banned organization under Israeli law. Palestinians, in countering the authorities' allegations, argue that they are a people without a government but that they consider the PLO as their legitimate representative. Logically therefore, unions in the Occupied Territories, like many Palestinian institutions and organizations, explicitly identify with the PLO in general and with one of its factions in particular, although their union programmes are clearly attuned to local conditions. At the same time, according to the PLO Charter, all Palestinians are automatically members of the PLO by virtue of birth, not by paying membership dues or carrying a membership card. It is therefore just as normal for the PLO to promote social, cultural, and trade union activities in the West Bank and Gaza and for trade unions to take positions close to PLO views, as it is easy for the Israeli authorities to accuse trade unions and other organizations of being 'terrorist fronts'.

The authorities do not need to resort to the 'PLO argument' to crack down on union activity, however. Historically they have banned any nationalist expression and interfered with any organized activity by Palestinians in the Territories, labelling such expressions and activities a threat to their security. The word 'security' has a very wide meaning in the official Israeli vocabulary, and seems to refer generally to Israeli 'interests'.[69] Nationalist expressions and organized activity by Palestinians run directly counter to Israeli interests in the Occupied Territories, and are therefore labelled threats to Israeli security.

The security concern has been cited with such frequency as to appear to be an excuse, which, however, has lost none of its effectiveness all the same. The relative lack of criticism from outsiders about the policies of the military authorities in the Territories, and especially in regard to the trade union movement, is partly to blame for this. It is also due, however, to the youth and inexperience of unionists who have only recently begun to develop the capability to record and publicize information in a more or less efficient way, and to link up to an international network which can act upon such information. It is only in the last two years, especially since the launching of the 'Iron Fist' policy, that the unions in the Territories have started to attract international attention. In 1987, the ILO observed in its annual report on the conditions of workers in the Occupied Territories that the unions were not political structures but indeed legitimate trade unions:

In the past, the Israeli authorities have on a number of occasions expressed the opinion that the activities of trade unionists in the occupied territories were

---

[69] M. Rishmawi, 'Finding Security in Subterfuge: The Uses of an Argument', unpublished articles, files of al-Haq/LSM (Ramallah, 1987). For further discussion of the reliance of the Israeli authorities on 'security' needs, see Ch. 6 in this volume.

concerned with political matters rather than trade union issues and that their meetings were devoted to discussions that could not be considered as trade union business. The Director-General's representatives were struck by the fact that, contrary to the many fears expressed by the Israeli authorities, no questions of a political nature were raised during their talks; the trade unionists they met confined themselves to matters relating to the difficulties involved in carrying out trade union activities aimed at promoting and defending the interests of Arab workers.[70]

Part of the difficulty unions face in parrying repressive measures has been the lack of legal recourse to decisions issued by the Israeli military commander. Such decisions are formulated in administrative orders from which there is no legal appeal, except through the Israeli High Court of Justice. The High Court, however, does not study a case on its merits but simply decides whether the military commander stayed within the bounds of his prerogative when he issued the order. It is only in rare cases that the Court rules against the military commander. The military authorities have therefore been singularly successful in closing down union offices and detaining, or even deporting, union activists.

In August 1986, al-Haq took up the case of the one-month closure of the general federation in Nablus earlier that month. This is a significant case because it elicited a lengthy response from the army justifying administrative measures like the closure of buildings. Al-Haq first sent a letter to the military commander protesting the closure, quoting international conventions concerning occupied territories, as well as the relevant ILO conventions.[71] The reply which the organization received from the legal adviser to the military government in the West Bank a few weeks later referred simply to the commander's right to close offices or buildings in order to 'maintain security and public order in the area'.[72] The legal adviser added: 'The activity which took place in that federation is as far removed from the activities in which a professional union should be involved as East is from West.'[73] Dissatisfied with such a categorical statement, al-Haq continued to intervene with the authorities on this issue, insisting that

[I]f the allegations made in [the legal adviser's] letter can be substantiated, they must be made public. Whereas in al-Haq's understanding a union itself cannot be guilty of any offence, those who are responsible for or active in the union can be. If any charges exist against any union representative or member, those in question must be informed of the charges against them without undue delay

---

[70] ILO, 'Report on the Situation of Workers', 32.
[71] Al-Haq/LSM, 'Closure of Trade Union Office', in *Newsletter 14* (July/Aug. 1986).
[72] Al-Haq/LSM, 'Closure of Nablus Trade Union Offices', in *Newsletter 15* (Sept./Oct. 1986), 5.
[73] Al-Haq/LSM, 'Protection of Trade Union Rights', in *Newsletter 15* (Sept./Oct. 1986), 1.

and be brought to trial. The union, which serves a large constituency, should not be closed as a punishment for individuals who are misusing a public responsibility in a way which is too serious to be overlooked.[74]

Al-Haq then requested that the closure orders be rescinded.

In a reply dated 8 December 1986, the legal adviser reiterated the military commander's prerogative to close down a union's office by administrative order if it was found that 'hostile activities' were taking place inside the union. Regardless of the administrative order, the authorities could still bring unionists to court on formal charges, the legal advisor added. He also claimed that unionists could appeal administrative measures to the Israeli High Court of Justice.[75] Al-Haq responded in February 1987, noting that administrative measures against unions and unionists are illegal under the ILO's Freedom of Association Convention, and arguing that the ILO has recognized that even political activities may be legitimate in a union context.[76] According to the ILO,

an outright prohibition of political activities . . . is not only incompatible with the principles of freedom of association, but it would also seem to be unrealistic in actual practice. Trade unions may wish to make publicly known their position on matters of economic and social policy, in relation to their task of furthering and defending the interests of their members.[77]

Al-Haq's insistence on being provided with specific legal clarifications about the authorities' closure of the trade union federation in Nablus eventually prompted a lengthy legal reply from the legal adviser, in July 1987. Quoting extensively from international law and conventions, and citing international legal experts as well as decisions of the Israeli High Court of Justice, the legal adviser affirmed the commander's right to close union offices: if he is convinced that 'hostile activities' take place in a union, 'it is incumbent upon the Military Commander to take preventive administrative measures'. The activities of a union must be 'within the bounds of the law and security legislation' and must fall within the 'stated legitimate aims of the organization'. The legal adviser also argued that 'political activities may include economic factors, but they should not, as political entities, include hostile activities.' To al-Haq's claim that the term 'hostile activities' is left undefined and can therefore be used by the authorities as a pretext to close down legitimate trade unions, the legal adviser responded:

[74] Al-Haq/LSM, 'Closure of Nablus Trade Union Offices'.
[75] Files of al-Haq/LSM, Ramallah. See also al-Haq/LSM, 'Closure of the Nablus Trade Union Federation'.
[76] Ibid.
[77] ILO, *ILO Principles, Standards, and Procedures Concerning Freedom of Association* (Geneva, 1978), 16.

To whom is the Military Commander obligated to substantiate his judgements? To al-Haq???!!! ... To the best of our understanding, your organization has no jurisdictional legitimacy.

The legal adviser ended his letter stating:

In light of all that has been said above, it is perfectly clear that preventive measures implemented by the IDF against different workers' associations, as referred to in your letter, are decidedly legitimate and 'to the letter of the law' governing the internal administration of the Territories, as well as in accordance with the principles of international justice. Understandably, the opportunity always exists to examine the validity of administrative sanctions, either through the Appeals Committee or the High Court of Justice, according to the nature of the matter under consideration.[78]

Despite the authorities' refusal to disclose the evidence they claim to have against the activities of individual unions or unionists, it is significant that at least they are being pushed toward clarifying their position, stating the criteria they employ in executing administrative measures. It is only when the authorities are on record as taking a particular position that unions can seek recourse in the international community.

In 1986 a number of trade unions in the West Bank submitted a representation to the ILO concerning the deportation of two trade union leaders and the administrative detention of seventeen others in the fall of 1985. The representation was, however, deemed not receivable by the ILO because, among other things, '[T]he occupation by Israel of Arab territories in 1967 cannot be considered as having extended to the Occupied Territories Israel's obligations under Conventions it has ratified.'[79] The status of the Territories in international law, complicated even to the expert, thus has thrown barriers in the path of those among the occupied population who seek recourse against unjust measures perpetrated by the occupying power. Theodor Meron has argued forcefully in favour of the applicability of ILO Conventions to the Occupied Territories, especially ILO Convention No. 87 concerning Freedom of Association and Protection of the Right to Organize, and Convention No. 111 concerning Discrimination in Respect of Employment and Occupation. Both conventions were ratified by Israel, and Convention No. 87 has been ratified by Jordan as well.[80]

At the end of 1986, the Palestine Trade Unions Federation, based outside the Territories, submitted a complaint against the Israeli

---

[78] Files of al-Haq/LSM (translated by al-Haq from Hebrew).
[79] Al-Haq/LSM, 'Representation of West Bank Trade Unions to the ILO', in *Newsletter* 15 (Sept./Oct. 1986), 3.
[80] T. Meron, 'Applicability of Multilateral Conventions to Occupied Territories', in M. Shamgar (ed.), *Military Government in the Territories Administered by Israel 1967–80*, I: *The Legal Aspects* (Jerusalem, 1982), 217–36. See also Chs. 9 and 16 in this volume.

Government to the ILO Committee on Freedom of Association.[81] The complaint, Case No. 1390, which was endorsed by the World Confederation of Labour, focused on several closures of trade unions and break-ins into union premises, as well as restriction orders against and deportations of trade unionists in the West Bank and Gaza. The complaint was deemed receivable by the ILO because the Freedom of Association Committee is not trammelled by restrictions on the applicability of international conventions as are other ILO bodies, since the right to organize is considered to be part of international customary law. In its ruling, the Committee, addressing the ILO's Governing Body, asked approval for the following recommendations: (*a*) that the Israeli authorities respect the inviolability of union premises; and (*b*) that the authorities 'ensure that such actions as house arrest or the expulsion of trade unionists are accompanied by the necessary judicial guarantees and, in addition . . . ensure that such measures are not employed in such a manner as to restrict trade union rights or constitute interference in the activities of the trade union organizations'.[82] In June 1987, Gaza unions submitted a complaint to the ILO's Freedom of Association Committee concerning the banning of union elections in Gaza in February and April 1987, and the subsequent repressive measures taken by the Gaza military authorities against individual unionists.[83]

When seeking outside assistance, unions hit upon an additional stumbling block in the form of the established alliances between western trade union federations and the Israeli federation, the Histadrut. Few western unions are willing to address the Israeli government, thereby bypassing the Histadrut, on issues relating to repression of the trade union movement in the Occupied Territories for fear of offending their Israeli counterpart. At the same time, the Histadrut itself has stated that it cannot intervene on behalf of trade unions and workers' rights in the Territories, if ever it was so inclined, because to do so would be tantamount to a recognition of the *de facto* annexation of the West Bank and Gaza by Israel, which the Histadrut has said it

---

[81] 'Case No. 1390: Complaint against the Government of Israel Presented by the Palestine Trade Unions Federation (PTUF) and the World Confederation of Labour (WCL)', in the *251st Report of the Committee on Freedom of Association* (Geneva, May 1987), 46–51.

[82] Ibid. 50–1.

[83] Gaza Building Workers, 'Violations against the Right to Organize' (complaint submitted to ILO, 2 June 1987). See also al-Haq/LSM, 'Banning of Gaza Union Elections', in *Newsletter 18* (Mar./Apr. 1987). The ILO ruling, issued after the due-date of this essay, constituted a victory for the Gaza unions. However, although the ILO ruled in favour of the Gaza unions, there has been no active enforcement of either this or the previous ILO decision, leaving Israel's repression of trade union activists essentially unaffected.

opposes.[84] The Palestinian unions are thus left with little effective recourse.

Despite such obstacles, unions have begun in the late 1980s to create precedents in the ILO that in the long term may produce a larger measure of international protection for Palestinian trade unions in the Occupied Territories. The fact that the ILO and international labour federations raised their profile during the *intifada* also points in this direction.[85]

Conclusion

Concerned with a deteriorating social infrastructure in the West Bank and Gaza, Palestinians began pooling community efforts in the 1970s to provide those basic services which were most sorely lacking, thus making a major contribution to the development of Palestinian society. During the past decade, a fully fledged popular movement emerged in the Territories which in its work could not avoid addressing the root cause of the Palestinians' current predicament, Israeli colonization efforts carried out under the guise of a military occupation.

In response, the Israeli military authorities, who deny the existence of a Palestinian society and a Palestinian identity, and who consider the mere existence of autonomous Palestinian organizations as hostile to their interests, have draped such organizations in an atmosphere of fear in an effort to deter potential members from joining. The subterfuge of 'security concerns', referred to above, has allowed the authorities to deflect criticism from within Israeli society and from the side of the international community against their repressive practices in the Territories.

Palestinian trade unionists succeeded nevertheless in forging a labour movement that has catered increasingly for the needs of workers. Toward the end of the 1980s, and especially after the outbreak of the *intifada*, they also began to mark success in mobilizing international opinion on their behalf, both in the ILO and in labour federations. Foreign delegations visited the Occupied Territories to study the conditions of workers and trade unions, reporting their findings to their governments and organizations once they returned home. This led to formal protests of Israel's violations of Palestinian rights to organize and associate. Although the military occupation continues to place obstacles in the path of Palestinian trade unions to organize and render

---

[84] Undated Histadrut circular signed by Yerucham Meshel, Histadrut secretary-general in the early 1980s.
[85] See J. Hiltermann, 'Workers' Rights during the Uprising', *Journal of Palestine Studies* 73 (Autumn 1989), 83–91.

services to workers, there are now growing hopes that international interventions will provide the checks and balances necessary to ensure the development of a vibrant labour movement in the Occupied Territories and therefore of Palestinian society generally.

11

Taxation under Belligerent Occupation

GERHARD VON GLAHN

THE five multilateral conventions comprising the modern international law of belligerent occupation display a fair-sized gap in failing to provide rules in the general subject area of economics, including such topics as central banks, exchange reserves, currency questions, and almost all other aspects of business and financial operations.[1] The silence of conventional law on these topics is doubly surprising: the subject matter in question is, and should be, of great importance both to an occupant and to his enemy, the ousted government; and any of the states that ratified or acceded to the instruments involved should have envisioned the possibility that it could at some time become an occupant or an ousted sovereign and as such might wish that the gaps in the rules had been filled at an earlier date. On the other hand, the major signatories of the treaties in question (1899, 1907, 1949, and 1977) may have seen themselves only as future occupants and as such may have wanted to avoid being restricted, by additional new rules, from acting in the manner in which they expected to behave.

At the edge of the gap in conventional regulation of belligerent occupation stands the subject of taxation. It has not been omitted, to be sure, but the relevant rules are few in number and the military manuals of the major Powers do not allow much space for the detailed coverage of the subject, despite its appearance in every belligerent occupation. The same paucity of treatment is encountered in the majority of scholarly works dealing, somewhere, with the subject of occupation, and even in books devoted entirely to occupation, the topic of taxes receives short shrift.[2]

---

[1] See G. von Glahn, *Law Among Nations*, 5th edn. (New York, 1986), 707–9, and his *The Occupation of Enemy Territory* (Minneapolis, 1957), 202–14, for brief coverage of the missing areas.

[2] Thus O. Debbasch, *L'Occupation militaire: Pouvoirs reconnus aux forces armées hors de leur territoire national* (Paris, 1962), covers the subject of taxation solely on pp. 38–9, out of a total of 424 pages in the book.

I. The Law

The law of belligerent occupation has been codified since 1907 (considering a Hague Convention of 1899 as having been replaced by one with virtually identical contents in 1907) in three multilateral instruments:

1. The Fourth Hague Convention Respecting the Laws and Customs of War on Land of 1907, and its annexed Regulations Respecting the Laws and Customs of War on Land (hereinafter cited as 'the Hague Regulations')
2. The Fourth Geneva Convention Relative to the Protection of Civilian Persons in Time of War of 1949 (hereinafter cited as 'Geneva IV')
3. Protocol I Additional to the Geneva Conventions of 12 August 1949, and Relating to the Protection of Victims of International Armed Conflicts of 1977 (hereinafter cited as 'Geneva Protocol I'). A second instrument, Protocol II Additional to the Geneva Conventions of 12 August 1949 Relating to the Protection of Victims of Non-International Armed Conflicts of 1977, entered into force on 7 December 1978.[3]

The use of the term 'armed conflicts' in the two Protocols in place of the usual 'war' or 'land warfare' reflected the growing realization on the part of diplomats and legal scholars that numerous recent (and some current) armed clashes did not fit precisely into the traditional concepts associated with 'war'.

It should be noted that as of this date, the United States and several other major Powers have chosen not to become parties to either Protocol.

As far as the subject of this report, taxation, is concerned, neither Geneva IV nor the two Protocols of 1977 treat anywhere with relevant financial matters. This means that unlike many other aspects of belligerent occupation covered by the 1949 and 1977 instruments mentioned, taxation is the subject only of part of the Hague Regulations (Articles 48, 49, and 51); only one article is devoted to taxes as such, the other two relate to contributions, which will be discussed subsequently, after taxes proper.

The two articles of the Hague Regulations basic to the subject of taxation and thus representing the body of international law regulating that subject read as follows:

Article 48
If, in the territory occupied, the occupant collects the taxes, dues, and tolls imposed for the benefit of the State, he shall do so, as far as is possible, in

---
[3] The texts of these instruments may be found in A. Roberts and R. Guelff, *Documents on the Laws of War* (Oxford, 1982), 43–57, 272–326, and 389–458.

accordance with the rules of assessment and incidence in force, and shall in consequence be bound to defray the expenses of the administration of the occupied territory to the same extent as the legitimate Government was so bound.

Article 49
If, in addition to the taxes mentioned in the above article, the occupant levies other money contributions in the occupied territory, this shall only be for the needs of the army or of the administration of the territory in question.

Article 51 supplies some of the operational details for the collection of contributions and is thus related to the two basic articles:

Article 51
No contribution shall be collected except under a written order and on the responsibility of a commander in chief. The collection of the said contribution shall only be effected as far as possible in accordance with the rules of assessment and incidence of the taxes in force. For every contribution a receipt shall be given to the contributors.

It may be of value, in view of the discussion to follow, to reproduce also the 'law' article of the Hague Regulations:

Article 43
The authority of the legitimate power having in fact passed into the hands of the occupant, the latter shall take all the measures in his power to restore and ensure, as far as possible, public order and safety, while respecting, unless absolutely prevented, the laws in force in the country.

All the articles above are found in every major military manual, usually followed by some additional statements that can easily trap the unwary reader into mistakingly assuming that they represent obligatory treaty provisions. In reality, the various statements and assertions following the reproduced text of the Hague Regulations represent nothing more than a national (say United States, British, or French) interpretation without legally binding force, as seen from the point of view of international law.

There are also judicial decisions, limited in number, dealing with taxation questions under occupation; many of them unfortunately reflect governmental views and policies of the occupant alone. It should be remembered, too, that in most instances of belligerent occupation, a suit by inhabitants against an occupant is prohibited by the latter: this may help to explain the limited number of cases dealing with the subject.

Finally there are the already mentioned writings of scholars and a few government documents (directives of basic import and letters by high officials to other similar individuals, dealing with taxation) that can be mentioned as interpretations of the law, not as sources thereof.

Several preliminary questions must be examined briefly before taxation under belligerent occupation can be explored in depth. It appears necessary to determine the extent to which the Hague Regulations actually apply to territory under occupation, and in second place the applicable laws under belligerent occupation must be ascertained, with particular reference to taxation. Only after those issues have been surveyed is it deemed to be possible to turn to the central theme of this report, taxation (including customs duties as well as monetary contributions in that rubric).

II. The Applicability of the Hague Regulations to Territory under Belligerent Occupation

It is regrettable that the interesting and much debated question of the applicability of Geneva IV to such complex belligerent occupations as that of Israel over its 'Administered Territories' falls outside the scope of this report, inasmuch as Geneva IV does not deal with the subject of taxation. But the general applicability of the Hague Regulations, as the only conventional law on the subject, is another matter.

It has been suggested that the Hague Regulations were not applicable in the territories occupied by Israel today (the West Bank and the Gaza Strip) as well as in the case of the Golan Heights and East Jerusalem, annexed by Israel in apparent violation of international law, because neither Israel nor Jordan, Egypt and Syria had ratified or acceded to the Fourth Hague Convention of 1907 and its annexed Regulations. None of the countries in question had existed as an independent subject of international law in 1907 and none of them had subsequently seen fit to become a party to the Hague Regulations. All of this, however, is quite immaterial, for the Hague Regulations have been accepted as declaratory of customary law rules, binding on all members of the family of nations. Only if a state had objected to a new rule from its very inception would that state not be bound by the rule, once it became part of customary law. None of the Middle Eastern states in question could have objected because they did not exist in 1907.

The international Military Tribunal at Nuremberg held that the rules found in Hague Convention IV and its Regulations were 'recognized by all civilized nations' and were 'regarded as being declaratory of the laws and customs of war',[4] and the International Military Tribunal

---

[4] *Trial of the Major War Criminals before the International Military Tribunal*, 1: 253–4, 6 FRD 69, 130 (1946). See also B. M. Claggett and O. T. Johnson Jr., 'May Israel as a Belligerent Occupant Lawfully Exploit Previously Unexploited Oil Resources of the Gulf of Suez?', *AJIL* 72 (1978), 560; Roberts and Guelff, *Documents on the Laws of War*, 44, and L. Oppenheim, *International Law*, 7th edn., ed. E. Lauterpacht (London, 1952), 234–5.

for the Far East expressed the same view in its judgment in 1948.[5]

The binding force of the Hague Regulations on all states has also been affirmed in numerous court decisions.[6] In the instance of Israel, the obligations imposed by the Hague Regulations as part of international customary law would date from the middle of May 1948, for no evidence has yet been found to the effect that Israel objected to the application of the corpus of rules laid down in the instrument. Israel has differed with the interpretations delineated by other states only on a few points, as will be shown below. And a number of Israeli court decisions confirm the customary law character of the Hague Regulations. Particularly the Supreme Court, sitting as a High Court of Justice, has dealt with this subject. In the *Beit El* case the Court stated in its judgment that international customary law constituted part of the municipal law of Israel. Later, in the *Elon Moreh* case, the Supreme Court stated that '... the Hague Rules... bind the military administration in Judea and Samaria, being part of customary international law'.[7]

It must be concluded, in view of general practice with respect to customary law and the court decisions in Israel and other countries that the Hague Regulations represent customary international law, applicable everywhere.

On the other hand, a minority view shared by the Israeli government and a few scholars holds that, while the foregoing statement represents a general conclusion, the correct interpretation would be that if a belligerent occupation should be of considerable duration, changes could be made by the occupant in the provisions of the Hague Regulations. In other words, an initially strict application of the Hague Regulations in territory under belligerent occupation should be permitted to be weakened in the case of a prolonged occupation. This concept is not new: it first appeared in print, to this writer's knowledge, as early as 1916 when Leurquin wrote:

When the occupation is prolonged and when, owing to the war, the economic and social position of the occupied country undergoes profound changes, it is perfectly evident that new legislative measures are essential sooner or later.[8]

The concept of permitted deviation from the Hague Regulations was supported very eloquently by Dr Yehuda Z. Blum, of the Hebrew

---

[5] *Judgment of the International Military Tribunal of the Far East, 1948*, United Nations War Crimes Commission, 15 *Law Report of Trials of War Criminals* (Tokyo, 1949), 13; see also T. Meron, 'On the Inadequate Reach of Humanitarian and Human Rights Law and the Need for a New Instrument', *AJIL* 77 (1983), 591.

[6] See Claggett and Johnson, 'May Israel', 560–1 for a list of such decisions handed down in Corfu, Rome, Trieste, etc.

[7] See Ch. 2 in this volume for a full review of these cases.

[8] M. Leurquin, 'The German Occupation in Belgium and Article 43 of the Hague Convention of the 18th October 1907', *Int. Law Notes* 1 (1916), 55, and von Liszt, *Das Völkerrecht*, 12th edn., ed. M. Fleischman (Berlin, 1925), 491.

University, before a subcommittee of the US Senate Judiciary Committee in 1977, when he said:

Belligerent occupation exceeding a long period of time simply cannot work under the same constraints as the normal belligerent occupation, if the term 'normal' can be applied to a situation of this kind. Obviously the Red Cross Convention [Geneva IV] and other international instruments have in view the 'normal' situation under which the hostilities are ceased or terminated and you have an interim period of a few weeks or months of belligerent occupation, followed by peace negotiations which finally dispose of the territory.[9]

The Government of Israel itself had suggested in a Memorandum of Law concerning new oilfields in Sinai and the Gulf of Suez[10] that certain doubts existed as to the relevance—and even validity—of the Hague Regulations in a situation in which the belligerents had ceased to engage in active hostilities.

Claggett and Johnson believed that this concept was based on the writings of a publicist who had maintained that a part of the Hague Regulations applied 'expressly' only to a situation in which the belligerent armies were 'still fighting in the field'.[11] It is impossible, however, to find such an 'express' limitation in the text of the Hague Regulations, while almost all courts and scholars are in agreement that the end of hostilities does not affect in any manner the obligations or the rights of a belligerent occupant.[12] In fact, Feilchenfeld contradicted the cited view when, later in the same work, he asserted that it was generally recognized that the Hague Regulations continued to apply beyond the conclusion of a cease-fire or of an armistice agreement, except as otherwise specified in such arrangements.[13]

If the plea for modification of the rules of customary law in the course of a prolonged belligerent occupation were to be considered favourably by the members of the family of nations, the entire fabric of safeguards for the protection of the indigenous population of occupied territory would be in tatters in no time at all. The Hague Regulations

---

[9] Reproduced in S. V. Mallison and W. T. Mallison Jr., *The Palestine Problem in International Law and World Order* (Harlow, 1986), 260.

[10] Government of Israel, *Memorandum of Law*, ILM 17 (1978), 432–3. That document was the reply to an earlier US Dept. of State *Memorandum of Law* (1 Oct. 1976) concerning exploitation of oil resources, ILM 16 (1977), 733. Amusing to this writer is the fact that both governments cited and quoted his *Occupation* in the documents.

[11] Claggett and Johnson, 'May Israel', referring to E. H. Feilchenfeld, *The International Economic Law of Belligerent Occupation* (Washington, 1942), 6.

[12] See the *Manual of Military Law, III: The Law of War on Land* (UK War Office, London, 1958), par. 447, at 130; E. Fraenkel, *Military Occupation and the Rule of Law* (London, 1944), 8–9; A. Gerson, 'War, Conquered Territory, and Military Occupation in the Contemporary International Legal System', HILJ 18 (1977), 528–9; see also Chs. 1 and 5 in this volume.

[13] Feilchenfeld, *International Economic Law of Belligerent Occupation*, 111.

would cease to play a vital part in restraining an occupant, once the latter had decided that the duration of his regime justified alterations in the rules, and the occupant would be able to carry out his unchecked will against a multitude of helpless civilians.[14]

It might be mentioned in passing that it may well be that the failure in 1907 to specify what might happen to the Hague Regulations in the course of a long occupation prompted the inclusion in Geneva IV of that part of its Article 6 that applied to occupied territory after the cessation of hostilities.

III. Applicable Laws under Belligerent Occupation

The rule relating to laws in territory under belligerent occupation is found in Article 43 of the Hague Regulations, reproduced earlier in this report. The article reproduced corresponding provisions in the Brussels Code of 1874 and the *Oxford Manual* of 1880.[15] Gerson cogently pointed out that the Hague Regulations emphasized the view that an eventual reversion of control, in whole or in part, would take place in favour of the displaced government. Hence any serious interference with that government's institutions and legislative system was forbidden, 'for fear of being inimical to the settlement process'.[16]

During a belligerent occupation the occupant acts as the substitute of the ousted government and as such is entrusted with the task of continuing the administration of the area—a task usually more easily accomplished with the utilization of existing laws. An exception would be such ordinances as represented dangers to the occupant (military training, right to bear arms, etc.) or that conflicted with the war aims of the occupant (laws concerning the Nazi Party and its institutions in Germany).

Ordinary civil law, pertaining to family life, inheritance, property, debts, contracts, and so on, may not be altered or suspended by an occupant, except as military necessity or the maintenance of public order and safety may require.[17] The latter exception does not mean, however, that an occupant had a free hand in providing the local population with ideal—or even only better—living conditions. The exception appears to have been intended only for restoring such order and public safety as were found in the area before the occupation, as

---

[14] On prolonged occupation and its effect, see other chapters in this volume, particularly those of Roberts, Greenwood, and Cassese.
[15] See the illuminating background coverage in D. A. Graber, *The Development of the Law of Belligerent Occupation 1863-1914: A Historical Survey* (New York, 1949), 1–36.
[16] Gerson, 'War, Conquered Territory and Military Occupation', 537.
[17] von Glahn, *Occupation*, 98–9.

well as to continue this level of order and safety for the duration of the occupation.[18]

Scholars still differ as to the primary purpose of the rules applicable to belligerent occupation. Some assert that the protection of the inhabitants (against excesses committed by the occupant) should be regarded as the primary purpose for the existence of the Hague Regulations and other later instruments, and that protection of the reversionary interests of the ousted government represented at most a secondary purpose for the existence of the rules. This outlook corresponds with the traditional outlook on the subject.[19] Others, including this writer, believe that the primary purpose incorporated in the Hague Regulations is military necessity—the security of the occupying forces, considering that the occupation is of the 'belligerent' type. Next would come the protection of the inhabitants against acts of the occupant, and lastly the reversionary interests of the ousted government. Admittedly the ranking given is a controversial one, but it can be asserted that (1) military necessity (security) cannot be omitted from consideration, and (2) no one today would maintain that such military necessity alone should be viewed as the sole purpose of a set of rules such as the Hague Regulations.[20]

Much more disagreement prevails among both governments and scholars as to the meaning of the phrase 'public order and safety' in Article 43. The original and governing text of the treaty reads '*l'ordre et la vie publics*': the common semi-official English translation of 'public order and safety' simply does not convey the meaning of the original wording. One learned author has suggested the use of 'public order and civil life'.[21] Others have favoured 'order and the social and economic life of the community',[22] while Lubrano-Lavadera believed that the phrase referred to 'safeguarding public order and the security of the army of occupation' (*sauvegarder l'ordre public et à assurer la securité de l'armée d'occupation*).[23] American and British military manuals all use

---

[18] See the succinct minority opinion of Judge Haim Cohn in the Israeli Supreme Court case of the *Christian Society for the Holy Places*, HC 337/71, at 588. The relevant portion of the opinion was reproduced in English in Israel National Section of the International Commission of Jurists, *The Rule of Law in the Areas Administered by Israel* (Tel Aviv, 1981), 7.

[19] For example, S. Boyd, 'The Applicability of International Law to the Occupied Territories', *IYHR* 1 (1971), in discussion section, 370.

[20] See A. Gerson, 'Trustee-Occupant: The Legal Status of Israel's Presence in the West Bank', *HILJ* 14 (1973), 13, and von Glahn, *Occupation*, 43.

[21] E. H. Schwenk, 'Legislative Power of the Military Occupant under Article 43, Hague Regulations', *Yale L. J.* 54 (1944–5), 393, n. 1.

[22] H. Wheaton, *Elements of International Law*, II, 6th Eng. edn., ed. A. b. Keith (London, 1929), 783.

[23] E. M. Lubrano-Lavadera, *Les Lois de la guerre et de l'occupation militaire* (Paris, 1956), 17.

the terminology of 'public order and safety',[24] just as von Schmoller held that the rights and duties of an occupant included the maintenance of law and order (*das Recht und die Ordnung aufrechtzuerhalten*).[25]

There can be no doubt about the lawful ability of a belligerent occupant to change the legal system existing in occupied territory by suspending or altering existing laws, and that the relevant military commander, as legislator for the area, can issue new legislation. (A subsequent section of this chapter will deal with the subject of new taxes in occupied territory.) Presumably such changes or new legislation will have to be related either to needs of the occupying army or to the maintenance of 'public life'.

In the case of the latter category, the question arises whether the motivation for the legislation arose out of a promotion of the occupant's own interests or out of a genuine desire to improve the social or economic life of the inhabitants of the territory, '*la vie publique*' of Article 43. The former situation, i.e. the occupant's own interests, would be illegal unless genuine problems justified the changes in law; the latter would be legal only if no constraints laid down in the Hague Regulations had been violated.[26]

In any case, the occupant, 'unless absolutely prevented' (Hague Regulations, Article 43), has to respect the bulk of the laws found in the occupied territory and may supplement them with ordinances and laws of his own.[27] If a given belligerent occupation extends over a long period of time, then, as several writers have asserted, it will invariably be necessary for the occupant to legislate on many matters in the field of economics. Such action is deemed by those in question as a permitted change, extensive though it may become.[28]

On the other hand, most scholars have refused to accept such a broad grant of authority and insist on linking new legislation to the test of the *motivation* involved. As Grassmann observed, ordinances

---

[24] Such as *US Field Manual FM 27–10, The Law of Land Warfare* (Washington, DC, 1956), par. 370, at 142.

[25] G. von Schmoller, H. Maier, and A. Tobler, *Handbuch des Besatzungsrechts* (Tübingen, 1951), I, para. 24a, at 36.

[26] See C. M. O. van Nispen Tot Sevenaer, *L'Occupation Allemande pendant la dernière guerre mondiale* (Tübingen, 1946), 233–5, concerning the difficulty of making such judgements.

[27] See again the *Christian Society for the Holy Places* case, HC 337/71, at 582.

[28] Feilchenfeld, *International Economic Law of Belligerent Occupation*, 86–7; Schwenk, 'Legislative Power', 393; and M. Greenspan, *The Modern Law of Land Warfare* (Berkeley, 1959), 221. See also Judge Sussman's comment in the *Christian Society* case, 582: 'In the event of a military occupation continuing for a long time until peace is achieved, the obligation of the occupant towards the civil population is to change the laws to suit the changing needs of the society with the passing of time and the law must answer this change of needs.' See also Chs. 1 and 7 in this volume.

that served exclusively the interests of the inhabitants have been rare indeed.[29]

IV. Taxation and Customs Duties under Belligerent Occupation

General Considerations

A belligerent occupant does not necessarily have to collect any taxes in occupied territory. But if he chooses to do so, he is limited in his ability fully to carry out his purpose. The governing principles on the subject, as laid down in Article 48 of the Hague Regulations, ordain that the occupant collecting taxes, dues, and tolls imposed for the benefit of the ousted government, must do so, as far as is possible, in accordance with the rules of assessment and incidence in force. In consequence of collecting such revenues, the occupant is then bound to pay for the expenses of the administration of the occupied territory to the same extent that the ousted government was so bound.

It is generally accepted that the wording of Article 48 bars the occupant from collecting taxes normally due to regional, district, county, and local government authorities, provided that such taxes had not been collected previously (i.e. before the occupation) by such lower level authorities for transfer to the ousted national government. Thus no old, nor new, 'local taxes' can be levied lawfully by an occupant.

If any funds remain after the occupant has collected the former 'national taxes' and has disbursed the appropriate sums to cover the expenses of the administration of the territory, such a surplus may be utilized by the occupant for the use of the army of occupation.[30]

Article 48 of the Hague Regulations specifically mentions holding the rates of assessments and incidence on national taxes, formerly collected for the benefit of the ousted government, at levels coincident with the beginning of the occupation: the occupant must maintain these rates at those levels as far as possible. However, should such tax revenues, now collected on behalf of the occupant to pay for the administration or the civil life of the population in the territory, prove to be insufficient to cover such administrative or other costs, the occupant would be free lawfully to change the rates in order to collect more revenue.[31]

---

[29] G. O. Grassmann, *Die deutsche Besatzungsgesetzgebung während des 2. Weltkrieges im Rahman des Volkerrechts* (Tübingen, 1958), 10.

[30] *British Manual*, para. 527, at 146; Greenspan, *Modern Law of Land Warfare*, 228; R. de Card, *La Guerre continentale et la propriété* (Paris, 1877), 69; A. Bustamente y Sirven, *Droit international public*, iv, trans. P. Goule (Paris, 1937), 374; J. W. Garner, *International Law and the World War* (London, 1920), 66; *US Field Manual* (1956), para. 425(b), at 157.

[31] J. Stone, *Legal Controls of International Conflict*, rev. edn. (New York, 1959), 712; von Glahn, *Occupation*, 151; Feilchenfeld, *International Economic Law of Belligerent Occupation*, 49.

Another alternative, adopted by very few occupants, would be for an occupant to meet the deficits involved out of his own resources;[32] and finally the occupant might levy new taxes. The last solution would be lawful only, however, if the purpose of the levies would be to meet the needs of the army (administration) or of financing the 'restoration' of the civil life of the inhabitants. Any new tax levied for other purposes or goals would be unlawful under Article 43.

Unlike most of the military manuals, the American *US Field Manual* dealt with one of the realities of modern warfare when, in discussing taxes, it suggested that:

> If, due to the flight or unwillingness of the local officials, it is impracticable to follow the rules of incidence and assessment in force, then the total amount of taxes to be paid may be allotted among the districts, towns, etc., and the local authorities required to collect it.[33]

A consensus exists among both governments and writers on the law that local taxes (districts, counties, communities) formerly not turned over to the ousted government but used for 'local' purposes cannot be collected lawfully by a belligerent occupant. The latter may, however,—and has done so in virtually all instances known to this writer—supervise such 'local' expenditures, and may forbid any that are deemed hostile to the forces or interests of the occupant. 'Local' authorities normally are free to change tax rates and even to introduce new local taxes for local purposes. This fact was discussed in considerable detail in the case of *Commune de Grace-Berleur v. Charbonnages de Gosson Lagasse et Consorts* (1919), in which a Belgian court decided that an order of the German Governor-General which made resolutions of communal councils levying communal taxes subject to the approval of the occupant was illegal. The court held that the order did not contribute to the restoration of public order and safety under Article 48 of the Hague Regulations.[34] The present writer does not know under what authority—if any—the Belgian court judged an order of the belligerent occupant!

If the local authorities have collected taxes for the ousted government (national taxes), then the tax collections paid to them by the inhabitants during occupation on the same basis are to be treated by the occupant's authorities as if the ousted government itself had been the tax-collecting agency.[35] On the other hand, if 'local' authorities in occupied territory had sent the tax revenues collected by them to the

---

[32] Israel has followed such a policy: see Israel National Section of the International Commission of Jurists, *The Rule of Law*, 94.
[33] Para. 426(a) at 157.
[34] See G. H. Hackworth, *Digest of International Law* (Washington, DC, 1943), 393–4.
[35] See W. P. Bordwell, *The Law of War between Belligerents: A History and Commentary* (Chicago, 1908), 329.

ousted government before the onset of the occupation with a view toward eventual redistribution at the regional, district, county or community levels, such revenues collected under occupation cannot be regarded as 'national' taxes by the belligerent occupant. The latter cannot, of course, permit such revenues to be forwarded to the ousted government but will insist that they be turned over to his own fiscal officers in the occupation administration.

As long as the major obligations of a belligerent occupancy are to restore and maintain order and public safety (civil life) in an occupied territory, it would appear to be fair that the beneficiaries of such activities pay for their cost.[36] If the 'national taxes' discussed earlier are insufficient to pay for administration expenses and/or the civil life of the inhabitants, then the burden of funding the deficit falls on the occupant in one of several ways, as mentioned earlier. But if the deficit in question would be caused by heavy capital outlays (a rare occurrence in occupied areas) initiated by local authorities, then the occupant who merely consented to expenditures outside his more lasting interests in the area should not be expected to pay for such extraordinary outlays.[37]

In this connection the present writer believes that a belligerent occupant may adjust existing 'national' taxes collected on his behalf in occupied territory to the level at which such taxes are being levied in the occupant's own country, provided such taxes are designated either for the costs of administration or for the restoration of the civil life of the inhabitants. Should a surplus result from such increased levels of taxation, it could be used for the army of occupation. A belligerent could, of course, suspend the collection of the 'national' taxes, should such revenues not be needed to cover administrative costs or the 'civil life' expenditures for the population.[38]

A subject already mentioned and one that is the cause of considerable disagreement among scholars and also among some governments is the imposition of *new* taxes by an occupant in territory administered by him. The present writer, at the risk of digressing briefly into the sphere of semantics, wishes to return to Article 43 of the Hague Regulations. In the English-language version, the article calls on the occupant to 'restore, and ensure, as far as possible, public order and safety'. Using the original and governing French-language version, i.e. 'public order and civil life', shifts the occupant's legislative authority

---

[36] Ibid.; see also [US] Judge Advocate General's School, *Law of Belligerent Occupation* (JAGS Text No. 11, 1944), 160–1.
[37] See also Great Britain, War Office, *Military Manual of Civil Affairs in the Field* (1944), 77.
[38] Judge Advocate General's School, *Law of Belligerent Occupation*, 187; British Manual, para. 372, n. 'A'.

and responsibility quite drastically from public order and the safety of his own forces to public order and the civil life of the inhabitants. A reasonable interpretation of the phrase would imply that public order refers not only to order among the indigenous population but also to the protection—through a stable social order—of the occupying forces.

A brief comment appears to be needed, however, concerning the word 'restore' in the English version of Article 43. The governing French text uses *rétablir*, or re-establish and also restore—yet this poses a semantic problem.[39] The present writer believes that to restore something means to re-establish, recreate, or restore something that existed before. The word 'restore' cannot mean the establishment of something new, something never before existing. Therefore it is held that an occupant's legislation restoring something that did not exist previously contravenes the provisions of Article 43, and exceeds his legal competence under the Hague Regulations.

Imposition of a new tax would therefore not be permissible *unless* it in fact was needed to meet administrative expenses of the occupant in the territory under occupation or was designed to restore (promote, re-establish) the civil (social, economic) life of the inhabitants.

Determination of the illegality of an occupant's proposed new tax would be in the domain of courts. Whose courts could rule on the question is a moot issue, beyond the scope of this chapter. However, in the case of Israel, while the domestic law of the occupant does not grant the country's Supreme Court explicit jurisdiction over the Occupied Territories—the Court being technically and legally outside those territories—the Court has agreed repeatedly since 1967 to hear applications and cases from those territories, sitting under those circumstances as a High Court of Justice.

The present writer believes that in any discussion of new taxes in occupied territory, Article 43 of the Hague Regulations must be regarded as the governing article. Most scholars and most governments grant the occupant a limited right to impose new taxes when 'required to do so by considerations of public order and safety'.[40] It must again be emphasized that the foregoing statement refers to a genuinely lawful purpose for imposing the new tax, as explained earlier. The Israel National Section of the International Commission of Jurists, elaborating on this question, stated that when receipts from a tax changed materially, when new needs demanded new revenues, when an occupation lasted for several years, then the lawful govern-

---

[39] See Schwenk, 'Legislative Power of the Military Occupant', 396, and C. Meurer, *Die volkerrechtliche Stellung der vom Feind besetzten Gebiete* (Tübingen, 1915), 18.
[40] *US Field Manual*, para. 426(b), at 157; *British Manual*, para. 529; Feilchenfeld, *International Economic Law of Belligerent Occupation*, 49; Stone, *Legal Controls*, 712–13.

ment would have found it necessary to modify tax legislation and introduce new taxation. Likewise the occupant, in place of the ousted government, would have to do so, for he could not disregard the realities of the situation. To do so 'may well interfere with the welfare of the country and ultimately with "public order and safety" as understood in Article 43'.[41]

The American interpretation, as stated in *US Field Manual*, asserts succinctly that 'unless required to do so by consideration of public order and safety, the occupant must not create new taxes'.[42] It should be pointed out at this point that a majority of the examples of new taxes imposed by occupants, as outlined below, represent unlawful interpretations of Article 43: the taxes in question did not exist to meet administrative expenses, nor did they contribute to the welfare (civil life) of the population in question.

Customs Duties

The literature dealing with belligerent occupation contains but few references to the subject of customs duties, even though the latter are a part of the 'national' revenue collected in many territories under belligerent occupation. The inclusion of 'dues' in Article 48 of the Hague Regulations is taken to mean that customs duties fall under the same rules as 'national taxes' in occupied territory.[43] If customs duties were collected by an occupant, they would, therefore, contribute to defraying the costs of administration and, like 'national' taxes, could be raised by the occupant if additional funds had to be found for lawful purposes. Application of these principles has varied greatly from occupation to occupation. In many instances, an occupant suspended customs duties altogether, in view of a ban imposed on all foreign trade of an occupied area; in virtually all instances, the occupant suspended all customs duties as far as they affected both the property of the occupant in occupied territory and the shipment of goods from his own country to the occupied territory, especially if such goods were intended for the use of the occupying forces.[44] Again, in some occupations exports from an occupied area to the occupant's own country were exempt from customs duties. And, as in the case of new taxes, the concept that an occupant may introduce *new* customs duties

---

[41] Feilchenfeld, *International Economic Law of Belligerent Occupation*, 49.
[42] *US Field Manual*, para. 426(b), at 157.
[43] von Glahn, *Occupation*, 150; Feilchenfeld, *International Economic Law of Belligerent Occupation*, 83.
[44] Bustamente y Sirven, *Droit international public*, 374–5, and Meurer, *Die völkerrechtliche Stellung*, 24.

in the occupied territory has been the subject of controversy among legal scholars.[45]

Selected Practices

Major Powers have supplied their armed forces with military manuals containing not only the texts of treaties applicable to warfare, including belligerent occupations, but also national interpretations of the meaning of the international rules. In almost every instance known, such national interpretations have displayed a perhaps understandable tendency to diminish some of the restraints imposed on an occupant by the Hague Regulations and subsequent instruments. This generalization also applies to the subject of taxation in occupied territory. The results of the application of national interpretations are illustrated by the examples below. It must be emphasized that in all too many cases, the permissive interpretation found in military manuals was so extensive that its application in the field resulted in the commission of what today would be termed war crimes.

It should be noted that military manuals such as those cited in this report must not be taken to be a source of rules of international law, as the US Military Tribunal at Nuremberg pointed out:

[A]rmy regulations are not a competent source of international law. It is possible, however, that such regulations, as they bear upon a question of custom and practice in the conduct of war, might have evidentiary value, particularly if the applicable portions had been put into general practice.[46]

Nevertheless the manuals were possessed of official standing, and occupying forces were expected to comply with the national interpretations set forth.[47]

World War I
Belgium. The German 'Zone of Occupation' was governed by one of the relatively rare mixed civilian–military organizations encountered

---

[45] See also Israel National Section of the International Commission of Jurists, *The Rule of Law*, 96.
[46] US Military Tribunals, *Trials of War Criminals Before the Nuernberg Military Tribunals*, XI (1950), 1237, reproduced in Roberts and Guelff, *Documents on the Laws of War*, 7.
[47] France, *Manuel de lois de la guerre continentale* (1913); *British Manual*; Great Britain, War Office, *A.M.G.O.T. Plan, Proclamations and Instructions*, 2nd edn. (Sept. 1943); Great Britain, War Office, *Manual of Military Law*, 6th edn. (1914); Great Britain, War Office, *Military Manual of Civil Affairs in the Field* (1944); *US Field Manual*; [US] Army and Navy, *Manual of Civil Affairs/Military Government* (14 Oct. 1947) (FM 27–5 and OPNAV P22–1115, superseded FM 27–5 of 1943); [US] Department of the Army, *Basic Manual of Land Warfare* (FM 27–10, 1940, superseded by *US Field Manual* in July 1956); and [US] Army and Navy, *Joint Manual of Civil Affairs/Military Government* (FM 41–5; OPNAV P 21–1; AFM 110–7; NAVMC 2500, 1940) (superseded by the Army and Navy *Manual* of 1947).

among modern belligerent occupations (Israel now has one of these hybrid structures governing its Administered Territories), even though at the time the German authorities referred to their creation as a military government.

The German Governor-General announced as early as 12 November 1914 that, in accordance with Article 48 of the Hague Regulations, the taxes, dues, fees, and customs existing in favour of the Belgian State would continue to be levied by the occupation authorities and that the cost of administering the occupied areas would be met by such revenues. Soon, however, taxes and customs duties proved to be insufficient and the German authorities, relying on Article 48 and 49 of the Regulations, increased the previous tax and customs rates and began to explore the possibilities of new sources of tax revenue.[48] However, in most instances the previous tax rates were still employed by Belgian tax collectors until May 1916, when various segments of the Belgian (national) tax acts were either repealed or altered by the German authorities.

The new tax structure was based on three main sources of revenue: a land tax (property tax), a trade licences tax (including both industry and agriculture), and an income tax.[49]

In 1916 the occupant ordered an expansion of the base of the property tax and of the tax levied on income from patents above a certain level of income; he also introduced an additional personal tax on executive and similar officials of incorporated enterprises.[50] In 1917 (and again for the fiscal year 1918) the tax system was revised, and in June 1917 a new excise tax on salt was instituted. On 29 July 1917, another new tax was introduced: a property tax based on the total movable property held in absolute ownership or belonging as a 'life estate' to any person who was an inhabitant of occupied Belgium on 1 January of each year. That tax was assessed on a sliding scale and was payable in two semi-annual instalments.[51]

It is not possible to determine now whether a rise in administrative costs, i.e. the needs of the army, or the ever-expanding costs involved in maintaining or promoting the civil life of the Belgian people, required the recorded increases in taxation. The present writer believes that neither purpose was involved but that enrichment of the occupant was the primary purpose. If such was the case, the tax increases were unlawful, even though the Governor-General originally invoked Article 48 of the Hague Regulations.

---

[48] L. Von Köhler, *Die Staatsverwaltung der besetzten Gebiete*, i: *Belgien* (Stuttgart, 1927), 60.
[49] J. Bisschop, 'German War Legislation in the Occupied Territory of Belgium', *Trans. Grotius Society* 4 (1919), 110, at 140.
[50] Von Köhler, *Die Staatsverwaltung*, 61.
[51] Bisschop, 'German War Legislation', 140.

Preceding the above new taxes had been a levy introduced by the occupant as early as 16 January 1915, which was judged by foreign commentators at the time to be in violation of the Hague Regulations: it had been instituted, not to help in defraying the costs of administration, but to punish individuals who had left the occupied territory. The tax was imposed on all Belgians who had left their country voluntarily after the beginning of the war, who stayed away more than two months after departing from Belgium and who refused to return before 1 March 1915. Such individuals were classified as 'absentees' or as 'refugees'. The actual amount of the tax was ten times the tax for which such a 'refugee' would have been liable in 1914. Also, on the same day that saw the introduction of this measure, a German Ordinance granted what amounted to a total remission of all taxes for German citizens and those of countries not at war with Germany, if the conflict had forced them to leave Belgium and had caused them considerable financial losses.[52]

The German administration in Belgium did not alter existing customs duties except in the case of tobacco. In April 1917, the duty on tobacco was increased and during the next summer, the old (1896) regulations were repealed, revised, and then re-enacted in their new version. In September 1917, however, all tobacco in the occupied territory was seized and its control and distribution placed under the administration of the occupant.[53] The comment of the present writer, given above, concerning tax increases appears also to relate to the tobacco issue.

Serbia. The Austro-Hungarian occupation authority in Serbia, the *Zivil-Landeskommissariat*, appears to have been another example of a hybrid military and civilian administration. All matters of levying taxes, assessment of customs rates, and the administration of Serbian national monopolies were placed in the jurisdiction of a Finance Department. Actual revenues from 'national' taxes were turned over to the county treasuries (*Kreiskassen*), by military personnel, accountants, and specially detailed invalid-status officers. Any surpluses above actual running expenses of the countries were remitted to a central occupation treasury agency. The latter had the duty, *inter alia*, to distribute portions of such surplus revenues to countries whose collections had proven to be insufficient to meet expenses. The costs of the military administration and of the occupation forces were covered by the Austro-Hungarian Government out of its own funds until the second half of 1916. Afterward the costs of the military forces were transferred to the revenues collected by the counties.[54]

---

[52] Ibid. 141–2.
[53] Ibid. 141.
[54] H. Kerchnawe, *Die Militärverwaltung in den von den österreichisch-ungarischen Truppen besetzten Gebieten* (New Haven, 1928), 239. Serbia is covered in pp. 253–69.

Receipts by the counties were composed of direct taxes, customs, stamped documents, and other fees, plus income from the various monopolies, and finally income from Serbian governmental enterprises. The last of these sources, comprising meat-packing (slaughterhouses), a cigarette factory, a soap factory, and a difficult-to-translate 'disposal of farm crops' (*Ernteverwertung*) brought in the greatest part of all income during the last year of the occupation.[55] The monopolies mentioned earlier included sugar, salt, petroleum, tobacco, and spirits. Finally, and interestingly enough, it should be noted that taxes in occupied Serbia remained at the pre-war levels throughout the occupation.[56]

Unlike most other belligerent occupations discussed here, the Austro-Hungarian tax situation in Serbia appears to have been consonant with the Hague Regulations.

The Rhineland. The Allied occupation of the German Rhineland after World War I was not a true belligerent occupation in the sense of the Hague Regulations. It had been imposed on a defeated Germany for a period of fifteen years in order to help ensure the fulfilment of the provisions of the Treaty of Versailles.[57]

Japan in China. Scanty and frequently undocumented reports available disclose that, prior to 1940, Japanese forces in the portions of China under their control operated not through a formally organized occupation regime, but rather through a number of regional puppet governments. The latter were always centred in an important urban community. They were subject to frequent 'suggestions' from the Japanese military commander of the region in question, and such suggestions appear to have been adopted as the price of survival of each such Chinese regime.

Taxation under these puppet governments, just like the agencies imposing it, did not fit into the pattern found elsewhere or laid down in the Hague Regulations. Hence a considerable variety of tax systems as well as tax problems emerged, prompted in part by the level of prosperity existing under wartime conditions in the different regions of occupied China.

Thus, in the Soochow region, the peasants resisted payment of rent on land and only one-twentieth of the pre-war sums was collected.

---

[55] Ibid. 243, 245.
[56] Ibid. 243.
[57] The interested reader should consult Allied and Associated Powers, *Military Occupation of the Rhine. Agreement between the United States, Belgium, the British Empire, France and Germany with regard to the Military Occupation of the Rhine*, signed at Versailles on 28 June, 1919 (Washington, DC, 1919), 7; and [US] War Department, *American Military Government of Occupied Germany, 1918–1920* (Report of the Officer in Charge of Civil Affairs, Third Army and American Forces in Germany [Hunt Report]) (Washington, DC, 1943), xiv, 365.

The shortages from this important revenue source were so great that at times the Japanese occupant had to advance funds to the regime based in Soochow. As early as 1958, an attempt had been made to start a Provincial Bank, envisaged as a lending agency for the Soochow authorities, but it never opened. The regime, desperate for funds, revived, then removed, then reintroduced the old transportation tax. It also imposed a licensing system which even included farmers bringing their produce to urban markets.[58]

In the case of the Hankow puppet regime (representing 'Wuhan'— an entity composed of Hankow, Hanyang, and Han Rivers), it was reported that, almost at once, those authorities introduced a total of eleven new taxes. The originators of this massive tax burden were nothing if not imaginative: the new taxes applied, among other things, to opium smoking, prostitution, bars, restaurants, salt, and meat. But the Hankow government went beyond mere taxation in its search for revenues. It established fifty opium-smoking houses, each with twenty beds, and rented these at 5 Chinese dollars per smoker. This was soon followed by the licensing of opium dens throughout Wuhan. The fees collected from this new source of income were said to have amounted to over a million Chinese dollars per month by 1939.[59]

In view of the employment of Chinese puppet governments by the Japanese occupation authorities, it is not possible today to evaluate the legitimacy of the taxes in question, at least based on the standard laid down in the Hague Regulations. However, if this could be done, the *kinds* of *new* taxes and the absence, assumed by the present writer, of any relation either to Japanese military needs or to the welfare of the indigenous population would lead to the conclusion that the taxes were not lawful.

World War II
Japan in Indonesia. Just as several of the Western Allies had spent much time and effort in planning belligerent occupation policies for various parts of Europe, so the Japanese authorities carefully prepared for the occupation of enemy territory. The ministers concerned with different aspects of occupation met and conferred on policies to be adopted in a particular region of the 'Greater East Asia Co-Prosperity Sphere', brought their proposals to a Liaison Conference between Imperial Headquarters and the Government, and finally submitted the results of that conference to the entire Cabinet.[60]

---

[58] Shu Hsi Hsu, *A New Digest of Japanese War Conduct* (Shanghai, 1941), 148.
[59] Ibid. 167.
[60] See H. J. Benda *et al.*, *Japanese Military Administration in Indonesia: Selected Documents* (New Haven, 1965), 17–25.

It is a matter of interest that most key Japanese ordinances and orders concerning the administration of occupied Indonesia (to give the Dutch East Indies their modern name) contain somewhere a reference to 'the acquisition of resources vital to the national defence and the self-sufficiency of occupation troops'. The Japanese realized that such policies would result in economic hardships imposed on the native livelihood, but it was apparently felt that such hardships had to be endured because of the objectives of the Japanese occupation.[61] This emphasis on the acquisition of major resources by Japan runs through confidential as well as published documents of the period and is unique, in this writer's opinion, among documentations of belligerent occupations.[62]

As far as finances, including taxes, were concerned, Japan forced local authorities to defray their own administrative expenses and at the same time to make maximum contributions toward financing the economic self-sufficiency of occupation troops.[63]

In the instance of the island of Java, local authorities could modify rates of tax assessments and collections only after obtaining the approval of the relevant Japanese Superintendent of Military Administration.[64]

In Sumatra, the principles of taxation laid down by the occupant provided that tax revenue had to cover not only local administrative costs but also 'defraying the necessary expenses of Army and Navy troops stationed in each occupied area'. Fiscal assessments, however, were to be kept at the limit of pre-war contributions made by each area to its respective metropolitan country.[65] As far as any special emphasis on spending for certain purposes (and on relevant taxes) and its ranking were concerned, the Japanese stated that, for Sumatra,

> Disbursements for the preservation of public peace and order, emergency repairs of roads, communications, and electric and water utilities, as well as for the acquisition of important commodities shall take precedence.[66]

While the documentation of Japanese orders and recommendations covering taxation under occupation is quite impressive, it is not possible to locate specific and detailed information on actual tax collections and disbursements. It is, therefore, not possible to determine whether

---

[61] See ibid. 1–3, for Point 7 of 'Principles Governing the Administration of Occupied Southern Areas', adopted by the Liaison Conference on 20 Nov. 1941.

[62] See ibid. 26, for a fascinating, down-to-earth outline of the principles governing the conduct of Japanese occupation governments, including a variety of proposals that would be ruled illegal under the Hague Regulations.

[63] Ibid. 32.

[64] Ibid. 77.

[65] Ibid. 173.

[66] Ibid. in 'Principles Governing the Military Administration of Sumatra' (Military Admin. Dept., 27 Apr. 1942), 171–5.

Japanese taxation practices were in accord with or in violation of customary international law. The present writer is somewhat ambivalent on this question but favours the belief that the rules of the law were observed for the most part.

World War II: German Occupations
Poland. The German administration of the occupied portions of Poland preserved the pre-conquest tax laws, but only in principle. New rulings and ordinances quickly raised the rates of assessments and most former exemptions were eliminated: for example, the Polish property tax for the fiscal year 1940 was raised by 50 per cent, and registration fees by 200 per cent, over pre-war levels.[67] The penalties previously imposed for late payment or non-payment of taxes were also increased to sizeable levels.[68] The occupant also introduced in 1940 a new tax, styled a 'population contribution' or a 'community tax'. It was in effect a capitation tax levied on every inhabitant of the occupied territory, regardless of a person's ability to pay or of levels of income; the tax was collected by each community from its inhabitants.[69]

While the occupation authorities retained the pre-war Polish Treasury offices as tax-collection agencies, they superimposed German inspectors on them, possessed of almost unlimited authority. This group of inspectors determined the rate of assessment of the 'population' capitation tax. Failure to pay the latter resulted in instant seizure of property equal in value to the sum due.

The German administration also retained in use the pre-war Polish state lotteries but introduced new games; it was reported at the time that substantial profits were made for the occupant through the operation of new gambling casinos.[70] The previous Polish national monopolies (alcohol, tobacco, saccharin, salt, and matches) were continued under the occupant, but a considerable increase in prices was mandated. According to contemporary accounts, in the Polish General Government area, taxes, excise revenue, and monopoly profits in 1942 were double the collection of those revenues in all of pre-war Poland.[71]

Despite the lack of detailed data on tax collections and disbursements under the German occupation authorities in Poland, available information such as that mentioned above indicates that the German taxation system was almost entirely in violation of Article 48 of the Hague Regulations. One clue to its illegality was the vast increase in

[67] R. Lemkin, *Axis Rule in Occupied Europe* (Washington, DC, 1944), 14, 228.
[68] H. S. Bloch and B. F. Hoselitz (eds.), *Economics of Military Occupation* (Chicago, 1944), 76.
[69] Ibid.; and Lemkin, *Axis Rule*, 228.
[70] Bloch and Hoselitz, *Economics of Military Occupation*, 76.
[71] Ibid. 77.

tax collections. All available sources agree that neither the needs of the occupying forces nor any claimed benefits to the population were involved in the rise in tax revenue. (See also the comment below under the section on Latvia.)

One of the interesting aspects of German tax policy in occupied Poland was the universal utilization of differential taxation. Thus income taxes, deducted at the wage source, were ranked or graded not only on an estimated ability to pay, but also according to the national or racial status of the individual taxed. Different tax rates were in force for German citizens in Poland (paying the lowest tax rates), Poles, and Jews (assessed at the highest rate).[72]

Latvia under German Occupation. After German forces occupied the Baltic Republics (Latvia, Lithuania, Estonia) and White Ruthenia, a special decree of the Reich Government (28 July 1941) proclaimed the combination of the areas in the new German province of *Ostland*. This did not mean, however, that the territory in question was an integral part of Germany; rather the occupied territories became part of 'German property'—to use a thoroughly non-scholarly term—under a German Reich Commissar, H. Lohse.

On 19 October 1941, the *Deutsche Zeitung im Ostland*, official organ of the Reich Commissioner, contained an announcement by Dr W. Zimmermann, press chief of the German administration, which outlined the new theory of a Soviet inheritance by Germany:

At the commencement of the German-Soviet war (22 June 1941) private property did not exist in the countries under Soviet rule, so nobody could claim to be a legal proprietor. By sacrificing the blood of German soldiers, all these countries were liberated. The German Reich, therefore, becomes the legal heir to the Soviet inheritance.[73]

That somewhat astonishing doctrine had been transformed into occupation policy two days earlier through several decrees of the Reich Commissioner. Even the former owners of real estate, buildings, and factories nationalized by the Soviet authorities during their control of the Baltic republics now had to pay rent for their properties. Similarly, industrial enterprises had to pay 'rent' for raw materials stocked. In the case of farmers, a new tax was introduced: they were assigned specific production and tax quotas, and a specified percentage of their total product had to be paid as a tax to the occupant. Similar taxes had been imposed on farmers in Poland and other Eastern occupied territories.

Even though the German occupation authorities had declared invalid all legislation passed under Russian rule in the Baltic republics, they

---

[72] Ibid. and Grassmann, *Die deutsche Besatzungsgesetzgebung*, 76, citing 'VO über Steuererleichterungen für Deutsche vom 4. 3. 1942'.

[73] Latvian Press Bureau (Washington, DC), *Latvia in 1939–1942* (1942), 55.

preserved intact the Soviet nationalization laws enacted in the region. All property previously owned by the Soviet Government through those laws was now regarded as the property of the German Reich. To be sure, promises of return of most of such property to its original owners were made, but no date was set for such a step. The return in question was also limited to individuals with 'satisfactory' professional and personal qualifications which, obviously, were to be determined by the German occupation authorities.[74]

There is no clue in the available documentation as to the true purposes of the new tax on farmers. It may be assumed that it was not intended to relieve needs of the army or to assist in maintaining or promoting the civil life of the inhabitants. It therefore would have to be held to have been in violation of the Hague Regulations.

Belgium under German Occupation. Lemkin recorded an interesting practice of the German occupant in Belgium during World War II: the granting of tax credits for metals. A German order of 20 October 1941 dealt with the surrender of non-ferrous metals. The order instituted tax credits for any Belgians turning in such metals. The Belgian Treasury was forced to co-operate in obtaining the desired scrap, and as a result of the tax credit granted under the order, it was in truth the Belgian Treasury that paid for the metals which, in turn, cost the Germans nothing at all.[75]

France under German Occupation. In the light of increasing metal shortages for its war effort requirements, Germany introduced a new metal tax in 1942/3. This required specified types of taxpayers in occupied France to meet a fixed portion of their tax obligation in the form of one of the desired metals.[76] The occupation authorities determined the unit value of the metal involved in order to arrive at the reduction in taxes to be paid in cash. The scheme was officially called a 'contribution' but did not correspond to the legal meaning of that term (see below), hence could not be regarded as a legal contribution. If the procedure had, more properly, been called a tax, it would have been illegal inasmuch as the metals were not collected for administrative costs (needs of the army) or for the benefit (welfare, civil life) of the population.

Germany under British Occupation. The reader should note that the following discussion of British tax policies in occupied Germany is limited to the period from first invasion to the German surrender of 8 May 1945, after which the Hague Regulations applied no longer to defeated Germany: see a brief comment on this in the following

---

[74] Ibid. 57.
[75] Lemkin, *Axis Rule*, 64.
[76] Bloch and Hoselitz, *Economics of Military Occupation*, 79.

section, dealing with the American occupation of Germany during World War II.

According to the *British Manual* of 1958 and its predecessors, the financial administration of occupied enemy territory passed into the hands of the occupant, but all fiscal laws remained in force. The occupant would be entitled to take for the use of his army of occupation any balance remaining after the expenses of the territory's administration have been met.[77]

When British forces invaded north-western Germany, it had already been decided that only discriminatory forms of revenue would be discarded from the corpus of German tax law. Normal expenditures would be met for pensions, allowances, and social security payments, unless these would be incompatible with military security or in conflict with agreed Allied policy. If there were deficits—and these were to be expected—the regional, district, or local agencies were expected to borrow from German banks or other normal financial sources. But all this represented mere dreaming, in view of the collapse of German institutions, disappearance of their assets, and quite often of many of their staff. When such realities became apparent, it was decided that only as a last resort would the Supreme Allied Commander agree to an advance.[78]

Finding all surviving banks closed, the British occupant improvised a 'central bank' at Issum, whose clerical work was undertaken by the staff of the local savings and loan bank,[79] while the cash of the 'central bank' was placed into two safes in the town hall, otherwise utilized as a British military hospital.

The Issum central bank then proceeded to make small cash advances to local authorities whose tax collections were insufficient for their needs. Eventually the major branches of the *Reichsbank* (Kiel, Hamburg, Hanover) became 'provincial' central banks.

Donnison pointed out that the smaller local authorities which had previously depended on grants from the national government, found very quickly that the proportion of local taxation given to them was totally insufficient. The British authorities thereupon permitted the tax-collecting units to keep and use for their own needs all former 'national' taxes collected by them. Should even this prove to be insufficient, the communities, etc. could borrow from savings banks and the large units could borrow from the branches of the *Reichsbank*.[80]

---

[77] *British Manual*, para. 527, at 146.
[78] F. S. V. Donnison, *Civil Affairs and Military Government, North-West Europe, 1944–1946* (London, 1961), 444.
[79] Earlier, Allied troops had broken into that bank and looted it of all cash in the till (RM 95,000) at gunpoint—a sign of the times; ibid. 446.
[80] Ibid.

The limited factual information indicates that British taxation policies in occupied Germany were in accordance with the relevant provisions of the Hague Regulations.

Germany under American Occupation. The 1907 Hague Regulations applied to Allied occupations in Germany (World War II) only to the date of the German military surrender. It is now generally agreed by both governments and scholars that the Hague Regulations ceased to be effective in Germany after 8 May 1945.[81] It should be noted that the Privy Council in the United Kingdom took a slightly different view as to the date of the end of hostilities, holding in 1953 in *Schiffahrt-Treuhand v. HM Procurator-General* that the Declaration of Berlin, of 5 June 1945, terminated hostilities and thus, in the German case only, the applicability of the Hague Regulations.[82] In this Chapter, however, discussion of taxation in Germany under belligerent occupation extends only to the surrender date.

While it is not generally known, it is true that the National Socialist Government of Germany had undertaken very few changes in the German tax system it had inherited from the Weimar Republic. Beginning in 1939, the government began to cover the ever heavier costs of the war effort by borrowing and by exploiting (better: looting) territories under its occupation.

From an organizational point of view, Germany contained, before the end of hostilities, some 500 tax collection offices and about 200 main customs offices (in charge of 1,300 customs houses). At the apex of the pyramid was the Central Treasury in Berlin.[83]

When American forces entered western Germany, the rules of law applicable to taxes were found in an early edition of a War Department Field Manual,[84] which, in essence, simply reproduced the textual provisions of the Hague Regulations. An interesting comment was appended, however, after Article 48:

Para. 296. What is included in taxes, tolls, etc.—The words 'for the benefit of the State' were inserted in the article to exclude local dues collected by local authorities. The occupant will supervise the expenditures of such revenue and prevent its hostile use.[85]

---

[81] See von Glahn, *Occupation*, 281–5; Judgment of the US Military Tribunal, Judgment No. III, in Case No. 3, *The United States of America v Josef Altstoetter et al.*, in *Trials of War Criminals, Nuernberg Military Tribunals* (1951), 960, reproduced in M. Whiteman, *Digest of International Law* (Washington DC, 1968), 595; and see Letter of 28 January 1953 from Chief of Legal Services Division, US High Commissioner for Germany, ibid., 595–6.
[82] [1953] 1 *All ER*, 394.
[83] H. Zink, *The United States in Germany, 1944–1955* (Princeton, 1957), 271.
[84] [US] War Department, *Rules of Land Warfare* (Basic Field Manual FM 27–10, 1940). That Manual contained few comments on the Hague Regulations, compared with the extensive commentary in the 1956 (and current) revision, cited herein as *US Field Manual*.
[85] Ibid. para. 296, at 78.

Once the American occupation began, the taxes called for by existing laws began to be collected by surviving state, provincial, and municipal agencies. National (Reich) taxes were collected by the appropriate civilian agents and turned over to the American officer in charge of the fiscal department of the civil affairs section. Such 'national' funds were used to pay for the expenses of civilian and military administration, including Allied Military Government. All transactions of the tax collectors and all disbursement of tax revenues in addition to proper inspection and audit, were subject to inspection and audit by the military government. All taxes deemed to be discriminatory in their effect were suspended and later abrogated.[86] The occupant supplied specific instructions to prevent the mingling or mixing of revenues derived from 'national' taxes with other revenues finding their way to the occupant's disbursing officers, for the revenues from the 'national taxes' were dedicated to meeting administrative expenses under occupation.[87]

It was pointed out earlier that the American interpretation of Article 48 asserted that if, for a variety of stated reasons, it was impracticable to follow the rules of incidence and assessment in force in an occupied territory, the occupant could allocate the total amount of the taxes due among the districts, towns, etc. The local authorities could then be required to collect the taxes as a single capitation tax, or otherwise.[88] It should be mentioned in passing that fairly soon *after* the German surrender (22 October 1945), the Allied Control Council ordered a sharp increase in the wage-based income tax, primarily because of low tax receipts from other sources.[89]

Insofar as the mechanics of tax collections were concerned, the occupant appears to have felt that the British system described earlier tended too much in the direction of centralization. In consequence of this suspicion, it was ordered in June 1945 (*after* the surrender) that locally collected non-national tax revenues were to be forwarded to the appropriate finance ministries of the *Lander* (states). The latter

---

[86] See the interesting and important 'Directive to Commander-in-Chief of United States Forces of Occupation Regarding Military Government of Germany' (JCS-1067) sent by the Joint Chiefs of Staff to General Eisenhower, 28 Apr. 1945. Text in *Department of State Bulletin* 13 (1945), 596–607, and in H. Holborn, *American Military Government, its Organization and Policies* (Washington DC, 1947), 157–72. See ibid. 177–94, for text of a similar directive concerning the operations of Military Government in Austria.

[87] See ibid. additional para. 13.5, for the prohibition in question.

[88] Ibid. para. 294, at 77–8.

[89] von Schmoller, *Handbuch*, ii, 40. In 1950, the West German Government reduced most tax rates sharply from the high levels set in 1946: the top income tax rate was cut from 95% to 70%, the top property tax rate from 2.5% to 0.75%, the alcohol tax from RM 11,470 to RM 1,000, and the beer tax from RM 35–118 to RM 2–15; see Zink, *The United States in Germany*, 272.

agencies, in turn, were ordered to distribute the revenues to the states, districts, counties, and communities.[90]

All available information indicates that the United States' taxation practices in occupied Germany complied with the provisions of the Hague Regulations.

Italy under Allied Occupation. Italy surrendered to the Western Allies on 3 September 1943, and until that day there existed an Allied belligerent occupation of portions of the kingdom. The directives for the operations of the military government during the occupation phase[91] were drawn up in accordance with the Hague Regulations. They provided, *inter alia*, that neither revenues collected from national taxes nor any other revenues collected by Italian tax agencies could be used for the payment of principal or interest in Italian national government obligations.[92] The earlier directives of 1943 were supplemented— and replaced in part—by General Order No. 2 of 13 August 1943, from AMG 22 Headquarters. That instrument included several items relating to taxes: it ordered prompt payment; ordered that all taxes be paid in cash; authorized Italian banks to pay to Italian tax collectors moneys held by taxpayers on deposit; and abolished taxes collected from the Syndicates, integral components of the centralized Fascist economic system.[93]

South Korea under American Occupation. Little has been published about the planning and operation of American Military Government in South Korea during its initial period.[94] In view of the fact that the Military Government operated only after the surrender of Japan, the American position in Korea cannot be described accurately as a belligerent occupation in the sense of the Hague Regulations.

The structure of the American military government appears to have followed the pattern of control left by the departed Japanese, except that an Interim Legislative Assembly was created. A very pronounced emphasis on Koreanization proved to be unusually successful, and that in a brief period of time. To be sure, for quite a period each Korean administrator had at his side an American adviser, and the latter

---

[90] Ibid.
[91] H. L. Coles and A. R. Weinberg, *Civil Affairs: Soldiers Become Governors* (Washington, DC, 1964), 177–80: 'CCS Directive, Organization and Operation of Military Government for Husky', CCS24, 7/5 D, 28 June 1943.
[92] Ibid. 179.
[93] Ibid. 202.
[94] See G. M. McCune, 'The Occupation of Korea', *Foreign Policy Reports* 23 (1947), 186–95, for a succinct account of how the military government came into being; see also E. G. Meade, *American Military Government in Korea* (New York, 1951), an expert analysis of military-government operations. Meade's work, however, is limited to the first year (late Sept. 1945–Oct. 1946) and to the province of Cholla Nam Do (South Cholla), then the centre of South Korea's agrarian economy.

normally exerted a considerable influence on his Korean colleague, particularly in the sphere of finance.

An income tax provided the largest amount of tax revenue in South Korea, followed by the land and property tax; the latter had been assessed irregularly under Japanese control, but the American authorities quickly saw to it that an annual assessment basis was adopted. Another major source of revenue was the family head-tax, a flat amount payable each year for each household member over the age of 25. South Korea also had a very high-rate entertainment tax: if a restaurant or hotel offered entertainment, the tax was levied at 300 per cent of the price of food charged to a customer. A general sales tax was levied on furniture as well as on clothing (the military government eliminated its application to salt), and a luxury tax was collected on furs, jewellery, and art objects. There also existed a tax on sake (rice wine), and a night-soil tax was said to enable local officials to hand out 'fat political plums'.[95]

National revenues from taxes were exceeded by far by the income derived by central Korean authorities from government monopolies (salt, tobacco, ginseng), even after a Japanese-introduced monopoly was outlawed at once by the Military Government. Each provincial Monopoly Bureau, under the central Finance Department, was totally independent of Military Government control, and the latter's only real connection with a Bureau was to prevent the property of that Bureau from being seized by some tactical command.[96]

Meade concluded that the most valuable assistance provided by the fiscal supervisors of the Military Government was in the field of tax collection. Such assistance, covering even such mundane policy decisions as determining key road repairs, was tied into the Korean tax system. The latter depended to a considerable extent on revenue-sharing, with many types of national revenue earmarked for provincial expenditures. The American advisers therefore helped to determine the distribution of such funds at the lower levels by pointing out to their Korean colleagues the nature and scope of projects in their jurisdiction that should and could be financed through revenue-sharing with the central authorities.[97]

The limited factual information available on the South Korean tax situation under US occupation indicates a general compliance with the Hague Regulations, with no significant violations of international law.

[95] Ibid. 140–1.
[96] Ibid. 141.
[97] Ibid. 146–7.

Israel's Occupied Territories.[98] Israel's occupation of the West Bank, the Gaza Strip, the Golan Heights, and East Jerusalem represents the latest example of true belligerent occupation to be found today.[99] Among many topics of disagreements about this series of occupations, among both governments and scholars, taxation issues have played a prominent role. One of many reasons for this can be found in the heady mixture of codes applying in whole or in part to what Israel likes to refer to as its 'Administered Territories': the Hague Regulations, Geneva IV, Jordanian law, Israeli law, Syrian law, regulations issued by the former Egyptian military government in the Gaza Strip, and anti-terrorist rules and directives drafted by British authorities in the days of the League of Nations mandate: a rich legal broth indeed!

The governing rules for taxation in the territories in question are to be found in the Hague Regulations (Articles 43, 48, 49–51). As has already been pointed out, these rules have already been accepted by Israel as binding, subject to certain special interpretations, particularly with respect to the subject of new taxes.

Regrettably, recent Israeli sources on the occupied areas, such as *Survey II*, no longer contain the details found in *Reports* of some twelve or more years ago and thus make it more difficult for an outsider to judge what has been the picture in the sphere of taxes.

The West Bank. The following taxes were in force when the occupation began in 1967: an Income Tax, a Municipal Property Tax, a Business Tax, a Village Property Tax, and a Property Tax on Industrial Structures. These taxes were collected on the basis of Jordanian laws. Of these taxes, only the Village Property Tax did not correspond to an equivalent Israeli tax; it represented a tax on land cultivated under irrigation, with the assessment based on the type of crop harvested.

Revenues from the income tax and the village property tax were assigned at once to the central administration of the occupied areas, while 90 per cent of the business tax and the municipal property tax were designated for the cities in which they were collected—the re-

---

[98] The following sources are cited repeatedly in this section of the report: Israel, Ministry of Defence (all by the Co-ordinator of Government Operations in the Administered Territories): *The Administered Territories 1971/1972, 1972/1973,* and *1973/1974* (hereinafter cited as *Reports* and appropriate year), as well as *Survey of the Administered Territories 1967–1975* (hereinafter cited as *Survey I*); Israel, Ministry of Defence (by Co-ordinator of Government Operations in Judea and Samaria and Gaza District), *An Eighteen Year Survey (1967–1985)* (July 1986) (hereinafter cited as *Survey II*). See also D. Shefi, 'Taxation in the Administered Territories', *IYHR* 1 (1971), 290.

[99] The list as given includes two areas annexed or incorporated by Israel; this writer believes that both actions represent violations of international law: see G. von Glahn, *Law Among Nations,* 5th edn. (New York, 1986), 323–6, and M. Crane, 'Middle East: Status of Jerusalem', *HILJ* 71 (1980), 784.

mainder being assigned again to the central occupation administration.

Parenthetically, no information on the Syrian tax system was available when the Golan Heights were occupied by Israel, while in the Gaza Strip, the pre-1948 British tax system had been perpetuated by the Egyptian Military Government. The Golan Heights problem was solved by having the Military Commander impose only one tax: an income tax based on the rules and rates then governing the collection of such a tax in Israel itself.[100]

Receipts (in the West Bank) from the taxes mentioned above increased sharply after minimal returns during the last part of 1967: by the end of the fiscal year 1971, collections had risen more than five times over those of 1968 and had doubled since fiscal year 1969. By the end of the budget year 1973–4, revenues from several taxes had risen significantly over estimates: the income tax receipts had increased by 8 per cent, the Urban Property Tax revenues by only 2 per cent, the Rural Property Tax by 24 per cent, and the Business Tax had risen by 22 per cent over estimates.[101]

Additional funds were collected from customs and excise taxes in the area. The opening of the Allenby and Adam bridges stimulated customs receipts, and in 1971 the occupant equalized customs tariffs with those prevailing in Israel itself. Excise taxes included a tax on most local production (paralleling the then purchase tax in Israel), a tax on tobacco products, and a stamp tax levied in accordance with the Jordanian stamp-tax law. During the first two years of occupation, revenues from customs and from the excise tax on tobacco products showed the greatest increase in yield.[102]

In 1972/73, the occupant authorized selected municipalities in the West Bank to increase the rates of fees charged by them.

The Gaza Strip. The economy of the Gaza Strip in 1967 was of such a nature that budget deficits were expected from the beginning of the occupation: a minimal industrial structure, agriculture in a primitive state of development, and over 200,000 refugees crammed into camps, several of which dated back to 1948. It was therefore not surprising that the budget for 1969/70 anticipated an estimated deficit equal to 90 per cent of expected expenditures, that for 1970/71 a deficit equal to 92 per cent of estimated disbursements, and for 1972/73 a deficit estimated at the same figure in terms of expenses.[103] The massive actual budget deficits were met by the Israeli Government; they included considerable development expenditures for this particular occupied area.

[100] Shefi, 'Taxation in the Administered Territories', 292.
[101] *Report 1971/72*, 50–1 and *Report 1973/74*, 72–3.
[102] *Report 1971/72*, 54–7.
[103] Ibid. 228.

Revenue in the Gaza Strip has been derived principally from three sources: an Income Tax, an Urban Property Tax, and a Rural Property Tax; the yields from the latter two sources declined dramatically for several years after the early period of occupation.

The Report 1972/73 contained the claim that 'All the revenue from taxation in the Gaza Strip is in addition to the budget and is returned to the population by way of various services.'[104]

In the subsequent fourteen years, the subsidization of the Gaza Strip by Israel has continued, at very high costs to the occupant. On the other hand, industrial production in the Strip (viewed as a source of tax revenue) has risen significantly and represented as early as 1975 not less than 10 per cent of Israel's national output.[105]

Returning to the overall picture of the 'Administered Territories', it should be noted that Israel's tax system is 'territorial'—incomes earned in Israel are subject to income tax. Thousands of individuals living in the occupied territory work regularly in Israel, but *their* tax regulations are based (in the West Bank and the Gaza Strip) on Jordanian regulations in force in 1967, subject to amendments by the occupant 'required by changes in price levels'. On the other hand, Israeli inhabitants of the Occupied Territories are, since March 1979, subject to the Israeli tax laws. In 1980, the Israeli tax law was amended to the effect that any income of Israeli settlers produced or received in the West Bank was to be regarded as produced in Israel. In 1984, an amendment to the Emergency Regulations permitted tax authorities to collect tax revenues in the 'region'. That manœuvre avoided any embarrassing reference to the Israeli settlements in the area.[106]

The latest available figures (October 1985) indicate that at the time inhabitants of the occupied areas were taxed (income tax) at a somewhat higher rate than was the case for persons living in Israel.[107]

The greatest amount of discussion relating to taxation by Israel began when, in 1981, the occupant ordered the enforcement in the West Bank and the Gaza Strip of certain tax orders previously promulgated by the occupation authorities on 1 June 1976. The orders in question instituted a new tax (8 per cent), parallel to the Value Added Tax (VAT) enacted in Israel itself in 1975.

Businessmen and others in the Occupied Territory objected strongly to what they viewed as a violation of the 1907 Hague Regulations and went to court to block the application of the tax to the occupied areas.

---

[104] *Report 1972/73*, 97.
[105] *Survey I*, 4.
[106] R. Shehadeh, *Occupier's Law: Israel and the West Bank* (Washington, DC, 1985), 66. See von Glahn, *Law Among Nations*, 692–3 concerning the illegality of the settlement policy, under IV Geneva Convention, Art. 49 (6), and Protocol I, Art. 85(4)(a).
[107] *Survey II*, 105.

In 1983, the Supreme Court of Israel, sitting as a High Court of Justice, handed down its verdict in *Abu Aita et al. v. Military Commander of the Judea and Samaria Region et al.; Kandil et al. v. Military Commander of the Gaza Strip Region et al.*, commonly referred to and cited as the *Kandil* or *VAT* case.[108]

The *VAT* case centred on the issue of whether a belligerent occupant could lawfully introduce a new tax in occupied territory. All traditional arguments were brought forth by petitioners and respondents, with both sides agreeing fully on the applicability of the Hague Regulations, as interpreted by them: the interpretation of Article 48 and its relation to Article 43; the primary responsibility of an occupant: for his own security or for the civil life of the inhabitants; the effects, if any, of a prolonged occupation on the law-making perquisites of an occupant, and so on. In the end the Court held that the financial measures (imposition of the VAT) were necessary in the light of the economic situation in the areas that faced the military government, and that there was really nothing to prevent the introduction of such a new tax, particularly if the occupation was one of long duration.

The present writer disagrees with the decision of the court as to the validity of the VAT under the rules of customary international law. He believes that the court's decision did not incorporate convincing evidence that the new tax actually served to improve (or even to maintain) the civil life of the population, nor that there was shown any evidence that the imposition of the new tax served the needs of the occupying Israel Defence Forces. In part his belief is based on the statistics included in the decision, since many of them related to years before the tax was imposed, and other data intimated that only a very small percentage of the total population would derive benefits from the tax, not the population as a whole. Furthermore, no mention was made in the 131 pages of the typewritten opinion of the fact that a very high percentage of the area's population (that is, in the West Bank and the Gaza Strip) consists of the residents of the various refugee camps. Those persons would not benefit from the imposition of the VAT. The present writer therefore is convinced that the Value Added Tax was imposed in violation of the Hague Regulations, of international law.

It should also be mentioned again that, despite repeated and un-

---

[108] HC 69/81 and HC 493/81. Key excerpts from the very long decision may be found in English in *PYIL* 4 (1987–8), 186–209. See also the relevant von Glahn *'Obiter Dictum*: An Unofficial Expression of Opinion on the *VAT* Case Judgment', ibid. 210–21, and the excellent summary in P. Sharon, 'A Digest of Recent Israeli Cases', *IsLR* 18 (1983, 3/4), 475–86. The Sharon review includes a substantial portion of the opinion requested of the present writer. An analysis of the nature and 'purposes' of the VAT tax may be found in Israel National Section of the International Commission of Jurists, *The Rule of Law*, 94–7.

equivocal assertions by the court in its decision, the passage of time involved in the duration of a belligerent occupation does not affect the validity of the rules laid down in the Hague Regulations. No occupant can deviate from limitations imposed by that instrument without committing an illegal act.

V. Contributions

A belligerent occupant may secure funds beyond those collected lawfully from taxes and customs duties by imposing monetary contributions on the inhabitants of an occupied territory. The relevant portions of the Hague Regulations read as follows:

Article 49
If, in addition to the taxes mentioned in the above article, the occupant levies other money contributions in the occupied territory, this shall only be for the needs of the army or of the administration of the territory in question.

Article 51
No contribution shall be collected except under a written order, and on the responsibility of a commander-in-chief. The collection of the said contribution shall only be effected as far as possible in accordance with the rules of assessment and incidence of the taxes in force. For every contribution a receipt shall be given to the contributors.

Thus, rather specific limits have been set for a belligerent occupant, outlining only two specific purposes as well as a mechanism for the levying of monetary contributions.[109] (It should be pointed out that Article 50 of the Hague Regulations has been omitted deliberately from both listing and discussion in this report. In the view of the present writer, the article in question relates to a prohibition of certain types of a general penalty imposed, illegally, by some occupants. The article belongs properly among provisions dealing with acts of inhabitants against the occupant, not in the section dealing with taxes and monetary contributions.)

The International Military Tribunal at Nuremberg made it clear that under the accepted rules of war (Hague Regulations, Articles 48, 52, 53, 55, and 56 in this connection), the economy of an occupied territory could only be required to bear expenses of the occupation no greater than that economy could be expected to bear.[110] That judgment must be viewed as erecting one more barrier against an occupant's unbridled

---

[109] See James Garner, 'Contributions, Requisitions, and Compulsory Service in Occupied Territory', *AJIL* 11 (1917), 74. Garner's introductory pages (74–7) represent a classic summary of the subject of contributions prior to 1898.
[110] International Military Tribunal (Nuremberg), *Trial of the Major War Criminals*, 22, 411, at 481–2.

urge to enrich himself at the expense of a population under occupation, to pay for war expenses in general, or for any purposes other than those approved in Article 49.[111] It should be noted, in this connection, that Israel has not levied contributions in the territories occupied by it, but has opted in favour of covering deficits in area budgets out of its own resources when necessary.[112] Most modern belligerent occupations show in fact an absence of monetary contributions after the excesses demonstrated during World War I by Germany.

German practices relative to the collection of contributions imposed on France and Belgium have been detailed by Garner.[113] Initially, soon after the occupations began, enormous sums were mentioned as 'war contributions'. In some instances immediate and drastic reductions were made, in other cases payment was arranged on an instalment plan. In most instances, especially in Belgium, the payments to the occupant were made by banks, each of which contributed an agreed-upon percentage of the total contribution levied. The actual mechanism by which the contribution was ordered was detailed carefully by Bisschop whose analysis can be summarized as follows.[114]

The German occupant levied the monetary contributions on the inhabitants through the then still-existing Provincial Councils, summoned by the Governor-General only when necessary, that is, when it was necessary to improve some financial matter. As early as 8 December 1914, a war contribution of 40 million francs per month was levied, to be paid for through the issue of provincial bonds. In November 1915, the Councils were again called into session to approve both the contribution for 1916 and the treasury bills (bonds) issued during the previous year. In November 1916, the contribution for 1917 was increased to 50 million francs per month. This time, however, five of the Councils denied their approval, and the Governor-General, citing his authority as 'sovereign power *de facto*', overrode the decision of the Councils and approved the 1917 contribution. In May 1917, the war contribution total was raised to 60 million francs per month, and this time all Provincial Councils refused to approve the proposal. The Governor-General, however, again invoked his legislative authority and approved the increase in the contribution, despite the demonstrated disapproval of the Councils.

---

[111] See also Oppenheim, *International Law*, ii, para. 148 at 412; Stone, *Legal Controls*, 713; Feilchenfeld, *International Economic Law of Belligerent Occupation*, 41; and von Glahn, *Occupation*, 161–2.
[112] See Israel National Section of the International Commission of Jurists, *The Rule of Law*, 93–4.
[113] Garner, 'Contributions', 77 ff.
[114] Bisschop, 'German War Legislation', 142–3.

The present writer believes that the contributions exacted by the German authorities in Belgium during World War I violated the limitations laid down in Article 49 of the Hague Regulations: money contributions could be levied only for the needs of the army or of the administration of an occupied territory. The needs of the German army in occupied Belgium or of the administration involved do not appear to have justified the enormous expansion of contributions levied. In retrospect, the situation then existing appears to the present writer to have been another instance of self-enrichment by an occupant.

Garner also noted a new—and obviously illegal under the Hague Regulations—German practice in Belgium: the imposition, in certain instances, of 'special contributions' on particular wealthy individuals or on particular enterprises,[115] citing a source to the effect that a contribution of one million francs had been levied on Baron Lambert de Rothschild and one of thirty million francs on a M. Solvay, apparently a well-known Belgian manufacturer. The practice in question was admitted by Meurer when he wrote that, heretofore, in practice, contributions had been laid on districts or cities, but according to newspaper reports heavy contributions had been imposed on individual firms or individuals in Belgium.[116] Articles 49 and 51 of the Hague Regulations do not specify the precise sources of the funds represented by a monetary contribution, but Garner pointed out that the French *Manuel de lois de la guerre continentale* of 1913 had stated specifically, in paragraph 108, that contributions could *not* be imposed on individuals, only on districts and communities.[117]

That lone reference to the *French Manual* points up the fact that few writers and even fewer governments have touched on the delicate question of who actually pays the contributions levied by a belligerent occupant. The usual procedure has been to have communal authorities transmit the sums allocated for their area to designated agencies of the occupant, and then collect reimbursement from the taxpayers in that area. Another method of raising such contributions was that used in Belgium during World War I: the various banks would pay appropriate portions of the total sum and be reimbursed through the issuance of bonds.

Payment of contributions falls equally on the native inhabitants of the occupied territory and on resident neutral citizens, unless the latter are exempt through treaty obligations of the occupant. Eventual repayment of sums paid toward an occupant's contributions can be expected only from a returned ousted government, unless the belligerent occu-

---

[115] Garner, 'Contributions', including n. 39.
[116] Ibid.
[117] Ibid.

pant had lost the war in question and would be obligated to repay such sums to the contributors as part of a peace settlement.

During World War II, Germany exacted enormous sums as 'occupation costs' from France in the form of forced contributions. Such collections were said to have totalled more than 72 billion francs by the end of December 1940, of which in excess of 41 billion had not been spent yet. A year later the unspent surplus was reported to amount to more than 62 billion francs, all deposited in the *Banque de France* to the credit of the *Reichskreditkasse*.[118]

Again, as in the case of Belgium during World War I, the German authorities in France during World War II must be judged to have resorted to illegal money contributions. Proof of this assertion is to be found in the existence of the enormous balances *not* spent on the needs of the army or administration.

Conclusion

It appears difficult to this writer to compose a summarizing conclusion to the subject of taxation under belligerent occupation. The applicable rules of law are brief and somewhat imperfect, whereas the practice of States is at best inconsistent and, on all too many occasions, thoroughly deplorable. Perhaps the most fitting observation on the subject is to reproduce in part the Preamble to the Fourth Hague Convention of 1907 and its Regulations:

Until a more complete code of the laws of war has been issued, the High Contracting Parties deem it expedient to declare that, in cases not included in the Regulations adopted by them, the inhabitants and the belligerents remain under the protection and the rule of the principles of the law of nations, as they result from the usages established among civilized peoples, from the laws of humanity, and the dictates of the public conscience.

---

[118] See J. Robinson, 'Transfer of Property in Enemy Occupied Territory', *AJIL* 39 (1945), 219, and especially 'Finance' in A. Toynbee and V. M. Toynbee (eds.), *Hitler's Europe*, iv: *Survey of International Affairs, 1939–1945* (London, 1954), 271–4 for illegal contributions in France and a breakdown of German collections by European countries.

12

Financial Administration of the Israeli-Occupied West Bank

HISHAM JABR

ALTHOUGH the Israeli occupation of the West Bank and Gaza has now continued for over twenty years, the financial administration of these territories by the Israeli military authorities and its implications for the development of the region have received scant attention. The purpose of this paper is therefore to give an overview of financial aspects of the administration of the West Bank under Israeli occupation.

I will focus especially on budgetary aspects, on sources of revenue and on expenditure, in an attempt to evaluate services rendered to the inhabitants of the West Bank as compared with taxes, customs, excise, fines, and other fees paid by them to the occupying authority. The legal issues regarding the levying of such taxes and other payments are also discussed. Comparison is made also with practices under Jordanian rule and with the taxation system in the Israeli settlements, illegally implanted in the Occupied Territories.[1]

The financial administration of the Occupied Territories has been little studied or documented, and there are almost no sources of analytic material to which to refer. A notable exception is the work of the West Bank Data Base Project, headed by Meron Benvenisti. Researchers on this project were able to obtain extensive access to Israeli official data which is difficult for Palestinian researchers to make use of for both practical and linguistic reasons, since most data is available only in Hebrew. The writer therefore acknowledges his indebtedness to this work, to which frequent reference will be made.

I. The Taxation System in the West Bank prior to 1967

According to the Israeli researcher Dov Shefi, 'an elaborate and modern system of taxation laws existed' in the West Bank when Israel occupied

---

[1] On legality of settlements see Ch. 1, text at n. 147 ff., and Ch. 14, text at n. 48 ff.

the area in June 1967.[2] Pre-1967 taxes included: (1) direct taxes, namely, income tax, property tax, and business tax; (2) indirect taxes, including customs duties and excise; and (3) several kinds of fees, payable to municipalities.

Taxation laws that existed in the West Bank prior to the occupation included:

1. *The Income Tax Law of Jordan No. 25* (1964). According to this law, a tax was levied on any income derived or earned by any resident from gains or profits from any work, business, profession, employment, interest, or rents of property.[3] All sources of income by residents were subject to tax; exempted were non-profit organizations, pensions, agricultural businesses, university fees paid by students, interest on public debt, and business firms exempted by virtue of the law promoting investment.[4] The purpose of these exemptions was: (*a*) to alleviate the burden of the taxpayer, especially if he was subject to multiple expenses such as maintenance of family, university fees for children, etc.; (*b*) to encourage investments that might enhance the country's economic development; and (*c*) to help non-profit organizations in promoting the social welfare of the community.

The income tax rate according to this law was progressive for employees and self-employed persons. The following table shows the tax on income of employees and self-employed persons according to the Income Tax Law of 1964:

	Income	Tax rate	Tax	Accumulated Tax
	JD		JD	
	400	5%	20	20
each additional	400	7%	28	48
"	400	10%	40	88
"	400	15%	60	148
"	400	20%	80	228
"	400	25%	100	328
"	400	30%	120	448
"	1200	35%	420	868
"	2000	40%	800	1668
"	2000	45%	900	2568
anything over this sum		50%		

Exemptions: JD 150 for a single taxpayer
JD 250 for a married taxpayer
JD 70 for each child up to four in number
JD 200 for an additional two dependants plus 15% of the income.

[2] D. Shefi, 'Taxation in the Administered Territories', *IYHR* 1 (1971), 291–2.
[3] Jordan Income Tax Law No. 25 of 1964, Art. 5.
[4] Ibid. Art. 8.

For example, a taxpayer with an income, after deducting all exemptions, of JD 8,000 a year was liable to pay JD 2,568, or an average tax rate of 32.1 per cent, while a proportional tax rate was charged to business corporations at a rate of 35 per cent of net income before dividends.[5]

2. *The Law of Buildings and Lands Inside Cities of Jordan No. 11* (1954). Under this law, a property tax was levied by municipalities on buildings and lands inside cities at a rate of 17 per cent of the estimated annual rent.

3. *The Land Tax Law of Jordan No. 30* (1955). According to this law, a tax was imposed on lands planted with fruits and vegetables at a nominal fee of about JD 1 per quarter of an acre.

4. *Education Rules of Jordan No. 1* (1956). According to these regulations, a tax was imposed on properties in municipal areas at a rate of 3 per cent of the equivalent annual rent of the property.

5. *Laws governing customs duties and excise on local goods*. Several laws of this kind existed in the West Bank before the occupation. Customs duties and excise were imposed according to specific laws on goods manufactured locally, such as the Customs and Excise Law No. 1 of 1962, the Law of Unification of Fees and Taxes Levied on Imported, Exported and Locally Manufactured Goods No. 25 of 1966; the Tobacco Law No. 32 of 1952; the Salt Law No. 16 of 1950; the Law of Fees on Local Products No. 16 of 1963, the Law of Excise on Petroleum Products No. 36 of 1960; the Profession Licensing Law No. 89 of 1966; and others.

6. *Laws governing fees and customs duties on government services*. Several laws existed that imposed fees, usually very low, or customs duties on government services. Government departments would charge for services rendered through revenue stamps, for example.

One will notice that the customs and tax laws of Jordan that were in force before the 1967 war were consistent with similar legislation in other states at that time. After 1967, these laws were regularly updated. For example, Jordan has amended the Income Tax Law of 1964 three times since 1967—in 1975, 1982, and 1985—each time improving the position of the taxpayer. Some examples of such amendments include:

1. Total exemption from tax. According to Article 7 of the 1985 Income Tax Law, the following incomes are totally exempted from tax: income of local authorities, unions, co-operatives, non-profit organizations, religious, charitable, educational, and athletic institutions, pensions, disability payments, and income derived from agricultural land and livestock.

2. Partial exemption from tax. Exemptions include, for example:

[5] Ibid. Art. 24.

(a) 30 per cent of rent in the Amman district, and 50 per cent of rent in other areas

(b) dividends on shares and on interest on Jordanian development bonds

(c) family and personal exemptions, which were increased, as of 1985, to the following levels:

— JD 400 for a single person
— JD 600 for a married person
— JD 200 for each child
— JD 100 for each dependant up to a maximum of JD 300
— JD 500 for each child studying at a university, provided that he/she has no scholarship[6]

(d) 50 per cent of salaries paid by governmental institutions, and 25 per cent of salaries paid by other institutions.

II. Taxation under the Israeli Occupation

Immediately after the occupation of the West Bank, the commander of the Israeli forces in the West Bank stated that, with certain specified exceptions, the pre-existing legal system would remain in force.[7] Observers understood this to mean that laws, including local tax laws, existing prior to the occupation would continue to be valid under Israeli military rule.[8]

However, Israel claimed that its efforts to restore and maintain the economic life of the Occupied Territories necessitated substantial financial resources.[9] This claim was used to justify the imposition and collection of more taxes from the inhabitants by virtue of the tax legislation that had existed prior to the war, and the imposition of new and additional taxes on the inhabitants.[10]

The resulting tax system as established in the territories occupied in 1967, including the West Bank, is indeed based upon the local tax law of the territories, i.e. Jordanian tax law in the case of the West Bank. However, this system has been extensively altered in the intervening years by orders promulgated by the military authorities amending the law. Some of the major changes made to existing taxes and the new

---

[6] Jordan Income Tax Law No. 57 of 1985, Art. 13.
[7] See Ch. 4.
[8] D. Kretzmer, *Israel and the West Bank: Legal Issues* (Jerusalem, 1984), and Shefi, 'Taxation in the Administered Territories', 292. See also Ch. 7 in this volume for discussion of relevant principles of international law.
[9] Shefi, 'Taxation in the Administered Territories'.
[10] Ibid.

taxes introduced to supplement revenue from the territories are examined below, following a detailed review of the fundamental changes made to the pre-existing income-tax provisions.

Income Tax

The Jordanian Income Tax Law No. 25 of 1964 and amendments to this law by means of military orders have provided the basis for the collection of taxes, customs, excise, fees, and fines. As mentioned above, the Law was amended three times in Jordan itself after 1967; the amendments were approved by the Jordanian Parliament and benefited the population. In contrast, the Israeli military authorities in the West Bank have made amendments to the Law after 1967 through military orders, all of which have benefited the occupying authorities and run counter to the interests of the local population. To date, more than forty such amendments have been made, examples of their effects including:

1. Changing the forum for income tax appeals initially to a lower-level court (MO 109 of 1967), and then to military committees (MO 406 of 1967).
2. Calculation of taxes on the basis of the Jordanian rather than the Israeli currency, even though the Israeli price structure prevails in the Occupied Territories (MOs 509, 586, and 612).
3. Changing the collection procedures: down-payments have to be made in ten monthly instalments, and tax officials have the right to increase or decrease the level of these advance payments; a fine of 10–25 per cent of the amount of taxes is imposed as a penalty for late payment (MOs 770 and 791).
4. Changing the rates, income brackets, and exemptions; none of those changes have been in favour of the taxpayer (MOs 545, 636, 725, 754, 782, 816, 835, 873, 900, 907, 920, 943, 958, 978, 1014, 1028, 1050, 1062, 1084, 1094, 1098 and 1185).
5. Changing tax collection procedures (MO 924), to permit confiscation of funds, prevention of inhibitants from travel, and closure of shops (for example, MO 770).
6. Authorizing the civilian administration to increase the maximum tax rates (MO 1106).

A comparison of the income tax paid by Jordanian, Israeli, and West Bank taxpayers is offered in Table 1. Such a comparison is useful because it shows, in the case of Jordan and the West Bank, the taxes which Palestinians in the West Bank would have paid had the West Bank remained part of Jordan. In the case of Israel and the West Bank, it shows how the Israeli authorities discriminate between Israeli citizens

TABLE 12.1. *Comparison of income tax paid by taxpayers in Jordan, Israel, and the Occupied Territories in 1986*

	Jordan		Israel		Occ. Territories	
Taxable Income	Income Tax	Tax Rate %	Income Tax	Tax Rate %	Income Tax	Tax Rate %
JD 1500	—	—	—	—	36.3	3.75
JD 3000	—	—	41	1.63	333.7	11.12
JD 6000	100	1.66	1,127	18.78	1,462.8	24.38
JD 12000	850	7.08	3,938	32.82	4,246.0	35.38
JD 24000	3,550	14.79	9,699	40.4	9,856.5	41.06

(Source: Atef Alawneh, 'The Income Tax Burden in the Occupied Territories, Jordan and Israel: A Comparative Study', (forthcoming))

and Palestinians in the West Bank, despite the presence of a *de facto* common market in the two areas. From Table 12.1 it is evident that:

1. The West Bank taxpayer pays a much higher income tax than his counterpart in Jordan or Israel, although he receives a much lower level of services.
2. The lowest income bracket (JD 1,500 or less) is totally exempted from income tax in Jordan and in Israel, while it is subject to about 3.75 per cent income tax in the Occupied Territories.
3. The minimum non-taxable income is reduced to a level below basic needs. It is a universally accepted practice that an income which meets basic needs only should not be taxed.[11] The Israeli authorities, however, charge taxes even on a monthly income of only $30 in the West Bank.[12]
4. The taxpayer in the Occupied Territories with an income of up to JD 3,000 pays a tax over eight times higher than that of his counterpart in Israel. This is especially noteworthy when it is realized that most West Bank taxpayers are located in this income bracket.
5. Taxpayers with incomes up to JD 6,000 pay 1.66 per cent income tax in Jordan, 18.78 per cent in Israel, and 24.38 per cent in the Occupied Territories.
6. Taxpayers with incomes up to JD 12,000 pay 7.08 per cent income tax in Jordan, 32.82 per cent in Israel, and 35.38 per cent in the Occupied Territories.

[11] 'Abd-al-Munim Fawzi, *Tax Systems* (Cairo, 1973), 29–30.
[12] N. Sabri, 'The Effects of Taxes Imposed on the Population of the Occupied Palestinian Territories'. Paper presented at the Seminar on Living Conditions of the Palestinian People, organized by Habitat in Vienna, March 1985.

Financial Administration

7. Taxpayers with incomes up to JD 24,000 pay 14.8 per cent in Jordan, 40.4 per cent in Israel, and 41 per cent in the Occupied Territories.
8. The highest tax rate in Jordan is 45 per cent, while it is 52.8 per cent in Israel, and 55 per cent in the West Bank.

From the above it is evident that taxpayers in the Occupied Territories pay appreciably more in income tax than their counterparts in Israel or Jordan.

Other Tax Laws Amended

In addition to changes in the Income Tax Law, other laws governing taxes have also been amended through military orders. For example:

1. Amendment of the Professions Licensing Law No. 89 of 1966 through MO 977, giving the authorities the right to change or amend tables (i.e. the rates payable) in the appendix of the Law.
2. Amendment of the Land and Building Law No. 30 of 1955 through MO 642, increasing the rates payable.
3. Amendment of the Law of Land Registration Fees No. 56 of 1958 through MOs 505, 693, and 1018, increasing existing fees and imposing new ones.
4. Amendment of Education By-law No. 1 of 1956, increasing education fees and the education tax from 3 to 7 per cent of the net rent (through MOs 501, 671, and 1195).
5. Changes in the Customs Duties the Excise Laws on local goods in relation to regulations, procedures, and tax rates (MOs 31, 643, and 740).
6. Amendment of Stamp Revenue Laws, increasing fees several times, with the result that they are currently fifteen times higher than those in Jordan.
7. Increasing court fees to 4 per cent of the sum claimed.
8. Amendment to the Public Health Law No. 43 of 1966, raising health services fees (for example, by MO 746).
9. Several amendments to the Transport on Roads Law No. 49 of 1958, including the raising of fees for driving licences, driving tests, licences for driving schools, and car ownership, registration, and inspection.

Finally, the Israeli military authorities imposed new taxes, including Value Added Tax.

The Value Added Tax (VAT)

VAT was imposed in early 1976. The military authorities introduced VAT in the form of a by-law entitled 'By-law Concerning Fees and

Excise on Local Goods No. 31 (West Bank) of 1976', which does not mention the words value added tax or consumption tax. The law was not published, was signed by a person without a title, and was distributed to public accountants only.[13] The VAT rate was 8 per cent in 1976, 12 per cent in 1978, and 15 per cent in 1982.

The method employed by the authorities in introducing VAT is interesting. Since VAT did not exist under Jordanian rule, the authorities, rather than introducing entirely new legislation, amended the first and last paragraphs of an existing Jordanian law (No. 16 of 1963), inserting clauses concerning VAT in between.[14] Law No. 16 had nothing to do with value added tax.[15] It appears from this that the military authorities prefer to introduce new legislation by amending existing laws rather than by passing new orders. In addition, by not publishing a new law, public announcement of its imposition was avoided.

Seen as an attempt to facilitate economic and administrative ties between the Occupied Territories and Israel,[16] the introduction of VAT met with widespread opposition in the West Bank and Gaza. The most strenuous opposition related to new bookkeeping obligations imposed on merchants and providers of services through special regulations, since people were not experienced and sophisticated enough to meet them. The problems caused to merchants by the imposition of VAT, especially in its collection procedures, will be discussed below. When in 1980 the authorities began to enforce the bookkeeping requirements, the merchants of the Occupied Territories decided to challenge the legality of the imposition of VAT before the Israeli High Court of Justice. Their main argument was that a belligerent occupant is forbidden by the rules of customary international law to introduce new taxes in occupied territories.[17] The state attorney's argument was that VAT was imposed in the Occupied Territories in 1976 at the same time as it was imposed in Israel itself. The merchants failed in their attempt to have this tax cancelled, as is discussed more fully elsewhere in this collection.[18]

It is not known whether the purpose of the VAT is to provide services to the taxpayers or to increase the revenues of the Israeli government. Available data show a very low level of services and almost no government investment in infrastructure and development in the Occupied Territories, either by the central military government or through local councils.[19]

[13] Ibid.
[14] Kretzmer, *Israel and the West Bank*, 34.
[15] Ibid.
[16] Ibid. 43.
[17] Ibid. 48–51.
[18] For discussion of the legality of the introduction of VAT and of the court's decision, see Chs. 2 and 11 in this volume.
[19] M. Benvenisti, *West Bank Data Base Project: Interim Report No. 1* (Jerusalem, 1982), 14.

Collection of the 15 per cent VAT in both the West Bank and Gaza renders about $50 million in revenue a year, while import duties total about $30 million annually.[20] According to Benvenisti,[21] after deduction of Israeli subsidies on Israeli agricultural produce consumed in the West Bank, residents of the West Bank alone have paid an 'occupation tax' conservatively estimated at $700 million over nineteen years of occupation, or about two and a half times the total government capital formation accumulated throughout the occupation, in the form of VAT and import duties only. These figures illustrate the extent to which residents of the West Bank and Gaza finance the occupation. Benvenisti concludes that

That fact refutes Israeli claims that the low level of public expenditure and investment derives from budgetary limitations. If net fiscal transfers had been invested in the area, rather than added to Israeli public expenditure, it would have been possible to improve local services significantly and, in particular, to develop local economic infrastructure.[22]

The Stamp Revenue Tax

This includes in particular the Jordan Bridges crossing tax. A stamp revenue tax existed in the West Bank before the occupation for daily transactions with governmental agencies, the rate being very low. In 1967, the occupying authorities imposed a new 'bridge-crossing tax' under the name of the Stamp Revenue Tax. This tax differs from the customary tax system in Israel.[23] It is imposed mainly on travel through the bridges, the airport, and other border crossings, and constitutes an important source of revenue for the occupying authorities. The tax is paid by inhabitants of the Occupied Territories who travel outside the Territories or who arrive from outside, the majority passing over the bridges across the Jordan River. According to Israeli statistics as shown in Table 12.2, more than 350,000 people travel out of the West Bank annually, and more than 60,000 people come as visitors through the border-crossing points, most of them to and from Jordan.

Whereas crossing the bridges before the occupation used to be free of charge, the 1987 bridge-crossing tax rates are as follows:

- NIS ('new Israeli shekel') 125.5 (about $74) on each exit permit
- NIS 147.5 (about $85) on each visit permit
- NIS 92 (about $55) for each renewal of an exit permit
- NIS 115 (about $70) for each renewal of a visit permit, in addition to NIS 32.5 (about $20) for infants, NIS 14 (about $8) for an escorted

---

[20] Benvenisti, *1986 Report*, 19.
[21] Ibid.
[22] Ibid.
[23] Benvenisti, *Interim Report*, 13.

TABLE 12.2. *Movements of residents and visitors by crossing points (departures only)*

	Visitors				Residents			
Year	Rafah	Damia Bridge	Allenby Bridge	Total*	Rafah	Damia Bridge	Allenby Bridge	Total*
1976	—	45,474	73,870	119,344	—	154,172	152,242	310,701
1978	—	50,471	81,041	131,512	—	158,758	168,808	331,471
1980	16,983	46,364	61,891	125,236	27,928	179,898	180,729	393,980
1982	17,695	20,525	37,048	75,268	83,622	171,594	190,391	451,882
1983	22,205	22,976	37,246	82,430	66,920	146,013	172,997	393,160
1984	22,458	28,150	38,818	89,426	61,842	160,910	194,761	419,125
1985	16,876	23,899	27,794	68,569	46,847	159,796	176,745	383,462
1986	16,983	21,015	24,649	62,647	44,850	142,623	167,748	355,221

* The total includes movements via Haifa Port and Ben-Gurion Airport.

(Source: Israel Central Bureau of Statistics, *Judea, Samaria & Gaza Area Statistics*, XVII (Jerusalem, 1987), 2)

child of less than 12 years of age, and NIS 37 (about $23) for each escorted child of more than 12 years and less than 16 years of age.[24]

A rough estimate of the travel tax for the year 1986 can be calculated as follows:

355,221 × 125.5 = NIS 44,580,235.5 (about $26 million) on exit permits;
62,647 × 147.5 = NIS 9,240,432.5 (about $5.4 million) on visitor permits;
NIS 326,802 (about $190,000) on renewal of permits by the 10 per cent of West Bank and Gaza residents working abroad;
NIS 72,047.5 (about $40,000) on renewal of visit permits, since about 10 per cent of visitors renew their permits.

Table 12.3 shows that a conservative estimate of the total amount charged as a travel tax in 1986 is NIS 54,219,517.9 (about $32 million). A further $3 million is paid annually by drivers of taxis and trucks for permits to drive to and cross the bridges.

In addition to these taxes, customs duties are payable at bridge crossings. Palestinians crossing the bridges are only allowed to carry clothes, shoes, etc. Electrical equipment, cameras, etc. are not allowed and if found will be confiscated. Customs duties are thus paid on clothes, whether gifts or for personal use. Total customs fees derived from inhabitants crossing the bridges are estimated conservatively at about $15–20 million a year, based on an estimated average of $30–40

---

[24] Rates are taken from instructions given to post offices.

TABLE 12.3. *Travel tax on movements of inhabitants of the West Bank through crossing points for the year 1986*

	No. of Persons Crossing	Tax rate	Total in Shekels
On exit permit	355,221	125.5	44,580,235.5
On visitor permit	62,647	147.5	9,240,432.5
Renewal of exit permit*	35,522	92	326,802.4
Renewal of visitor permit*	6,265	115	72,047.5
TOTAL			54,219,517.9

Total in US dollars: $31,893,834 (based on an exchange rate of 1.7 Israeli shekels per US dollar).

* Estimated on the basis of 10% of the persons who travel.

(Source: compiled by the author, based on statistics from Table 2 and interviews with Nablus postal authorities)

charged as a customs fee for each person crossing the bridges.[25] These are payable in Jordanian dinars, the Israeli authorities refusing to accept customs fees in Israeli shekels.

The customs fees imposed on residents and Palestinian visitors crossing the bridges are frequently arbitrary and excessive. A typical experience was related by a woman on the Israeli radio programme 'Studio One' on 5 December 1987. She recounted how, when she crossed the bridge from Jordan into the West Bank, the Israeli customs officer asked her to pay NIS 130 (about $80) as a customs fee on clothing belonging to herself and her son. When she complained that this amount was very high, the official raised the amount to NIS 150. When she said that she did not have the amount, the customs officer confiscated her luggage and told her that she could pass but would have to collect her luggage in Jericho later. She went home without her luggage and later paid the dues in the customs department. When she went to Jericho to collect her belongings, she found that many of her and her son's clothes were missing.

Despite the high cost of crossing the bridges, no meaningful service is rendered. On the contrary, crossing the bridge is a humiliating experience for Palestinians due to elaborate inspection of belongings and body searches; the bridges are open for only a limited period each day, and are closed for a total of about seventy days a year.

The total amount paid by inhabitants of the Occupied Territories in crossing the bridges therefore amounts to some $50–55 million an-

[25] This figure is an estimate, based on personal interviews by the author.

nually. It consists of: (a) the bridge-crossing tax, about $32 million; (b) permits for taxis and trucks, about $3 million; and (c) customs dues, about $15–20 million.

Tax on the purchase of foreign currency

This is imposed by means of MO 1055. This tax amounts to 1 per cent of the total value of the currency purchased, to be paid to the Civil Administration.

Fines for security offences

These are imposed through a number of military orders, for instance MOs 378, 845, 865, 948, 1071, etc. With maximum fines ranging from NIS 9,000 to NIS 13,000 ($3–5,000), these fines constitute a considerable source of revenue for the occupying authorities.

III. Tax Assessment and Collection in the West Bank

Arbitrary methods of assessment and collection of tax exacerbate the burden of high and discriminatory taxation already examined above. Tax officers are mostly Israeli and often not only lack adequate professional qualifications but are unable to read balance sheets and income statements in Arabic.[26] This routinely leads to arbitrary estimations of taxable income. While, at the time of writing, no systematic documentation or examination of these practices has been published, the following accounts cited from local newspaper sources, typical of similar reports published daily in the local press, illustrate some of the problems.

1. No consideration is given to losses incurred by merchants in estimating the tax. It is always assumed that the merchant is making a profit. For example, *Al-Mithaq* newspaper reported that tax officers entered Aqabat Jaber Refugee Camp near Jericho on 23 May 1986 and, using violence, forced shop-owners to pay taxes ranging from NIS 10–50 million, while the assets of most of the shops were only about NIS 2–4,000.[27] In another example, the daily *Al-Nahar* reported that a person was asked to pay about NIS 27,000 for the years 1981, 1982, and 1983, while his total revenues were much less than this figure.[28]

---

[26] A. Alawneh, 'Tax Administration in the West Bank and its Role in Achieving Tax Goals' (forthcoming).
[27] *Al-Mithaq*, 24 May 1986.
[28] *Al-Nahar*, 18 Apr. 1986.

2. *Al-Fajr* newspaper reported in July 1986 that the tax authorities had imposed a strange new tax on an inhabitant from Qalqiliya, when he went to the tax department for a declaration that he had paid his taxes in order to license his car. The official asked him to pay JD 85 (approximately $220) as a 'Driver's Tax'.[29] Examples of such arbitary taxes abound. Several protests were lodged by chambers of commerce in the West Bank, but with no response.[30]

3. In March 1987, tax authorities levied a tax of NIS 10 million on shops in Kalandiya Refugee Camp, prompting protests from the United Nations Relief and Works Agency for Palestinian Refugees (UNRWA).[31]

4. Taxes were imposed on water usage in Qalqiliya in January 1987, even though the wells there are exempt from taxes since the water is used for irrigation.[32]

5. A tax of JD 580 was imposed on a shop-owner in the centre of Hebron in November 1986 after the army had blocked access to his and others' shops for so-called 'security' reasons, making it difficult for the shopkeepers to conduct any business at all.[33]

Examples of the type of practices enumerated above abound,[34] with a destructive impact on the economy of the territories. On more than one occasion such practices have forced shop-owners to close their shops as, for instance, in Beit Jala and Jenin in the autumn of 1986.[35] Many such instances are summarized in a memorandum of July 1986 submitted by the Chamber of Commerce in Nablus to the Israeli Minister of Defence on behalf of all chambers of commerce in the West Bank, regarding income tax, VAT, and the behaviour of tax officials.[36] No reply was ever received to this memorandum.

IV. The West Bank Budget and its Role in Development

In parliamentary democracies, the executive branch of the government is responsible for a country's budget, and is accountable to the legislative branch. In the case of the Occupied Territories, however, the

---

[29] *Al-Fajr*, 2 July 1986.
[30] See, for example, *al-Ittihad*, 2 July 1986; *al-Fajr*, 1 and 22 July 1986; *al-Mithaq*, 1 July 1986; *al-Quds*, 22 May, 21 and 24 June, and 20 July 1986; *al-Sha'ab*, 12 Mar. 1987.
[31] *Al-Sha'ab*, 12 Mar. 1987.
[32] *Al-Fajr*, 30 Jan. 1987.
[33] *Al-Sha'ab*, 11 Nov. 1986.
[34] See, for example: *al-Mithaq* 10 Feb. 1986; *al-Quds* 22 May, 5 Sept., 16 Oct., 27 Nov. 1986, and 13 Jan. 1987; *al-Ittihad* 22 July 1986; *al-Sha'ab* 16 Dec. 1986; *al-Fajr* 2 Oct., 6 Nov., 12 Dec. 1986, and 25 Feb., 2 and 6 Mar. 1987. See also Alawneh, 'Tax Administration in the West Bank'.
[35] *Al-Sha'ab*, 24 Dec. 1986, and *al-Quds*, 18 Sept. 1986.
[36] *Al-Quds*, 20 July 1986.

military authorities estimate and implement the budget without any input from the local population and without being accountable to that population.

Revenues derived from and sums invested in the West Bank are not easy to calculate, since reliable statistics are difficult to obtain.[37] The Israeli government's budget for the Occupied Territories consists of two separate components: the military government's civilian budget (included in the budget of the Ministry of Defence), and items in the budgets of individual Israeli government ministries.[38] Generally speaking, the military government's budget is designed for the Arab population and the ministries' budgets are designed for the Jewish population, especially Israeli settlements and roads in the Occupied Territories.

In 1980, the total Israeli government expenditure on the West Bank (for the Arab population) amounted to NIS 211.7 million. Eleven per cent of this budget was for capital investment ('the development budget'), and the remainder was for current expenditures.[39]

Yossi Sarid, a member of the Israeli Knesset from the Citizens' Rights Movement, claimed in 1987 that the Israeli treasury had allocated $25 million for development to the civilian administration in the Territories the previous year, while it netted $170 million in the form of VAT, customs, dues, and compulsory deductions from salaries of West Bank and Gaza workers employed inside Israel.[40]

The budgetary policies of the authorities further depress conditions in the Palestinian sector,[41] especially since foreign aid programmes make it less urgent for the military government to invest in fixed assets. And even these programmes, sponsored by foreign funding organizations, are directed mainly toward consumption-oriented projects because of the difficulty of obtaining permits for productive projects.[42]

Tables 12.4 and 12.5 show the development and regular budgets of 1984, 1985, and 1986 for the West Bank. The following comments can be made:

1. The total development budget was about $18.7 million in 1984, reduced to $14.7 million in 1985, and then raised to $28.5 million in 1986. It is apparent from Table 12.4 that most of the expenditure in this budget is directed towards human capital formation services (education, health, industry, and agriculture). Ongoing consumption expen-

---

[37] Statement by Israeli Finance Minister Moshe Nissim, *Jerusalem Post*, 16 June 1987.
[38] Benvenisti, *Interim Report*, 14.
[39] Ibid.
[40] *Jerusalem Post*, 16 June 1987.
[41] Benvenisti, *1986 Report*, 16.
[42] Ibid.

TABLE 12.4. *West Bank Development Budget 1986 ('000 NIS)*

	1984 Actual Figures	1985 Budget	1986 Budget
TOTAL	5,471	17,384	42,385
1. Dev. of water resources	535	2,200	4,700
2. Loans and grants to local authorities	1,634	3,500	8,700
3. School buildings	266	1,200	3,200
4. Dev. of post offices	10	75	100
5. Electric grids	668	1,400	2,600
6. Telephones	556	1,800	4,900
7. Roads	563	2,800	6,100
8. Health	634	2,490	9,540
9. Civilian Administration	6	520	400
10. Archaeology	58	108	280
11. Natural reserves	20	16	20
12. National parks	40	20	35
13. Bedouin settlement	55	120	140
14. Quarries	—	60	—
15. Buses	8	170	300
16. Industry & agriculture	405	60	100
17. Reserve for inflation	—	845	1,270
18. Non-recurring items	13	—	—
Exchange rates:	1984	1985	1986
US$1 = NIS	0.2925	1.1785	1.4879

(Data obtained from Meron Benvenisti)

diture ought to be higher, while there is no promotion of capital formation aimed at encouraging growth.

Moreover, expenditures allocated to what is called the development budget are minimal. The share of the development-related budgets actually implemented has been reduced from almost half of the original programme to less than one-third. It can be concluded that the Israeli authorities have obstructed efforts to foment development in the Occupied Territories.

A study conducted by Meron Benvenisti in 1984 examined the way in which the military authorities dealt with the 358 proposed projects with a total budget of $66 million generated by USAID financing in 1977–83 when they were submitted to the authorities for approval. Many could not be carried out because the authorities failed to grant a permit, prompting a shift from development projects to services and charity by systematically giving permits to consumption-oriented projects while withholding them from development-oriented projects.[43] By the end of 1984 (eight years after the introduction of US-funded projects), 54 per cent of the amount had been spent, 32.1 per cent had been disapproved, and 13.8 per cent was pending.[44] Furthermore, the authorities tended to delay responding to project proposals. The average response time ranged from 3.8 months for water-pipe projects to 48 months for industrial projects. The overall average was 12.2 months per project.

The approval of foreign-aid support for consumption-oriented public works reduces the budgetary burden on the Israeli government. The building of classrooms, internal roads, and water and electricity grids ought normally to be provided by the government (including a military government), or at least financed by the taxpayers' money. Directing foreign aid mainly to such projects, however, has enabled the authorities to free the military government's own public funds for other purposes.[45]

In short, as Benvenisti concluded, the actual contribution of US aid to the Occupied Territories, contrary to the original intention, helps to strengthen the 'pacification alternative' pursued by Israel. Israeli intervention, through its permits policy, alters the emphasis and use of US economic aid in the Territories to implement Israel's own economic policies.

2. Table 12.5 shows the regular budget of the West Bank for the years 1984, 1985, and 1986 in which about $112.6 million is allocated for 1984, $53.7 million for 1985 and $98.5 million for 1986. This table reveals the same trend in the regular as appears in the development budget, that is directing expenditures towards consumption, primarily education and health.

Some general conclusions about both the regular and development budgets of the West Bank can now be made:

(a) Low amounts are allocated. Maximum amounts totalled $131.3 million in 1984 ($112.6 million regular budget, $18.7 million development budget), reduced to about half in 1985, then partially restored in 1986.
(b) Even though part of the budget is labelled developmental, it is actually a consumption-oriented budget.
(c) The rate of public expenditure does not meet the growth demands of the economy and indicates a very low level of services.
(d) Budgetary policies of the authorities depress conditions of Pales-

---

[43] M. Benvenisti, *US Government Funded Projects in the West Bank and Gaza (1977–1983) (Palestinian Sector)* (Jerusalem, 1984), 12–14, and table 13.
[44] Ibid. table 8.
[45] Ibid. 14.

TABLE 12.5. *West Bank Regular Budget for 1986—by Unit ('000 NIS)*

Unit	Actual Figures 1984	Budget 1985	Budget 1986
TOTAL	32,931	63,250	147,784
1. Civilian Administration	251	1,048	5,308
2. Statistics	101	198	538
3. Finance	1,355	5,306	12,166
4. Customs	541	932	2,158
5. Tax	1,364	2,648	5,792
6. Interior	1,151	2,968	6,911
7. Justice	366	545	1,406
8. Land	75	152	320
9. Assessment	14	27	60
10. Education	16,119	27,311	55,876
11. Archaeology	93	187	445
12. Religion	26	57	126
13. Labour	480	808	1,295
14. Employment	111	217	1,003
15. Health	6,101	10,873	31,149
16. Welfare	1,308	2,746	6,443
17. Housing	53	83	156
18. Public work	1,065	2,614	6,546
19. Surveying	42	95	205
20. Agriculture	692	1,171	2,586
21. Water-expenditure income	1,331 (1,414)	2,400 (2,400)	8,400 (8,400)
22. Natural reserves	20	41	240
23. Industry and trade	282	441	919
24. Quarries	8	14	33
25. Tourism	23	37	80
26. Energy	23	34	76
27. Transportation	163	413	888
28. Postal services	504	1,023	2,419
29. Telecommunications	394	741	1,619
30. State and absentee property	289	464	1,021
Exchange rates: US$1 = NIS	1984 0.2925	1985 1.1785	1986 1.4879

(Data obtained from Meron Benvenisti)

tinians by the small amount allocated to the West Bank budget, and the great reliance on the consumption budget rather than the development budget. The result is that very few, if any, development projects are implemented. This in turn contributes to an increase in the unemployment rate in the West Bank, and to a large deficit in the balance of trade.[46]

V. Revenues Collected, Services Rendered

It is difficult to calculate the exact amount of revenues which the occupying authorities collect annually. Figures are not made public, and the explanation given by the Israeli Minister of Finance, Moshe Nissim, that 'statistics are hard to collect',[47] is itself hard to accept. A more probable explanation for this reticence is the belief, held by many analysts, that not only is the occupation financed by the inhabitants, but that the fiscal burden of occupation of the West Bank is negative, and that Israel has in fact benefited from the occupation.[48] Moreover, as shown above, foreign aid has reduced the budgetary burden on the Israeli government because of the methods used by Israel to direct these funds into consumption-oriented public works.

Although precision is impossible, the following will give an indication of the elements of the revenue collected from the West Bank:

1. The VAT is estimated by Benvenisti at about $40–50 million annually, as mentioned above.
2. The bridge-crossing tax and customs paid by inhabitants crossing the bridges are estimated conservatively at about $50–55 million annually.
3. Total revenue from income tax is hard to calculate, but based on the national disposable income of the West Bank it could be estimated at around $100 million a year.
4. It is difficult to list all other taxes, customs, and fees, and impossible to even estimate the revenue from some. What follows is therefore only a sampling:

    (a) Fees for entering public parks (MO 89 of 1967).
    (b) Education tax: 7 per cent of net annual rent.
    (c) Fees for land registration (MOs 505 and 693).
    (d) Land tax (MO 642).
    (e) Professional licensing fees (MO 977); rates range from JD 10 to about JD 750 a year.

---

[46] Benvenisti, *1986 Report*, 14–15.
[47] *Jerusalem Post*, 16 June 1987.
[48] See for instance Benvenisti, *1986 Report*, 18.

(f) Tax on imported services: 20 per cent of an airplane ticket value, 15 per cent of the ground services at airports (MO 1142).
(g) Court fees: 4 per cent of the value of the case (MO 808).
(h) Vehicle registration fees (MO 1150). The total number of vehicles registered until the end of May 1987 in the West Bank was 57,049. If we assume an average amount paid, according to the table attached to the Order, of about $500 for each vehicle, the total amount would be $28 million annually.
(i) Drivers' licensing fees. There were about 67,238 licensed drivers in the West Bank by the end of May 1987. The licensing fee is NIS 11 a year or about $6.5 per driver. This amounts to about $0.5 million annually.
(j) Identity-card fees: NIS 14 (about $8) is charged per identity card issued. Each person over 15 years of age is obliged to have an identity card. Statistics show that more than 500,000 persons in the West Bank are 15 years and above, which means that approximately $4 million is collected annually. The occupation authorities so far have required residents to renew their identity cards three times since 1967.
(k) Driving-test fees. Driving tests consist of two parts: oral and practical. On the average, about 5,000 persons sit annually for the test and repeat both parts of the test at least once. It is estimated that a person pays an average of $300 for taking these tests, which makes the total amount levied about $1.5 million annually.
(l) Fees for registration of births and deaths, which range from NIS 10–19.

5. Finally, large sums, consisting of 20 per cent of the income of Palestinian workers from the Territories officially employed in Israel, as well as employers' contributions, have since 1970 been collected by the Government Employment Service to cover various social benefits. In the case of the most important of these deductions, the National Insurance Tax, whereas the Israeli workers' payments are transferred to the National Insurance Institute, those made in the name of the Palestinian workers are transferred directly to a special Deduction Fund. Palestinian workers are not entitled to receive many of the benefits provided by the National Insurance, including payments for widowhood, dependent children, general disability, and unemployment, since these benefits are only paid to Israeli residents. This is in spite of the fact that the same sums are deducted from the Palestinian workers' wages as from the Israeli workers. The sums deducted from Palestinian workers, for which

they do not receive any benefit, are estimated at a cumulative total of about $1 billion since 1970.[49]

As mentioned earlier, the annual budgetary expenditure of the occupying authorities in the West Bank (both regular and development) is between $100–130 million annually. Although no precise figure can be given for the total revenue collected, it will be noted that the sums estimated in (1) and (2) above together more or less cover the authorities' annual budgetary expenditures. The revenue listed in items (3), (4), and (5) therefore constitutes almost total gain to the occupying authorities.

As to services rendered, the following comparison between the services rendered to Israeli settlers in the West Bank and those rendered to the local population will be illustrative. A substantial part of the Israeli budget for the Occupied Territories is allocated to Israeli settlements in the territories, whose presence is illegal under international law.[50] Annual capital investment in West Bank settlements is estimated at about $200–250 million,[51] or more than double the amount allocated to the local population. Benvenisti has noted that these allocations enable the local authorities to employ a large staff and provide a range of services. Regular and development government budgets have allowed the settlements to amass considerable independent economic strength. Comparing the standard of services in Jewish and Palestinian local authorities in the West Bank, one can easily conclude the priority status of Jewish councils in the West Bank.[52]

In 1982, per capita expenditure on the Palestinian population was at a ratio of 1:6.6 compared to Israel. Per capita expenditure on health was 8 per cent of that in Israel. Per capita expenditure on education was 12–15 per cent of that in Israel. The standard of living of Palestinians in the West Bank is lower than the Israeli standard of living by a ratio of 1:4.[53]

The following table sets out examples of per capita public service expenditures in 1983 in selected West Bank districts:[54]

Jewish District	Palestinian District
Kiryat Arba $260	Hebron $54
Shomron $568	Jenin $12
Mateh Benyamin $406	Ramallah $8.5

[49] Benvenisti, *1987 Report*, 31.
[50] See Ch. 1, text at n. 147 ff., and Ch. 14, text at n. 48 ff.
[51] Benvenisti, *1986 Report*, 51. See also Ch. 8 in this volume.
[52] Benvenisti, *1986 Report*, 56.
[53] Ibid. 15–18.
[54] WBDP, 'Press Release: Study on Population and Public Funding on the West Bank' (Jerusalem, 1985), 10.

The preferential status of Jewish settlements is reflected clearly in the statement by the researcher Haim Ramon: 'In 1981 alone, when 30,000 settlers lived in Judea and Samaria and Gaza, more money was invested on their behalf than had been invested for all the Arabs in the previous decade and a half'.[55]

A comparison of per capita public expenditures in Jordan, Israel, and the West Bank is offered in Table 12.6. This Table makes it clear that

TABLE 12.6. *Per capita public expenditure in Jordan, Israel, and the Occupied Territories*

	Jordan*	Israel	West Bank	Gaza
1983	761	n.a.	n.a.	n.a.
1984	777	1218	136	100
1985	825	1732	65	50
1986	n.a.	2413	120	90

* Figures for Jordan are of 1983, 1984, and 1985 respectively, and are taken from the Central Bank of Jordan, *Annual Report 1986*.

(Source: Atef Alawneh, 'The Income Tax Burden in the Occupied Territories, Jordan and Israel: A Comparative Study' (forthcoming)).

there is a substantial difference in the services rendered to Israeli inhabitants as compared to those provided to inhabitants of the Occupied Territories. While the occupying authorities spent about $120 per capita in the West Bank in 1986, they spent approximately $2,413 per capita in Israel itself in the same year. The per capita public expenditure of Israel was thus more than twenty times that of the West Bank, and more than twenty-six times that of Gaza; this, while both West Bank and Gaza residents pay income taxes that are significantly higher than those paid by inhabitants of Israel.

As is evident from the above discussion, the low level of services for the Palestinian population of the West Bank is due not to any lack of financing but to Israeli policies of maintaining low levels of professional staff and committing low levels of public expenditure. In sum, the figures given above indicate that the occupation does not constitute a fiscal burden on the Israeli Treasury but, on the contrary, that Palestinians contribute large sums to Israeli public expenditure.[56] Conservative estimates of revenues indicate that Israel levies more revenues than it spends. Once more according to Benvenisti, 'In 1987 alone . . . at least US$80 million of Palestinian contributions were

---

[55] Ibid.
[56] Benvenisti, *1986 Report*, 18.

directed to Israeli public expenditure ... The 1986/1987 'occupation tax' could have doubled the territories' development budget of that year.'[57]

Conclusion

It appears to the observer that it has been Israel's policy since 1967 to block development of the Palestinian economy in the Occupied Territories, and to turn the occupation into a profitable enterprise. The Civilian Administration has stated officially that it does not demand any Israeli government contributions to its budget and that the present level of public expenditure and investment is the maximum it can use.[58]

What this implies is that the Israeli authorities do not intend to develop the territories, and do not wish to use money generated from the Occupied Territories in the territories themselves. In sum, the net result of the policies, practices, and behaviour of the occupying authorities in their financial administration of the West Bank is that the economy of the West Bank has become unbalanced, distorted, and subservient.[59]

[57] Benvenisti, *1987 Report*, 32.
[58] Ibid. 30.
[59] Ibid.

13

Israel's Economic Policies in the Occupied Territories: A Case for International Supervision

Hisham Awartani

Introduction

THE predominantly agricultural economy of Mandatory Palestine centred around the rich coastal plain and the sea ports on the Mediterranean coast, with subsistence farming in the hills now known as the West Bank. Following the 1948 war, with the loss of virtually all the coastal plain and all but one port, the Palestinian economy was decimated and fragmented. The two segments of Palestine remaining under Arab control, together constituting less than one-quarter of the original land area, fell under separate administration. Bordering Egypt, the Gaza Strip was placed under Egyptian administration, while the West Bank fell under Jordanian rule and later annexation.

Following the end of armed hostilities, the economies of each of the two segments underwent separate evolution. The Gaza Strip, its population tripled by refugees, was ignored rather than exploited under Egyptian control. No effort was made to undermine or disguise the Palestinian identity of the Strip nor to impose disadvantageous economic relations between the Strip and Egypt; but, deprived of the hinterland which it served and distanced by the Sinai from alternative Egyptian markets, the economy did not take full advantage of its affiliation with the largest Arab state. The West Bank, on the other hand, was better developed in 1948 than Jordan and its agricultural land richer. Although its economy was severely hurt by the devastating consequences of the 1947–8 war, yet the West Bank achieved a fairly high growth rate during Jordanian rule. Growth could have been much higher had it not been for Jordan's official policy of giving priority to the East Bank.

In 1967, when the two territories were occupied by the Israeli army, neither had a viable integral economy. The Gaza Strip had been weakened by neglect, over-population, and the loss of its natural hinterland, while the West Bank formed but one unbalanced part of the national economy of Jordan. This was the situation when these two economies were suddenly thrust into close relation with the Israeli economy, which in contrast was comparatively well-developed, but suffering from the absence of local markets due to the Arab boycott.

The economies of the West Bank and Gaza Strip have witnessed far-reaching transformations since both territories fell under Israeli occupation in June 1967. The economic consequences of occupation are so diversified and complex that they have been viewed very differently by different sides. Official Israeli sources portray the economic aftermath of occupation in an overwhelmingly positive and rosy context.[1] Their judgement is supported, as we shall see later, by marked achievements on a number of macro-economic indicators. Most independent economists, on the other hand, project a considerably more reserved assessment of the economic outcome of Israeli occupation.[2] Despite certain visible achievements, they express great concern for the ultimate impact of Israeli policies on the long-term interests of the indigenous population.

This chapter is not intended to provide a comprehensive examination and evaluation of economic transformation and policies as they emerged during two decades of Israeli occupation. Instead, it provides a brief evaluation of change along major economic indicators, and focuses attention on some practical manifestations of Israel's tacit economic policies in the Occupied Territories, indicating the means by which these policies are implemented by changes in pre-existing law or regulations.

From the outset, the Israeli government has treated both territories as distinct economic entities, and has assumed sole responsibility for determining the development of all three economies, for Israel as the elected government and for the West Bank and Gaza as military ruler. The arrangement whereby the Israeli government acts as its own negotiating partner in the establishment of bilateral economic relations between its own state and the territories it occupies is the focus of the anomalous relationship which this paper will examine. The author will examine the consequences of Israel's position as sole determinator of its own population's development and that of its neighbours. No mention is made of policies relating to land and water resources nor

---

[1] See, for instance, the chapter on economic development and standard of living in the report by the Israel Ministry of Defence, *Judea, Samaria and the Gaza District 1967–1987: Twenty Years of Civil Administration* (Jerusalem, 1987).

[2] For prominent examples of such views, see B. Van Arkadie, *Benefits and Burdens: A Report on the West Bank and Gaza Strip Economies since 1967* (New York, 1977); UK Economic Commission for Western Asia, *The Industrial and Economic Trends in the West Bank and Gaza Strip* (New York, 1981); M. Benvenisti, *West Bank Data Base Project Report, 1987* (Jerusalem, 1987).

to fiscal relations between the Territories and Israel, as those topics will be covered in other chapters in this collection.

I. Economic Growth

The economy of the West Bank and Gaza Strip achieved a relatively high rate of growth during the early years of occupation. According to data published by the Central Bureau of Statistics,[3] gross domestic product (GDP) grew during the years of 1969–75 at 12.2 per cent per annum.[4] Because of total dependence on Israel's economy, however, growth in the Territories slowed down considerably after Israel plunged into recession and spiralling inflation. GDP grew at only 5.3 per cent per annum during the period of 1975–9.[5]

Economic growth has slowed further since 1980, rising by only 3.2 per cent per annum during 1980–5. With a population increase of aroung 2.5 per cent, GDP per capita has therefore risen by less than 1 per cent per annum.

Following economic recovery in Israel during the mid-1980s, and as a consequence of an unusually good olive crop, GDP of the Territories picked up again at a marked pace. The combined GDP of both territories was estimated for 1986 at $1,494 million, equalling 72 per cent of their GNP ($2,073 million).[6] However, the Territories' GDP for 1986 amounted only to 5.4 per cent that of Israel, whereas their population at the end of 1986 amounted to 32 per cent that of Israel (1.382 million as against 4.331 million).[7]

Analysis of data on economic growth reveals the following:

1. The average annual rate of growth achieved in the West Bank following Israeli occupation (1969–86) is estimated at 8 per cent.[8] This rate is lower than that achieved in Jordan, the West Bank included, during the pre-war period of 1954–66, estimated at 10 per cent.[9]
2. Despite a relatively high overall rate of growth, productive sectors

---

[3] It should be noted that CBS data on economic transformations in the Occupied Territories are known for their poor reliability. Strong reservations as to their reliability are expressed even by the staff of the CBS themselves (see *National Accounts of Judea, Samaria and Gaza Area Statistics 1977–83*, xi).

[4] *National Accounts of Judea, Samaria and Gaza Area 1968–1986*, No. 818 (Jerusalem, 1988), 56.

[5] Ibid.

[6] *Statistical Abstract of Israel 1987*, 709. Conversion to US dollars is made at the official exchange rates of NIS 1.1785 and NIS 1.4879 per dollar for 1985 and 1986 respectively.

[7] Ibid. 30, 174, 701.

[8] *National Accounts 1968–1986*, 77.

[9] Jordan Development Board, *Development Plan 1976–1980*, 9.

have played a noticeably minor role in the national economy. Agriculture and industry together contributed only 30 per cent of the Territories' GDP in 1986.[10]
3. The economy of the Territories is heavily dependent on external sources of income. Representing a share of 24 per cent of the GNP (1986), factor payments from abroad, in this case consisting mainly of labour remittances from Palestinians employed in Israel, constitute the most important single component of national product. Income from external factor payments is in fact only a little lower than the combined share of agriculture and industry (for 1986 only 8 per cent lower[11]). Noting the particularly significant role of labour remittances from Israeli sources, Van Arkadie points out that '50 per cent of the Territories' growth of income since 1967 is attributable to wages earned in Israel'.[12]
4. All major economic sectors are directly or indirectly dependent on the Israeli economy, and are generally subservient to that economy. As will be demonstrated later in this paper, the creation of an indigenous economic base and the emergence of effective competition to Israeli firms are deliberately discouraged and resisted.

II. Standard of Living

Inducing a marked rise in the standard of living was an important objective on the list of Israeli economic policies in the Territories during the period 1967–87.[13] In addition to improving the tarnished image of Israel's oppressive rule, Israeli authorities envision that a higher standard of living may render Palestinian residents increasingly concerned to preserve or even improve their life-style which, expectedly, will leave them little time to worry about the occupation. Excessive consumerism will also create a larger market for Israeli goods.

The past twenty years have undoubtedly witnessed a pronounced rise in the standard of living of the Palestinian population in the West Bank and Gaza Strip. This is clearly evidenced by a number of indicators relating to food intake, housing conditions and ownership of private cars and household durable goods. Improvements on these criteria of living standards have been buttressed by a marked rise in

---

[10] *Statistical Abstract of Israel 1987*, 709.
[11] *National Accounts 1968–1986*, 58, 70.
[12] Van Arkadie, *Benefits and Burdens*, 144.
[13] Obviously, Israeli policies in this connection were reversed in the wake of the *intifada*, since pressures on living standards were employed in the context of other measures aimed at quelling the Palestinian uprising.

levels of income. Private consumption per capita rose during 1969–86 at an overall rate of 5 per cent per annum.[14] In 1985 it was estimated at $1,117, or about one-third of per capita private consumption in Israel ($3,320). Similarly, GNP per capita rose in the Territories to approximately $1,124 (1986), as compared to $4,950 in Israel.[15]

There are two important qualifications relevant to the rise in standard of living following the onset of Israeli occupation. Firstly, it must be noted that the rise in disposable income has not been underlain by a genuine growth in the domestic economic base. Instead, it has actually been precipitated as a consequence of parasitic subordination to the Israeli economy. Private consumption has in fact consistently exceeded gross domestic product by a considerable margin, estimated at an average of 38 per cent during the last three recorded years (1984–6).[16] This is a clear indication that consumption in the Occupied Territories has considerably outstripped domestic production. Secondly, it is important to note that, despite the marked rise in per capita income, it still lags far behind that of Jordan, which is estimated for 1986 at $1,956.[17] Consequently, it is unjustifiable to claim phenomenal improvements in the standard of living in the West Bank and Gaza Strip since Israeli occupation.

III. Employment

Because of a chronically weak economic base and a high rate of population growth, the local absorptive capacity of the domestic labour market is noticeably limited. For many years prior to occupation, these factors had given rise to certain forms of unemployment and stimulated vigorous emigration to neighbouring countries, particularly to Jordan and the Gulf States.

Shortly after the onset of occupation, Israeli authorities permitted Palestinians from the Territories to seek employment in Israel. This immediately triggered an influx of labourers into the Israeli labour market. In 1986 the number of workers from the Territories (East Jerusalem included) employed in Israel was estimated at 114,000, i.e. 36 per cent of the total labour force in the West Bank and Gaza Strip.[18]

The economic and social consequences of the employment of

---

[14] *National Accounts 1968–1986*, 60.
[15] Benvenisti, *1987 Report*, 12–13.
[16] *National Accounts 1968–1986*, 58.
[17] Derived from Central Bank of Jordan, *Annual Report 1986* (Amman, 1987), 4.
[18] *Statistical Abstract of Israel, 1987*, 723. The number of workers from East Jerusalem is added (around 18,000). On Palestinian migrant labour in Israel, see also Ch. 10 in this book.

Palestinians in Israel are too complex to be evaluated in the present context. It is clear, however, that the *de facto* rate of employment has risen so substantially that visible unemployment has dropped to less than 5 per cent since 1970.[19] And, as has been noted earlier, remittances from Israel have long since become the backbone of the economy in both territories.

Gains accruing to the Israeli side, however, have been more substantial. Wages paid to Palestinian labourers are considerably lower than those paid to their Jewish counterparts. A recent study has estimated that wage differentials between Israeli and Palestinian workers employed in Israel add up to a cumulative total of $3,049 million during the period 1968–85.[20] Furthermore, Palestinian workers are characterized by high spatial and occupational mobility, which offers great flexibility to business firms and improves their competitive standing in international markets.[21]

It is important to note that wages paid to Palestinian workers employed in Israel are subject to a variety of deductions which amount to approximately 20 per cent of their nominal pay. They do not, however, qualify for most of the benefits for which these deductions are supposed to pay. In the case of one of these deductions, National Insurance, deductions from Israeli workers are transferred to the National Insurance Institute where they are used to finance a wide range of services and benefits which are accorded to workers and their families. Comparable deductions from Palestinian workers are placed in a special fund, called 'the Deduction Fund'. In contrast to Israeli workers, however, Palestinian workers from the Occupied Territories employed in Israel are not entitled to receive the same benefits as Israeli workers, due to discriminatory residency requirements contained in the National Insurance Law. Since the workers only qualify for a small percentage of the benefits, only a small part of the Deduction Fund is therefore used to pay for the meagre level of services accorded to Palestinian workers. The bulk of the funds is divided between the military government budget (about three-quarters) and the Treasury of Israel.[22] The cumulative value of sums accruing to the Deduction Fund is a well-guarded secret, but it is estimated to have exceeded $1 billion.[23]

---

[19] *Statistical Abstract of Israel, 1987*, 718.

[20] T. Arouri, 'The Economic Gains Accruing to Israel from the West Bank and Gaza Strip', *al-Kateb* No. 86, 99.

[21] E. Farjoun, *Palestinian Workers in Israel: A Reserve Army of Labour* (Jerusalem, 1976).

[22] Benvenisti, *1987 Report*, 31.

[23] Ibid. Other researchers put the value of the Deduction Fund during the same period at $1,489 million. Arouri, 'The Economic Gains Accruing to Israel', 102.

IV. Development Planning

Planning of development in the West Bank and Gaza Strip was performed prior to occupation through a number of specialized bodies, managed mainly by Palestinian experts, sometimes with the participation of Jordanian or Egyptian officials. Although it may have been riddled with grave technical deficiencies and administrative inefficiencies, the planning process in the Gaza Strip was not underlain by alien political objectives or conflicting national interests. In the case of the West Bank, a pronounced degree of bias to the favour of the East Bank was consistently maintained at top levels. This had stunted indigenous economic growth and facilitated subsequent annexation to the Israeli economy. Yet one should admit that the West Bank economy had achieved a noticeably high rate of growth while under Jordanian rule.

The situation in regard to planning of economic development has undergone profound changes in the wake of Israeli occupation. All development-related departments (for example, agriculture, trade and industry, quarries, and taxes) have been transferred into Israeli hands.[24] Each of these departments is assigned an officer-in-charge who has been bestowed with the duties and legal status of a minister, as prescribed in the laws in effect prior to the occupation. Each of these departments is staffed by a small number of senior Israeli officials who hold all key positions in the hierarchy of their respective departments.

The officers-in-charge and their senior assistants are often recruited from the staff of respective ministries in Israel. Planning in any sector, as will be demonstrated in the few examples discussed below, is performed in close co-ordination with concerned Israeli organizations and in line with their explicit and tacit interests. And as Israeli officials have the last word, any conflict of interests is resolved in Israel's favour.[25] This was openly and vividly expressed in Israeli Defence Minister Rabin's infamous oath in which he pledged that 'There will be no development in the territories initiated by the Israeli government, and no permits given for expanding agriculture or industry which may compete with the state of Israel.'[26]

There are numerous instances where conflict of interest has come to bear heavily on the way Israeli officials 'plan' for the development of the Occupied Territories. Some notable examples are reviewed here.

---

[24] The Civil Administration in Judea and Samaria, *Annual Report 1984* (1985), iv. For a detailed description of all changes made in the West Bank, see Ch. 8 in this book.

[25] On whether international law permits an occupier to take its own interest into account in administering the economy of the occupied territory, see Chs. 7 and 14.

[26] *The Jerusalem Post*, 15 Feb. 1985.

The Arab Cement Factory

All West Bank needs for cement were satisfied prior to the onset of Israeli occupation by the Jordan Cement Factory which was located in the East Bank of Jordan. This factory was an incorporated firm in which many West Bank residents had invested much of their savings. Following occupation, the entry of cement from Jordan was prohibited and all West Bank and Gaza cement needs were supplied by Nesher, Israel's sole cement manufacturer.

In 1977, a group of entrepreneurs from the West Bank and Gaza Strip launched efforts aimed at establishing a cement factory, the first of its kind in the Territories. The founding committee commissioned a consortium of European firms to conduct the necessary feasibility study and to formulate implementation plans. The results of initial investigations demonstrated a clearly positive viability. Full production capacity of the proposed factory was projected at 1,250 tons a day, which was not significantly higher than current demand, estimated then at 900 tons a day. Consequently, the proposed firm was registered in 1980 under the name of 'Arab Cement Company' (ACC), with an initial share capital of $42 million. Subscription to the public was opened, and demand for the shares of the new firm was unusually high.

But when ACC commenced actual implementation of its plans, its management was informed of Israel's refusal to issue the permits needed to initiate mining operations and to import production machinery. Israeli opposition thus froze the project before it even got off the ground. On the surface, the Israeli authorities rationalized their stand by claiming that the project was not economically viable. But it was abundantly clear that Israeli opposition to the Palestinian cement project was underlain by the desire to safeguard the interests of the Israel Cement Corporation (Nesher) by maintaining its uncontested access to the Occupied Territories. This was made clear when the Minister of Defence notified ACC's founders that his approval to license the new factory would be contingent on obtaining a solid guarantee that 70–80 per cent of its output would be channelled to Jordan.[27]

A Poultry Hatchery Refused

The poultry industry in the Occupied Territories achieved a pronounced level of development several years prior to Israeli occupation.

---

[27] Information given to the writer by the chairman of the Arab Cement Company board.

West Bank producers were by 1967 coming close to meeting all domestic demand for poultry-meat and eggs. Baby chicks and feed concentrates were purchased from hatcheries and feedmills located in the East Bank of Jordan.

Following occupation, the importation of baby chicks across the bridges was immediately discontinued, presumably because it violated Israeli quarantine regulations. Consequently, poultry raisers in the West Bank and Gaza were obliged to procure their replacement chicks from Israeli hatcheries. Similarly, they purchased feed concentrates from Israeli feedmills, because it was not feasible to bring it in from Jordan or Egypt.

A few years after the onset of occupation, Palestinian poultrymen began attempts to produce their own major production inputs. Several local feedmills were established without undue opposition from Israeli authorities. But when some poultry-raisers and dealers of production inputs attempted to set up a local hatchery, Israeli opposition was fierce. Finding great difficulty in substantiating their stand, Israeli officials raised doubts about the technical capabilities available locally, and at other times questioned the viability of the project.

The real motives behind Israel's firm opposition, however, apparently bear on remote vested interests. Acting on directives received from Israel's Poultry Board, the Ministry of Agriculture has placed a rigid quota on the number of replacement chicks which are to be supplied to poultry-raisers in the Occupied Territories.[28] By so doing, local production is maintained well below expected demand, so that a substantial proportion of the end products (meat and eggs) is still procured from Israeli producers. By not permitting the establishment of a local hatchery, Israeli authorities can maintain their grip on local poultry production in the Territories and direct this industry as deemed appropriate by Israel's Poultry Board.

The Bank of Palestine

The Bank of Palestine was established in 1960 in the city of Gaza, and by June 1967 it had opened one other branch in Khan Yunis, a city of 60,000 residents. A third branch was scheduled to open in Rafah later in 1967, but so far has not done so.

Immediately following the occupation, all banks and financial institutions in the West Bank and Gaza were closed in accordance with Military Order No. 7, which was issued only four days after the onset of occupation. A few months later, on the other hand, Israeli banks were permitted and encouraged to open branches in all major towns.

---

[28] Information given to the writer by a senior official in the Dept. of Agriculture.

By 1984, there were thirty-six such branches in the West Bank and five in the Gaza Strip.[29] For a variety of reasons, however, Israeli banks have not succeeded in providing normal banking services to Palestinian residents and firms, especially in the area of credit and foreign trade.

Prompted by the sore need for full-fledged banking services, the managers of the Bank of Palestine entered into a lengthy dialogue with Israeli authorities in an effort to resume functioning. After painstaking efforts, the Bank was permitted to reopen its main branch in 1981. That was conceived of as a first step towards restoring and later expanding the Bank's services to residents in the Gaza Strip.

Six years after its reopening, the Bank of Palestine has only achieved a fraction of its cherished goals. From the day it resumed its operations, the Bank was bogged down by numerous restrictions which were aimed at circumventing its normal functioning. The list of Israeli vetos included the following:

1. The Bank was not permitted to hold or conduct transactions in foreign currencies, which pre-empted its role in facilitating international trade.
2. The Bank of Palestine was not permitted to reopen its Khan Yunis branch, nor was it permitted to restore the building it owned in Rafah which, ironically, had been occupied by the Israeli Hapoalim Bank since the early years of occupation. Consequently, both cities of Khan Yunis and Rafah remain under the domain of Israeli banks, which continue to operate under monopolistic conditions.
3. The Bank of Palestine has been prevented from issuing new shares and raising its capital. Measured at fixed prices, the Bank's share capital in 1986 was estimated at $1.5 million,[30] which is equivalent to what it was when the Bank was opened in 1960.

The openly hostile attitude of Israeli authorities towards the Bank of Palestine has considerably undermined its ability to provide normal banking services to the 550,000 Palestinian residents of the Gaza Strip. This in turn has been another predisposing factor for perpetuating weakness in the local economic base and for maintaining the Strip as a reservoir of cheap labour to the advantage of Israeli firms.

The Demise of the Fish Industry in the Gaza Strip

With scarce natural resources and a coastline of 43 kilometres, fishing was for a long time an important economic sector in the Gaza Strip. In

---

[29] Bank of Israel, *Annual Statistics of Israel's Banking System 1980–1984* (Jerusalem, 1985), 35.

[30] Bank of Palestine, *The Annual Report of Balance Sheet 1988*, 9.

addition to satisfying local demand for an important food item, the fishing industry employs around 1,000 workers.[31]

Fishing in the Gaza Strip was for many years a flourishing industry, both before and after Israeli occupation. The main reason for that was that local fishermen were permitted access to all the sea area lying opposite the Gaza Strip and the Egyptian Sinai Peninsula. This situation changed abruptly after the signing of the Egyptian–Israeli peace treaty of 1978, which resulted in the return of Sinai to Egypt. Because the interests of the Gaza fishermen do not seem to have been considered, those fishermen were suddenly denied access to Egyptian sea waters, thereby reducing the fishing area from 7,500 square kilometres to only 600.[32]

The fishing industry was victimized still further by restrictions imposed by Israel in the name of security. Showing no concern for the drastic drop in the fishing area after withdrawal from Sinai, Israeli authorities imposed a 12-mile limit on the width accessible to Gaza fishermen. No such limits are imposed on Israeli fishermen. Furthermore, local fishermen were permitted to conduct their work only at night, being required to return to shore by 5 a.m. To further exacerbate the hardship to Gaza fishermen, the Israeli authorities have permitted Israeli fishing boats free access to Gaza waters, without being subject to the restrictions imposed on local fishermen.

The above-mentioned transformations have resulted in a sharp decline in the volume of fish catches by Gaza Strip fishermen, which dropped from 3,000 tons in 1977 to 500 tons in 1985.[33] Furthermore, income earned by fishermen has dropped so sharply that most of them have ultimately opted to abandon fishing and join the 46 per cent of the Gaza labour force employed in Israel.[34] The fishing industry has thus been reduced from a thriving sector to a minor activity, thereby depriving the Gaza Strip of what could be a major economic resource.

Physical Planning

In the first few years after occupation, Israeli authorities displayed little interest in issues relating to the physical planning of the Occupied Territories. As their intentions grew more permanent, they began to exercise stringent control of physical planning, enabling them to expedite greatly the creeping annexation of the newly occupied

---

[31] M. Awad, *Fishing Resources in Gaza Strip* (Nablus, 1987), 18.
[32] Ibid. 6.
[33] Ibid. 7.
[34] *Statistical Abstract of Israel 1987*, 723.

territories.[35] In order to do so, a series of military orders was issued, all aimed at restricting construction pertaining to Palestinian residents to the bare minimum. As expressed by Benvenisti, 'The physical planning process reflects Israeli interests exclusively, while the needs and interests of the Palestinian population are viewed as constraints to be overcome.'[36]

The way in which the Israeli authorities amended the Jordanian Planning Law No. 79 of 1966, to the point where it has been remoulded in the light of Israeli interests, has been reviewed by Mona Rishmawi in her chapter in this book. Most strikingly, the amendments were aimed at transferring almost all authority from local and regional planning committees to the Higher Planning Council (HPC). This Council is given total authority on all matters relating to physical planning, such as amending, revoking, and even issuing construction licences. The HPC has exercised its authority through its own offices in areas which lie outside municipal boundaries, but it has also assumed full overriding power on licensing by municipal councils.

The composition of the HPC has also been restructured so that it consists entirely of Israeli officials and settlement organizations. Until 1985, the Higher Planning Council was affiliated to the Israeli officer in charge of the interior, but since then it has been transferred to the Infrastructure Branch in the Civil Administration, which also assumes direct responsibility for the confiscation of land. The change renders physical planning in the West Bank even more vulnerable to Israel's immediate and long-term settlement aspirations.

The consequences of the sweeping amendments in physical planning regulations reflect most clearly the tacit intentions they are originally designed to serve. Procuring a building licence has become an extremely complicated and expensive process. In areas which lie outside municipal boundaries of Arab cities and in East Jerusalem the rate of approvals drops sometimes below 10 per cent of submitted applications.[37]

The consequences on the Israeli side are diametrically different. Having assumed full control of the physical planning process, Israeli authorities proceeded to formulate and implement massive regional plans which invariably entail grave consequences to the indigenous population.

A prominent example of planning abuse is manifest in the so-called Mateh Binyamin Regional Council Master Plan No. 200. The area

---

[35] For a detailed analysis of Israeli planning policies in the Occupied Territories, see M. Rishmawi, *Planning: In Whose Interest?* (Ramallah, 1986), and Ch. 8 in this book.
[36] Benvenisti, *1986 Report*, 33.
[37] Interview with the Chairman, West Bank Engineers' Syndicate.

encompassed by that plan is around one million dunums, of which only 24,000 dunums are under the control of the Jewish settlers living in the region, estimated in 1985 at 6,180 persons.[38] Notwithstanding the relatively very small number of resident Jewish settlers, the plan designates an area of 220,000 dunums, or almost one-quarter of the total land area, to satisfy their potential needs. On the other hand, no mention is made of the 95 Arab towns and villages in which lives nearly 96 per cent of the total population covered by the plan, except in relation to the need to expropriate land for 'public purposes'.[39]

V. Bilateral Trade

Immediately following occupation, local markets of the Occupied Territories were unconditionally opened to Israeli industrial and agricultural products. The flow of produce from the Territories to Israel, on the other hand, has been governed by stiff regulations, laid down in the light of Israel's own interests.

Industrial goods from the West Bank and Gaza Strip are in principle permitted entry to Israeli markets, subject to compliance with prescribed labelling and hygiene regulations. This rather relaxed stand can be explained by the fact that the vast majority of firms in key industries, such as cloth and shoe manufacturers, have flourished only by virtue of performing a subservient role to Israeli firms through inequitable subcontractual arrangements.[40] Furthermore, Israeli authorities still maintain effective control on the scale and magnitude of indigenous industrial development through other means, most noticeably through rigid licensing procedures.

Unlike industrial goods, the entry of Palestinian farm produce to Israel is possible only after obtaining special permits from relevant *Israeli* marketing boards. In an effort to safeguard their delicate price stabilization schemes, marketing boards use these permits to keep the entry of Palestinian produce to a minimum, and then only when needed to alleviate occasional shortages in local supply. Under no circumstances is this form of trade permitted to undermine the interests of Israeli growers.[41]

Inequitable bilateral terms of trade between Israel and the Occupied Territories have given rise to a typically colonial subjugation of their economy to that of Israel. The Territories procure 90 per cent of their

---

[38] Benvenisti, *1986 Report*, 34.
[39] Ibid. 34.
[40] UN Economic Commission for Western Asia, *Industrial and Economic Trends*.
[41] *Jerusalem Post*, 15 Feb. 1985.

imported goods from Israel.[42] The value of Israeli goods channelled in 1986 to the Occupied Territories, including East Jerusalem, amounted to $917 million, making the territories the second largest importer from Israel, after the United States. At a time when Israeli exporters have to face fierce competition in foreign markets and suffer a substantial trading deficit, Israel has managed to transform the West Bank and Gaza Strip into a backyard market with which it enjoys a steady and lucrative surplus, estimated for 1986 at $538 million.[43]

The consequences for the Palestinian side, on the other hand, have been disastrous. Competition with Israeli firms is extremely difficult, because Palestinian entrepreneurs are categorically denied all the lavish incentives accorded to Israeli firms. The reason for that, as explained by Israeli officials, is that Palestinian businessmen from the West Bank and Gaza are not Israeli citizens, and therefore they are not eligible for the same rights.[44] The adverse impact of this anomalous policy on local industries has been overwhelming, but it is especially disastrous for fledgling industries where Palestinians are incapable of fostering any form of protection for firms which are in severe need of it during the critical initial growth-stages. The emergence of pioneering industries is rendered more difficult by having to cope with rigid licensing problems, and by the total lack of institutional sources of credit.

The impact of differential terms of trade entails even more serious consequences for the indigenous economy of the Occupied Territories. Local producers are obliged to compete in their own market with Israeli producers who enjoy massive support, ranging from subsidized production inputs and credit facilities to generous price-stabilization schemes.[45] This has led to a drastic set-back for some major farming patterns. Local production of dairy and poultry products, for instance, amounted to 35 per cent of domestic consumption,[46] the rest being imported from Israel. In the few cases where Palestinian producers have succeeded in acquiring certain forms of comparative advantage (as with grapes, plums, and vegetable crops), local farmers are pre-

---

[42] Five years' average (1982–6), computed from the *Statistical Abstract of Israel 1987*, 711. Estimates include trade with East Jerusalem.

[43] Ibid. The figure includes a 15% increment to the figure reported in the *Statistical Abstract of Israel* to account for Israeli goods sold in East Jerusalem. This addition corresponds to the ratio of Jerusalem's Arab population to that of the West Bank and Gaza Strip.

[44] Interview with the Officer-in-Charge of Economics.

[45] Irrigation water, for instance, is sold by Mekorot to Israeli farmers at 23 Israeli *agorot* per cu.m., as against 50 *agorot* for Arab farmers. Direct subsidies on agricultural produce and irrigation water amounted in 1981 to $1.5 billion.

[46] Israel Central Bureau of Statistics, *Judea, Samaria and Gaza Area Statistics 1986* (3), 110, 112.

vented from sending their produce into Israel, except when that serves Israeli interests.

Inequitable terms of trade between Israel and the Occupied Territories impede genuine economic growth in those territories. The consequences of this odd connection include:

- the inhibition of the emergence of a vigorous local industrial base and the fostering of a subordinate form of integration of the local economy into that of Israel;
- the undermining of local employment potential, and consequently the initiation of a massive drain of workers to Israeli and external labour markets; and
- ultimately, all this has led to a severe set-back for certain farming patterns and to a tangible decline in the farming area, estimated for the West Bank at 21 per cent since the occupation began.[47]

VI. Export Trade

The economy of the West Bank and Gaza Strip depended heavily, prior to Israeli occupation, on a narrow range of exported goods which included, most importantly, citrus, vegetables, olive oil, samneh (margarine), and building stones. The small size of domestic markets (the combined population of both territories is just about 1.6 million), has rendered export trade indispensible, more so after the influx of Israeli produce to these markets. In essence, therefore, facilitating the export trade of Palestinians in the Occupied Territories can serve Palestinian interests, and indirectly those of Israeli producers, by reducing surpluses in local markets. But Israeli authorities seem to believe otherwise, as evidenced by the measures and policies which they promulgated in this connection, almost exclusively to Israel's unilateral interests. The following are examples of such measures:

1. Gaza citrus-growers have for a long time prior to occupation channelled most of their produce to Western European countries. Fearing that Gazan exporters may eventually compete with the Israeli Citrus Marketing Board, Palestinian firms were prevented direct access to those markets and were permitted only to maintain their links with the much less lucrative markets of Eastern Europe, where Israel had no vested interests. This has been one of the principal factors in the severe marketing crisis which afflicted Gaza's citrus industry and caused its steady decline. The area of citrus groves reportedly dropped

[47] H. Awartani, *The Economies of the West Bank and Gaza Strip* (Nablus, 1987).

by 27 per cent between 1979 and 1988, from 75,000 to 55,000 dunums.[48]

2. A similar situation has emerged over the past two years in relation to vegetables and fruits destined for export to countries of the European Community. Channelling part of the surplus produce to EC markets was viewed with great hope as an effective means for alleviating surplus problems, which to a large extent have been precipitated by the unrestricted inflow of Israeli produce to local markets.

Not surprisingly, Israeli authorities repeatedly encouraged Palestinian growers to identify new markets, especially as the latter faced increasing problems and restrictions in neighbouring traditional Arab markets. Prompted by soaring surpluses and encouraged by the initial Israeli stand, Deir el-Balah Co-operative in the Gaza Strip launched exploratory efforts which culminated in a firm trial order from a Norwegian client. But when the manager of the co-operative applied to Israeli authorities for the necessary export permit, his request was turned down. He was advised instead to refer the Norwegian client to Agrexco, the sole Israeli vegetable-exporting firm, on the basis that this firm was granted exclusive rights over Israel's vegetable exports.[49]

After enormous pressure from the European Community, Israel signed a memorandum agreeing to permit direct export from the Occupied Territories to the markets of member countries. Even then Israeli authorities incorporated vague conditions which would permit delay and obstruction. For instance, the agreement stipulates that exports will be permitted only 'after a plan is agreed upon with the Israeli Ministry of Agriculture' and only in the absence of 'special circumstances' which would prevent the issuance of required permits. Furthermore, 'security inspection will be co-ordinated with the security authorities according to established procedures'.[50] It is clear that such loose conditions offer Israel enough leeway to exercise full control over Palestinian farm exports to Europe or even to stall the process completely.

3. Restrictions on the number of lorries permitted to cross the bridges to Jordan to those which were in service prior to the occupation, all of which are by now over 20 years old, and imposition of exorbitant fees on traffic across the bridges have resulted in a sharp rise in transportation costs. Consequently, those measures have severely undermined the competitiveness of Palestinian exporters. A truckload of around 12 tons transported from Nablus to Amman may entail a total cost outlay of around $700, i.e. $58 per ton. Obviously, this results in a sharp drop in the viability of export trade to Jordan and

---

[48] *Export of Agricultural Produce from the West Bank and the Gaza Strip*, Report of the Netherlands Government Mission (1988), 11.

[49] Copies of this correspondence are in the author's possession.

[50] Netherlands Government Mission, *Export of Agricultural Produce*, Annexe 2.

neighbouring Arab markets, which is clearly evidenced by the pronounced and steady decline in the volume of Palestinian farm produce shipped to Jordan over the past few years.[51]

In addition to limiting the number of trucks permitted to shuttle across the bridges, the main reason for the excessively high trucking costs relate to the very high rates of fees imposed on traffic across the bridges, which amounted in February 1988 to a total of around $140 per trip, itemized as follows:[52]

	New Israeli Shekel	US$
Exit permit for owner of merchandise (per trip)	111	74
Permit for lorry driver (per month— a truck makes around 5 trips a month)	231	154
Inspection fee of truck on return (per trip)	30	20
Custom service fee (per trip)	21	14

Depending on the market value of transported goods, it is estimated that the cost of fees charged on a truckload destined to Amman adds up to 5-10 per cent of sale proceeds. This entails a heavy restrictive burden, which obviously contrasts sharply with the liberal incentives accorded to Israeli exporters. Furthermore, not only does the use of very old lorries for heavy duty on the narrow and steep roads connecting the West Bank with Amman result in a sharp rise in repair costs; it also poses serious traffic hazards to drivers and pedestrians.

4. Israeli authorities have instituted a wide range of measures which they claim to be imperative for security reasons,[53] but which entail damaging consequences on Palestinian foreign trade. Examples of such measures include the following:

- Palestinian businessmen (except those in East Jerusalem) are not permitted to install their own telecommunication facilities, hence they are obliged to use facilities owned by Israeli firms in neighbouring cities or those present in East Jerusalem. Soliciting telecommunication services through other intermediaries entails undue delay and extra costs, and may cause communication leaks.
- Goods imported directly by Palestinian businessmen are subject to elaborate inspection measures which require a much longer time

---

[51] According to official Jordanian data from the Ministry of Agriculture in Amman, the total quantity of fruits and vegetables procured from the Occupied Territories dropped from 225,000 tons in 1984 to 164,000 in 1986.
[52] Derived from instructions issued to post offices.
[53] On use of security to justify Israeli actions in the Occupied Territories, see Ch. 6.

and a higher cost in comparison with goods imported by Israelis. In practice, as a result, most Palestinian firms find it cheaper and more expedient to procure their imported goods via Israeli middle firms.
- Wooden boxes used in sending farm produce to Jordan are not permitted re-entry to the Occupied Territories, presumably for security reasons. This measure results in a sharp increase in marketing expenses, which further reduces the competitive position of Palestinian growers in their major export markets.

Conclusions

The foregoing exposition demonstrates that Israel's occupation of the West Bank and Gaza Strip has entailed an exploitative net of relations, structured to benefit a wide range of Israel's economic and political interests, but often at the cost of the national aspiration of the indigenous Palestinian population. In the course of implementing Israeli economic policies in the Occupied Territories, the occupying power has regularly encountered situations where Israeli interests have to be weighed against those of the indigenous population. By inequitable weighing of interests and abuse of an occupier's wide authority, the Israeli occupying power has succeeded in 'freezing the economic development of the Palestinian (economic) sector' and 'discouraging independent economic development that would enter into competition with the Israeli economy', and has 'create[d] greater dependence on Israel'.[54]

The potential impact of Israel's economic policies in the Occupied Territories is immensely grave, and bears on the national aspirations of the Palestinians no less seriously than on their economy. The anomalous relationship referred to at the start of this paper, whereby Israel is its own negotiating partner in the formation of linkages and the development of comparative strengths and weaknesses between its own state and that of the territories it occupies, inevitably leads to injustice. International law regulating relations between the occupier and the occupied has not been able to prevent this situation, nor provided any protection for the economy of the occupied land to ensure its independence from that of the occupier.

It is imperative that every effort be exerted to restructure bilateral economic relations between Israel and the Occupied Territories on more respectful and equitable grounds. By so doing we may succeed

---

[54] M. Benvenisti et al., *The West Bank Handbook: A Political Lexicon* (Jerusalem, 1986), 67.

in paving the way for other courageous steps along the course to a just peace. In the light of the long history of mistrust and unilateral dominance, the writer suggests that bilateral economic relations between the Occupied Territories and Israel be restructured under the aegis of a specialized and neutral third party.

14

Powers and Duties of an Occupant in Relation to Land and Natural Resources

ANTONIO CASSESE

Introduction

BEFORE considering the subject of this chapter, it may prove useful briefly to touch on a preliminary issue: what legal rules govern a military occupation such as that of Israel over the Arab territories invaded in 1967?

It has been contended by a distinguished scholar,[1] and was also suggested in an official Israeli document,[2] that the long duration of that occupation makes it quite unique; as a consequence, not all the legal constraints concerning 'normal' belligerent occupation could apply in the case of the Israeli 'administration' of the Arab territories.

This view has already been authoritatively criticized by von Glahn.[3] I see two basic objections to it. First, it fails to specify which of the customary and conventional rules on belligerent occupation should be set aside, and which should continue to apply to the Israeli occupation. It is plain that in a matter so delicate and controversial as the one with which we are here concerned, one cannot rest content with vague and loose suggestions.

Second, it is true that the existing body of law proceeds from the assumption that belligerent occupation is, or should be, of short duration. But in order to establish whether instances of prolonged occupation are governed by different rules from the traditional ones, one should inquire into whether new rules have evolved through the traditional law-making processes of international law: custom and treaty. Can we argue that *new rules* of customary or treaty law have recently emerged for the specific purpose of regulating prolonged

---

[1] Y. Z. Blum, quoted in S. V. Mallison and W. T. Mallison Jr., *The Palestine Problem in International Law and World Order* (Harlow, 1986), 260.
[2] Memorandum of Law, in *ILM* 17 (1978), 432–3.
[3] See Ch. 11 in this volume, and also Chs. 1 and 7.

military occupations? As is apparent from the attitude of all states *vis-à-vis* the Israeli occupation of the Arab territories, states have consistently taken the view that customary law as embodied in the 1907 Hague Regulations, as well as the Fourth Geneva Convention of 1949, apply to that situation. Attempts by Israel to propound the idea that her occupation does not fit into those rules have been firmly and consistently rejected by states as well as by the United Nations. In these circumstances it was impossible for new customary rules to evolve in the matter: unilateral statements by one state are not sufficient to form a customary rule.

It follows that, however unique and new its features may be, the Israeli occupation remains subject to the body of law to which I have just made reference. On the other hand, I shall show, in Part III, that it is possible to make allowance for the novelty of the Israeli occupation, without departing from the legal framework offered by traditional international law. This 'adjustment', as I shall show, can be made on the strength of an 'evolutive' interpretation of the existing rules. (By an 'evolutive' interpretation I mean a dynamic one, which takes account of the changing context in which the rules operate).

I. General Principles Governing Belligerent Occupation

Before examining the legal principles governing the use of natural resources in occupied territories, it is fitting to point to the general context in which they must be viewed, that is, the general principles governing belligerent occupation. The latter principles ought always to be borne in mind when considering specific problems. In many instances they may prove of great help in reaching the right solution.

Belligerent occupation, as is well known, is based on four fundamental principles. First, the occupant does not acquire any sovereignty over the territory; it merely exercises *de facto* authority. Second, occupation is by definition a provisional situation. The rights of the occupant over the territory are merely transitory and are accompanied by an overriding obligation to respect the existing laws and rules of administration. Third, in exercising its powers, the occupant must comply with two basic requirements or parameters: fulfilment of its military needs, and respect for the interests of the inhabitants. International rules strike a careful balance between these two (often conflicting) requirements: while military necessities in some instances may gain the upper hand, they should never result in total disregard for the interests and needs of the population. Fourth, the occupying Power must not exercise its authority in order to further its own interests, or to meet the needs of its own population. In no case can it exploit the inhabitants, the resources or other assets of the territory under its control for the benefit of its own territory or population. Linked with this is the principle that the occupying Power cannot force the occupied territory—both its inhabitants and its resources—to contribute to, or in any way assist, the occupant's war effort against the displaced government and its allies.

II. Principles Governing the Use of Land and Other Natural Resources in Occupied Territories

Customary rules governing the powers and duties of the occupant in the field of economic activities are fairly simple. The occupant must respect *private property*. Thus, Article 46(2) of the Hague Regulations provides that 'private property may not be confiscated'. This is, however, subject to Article 53(2), whereby all kinds of privately-owned war materials may be seized, 'but must be restored at the conclusion of peace, and indemnities must be paid for them'. Private property may only be requisitioned 'for the needs of the army of occupation', upon payment in cash or the provision of a receipt, with payment as soon as possible (Article 52). Alternatively, private property may be expropriated in the public interest of the whole of the inhabitants of the occupied territory (ex. Article 46). The property of local authorities, as well as that of institutions dedicated to public worship, charity, education, science, and art, is assimilated to private property (Article 56(1)). As for *public property*, that is, assets belonging to the state, the occupant can seize movables 'which may be used for military purposes' (Article 53), whereas it can only use immovables as 'administrator and usufructuary' (Article 55: it can benefit from the use of these assets, but 'must safeguard the capital').

Two general remarks are called for. First, as has been noted by a few authorities,[4] and also stressed by the Supreme Court of Israel in a judgment in 1984,[5] this legal regulation reflects the approach to economic organization prevailing in the nineteenth century. Private property was sacred. As was pointed out in 1921 by the US Arbitrator W. D. Hines in the *Cession of vessels and tugs for navigation on the Danube* case: '[T]he purpose of the immunity of private property from confiscation is to avoid throwing the burdens of war upon private individuals, and is, instead, to place those burdens upon the States

---

[4] E. Feilchenfeld, *The International Economic Law of Belligerent Occupation* (Washington DC, 1942), 87; J. Stone, *Legal Controls of International Conflict* (New York, 1959), 729.

[5] HC 393/82, *A Teachers' Housing Cooperative Society v. The Military Commander of the Judea and Samaria Region et al.*, excerpted in *IYHR* 14 (1984), 301, esp. 306–7.

which are the belligerents.[6] On the other hand, since, in that period, state involvement in economic activity was still limited, no account was taken of possible forms of state intervention in the economic sphere (which have become so widespread and multifarious this century).

My second remark relates to the limits within which the occupying Power can exercise the rights and fulfil the duties deriving from customary law. In my view it follows from the provisions of the Hague Regulations referred to above that the occupant can interfere in the economic activity of the territory under its control (by requisitioning private property, seizing public movables, or using state-owned immovables) only for the following purposes: (*a*) to meet its own military or security needs (i.e. the exigencies posed by the conduct of its military operations in the occupied territory); (*b*) to defray the expenses involved in the belligerent occupation; (*c*) to protect the interests and the well-being of the inhabitants.

These are indeed very strict limitations upon the powers of the occupant. Any interference with enemy private or state-owned property must be effected for one of these purposes. It is strictly forbidden for the occupant to resort to one of the aforementioned measures for other purposes, e.g. with a view to drawing economic benefits for himself (that is, for his inhabitants, or for the national economy, etc.).

The above view is borne out by recent state practice, which tends to uphold a *strict* approach to the rights of belligerent occupants. The opposition of the British Government to the projected building by Israel of a canal between the Mediterranean and the Dead Sea illustrates this kind of approach and provides support for a number of the limitations noted above. On 18 November 1981, replying in writing to a question in the House of Commons, the British Minister of State, Foreign and Commonwealth Office, stated that:

[T]he project as planned is contrary to international law, as it involves unlawful works in occupied territory and infringes Jordan's legal rights in the Dead Sea and neighbouring regions. No official support will be given by Her Majesty's Government in respect of the project.[7]

On 4 December 1981, in the UN General Assembly, the British representative, speaking also on behalf of the European Community, restated the opposition to the Israeli project, because, among other things,

the plan as announced by the Israeli Government would involve construction work across the Gaza Strip. The Ten consider that under general international law, and with reference to the Fourth Geneva Convention, *such construction and*

---

[6] *UN Reports of International Arbitral Awards*, 1, 107.
[7] See *BYIL* (1981), 515.

alteration of property would exceed Israel's right as an occupying power. Under international law an occupant exercises only a temporary right of administration in respect of territory occupied by it. *The proposed canal can in no way be considered an act of mere administration*. In addition, the Ten believe that the project as planned could serve to prejudice the future of Gaza which should be determined as part of a general peace settlement. In the circumstances the Ten wish to reiterate their opposition to the project.[8]

The canal project has, in the event, been scrapped, but the statement nevertheless shows that the (then) ten member states of the European Community adhered to the general concept that alterations to property carried out by an occupant in the territory under his control (1) must not have permanent effects and (2) must not be undertaken to the detriment of the displaced government or, at any rate, the local population.

III. Should Traditional Customary Law on Belligerent Occupation be Construed in Light of Present Circumstances (the so-called 'Evolutive Interpretation')?

I now wish to raise a general question, which has some impact on the specific issues addressed in this paper. I mentioned before that the Hague Regulations were drafted in a period when state intervention in the economy was minimal, whereas private property was regarded as sacred. In addition, those rules were conceived on the assumption that the belligerent occupation of foreign territories should be of short duration. It is obvious that things have greatly changed since then. State authorities have become more and more 'interventionist' in the realm of the economy; at present it is often hard to distinguish in many countries between the 'private' and 'public' sector of the economy. In addition, the financial requirements of modern occupants have increased at a staggering pace, on account of the growing demands of modern armies. This became particularly apparent during World War II. On top of all this, one may mention that one of the most conspicuous instances of modern belligerent occupation is the prolonged occupation begun by Israel in 1967.

The question therefore arises whether one should interpret the body of traditional customary rules on occupation in the light of the present circumstances surrounding belligerent occupation. This sort of interpretation has been upheld by the Supreme Court of Israel in at least two cases.[9] In the first, Judge Shamgar stated that the scope of an

---

[8] Ibid. 516 (emphasis added).
[9] Case HC 69/81, *Abu Aita et al. v. The Military Commander of the Judea and Samaria Region*, excerpted in *IYHR* 13 (1983), 348; HC 393/82, *A Teachers' Housing Cooperative Society v. The Military Commander of the Judea and Samaria Region et al.*, *IYHR* 14 (1984), 301.

occupant's authority is influenced by the time factor; hence, a prolonged occupation cannot be totally governed by rules envisaging an occupation of short duration. In the second case, Judge Barak ruled that the High Court, though bound to apply the Hague Regulations, ought to consider the tasks and duties of an occupant according to the prevailing norms present among civilized countries. As he put it with reference to a specific customary rule:

[T]he concrete content that we shall give to Article 43 of the Hague Regulations in regard to the occupant's duty to ensure public life and order will not be that of public life and order in the nineteenth century, but that of a modern and civilized State at the end of the twentieth century.[10]

The same judge stated that one should also make allowance for the duration of the belligerent occupation. According to him, although the Hague Regulations were adopted against the background of a short duration occupation,

nothing prevents the development—within their framework—of rules defining the scope of a military government's authority in cases of prolonged occupation.

He drew the following specific conclusion:

Long-term fundamental investments [made by the occupant] in an occupied area [in the course of a prolonged occupation] bringing about permanent changes that may last beyond the period of the military administration are permitted if required for the benefit of the local population—provided there is nothing in these investments that might introduce an essential modification in the basic institutions of the area.[11]

I submit that both the 'evolutive' interpretation advocated by the Supreme Court of Israel, and the practical inference the Court drew from that interpretation, are correct. The following considerations are intended to support and expand them.

That in certain instances international rules should be interpreted so as to take account of current circumstances, has been pointed out by the International Court of Justice, in the advisory opinion delivered in 1971 on *Legal Consequences for States of the Continued Presence of South Africa in Namibia (South West Africa)*. The Court held that: '[A]n international instrument has to be interpreted and applied within the framework of the entire legal system prevailing at the time of the interpretation.'[12] The Court inferred from that, that the concept of 'sacred trust' embodied in Article 22 of the Covenant on the League

---

[10] Ibid. 307.
[11] Ibid. 310.
[12] ICJ *Reports* (1971), 31–2 (para. 53).

of Nations (1919) was to be interpreted in the light of the current situation. As the Court put it:

[V]iewing the institutions of 1919, the Court must take into consideration the changes which have occurred in the supervening half-century, and its interpretation cannot remain unaffected by the subsequent development of law, through the Charter of the United Nations and by way of customary law.[13]

This principle of interpretation entails for our purposes that the relevant international rules (the Hague Regulations) can be somewhat 'adjusted' both to the present legal system and to current political and historical realities. This process of 'adjustment' should not, however, result in thwarting the underlying objectives of the rules at issue. It should rather aim at applying the rules in a flexible way, adapting their scope and purpose to the new general context in which they now operate. Two consequences follow. First, the Hague Regulations should be viewed in the light of developments in international law since 1907 (and particularly since the adoption of the UN Charter). Second, they should be so construed in the light of factual developments since 1907, particularly cases of prolonged occupation.

From the first vantage point, it is appropriate to mention an argument advanced by the US State Department in the legal memorandum concerning the alleged right of Israel to develop new oilfields in Sinai and the Gulf of Suez. One may recall that it was stated there that the Hague Regulations should be taken to mean that the occupant can use the economic resources of the enemy state, in particular state-owned immovables, within the limits of what is required for the army of occupation and the needs of the local population. The legal memorandum goes on to state that:

[T]hese limitations are entirely consistent with, if not compelled by, the limited purposes for which force may be used under the UN Charter. It is difficult to justify a rule that the use of force in self-defence may, during any resulting occupation, give the occupant rights against the enemy sovereign not related to the original self-defence requirement, or not required as concomitants of the occupation itself and the occupant's duties. A rule holding out the prospect of acquiring unrestricted access to the use of resources and raw materials, would constitute an incentive to territorial occupation by a country needing raw materials, and a disincentive to withdrawal.[14]

It is submitted that this view is illustrative of the right way to interpret the Hague Regulations in the light of the general legal principles currently prevailing in the world community.

Aside from the prohibition on the use of force except in self-defence

---

[13] Ibid.
[14] Memorandum of Law, *ILM* 16 (1977), 745–6.

referred to in the above-mentioned US legal memorandum, another recent legal development which has an important impact on the interpretation of the Hague Regulations (and particularly those provisions relating to state-owned immovable property) is the notion of 'permanent sovereignty over natural resources'.

This principle, which has been established by, *inter alia*, a series of resolutions of the United Nations,[15] as well as by the International Covenants on Human Rights adopted in 1966,[16] recognizes the universal right fully and freely to use and exploit the natural wealth and resources of one's own territory for one's own ends. This is seen as both an 'inalienable right of all States'[17] (that is, an aspect of state sovereignty), and, at the same time, an 'inherent right of all peoples'[18] (that is, an aspect of the right of peoples to self-determination).

In the context of belligerent occupation, this, of course, tends to support a restrictive interpretation of the occupant's powers to exploit and dispose of immovable property. Even if the occupant has reservations about the 'statehood' of its enemy, this principle should serve to restrain the occupant from exploiting resources in contravention of the rights of an alien people in occupied territory.

Customary rules should also be construed so as to take account of new practical developments. The long duration of the Israeli occupation is a fact that cannot but impinge upon the relevant rules. But what is its precise impact on those legal rules? To my mind, the right approach was suggested by Dinstein[19] and the Israeli Supreme Court[20] when they stated that the prolongation of military occupation makes it increasingly necessary to take into consideration the social and economic needs of the local population. Indeed, as a result of a drawn-out occupation, the provisional nature of the administration by

---

[15] See, *inter alia*, GA Res. 626 (VII) of 21 Dec. 1952, Res. 1803 (XVII) of 14 Dec. 1962 (the so-called 'landmark resolution' on permanent sovereignty over natural resources), Res. 2994 (XXVII) of 15 Dec. 1972 (noting with satisfaction the Report of the UN Conference on the Human Environment, Stockholm, 5–16 July 1972, UN Doc. A/CONF.48/14; see esp. Princ. 21), Res. 3171 (XXVIII) of 17 Dec. 1973, Res. 3021 (S–VI) of 1 May 1974 ('Declaration on the Establishment of a New International Economic Order'; see esp. para. 4(e)), Res. 3281 (XXIX) of 12 December 1974 ('Charter of Economic Rights and Duties of States'; see esp. Art. 2). See also SC Res. 330 (1973) of 21 Mar. 1973.

[16] See common Art. 1(2) of the International Covenant on Economic, Social, and Cultural Rights (ICESCR) and the International Covenant on Civil and Political Rights (ICCPR), adopted by the UNGA on 16 Dec. 1966. See also Art. 25 of the first-mentioned Covenant.

[17] GA Res. 1803 (XVII) of 14 Dec. 1962 (preamble).

[18] ICESCR, Art. 25.

[19] Y. Dinstein, quoted in *IYHR* 14 (1984), 307, and also his article, 'The International Law of Belligerent Occupation and Human Rights', *IYHR* 8 (1978), 112.

[20] See HC 337/71 The *Christian Society for the Holy Places* case, ibid. 112, and HC 393/82, *Teachers' Housing Cooperative Society* case, *IYHR* 14 (1984), 307–9; and see also discussion of both cases in Ch. 2 in this volume, and in Chs. 1 and 6.

a military authority tends to fade away, and the occupying force tends to turn into a fully-fledged administrative entity, without there being any of the safeguards of ordinary government (political representation, etc.). Consequently, to avoid frustrating the purpose and the spirit of the Hague Regulations, one should give pride of place to those limitations upon the powers of the occupant that are explicitly or implicitly set out in the Hague Regulations. The strengthening of these limitations is the only safeguard against the turning of the occupant (a transitory military administration) into a political and administrative government in disguise.

It is suggested that the view propounded by Dinstein and the Israeli Supreme Court should be upheld and should be applied to, *inter alia*, uses by the occupant of enemy state-owned movables or immovables. The use of locally-owned property during a prolonged occupation is obviously particularly susceptible of producing permanent—and potentially detrimental—effects.

IV. The Occupant's Use of Enemy State-owned Immovable Property

The general proposition stated in Part II above, concerning the limited purpose for which the occupant is allowed to use the resources of the territory under his control, is based on the text of a number of provisions of the Hague Regulations, including those relating to the levying of taxes and other 'money contributions' (which, under Article 49, can only be done for 'the needs of the army or of the administration of the territory') and those relating to requisitions in kind, services and contributions (which, under Article 52(1), can be demanded from local authorities or inhabitants only 'for the needs of the army of occupation').

That proposition also follows from the provisions relating to movable property belonging to the enemy state, although it must be acknowledged that the matter is not without controversy. A number of learned commentators (including Dinstein[21]) take the view that the expression 'which may be used for military operations' in Article 53(1), refers to all goods susceptible of military use; the actual use to which the occupant puts them is seen as immaterial and may be non-military. To put it differently, according to those commentators the proviso '[movable property] which may be used for military operations' is only intended to identify the class of property of which the occupying army can take possession (the army is allowed to seize only property susceptible of use for military operations). The expression at issue is not intended—

---

[21] Dinstein, 'The International Law of Belligerent Occupation', 131.

so they argue—to demand that the occupant should actually use that property solely for military operations. However, reading Article 53 in the context of the other provisions to which reference has already been made, it seems clear to me that such *potential* military use is not sufficient to justify a taking under that Article.

The principal provision relating to the power of the occupant to exploit the resources of the occupied territory is Article 55 (concerning 'immovable property belonging to the hostile State'). This contains no such explicit reference to purpose. Should one infer from this omission that, acting as the 'usufructuary' of those assets, the occupant is allowed to use the fruits of all state-owned immovable property *for any purpose whatsoever*, provided only that it does not want only to dissipate them? In particular, should one infer that the occupant is allowed to sell those 'fruits' with a view to boosting the home economy, or even to transfer them to the national territory of the occupying state? This is precisely the view taken by a few distinguished scholars (von Glahn, McDougal and Feliciano, Gerson, Dinstein)[22] as well as by the Israeli authorities.[23] Other scholars (for example, Oppenheim–Lauterpacht and Greenspan) merely state[24] that the produce of public immovables belonging to the enemy state may be appropriated by the occupant, without adding any restriction as to purpose. However, the fact that those authors point out that the occupant, being only a 'usufructuary', 'is prohibited from exercising his right in a wasteful or negligent way so as to decrease the value of the stock and plant'[25] indicates that, in their view, no other restriction is imposed on the use of the 'fruits' of the immovables at issue.

This view is clearly based on a *textual* or *literal* interpretation of Article 55. Admittedly, such an interpretation may have been appropriate at the time the Hague Regulations were drafted, in spite of what today can turn out to be an inconsistency with other provisions of the same Regulations. Indeed, the textual or literal interpretation of Article 55 can appear illogical if one considers that this interpretation leads to *greater* limitations being imposed on the use of that class of property (movables) which the occupant can go as far as to appropriate, than are imposed on the use of that class of property (immovables) which the occupant can only administer as 'usufructuary'. Why demand

---

[22] G. Von Glahn, *The Occupation of Enemy Territory* (Minneapolis, 1957), 177; M. McDougal and F. P. Feliciano, *Law and Minimum World Public Order* (New Haven, Conn., 1961), 812–13; A. Gerson, 'Off-shore Oil Exploration by a Belligerent Occupant—the Gulf of Suez Dispute', *AJIL* 71 (1977), 730–1; Dinstein, 'The International Law of Belligerent Occupation', 129–30.

[23] Memorandum of Law, in *ILM* 17 (1978), 432–3.

[24] L. Oppenheim, *International Law: A Treatise*, ii: *Disputes, War and Neutrality*, ed. H. Lauterpacht, 398; M. Greenspan, *The Modern Law of Land Warfare* (Berkeley, 1959), 288.

[25] Oppenheim, *International Law*, 398.

that a certain use be made of assets of which the occupant can take possession, while leaving that occupant free to do whatever he pleases with respect to property over which he holds only limited rights? This illogicality probably stems from the historical origin of the provisions at issue. It should be borne in mind that, when the provision under consideration was drafted (and indeed Article 55 takes up Article 7 of the Brussels Declaration of 1874), immovable property owned by states was of limited relevance compared to state-owned movables; in particular, state-owned factories were almost non-existent. In short, at that stage seizure of movables was far more important than the exercise of rights of use over state-owned immovables. If that was so, the fact that those limitations upon the occupant concern only the more important category can be easily understood.

Today, however, the illogicality is glaring. This was graphically shown, of late, with reference to a specific case. In the US legal memorandum referred to above, it was pointed out, that

certainly there would be no basis for arguing that an occupant had greater freedom regarding the use or disposition of oil found in the ground (public immovable property) than of oil he found already lifted (public movable property).[26]

This reasoning is compelling: would it make sense to claim that the same resource (oil) could in one case be sold or used only for the military operations of the occupant, while in the other case it could be sold for any purpose, including that of enriching the occupant's home economy?

While a distinction between the two classes of property would be illogical from the particular vantage point we are discussing, resort to *systematic interpretation* and the consequent extension to immovable property of the same restrictions required for state-owned movables render the whole legal regulation of this matter fully coherent. The occupant cannot appropriate immovables belonging to the enemy state, for to do so would run counter to the provisional nature of belligerent occupation. It can, however, enjoy their fruits to the extent that this is made permissible by other provisions concerning the exploitation of enemy natural resources by the occupant.

As indicated above (Part III), the textual interpretation of Article 55 has, in any event, been overtaken by a number of very significant legal and factual developments. These developments call for a new 'evolutive' interpretation that limits an occupant's rights to exploit and dispose of the resources of the occupied territory.

In addition to the developments already referred to in Part III,

---

[26] Memorandum of Law, *ILM* 16 (1977), 742.

mention should be made, in this regard, of a series of cases that point in what I consider to be the correct direction. I shall first of all refer to the judgment delivered in 1947 by the International Military Tribunal at Nuremberg in the case *Goering et al*. The Tribunal, after quoting Articles 49 and 52 of the Hague Regulations, stated that:

[T]hese articles, together with Article 48, dealing with the expenditure of money collected in taxes, and Articles 53, 55, and 56 dealing with public property, make it clear that under the rules of war, the economy of an occupied country can only be required to bear *the expenses of the occupation*, and these should not be greater than the economy of the country can reasonably be expected to bear.[27]

A similar view was taken in 1948 by the US Military Tribunal at Nuremberg, in the *Flick*, *Krupp*, and *Krauch* cases.[28] The same view was also taken in 1956 by the Court of Appeal of Singapore in the famous *N.V. De Bataafsche Petroleum Maatschappij v. The War Damage Commission* case.[29] Equally, the US and the British manuals on the law of land warfare, as well as the aforementioned legal memorandum of the US State Department, submitted in 1976,[30] contain the same overriding requirement.

This authoritative body of legal opinion, which should be taken to reflect the right interpretation of Article 55, is corroborated by legal authors. In this connection reference may be made to the resolution adopted in London on 12 July 1943 by the International Law Conference[31] (a resolution that, according to von Glahn, 'can be said to represent the latest word on the problem, comprising as it did the considered opinion of outstanding jurists'),[32] and to the views of such authorities as Capotorti, Balladore Pallieri, and Stone.[33]

V. Applicability of the Previous Considerations to Land, Water, and Oil

The comments so far enunciated apply in particular to such natural resources as land, water, or oil.

---

[27] *Trial of the Major War Criminals Before the International Military Tribunal*, 1 (1947), 238–9 (emphasis added).

[28] These cases are quoted in the case mentioned in the following note.

[29] Text in *AJIL* 51 (1957), 808.

[30] See US Dept. of the Army, *Field Manual FM 27–10, The Law of Land Warfare* (Washington, 1956), para. 364, and UK War Office, *Manual of Military Law*, iii: *The Law of War on Land*, para. 526, as well as the US Memorandum of Law, *ILM* 16 (1977), 742–6.

[31] Text reproduced in von Glahn, *Occupation*, 194–6 (the relevant passage is para. 3, at 194).

[32] Ibid. 194.

[33] F. Capotorti, *L'occupazione nel diritto di guerra* (Naples, 1949), 118–19, 126–7, and 166–7; G. Balladore-Pallieri, *Diritto bellico* (Padua, 1954), 325–32; and *Diritto internazionale pubblico* (Padua, 1962), 662–5; Stone, *Legal Controls of International Conflict*, 697.

In the next section I shall consider in some detail some problems that arise concerning land. At this juncture, I shall confine myself to the following remark. The prohibition on using land belonging to the occupied state or to its inhabitants for purposes other than those referred to above (military needs of the occupant, etc.), is strengthened by Article 49(6) of the Fourth Geneva Convention of 1949, which provides that 'the Occupying Power shall not deport or transfer parts of its civilian population into the territory it occupies'. This provision is but the logical corollary of the requirement of customary international law whereby the occupant is not allowed to use the property of the occupied country, or of its inhabitants, for the furtherance of its own economic or other interests. Plainly, the transfer of civilians from the occupying state into the occupied territory cannot but serve economic, social, or 'strategic' needs of the occupying state as such. To this extent it is strictly prohibited.

Similar principles to those applying to land apply also to water. Water sources (rivers, wells, other natural springs) constitute assets that can be either private or public depending on the legal classification made in each particular state. In any case, water usable for drinking or irrigation purposes should be regarded as immovable property, like all 'appurtenances to real estate'. This seems to be the better view, and it is confirmed by the provisions of the civil code of a number of countries.[34] Reliance on these codes is warranted in view of the fact that the Hague Regulations are largely based on Roman law concepts ('usufruct', Article 55; 'movable property', Article 53; 'landed property'—'immeubles' in the original French—Article 54) and it is common knowledge that these concepts, in turn, have been taken up in many civil law countries.

A different view might be reached if one were to apply to water, by analogy, what has been stated by a distinguished scholar[35] with reference to oil: that unlike coal, which 'must be literally extracted from rock, namely carved out of it', oil 'is in a liquid state within a natural pocket underground, and drilling from it merely means that it is made possible for the oil to gush—or to be drawn up—on to the ground'. Whatever the value of these considerations concerning oil, the better view, as stated above, is that water is to be regarded as immovable property.

In the case of state-owned water, the occupant has therefore the legal position of a 'usufructuary': it has the right to use the fruits of the property without any right of ownership (including the right of disposal). The exercise of this right of use is, however, clearly restricted

[34] See e.g. Art. 812 of the Italian Civil Code, Art. 2119 of the French Civil Code; Art, 526 of the Belgian Civil Code.
[35] Dinstein, 'The International Law of Belligerent Occupation and Human Rights', 130.

in that it can only serve the military needs of the occupying army, or the needs of the population. It follows that the occupant is not allowed to use water to promote its own economy or to pump it into the home country.

Mention should now be made of the particular problem of the use of water in the Arab territories occupied by Israel. According to a reliable document on water resources in the West Bank and Gaza, a large part of the West Bank's water resources is utilized by the Israeli settlements:

The Israeli settlements of the Jordan Valley and North Dead Sea utilize over 30,646 million cu.m. Most of this water is pumped from boreholes. The total demand for water by the Arab villages of the valley is 44 million cu.m. (1983 consumption levels). In the region, the consumption of water for the irrigation of one dunam measures 1,342 million cu.m. in the Israeli settlements and 712 million cu.m. in the Arab villages. These figures reveal the contrasting levels of intensity of water use.[36]

I have pointed out above that the numerous civilian settlements established by Israel in the West Bank are illegal, for they are not intended to meet the military needs of the occupant but are designed to expand the economic and political penetration of Israel in the occupied territories. Consequently, the use by these settlements of a large quantity of the (limited) water resources available in the West Bank and the Gaza Strip cannot but confirm and accentuate the unlawful character of those settlements.

Similar considerations also apply to state-owned oil in the occupied territory. If oil is regarded as movable (the view taken by such scholars as Dinstein),[37] then it is obviously bound by the restrictions laid down in Article 53(1), and it can only be used for the purposes of the military operations of the occupying army. However, even if the better view is taken that at least oil in the ground should be regarded as immovable, the same limitations apply, for the reasons set forth above (Part IV). Consequently, use of oil by the occupant for the general benefit of its own economy, or its sale for commercial or military use, is prohibited.[38]

---

[36] D. Kahan, *Agriculture and Water Resources in the West Bank and Gaza (1967–1987)*, (Jerusalem, 1987), 113. See generally pages 110–14. See also Ch. 15 in this book.

[37] Dinstein, 'The International Law of Belligerent Occupation and Human Rights' 130.

[38] On the question of oil, in addition to the memoranda of law of the US and Israel quoted before, see Gerson, 'Off-shore Oil Exploration by a Belligerent Occupant', and B. M. Claggett and O. T. Johnson Jr., 'May Israel as a Belligerent Occupant Lawfully Exploit Previously Unexploited Oil Resources of the Gulf of Suez?', *AJIL* 72 (1978), 558 ff.; J. J. Paust, 'Oil Exploitation in Occupied Territory: Sharpening the Focus of Appropriate Legal Standards', *Houston Jnl. of Int. Law* 1 (1979), 147 ff.; and *Procs. of the ASIL* (1978), 118–42.

VI. Case-Law on the Use of Land in the Occupied Arab Territories

I propose at this point to make some observations about a number of decisions of the Israeli Supreme Court relating to the use of land in the West Bank. The reason why I shall concentrate on decisions concerning land use is that, to my knowledge, the Supreme Court has not, so far, dealt with other natural resources in the Occupied Territories. I am not familiar with all the recent jurisprudence of the Israeli Supreme Court and certainly do not propose any complete survey of its judgments on this matter. Rather, I shall confine myself to first drawing attention to some important features of the Court's pronouncements, and then raising doubts about some other points made in those pronouncements.

The Importance of the Supreme Court's Judicial Review

The Court's judicial review of decisions of the military authorities in the West Bank and Gaza deserves to be praised in many respects. I shall begin by briefly underscoring some points of general interest, although they do not relate directly to the subject of this paper.

First, the Court has rightly upheld its power of judicial review over official measures taken with respect to the Occupied Territories, '[T]he ground for this review being that the Military Commander [in the Occupied Territories] and his subordinates are public officials exercising public functions by virtue of law.'[39] Clearly, resort to judicial safeguards against abuses by the occupant should be regarded as an important step taken in the interests of the inhabitants of the Occupied Territories.

Second, the Court has consistently stated (contrary to the position of the Israeli political and military authorities) that the occupation of the Arab territories is a *belligerent occupation* governed by the Hague Regulations (which are seen to reflect customary international law) and by the Fourth Geneva Convention of 1949 (to which Israel and the relevant Arab States are parties). Admittedly, on a number of occasions the Court has ruled that the Geneva Convention cannot be relied upon by individual petitioners.[40] This, however, appears to be due to the particular legal system of Israel, where international treaties for which

---

[39] See the various cases quoted in *IYHR* 14 (1984), 312.
[40] See, for instance, case HC 500/72, *Abu el-Tin v. Minister of Defence et al.*, excerpted in *IYHR* 5 (1975), 376; HCJ 606/78 and 610/78, the *Beit El* case, jointly reproduced in Mallison and Mallison, *The Palestine Problem*, 371, at 388; HC 390/79, the *Elon Moreh* case, *PYIL* 1 (1984), 134 at 156, and excerpted in *IYHR* 9 (1979), 345; and HC 629/82, *Mustafa et al. v. The Military Commander of the Judea and Samaria Region*, excerpted in *IYHR* 14 (1984), 313 at 315. See also Ch. 2 in this volume.

no implementing legislation has been passed are not incorporated into national law and cannot therefore be invoked or relied upon by individuals before domestic courts. While, of course, disregard for this treaty amounts to an international wrong *vis-à-vis* the other contracting states, the failure of the Court to apply the Convention cannot *per se* be regarded as an international wrong—contrary to what has been recently stated.[41] And at any rate one should not downplay the importance of the ruling by the Court that,

> ... towards the international community of States, an Occupying State in an occupied territory must observe and apply both the rules of customary international law and the rules embodied in international conventions to which it is a party.[42]

I shall now move on to my third remark, which, like following ones, has a more direct connection with the subject of this paper. The Court must be commended for having rightly stressed the *restrictions* imposed by international law on the occupant: *dicta* appear in two judgments, observing that

> the Military Commander [of the Israeli forces in the Arab territories] is not allowed to consider any national economic or social interests of his own State; not even national security interests, but only his own military needs and those of the local population.[43]

The Court has also pointed out that an occupied territory is not an 'open field for economic or other exploitation' and has consequently held that, for example, it is forbidden for a military administration to impose taxes on the inhabitants of an occupied territory in order to fill the coffers of the occupying State.[44] It would seem that this interpretation supports the construction of Article 55 of the Hague Regulations put forward above (see Part IV).

Fourth, the Court appears to have adopted an evolutive interpretation of the Hague Regulations, for the purpose of taking account of a prolonged occupation such as that of Israel. To this effect the Court has stated that the occupant can plan and carry out fundamental investments likely to produce permanent modification in the occupied territory on condition that this be to the benefit of the inhabitants of the territory.[45] In other words, the Court appears to be applying, as a basic test, the *protection of the interests of the local population*, to the exclusion of any other criteria.

---

[41] *PYIL* 2 (1985), 134–5 (editor's note).
[42] See HC 393/82, the *Teachers' Housing Cooperative Society* case, *IYHR* 14 (1984), 303.
[43] See HC 390/79, and HC 393/82, 304.
[44] Ibid.
[45] See HC 393/82, 309–13; see also Ch. 6 in this volume.

At the same time, it should be mentioned in this context that the Court has also used this 'evolutive' approach to permit the establishment of 'permanent' settlements in occupied territory; that is, settlements apparently intended to remain in existence after the occupation has ended. Given the already prolonged occupation and the fact that 'the prospect of a comprehensive peace with all [Israel's] neighbours still lies hidden in the unknown future', the Court has held that 'the word "permanent" must be taken in a relative sense'.[46]

Fifth, it should be emphasized that in at least one case (the famous *Elon Moreh* case),[47] the Court has declared null and void the measures taken by the occupying army (namely the creation of a Jewish settlement not justified by military needs).

Issues and Findings in the Supreme Court's Case-Law on which Doubts can be Raised

Along with important and innovative interpretations that deserve full commendation, one can however also discern rulings that may give rise to misgivings. I shall refer to some of them.

1. Disregard for the Fourth Geneva Convention First, one may wonder whether the Court could not have gone beyond its 'Pontius Pilate' attitude with regard to the question of the applicability, in the Israeli legal system, of the Fourth Geneva Convention of 1949. It is clear that in Israel, as in many other countries, treaties ratified but not 'incorporated' by dint of implementing legislation do not become part and parcel of Israeli law; consequently, they cannot be relied upon by individuals in Israeli courts. Yet this would not seem to preclude the Court from taking account of the Convention in the course of interpreting and applying the customary rules of international law on belligerent occupation, as reflected particularly in the Hague Regulations.

Thus, the Court could have taken into consideration Article 49(6) of the Fourth Geneva Convention (prohibiting the transfer of parts of the occupant's civilian population into the occupied territory) for the purpose of restricting the use of land in the Arab territories by the Israeli military authorities. Whenever the requisition of private land or seizure of public land had been carried out by the occupying army for military needs, the Court could have demanded that those needs be met, to the consequent exclusion of any civilian Jewish settlement in

---

[46] See HC 606/78 and 610/78, the *Beit El* case, jointly reproduced in Mallison and Mallison, *The Palestine Problem*, 371.

[47] HC 390/79, the *Elon Moreh* case, PYIL 1 (1984), 134 at 156, excerpted in *IYHR* 9 (1979), 345.

the areas; only the use of land by members of the army should have been allowed.

By contrast, the Court's approach when dealing with petitions regarding civilian settlements in occupied areas has been generally to exclude Article 49 from consideration and even give to the Hague Regulations a rather 'loose' interpretation as regards the occupant's rights to use land in occupied territory. (In at least one case—the *Beit El* case—the court upheld the lawfulness of certain civilian settlements in the West Bank on the basis, *inter alia*, that their existence contributed 'to security in that territory and [made] it easier for the army to carry out its task'.[48] Thus the Court characterized the function of the settlements (admittedly for the purposes of certain domestic law) as military.)

The method of relying upon international treaties, particularly when applying customary rules of international law, is certainly not unusual. Suffice it to recall, first, that, as pointed out by a learned author, Ruth Lapidoth,[49] Israeli courts have long applied treaties ratified by Israel but not attended by any implementing legislation. Indeed, in other countries with the same system as Israel, treaties which have not been incorporated by means of national legislation are regularly applied by domestic courts—usually for the purpose of interpreting national statutes consistently with the relevant state's international obligations. (In England, the rule whereby treaties are not part of English law if no enabling Act of Parliament has been passed exceptionally does not apply to treaties relating to the conduct of war or treaties of cession).[50]

If this approach is well established with respect to a state's national legislation, there seems to be no reason in principle why resort to it should not also be had for the purpose of interpreting other rules of international law (which form part of the state's domestic law) as well. Were one then to object that the application of Article 49(6) goes further than mere interpretation of the relevant customary rule, I would rebut that this is not correct. As was pointed out above (Part V), Article 49(6) of the Fourth Geneva Convention is simply a corollary or a necessary implication of the general principle laid down in the Hague Regulations, whereby the occupant is not allowed in the territory under its control to further economic, social, or political interests of its own state. In other words, the Fourth Geneva Convention in this respect merely specifies this general principle. For reasons of security

---

[48] See HC 606/78 and 610/78, the *Beit El* case, jointly reproduced in Mallison and Mallison, *The Palestine Problem*, 377.

[49] R. Lapidoth, *Les Rapports entre le droit international public et le droit interne en Israel* (Paris, 1959), 118–27.

[50] See I. Brownlie, *Principles of Public International Law* (Oxford, 1979), 49; and see Ch. 2 in this book.

for the occupying army, the occupant can establish military camps or military installations. It is not allowed, however, to move a great number of its own civilians into the occupied territory, for due to their presence, the military or security grounds would be considerably outweighed by other (economic, political, etc.) considerations.

I shall add that, should one consider the above observations as unsound, or inapplicable to the Israeli legal system, due to the particularities of that system, the Court could perhaps have taken a different step. That is, it could have urged the Knesset to take the necessary measures for passing implementing legislation. It is not unusual for Supreme Courts to call upon other state agencies to take measures that, although beyond the province of the judiciary, are strictly required by international law.

The Court has rightly held that the Fourth Geneva Convention is applicable to the Israeli occupation. It has also stated that 'enforcement [of the Convention] is a matter for the States parties to the Convention'.[51] By themselves, these holdings may be seen as a clear reprimand to the Israeli Government, which has consistently denied the applicability of the Convention. And yet, this sort of implicit criticism would seem insufficient. I would submit that the Court should have gone further and made it clear to the Israeli Government that it does not make sense to ratify a treaty and then leave it in abeyance or, even worse, totally disregard some of its basic provisions.

There are also moral reasons for complying with the Convention: after all, it was a distinguished Israeli scholar, H. Klinghoffer, who remarked that whatever legal reasons may justify the non-application of unincorporated treaties, from a moral point of view a court should not refuse to take account of a treaty regularly signed and ratified by the Government.[52]

2. *The Presumption that Enemy Property in the Occupied Territories is Public*
In the case of *Al-Nawar v. The Minister of Defence et al.*, the Supreme Court stated that: '[W]hen doubt arises concerning whether a given property [in an occupied territory] is governmental or private, it is presumed to be governmental until the contrary is proved.'[53] Although the case at issue related to an enterprise which manufactured plastic products, situated near the village of Damur in South Lebanon, the ruling made by the Court might be taken to have a general import, so as to apply to property in the West Bank as well.

---

[51] HC 606/78 and 610/78, the *Beit El* case, jointly reproduced in Mallison and Mallison, *The Palestine Problem*, 389.
[52] H. Klinghoffer, *Administrative Law* (in Hebrew), quoted by Lapidoth, *Les rapports*, 131–2.
[53] HC 574/82, excerpted in *IYHR* 16 (1986), 326.

I submit that this ruling is questionable. I am aware that some authors (for example, von Glahn)[54] take the same view as the Court, and that support for it can be found in the US and UK military manuals currently in force.[55] One fails to see, however, the justification for this view. Indeed, the only argument in its support is suggested by the British Military Manual, where it is recalled that, in many instances, when an enemy belligerent occupation is impending, governments transfer public property to private individuals, in order to shelter it from any take-over by the occupant. If this were to be the only sound justification for such presumption, it would be correct to rely upon the presumption only when there is sufficient evidence of abuses committed before the occupation. Whenever no such legal expedients have been resorted to, one fails to see why, by propounding the presumption referred to, one should in fact broaden the powers of the occupant.

It appears from the *al-Nawar* judgment that in that case the parties concerned had indeed resorted to a legal expedient for the transfer of ownership. According to Judge Shamgar, the enterprise seized by the IDF belonged to the PLO but had been sold to an individual after its seizure by the occupying force. In that case the presumption might therefore have been justified, were PLO property to be deemed, for the purposes of the Hague Regulations, property belonging to the hostile state. In fact, however, Judge Shamgar was equivocal in his characterization of the status of PLO property for this purpose.[56]

In any case, what seems dubious is the possible extension of this presumption to other instances. It is to be hoped that the Court's above-mentioned ruling will be applied in the light of the particular circumstances of each case.

3. *The Presumption in Favour of the Occupant's Appraisal of the Military Necessity Justifying Requisition of Privately-Owned Property* Another ruling by the Supreme Court which is open to doubt is that in the *Amira et al. v. Minister of Defence et al.* case.[57] The Military Commander in the West Bank had requisitioned privately-owned land situated in the Ramallah District. In the opinion of the occupying authority, the requisition was necessary for military needs. The land was designed

---

[54] Von Glahn, *Occupation*, 179.

[55] *US Field Manual*, para. 394(c); *British Manual*, para. 614. (According to this manual, 'cases of Government property being transferred to private ownership to avoid seizure have occurred in various wars'.)

[56] Characterizing the PLO as 'a comprehensive organization engaged in terrorist and military activity', he held that the property of its economic arm should be treated as either 'property of a belligerent enemy state *or* . . . private property serving the enemy' (my emphasis). See HC 574/82, excerpted in *IYHR* 16 (1986), 327–8.

[57] HC 258/79, excerpted in *IYHR* 10 (1980), 331 ff.

to form part of a defensive line, based on three settlements, which together would constitute a system protecting the Ben Gurion International Airport. The statement of the military commander was disputed by the petitioner, who produced an affidavit submitted by a military expert to the effect that the needs of the military did not warrant the requisitioning.

The Court held that it was faced with a 'factual and professional' issue, and then stated the following:

> In a dispute such as this, involving questions of a military-professional character in which the Court does not have its own founded knowledge, it will presume that the professional arguments ... of those actually responsible for security in the occupied areas and within the Green Line [the border dividing Israel from the West Bank] are valid. This presumption may only be rebutted by very convincing evidence to the contrary.[58]

Again, one fails to see the legal justification for such a presumption. In order to establish it, one has to proceed from the assumption that in principle the allegations of the occupant are right, unless refuted by the petitioner on the strength of strong evidence. But why should one proceed from this assumption? Arguably, the presumption should be *inverted* to the effect that it is incumbent on the *occupying army* convincingly to prove that military requirements justify the requisitioning of private land. This proposition rests on the following reasons. Since, as pointed out above (Part IV), in a prolonged occupation the necessity of safeguarding the needs and interests of the civilian population becomes more imperative than before, one should place severe limitations on the power of the occupant to requisition privately-owned land or to use public land for military needs.

Whereas in a short occupation, taking place during a fully-fledged war, international law can be less demanding on the occupant, in the case of a prolonged occupation greater restraint should be exercised in allowing the occupant to take measures tampering with property in the occupied territory. In a drawn-out occupation the occupant is tempted to expand the concept of 'military needs' so as to cover a wide range of actions which fall more in the province of the military activity of an *ordinary government* than in the field of the *provisional administration, by a military force*, of a foreign territory.

4. *The Court's Power to Determine Whether or not Certain Actions of the Occupant Serve the Interests of the Local Population or are at any rate Beneficial to such Population* I have mentioned above the rulings of the Supreme Court to the effect that a prolonged occupation such as that of

---

[58] Ibid. 332.

Israel in the Arab territories entails among other things the following consequence: greater care must be taken in ascertaining whether or not the actions of the occupant are either justified by military exigencies or are designed to meet the needs of the inhabitants.

In a very important case (*A Teachers' Housing Cooperative Society v. The Military Commander of the Judea and Samaria Region et al.*),[59] the Court was called upon to pass judgment on the lawfulness of the requisition of private lands for the purpose of constructing a network of metropolitan highways. In view of the permanent modifications in the occupied territory these works would entail, the Court asked itself whether they were lawful, and answered in the affirmative, on the basis of the 'test of the benefit for the local population'.

Resort to this test is undoubtedly correct, and the Court must be praised for making use of it. It appears, however, that in the view of the Court the test must be applied by the Court itself; so the Court remains the only body to pronounce on whether or not certain measures benefit the inhabitants of the Occupied Territories. Is this conclusion warranted? I respectfully submit that it is not.

It seems to me that the Court is not the best-placed body for determining whether or not certain measures of the occupant meet the needs of the local population. In a democratic country such a determination would naturally fall on the various representative bodies of the community concerned. In the Occupied Territories, local administrations run by the inhabitants or their representatives would seem to be the most appropriate bodies for making this sort of decision. These administrations could be requested to provide—ideally at the stage when the measures are being considered by the occupation authorities but, if not then, at least when they are being challenged in Court—a statement as to whether in their view the measures in question serve their interests, meet their needs. This statement would then (save in exceptional circumstances involving, for instance, bad faith) be treated as conclusive on the matter. In any case, whatever local body may be selected and however its views may be elicited, what should be surely ruled out is the power of the Court to decide on behalf of, or in lieu of the local population, in cases where there may be conflicting values, patterns of judgement, psychological approaches, and so on.

That such conflicts can and do arise, is apparent from the facts of the case referred to above. The Israeli occupying forces claimed that the highways project was intended to serve the needs of the local population, for it would considerably facilitate transportation between populated settlements, towns, and villages of the West Bank. The occupant conceded that the highways would also facilitate connection

---

[59] HC 393/82, excerpted in *IYHR* 14 (1984), 301 ff.

between the West Bank and Israel, but drew attention to the fact that thousands of Arab workers employed in Israel travelled daily to their places of work and back to their homes in the West Bank. The occupying forces also pointed out that if they were to refrain from improving the existing outdated roads, they surely would be blamed for 'freezing' the development of the West Bank and of its population. These allegations should be contrasted with those of the petitioning Arab co-operative society, which saw the highways project—developed in Israel and partly financed by it—as one which would exclusively serve the transportation requirements of Israel. In its view the West Bank did not need such a 'luxurious and showy' highways scheme.[60]

I should like to add that the test concerning the interests of the local population cannot be applied by the Court on its own, not even if it is supplemented by some sort of fairly 'objective' standard. One such standard or yardstick was suggested by Dinstein.[61] In his view, although

there is no objective criterion in practice for drawing a distinction between sincere and insincere concern [by the occupant] for the civilian population, in most cases the criterion may be simple enough, namely whether or not the occupant is equally concerned about his own population. In other words, if the occupant enacts, for example, a law for the prevention of cruelty to animals in an occupied territory, the proper question is whether there is a similar (not necessarily an identical) law in his own country. If the answer is affirmative, there can usually be no objection to the legislation under Article 43 [of the Hague Regulations]; if it is in the negative, an objection is definitely in order.

It is apparent that his criterion can only work in extreme cases; in normal situations, the comparison with the home state of the occupant may prove misleading, on account of the possible huge differences in social and economic conditions, in psychological outlook, customs, etc. Thus, for example, with reference to the case brought before the Court and discussed in this section, Dinstein's criterion would have been of little consequence.

Concluding Remarks on the Case-Law Previously Surveyed

Undoubtedly the judicial review of the occupant's acts, undertaken by the Israeli Supreme Court, has had a restraining impact and has also served to delineate the parameters within which the occupant is allowed to operate. It seems, however, that, in spite of its important contribution to the scrutiny of military action by Israel in the Occupied Territories, the Court has frequently shown excessive self-restraint

---

[60] Ibid. 301–2; and see generally Chs. 2 and 6 in this book.
[61] Dinstein, 'The International Law of Belligerent Occupation and Human Rights', 113.

towards the other Israeli authorities, or has indulged in some sort of legal formalism that ultimately diminishes its bearing on the action of the occupying forces. Very often, the Court has made great strides towards the abstract affirmation of the need to respect the interests of the local population, while *in concreto* it has refrained from actually catering for those interests.

One can only hope that the Court will take a more incisive approach by being less deferential to the political and military authorities of Israel.

15

Exploitation of Land and Water Resources for Jewish Colonies in the Occupied Territories

IBRAHIM MATAR

Introduction

THE June war of 1967 brought the West Bank and Gaza Strip under the occupation of the Israeli armed forces. Since then, the 1.7 million Palestinians of the territories have been submitted to a variety of repressive measures. Oppression and violation of human and political rights are perhaps inherent in an alien occupation. However, a distinctive distressing feature of this occupation is the occupying power's determination to maintain permanent control over the territories by a systematic policy of colonization and Judaization.

This policy of colonization is being implemented by a systematic practice of seizing private Christian and Muslim Palestinian property, and the transferring of such properties to exclusively Jewish control.[1] This amounts to another form of apartheid, based on religious discrimination rather than on colour as in South Africa. Some of these land seizures are for the purpose of establishing and expanding Jewish colonies in the Occupied Territories. These colonies are euphemistically called 'settlements' in the Gaza Strip and the West Bank, and 'neighbourhoods' in East Jerusalem.

In the resource-poor Occupied Territories, water is a second vital commodity for Palestinians. The area has sporadic shortage of water for geographic, meteorological, and demographic reasons. Droughts have been common since biblical times and are worsening now. In this context, the Israeli occupation authorities have virtually halted water-resource development for the Palestinians and rapidly expanded it for Jewish use in and outside of the Occupied Territories.

---

[1] The use of the term 'Jewish', as opposed 'Israeli', here and below is accurate, since many of the Jewish colonizers of the Occupied Territories are not Israeli citizens, though they could become so under Israel's Law of Return.

Whereas the Israeli Likud Party, other right-wing parties, and some ultra-orthodox religious parties have made their intentions clear never to withdraw from the Occupied Territories, some Israeli Labour Party leaders debate the hypothetical possibility of a 'land for peace' trade to be negotiated with Jordan under what is called 'the Jordan Option'. But even these Labour Party politicians accept the predicates that the West Bank, which they also refer to by its Biblical name, 'Judea and Samaria', belongs fundamentally to the Jewish people, to be partly disposed of tactically in accordance with what is called 'the Allon Plan',[2] and East Jerusalem in any event is never to be relinquished. Meanwhile (and the issue of interest in this chapter) the ongoing land and water practices of the Israeli occupation authorities in the Occupied Territories have the practical effect of slamming the door on a negotiated peaceful resolution to the Palestinian–Israeli conflict.

The following sections will describe post-1967 Israeli policies of colonization of the West Bank and Gaza Strip, pretexts for seizure of land, exploitation of water resources, and the impact of these land and water policies on the indigenous Palestinian population. Concluding remarks will then be made regarding attempted remedies.

II. Chronology of Development of Israeli Policies Regarding Seizure of Palestinian Property for Jewish Colonies 1967–1988

Land has been at the core of the Palestinian–Jewish Zionist conflict since the turn of this century. The objectives and motivations of the early Jewish Zionist immigrants to Palestine are the same as those of the Zionist activists of today. These objectives can be best summarized by the phrase: 'dunum after dunum' of Palestinian land for Jewish colonies.

If history be the guide, this process will entail further displacement and uprooting of the indigenous Palestinian population. I will describe briefly below the different policies of the successive Israeli occupation governments which have ruled the West Bank and Gaza Strip for the past twenty-one years.

Israeli Labour Government Policies 1967–1977

The Israeli Labour Government concentrated its land acquisition policies in the annexed areas of East Jerusalem and in the Jordan Rift,

---

[2] For full text of the Allon plan, see Y. Cohen, *The Allon Plan* (Tel Aviv, 1972) (in Hebrew), trans. in L. Fabian and Z. Schiff (eds.) *Israelis Speak* (New York, 1977), 207; see below and also Ch. 8 in this volume for details of the plan.

in accordance with 'the Allon Plan'. This Plan was conceived by the late Labour Party Government Minister, Yigal Allon, and served as a guide-line for the deployment of Jewish colonies in the Occupied Territories. The purpose of the land confiscations in occupied East Jerusalem was for the construction of Jewish residential fortress colonies to encircle, from all directions, the 137,000 Palestinian population of Jerusalem. These large colonies are located as follows: Ramot to the west, Neve Yaacov to the north, Pisgat Ze'ev to the north-east, French Hill to the central east, East Talpiot to the south-east, and Gilo to the south.[3]

In the Jordan Rift, the land was seized for establishing two series of Jewish colonies along the north-south length of the eastern border of the West Bank. The first belt is located in the Jordan Valley plains. The second is in the highlands overlooking the Jordan Valley.[4] For the colonization of the Jordan Rift, the Settlement Department of the Jewish Agency formulated a twenty-year plan extending from 1975 to 1995. The writer obtained a copy of this plan translated into English, which stated as its two major goals: (*a*) to populate the area with at least 8,000 Jews by 1995; and (*b*) to exploit the natural resources of the area—mainly land, water, and climatic conditions—for the exclusive benefit of the Jews.

These plans are in an advanced stage of implementation. The Jewish colonies are already in control of approximately 50 per cent of the cultivable land in the Jordan Valley plains, according to my on-site physical survey of the areas under the control of these colonies. An extensive infrastructure to serve only the Jewish colonies has been established, consisting of an electric grid, telephone lines, access roads, deep-bore wells, irrigation reservoirs, and pipelines and irrigation systems.

These policies are consistent with the explicit political objectives of the Israeli Labour Government which, in June 1967, annexed occupied East Jerusalem, and, in accordance with the Allon Plan, called for imposing permanent Israeli sovereignty over one-third of the area of the West Bank, namely the Jordan Valley and the strategic highlands overlooking the valley. This plan leaves very little land for the Palestinians, but it purports conveniently to solve the so-called Palestinian 'demographic problem', by proposing to return those areas of the West Bank most heavily populated by Palestinians to Jordanian

---

[3] For more information and maps on Israeli policies to encircle the Palestinian population of East Jerusalem see I. Matar, 'From Palestinian to Israeli: Jerusalem 1948–1982', *Journal of Palestine Studies* 48 (Summer 1983), 57–63.

[4] For more information and maps about Israeli settlement policies on the West Bank see I. Matar, 'Israeli Settlements in the West Bank and Gaza Strip', *Journal of Palestine Studies* 41 (Autumn 1981), 93–110.

administration. This avoids the annexation of these areas to the Jewish State, which would mean giving equal voting rights to the Christian and Muslim Palestinians, and consequently, in the view of Labour party leaders, endangering the purity of the Jewish State.

Israeli Likud Government Policies 1977–1984

For the Likud, the seizure and control of Jerusalem plus one-third of the West Bank was insufficient. The Likud Party wanted all the West Bank and Gaza Strip. According to its ideology, the West Bank, or 'Judea and Samaria' as they call it, is the liberated land of the Jewish people and an inseparable part of Greater Israel. Based on this ideology, the Likud Government began seizing land in the Palestinian populated areas of the highlands of the West Bank, mainly around and in between the major Palestinian cities and towns. In 1980, the Settlement Department of the World Zionist Organization published its first five-year plan 1980–5,[5] for comprehensive Jewish 'settlement' of the Occupied Territories. This plan clearly stated the purpose for this new policy of land seizure and colonization:

The best and most effective way of removing every shadow of doubt about our intention to hold on to Judea and Samaria forever is by speeding up the settlement momentum in these territories. The purpose of settling the areas between and around the centers occupied by the minorities [that is the Palestinian majority in the West Bank] is to reduce to the minimum the danger of an additional Arab state being established in these territories. Being cut off by Jewish settlements, the minority population will find it difficult to form a territorial and political continuity.[6]

To complete this new *de facto* policy of creeping annexation, the Likud Government issued Military Order No. 783, establishing four Jewish Regional Councils in the West Bank which would include only the Jewish colonies and exclude all the Palestinian cities, towns, and villages. These regional councils are an extension of the regional councils within Israel and fall under the jurisdiction of the Israeli Ministry of Interior.[7] Thus this military order effectively brought the Jewish colonies in the West Bank under Israeli law while keeping the Palestinian communities under military government law and rule.

Under this policy of segregation and creeping annexation, what would be the political future of the 1.7 million indigenous Palestinian population? They are apparently to be given three choices: to accept

---

[5] M. Drobles, *Master Plan for the Development of Settlement in Judea and Samaria* (Jerusalem, 1980).

[6] Ibid.

[7] On the structure of regional councils, see Ch. 8.

permanent Israeli rule without political and civil rights; or to leave home and country voluntarily; or to be forcibly expelled—'transferred' as an increasing number of Israeli officials are now openly putting it.

Policies of the 'National Unity' Coalition Government Likud and Labour 1984–1988

The policy of the Israeli coalition government at the time of writing is to continue the land-acquisition process for a limited number of Jewish colonies agreed upon by the coalition parties and for expanding or thickening existing Jewish colonies. This expansion policy consists of quietly increasing the construction rate of new houses and apartments in existing colonies, in order to increase as fast as possible the number of Jews who would be moved to inhabit them in the Occupied Territories, rather than just increasing the number of Jewish colonies. This would make the Jewish population in the Occupied Territories a significant minority and would effectively prevent any so-called territorial compromise in any future negotiated settlement of the Palestinian Israeli conflict.

Overall Results of the Above-Mentioned Jewish Colonization Policies

The cumulative results of these Israeli policies of colonization of the Occupied Territories over the past twenty-one years have produced the following:

1. Control by Israel of over 52 per cent of the land areas of the West Bank, divided into three blocks: 25 per cent of West Bank area closed to Palestinians for security and military reasons, 20 per cent declared by the occupation authorities to be so-called 'state lands' and therefore allocated for Jewish use only, and 7 per cent of the land area seized and in actual use by the Jewish colonizers, either built on for housing purposes or used for agricultural purposes particularly in the Jordan Valley area. In the Gaza Strip, the occupation authorities are in control of over 40 per cent of the land area of the Gaza area, most of it declared by the occupation authorities to be 'state land' and therefore under the control of the Jewish state.[8]

2. On the 7 per cent of the land area of the West Bank referred to above and seized for direct Jewish colonization, the following Jewish colonies had been built by early 1988:[9]

---

[8] For a complete analysis of the number of dunums confiscated and areas controlled by the Israeli occupation authorities in the West Bank, see U. Halabi, *Land Alienation in the West Bank, A Legal and Spatial Analysis* (Jerusalem, 1985).

[9] For more detailed information about the number of Jewish colonies, types of colonies, Jewish population in the colonies, etc., see M. Benvenisti, *West Bank Data Base Project Report 1987* (Jerusalem: 1987).

(a) 117 Jewish colonies in the West Bank (excluding East Jerusalem), with a population of over 67,000.

(b) 8 large Jewish residential colonies, built in fortress-style in the annexed part of East Jerusalem, with a total population of 100,000.

3. In the Gaza Strip, fourteen Jewish colonies have been established with a population of some 2,500.

The price paid by the indigenous Palestinian population as a result of Jewish colonization of the Occupied Territories and land seizures has been immense. Since 1967, several thousands of Palestinian landowners and farmers have been dispossessed, displaced, and impoverished. In a poll sponsored in 1986 by the Australian Broadcasting Corporation, the US *Newsday*, and the Palestinian newspaper *al-Fajr*,[10] 22.8 per cent of those polled indicated that they had experienced property and land confiscation. This suggests that approximately a quarter of the population of the West Bank and Gaza have been dispossessed of all or part of their lands. And the process continues.

II. Israeli Pretexts or Devices for Seizure of Palestinian Property

Jewish colonies are not built in a vacuum. They are built on lands taken from their rightful Palestinian owners by means of a number of ostensibly legal devices.[11] There are three main pretexts that have been used by the occupation authorities for seizing private property from Palestinians:

1. In the annexed areas of East Jerusalem, Palestinian property is confiscated for 'public purpose' in accordance with Israeli law. The public referred to here is the Jewish public and the purpose is the construction of residential Jewish colonies in annexed areas of Jerusalem. These land confiscation orders are signed by the Minister of Finance. Since 1967, the Palestinian, Christian, and Muslim residents of the occupied part of East Jerusalem have been dispossessed of extremely valuable private real estate property in the heart of the Holy City by three waves of land confiscation orders. The first, in January 1968, was for 1,500 dunums for the construction of two residential colonies, French Hill and Ramat Eshkol, and an industrial park in the

---

[10] This poll, conducted under the supervision of Professor M. Shadid, Professor of Political Science at an-Najah National University in Nablus, was first published on 8 Sept. 1986 in *al-Fajr* Arabic daily newspaper and by *Newsday*, then summarized in *al-Fajr*'s English weekly edition on 12 Sept. 1986.

[11] R. Shehadeh, *Occupier's Law* (Washington, 1985), part 1.

Kalandiya area. The second, in August 1970, was for 14,500 dunums for the construction of four residential Jewish colonies: Ramot, Neve Yaacov, East Talpiot, and Gilo. The third, in March 1980, was for 1,500 dunums for the construction of the large residential fortress colony of Pisgat Ze'ev.

In the rest of the Occupied Territories which are under military rule, private Palestinian property has been seized by the occupation authorities by using two additional devices.

2. Closure or requisition of private Palestinian land for security reasons, by military orders issued by the military governor of the West Bank or Gaza. Initially, this land is used by paramilitary Israeli units called the *Nahal*, for the establishment of the nucleus of Jewish colonies. Subsequently, these paramilitary bases are transferred by a decision of the Israeli government for civilian Jewish use.[12]

3. Seizure of Palestinian property by designating certain land areas to be 'state lands' in accordance with Ottoman law. This law states that any piece of land which is not cultivated for three consecutive years or is not cultivated more than 50 per cent reverts back to the Ottoman ruler or the Sultan. The Ottomans passed this law to encourage farmers to cultivate the land. The Israelis are today using that same law to take away land from their legitimate owners for Jewish colonization. By using this Ottoman law the Israeli occupation authorities have also earned for themselves the title of the new 'Sultan' of Palestine.

This device has been used extensively by the Israeli occupation authorities in the West Bank and Gaza, after the security pretext mentioned above was successfully challenged by Palestinians in the Israeli High Court in the *Elon Moreh* land case of 1980.[13] Suffice it here to emphasize one vital point concerning so-called 'state land'. The actual practice of Ottoman, British, and Jordanian government rule in Palestine treated by far the majority of what Israel now routinely calls 'state land' to be privately entitled land.

III. Impact of Land Seizures on Palestinian Population

Since 1967, from evidence obtained by myself in on-site surveys of Jewish colonies and interviews with village leaders and *mukhtars* in the West Bank, thousands of dunums have been seized from Palestinians by the occupation authorities. As a result, several thousand Palestinian landowners and farmers have been displaced, dispossessed of their

---

[12] On requisition of land for security reasons, see also Ch. 6 in this volume.
[13] HC 390/79 *Dweikat et al. v. State of Israel et al.*; and see Ch. 8 in this volume.

property, and impoverished, and many farmers have also lost their source of livelihood. Yet the Israelis continue to claim that no Palestinians have been displaced from their property. In order to test these assertions I have carried out a number of studies and on-site surveys on all lands seized and in actual use for Jewish colonies, and have published the results,[14] indicating previous status of the land and how Palestinian villagers were dispossessed of their property.

In the first survey, I wanted to verify whether the land seized had in fact been private and cultivable, or was 'state land' in the strict sense of non-cultivated and unused areas. More specifically, the categories of land ownership considered 'private' for the purposes of the survey included: (a) *'mulk'* land, or private lands having clear title deeds; (b) *'miri'* land, which has been actively cultivated for generations by the farmers and registered during the British Mandate at the Finance Department for land-tax purposes; and (c) *'Jiftlik'* or *'mudewwara'* lands, which have also been actively cultivated by Palestinian farmers and which in the nineteenth century were nominally under the title of the Ottoman Sultan and have been recognized by the British and Jordanian governments as private lands. (Prior to the occupation of the West Bank in 1967, the Jordanian Government was in the process of carrying out surveys in the West Bank to issue title deeds to the farmers who were cultivating these lands, so as to recognize explicitly their ownership.)

The categories of land included in the survey under 'state' included the following: (a) *'mawat'* land, or waste land, including deserts, forests, and rocky uncultivated mountain tops not owned by individuals; (b) lands which were once the sites of British Mandate 'Taggart' forts and Jordanian police or army camps; and (c) lands which have been designated for community purposes and hospitals.

Based on the above criteria and categories of land ownership, I found that 95 per cent of all lands seized from Palestinians and transferred for the exclusive use of the Jewish colonies are in fact *private* lands belonging to individual Palestinian landowners and farmers, while only 5 per cent of the seized land could be considered public land.[15]

In the course of my studies, the human impact of the seizures became apparent. I found that, prior to seizure of cultivated lands, the occupation authorities have systematically bulldozed wheatfields, ploughed under crops, used defoliants to burn crops, and have cut down thousands of fig, olive, grape, plum, and other fruit trees. Some

---

[14] See Matar, 'From Palestinian to Israeli', and 'Israeli Settlements in the West Bank and Gaza Strip'.

[15] On the legality of this action, see Ch. 14.

examples of destruction of agricultural crops to which I have personally been a witness include:

1977: Wheatfields belonging to the farmers from Tubas in the northeastern part of the West Bank were bulldozed by the Israelis. These same lands are now being cultivated by the Jewish colony of Roi.

1978: Wheatfields belonging to the farmers of Beit Furik, east of Nablus, were bulldozed by Israelis. These lands have been planted with avocado trees for the Jewish colony of Mekhora.

1980: Grape-vines belonging to the farmers of Beit Iskaria were uprooted for the expansion of the land for the Jewish colonies of Rosh Tzurim and Alon Shevot in the Beit Ummar area, half-way between Bethlehem and Hebron.

1981: 400 fig and 20 olive trees were uprooted by Jewish colonizers from Ofra, for expanding their colony. The trees belong to the Fare'h family from the village of 'Ain Yabroud in the area. This incident was prominently displayed in a documentary by ABC *20/20*, shown in the US in February 1982.

1984: 400 grape-vines were uprooted and lands seized from farmers in the village of Al-Khadr, near Bethlehem, for the construction of the Jewish colony of Efrat.

1985: Fig and olive trees belonging to the farmers from the village of Al-Jib in the Ramallah area were uprooted and land seized for the construction of the Jewish colony of Givat Ze'ev.

1987: Grape-vines belonging to the farmers in the village of Al-Khadr in the Bethlehem area were bulldozed by the Israelis for the expansion of the Jewish colony of Daniel.

In fact, the destruction of Palestinian villages, homes, orchards, and crops began right after the 1967 war. The most blatant example (in June 1967) was the complete destruction of three villages in the Latroun salient. Yalu, Beit Nuba, and Imwas, consisting of over 6,000 homes. Now the colony of Mevo Horon is cultivating the lands of these razed villages estimated to consist of more than 20,000 dunums. In July of 1967, three more villages were destroyed in the Jordan Valley, al-Ajajreh, Sattariyeh, and Makhrouq. Now the colony of Massua rests on the ruins of the village of al-Ajajreh.

Based on the above, Israeli claims that no private Palestinian lands have been seized and transferred for use to Jewish colonies are belied literally by the evidence in the field.

In my second survey, consisting mainly of interviews with village leaders and *mukhtars* most affected by seizure of land, I wished to ascertain whether any Palestinian farmers have been displaced and dispossessed of their lands for Jewish colonies. As a result of this study, I discovered that thousands of farmers have, in fact, been made totally or partially landless. The villages most affected by land seizures are the villages in the eastern highlands of the West Bank, overlooking the Jordan Valley, mainly Majdal Bani Fadel, Akraba, Beit Furik, Beit Dajan, Tammoun and Tubas. For example, the village of Beit Dajan has lost an estimated 60 per cent of its cultivable land to the Jewish colony of Hamra, and 90 per cent of the village population of 2,000 inhabitants have as a result become partially or totally landless. In the nearby village of Beit Furik an estimated 60 per cent of its lands have been seized or closed off for the Jewish colony of Mekhora and some 80 per cent of the village population of 7,000 have also become partially or completely landless. In the Jerusalem area, the village of Beit Hanina has lost more than 50 per cent of its land to three Jewish residential fortresses: Neve Yaacov, Pisgat Ze'ev, and Ramot.

The above examples again completely refute Israeli claims that no Palestinian farmers have been displaced, and confirm that Jewish land-acquisition policies have not only violated Palestinian property rights but have also brought severe economic and social hardships to the Palestinian proprietors, for whom land and house are culturally essential.

Finally, the impact of having more than half of their land expropriated (40 per cent in the very densely populated Gaza Strip) affects more than personal, cultural, and community development. The policy of Israel, from a land-use planning point of view, has been to fragment the Palestinian communities.

While no rigorous studies have been done on the effect on Palestinian economic development of the land and water policies of the occupation authorities, the qualitative impact is evident. Land is an essential factor of production. The heavily agrarian Palestinian economy depends disproportionately on land and water. These two physical resources have been gradually shrinking and, as a result, limiting the potential growth of the agriculture sector in the economy of the Occupied Territories.

IV. Exploitation of Water Resources

The colonization process of the West Bank and Gaza Strip does not only involve the seizure of Palestinian land, but also the exploitation or, more precisely, expropriation of the scarce underground water resources for the virtual exclusive use of the Jewish colonies. This has been done by drilling deep-bore wells in all areas of the West Bank and, in particular, in the Jordan Valley where the Jewish agricultural colonies are completely dependent on these wells for their domestic and irrigation purposes.

According to the report by the State Comptroller of the Israeli government for 1987, the Jewish water company, Mekorot, has drilled more than 40 deep-bore wells and is pumping some 42 million cubic metres (MCM) per year from West Bank underground water supplies for Jewish colonies. This quantity already exceeds by 40 per cent the quantity of water being pumped by Palestinians from some 300 pre-1967 shallow wells, the volume of which is estimated to be 20 MCM per year.[16] Furthermore, the 42 MCM being pumped by Mekorot for Jewish use in the colonies of the West Bank is now almost equal to 50 per cent of the total water consumption by the entire Palestinian population in the West Bank for all purposes—domestic, agricultural, and industrial—estimated at 90 MCM per year. This is the water used by Palestinians from all sources which include wells, springs, and cisterns.

In some cases, the Israeli wells have been drilled in close proximity to local Palestinian springs, contrary to the Jordanian water authority regulations regarding drilling of wells. This has been the case particularly in the Jordan Valley, where Palestinian agriculture is mainly dependent on spring water for irrigation. The impact of these well-drilling practices has already been devastating economically for two areas in the valley, as I have personally witnessed. In the first case, in the northern end of the valley, in the mid-1970s, all springs and wells belonging to Palestinian farmers from the villages of Bardala and 'Ain el-Baida dried up as a direct consequence of two deep-bore Jewish wells drilled in the area by Mekorot to supply water to the Jewish colony of Mehola. After the Palestinian farmers suffered extensive crop losses due to lack of water, and as a result of pressure from the world community, Mekorot agreed to substitute local water losses with limited quantities of water from the new wells. As a result, the Palestinian farmers are now completely dependent on the Israelis for their water needs, and their status has been changed from owners to renters of their own resource. This case was given prominence in a documentary called 'Whose Hand on the Tap?', produced by ITV in 1981 and shown on British television.

In the second case, water dried up because of Israeli wells dug near the site of a spring in the village of al-Auja, 10 kilometres north of Jericho. In the autumn of 1987, in spite of the previous year's heavy rains, the village springs dried up, and cultivation in the winter of 1988 was almost totally destroyed. This is the third time the al-Auja spring has dried up since 1979, when a shortage of water destroyed

---

[16] For a more thorough analysis of the issue of exploitation of the West Bank water resources by the occupation authorities, see H. Awartani, 'Water Resources and Policies in the West Bank', *Samed el Iktisadi* 3 (Aug. 1980).

crops with an estimated loss of $3 million. Informed hydrologists link this water depletion of the al-Auja spring to the two Israeli wells dug near the site of the spring.

Not only have the Israelis been freely developing new wells in the West Bank and Gaza for their own exclusive use, but, with a few exceptions, the military authorities have not issued any new licences for Palestinians to drill new wells for irrigation purposes. The occupation authorities have also restricted the amount of water pumped by Palestinians from pre-1967 wells by enforcing quotas on the quantity of water that can be pumped from these wells. In fact, the Israeli water commissioner in a television interview for the British documentary, 'Whose Hand on the Tap?', stated quite categorically that Palestinian water consumption in the West Bank will not be allowed to exceed 100 MCM per year for all purposes.

This Israeli limitation on use of water by the Palestinian communities gives Israel complete control of the West Bank underground water supplies which are estimated at 600 MCM per year, and opens the way for the exclusive exploitation of this vital resource by Israel and only for its own purposes. It is estimated that pre-1967 Israel pumps a full one-third of its annual needs of 1.8 billion cubic metres from underground West Bank basins, which extend inside the 1967 Israeli borders to the coastal plains to the west and the Gilboa plains in the north, and also to the north-east. Thus, limiting Palestinian use of their own West Bank underground water supplies permits the Israelis to exploit this water for two objectives: first, to provide water for Israel proper, and, second, to provide water to the Jewish colonies in the Occupied Territories.[17] Meanwhile, the Palestinians have to pay the price. They are prevented from developing their own water resources for their own welfare and economic survival—let alone from having a say in their own water-resource management policy.

V. Conclusion

In the face of these continuous Israeli official policies to dispossess Palestinians from their property and physical resources, the Palestinians under occupation have used various means to attempt to slow down this process and protect their property.

They have challenged in Israeli-controlled courts the occupation authorities' land policies. In the early years of the occupation Palestinian farmers and landowners tried physically to block Jewish attempts to seize their land by sitting in front of bulldozers or preventing

---

[17] On the legality of these measures, see Ch. 14.

Israeli surveyors from surveying their property. They protested to the military governors in their areas. They appealed to local courts. However, these methods did not prove fruitful until May 1978, when landowners from the village of Nabi Saleh, in the Ramallah District, challenged in the Israeli High Court the seizure of their land by the colonizers from the colony of Nevi Tsuf[18]. In this particular case, the Israeli High Court ordered the removal of the fence set up by the Jewish colonizers and the return of the land to their rightful owners. This was the first taste of victory for Palestinians. In 1979, it was followed by the *Toubas and Beit El* case.[19] Although the Palestinian owners lost their case on security grounds, yet the Israeli High Court established that civilian Jewish colonies are temporary and by implication should be dismantled should the state of belligerency end. In 1980, the case of the Jewish colony of *Elon Moreh* became prominent.[20] The Palestinian owners from Rujeib challenged the seizure of their land on alleged security grounds for the establishment of the Jewish colony of Elon Moreh. In this case, the Israeli High Court ordered the return of the land to the Palestinian landowners and the dismantlement of the Jewish colony after it had been established for some three months. This was the peak of success for the Palestinians in their attempts to use legal remedies to defend their rights and property.

The success, however, did not last long. The occupation authorities revised their tactics and stopped using the security pretext for seizing land. Instead, in 1981 they began using Ottoman laws, declaring the intended lands to be seized as 'state lands' and giving the landowners thirty days to prove the contrary. Futhermore, in 1983 the military authorities passed MO 1060, denying local civil courts the right to judge any dispute concerning land, and transferring this authority to Israeli military review boards. This new technique also served the purpose of preventing cases from directly reaching the Israeli High Court, as all cases had to be reviewed first by these boards.

Despite these legal obstacles set up by the occupation authorities to block a fair hearing of Palestinian grievances in defence of their land and property, Palestinian landowners continued to bring cases to these review boards in almost all instances where land was declared as state land. Many land cases, however, were never filed or were discontinued for lack of funds or disillusionment.

In short, the court cases have been instrumental in some cases in regaining some lands or in preventing the expansion of existing colonies. They have also forced the occupation authorities to change

---

[18] The petitioners in this case were villagers from the village of Nebi Saleh in the Ramallah area, represented by Advocate Elias Khoury.
[19] HC 606/78 *Ayyoub et al. v. Minister of Defence et al.*
[20] HC 390/79 *Dweikat et al. v. State of Israel et al.*

their tactics regarding seizure of Palestinian property, which helped to expose the occupation realities to world public opinion.[21]

To hold and protect their lands, Palestinians have also used other non-violent means. Planting olive and other fruit trees has been one means, as where land is planted with trees, it is more difficult for the occupation authorities to claim that the land is not cultivated and therefore 'state land' in accordance with the Ottoman laws referred to above. In 1976, the Mennonite Central Committee initiated a project of mass distribution of olive seedlings to farmers, and in a period of five years together with another non-government organization, Save the Children, distributed over 1.5 million olive seedlings. This created a momentum for tree-planting which brought the number of olive trees planted in the last ten years to over 4 million.

Another method of preventing land seizure has been the reclamation of rocky lands by clearing rock from the land and planting it with fruit trees. Over 20,000 *dunums* of land have been reclaimed over the past 10 years. Building houses on the land has also been used as another tactic to protect Palestinian property.

Palestinians have also resorted to the media as a means to inform the world community of the facts of the occupation and in particular of the violation of property rights of the Palestinian people. A number of documentaries have been produced by American and British TV networks about Jewish colonization of the Occupied Territories.[22] Though the above measures have not been able to stop Jewish colonization in the Occupied Territories, they have been able to slow down the process. Such are the Palestinians' definition of success.

In conclusion, an ongoing battle over the land is taking place daily in the Occupied Territories. On one side, the Israeli occupation authorities have been and are working feverishly to dispossess the Palestinians and to possess definitively and integrate *de facto* into Israel what remained in 1948 of the historical lands of Palestine, that is the West Bank and Gaza Strip. In 1948, the Israelis succeeded in uprooting one million Palestinians from their homes and land, destroying over 350 Palestinian villages, erasing virtually every trace of Palestinian presence from the areas and villages from which they were uprooted, and consequently gaining control of 78 per cent of the historical land of Palestine. In 1988, the Israeli occupation authorities are now trying to gain permanent control of the remaining 22 per cent of the land of Palestine. On the other side, the Palestinians continue their struggle

---

[21] For further review of these cases, see Ch. 8.
[22] 'Whose Hand on the Tap?' (1981, ITV, UK); 'Under the Israeli Thumb' (1982, ABC, USA); 'A People without a Land' (1984, Granada, UK); 'The Promised Land' (1985, Yorkshire TV, UK).

to protect their property, their resources, their country, and their survival on their own land. Despite twenty-one years of occupation, the Palestinian people have not given up. The uprising of the Palestinians of the Occupied Territories testifies to this effect.

Part Three

Enforcement of International Law

16

Enforcement of Human Rights in the West Bank and the Gaza Strip

JOHN DUGARD

WHATEVER the correct legal status of the Occupied Territories of the West Bank and the Gaza Strip may be, it is accepted by both Israel and her critics that the conduct of the military administration in the Occupied Territories is to be judged by the standards of international law. The most obvious standards are those contained in the humanitarian provisions of the Hague Regulations of 1907 and the Fourth Geneva Convention Relative to the Protection of Civilian Persons in Time of War of 1949. However, it is also suggested that Israel's administration should be judged by wider standards, such as those contained in the Universal Declaration of Human Rights of 1948.[1]

That Israel has violated a number of basic human rights in the Occupied Territories has been established by investigations carried out, *inter alia*, by Amnesty International,[2] *The Sunday Times* of London,[3] the United Nations Special Committee to Investigate Israeli Practices Affecting Human Rights of the Population of the Occupied Territories, al-Haq,[4] and the Israeli International Center for Peace in the Middle East.[5] These investigations have focused particular attention on deportation, collective punishments, detention without trial, house (and town) arrest, torture, arbitrary lethal shootings, and the restrictions imposed on the freedoms of speech, press, association, and assembly

---

[1] The United Nations General Assembly has on several occasions referred to the Universal Declaration of Human Rights as providing the law applicable to the Occupied Territories: Res. 2443 (XXIII), 2727 (XXV), 2765 (XXV). See, too, the International Center for Peace in the Middle East (ICPME), *Human Rights in the Occupied Territories 1979–1983* (Tel Aviv, 1985), 5, 9–10.
[2] *Report and Recommendation of an Amnesty International Mission to the Government of the State of Israel, 3–7 June 1979.*
[3] 19 June 1977.
[4] R. Shehadeh and J. Kuttab, *The West Bank and the Rule of Law* (Geneva, 1980); *In Their Own Words: Human Rights Violations in the West Bank* (Geneva, 1983); R. Shehadeh, *Occupier's Law: Israel and the West Bank* (Washington, 1985); E. Playfair, *Administrative Detention in the Occupied West Bank* (Ramallah, 1985); J. Hiltermann *Israel's Deportation Policy in the Occupied West Bank and Gaza* (Ramallah, 1986).
[5] ICPME, *Human Rights in the Occupied Territories 1979–1983*.

in the Occupied Territories. Probably the most telling of these reports is that of International Center for Peace in the Middle East which, according to its Preface, 'was written by Jews who grew up in Israel, and whose beliefs were shattered before their eyes by their findings in the Occupied Territories'.[6]

That Israel has violated and violates human rights in the Occupied Territories is therefore a matter of record. The events of late 1987 and early 1988 emphasize the extent to which Israel is prepared to suppress human rights in its determination to maintain its control over the Occupied Territories. The purpose of this enquiry is to examine how the situation is to be remedied; that is, how respect for human rights in the West Bank and the Gaza Strip is to be enforced.

In essence there are two models for the enforcement of human rights in the Occupied Territories. The first—which I shall call the Direct Enforcement Model—seeks to enforce human rights in the Occupied Territories by means of enforcement action under Chapter VII of the UN Charter, or by means of the Uniting for Peace Resolution. The second—the Indirect Enforcement Model—aims to secure the enforcement of human rights by means of less direct, but probably more practicable, methods involving the use of the International Court of Justice, the United Nations, specialized agencies, non-governmental organizations, and the domestic courts of the Occupied Territories and Israel.

I. The Direct Enforcement Model

The Palestinian jurist Henry Cattan has advocated the use of enforcement action under Chapter VII of the UN Charter, premised on a finding that the situation in the Occupied Territories constitutes a threat to international peace under Article 39 of the Charter.[7] He is, however, compelled to concede that there is little likelihood of such action materializing in the light of the close relationship between Israel and the United States and the near certainty that any attempt to impose mandatory economic sanctions (or military sanctions) against Israel would be vetoed by the United States. This prediction is borne out by the South African experience. Despite the clearly articulated opposition of the United States administration to the policies of the

---

[6] Ibid. 5. See also E. R. Cohen, *Human Rights in the Israeli Occupied Territories 1967–1982* (Manchester, 1985).

[7] *Palestine and International Law*, 2nd edn. (London, 1976), 244–9; and 'The Implementation of United Nations Resolutions on Palestine' in I. Abu-Lughod (ed.), *Palestine Rights: Affirmation and Denial* (Illinois, 1982), 39–43. A similar suggestion is made by S. V. Mallison and W. T. Mallison in 'The Juridical Bases for Palestinian Self-Determination', PYIL 1 (1984), 62–3.

South African government, the adoption by Congress of sanctions measures against South Africa,[8] and the absence of bonds between South Africa and the United States of the kind that bind Israel and the United States, the United States has shown a determination—together with Britain—to veto Chapter VII action against South Africa.[9] *A fortiori* such action would be vetoed in the case of Israel.

In the alternative, Cattan suggests[10] that the General Assembly might take action against Israel to enforce compliance with international law under the Uniting for Peace Resolution of 1950.[11] This proposal is politically unrealistic and legally unsound. The history of the United Nations shows that the Uniting for Peace Resolution is not a substitute for Security Council action. Although recommendations have been made in terms of this Resolution where the veto has paralysed the Security Council, no real attempt has been made to mobilize international enforcement *action*—as opposed to rhetoric—under its auspices. One reason for this is that the power of the General Assembly to recommend enforcement action has been seriously questioned by the International Court of Justice in the *Expenses Case*,[12] which in effect holds that enforcement action under the Charter remains the prerogative of the Security Council.

The General Assembly has already adopted resolutions on the subject of the Occupied Territories under the Uniting for Peace Resolution. A resolution adopted in 1980[13] requests the Security Council, in the event of Israel failing to withdraw from the Occupied Territories, to adopt measures under Chapter VII of the Charter; and a later resolution, adopted in 1982,[14] 'calls upon' states to terminate economic, military, and diplomatic ties with Israel. Neither of these resolutions, however, has had any real effect as resolutions of the General Assembly remain recommendatory even if adopted in terms of the Uniting for Peace procedure.

The Direct Enforcement Model therefore offers no real prospect of success in the enforcement of human rights in the Occupied Territories.

II. The Indirect Enforcement Model

Unfortunately there is no easy solution to the problem of human rights violations in the Occupied Territories. All avenues must be

---

[8] Comprehensive Anti-Apartheid Act of 1986.
[9] In 1977, the Security Council did, however, impose an arms embargo against South Africa under Chapter VII: Res. 418 (1977).
[10] *Palestine and International Law*.
[11] Res. 377 (V).
[12] ICJ *Reports* (1962), 151.
[13] ES–7/2.
[14] ES–9/1.

explored and the assistance of a wide range of institutions invoked in order to secure the advancement of human rights in the West Bank and the Gaza Strip. Before these methods are examined, however, it is necessary to consider the status of the Occupied Territories with a view to determining the human rights regime that is to govern the territory. In particular it is necessary to consider the question of whether Israel is bound to comply only with the humanitarian standards contained in the Hague Regulations and the Fourth Geneva Convention or whether there are additional higher standards with which Israel must comply. The characterization of the governing human rights regime[15] is therefore an essential starting point in any enquiry into the methods that may be employed to enforce human rights.

The Classification of the Human Rights Regime Applicable to the Occupied Territories

The precise legal status of the Occupied Territories (including East Jerusalem) is subject to debate and dispute. Briefly, the following legal regimes have been suggested.

1. *The Territories form part of Israel* Although Israel has not formally annexed the Occupied Territories (except for East Jerusalem and the Golan Heights) there are reactionary forces in Israel that lay claim to the territories—especially to the West Bank, renamed Judea and Samaria—on politico-religious grounds.[16] However untenable these claims may be in law, there is no ignoring the fact that Israel has consciously implemented a policy of *de facto* annexation by establishing and extending settler communities in the West Bank and in the Gaza Strip.

The extent to which this policy has changed the character of the West Bank has been fully documented by Dr Meron Benvenisti.[17] Some legal justification for this policy in regard to the West Bank is possibly to be found in the argument that Israel's title to the West Bank is better in law than that of Jordan on the ground that Israel acquired the West

---

[15] T. Meron, *Human Rights in Internal Strife: Their International Protection* (Cambridge, 1987), 43–4, 161–2.

[16] See D. S. Will, 'Zionist Settlement Ideology', *JPS* 11 (1982), 37. See too the arguments presented in the *Elon Moreh* case, *PYIL* 1 (1984), 134 by Gush Emunim, reported in M. Shamgar (ed.), *Military Government in the Territories Administered by Israel 1967–1980*, 1: *The Legal Aspects* (Jerusalem, 1982), 414–15, 435.

[17] M. Benvenisti, *The West Bank Data Project, A Survey of Israel's Policies* (Washington, DC, 1984); and *The West Bank Data Base Project Report 1987* (Jerusalem, 1987)

Bank in a defensive operation in 1967 whereas Jordan acquired it by aggression in 1948.[18]

2. The Status of the Territories is sui generis In broad outline, the official position of the Israeli government,[19] which is echoed by its courts,[20] may be summarized as follows. Jordan and Egypt were not the sovereign powers over the West Bank and Gaza, respectively, between 1948 and 1967. Israel's occupation of these territories cannot therefore be classified as one of belligerent occupancy under the Fourth Geneva Convention because there is no ousted sovereign as required by Article 2(2) of this Convention. Israel is accordingly under no legal obligation to comply with the humanitarian standards contained in the Fourth Geneva Convention. As a matter of policy, however, Israel complies with these standards—except insofar as they are irreconcilable with Israel's security interests. In pursuance of this policy, Israel permits the International Committee of the Red Cross (ICRC) to monitor the actions of the Israeli military government in the Occupied Territories.

3. Trustee Occupation Allan Gerson has advanced the view that the population of the Occupied Territories is the sovereign body and that Israel's role is therefore that of a trustee-occupant, obliged to comply with higher standards of fairness and justice in its administration than those required by the Fourth Geneva Convention.[21] This is not really a novel suggestion for, as Adam Roberts has pointed out, there is an element of trusteeship in all occupation law.[22]

4. Belligerent Occupation The United Nations,[23] supported by the community of states,[24] maintains that Israel is in belligerent occupation of the West Bank and the Gaza Strip and thus bound to comply with the

---

[18] E. Lauterpacht, *Jerusalem and the Holy Places* (London, 1968), 48; E. V. Rostow, 'Palestinian Self-Determination: Possible Futures for the Unallocated Territories of the Palestine Mandate', *Yale Studies in World Public Order* 5 (1979), 147; Y. Z. Blum, 'The Missing Reversioner: Reflections on the Status of Judea and Samaria', *IsLR* 3 (1968), 279; S. M. Schwebel, 'What Weight to Conquest?', *AJIL* 64 (1970), 344.

[19] Israel National Section of the International Commission of Jurists, *The Rule of Law in the Areas Administered by Israel* (Tel Aviv, 1981), vii–viii; Shamgar (ed.), *Military Government*, 31–43. For criticism of this position, see Y. Dinstein, 'The International Law of Belligerent Occupation and Human Rights', *IYHR* 8 (1978), 107.

[20] *Mil. Pros. v. Suhadi S. H. Zuhad*, 47 *IsLR* (1974), 490. For a review of other cases, see Ch. 8 in this volume.

[21] 'Trustee-Occupant: The Legal Status of Israel's Presence in the West Bank', *HILJ* 14 (1973), 1; and *Israel, The West Bank and International Law* (London, 1978), 81–2, 237–8.

[22] 'What is Military Occupation?', *BYIL* 55 (1984), 295.

[23] See, for example, SC Res. 446 of 22 Mar. 1979 and 465 of 1 Mar. 1980; and GA Res. 32/91A of 13 Dec. 1977 and 37/123A of 16 Dec. 1982.

[24] Including the US. See S. M. Boyd, 'The Applicability of International Law to the Occupied Territories', *IYHR* 1 (1971), 258.

Hague Regulations of 1907 and the Fourth Geneva Convention of 1949, which together establish the legal regime of belligerent occupation. This view is supported by scholars, both within Israel[25] and outside,[26] and by the ICRC, which is charged with the task of monitoring compliance with the Fourth Geneva Convention.

This approach, which may be described as the orthodox one, 'freezes' the legal system of the Occupied Territories as it requires Israel to administer the territories in accordance with the law in force at the time of occupation[27] and the Hague Regulations and Fourth Geneva Convention. This means that Israel is not compelled to comply with wider obligations in the human rights field. In particular, no obligation is placed upon Israel to advance the right of self determination.

5. *Non-Self-Governing Territory* Mahnoush Arsanjani has persuasively argued[28] that the West Bank and the Gaza Strip are non-self-governing territories within the meaning of Chapter XI of the Charter and the Declaration on the Granting of Independence to Colonial Countries and Peoples of 1960.[29] She argues that:

They have been ruled by political entities which are distinct from the rank and file, are alien to the inhabitants of the territories and have only assumed responsibility for the administration of the West Bank and the Gaza Strip. In fact the status of the West Bank and the Gaza Strip is analogous to Namibia's. Both are former colonial territories and both were subjected to some forms of international supervision delegated to foreign entities.[30]

She accordingly contends that the United Nations should declare the Occupied Territories to be the concern of the United Nations under Chapter XI of the UN Charter.

The above brief survey of the different views relating to the status of the Occupied Territories highlights the wide divergence of opinion on this subject and emphasizes the need for greater clarity.

There is undoubtedly much validity in the argument that belligerent occupancy is intended as a temporary, provisional measure and not one that continues for over twenty years. In its study of *Human Rights in the Occupied Territories 1979–1983* the International Center for Peace in the Middle East rightly declares:

---

[25] Y. Dinstein, 'The International Law of Belligerent Occupation and Human Rights', *IYHR* 8 (1978), 107; N. Feinberg, 'Legal Status of the West Bank', in *Ha'aretz*, 9 Oct. 1987.

[26] See, for example, S. V. Mallison, 'The Application of International Law to the Israeli Settlements in Occupied Territories' in Abu-Lughod (ed.), *Palestine Rights*, 55; Boyd, 'The Applicability of International Law to the Occupied Territories'.

[27] Gerson, *Israel, the West Bank and International Law*, 9.

[28] 'United Nations Competence in the West Bank and Gaza Strip', *ICLQ* 31 (1982), 426.

[29] Res. 1514 (XV).

[30] Arsanjani, 'United Nations Competence', 442.

The birth of the [Geneva] Conventions after World War Two and the original intention of creating rules and norms practised in territories captured in war was for a relatively short period of time, to be used until the time when the antagonists reached agreement on the future of the territories. These assumptions no longer exist regarding 'occupied territories': Israel has ruled these territories for over sixteen [now twenty] years; actually, there has been no war between the two sides during most of this period, and a political agreement does not appear in sight. The Geneva Conventions are not suited to such a prolonged period of occupation. There are no regulations or rules in international law for a situation such as that in the West Bank and Gaza Strip.[31]

In these circumstances there is clearly room for the argument that the status of the Occupied Territories is 'special' or *sui generis*. However, this argument does not lead to a conclusion that greater powers are vested in the Israeli military administration.[32] On the contrary, if regard is had to the length of the occupation, to the convergence of humanitarian law and human rights law,[33] and to the international status of the territories as a result of the unfulfilled mandate of the League of Nations, it would appear that the territories are to be accorded a status involving a greater degree of international supervision than that contemplated by the Fourth Geneva Convention (without detracting from the minimum obligations contained in this Convention), and one in which the advancement of a wider range of human rights becomes obligatory for the occupying power.

The Hague Regulations and the Fourth Geneva Convention prescribe minimum rules of humanitarian conduct to be observed by the occupant. They are not intended to be exhaustive. Where a territory enjoys a status which entitles it to be governed in accordance with additional standards rooted in the concepts of human rights and self-determination, the occupant is obliged to act in accordance with both these standards and the minimum rules contained in the law of occupation.[34]

---

[31] At 9–10. According to Roberts, '[O]ccupations of exceptional length do expose certain inadequacies in a body of law essentially intended for much briefer and more precarious periods of foreign military control' ('What is Military Occupation?', 273).

[32] Benvenisti argues that, although Israel has not annexed the West Bank and the Gaza Strip, it has, over the years, extended 'permanent control' over them. 'Permanent control', he says, 'means any form of administration, under whatever legal disguise, by which exclusive or ultimate control of the territories is retained and perpetuated' (Benvenisti, *The West Bank Data Base Project: A Survey of Israel's Policies* (Washington, DC, 1984), 38).

[33] Meron, *Human Rights in Internal Strife*, Ch. 1. The merging of humanitarian law and human rights law is particularly apparent in a series of UNGA resolutions adopted after 1968 on 'Respect for Human Rights in Armed Conflicts'. See, in particular, GA Res. 2675 (XXV).

[34] Roberts states:

Indeed, while it is certainly based on some clear minimum standards, there is an extent to which it is wrong to conceive of the law on occupations as a single set of

Two methods might be employed in order to obtain acceptance of the notion that Israel's legal obligations extend beyond the Hague Regulations and the Fourth Geneva Convention: a solemn declaration of the General Assembly or an advisory opinion of the International Court of Justice. The former method is unlikely to achieve the desired result of persuading the international community *and Israel* to accept such a status, as the credibility of the General Assembly in matters affecting Israel is suspect, to put it mildly, among Western nations, and would have no impact on Israel itself. An advisory opinion of the International Court of Justice on the status of the Occupied Territories might, however, have more positive results[35] and provide the necessary legal basis for the enforcement of human rights in the Occupied Territories. Such an opinion would also serve to confirm the minimum obligation imposed upon Israel 'to respect and to ensure respect' for the Fourth Convention 'in all circumstances' and upon other signatory States to ensure compliance with the Convention on the part of Israel.[36]

Obviously there are problems associated with the suggestion of an advisory opinion which must be considered. First, would the International Court of Justice be likely to give such an opinion if requested? Secondly, would the Court be likely to give an opinion that accords to the Occupied Territories a special status? Thirdly, would an opinion that subjects Israel to greater legal obligations than at present be acceptable to Western states and Israel? Fourthly, what would such an opinion achieve?

III. Advisory Opinion of the International Court of Justice

Would the International Court of Justice give an Advisory Opinion if Requested?

The Security Council is unlikely to request an advisory opinion on the legal status of the Occupied Territories. It has only once before made

---

rules. True, its basic principles and provisions are set out in concise form in the Hague Regulations and the Geneva Civilian Convention, but to these must be added other elements, involving State practice, case law and writings, as well as other conventions of a more general character. In addition, the parallel stream of the international law of human rights has not only influenced the recent development of the laws of war in the shape of the 1977 Geneva Protocol I, but has also been increasingly recognized as having some applicability to occupations in its own right.

('What is Military Occupation?', 305). See, too, Cohen, *Human Rights in the Israeli Occupied Territories*, 9, 28, 289.

[35] An advisory opinion has been suggested by Hassan bin Talal in *Palestinian Self-Determination: A Study of the West Bank and Gaza Strip* (New York, 1981), 87.

[36] In accordance with Art. 1 of the Convention.

such a request[37] and it is improbable that the United States would give its support to such a strategy. Consequently such a request would have to emanate from the General Assembly, acting under Article 96(1) of the Charter.

The International Court has indicated that it will not give an opinion in circumstances in which this would amount to deciding a dispute between states.[38] However, a request for an opinion on the legal status of the Occupied Territories would not fall into this category as the purpose of such an opinion would not be to settle a dispute between states but rather to guide the General Assembly in respect of its own actions. The Court would therefore in all likelihood follow the precedent of the 1971 *Namibia Opinion*[39] and render such an opinion.

What Type of Opinion could be Expected?

There should be little difficulty in persuading the International Court that the Fourth Geneva Convention applies to Israel's administration of the Occupied Territories. Article 1 of the Convention, which provides that 'The High Contracting Parties undertake to respect and to ensure respect for the ... Convention in all circumstances', has been held by the Court in the *Nicaragua* case to impose an obligation which derives not only from the Convention, 'but from the general principles of humanitarian law',[40] which suggests a determination on the part of the Court to ensure that the Geneva Conventions are widely enforced. It is highly unlikely therefore that the 'excessively legalistic'[41] arguments raised by Israel against the applicability of the Fourth Geneva Convention would find favour with the Court.

Although it is essential to obtain judicial approval for the applicability of the Fourth Geneva Convention to the Occupied Territories, it is necessary to go beyond such a finding and to persuade the Court that Israel's obligations in the human rights sphere are more extensive than those minimum obligations contained in the Fourth Geneva Convention, on account of the special international status of Palestine.

There are important similarities between Namibia and Palestine. Both were mandated territories of the League of Nations; both mandates were confronted with the problem of legal succession after the demise

---

[37] In Res. 284 (1970) it requested an advisory opinion on Namibia.
[38] *Eastern Carelia Case*, PCIJ Reports, Ser. B, No. 5 (1923).
[39] *Legal Consequences for States of the Continued Presence of South Africa in Namibia (South West Africa) notwithstanding Security Council Resolution 276 (1970)* (hereinafter referred to as the *Namibia Opinion*), ICJ Reports (1971), 16 at 23–4. See, too, the Court's opinion in the *Western Sahara* case, ICJ Reports (1975), 12 at 21–9.
[40] *Military and Paramilitary Activities in the against Nicaragua, Merits*, ICJ Reports (1986), 14 at 114.
[41] Roberts, 'What is Military Occupation?', 282.

of the League of Nations; both mandates were terminated by resolutions of the General Assembly of the United Nations;[42] and both territories are still in full (Namibia) or in part (Palestine) under alien occupation. In these circumstances it is acknowledged by many jurists that the key to the legal conundrum of the status of the Occupied Territories is to be found in the 'law of Namibia'.[43] It is not improbable therefore that the Court would be led by the guiding principles of the *Namibia Opinion* of 1971 in its assessment of the legal status of the Occupied Territories. These principles are:

1. Non-annexation.[44] *A fortiori* this principle applies to Palestine as an A-type mandate.
2. The principle that the well-being and development of the peoples of the mandated territory is to form a 'sacred trust of civilization'.[45]
3. The interests of humanity and respect for human rights.[46]
4. The principle of self-determination, as developed in the United Nations, which views independence as the ultimate goal.[47]
5. The international character of the territory until the fulfilment of the sacred trust,[48] by the proper exercise of self-determination.

If these principles are applied to the Occupied Territories, it is probable that the Court would find that those parts of the mandated territory of Palestine which have not yet exercised their right to self-determination (West Bank and the Gaza Strip) as a result of alien occupation (initially by Jordan and Egypt, respectively, and later by Israel) are not susceptible to annexation and that the peoples of these territories should be permitted to exercise their human rights to the full, particularly their right to self-determination. Moreover the human rights regime most likely to be identified as the governing order for the territories pending the exercise of the right of self-determination is that contained in the International Bill of Rights.[49] Such a finding

---

[42] Res. 2145 (XXI) in the case of Namibia; and Res. 181 (II) in the case of Palestine.

[43] Gerson, *Israel, the West Bank and International Law*, 47–8; J. H. Weiler, 'Israel and the Creation of a Palestinian State: The Art of the Impossible and the Possible', *Texas Int. L. J.* 17 (1982), 316; Rostow, 'Palestinian Self-Determination', 154–9.

[44] ICJ *Reports* (1971), 28, 30.

[45] Ibid. 28.

[46] Ibid. 29, 57.

[47] According to the Court, '[T]he ultimate objective of the sacred trust was the self-determination and the independence of the peoples concerned' (Ibid. 31).

[48] This principle is the basis of both the 1971 *Namibia Opinion* and the 1950 Opinion on the *International Status of South West Africa*, ICJ *Reports* (1950), 128.

[49] Universal Declaration of Human Rights, the International Covenant on Civil and Political Rights, and the International Covenant on Economic, Social, and Cultural Rights. Support for the view that such a human rights regime is to apply in the case of prolonged belligerent occupation is to be found in Cohen, *Human Rights in the Israeli Occupied Territories*, 9, 28.

would not undermine in any way the applicability of the humanitarian provisions of the Hague Regulations and the Fourth Geneva Convention, but would expand the rights of inhabitants of the Occupied Territories and thereby give acknowledgement to the growing convergence of human rights and humanitarian law.

There is a debate among international lawyers over the effect of General Assembly Resolution 181 (II) which purported to terminate the mandate for Palestine. While some claim that it had full legal force,[50] others argue that, as a resolution of the General Assembly, it was only recommendatory,[51] with the result that the mandate has not yet been fully terminated. The 1971 *Namibia Opinion* does not give the final answer to this question as it is not absolutely clear from the Court's Opinion whether it found General Assembly Resolution 2145 (XXI), which purported to terminate the mandate for South West Africa, to be legally binding *per se* or whether it acquired its full effect from subsequent Security Council resolutions.[52]

On either interpretation the rights of the Palestinian people in the Occupied Territories remain protected. If Resolution 181 (II) terminated the mandate, it is clear that the people of Palestine in the Occupied Territories have not yet exercised their right to self-determination as envisaged by that resolution. Alternatively, if the mandate still survives in respect of the Occupied Territories, the people are protected by Article 80 of the UN Charter which preserves their rights to international supervision.

Would such an Opinion be Accepted by Western Nations and Israel?

At present Israel is able to rely on Western states, and particularly the United States,[53] for support. The main purpose of an advisory opinion is therefore to gain support among these nations for a greater degree of international supervision of the West Bank and the Gaza Strip and, ultimately, for the full exercise of the right of self-determination in these territories. As the Western nations pride themselves on their respect for the rule of law in international affairs, and therefore for decisions and opinions of the International Court of Justice, there is a greater likelihood that they will accept an opinion of the Court than a declaration of the General Assembly. The United States has in recent times raised doubts about its willingness to honour decisions of the

---

[50] S. V. Mallison and W. T. Mallison Jr., *An International Law Analysis of the Major United Nations Resolutions Concerning the Palestine Question* (United Nations, 1979), 9–27.
[51] Gerson, *Israel, the West Bank and International Law*, 48–9.
[52] *Namibia Opinion*, ICJ Reports (1971), 51.
[53] See J. Quigley, 'United States Complicity in Israel's Violation of Palestinian Rights', PYIL 1 (1984), 95.

International Court, as evidenced by its refusal to accept the decision of the Court in the *Nicaragua* case. However, it must be appreciated that administrations change and that there is strong domestic support in influential quarters in the United States for compliance with judgments of the International Court.

Although Western nations may be cautious in their response to an opinion that asserts the right of Palestinian self-determination, there is no doubt that they would accept a ruling on the applicability of the Fourth Geneva Convention as this coincides with their own present stated positions. The effect may be to encourage these States—particularly the United States—to bring greater pressure to bear upon Israel to observe the obligations contained in the Fourth Geneva Convention and to desist from such practices as collective punishments, deportations, and Jewish settlement. This would accord with the obligation imposed on these states under the Convention to take positive action to ensure compliance with the Convention.[54] In principle, this obligation encompasses the institution of criminal proceedings under Article 146 of the Fourth Geneva Convention against those guilty of grave breaches of the Convention under Article 147.[55] Although it is unlikely that Western states would take action against those responsible for torture, arbitrary killings, and deportations in the Occupied Territories if they came within their territorial jurisdiction, the assertion of such an obligation would probably do much to curb the excesses of the military authorities in the Occupied Territories.

It is difficult to predict Israel's response to an opinion of this kind. Although reactionary forces in Israel deny the relevance of international law, there are other forces that favour compliance with international law. Israel has inherited a Jewish tradition and set of values in which compliance with international law plays an important part.[56] According to Amnon Rubinstein, a distinguished constitutional lawyer and leader of the Shinui party in the Knesset:

In 1948 the State of Israel was born, clinging to the original Zionist vision. Independence was granted according to international law and with the assistance of the great majority of nations, including the big superpowers—all in accordance with Herzl's foresight. The drafters of Israel's Declaration of Independence in 1948 saw Israel in the image of early Zionist Congresses; a secular state based on Jewish national history; a model society embracing

---

[54] See further on this obligation M. Stephens, *Enforcement of International Law in the Israeli-Occupied Territories*, al-Haq Occasional Paper No. 7 (Ramallah, 1989). Cf. T. Meron, 'The Geneva Conventions as Customary Law', *AJIL* 81 (1987), 348.
[55] Stephens, *Enforcement of International Law*
[56] M. I. Dimont, *Jews, God and History* (New York, 1962), 258; A. Nussbaum, *A Concise History of the Law of Nations* (New York, 1947), 9.

equality regardless of religion or race; a people inspired by the prophet's vision of justice to all; a dutiful member in the family of nations.[57]

This tradition has been fostered by the writings of Jewish jurists, in both the Diaspora and Israel, who have played a major role in the development of international law in general and human rights law in particular. Today Israeli lawyers are fully conscious of this heritage and, as shapers of public opinion, they endeavour to ensure that Israel conducts itself within the parameters set by international law.

Although there is considerable hostility to the United Nations in Israel, the same cannot be said of the International Court of Justice. It is therefore at least a possibility, if somewhat remote, that an advisory opinion will be seriously considered, and perhaps accepted, by Israel.

The history of Namibia since the 1971 Opinion is relevant to this discussion. Initially the South African government rejected the Court's Opinion as 'untenable'.[58] However, as it became clear that the entire international community—*including Western nations*—accepted the Opinion, South Africa changed its stance. While it did not accept the illegality of its presence in Namibia, it accepted that it was obliged to grant independence to the territory as one unit—and not in the form of a number of Bantustans as was originally intended. The implementation of Namibian independence was slow however, as the presence of Cuban forces in the conflict in Angola was raised by both South Africa and the United States as a pretext for delaying independence, but international pressure *premised on the Court's Opinion* did much to accelerate the preparation of the territory for independence.[59]

It is not inconceivable that Israel's response to an advisory opinion would be more positive than that of South Africa for two reasons: firstly, Israel's occupation of the West Bank and Gaza is not as entrenched as was South Africa's occupation of Namibia; secondly, Israeli public opinion is possibly likely to be more sensitive to international opinion premised on a judicial opinion than that of South Africa.

What could an Advisory Opinion Achieve?

In the long term it is possible that an opinion of the kind predicted might lead to the exercise of self-determination in the Occupied Territories, the withdrawal of Israel, and the creation of a Palestinian state.

---

[57] *The Zionist Dream Revisited. From Hertzl to Gush Emunim and Back* (New York, 1984), 72. See too, the foreward by Shulamit Aloni MK to ICPME, *Human Rights in the Occupied Territories 1979–1983*, 1–2.

[58] J. Dugard, *The South West Africa/Namibia Dispute* (Berkeley, CA, 1973), 490.

[59] Namibian independence was ultimately achieved in 1990, *in terms of United Nations resolutions premised on the Court's opinion of 1971*. SC Res. 435 of 1978 and subsequent resolutions aimed at securing and implementing Namibian independence were all

It would, however, be naïve to believe that this could be achieved without considerable pressure and a measure of coercion. These forms of pressure will be discussed below. It must, however, be stressed that strategies such as economic coercion, exclusion from international organizations, and non-recognition—which are employed today without much effect—will inevitably gain more support, and hence effectiveness, when they are premised on an advisory opinion.

In the short term, while attempts were made to implement the Court's opinion, it is not improbable that Israel would itself implement directions from the court relating to human rights and humanitarian law. This might result in:

1. a recognition of the *de jure* applicability of the Fourth Geneva Convention;
2. an extension of human rights as Israel attempts to implement higher human rights standards than those contained in the Fourth Geneva Convention;
3. a cessation of Israeli settlements in the West Bank and Gaza and the gradual dismantling of the existing settlements as both government and settlers come to appreciate the incompatibility of Israeli settlements with the notion of self-determination for the Palestinian people;
4. the recognition of the right of Palestinian self-determination in the Occupied Territories.

At present the Israeli government refuses to accept the very idea of Palestinian self-determination. Reasons advanced for this policy vary from a complete denial of the existence of a Palestinian entity[60] to the argument that Palestinians must exercise their right to self-determination in Jordan, which, so it is contended, is already a Palestinian state.[61] Although perceptions of the import of the Camp David

---

premised on the principal findings of the International Court in the 1971 advisory opinion. For a brief survey of the final implementation of Res. 435, see 'Human Rights Index', *South African Journal on Human Rights* 6 (1990), 141–150.

[60] This denial finds its inspiration in the oft-quoted remark of Golda Meir: 'There was no such thing as Palestinians... It was not as though there was a Palestinian people in Palestine considering itself as a Palestinian people and we came and threw them out and took their country away from them. They did not exist.' (Quoted in David Gilmour, *Dispossessed: The Ordeal of the Palestinians* (London, 1982), 12.) According to Julius Stone, 'To present, in 1980, a 'Palestinian Nation' as having been displaced by Israel in Palestine, when no such distinctive entity recognized itself or existed at the time of the allocation between the Jewish and Arab peoples after World War I, is an impermissible game with both history and justice.' (*Israel and Palestine: Assault on the Law of Nations* (Baltimore, 1981), 16.)

[61] This argument is neatly summed up in an 'Information Briefing' entitled *The Palestine Liberation Organization: Liberation or Liquidation?*, published by the Israel Information Centre in 1979: 'Since the majority of Palestinian Arabs are citizens of

Accords may differ, it must be accepted that the Israeli government's interpretation of the Accords does not envisage the creation of an independent Palestinian state in the West Bank and the Gaza Strip.[62] The Israeli government's attitude is supported by the Israeli public at large, although there is growing recognition of the Palestinian right to self-determination in liberal circles.[63]

On the international plane there is growing recognition of the right of Palestinian self-determination and since 1974 recognition of this right has featured prominently in resolutions of the General Assembly.[64] The Security Council has, however, been restrained from following this course by the veto of the United States.[65]

Today there is an urgent need to educate public opinion in Israel and the United States about the validity of Palestinian claims to self-determination. An advisory opinion stressing the applicability of this legal principle to the Palestinian peoples in the Occupied Territories might serve this purpose admirably.

IV. Additional Methods to Secure the Protection of Human Rights in the Occupied Territories under the UN Charter

To date the United Nations has invoked a number of methods to secure human rights and to halt Israel's expansionism in the West Bank and the Gaza Strip. These are non-recognition, economic coercion,

Jordan ... and the majority of Jordanian citizens are Palestinians, it seems only logical to acknowledge that the ultimate solution to the problem of Palestinian self-determination lies in the recognition of Jordan as the Palestinian Arab homeland.'

[62] Y. Dinstein (ed.), *Models of Autonomy* (New Brunswick, NJ, 1981), 256, 269–70.

[63] See A. Hareven (ed.), *Can the Palestinian Problem be Solved?* (Jerusalem, 1983). In his essays in *In the Land of Israel* (New York, 1983), the Israeli writer Amos Oz states:

And ... let me move on to the problem that you prefer to leave unnamed: the Palestinian problem. Alongside Zionism, parallel to it and perhaps a by-product of it, flowered the Palestinian experience. It may be a reflection of our own, a shadow. Perhaps it is a caricature, borrowing our symbols, emotional motifs, military and political techniques, our style and even our poetic sensibilities. There is no copyright law for national experience, and one cannot sue the Palestinian national movement for plagiarism. Even if one were to claim that the Palestinian experience is nothing more than a parody, this would not suffice to nullify the fact of its existence. It has germinated and its growth presents a moral problem to us. One can find some kind of answer or even ignore it, but the price of ignoring it is heavy indeed. (p. 144)

[64] Res. 3236 (XXIX) of 22 Nov. 1974. See, further, *The Right of Self-Determination of the Palestinian People*, ST/SG/SER: F/3 (UN 1979); H. Gros Espiell, *The Right to Self-Determination: Implementation of United Nations Resolutions*, E/CN 4/Sub/2/405/Rev.1 (UN, 1980); Mallison and Mallison, *An International Law Analysis*. On self-determination generally, see Chs. 1, 3, and 5 in this volume.

[65] In 1976, the US vetoed a resolution recognizing the right of the Palestinian people to self-determination: see Gros Espiell, *The Right of Self-Determination*. See also, M. K. Shadid, *The United States and the Palestinians* (1981), 188.

and exclusion from international organizations and investigative committees. At present all these methods suffer from an absence of a clear statement of the law on the status of the Occupied Territories. An advisory opinion would undoubtedly remedy this defect and lend weight to the credibility and effectiveness of these methods.

Non-Recognition of the Annexation of East Jerusalem

Israel has purported to annex both East Jerusalem (1980) and the Golan Heights (1981). As the Golan Heights lay outside the Palestine mandate and were part of Syria until 1967, no attention will be directed to this unlawful annexation.[66] East Jerusalem, however, forms part of the West Bank with the result that its position cannot be ignored in any study of the legal status of the Occupied Territories.

The precise legal status of East Jerusalem is unclear.[67] In 1967, in the wake of the Six Day War, Israel asserted its jurisdiction over East Jerusalem by placing the entire city under a common civil administration.[68] Although Israel denied that this measure constituted annexation,[69] it was strongly condemned as 'invalid' by both the Security Council[70] and the General Assembly[71] on the ground that it purported to alter the status of Jerusalem. In 1980, Israel took a further step towards the full incorporation of East Jerusalem when the Knesset enacted a 'basic law' declaring 'Jerusalem united in its entirety' to be the capital of Israel.[72] This action, which has been widely hailed as the final annexation of East Jerusalem,[73] was condemned by the Security Council in Resolution 478 (1980)[74] as a 'violation of international law'

---

[66] See J. Dugard, *Recognition and the United Nations* (Cambridge, 1987), 115.

[67] For a comprehensive, albeit partisan, account of the present legal status of the city, see H. Cattan, *Jerusalem* (New York, 1981). A more objective analysis of the situation is provided by Melinda Crane, 'Middle East: Status of Jerusalem', *HILJ* 21 (1980), 784.

[68] Gerson, *Israel, The West Bank and International Law*, 210–11; Shlomo Slonim, 'The United States and Jerusalem 1947–1984', *IsLR* 19(2) (1984), 179, 210–11.

[69] In 1967 Israel's Foreign Minister, Abba Eban, informed UN Secretary-General U Thant: 'The term "annexation" used by supporters of the resolution is out of place. The measures adopted relate to the integration of Jerusalem in the administrative and municipal spheres, and furnish a legal basis for the protection of the Holy Places in Jerusalem.' UN Docs. A/6753; S/8052 (1967). But see Cattan, *Jerusalem*, at 71, who argues that the unification of Jerusalem amounted to annexation. Significantly, in *Iwad and Maches v. Hebron Military Court*, ILR 48 (1975), 63, two judges of the Israeli Supreme Court accepted that East Jerusalem had been annexed by Israel.

[70] Res. 252 (1968), 267 (1969), 298 (1971), 446 (1979), 465 (1980).

[71] Res. 2253 (ES–V) (1967), 2254 (ES–V) (1967), 31/106A (1976); 33/113 (1978).

[72] Basic Law: Jerusalem Capital of Israel, 5740–1980 (31 July 1980). See Slonim, 'The United States and Jerusalem'.

[73] Crane, 'Middle East: Status of Jerusalem', 789, 792; Hassan bin Talal, *Palestinian Self-Determination*, 70.

[74] See, too, SC Res. 476 (1980), which anticipated the enactment of Israel's 'Basic Law' on Jerusalem. Res. 478 (1980) has been endorsed by the General Assembly in Res. 36/120E of 10 Dec. 1981; 37/123C of 16 Dec. 1982; 39/146C of 14 Dec. 1984.

and 'null and void'. The Council also decided 'not to recognize the basic law' and such other actions by Israel that, as a result of this law, seek to alter the character and status of Jerusalem. Although Resolution 478 (1980) was not adopted under Chapter VII of the Charter, it is at least arguable that it is binding on Member States under Article 25 as the language of the resolution, particularly the use of the word 'decide' in relation to the decision 'not to recognize the basic law', suggests an intention on the part of the Security Council to bind States—within the meaning of the test expounded in the 1971 *Namibia Opinion*.[75] In the event, no State has recognized Israel's annexation of Jerusalem.

The principal reason advanced for the non-recognition of Israel's claims to sovereignty over East Jerusalem is that Israel acquired jurisdiction over the Old City by the use of force in the course of the Six Day War. Resolutions of both the Security Council[76] and the General Assembly on Jerusalem repeatedly reaffirm 'that the acquisition of territory by force is inadmissible' and draw no distinction between territory acquired by the *lawful* use of force and the *unlawful* use of force.[77] Thus the United Nations expressly refuses to accept the argument that territory may be permanently acquired as a result of action taken in lawful self-defence, as Israel claims she acted in 1967.[78] By necessary implication, resolutions of the political organs of the United Nations also reject arguments that Israel may exercise sovereignty over East Jerusalem on the grounds that her title to the city, based on action taken in self-defence, is better founded than that of Jordan, which acquired control over the city in an aggressive operation in 1948, and that Israel may therefore fill the vacuum of sovereignty in Jerusalem arising from the termination of the mandate.[79]

Two other important norms weigh heavily with the United Nations

---

[75] ICJ *Reports* (1971), 16, 52–4. In 1982, the General Assembly declared in its preamble to Res. 37/123A (1982) that Israel had 'refused, *in violation of Article 25 of the Charter*, to accept and carry out the numerous relevant decisions of the Security Council' (emphasis added).

[76] Res. 242 (1967), 252 (1968), 267 (1971), 476 (1980).

[77] The refusal to draw such a distinction is in line with the Declaration on Principles of International Law Concerning Friendly Relations and Co-operation among States in Accordance with the Charter of the United Nations, adopted by the General Assembly in 1970 (Res. 2625 (XXV)) which provides: 'No territorial acquisition resulting from the threat or use of force shall be recognized as legal'. See, M. Akehurst, *A Modern Introduction to International Law*, 4th edn. (London, 1982), 147–8; D. W. Bowett, 'International Law Relating to Occupied Territory: A Rejoinder', *Law Quarterly Review*, 87 (1971), 473.

[78] Stone, *Israel and Palestine*, 51–3; A. Shapira, 'The Six-Day War and the Right of Self-Defence', *IsLR* 6 (1971), 65.

[79] Several arguments have been advanced along these lines. See Stone, *Israel and Palestine*, 116–23; Lauterpacht, *Jerusalem and the Holy Places*, 48, 52; S. M. Schwebel, 'What Weight to Conquest?', *AJIL* 64 (1970), 344; Blum, 'The Missing Reversioner'.

in its approach to Jerusalem. First, both the Security Council[80] and the General Assembly[81] maintain that Israel is in belligerent occupation of East Jerusalem and thus bound to comply with the Fourth Geneva Convention, an obligation which is irreconcilable with the exercise of complete jurisdiction over the City in terms of the Israeli 'basic law' of 1980. Secondly, the General Assembly[82] clearly views Jerusalem as forming part of a Palestinian self-determination unit embracing Jerusalem, the West Bank and the Gaza Strip. Thus, in Resolution 39/146A of 14 December 1984, the General Assembly declared that:

[P]eace in the Middle East is indivisible and must be based on a comprehensive, just and lasting solution of the Middle East problem, under the auspices of the United Nations and on the basis of relevant resolutions of the United Nations, which ensures the complete and unconditional withdrawal of Israel from Palestinian and other territories occupied since 1967, *including Jerusalem*, and which enables the Palestinian people, under the leadership of the Palestine Liberation Organization, to exercise its inalienable rights, including the rights to return and the right to self-determination, national independence and the establishment of its independent sovereign State in Palestine.... (emphasis added)

Consequently a cluster of principles inherent in the two fundamental norms of the prohibition on the use of force and the right to self-determination provide a legal basis for the refusal of the United Nations to recognize Israel's sovereignty over East Jerusalem. More specifically, the annexation of East Jerusalem violates three peremptory norms having the character of *jus cogens*, namely: (*a*) the prohibition on the acquisition of territory by force; (*b*) principles of humanitarian law contained in the Hague Regulations and the Fourth Geneva Convention; and (*c*) the right of self-determination.

The annexation is therefore null and void and States are under a duty not to recognize it.[83] In essence, non-recognition is employed as a sanction by the international community, as a result of Israel's violation of international law, in the same way that non-recognition was invoked against South Africa in respect of its administration of Namibia and its creation of Bantustan states.

The consequences of non-recognition are of the kind spelt out by the

---

[80] Res. 476 (1980), 478 (1980). See also Crane, 'Middle East: Status of Jerusalem'.

[81] Res. 36/120E (1981), 39/146A (1984).

[82] Since 1974, when the General Assembly reaffirmed 'the inalienable right' of the Palestinian people to self-determination (Res. 3236 (XXIX)), resolutions of the General Assembly have increasingly approached the question of Palestine from the perspective of self-determination. See *The Right of Self-Determination of the Palestinian People*, ST/SG/SER/F/3 (UN 1979); Mallison and Mallison, *An International Law Analysis*.

[83] See on this subject, Dugard, *Recognition and the United Nations*, Ch. 6. On the illegality of annexation under belligerent occupation, see also Chs. 5 and 7 in this volume.

International Court of Justice in the 1971 *Namibia Opinion* and range from the severance of treaty relations to the termination of diplomatic and consular relations.[84] Although the law on this subject is fairly clear, this matter is one that might specifically be referred to the International Court of Justice in a request for an advisory opinion in order to obtain a judicial direction to states on the consequences of the non-recognition of Israel's annexation of East Jerusalem.

Economic Coercion

The General Assembly has already adopted a number of resolutions recommending economic sanctions against Israel on account of its violation of international law—including its refusal to withdraw from Palestinian territories occupied in 1967.[85] Resolutions of this kind are likely to increase in frequency and scope if the International Court hands down an advisory opinion along the lines predicted and Israel refuses to comply with it.

In some quarters economic coercion of this kind, not authorized by the Security Council, is viewed as contrary to international law. It is therefore necessary to consider the validity of this argument in the context of sanctions against Israel.

The traditional view is that the Charter of the United Nations prohibits the use of armed force alone in Article 2(4); and that economic coercion does not fall within this prohibition. This view is supported by the negotiating history of Article 2(4), the qualification of the term 'force' as 'armed force' in other provisions of the Charter,[86] the practice of states, and the writings of jurists.[87] Despite this, socialist and Third World states maintain that, as economic coercion may destroy the political independence of a state as effectively as armed force, it is essential to interpret Article 2(4) to encompass all forms of force. This interpretation received little support from Western nations until the 1973 Arab oil boycott shook the economies of the West. This led some

---

[84] ICJ *Reports* (1971), 54–6.

[85] In Feb. 1982, in Res. ES-9/1, the UNGA 'called upon' member states to apply the following measures: (*a*) To refrain from supplying Israel with any weapons and related equipment and to suspend any military assistance which Israel receives from them; (*b*) To refrain from acquiring any weapons or military equipment from Israel; (*c*) To suspend economic, financial, and technological assistance to and co-operation with Israel; and (*d*) To sever diplomatic, trade, and cultural relations with Israel. See too Res. 38/180A of 19 Dec. 1983.

[86] Preamble, Art. 46.

[87] D. W. Bowett, *Self Defence in International Law* (Manchester, 1958), 148; R. B. Lillich, 'The Status of Coercion under International Law', *Texas Int. L. J.* 12 (1977), 18–19; Y. Z. Blum, 'Economic Boycotts in International Law', *Texas Int. L. J.* 12 (1977), 10–12; R. B. Bilder, 'The Legality of the Arab Oil Boycott', *Texas Int. L. J.* 12 (1977), 41.

American international lawyers to support the view that economic coercion was contrary to the Charter.[88]

Although the argument that economic coercion is prohibited by Article 2(4) remains largely discredited, there is considerable support for the view that economic coercion is an unlawful intervention in the domestic affairs of a state when it is not authorized by the Security Council acting under Chapter VII of the Charter.[89] Here reliance is placed on two important resolutions of the General Assembly, the Declaration on the Inadmissibility of Intervention in the Domestic Affairs of States and the Protection of their Independence and Sovereignty of 1965[90] and the Declaration on Principles of International Law Concerning Friendly Relations and Co-operation among States in Accordance with the Charter of the United Nations of 1970,[91] which declare that:

> No state may use or encourage the use of economic, political or any other type of measures to coerce another state in order to obtain from it the subordination of the exercise of its sovereign rights or to secure from it advantages of any kind.

Even if it is accepted that economic coercion constitutes an unlawful form of intervention under international law,[92] it is clear that not every form of economic pressure is illegal. It must take the form of pressure that seeks to 'subordinate' the exercise of the target state's sovereign rights. According to Professor Bowett, of Cambridge University: 'This suggests that it will be necessary to characterize unlawful economic measures by their intent rather than by their effect. In other words, measures not illegal *per se* may become illegal only upon proof of an improper nature or purpose.'[93]

The categorization of economic coercion as an unlawful intervention has led some writers to argue that economic sanctions imposed by states and international organizations against a state in order to promote human rights—without Security Council authorization under Chapter VII of the Charter—are illegal.[94]

This view is clearly without substance in the context of Israel and the Occupied Territories, for, even if economic coercion is prohibited by an emerging norm of international law on non-intervention, it can hardly

---

[88] J. J. Paust and A. P. Blaustein, 'The Arab Oil Weapon—A Threat to International Peace', *AJIL* 68 (1974), 410–39.

[89] Blum, 'Economic Boycotts', 12–15.

[90] Res. 2131 (XX).

[91] Res. 2625 (XXXV).

[92] The prohibition on economic coercion under international law is still questioned by many writers: see, for example, Bilder, 'The Legality of the Arab Oil Boycott', 41–3.

[93] 'Economic Coercion and Reprisals by States', *Virginia Jnl. of Int. Law* 13 (1972), 5.

[94] G. N. Barrie, 'International Law and Economic Coercion—A Legal Assessment', *South African Ybk. of Int. Law* 1 (1985–6), 40–54; G. N. Barrie and P. C. Szasz, 'Agora: Is the ASIL Policy on Divestment in Violation of International Law?', *AJIL* 82 (1988), 311.

be maintained that the collective and unilateral economic measures taken against Israel are not justifiable under contemporary international law. Justification for such action can be found on two grounds:

1. Humanitarian Intervention Humanitarian intervention involving the use of armed force is prohibited by Article 2(4) of the UN Charter, but there is no such prohibition on humanitarian intervention that takes the form of economic coercion. The legal position is correctly stated in the following terms in a recent study:

> Unlike the use of armed force, resort to economic measures is not *per se* illegal. The complaining state must show that a particular use of economic force is unlawful because of improper intent. But a state that could cite violations of accepted norms of international human rights law as the motivation for the imposition of trade restrictions would have a defence to any charge of illegal motive and thus be justified in the imposition of economic sanctions.[95]

Israel's policies and practices in the Occupied Territories have been condemned as contrary to international human rights norms by the General Assembly of the United Nations.[96] Economic coercion against Israel taken in response to the violation of human rights could thus be properly justified as humanitarian intervention.

2. United Nations Authorization Although the Security Council has not taken action against Israel under Chapter VII of the Charter, the General Assembly has recommended to states that they impose economic sanctions against Israel.[97] According to Judge Hersch Lauterpacht, such recommendations may 'on proper occasions... provide a legal authorization for members determined to act upon them individually or collectively'.[98] Although the authorization of armed force by the General Assembly is contrary to the UN Charter, this is not the case with economic coercion which is not prohibited by the Charter. Here authorization by the General Assembly transforms what might have been an 'improper purpose' into a 'proper purpose', thereby rendering the economic sanctions employed lawful.

Recommendations of the General Assembly authorizing economic sanctions may also serve to release a state from its obligations under a

---

[95] W. C. Maddrey, 'Economic Sanctions against South Africa: Problems and Prospects for Enforcement of Human Rights Norms', *Virginia Jnl. of Int. Law* 22 (1981), 365, 373–5. See, too, S. C. Neff, 'The Law of Economic Coercion', *Columbia Jnl. of Transnational Law* 20 (1981), 435; Tom J. Farer, 'Political and Economic Coercion in Contemporary International Law', *AJIL* 79 (1985), 413.
[96] For example, Res. 38/79D of 1983.
[97] See n. 85.
[98] Separate opinion, *Voting Procedure Case*, ICJ *Reports* (1955), 115. See, too, Bowett, 'Economic Coercion', 6; P. C. Szasz, 'The Action does not Violate International Law', *AJIL* 82 (1988), 314.

trade agreement with Israel. Article 103 of the UN Charter absolves states from their treaty obligations where a conflict arises between such obligations and their obligations under the Charter. Although a state normally incurs 'obligations' under the Charter only in the case of a binding decision by the Security Council, there is some support for the view that recommendations of the General Assembly create such 'obligations' for the purpose of Article 103 and thereby release states from conflicting treaty commitments.[99]

Exclusion from International Organizations

Attempts have been made to exclude Israel from participation in specialized agencies[100] and, in 1982, an attempt was made to reject the credentials of Israel in the General Assembly of the United Nations on the ground that it had violated international law and refused to abide by decisions of the United Nations.[101]

This is a sanction that has been extensively employed against South Africa, which has been excluded from many specialized agencies and been denied the right to participate in the work of the General Assembly.[102] However, it is doubtful whether it is an effective method of persuading or coercing a state into complying with its international obligations, for a number of reasons. First, the effect of full expulsion is to release a state from its obligations under the constitution of the organization from which it is expelled without remedying the breach of international law. Secondly, it removes a state from the arena of criticism and thereby immunizes it from criticism. Thirdly, procedures of dubious legality are frequently employed to secure the exclusion,[103] and this produces sympathy for the state in question among Western nations and undermines respect for the international organization among opponents of the regime in its own state. Certainly the South African experience suggests that the exclusion of South Africa from the General Assembly has been counter-productive for the above reasons. In the Israel/Palestine context resort to illegal procedures to secure the exclusion of Israel from international organizations would be par-

---

[99] See generally on this subject, Dugard, 'The Legal Effect of UN Resolutions on Apartheid', *South African L. J.* 83 (1966), 56–9.

[100] In 1982 an attempt was made to exclude Israel from the ITU: see 1983 *Proceedings of the American Society of International Law*, 358.

[101] For an examination of this attempt, see M. Halberstam, 'Excluding Israel from the General Assembly by a Rejection of Credentials', *AJIL* 78 (1984), 179.

[102] See R. Bissell, *Apartheid and International Organizations* (Boulder, Col., 1977); J. C. Heunis, *United Nations versus South Africa* (Johannesburg, 1986), 148–75, 486–91.

[103] Halberstam, 'Excluding Israel'; Heunis, *United Nations*; D. Ciobanu, 'Credentials of Delegations and Representation of Member States at the United Nations', *ICLQ* 25 (1976), 351.

ticularly damaging to an enforcement strategy based on a sound legal foundation and judicial opinion. There is therefore much substance in the warning given by C. Wilfred Jenks in 1945 that '[A]t best [expulsion] is merely an alibi for the failure of other states to devise effective means of enforcing the provisions which have been flouted'.[104]

Investigative Committees

In 1968, the General Assembly decided to establish a Special Committee to investigate alleged violations of human rights in the territories occupied by Israel.[105] The Committee has not been permitted by Israel to carry out its investigations in the Occupied Territories so it has been obliged to rely on the testimony of witnesses outside the territories and on written submissions. The regular annual reports of this Committee have provided a basis for General Assembly resolutions condemning Israel's violation of human rights in the Occupied Territories.[106]

A number of criticisms have been directed at the Special Committee.[107] These include:

1. Improper constitution of the Committee.
2. Bias arising from the membership of the Committee, as the members are all representatives of countries hostile to Israel.
3. Prejudging of the issue by the General Assembly.[108]
4. Doubts as to the applicability of the human rights standards applied. The Special Committee has relied on the Fourth Geneva Convention, the Hague Conventions of 1899 and 1907, and the Universal Declaration of Human Rights.
5. Questions about the methods employed to verify the information received.
6. Undue politicization of the work of the Special Committee.

Unfortunately there is substance in some of these criticisms and this has detracted from the value of the work of the Special Committee. The purpose of such a committee must surely be to establish facts in a fair manner so that this information may be used to educate international opinion with a view to bringing pressure to bear upon

---

[104] 'Some Constitutional Problems of International Organizations', BYIL 22 (1945), 25.
[105] Res. 2443 (XXIII).
[106] See, for example, Res. 3240 (XXIX), 3525 (XXX), 38/79 of 1983.
[107] T. J. M. Zuijdwijk, *Petitioning the United Nations* (Aldershot, 1982), 281–303; D. Shefi, 'Reports of the Special Committees on Israeli Practices in the Territories' in M. Shamgar (ed.), *Military Government in the Territories Administered by Israel 1967–80*, 1: *The Legal Aspects* (Jerusalem, 1982), 285–331; and see note in *HILJ* 15 (1974), 470.
[108] Res. 2546 (XXIV).

the delinquent state. This exercise, which has been described as the mobilization of shame, is dependent upon the fairness and accuracy of the investigations. Due process of law is as important on the international level as it is on the national level.[109] Unfortunately the effectiveness of the Special Committee has suffered from its failure to have regard to this consideration.

Non-governmental organizations (NGOs)—such as the ICRC, Amnesty International, and the International Commission of Jurists—are not subject to the same political pressures as UN Committees, and are moreover able to draw on the professional expertise of persons better qualified to conduct investigations than those appointed by the United Nations to its investigative committees. In these circumstances, it is suggested that greater use should be made of NGOs[110] in the conducting of investigations and the mobilization of shame against Israel in respect of her administration of the Occupied Territories.

V. Applicability of ILO Conventions

There is a dispute over the applicability of ILO multilateral conventions to the Occupied Territories.[111] The two main conventions in dispute are ILO Convention No. 87, concerning Freedom of Association and Protection of the Right to Organize of 1948 (ratified by Israel but not Jordan), and ILO Convention No. 111, concerning Discrimination in Respect of Employment and Occupation of 1958 (ratified by both Israel and Jordan before 1967). The ILO appears to take the position that the extension of these conventions to the Occupied Territories by Israel will amount to an extension of Israel's 'sovereignty' over the Occupied Territories. This is ridiculous. The interests of humanity require that conventions of this kind be extended to Occupied Territories. As Meron states:

International labour conventions, as distinguished from the labour laws of a particular country, are evidence of generally agreed labour standards and may therefore be regarded as being in the interests of the population of an occupied territory.[112]

This is another issue on which legal clarification is required by the International Court of Justice. A question on the applicability of multi-

---

[109] See J. Carey, *UN Protection of Civil and Political Rights* (New York, 1970), 109.
[110] See further on this subject, D. Weissbrodt, 'The Contribution of International Nongovernmental Organizations to the Protection of Human Rights', in T. Meron (ed.), *Human Rights in International Law: Legal and Policy Issues* (Cambridge, 1984), 403–38.
[111] T. Meron, 'Applicability of Multilateral Conventions to Occupied Territories', *AJIL* 72 (1978), 542; *al-Haq Newsletter* 15 (Sept./Oct. 1986); and see Ch. 9 in this volume.
[112] Meron, 'Applicability of Multilateral Conventions', 550.

lateral ILO conventions to the Occupied Territories should therefore be included in a request for an advisory opinion from the International Court of Justice.

VI. The Advancement of Human Rights through Domestic Courts

Israel follows the same approach as England in respect to the relationship between municipal law and international law. Treaties do not form part of municipal law unless incorporated by legislative act, but customary law automatically forms part of municipal law. The Israeli High Court of Justice, which exercises review powers over the acts of the Israeli authorities in the Occupied Territories,[113] has applied this principle to the territories.[114]

In recent times attempts have been made by human rights activists in a number of countries, including the United States, England, and South Africa, to persuade domestic courts to apply the principal human rights norms *as customary international law*.[115] United States courts have held the prohibition on torture[116] and detention without trial[117] to be customary rules which may be applied by domestic courts. Similarly international standards on the treatment of prisoners have been applied by domestic courts.[118] In England, courts have acknowledged the guidance of the European Convention of Human Rights although the convention has not been incorporated into domestic law.[119] In South Africa and Namibia, attempts have been made to persuade courts that the Geneva Protocol I of 1977, extending prisoner-of-war status to members of liberation movements, now forms part of customary law—with mixed success.[120]

It is suggested that human rights groups in the Occupied Territories—notably al-Haq—might make greater use of these develop-

---

[113] On this review power, see Y. Butovsky, 'Law of Belligerent Occupation: Israeli Practice and Judicial Decisions Affecting the West Bank', *Canadian Ybk. of Int. Law* 21 (1983), 217; E. R. Cohen, 'Justice for Occupied Territory? The Israeli High Court of Justice Paradigm', *Columbia Jnl. of Transnational Law* 24(3) (1986), 471.

[114] See the *Elon Moreh* case reported in *PYIL* 1 (1984), 156; and the *Beit El* case reported in *PYIL* 2 (1985), 140–2. See further, Cohen, 'Justice for Occupied Territory?', 484–90; and Ch. 2 in this volume.

[115] See J. Dugard, 'International Human Rights Norms in Domestic Courts: Can South Africa Learn from Britain and the United States?' in E. Kahn (ed.), *Fiat Justitia: Essays in Memory of O. D. Schreiner* (Cape Town, 1983), 221.

[116] *Filartiga v. Pena-Irala* 630 F 2d 876 (2d Cir 1980).

[117] *Fernandez v. Wilkinson* 505 F Supp 787 (1980).

[118] *Lareau v. Manson* 507 F Supp 1177 (1980); *Sterling v. Cupp* Oregon 625 P 2d 123.

[119] For example, *Att.-Gen. v. BBC* [1981] AC 303 (HL) at 352–3.

[120] C. Murray, 'The Status of ANC and SWAPO and International Humanitarian Law', *South African L. J.* 100 (1983), 402. See, too, the judgment of Conradie J. in *S v. Petane* 1988(3) SA 51(C).

ments and precedents. Although it is unlikely that the military courts will be influenced by such arguments, it is possible that the High Court of Justice might be prepared to accept the following propositions:[121]

1. The principal human rights norms contained in the Universal Declaration of Human Rights form part of customary law and may therefore be applied in the absence of an overriding statute.[122]
2. In interpreting ambiguous statutes a court may be guided by unincorporated treaty obligations such as those contained in the Fourth Geneva Convention, which has not been incorporated into Israeli law,[123] and the human rights clauses in the UN Charter.
3. The administrative acts of the military authorities may be reviewed against the standards of Israel's international commitments.

While the acts of ordinary administrative officials cannot be judged against international norms,[124] there is no reason why the acts of the Military Commander should not be required to conform to rules of international law—both customary *and conventional*. The High Court has held that the Military Commander's actions may be tested against the standards of Israeli administrative law—that is, the notions of reasonableness and fairness that Israel has inherited from the legal systems of Western democracies.[125] It might be argued that the standard of reasonableness requires that a senior administrative officer—such as the Military Commander—act in accordance with Israel's international obligations, whether incorporated into Israeli municipal law or not.[126] In this way it may be possible to overcome the obstruction to the application of the Fourth Geneva Convention that results from the High Court's finding that only treaties incorporated into municipal law may be directly invoked before an Israeli court.

---

[121] For a discussion of these propositions, see Dugard, 'International Human Rights Norms in Domestic Courts', 233–9.

[122] This view is supported by Meron, 'West Bank and Gaza: Human Rights and Humanitarian Law in the Period of Transition', *IYHR* 9 (1979), 112–13. See Ch. 2 in this volume for a review of Israeli Supreme Court views on this issue.

[123] *Elon Moreh* case reported in PYIL 1 (1984), 134.

[124] In *R v. Sec. of State for Home Affairs: Ex Parte Bhajan Singh* [1976] QB 198 (CA), Lord Denning MR held that immigration officers ought to be guided by the unincorporated European Convention on Human Rights in exercising their powers under the immigration laws, 'because, after all, the principles stated in the Convention are only a statement of the principles of fair dealing; and it is their duty to act fairly' (at 207). However, he later retracted this view in *R v. Chief Immigration Officer, Heathrow Airport: Ex parte Salamat Bibi* [1976] All ER 843 (CA) at 847–8.

[125] Cohen, 'Justice for Occupied Territory?', 490–2.

[126] South African courts have left open the question whether administrative acts may be set aside if they conflict with the mandate for South West Africa—a treaty that has never been incorporated into municipal law. See *Winter v. Min. of Defence*, 1940 AD 194 at 198; *S v. Tuhadeleni*, 1969 (1) SA 153 (AD) at 176, 173–4. See further on this argument, Dugard, 'International Human Rights Norms in Domestic Courts', 237–9.

The use of the Israeli High Court of Justice to promote human rights is a controversial strategy as some argue that this confers legitimacy on the Israeli system of justice and constitutes an acknowledgement of the correctness of that court's exercise of jurisdiction over the Occupied Territories. This controversy raises a wide range of political and jurisprudential issues that fall outside the purview of this paper. However, it is interesting to record that this debate is paralleled in South Africa. There, utilitarian considerations have so far prevailed over ideological arguments and progressive forces have not hesitated to use the courts established by the National Party to promote human rights. Obviously when municipal courts lean too strongly in favour of the executive or are too easily influenced by arguments of military necessity,[127] the utility of such a strategy becomes questionable and considerations of legitimacy assume a greater importance.

Conclusion

The task of advancing human rights in the Occupied Territories of the West Bank and Gaza Strip is a difficult one as much depends on the prospects of an overall peace settlement in terms of Security Council Res. 242 providing for the withdrawal of Israel from the territories. This does not mean that those concerned about human rights in the Occupied Territories can sit back and wait for such a settlement. They must take action by employing all the means at their disposal. In this paper I have suggested that the present attempts to persuade the Security Council to take enforcement action are doomed to fail. I have suggested a multiple strategy instead, in which an advisory opinion from the International Court of Justice features prominently. Such an opinion could serve to answer a number of unanswered legal questions that at present obstruct the advancement of human rights; to lay a sound legal basis for political actions against Israel; and to provide an impetus for peace talks to secure the withdrawal of Israeli forces from the Occupied Territories. Only the full exercise of the right of self-determination by the Palestinian people will secure the real advancement of human rights in the West Bank and the Gaza Strip. An advisory opinion emphasizing this obvious truth might help to advance the implementation of this ideal—which has so long been denied the people of Palestine.

---

[127] For a discussion of the history of arguments based on military necessity before the Israeli High Court, see Cohen, 'Justice for Occupied Territory?', 497–506.

17

Avenues open for Defence of Human Rights in the Israeli-Occupied Territories

JONATHAN KUTTAB

PALESTINIANS in the Occupied Territories face a wide variety of human rights violations. Some pertain to their collective rights, such as the right of self-determination, others pertain to individual rights such as freedom of speech, freedom of assembly, freedom of movement, as well as the property rights and their rights to life and security of the person.

The perpetrators of these violations range from the Israeli military government and its different constituent parts, to Jewish settlers in the Occupied Territories and even Palestinian collaborators with the authorities (such as the Village Leagues) who have also been guilty of a wide variety of abuses and human rights violations.[1]

Some of the violations are incorporated in legislative enactments such as military orders. Others pertain to administrative actions and procedures followed by the authorities. Yet others pertain to specific actions and behaviour on a day-to-day basis. Some relate to patterns and forms of behaviour of authorities while others are clearly individual actions and deviations from internal regulations mandated by the Israeli authorities themselves.

The existence and extent of such violations has already been amply documented by international, Israeli, and Palestinian organizations. Al-Haq has an extensive amount of documentation on these violations. This paper will not repeat the findings or conclusions of these bodies but will proceed to describe the avenues available to human rights advocates who attempt to redress and put an end to these violations.

---

[1] See al-Haq, *In Their Own Words: Human Rights Violations in the West Bank* (Geneva, 1983) and other al-Haq publications.

I. Jordanian Law

The first avenue that presents itself, particularly to a local practitioner, is the Jordanian law. It must be recalled here that the Israeli authorities have inherited from the previous regime an existing legal system of Jordanian laws in the West Bank (and Egyptian and Mandate laws in the Gaza Strip). These laws have been very extensively altered through over 1,200 military orders issued by the Israeli military commander which are given precedence over the existing law. None the less, the basic framework of law continues to be that of Jordanian law in the West Bank and of Egyptian and Palestinian laws in the Gaza Strip. That is not the case in the Golan Heights and the expanded East Jerusalem region where Israeli laws have been applied.[2]

Jordanian law, like most legal systems, contains in its criminal code specific provisions prohibiting various forms of assault, robbery, trespass, kidnapping, and other attacks on the person and property.[3] A Palestinian who is subjected to human rights violations which fall within these categories may well consider whether local law does not provide him with a remedy.

The first obstacle that a practitioner who chooses this route will face is a practical one: judicial and executive organs, such as the police, the execution department, the attorney-general and his assistants, are extremely reluctant to consider any complaints against the Israeli authorities, against Jewish settlers, or against known collaborators. In fact, in this they are assisted by the lack of tradition and experience within the rule of law whereby the authorities and their friends are expected to be accountable to law. Brave individuals (or naïve and stupid ones) who have attempted to file such complaints with the police or to initiate criminal action against such perpetrators have been met with ridicule, threats, counter-accusations, and outright refusal to take their statements.

The author has himself met with all except the last of the above reactions in attempting to file complaints at police stations against settlers.[4] Al-Haq has also documented similar incidents where Palestinians who attempted to file complaints against border police were physically and elaborately beaten up.[5] In 1982, a study was prepared, following complaints by law professors at the Hebrew University, of seventy-five cases of violent attacks by Jewish civilian settlers on the Palestinian population in the Occupied Territories. The secret

---

[2] See R. Shehadeh and J. Kuttab, *The West Bank and the Rule Of Law* (Geneva, 1980), and Raja Shehadeh, *Occupier's Law* (Washington, 1985) for a full treatment of the subject.
[3] Jordanian Penal Law of 1960.
[4] Mostly at the Ramallah Police Station, but also at Bethlehem, and once in Tulkarem.
[5] Al-Haq affidavits Nos. 1085, 1059, and 1060.

report, prepared by the Israeli Justice Department's Judith Karp, revealed that complaints of this sort are routinely ignored by the police and the army, and that structural deficiencies prevented the proper investigation and prosecution of the perpetrators. The report itself and its recommendations were ignored until two years later, when they were leaked to the press and became known as 'the Karp Report'.[6] None the less, the recommendations were not adopted, and after a short furore, things returned to normal, and the settlers continue to enjoy virtual immunity in their harassment of the local population.[7]

Individuals who persist in making their complaints may next face unpublished internal regulations which prohibit the local police from taking complaints against Israeli individuals. This author once obtained a copy of an internal memorandum circulated to the prosecutors in the West Bank indicating that they are not to accept any complaints against an Israeli individual at all.[8] Pursuing the above matter, the writer was later told that this was a misunderstanding, that the police are in fact authorized to take complaints, but that only a particular police officer (the Jewish Israeli officer on the 'Upper Floor' of the Police Station) was specifically authorized to handle and take such complaints, not the Arab police officers sitting at the reception desk. An ordinary individual would have been deterred from pursuing the complaint at this point, and anyhow cannot have access to the upper floor unless specifically invited by one of the Jewish officers working there.

Once a criminal complaint has been successfully filed, it is within the total discretion of the authorities to refer it to a military court or to the civilian Arab courts or to postpone action on it indefinitely. In one instance, a complaint was filed by the author against Jewish settlers who kidnapped his Palestinian client and assaulted him severely. The Palestinian client had managed to obtain the licence number of the car in which the kidnappers travelled. The complaint has been with the authorities for over five years and all his attempts to obtain the name of the settlers (known to the police) in order to pursue civil remedies against them in Israeli courts have met with no success to this date.[9]

In addition to these practical problems, Military Order 164 explicitly

[6] *Karp Report*, reprinted in *PYIL* 1 (1984), 185.
[7] One exception to this is the trial of the 'Jewish Underground' terrorists, some of whom received life sentences for their actions. Others received lighter sentences or pardons, and political agitation is aimed at the time of writing at granting amnesty to the others.
[8] Unpublished circular kept at the offices of al-Haq in Ramallah.
[9] The case of Abdallah Dagash, Police File No. 1249/85. The investigation was dropped by the police and they have refused to give him the names or addresses of the settlers to pursue his remedies. The latest refusal was from the State Prosecutor, Dorit Benish.

prohibits the bringing of any action against the authorities or their constituent parts or even calling them to witness without obtaining a specific permit from the officer in charge of judiciary. Such permits, if given at all, take months to obtain. A circular was issued last year indicating that no such permits will be given when the complaint or the action is against the military government itself. Instead, the individual must go directly to the Israeli High Court. The High Court will be discussed at a later point in this chapter.

In addition to all the above, many of the military orders have altered Jordanian law in a fashion that is detrimental to the rights of the Palestinian population. New military orders granted the authorities extensive powers to violate the freedoms and human rights of Palestinians.[10] Other military orders provided a legal cover for the acquisition of Palestinian lands and water rights.[11] Other military orders granted the military government wide authority in controlling all aspects of Palestinian economy,[12] organization, and social life.[13] Yet others grant broad discretion to take preventive measures against the population at large in the name of security, which are then used punitively, or as collective punishments, or as extra-legal sanctions.[14] Such orders themselves are violative of the human rights of Palestinians, but it is clear that no recourse to local law can correct or remedy a violation that is inherent in the military orders which, as stated above, are given precedence over local law.

An extreme example of this is MO 160, the order on interpretations, reviving the British Defence (Emergency) Regulations of 1945 permitting, among other things, the practice of deportation.[15] Deportation had been specifically outlawed by the Jordanian Constitution. The Israeli High Court however has upheld the military government's view that military orders take precedence over every other Jordanian law including the Jordanian Constitution and have upheld the legality of deportations.[16]

---

[10] For example, MO 101 Concerning the Prohibition of Incitement and Adverse Propaganda prohibits 'the meeting of ten or more people in a place where a speech is heard on a political subject or on a subject which may be considered political', or marches of ten or more, or trying 'verbally or in any other manner to influence public opinion in a manner which might endanger public security or order'.

[11] For example, MO 58 on absentee property, MO 59 on state land, MO 291 which suspended the procedure for settlement of disputes over land and water, by which such rights could be registered.

[12] For example, MO 47, prohibiting exports without permits.

[13] Extensive use was made of the British Defence (Emergency) Regulations of 1945, with their sweeping authorities, which had been specifically revived by Israeli military orders. See M. Moffett, *Perpetual Emergency* (Ramallah, 1989).

[14] See Shehadeh, *Occupier's Law*, generally, and Chapters 2 and 6 in this volume.

[15] For an analysis of the Emergency Regulations and an argument that they are no longer legally permitted, see Moffett, *Perpetual Emergency*.

[16] HC 97/79 *Abu Awad v. The Commander of the West Bank Region* PD 33 [3] 309.

II. The Israeli High Court

The second avenue that presents itself to the practitioner is the Israeli High Court of Justice. Much has been made by the Israeli authorities of the fact that they have allowed the residents of the Occupied Territories access to their highest court, the Israeli Supreme Court. It has also often been claimed in Israeli apologetics that the Israeli High Court of Justice acts as a watch-dog and provides judicial oversight of activities of the military government.[17]

Since the beginning of the occupation, Palestinians have had mixed views about going to the High Court. On the one hand, there were serious legal objections to its jurisdiction over matters occurring in the West Bank. After all, the West Bank and Gaza belong to a different juridical entity and enjoy a separate legal status. The Israeli High Court has no jurisdiction over the Occupied Territories. Early in the occupation, however, the Israeli justice department, at the instructions of the then attorney-general, now president of the High Court, Mr Meir Shamgar, decided not to raise any jurisdictional objection of this nature and to accept the jurisdiction of the High Court over the military governor and his employees by virtue of their *in personam* jurisdiction over Israeli citizens, regardless of where they are. Since that time, the representatives of the Israeli government have maintained that position and deliberately refrain from any challenge to the jurisdiction of the High Court or the standing of Palestinians from the Occupied Territories who appeal to it.

That jurisdictional solution, however, did little to assuage the concerns of Palestinians who were facing a policy of creeping annexation and virtual incorporation into Israel. Some were concerned that access to the High Court was yet another politically injurious step. It also entailed a political cost of lending legitimacy and strength to the Israeli contention that, in fact, the High Court was a suitable remedy and resolution for their problems, and that if they failed to prevail there, they had no right to complain of injustice.

Yet others were reluctant to approach the High Court because practitioners in the Occupied Territories had no knowledge of the Hebrew language or the Israeli law and precedents applicable in that court, and were in any case prohibited from arguing before that court. To go to the High Court necessitates employing or obtaining the assistance of Israeli attorneys, or those admitted to the Israeli bar, and is an expensive and uncertain proposition.

For most, however, the determining factor was practical. It was

---

[17] Israel National Section of the International Commission of Jurists, *The Rule of Law in the Areas Administered by Israel* (Tel Aviv, 1981), 4–6, 35–41.

the proven inefficacy of the Israeli High Court of Justice. Out of tens, if not hundreds of cases before it, there have been an insignificant number where Palestinians obtained satisfaction and can claim that the Israeli court gave them the recourse that they sought in matters pertaining to the military government or its agents.

The reason for this disappointing outcome was not because of lack of independence of the Israeli High Court. All indications point to the fact that the High Court acts independently of the military government and is not dictated to by any Israeli governmental authority. The real reason was that the High Court itself often shared the same perspectives as the military government, politically or ideologically, and that it had voluntarily placed upon itself a number of restrictions that prohibited it from playing an effective role as a check on the behaviour of the military government or that of a neutral arbiter of its actions and legislation.

This matter is discussed in detail in another chapter of this book,[18] but I would like to summarize here a number of the restrictions the High Court placed upon itself which severely limited its power to intervene actively in human rights violations in the Occupied Territories.

1. *Sitting as High Court of Justice, rather than as Court of Appeal*. The Israeli High Court reviews cases arising from the West Bank not as a Court of Appeal but rather as a High Court of Justice exercising its authority under paragraphs 15 and 7 of the Israeli Basic Law (Judiciary). As such, it holds itself strictly to principles of equity, including the requirement of clean hands, exhaustion of administrative remedies, the requirement of bringing an action promptly, and the like. One particularly onerous restriction was articulated in the *Burkan* case:[19] an individual who approaches the media or the political levels and tries to obtain public support for his position is prohibited from appearing before the High Court. A strict interpretation of this doctrine of *sub judice* makes the appeal to the High Court, in the light of its limited possibility of success, a dangerous course since it blocks the opportunity for resolving the situation through appeal to the public. In many cases, individuals deliberately refrain from going to the High Court in order not to be foreclosed from seeking other remedies. One recent example of this is the case of Dr Mubarak Awad, founder of the Palestinian Center for the Study of Non-Violence, who refused to appeal to the High Court concerning his deportation in order to leave

---

[18] Ch. 2.
[19] HC 114/78 *Mohamed Sa'id Burkan v. The Minister of Finance et al.*

himself the freedom to work by other means which were initially more successful in preventing his deportation.[20]

2. *Refusal to apply the Geneva Conventions.* One of the most specific and useful conventions for the protection of the population of the Occupied Territories is the Fourth Geneva Convention pertaining to the treatment of civilians who fall under the military occupation of a country other than their own. This convention clearly and unambiguously prohibits deportation,[21] the settlement of civilians from the occupying power into the Occupied Territories,[22] collective punishment,[23] and the alteration of the existing legal and physical structures of the Occupied Territories.

Yet the position of the Israeli government has been that the Fourth Geneva Convention does not apply in the Occupied Territories. A variety of excuses have been given to avoid the application of this convention. One of them was to claim that the convention only applies to territories taken from a legitimate recognized sovereign, and that neither Jordan nor Egypt were prior legitimate sovereigns in the Occupied Territories.[24] Another argument adopted by the Israeli High Court is that the Geneva Conventions are treaty laws which have not been enacted by the Israeli Knesset and therefore the High Court is not authorized to apply them as part of its domestic legislation, even if they are binding on the State of Israel. The court has thereby limited its own authority to restrict the behaviour of the military government under the specific provisions of this Convention.[25]

3. *Broad interpretation of security.* The Israeli High Court gives a very broad interpretation to the requirements of security.[26] It is highly responsive to the political atmosphere in Israel which makes security something of an absolute. Furthermore, the justices frequently state that in matters of security they will not substitute their judgement for the judgement of the experts, namely the military government itself. In the *Elon Moreh* case,[27] the judges were faced with a situation where top-level Israeli officers, including a former chief of staff whose party

---

[20] Since the time of writing, Dr Awad was arrested for immediate deportation. At that point, he did appeal, unsuccessfully, to the High Court, thereby postponing his deportation for two months. He spent this time in prison, until the Court heard his appeal and confirmed his deportation which took place in June 1988.

[21] Art. 49, IV Geneva Convention.

[22] Ibid.

[23] Ibid. Art. 33.

[24] This argument was made full in Y. Z. Blum 'The Missing Reversioner: Reflections on the Status of Judea and Samaria', *IsLR* 3 (1968), 279.

[25] For full discussion of the case law, see Ch. 2; see also Chs. 1, 3, and 5, and other chapters in this book.

[26] On Israel's use of security to justify its actions, see Ch. 6.

[27] HC 390/79 *Dweikat v. State of Israel*, PD 34 [1] 1.

was then in opposition, presented affidavits contradicting the views of the then Minister of Defence. In this case, the court therefore permitted itself to question the judgement of the existing Minister of Defence. However, such a situation is so rare as to be unique. In almost all other cases, the court deliberately refrains from questioning the judgement of the military government whenever a security claim is made. The balancing of security against other interests, which should have been the province of the court, is left largely to the security forces themselves. Even secret evidence supporting the claims of security is routinely accepted in cases of deportation and other instances of the exercise of discretion by the military authorities.[28]

4. *Record of the court's efficacy.* For these and other reasons the court has accumulated a very disappointing record in terms of the rights of the Palestinians. Of the fifty-eight reported cases, only two and a half cases were ruled in favour of the Palestinians: the *Elon Moreh* case, the first *Qawassmeh* case, and half of the second *Jerusalem District Electricity* case.[29] Each of these victories came under very limited and special circumstances and is unlikely to serve as an effective precedent of the willingness of the High Court to champion the human rights of the Palestinians.

For all the above reasons, most Palestinian practitioners have very little faith in the court. Nonetheless, the High Court does continue to offer useful relief in three separate types of situation:

1. Where Israeli authorities violate their own procedures in carrying out different activities. Here, the High Court can be an effective forum to force the authorities to follow their own procedures. Once they do that, however, there is very little that the Court can offer substantively. This is illustrated in the case of the deportation of three mayors, who were deported without first being given an opportunity to appear before a military objections committee. In appealing to the High Court, they were allowed to return solely for the purpose of appearing before such a committee, after which they were promptly deported.[30] In fact they were allowed only just inside the border as the objections committee met near the border at the Allenby Bridge. Further appeal in that case to the High Court on substantive arguments was rejected.

2. In obtaining temporary injunctions against pending house demolitions or other activities. The court does routinely grant temporary injunctions which give individuals some time to organize their affairs

---

[28] On the High Court's attitude to security issues, see Chs. 6 and 14.
[29] HC 390/79 *Dweikat v. State of Israel*, HC 698/80 *Qawassmeh et al. v. Minister of Defence et al.*, and HC 351/80, HC 764/80 *The Jerusalem District Electricity Co. v. Minister of Energy and Planning*. See also Ch. 2, n. 25 in this book.
[30] HC 698/80.

before the demolition or other measure is actually carried out. While such an *order nisi* is generally routinely granted, it is rarely made absolute.

3. The court also has functioned in the past as a useful threat against actions by the authorities. In a few cases, Palestinian practitioners have been able to obtain partial or complete relief by threatening to go to the High Court. However, given the success rate of the authorities in convincing the court to accept their actions and arguments, this threat is increasingly less effective.

III. The International Court of Justice

Practitioners, as well as lay people who are thoroughly frustrated by their failure to obtain redress through the Israeli High Court of Justice and faced with a situation where clearly recognized international human rights are being violated by that court and by the Israeli government, naturally look to the International High Court of Justice sitting at the Hague to see if it is possible to appeal the decisions of the Israeli High Court of Justice or otherwise to complain to that court concerning violations of human rights.

For Palestinians living in the Occupied Territories, however, there are major obstacles to overcome before they can obtain redress before that august forum. I will not address myself here to the efficacy of that forum or to the effect it is likely to have in actually obtaining redress, since these are more than amply covered in the preceding chapter by John Dugard. I would only like to point out the practical obstacles that are faced by Palestinians who consider moving in that direction:

1. The International Court of Justice ordinarily takes claims and cases brought by one state against another. The Palestinians do not yet have a state of their own, and the Palestine Liberation Organization, which has been leading the Palestinian movement and is considered by Palestinians to be their sole legitimate representative, enjoys no standing before the International Court of Justice.

2. In addition, the Arab states that are generally thought of as supporting the Palestinian people do not (with the exception of Egypt) have any diplomatic relations with the State of Israel. The State of Israel has deposited a derogation or qualification to its acceptance of the jurisdiction of the International Court of Justice which stated that it does not accept the jurisdiction of the Court in cases brought against it (Israel) by states which do not have diplomatic relations with Israel. Since the Arab states (with the exception of Egypt) have themselves refused to recognize Israel or have diplomatic relations with

it, none of them has any standing to bring actions on behalf of the Palestinians before the ICJ.

This does, of course, leave two possibilities. The first is that the UN Security Council can bring a request for an Advisory Opinion. This, however, is highly unlikely because of the veto exercised by the US in matters that are of great concern to Israel. The other possibility would be for the UN General Assembly to bring such a request for an Advisory Opinion, similar to the one brought concerning the South African occupation of Namibia.[31] Such a proposal has been considered on more than one occasion.[32]

To bring about such a case requires a major political and diplomatic initiative at the UN but I think it is a worthwhile possibility. How useful it will be in defending human rights is studied in depth in Chapter 16.

IV. The Court of Public Opinion

The experience of practitioners as well as human rights activists, including al-Haq, has shown conclusively that the most effective forum for defending Palestinian human rights in the Occupied Territories has been the appeal to the 'court of public opinion' and the engagement, through implication, of major segments of the international public, foreign governments, international human rights organizations, and even sectors and organizations in the Israeli public itself. Israel has shown itself as vulnerable, if not more vulnerable than other states, to international pressure but there have always been a number of serious and important qualifications surrounding this aspect. Individuals and organizations who attempt to work in this direction must keep in mind a number of factors that will determine the effectiveness of this method. Without them, this will not be a useful avenue for defending human rights.

Accurate Documentation

Defence of human rights requires specific, detailed, and accurate documentation of the incidence of human rights violations and a

---

[31] ICJ Advisory Opinion, *Legal Consequences for States of the Continued Presence by South Africa in Namibia (South West Africa) notwithstanding Security Council Resolution 276 of 1970*, *ICJ Reports* 16 (1971), 453.

[32] Al-Haq has studied in depth the possibility of bringing such a case in the matter of a road-plan proposed for the West Bank. See A., F., and R. Shehadeh, *Israeli Proposed Road Plan for the West Bank: A Question for the International Court of Justice?* (Ramallah, 1984).

detailed account of the responsibility of the Israeli government or the military authorities in causing or failing to curb such violations. For a long time, the Israeli government and its many apologists abroad have had to contend only with generalized, exaggerated, and heartfelt but inaccurate descriptions of the human rights situation. Such appeals came in highly politicized and emotional tones and were easily countered and dismissed by the Israeli government and its friends abroad and not treated seriously by international bodies. Israel and its Jewish and non-Jewish friends abroad had easy access to the international media and were highly represented in international organizations working for human rights. Palestinians and their Arab and non-Arab friends, on the other hand, were not fully familiar with the international concepts of human rights and the rule of law and tended to state their claims in political terms. As such they were often dismissed by public opinion in a West already predisposed to support Israel and the Jewish people because of guilt over the Holocaust, as well as a general cultural affinity to Israel's Western-style legal and governmental system.

Al-Haq has therefore worked hard since its establishment towards obtaining international credibility by careful documentation through affidavits, medical and other records, and a sober listing of human rights violations that has successfully obtained for it international recognition as a credible source of information.

Tone and Political Content

The Middle East question and the Palestinian–Israeli conflict are highly charged emotional issues. Individuals and countries are quick to line themselves on one side or the other of this dispute. Those who have a predisposed idea or a political position on these issues are often emotionally involved and have a serious psychological commitment to the side they support.

Proper work for human rights, however, requires an objective and dispassionate appeal to internationally recognized principles which apply to friend and foe alike. Organizations like Amnesty International, the International Commission of Jurists, and others have staked their reputation on an even-handedness and a commitment to universal principles regardless of political bias toward a particular victim or perpetrator of the human rights violation. The entire fabric of international law is also based on the same premises that law and legal principles must be stated in universal and general terms and be applied impartially to all alike.

Appeals and attempts to defend human rights by working through the 'court of public opinion' require that the issue not be stated in political terms but rather stated in terms of universal principles coupled with a willingness to apply these same principles to all parties in the dispute. Palestinian activists who attempt to exonerate Arab countries for their own violations of human rights cannot expect a sympathetic response to their complaints against Israeli violations of these same rights. The temptation to utilize human rights only when it is in one's own interest must be resisted by those genuinely concerned about human rights and the international community.

The phenomenon of Anatoly Sharansky must be avoided. For thirteen years, Sharansky was hailed in the West as a champion of human rights in the Soviet Union because of his struggle for the right of Soviet Jews to emigrate from Russia. This right is enshrined in Article 14 of the Universal Declaration of Human Rights. However, upon succeeding in achieving this right he publicly refused to defend the application of that same provision to the Palestinian people whose right to leave their country and to return to it is safeguarded by the same article in the Universal Declaration of Human Rights. Instead, Mr. Sharansky's politics took a sharp turn to the right and he allowed his Zionist ideology to supersede his human rights position. He thereby forfeited his right to be considered as a champion of human rights.

Use of Publicity

The essence of working for human rights in the court of public opinion is basically different from the propaganda war in which an individual or a party attempts to score points against its opponent. Although wide publicity is often utilized, its main aim is to bring to light the violations that are being perpetrated with a view to ending them. Every regime, no matter how brutal, claims openly to adhere to international standards and to carry out its activities in a much more humane fashion than it actually does. The most brutal actions of torture and deprivation and the worst violations of human rights occur in the dark, in secret and away from public attention. Wide publicity sheds the light of truth upon the purported violations and denies the perpetrator the luxury of committing those violations in the dark, away from public scrutiny. It denies the perpetrator the right to claim, contrary to the reality on the ground, that it is in fact abiding by principles and standards which it is violating.

In this respect our own experience as a human rights organization confirms the truth that is known world-wide that the mere presence of foreign observers and access to international media has an ameliorating effect on human rights violations. Our observations have shown that the human rights situation is progressively worse in areas that are further away from international scrutiny and publication. In Gaza it is worse than the West Bank, in the refugee camps and outlying villages worse than in the cities, in Nablus and Hebron worse than Ramallah, Bethlehem, and Jerusalem. During the current uprising, a marked improvement in the conduct of soldiers and a proper restraint and reluctance to act brutally and arbitrarily is felt whenever television cameras or other reporters are present. When observers from the US Consulate and the Association for Civil Rights in Israel were present at 'speedy trials' in the Nablus military courts, much more lenient sentences were given and two boys were actually released on bail which is almost unheard of in military court cases. Interventions by al-Haq which were copied to international organizations received more prompt and positive results than otherwise.

Implicating Other Groups

In addition to shedding light on the practices themselves, defence of human rights often takes the form of challenging significant players in the international game to face their responsibilities and obligations towards the human rights violations that are occurring. In this sense, we must recall that the international legal system is built on the concept of the stake that every nation has in peace and in the value of adherence to human rights by every other nation. The theory is that violations of human rights create tension and inevitably lead to breaches of peace and disruption of public order which affect all nations. Each country has an interest and a responsibility to prevent human rights violations by every other country.

This concept is enshrined, among other places, in Article 1 of the Geneva Convention, which mandates and requires every signatory to the Geneva Conventions not only to comply, but also to ensure compliance by every other signatory with their obligations under the Geneva Conventions. A state that fails to ensure compliance by other states is itself violative of international law.[33]

Yet the nature of relations between states is such that protests of this kind are rarely undertaken with seriousness, especially among friendly nations and allies. Part of the work of a human rights organization is to challenge the outside participants to take up their responsibilities and to implicate them directly in the violations of human rights that are taking place. Recent efforts to point out, particularly to European nations, their responsibility under Article 1 of the Geneva Conventions seems to have borne fruit. As a result of a new aware-

---

[33] See M. Stephens, *Enforcement of International Law in the Israeli-Occupied Territories* (Ramallah, 1989).

ness of their obligations under Article 1 of the Geneva Conventions, bolstered by the massive publicity given in their countries to the human rights violations apparent in the recent events of the uprising, European states have protested strongly to Israel with respect to its policies in the Occupied Territories. These protests culminated in threats to suspend or delay ratification of trade agreements between Israel and the EEC precisely because of deportations and other human rights violations in the territories. In the past, the EEC had also delayed for three years its ratification of trade arrangements with Turkey because of its violations of human rights.[34]

The Israeli Court of Public Opinion

Defence of human rights by appealing to structures that have influence over the perpetrators of human rights violations is not limited to outside forces or foreign powers. Some success can be achieved by appealing directly or indirectly to elements within the Israeli public itself or even the Israeli establishment. To do this, however, a human rights activist must obtain a full understanding of the structure and true goals and interests of Israeli society, and must avoid thinking of Israelis or even of the military government as a monolith, or a totally evil structure, and must be able to address it on its own terms, while being aware of the dangers inherent in this approach.

1. The first point in the appeal here is to the relevant authority in the military government, i.e. the military officer in charge of education, or health, or the chief of police, or the commander of a prison, or the military commander in a certain area, or some other such official. It occasionally happens that the individual filling that particular post may be a genuinely decent human being, or at least a person of integrity, whose own values, or at least whose own understanding of his office, allows him, when properly approached, to take action to put a stop to a particularly outrageous violation. Unfortunately, such appeals are rarely effective, and have become even less so in recent times. None the less, such a step is often a necessary prerequisite to further intervention. Also if the official involved is aware that the complaint, and his response to it, are going to be carried up to a higher authority, and may end up being widely publicized, he may consider it more seriously. At any rate, such an appeal is indispensible in cases of an ongoing violation. An example of this is when there are reports

---

[34] Shortly after this was written, the European Parliament suspended scientific cooperation between the EC countries and Israel until the West Bank universities, which have been closed since before the start of the *intifada*, are allowed to reopen. See 'European Parliament Votes to Punish Israel', *Jerusalem Post*, 21 Jan. 1990.

of shooting incidents where the authorities are prohibiting ambulances from entering the area of the incident to evacuate the wounded; this occurred several times at Birzeit University.[35]

2. It has also been possible to appeal to the legal adviser of the military government. When Palestinians began appealing to the Israeli High Court on a large variety of issues, it became the habit of the different constituent parts of the military government, and the civil administration, to refer any complicated or controversial issue to the office of the legal adviser. Any request or complaint by a lawyer on behalf of Palestinian clients was also similarly referred to that office. This author was informed on more than one occassion by employees of the civil administration that they would not deal directly with him as a lawyer, but were instructed to refer all requests by lawyers to the legal adviser.[36]

To the extent that the holder of that office was conversant with international humanitarian law, and valued the concept of the rule of law, such appeals could be useful. At least a reasoned response would be forthcoming that is aware of the possibility of adverse publicity in case of a totally unintelligent response. For this reason, it became an almost routine procedure for al-Haq, after carefully investigating and adequately documenting a human rights violation that came to its attention, first to write a carefully worded intervention to the legal adviser, and await his response, both as to the factual accuracy of our statements, and for his legal response to the arguments we make.

Unfortunately, the present staff of the legal adviser's office do not seem to be concerned about the values of the rule of law, and protection of human rights. Their responses are very delayed, perfunctory, and lacking in substance. None the less, we feel more comfortable in addressing the 'court of public opinion' after we have first served our papers upon the legal representative for the other side. Unfortunately, we can no longer see in the legal adviser, even remotely, a possible avenue for redress.

Conclusion

A friend of mine who works in the Middle East desk at the American Friends Service Committee told me that he overheard his teenage son talking to a friend outside his window. The friend asked, 'What does your dad do for a living?' His son replied, 'He works for peace

---

[35] Documentation of these and other such incidents is held at al-Haq's offices in Ramallah.
[36] The officer for planning and inspection in Bethlehem first stated this rule to the author in 1985, and it was later confirmed by the legal adviser.

between Israelis and Palestinians'. Then he added, wistfully, 'But I don't think he's very good at it. He's been doing it for fifteen years, and they're still fighting.'

Those of us working in the field of human rights protection not only in the Occupied Territories, but elsewhere throughout the world, must often feel the same way. Many of us have dedicated our lives and careers to the cause of human rights. Much effort, energy, and brilliant thought has gone into this work, yet human rights violations continue to occur, and they often seem to be on the increase throughout the world.

And in fact the fight does seem unequal and unfair. Violators of human rights appear to have unlimited resources at their disposal, not to mention the coercive power of the State, and the leeway they are given under international law. The inadequacy of the international system in dealing with violators, the cynical use of the veto by the superpowers, the maddeningly slow pace of evolution of international law and accession to human rights protocols and conventions that have any effective enforcement mechanisms—all these and much more can easily provoke depression, cynicism, or at least severe frustration.

Yet all of us persist in our efforts for the protection of human rights because, in the final analysis, we cannot do otherwise. We may draw some solace from speculating how much *worse* things might be were it not for our feeble and seemingly ineffective efforts. Yet the real strength that keeps us going comes from a deeper source. Whether based on religious or philosophical viewpoints, we draw sustenance from the knowledge that we are on the side of Good against Evil, of Right against Wrong, and from the belief that ultimately Justice will prevail and that the forces of darkness will eventually be driven away before the rays of the coming dawn.

Bibliography

ABI SAAB, GEORGES, 'Les Guerres de libération nationale et la Conférence diplomatique sur le droit humanitaire', *Annales d'Ets.* 8 I (Geneva, 1977), 63–78.
—— 'The Implementation of Humanitarian Law', in Antonio Cassese (ed.), *The New Humanitarian Law of Armed Conflict* (Naples, 1980), 310–416.
ABU LUGHOD, IBRAHIM, *The Transformation of Palestine* (Illinois, 1971).
—— (ed.), *Palestine Rights: Affirmation and Denial* (Illinois, 1982).
AKEHURST, MICHAEL BARTON, *A Modern Introduction to International Law*, 4th edn. (London, 1982).
ALAWNEH, ATEF, 'Tax Administration in the West Bank, and its Role in Achieving Tax Goals' (forthcoming).
—— 'The Income Tax Burden in the Occupied Territories, Jordan and Israel: A Comparative Study' (forthcoming).
ALDERSON, R. Z., CURTIS, J. W., SUTCLIFFE, R. J., and TRAVERS, P. J., 'Protection of Human Rights in Israeli-Occupied Territories', *HILJ* 15 (1974), 470.
AL-HAQ, *In Their Own Words: Human Rights Violations in the West Bank* (Geneva, 1983).
—— *Jnaid: The New Israeli Prison in Nablus—an Appraisal* (Ramallah, 1984).
—— *Torture and Intimidation in the West Bank: The Case of al-Fara'a Prison* (Ramallah, 1985).
—— *Briefing Papers on Twenty Years of Israeli Occupation of the West Bank and Gaza* (Ramallah, 1987).
—— *Punishing a Nation: Human Rights Violations during the Palestinian Uprising, December 1987–December 1988* (Ramallah, 1988).
—— *Israel's War against Education in the Occupied West Bank: A Penalty for the Future* (Ramallah, 1988).
—— *Dahriyyeh: Centre for Punishment* (Ramallah, 1988).
—— *Ansar 3: A Case for Closure* (Ramallah, 1988).
—— *A Nation under Siege: Al-Haq Annual Report on Human Rights in the Occupied Palestinian Territories, 1989* (Ramallah, 1990).
—— *Al-Haq Newsletters* (Ramallah, 1984–90).
AMNESTY INTERNATIONAL, *Report and Recommendation of an Amnesty International Mission to the Government of the State of Israel 3–7 June 1979*.
—— *Amnesty International Report 1987* (London, 1987).
—— *Israel and the Occupied Territories—The Misuse of Tear Gas by Israeli Army Personnel in the Israeli Occupied Territories* (AI Index: MDE/15/26/88) (June 1988).
—— *Israel and the Occupied Territories—Excessive Force: Beatings to Maintain Law and Order* (AI Index: MDE/15/32/88) (Aug. 1988).
ARONSON, GEOFFREY, *Creating Facts: Israel, Palestinians and the West Bank* (Washington, DC, 1987).
AROURI, TAYSEER, 'The Economic Gains Accruing to Israel from the West Bank and Gaza Strip', *Al-Kateb* No. 86.
ARSANJANI, MAHNOUSH, 'United Nations Competence in the West Bank and

Gaza Strip', *International and Comparative Law Quarterly* 31 (1982), 426.
ARURI, NASEER (ed.), *Occupation: Israel over Palestine*, 2nd edn. (Belmont, 1989).
AWAD, MUNIR, *Fishing Resources in the Gaza Strip* (Nablus, 1987).
AWARTANI, HISHAM, 'Water Resources and Policies in the West Bank', *Samed el Iktisadi* 3 (Aug. 1980).
—— *The Economies of the West Bank and Gaza Strip* (Nablus, 1987).
BALLADORE-PALLIERI, GIORGIO, *Diritto bellico* (Padua, 1954).
—— *Diritto internazionale pubblico* (Padua, 1962).
BARRIE, GEORGEN N., 'International Law and Economic Coercion—A Legal Assessment', *South African Yearbook of International Law* 11 (1985–6), 40–54; 'AGORA: Is the ASIL Policy on Divestment in Violation of International Law? Further Observations', *AJIL* 82 (1988), 311.
BAVLY, DAN, *An Experiment in Coexistence* (London, 1971).
BAXTER, RICHARD R., 'Criteria of Prohibition on Weapons in International Law' in *Festschrift für Ulrich Scheuner zum 70 Geburstag* (Berlin, 1973), 41–52.
—— 'The Duty of Obedience to the Belligerent Occupant', *BYIL* 27 (1950), 235–67.
BENDA, H. J. et al., *Japanese Military Administration in Indonesia: Selected Documents* (New Haven, Conn., 1965).
BEN-MEIR, YEHUDA, *National Security Decision-Making: The Israeli Case* (Tel Aviv, 1985).
BENVENISTI, MERON, *West Bank Data Base Project: Interim Report No. 1* (Jerusalem, 1982).
—— *Israeli Rule in the West Bank: Legal and Administrative Aspects* (Jerusalem, 1983).
—— *US Government Funded Projects in the West Bank and Gaza (1977–1983) (Palestinian Sector)* (Jerusalem, 1984).
—— *The West Bank Data Project: A Survey of Israel's Policies* (Washington, DC, 1984).
—— *West Bank Data Base Project Report 1986* (Jerusalem, 1986).
—— *West Bank Data Base Project Report 1987* (Jerusalem, 1987).
with ABU ZAYED, ZIAD, and RUBINSTEIN, DANNY, *The West Bank Handbook: a Political Lexicon* (Jerusalem, 1986).
with KHAYAT, SHLOMO, *The West Bank and Gaza Atlas* (Jerusalem, 1988).
BERNHARDT, RUDOLF (ed.), *Encyclopaedia of Public International Law* (Amsterdam, 1982).
BILDER, RICHARD, 'The Legality of the Arab Oil Boycott', *Texas International Law Journal* 12 (1977), 41–3.
BINDSCHEDLER-ROBERT, DENISE, 'A Reconsideration of the Law of Armed Conflicts' in Carnegie Endowment for International Peace, *The Law of Armed Conflicts* (New York, 1971).
BIN TALAL, HASSAN, *Palestinian Self-Determination: A Study of the West Bank and Gaza Strip* (New York, 1981).
BISHOP, WILLIAM W. Jr., *International Law: Cases and Materials*, 3rd edn. (Boston, 1971).
BISSCHOP, JAMES, 'German War Legislation in the Occupied Territory of Belgium', *Transactions of the Grotius Society* 4 (1919).
BISSELL, RICHARD E., *Apartheid and International Organizations* (Boulder, Col., 1977).
BLOCH, HENRY SIMON, and HOSELITZ, BERT F. (eds.), *Economics of Military*

Occupation, Selected Problems (Chicago, 1944).

BLUM, YEHUDA, 'The Missing Reversioner: Reflections on the Status of Judea and Samaria', *IsLR* 3 (1968), 279.

—— 'Zion Ransomed by International Law' (in Hebrew), *Hapraklet* 27 (1971) 315.

—— 'East Jerusalem is not Occupied Territory' (in Hebrew), *Hapraklet* 28 (1972) 182.

—— *The Juridical Status of Jerusalem,* Jerusalem Papers on Peace Problems No. 2, Hebrew University (Jerusalem, 1974).

—— 'Economic Boycotts in International Law', *Texas International Law Journal* 12 (1977), 12–15.

BORDWELL, WALTER PERCY, *The Law of War between Belligerents: A History and Commentary* (Chicago, 1908).

BOTHE, MICHAEL, PARTSCH, KARL JOSEF, and SOLF, WALDEMAR A., *New Rules for Victims of Armed Conflicts* (The Hague, 1982).

BOWETT, DEREK W., *Self Defence in International Law* (Manchester, 1958).

—— 'International Law Relating to Occupied Territory: A Rejoinder', *Law Quarterly Review* 87 (1971).

—— 'Economic Coercion and Reprisals by States', *Virginia Journal of International Law* 13 (1972).

—— 'Reprisals Involving Recourse to Armed Force', *AJIL* 66(1) (1972), 581–96.

BOYD, STEPHEN M., 'The Applicability of International Law to the Occupied Territories', *IYHR* 1 (1971), 258–61.

BOYLE, FRANCIS, 'Create the State of Palestine!', 25 *American–Arab Affairs* (Summer 1988), 86–105.

BRETTON, PHILIPPE, 'L'Incidence des guerres contemporaines sur la réaffirmation et le développement du droit international humanitaire applicable dans les conflits armés internationaux et non internationaux', *JDI* 105(2) (1978), 208–71.

BROWNLIE, IAN, *Principles of Public International Law* (Oxford, 1979).

BRZEZINSKI, ZBIGNIEW, *Power and Principle: Memoirs of the National Security Adviser, 1977–1981,* rev. edn. (New York, 1985).

BUERGENTHAL, THOMAS, 'To Respect and to Ensure: State Obligations and Permissible Derogations', in Louis Henkin (ed.), *The International Bill of Rights: The Covenant on Civil and Political Rights* (New York, 1981), 72.

BUSTAMENTE Y SIRVEN, ANTONIO, *Droit international public,* iv, trans. Paule Goulé (Paris, 1937).

BUTOVSKY, YARON, 'Law of Belligerent Occupation: Israeli Practice and Judicial Decisions Affecting the West Bank', *Canadian Yearbook of International Law* 21 (1983), 217–34.

CAHIN, GERARD, and CARKACI, DENIZ, 'Les Guerres de libération internationale et le droit internationale', in *Annuaire du Tiers Monde* 2 (Paris, 1976), 32–56.

CAIRE, GUY, *Freedom of Association and Economic Development* (Geneva, 1977).

CAPOTORTI, FRANCESCO, *L'occupazione nel diritto di guerra* (Naples, 1949).

CAREY, JOHN, *UN Protection of Civil and Political Rights* (New York, 1970).

CASSESE, ANTONIO (ed.), *The New Humanitarian Law of Armed Conflict* (Naples, 1980).

—— 'A Tentative Appraisal of the Old and the New Humanitarian Law of

Armed Conflict' in Cassese (ed.), *The New Humanitarian Law of Armed Conflict*, 478.
—— 'Commentaire de l'Article 1, 2', in J. P. Cot and A. Pellet (eds.), *La Charte des Nations Unies* (Paris, 1985).
CATTAN, HENRY, *Palestine and International Law*, 2nd edn. (London, 1976).
—— *Jerusalem* (New York, 1981).
—— 'The Implementation of United Nations Resolutions on Palestine' in Ibrahim Abu-Lughod (ed.), *Palestine Rights: Affirmation and Denial* (Illinois, 1982).
—— *The Palestine Question* (London, 1988).
CHAUMONT, CHARLES, 'Le Droit des peuples à temoigner d'eux-mêmes', *Annuaire du Tiers Monde* (1976).
CHOMSKY, NOAM, *The Fateful Triangle: The United States, Israel and the Palestinians* (Boston, 1983).
CIOBANU, DAN, 'Credentials of Delegations and Representation of Member States at the United Nations', *International and Comparative Law Quarterly* 25(2) (1976), 351–81.
CLAGGETT BRICE M., and JOHNSON O. THOMAS Jr., 'May Israel as a Belligerent Occupant Lawfully Exploit Previously Unexploited Oil Resources of the Gulf of Suez?', *AJIL* 72(3) (1978), 558–85.
COHEN, ESTHER R., *Human Rights in the Israeli-Occupied Territories 1967–1982* (Manchester, 1985).
—— 'Justice for Occupied Territory? The Israeli High Court of Justice Paradigm', *Columbia Journal of Transnational Law* 24(3) (1986), 471–507.
COHEN, YORAM, *The Allon Plan* (in Hebrew) (Tel Aviv, 1972), trans. in L. Fabian and Z. Schiff (eds.), *Israelis Speak* (New York, 1977).
COHN, HAIM H., Foreword to the Israel National Section of the International Commission of Jurists, *The Rule of Law in the Areas Administered by Israel* (Tel Aviv, 1981).
COLES, HARRY LEWIS, and WEINBERG, ALBERT K., *Civil Affairs: Soldiers Become Governors* (Washington, DC, 1964).
COLIN, JEAN-PIERRE, and PETIT, GERARD, 'L'Organisation de Libération de la Palestine', *Annuaire du Tiers Monde* (1975).
COT, JEAN-PIERRE, and PELLET, ALAIN (eds.), *La Charte des Nations Unies* (Paris, 1985).
COUNCIL OF EUROPE, European Commission of Human Rights, *Decisions and Reports*.
COUSSIRAT-COUSTÈRE, VINCENT, 'Israël et le Golan—Problèmes juridiques résultant de la loi du 14 décembre 1981', *AFDI* (1981).
CRANE, MELINDA, 'Middle East: Status of Jerusalem', *HILJ* 21 (1980), 784.
CRISTESCU, AURELIU, and GROS ESPIELL, HECTOR, *Le Droit à l'autodetermination*, E/CN.4/Sub.2/Rev. 1 and 405/Rev.1. (UN, 1979).
DEBBASCH, ODILE, *L'Occupation militaire: Pouvoirs reconnus aux forces armées hors de leur territoire national* (Paris, 1962).
DE CARD, ROUARD, *La Guerre continentale et la propriété* (Paris, 1877).
DE MULINEN, FREDERIC, *Handbook on the Law of War for Armed Forces* (Geneva, 1987).

DE VISSCHER, CHARLES, 'Les Lois de la guerre et la théorie de la necessité', *RGDIP* (1917).
DIMONT, MAX I., *Jews, God and History* (New York, 1962).
DINSTEIN, YORAM, 'And the Ransom has not been Redeemed, or Not Demonstrations but Action' (in Hebrew), *Hapraklet* 27 (1971), 519–22.
—— *International Law and the State* (in Hebrew) (Tel Aviv, 1971).
—— 'Zion to be Ransomed by International Law' (in Hebrew), *Hapraklet* 27 (1971), 5–11.
—— 'Legislative Authority in the Administered Territories' (in Hebrew), *Eyunai Mishpat* (*Tel Aviv University Law Review*) 2 (1972), 505–12.
—— 'Judicial Review of the Actions of the Military Government in the Administered Territories' (in Hebrew), *Eyunai Mishpat* (*Tel Aviv University Law Review*) 3 (1973), 330–6.
—— 'Judgment Regarding Pithat Rafiah' (in Hebrew), *Eyunai Mishpat* (*Tel Aviv University Law Review*) 3 (1973), 934–41.
—— 'The International Law of Belligerent Occupation and Human Rights', *IYHR* 8 (1978), 104–43.
—— 'Settlements and Deportation in the Administered Territories' (in Hebrew), *Eyunai Mishpat* (*Tel Aviv University Law Review*) 7 (1979), 188–94.
—— 'The Deportation of the Mayors from Judea' (in Hebrew), 8 *Eyunai Mishpat* (*Tel Aviv University Law Review*) 8 (1981), 158–71.
—— (ed.) *Models of Autonomy* (New Brunswick, NJ, 1981).
—— 'Refugees and the Law of Armed Conflict', *IYHR* 12 (1982), 94–109.
—— *The Laws of War* (in Hebrew) (Tel Aviv, 1983).
—— 'Value Added Tax in the Administered Territories' (in Hebrew), *Eyunai Mishpat* (*Tel Aviv University Law Review*) 10 (1985), 159.
—— 'The Israeli Supreme Court and the Law of Belligerent Occupation: Reunification of Families', *IYHR* 18 (1988), 173.
DOMB, FANIA, 'Judgments of the Supreme Court of Israel Relating to the Administered Territories', *IYHR* 11 (1981), 344–56.
DONNISON, F. S. V., *Civil Affairs and Military Government, North-West Europe, 1944–1946* (London, 1961).
DRAPER, G. I. A. D., *The Red Cross Conventions (Commentary and Text)* (London, 1958).
—— 'The Geneva Conventions of 1949', *RCADI* (1965–I), 59–165.
DROBLES, MATTITYAHU, *Master Plan for the Development of Settlement in Judea and Samaria* (Jerusalem, 1980).
DRORI, MOSHE, 'The Israeli Settlements in Judea and Samaria: Legal Aspects', in Daniel J. Elazar (ed.), *Judea, Samaria and Gaza: Views on the Present and Future* (Washington, DC, 1982).
DUGARD, JOHN, 'The Legal Effect of UN Resolutions on Apartheid', *South African Law Journal* 83 (1966), 56–9.
—— *South West Africa/Namibia Dispute* (Berkeley, Calif., 1973).
—— 'International Human Rights Norms in Domestic Courts: Can South Africa Learn from Britain and the United States' in Ellison Kahn (ed.), *Fiat Justitia: Essays in Memory of O. D. Schreiner* (Cape Town, 1983), 221.
—— *Recognition and the United Nations* (Cambridge, 1987).

EIDE, ASBJORN, and SCHOU, AUGUST, *International Protection of Human Rights: Proceedings of the Seventh Nobel Symposium, Oslo 1967* (New York, 1968).
ELAZAR, DANIEL J. (ed.), *Judea, Samaria and Gaza: Views on the Present and Future* (Washington, DC, 1982).
FABIAN, L., and SCHIFF, Z., *Israelis Speak* (New York, 1977).
FALK, RICHARD A., *Reviving the World Court* (Charlottesville, 1986).
—— 'Some Legal Reflections on Prolonged Israeli Occupation of Gaza and the West Bank', *Journal of Refugee Studies* 2 (1989), 40–51.
KOLKO G., and LIFTON R. (eds.), *Crimes of War: A Legal, Political, Documentary and Psychological Inquiry into the Responsibility of Leaders, Citizens and Soldiers for Criminal Acts in Wars* (New York, 1971).
FALLOON, VIRGIL, *Excessive Secrecy, Lack of Guidelines: A Report on Military Censorship in the West Bank* (Ramallah, 1986).
FARER, TOM J., 'Political and Economic Coercion in Contemporary International Law', *AJIL* 79 (1985), 405.
FARHI, CAROL, 'On the Legal Status of the Gaza Strip', in Meir Shamgar (ed.), *Military Government in the Territories Administered by Israel 1967–1980, i: The Legal Aspects* (Jerusalem, 1982).
FARJOUN, EMANUEL, *Palestinian Workers in Israel: A Reserve Army of Labour* (Jerusalem, 1976).
FASHEH, MOUNIR JAMIL, 'Education as a Praxis for Liberation: Birzeit University and the Community Work Program', Ph.D. Thesis (Harvard University, 1987).
FAUCHILLE, PAUL, *Traité de droit international public*, 2: *War and Neutrality* (Paris, 1921).
FAWZI, 'ABD-AL-MUNIM, *Tax Systems* (Cairo, 1973).
FEILCHENFELD, ERNST H., *The International Economic Law of Belligerent Occupation* (Washington, DC, 1942).
FEINBERG, NATHAN, 'Legal Status of the West Bank', *Ha'aretz*, 9 Oct. 1987.
FEINSTEIN, BARRY A., *The Sources of Public International Law* (Jerusalem, 1973).
FLAPAN, SIMHA, *The Birth of Israel: Myths and Realities* (New York, 1987).
FLORY, M. (ed.), *La formation des normes en droit international du développement* (Paris, 1984).
FRAENKEL, ERNST, *Military Occupation and the Rule of Law: Occupation Government in the Rhineland, 1918–1923* (London, 1944).
FRANCE, GOVT. OF, *Manuel de lois de la guerre continentale* (Paris, 1913).
GAINSBOROUGH, J. RUSSELL, *The Arab–Israeli Conflict: A Politico-Legal Analysis* (Aldershot, 1986).
GARNER, JAMES WILFORD, 'Contributions, Requisitions, and Compulsory Service in Occupied Territory', *AJIL* 11(1) (1917), 74–112.
—— *International Law and the World War* (London, 1920).
GASPAR, LORAND, *Histoire de la Palestine* (Paris, 1968).
GERSON, ALLAN, 'Trustee-Occupant: The Legal Status of Israel's Presence in the West Bank', *HILJ* 14 (1973), 1.
—— 'War, Conquered Territory, and Military Occupation in the Contemporary International Legal System', *HILJ* 18(3) (1977), 525–56.
—— 'Off-shore Oil Exploration by a Belligerent Occupant—the Gulf of Suez Dispute', *AJIL* 71 (1977), 725.

—— *Israel, the West Bank and International Law* (London, 1978).
GILMOUR, DAVID, *Dispossessed: The Ordeal of the Palestinians* (London, 1982).
GRABER, DORIS APPEL, *The Development of the Law of Belligerent Occupation 1863-1914: A Historical Survey* (New York, 1949).
GRAHAM-BROWN, SARAH, 'The Economic Consequences of the Occupation', in Naseer Aruri (ed.), *Occupation: Israel over Palestine*, 2nd edn. (Belmont, 1989), 167.
GRASSMANN, GERHARD OTTO, *Die deutsche Besatzungsgesetzgebung während des 2. Weltkrieges im Rahman des Völkerrechts* (Tübingen, 1958).
GREENSPAN, MORRIS, *The Modern Law of Land Warfare* (Berkeley, Calif., 1959).
GREENWOOD, CHRISTOPHER, 'The Relationship between Ius ad Bellum and Ius in Bello', *Rev. Int. Studies* 9(4) (1983), 221-34.
GRESH, ALAIN, and VIDAL, DOMINIQUE, *The Middle East: War Without End?* (London, 1988).
GROS ESPIELL, HECTOR, *The Right to Self-Determination: Implementation of United Nations Resolutions*, E/CN 4/Sub/2/405/Rev. 1 (United Nations, 1980).
GROSSMAN, DAVID, *The Yellow Wind* (New York, 1988).
GUILHAUDIS, JEAN-FRANÇOIS, *Le Droit des peuples à disposer d'eux-mêmes* (Grenoble, 1976).
HACKWORTH, GREEN H., *Digest of International Law*, vi (Washington, DC, 1943).
HADAR, ZVI, 'The Military Courts', in Meir Shamgar (ed.), *Military Government in the Territories Administered by Israel 1967–1980*, 1: *The Legal Aspects* (Jerusalem, 1982).
HALABI, USAMA, *Land Alienation in the West Bank, A Legal and Spatial Analysis* (Jerusalem, 1985).
HALBERSTAM, MALVINA, 'Excluding Israel from the General Assembly by a Rejection of Credentials', *AJIL* 78 (1984), 179-92.
HAMMAD, M. BURHAN W., 'The Culprit, the Targets and the Victims', in John Norton Moore (ed.), *The Arab–Israeli Conflict: Readings and Documents 2*, (Princeton, NJ, 1974), 361.
HAREVEN, ALOUPH (ed.), *Can the Palestinian Problem be Solved? Israeli Positions* (Jerusalem, 1983).
HARKABI, YEHOSHOFAT, *The Palestinian Covenant and its Meaning* (London, 1979).
—— *Israel's Fateful Decisions* (London, 1988).
HARRIS, WILLIAM WILSON, 'War and Settlement Change: The Golan Heights and Jordan Rift 1967–1977', *Trans. Inst. of British Geog.*, NS, III, 3 (1978).
—— *Taking Root: Israeli Settlement in the West Bank, the Golan and Gaza–Sinai 1967–1980* (Chichester, 1980).
HENKIN, LOUIS (ed.), *The International Bill of Rights: The Covenant on Civil and Political Rights* (New York, 1981).
HERTZBERG, ARTHUR, 'Israel and the West Bank: The Implications of Permanent Control', *Foreign Affairs* 61 (1983), 1064.
HEUNIS, J. C., *United Nations versus South Africa* (Johannesburg, 1986).
HIGGINS, ROSALYN, 'Derogations under Human Rights Treaties', *BYIL* 48 (1976–77), 281–320.
HILTERMANN, JOOST R., *Israel's Deportation Policy in the Occupied West Bank and Gaza* (Ramallah, 1986).

—— 'Palestinian Unions: Force for Change in the West Bank', *The Nation*, 3 Oct. 1987, 338.
—— *Behind the Intifada: Labor and Women's Movements in the Occupied Territories* (Princeton, NJ, 1991).
HIRST, DAVID, *The Gun and the Olive Branch* (London, 1977).
HOLBORN, HAJO, *American Military Government, its Organization and Policies* (Washington, DC, 1947).
HOWARD, MICHAEL, 'The UN and International Security', in Adam Roberts and Benedict Kingsbury (eds.), *United Nations, Divided World* (Oxford, 1988).
HSU, SHU HSI, *A New Digest of Japanese War Conduct* (Shanghai, 1941).
HUBER, MAX, 'Die Kriegsrechtlichen Verträge und die Kriegsraison', *Zeitschrift für Völkerrecht* (Geneva, 1913).
HUMPHREY, JOHN, 'The Universal Declaration of Human Rights: Its History, Impact and Juridical Character', in B. G. Ramcharan (ed.), *Human Rights: Thirty Years after the Universal Declaration* (The Hague, 1979), 33.
HUNT, PAUL, *Justice? The Military Court System in the Israeli-Occupied Territories* (Ramallah, 1987).
INTERNATIONAL CENTER FOR PEACE IN THE MIDDLE EAST, *Research on Human Rights in the Occupied Territories 1979–1983* (Tel Aviv, 1985).
INTERNATIONAL COMMITTEE OF THE RED CROSS, *Annual Reports*.
INTERNATIONAL LABOUR ORGANISATION, *The Trade Union Situation in Chile: Report of the Fact-Finding and Conciliation Commission on Freedom of Association* (Geneva, 1975).
—— *ILO Principles, Standards and Procedures Concerning Freedom of Association* (Geneva, 1978).
—— *Freedom of Association. Digest of Decisions and Principles of the Freedom of Association Committee of the Governing Body of the ILO*, 3rd edn. (Geneva, 1985).
—— *Report on the Situation of Workers of the Occupied Arab Territories* (Geneva: ILO, 1987).
ISRAEL NATIONAL SECTION OF THE INTERNATIONAL COMMISSION OF JURISTS, *The Rule of Law in the Areas Administered by Israel* (Tel Aviv, 1981).
JENKS, CLARENCE WILFRED, 'Some Constitutional Problems of International Organizations', *BYIL* 22 (1945), 11–72.
—— *Human Rights and International Labour Standards* (London, 1960).
JENNINGS, R. Y., 'Government in Commission', *BYIL* 23 (1946), 112.
JONES, F. LLEWLLYN 'Military Occupation of Alien Territory in Time of Peace', *Trans. of the Grotius Society* 9 (London, 1924).
JOUVE, EDMOND, *Le Droit des peuples* (Paris, 1986).
KAHAN, DAVID, *Agriculture and Water Resources in the West Bank and Gaza (1967–1987)* (Jerusalem: WBDP, 1987).
KAHN, ELLISON (ed.), *Fiat Justitia: Essays in Memory of O. D. Schreiner* (Cape Town, 1983).
KALADHARAN NAYAR, M. G., 'Human Rights: The United Nations and United States Foreign Policy', *HILJ* 19 (1978), 813.
KALSHOVEN, FRITS, *Belligerent Reprisals* (Leiden, 1971).
KARP, JUDITH et al., *Report of the Inquiry Team re Investigation of Suspicions against Israelis in Judea and Samaria* ('Karp Report'), submitted by Judith Karp

(Deputy Attorney-General of Israel) to the Attorney-General, reprinted in *PYIL* 1 (1984), 185.
KASSIM, ANIS F., 'The PLO's Claim to Status—A Juridical Analysis Under International Law', *Denver Journal of International Law and Policy* 9 (1980), 1–33.
—— 'Legal Systems and Developments in Palestine', *PYIL* 1 (1984), 19–35.
KEESINGS'S CONTEMPORARY ARCHIVES (London).
KERCHNAWE, HUGO, et al., *Die Militärverwaltung in den von den österreichisch-ungarischen Truppen besetzten Gebieten* (New Haven, 1928).
KHALIDI, WALID, *From Haven to Conquest: Readings on Zionism and the Palestinian Problem until 1948* (Beirut, 1971).
KHOURY, FRANK J., *The Arab–Israeli Dilemma*, 3rd edn. (Siracusa, 1989).
KLINGHOFFER, H. *Administrative Law* (in Hebrew) (Tel Aviv, 1957).
KOCHLER, H. (ed.), *The Legal Aspects of the Palestine Problem* (Vienna, 1981).
KRETZMER, DAVID, *Israel and the West Bank: Legal Issues* (Jerusalem, 1984).
KUTTAB, JONATHAN, *Analysis of Military Order No. 854 and Related Orders Concerning Educational Institutions in the Occupied West Bank* (Ramallah, 1980).
—— and SHEHADEH, RAJA, *Civilian Administration in the Occupied West Bank: Analysis of Israeli Military Government Order No. 947* (Ramallah, 1982).
KUTTNER, THOMAS S., 'Israel and the West Bank—Aspects of the Law of Belligerent Occupation', *IYHR* 7 (1977), 166–221.
LANDAU REPORT—Findings summarized in *Jerusalem Post* International Edition, 7 Nov. 1987.
LAPIDOTH, RUTH, *Les Rapports entre le droit international public et le droit interne en Israël* (Paris, 1959).
LAQUEUR, WALTER, *A History of Zionism* (London, 1972).
LATVIAN PRESS BUREAU, *Latvia in 1939–1942* (Washington, DC, 1942).
LAWYERS COMMITTEE FOR HUMAN RIGHTS, *An Examination of the Detention of Human Rights Workers and Lawyers from the West Bank and Gaza and Conditions of Detention at Ketziot* (New York, 1988).
LAUTERPACHT, ELIHU, *Jerusalem and the Holy Places* (London, 1968).
LEMKIN, RAPHAEL, *Axis Rule in Occupied Europe: Laws of Occupation, Analysis of Government, Proposals for Redress* (Washington, DC, 1944).
LESCH, ANN MOSELY, and TESSLER, MARK, *Israel, Egypt and the Palestinians: From Camp David to the Intifada* (Bloomington, Ind., 1989).
LEURQUIN, M., 'The German Occupation in Belgium and Article 43 of the Hague Convention of the 18th October 1907', *International Law Notes* 1 (1916), 55.
—— 'The Status of Coercion under International Law', *Texas International Law Journal* 12 (1977), 17.
LILLICH, RICHARD B. (ed.), *Humanitarian Intervention and the United Nations* (Charlottesville, 1973).
LITCHFIELD, EDWARD HAROLD, *Governing Postwar Germany* (New York, 1953).
LUBRANO-LAVADERA, EUGÈNE MICHEL, *Les Lois de la guerre et de l'occupation militaire* (Paris, 1956).
LUSTICK, IAN, 'Israel and the West Bank after Elon Moreh', *Middle East Journal* 35 (Autumn 1981), 557–77.

—— For The Land and the Lord: Jewish Fundamentalism in Israel (New York, 1988).
MADDREY, W. C., 'Economic Sanctions against South Africa: Problems and Prospects for Enforcement of Human Rights Norms', *Virginia Journal of International Law* 22 (1981), 345.
MAGNUS, RALPH H. (ed.), *Documents on the Middle East* (Washington, DC, 1969).
MALLISON, SALLY V., 'The Application of International Law to the Israeli Settlements in Occupied Territories' in Ibrahim Abu-Lughod (ed.), *Palestinian Rights: Affirmation and Denial* (Illinois, 1982).
—— and MALLISON, W. THOMAS Jr., *An International Law Analysis of the Major United Nations Resolutions Concerning the Palestine Question*, ST/SG/SER. F/4 (United Nations, 1979).
—— 'The Juridical Bases for Palestinian Self-Determination', *PYIL* 1 (1984), 36–67.
—— *The Palestine Problem in International Law and World Order* (Harlow, 1986).
MANN, F.A. 'The Enforcement of Treaties by English Courts', *Trans. of the Grotius Society* 44 (1958–9).
MA'OZ, MOSHE, *Palestinian Leadership on the West Bank: The Changing Role of the Mayors under Jordan and Israel* (London, 1984).
MATAR, IBRAHIM, 'Israeli Settlements in the West Bank and Gaza Strip', *Journal of Palestine Studies* 41 (Autumn 1981), 93–110.
—— 'From Palestinian to Israeli: Jerusalem 1948–82', *Journal of Palestine Studies* 48 (Summer 1983), 57–63.
MCCUNE, GEORGE M., 'The Occupation of Korea', *Foreign Policy Reports* 23 (1947), 186–95.
MCDOUGAL, MYRES S., and FELICIANO, FLORENTINO P., *Law and Minimum World Public Order: The Legal Regulation of International Coercion* (New Haven, Conn., 1961).
MCDOWALL, DAVID, *Palestine and Israel: The Uprising and Beyond* (London, 1989).
MCNAIR, ARNOLD DUNCAN, *The Law of Treaties* (Oxford, 1961).
—— and WATTS, A. D., *The Legal Effects of War*, 4th edn. (Cambridge, 1966).
MEADE, EDWARD GRANT, *American Military Government in Korea* (New York, 1951).
MERON, THEODOR, 'The International Convention on the Elimination of All Forms of Racial Discrimination and the Golan Heights', *IYHR* 8 (1978).
—— 'West Bank and Gaza: Human Rights and Humanitarian Law in the Period of Transition', *IYHR* 9 (1979), 106–20.
—— 'Applicability of Multilateral Conventions to Occupied Territories', *AJIL* 72(3) (July 1978), 542–57.
—— 'On the Inadequate Reach of Humanitarian and Human Rights Law and the Need for a New Instrument', *AJIL* 77(3) (1983), 589–606.
—— *Human Rights in International Law: Legal and Policy Issues* (Oxford, 1984).
—— *Human Rights Law-Making in the United Nations* (Oxford, 1986).
—— 'The Geneva Conventions as Customary Law', *AJIL* 81 (1987), 348–70.
—— *Human Rights in Internal Strife: Their International Protection* (Cambridge, 1987).
METZGER, JAN, ORTH, MARTIN, and STERZING, CHRISTIAN, *This Land is Our Land* (London, 1983).

MEURER, CHRISTIAN, *Die völkerrechtliche Stellung der vom Feind besetzten Gebiete* (Tübingen, 1915).
MIGLIAZZA, ALESSANDRO, 'L'Évolution de la réglementation de la guerre à la lumière de la sauvegarde des droits de l'homme', *RCADI* 137 (1972–III), 143–242.
MOFFETT, MARTHA, *Perpetual Emergency: A Legal Analysis of Israel's Use of the British Defence (Emergency) Regulations, 1945, in the Occupied Territories* (Ramallah, 1989).
MOORE, JOHN NORTON (ed.), *The Arab–Israeli Conflict: Readings and Documents* (Princeton, NJ, 1974).
MORGENSTERN, FELICE, 'Validity of the Acts of the Belligerent Occupant', *BYIL* 28 (1951), 291–322.
MORRIS, BENNY, *The Birth of the Palestine Refugee Problem, 1947–1949* (Cambridge, 1987).
MOSSNER, J. M., 'Military Government' in R. Bernhardt (ed.), *Encyclopaedia of International Law* (Amsterdam, 1982).
MURRAY, CHRISTINA, 'The Status of ANC and SWAPO and International Humanitarian Law', *South African Law Journal* 100(3) (1983), 402–10.
NAHLIK, STANISLAW E., 'Droit dit "de Genève" et droit dit "de la Haye": unicité ou dualité?', *AFDI* 24 (1978), 1–27.
NATHAN, ELI, 'The Power of Supervision of the High Court of Justice over Military Government', in Meir Shamgar, *Military Government in the Territories Administered by Israel 1967–80*, i: *The Legal Aspects* (Jerusalem, 1982), 109.
NATIONAL LAWYERS' GUILD, *Report of the National Lawyers' Guild 1977 Middle East Delegation: Treatment of Palestinians in Israeli-Occupied West Bank and Gaza* (Washington, DC, 1978).
—— *1988 Report of the National Lawyers' Guild: International Human Rights Law and Israel's Efforts to Suppress the Palestinian Uprising* (Washington, DC, 1989).
NEFF, S. C., 'The Law of Economic Coercion', *Columbia Journal of Transnational Law* 20 (1981), 411.
NEGBI, MOSHE, 'The Israeli Supreme Court and the Occupied Territories', *Jerusalem Quarterly* 27 (Spring 1983), 33.
NETHERLANDS GOVERNMENT MISSION, *Export of Agricultural Produce from the West Bank and the Gaza Strip* (1988).
NISAN, MORDECHAI, *Israel and the Territories: A Study in Control (1967–1972)* (Ramat Gan, 1978).
NISPEN, TOT SEVENAER, and CAREL, M. O. VAN, *L'Occupation Allemande pendant la dernière guerre mondiale* (Tübingen, 1946).
NIXON, ANN, *The Status of Palestinian Children during the Uprising in the Occupied Territories*, i: *Child Death and Injury* (Jerusalem, 1990).
NGUYEN QUOC, DINH, DAILLIER, PATRICK, and PELLET, ALAIN, *Droit international public* (Paris, 1987).
NUSSBAUM, ARTHUR, *A Concise History of the Law of Nations* (New York, 1947).
OBRADOVIC, KONSTANTIN, 'La Protection de la population civile dans les conflits armés internationaux', in Antonio Cassese (ed.), *The New Humanitarian Law of Armed Conflict* (Naples, 1980), 128–160.
O'BRIEN, WILLIAM V., 'Legitimate Military Necessity in Nuclear War', *World*

Polity 2 (1960), 35–120.

—— *The Conduct of Just and Limited War* (New York, 1981).

OPPENHEIM, LASSA, *International Law: A Treatise*, ii: *Disputes, War and Neutrality*, edited by H. Lauterpacht (6th edn., London, 1944; 7th edn. 1952; 8th edn. 1955).

—— 'The Legal Relations between an Occupying Power and the Inhabitants', *Law Quarterly Review* (1917).

OTT, DAVID H., *Palestine in Perspective: Politics, Human Rights and the West Bank* (London, 1980).

OZ, AMOS, *In the Land of Israel* (New York, 1983).

PAUST, JORDAN J., 'The Human Right to Participate in Armed Revolution and Related Forms of Social Violence: Testing the Limits of Permissibility', *Emory Law Journal* 32 (1982), 545–81.

—— and BLAUSTEIN, A. P., 'The Arab Oil Weapon—A Threat to International Peace', *AJIL* 68 (1974), 410–39.

—— 'Oil Exploitation in Occupied Territory: Sharpening the Focus of Appropriate Legal Standards', *Houston Journal of International Law* 1 (1979).

PELLET, ALAIN, 'Note sur quelques aspects juridiques de la notion de droit au développement' in M. Flory (ed.), *La formation des normes en droit international du développement* (Paris, 1984).

—— 'Qui a peur du droit des peuples à disposer d'eux-mêmes?', *Critique socialiste* (1984), 89–103.

PERETZ, DON, 'Intifadeh: The Palestinian Uprising', *Foreign Affairs* 66(5) (1988) 964–80.

PHYSICIANS FOR HUMAN RIGHTS, *The Casualties of Conflict: Medical Care and Human Rights in the West Bank and Gaza Strip* (Boston, 1988).

PICTET, JEAN, *Commentary on Geneva Convention IV of 1949, Relative to the Protection of Civilian Persons in Time of War*, trans. Ronald Griffin and C. W. Dumbleton (Geneva, 1958).

—— *Humanitarian Law and the Protection of War Victims* (Leiden, 1973).

—— *Développement et principes du droit international humanitaire* (Paris 1983).

PLAYFAIR, EMMA, *Administrative Detention in the Occupied West Bank* (Ramallah, 1986).

—— *Demolition and Sealing of Houses as a Punitive Measure in the Israeli-Occupied West Bank* (Ramallah, 1987).

—— 'Israel's Security Needs in the West Bank: Real and Contrived', *Arab Studies Quarterly* 10(4) (1988), 406.

—— 'Legal Aspects of the Occupation: Theory and Practice', in Naseer Aruri (ed.), *Occupation: Israel over Palestine*, 2nd edn. (Belmont, 1989), 101–26.

POMERANCE, M., *Self-Determination in Law and Practice: The New Doctrine in the United Nations* (The Hague, 1982).

PORATH, YEHOSHUA, *The Emergence of the Palestinian–Arab National Movement 1918–1929* (London, 1974).

QUIGLEY, JOHN, 'United States Complicity in Israel's Violation of Palestinian Rights', *PYIL* 1 (1984), 95–120.

—— 'The Relation between Human Rights Law and the Law of Belligerent Occupation: Does an Occupied Population Have a Right to Freedom of

Assembly and Expression?', *Boston College Int. and Comp. Law Rev.* 12 (1989), 1.

—— *Palestine and Israel: A Challenge to Justice* (Durham, 1990).

RAMCHARAN, B. G. (ed.), *Human Rights: Thirty Years after the Universal Declaration* (The Hague, 1979).

RIDEAU, JOEL, 'Le problème du respect des droits de l'homme dans les territoires occupés par Israel', *AFDI* 16 (1970), 204–32.

RIGO-SUREDA, V. A., *The Evolution of the Right of Self-Determination* (Leiden, 1973).

RISHMAWI, MONA, *Planning: In Whose Interest? Land Use Planning as a Strategy for Judaization* (Ramallah, 1986).

—— 'Finding Security in Subterfuge: The Uses of an Argument', unpublished article.

ROBERTS, ADAM, 'What is Military Occupation?', *BYIL* 55 (1984), 249–305.

—— 'The Applicability of Human Rights Law during Military Occupations', *Review of International Studies* (1987).

—— 'Decline of Illusions: The Status of Israeli Occupied Territories over 21 Years', *Int. Aff.* 64(3) (1988), 347–59.

—— 'The Palestinians, the Uprising and International Law', *Journal of Refugee Studies* 2 (1988), 26–39.

—— and GUELFF, RICHARD, *Documents on the Laws of War* (Oxford, 1982; 2nd edn. 1989).

—— and JOERGENSEN, BOEL, and NEWMAN, FRANK, *Academic Freedom under Israeli Military Occupation* (London, 1984).

—— and KINGSBURY, BENEDICT (eds.), *United Nations, Divided World* (Oxford, 1988).

ROBINSON, JACOB, 'Transfer of Property in Enemy Occupied Territory', *AJIL* 39(2) (1945), 216–30.

ROELING, BERT V. A., 'Aspects of the Criminal Responsibility for Violations of the Laws of War' in Antonio Cassese (ed.), *The New Humanitarian Law of Armed Conflict* (Naples, 1980), 199–231.

ROSTOW, EUGENE V., 'Palestinian Self-Determination: Possible Futures for the Unallocated Territories of the Palestine Mandate', *Yale Studies in World Public Order* 5 (1979), 147.

ROUSSEAU, CHARLES, *Droit international public*, iii: *Les compétences* (Paris 1977).

—— *Le Droit des conflits armés* (Paris, 1983).

RUBIN, BENYAMIN, 'The Adoption of International Conventions by Israel in Israeli courts' (in Hebrew), *Meshpatiem* 13 (1983), 210.

RUBINSTEIN, AMNON, *The Zionist Dream Revisited. From Hertzl to Gush Emunim and Back* (New York, 1984).

—— 'The Changing Status of the Occupied Territories' (in Hebrew), *Eyunai Mishpat (Tel Aviv University Law Review)* 11 (1986), 439.

SABRI, NIDAL, 'The Effects of Taxes Imposed on the Population of the Occupied Palestinian Territories' (Paper presented at the Seminar on Living Conditions of the Palestinian People, organized by Habitat in Vienna, March 1985).

SAHLIYEH, EMILE, *In Search of Leadership: West Bank Politics since 1967* (Washington, DC, 1988).

SAID, EDWARD, *The Question of Palestine* (New York, 1979).

SALMON, JEAN J. A., 'La Conférence diplomatique sur la réaffirmation et le développement du droit international humanitaire et les guerres de liberation nationale', *Revue Belge de Droit International* 12(1) (1976), 27–52, and 13(1/2) (1977), 353–78.

SANDOZ, YVES, SWINARSKI, CHRISTOPHE, and ZIMMERMANN, BRUNO (eds.), *Commentary on the Additional Protocols of 8 June 1977 to the Geneva Conventions of 12 August 1949* (Geneva, 1987).

SANGUINETTI, ANTOINE, 'Rapports entre la notion de securité et les atteintes aux droits des hommes et des peuples', in Georges Fischer and Eugene Schaeffer (eds.), *Armement—développement—droits de l'homme—desarmement* (Brussels, 1985).

SCHINDLER, DIETRICH, and TOMAN, JIRI (eds.), *The Laws of Armed Conflicts* (Alphen, 1982).

SCHWARZENBERGER, GEORG, *International Law as Applied by International Courts and Tribunals*, ii: *The Law of Armed Conflict* (London, 1968).

SCHWEBEL, STEPHEN M., 'What Weight to Conquest?', *AJIL* 64 (1970).

SCHWELB, EGON, 'Some Aspects of the International Covenants on Human Rights of December 1966', in Asbjorn Eide and August Schou (eds.), *International Protection of Human Rights: Proceedings of the Seventh Nobel Symposium, Oslo 1967* (New York, 1968), 103.

SCHWENK, EDMUND H., 'Legislative Power of the Military Occupant under Article 43, Hague Regulations', *Yale Law Journal* 54 (1944–5), 393–416.

SCOTT, JAMES BROWN, *The Hague Conventions and Declarations of 1899 and 1907*, 3rd edn. (New York, 1918).

SHADID, MOHAMED, *The United States and the Palestinians* (London, 1981).

SHAMGAR, MEIR, 'The Observance of International Law in the Administered Territories', *IYHR* 1 (1971), 262.

—— (ed.), *Military Government in the Territories Administered by Israel 1967–1980* 1: *The Legal Aspects* (Jerusalem, 1982).

—— 'Legal Concepts and Problems of the Israeli Military Government: The Initial Stage', in Shamgar, Meir (ed.), *Military Government*.

SHAPIRA, AMOS, 'The Six-Day War and the Right of Self-Defence' *IsLR* 6(1) (1971), 65–80.

SHARON, PAUL, 'A Digest of Recent Israeli Cases', *IsLR* 18(3/4) (1983), 475–86.

SHEFI, DOV, 'Taxation in the Administered Territories', *IYHR* 1 (1971), 290.

—— 'The Reports of the UN Special Committees on Israeli Practices in the Territories' in Shamgar, Meir (ed.), *Military Government in the Territories Administered by Israel 1967–1980*, 1: *The Legal Aspects* (Jerusalem, 1982).

SHEHADEH, AZIZ, FU'AD, and RAJA, *Israeli Proposed Road Plan for the West Bank: A Question for the International Court of Justice?* (Ramallah, 1984).

SHEHADEH, RAJA 'Legal System of Israeli Settlements', International Commission of Jurists, *The Review* 27 (Dec. 1981), 59–74.

—— 'The Land Law of Palestine: An Analysis of the Definition of State Lands', *Journal of Palestine Studies* 42 (1982), 82–99.

—— 'An Analysis of the Legal Structure of Israeli Settlements in the West Bank', in Ibrahim Abu-Lughod, *Palestinian Rights: Affirmation and Denial* (Illinois, 1982), 79–94.

—— *Occupier's Law: Israel and the West Bank*, rev. edn. (Washington DC, 1988). DC, 1988).

—— 'The Changing Juridical Status of Palestinian Areas under Occupation: Land Holdings and Settlements', in Naseer Aruri, *Occupation: Israel Over Palestine*, 2nd edn. (Belmont, 1989), 173–93.

—— and KUTTAB, JONATHAN, *The West Bank and the Rule Of Law* (Geneva, 1980).

SHIPLER, DAVID K., *Arab and Jew: Wounded Spirits in a Promised Land* (New York, 1986).

SINGER, JOEL, 'The Establishment of a Civilian Administration in the Areas Administered by Israel', *IYHR* 12 (1982), 259–89.

SLONIM, SHLOMO, 'The United States and the Status of Jerusalem 1947–1984', *IsLR* 19(2) (1984), 179–252.

SOFER, SASSON, *Begin: An Anatomy of Leadership* (Oxford, 1988).

SOMMER, HILLEL, 'In spite of this, the provisions should be applied' *Eyunai Mishpat (Tel Aviv University Law Review)* 11 (1986), 263.

STEIN, ERIC, 'Application of the Law of the Absent Sovereign in Territory under Belligerent Occupation: The Schio Massacre', *Michigan Law Review* 46(3) (1948), 341–70.

STEPHENS, MARC T. R., *Enforcement of International Law in the Israeli-Occupied Territories* (Ramallah, 1989).

—— *Taxation in the Occupied West Bank 1967–1989* (Ramallah, 1990).

STONE, JULIUS, *The Middle East Under Ceasefire: Notes on the Legal Position before the Security Council in October 1967* (Sydney, 1967).

—— *No Peace—No War in the Middle East: Legal Problems of the First Year* (Sydney, 1969).

—— *Legal Controls of International Conflict: A Treatise on the Dynamics of Disputes and War Law* (New York, rev. edn. 1973).

—— *Israel and Palestine: Assault on the Law of Nations* (Baltimore, 1981).

SZASZ, PAUL C., 'The Action does not Violate International Law', *AJIL* 82 (1988), 314–18.

—— and BARRIE, GEORGE, 'AGORA: Is the ASIL Policy on Divestment in Violation of International Law?', *AJIL* 82 (1988), 311.

TABORY, MALA, 'Universality at the UN: The Attempt to Reject Israel's Credentials', *IYHR* 18 (1988), 189.

TESSLER, MARK, 'The Camp David Accords and the Palestinian Problem', in Ann Lesch and Mark Tessler (eds.), *Israel, Egypt and the Palestinians: From Camp David to the Intifada* (Bloomington, Ind., 1989), 3–22.

TEVETH, SHABTAI, *The Cursed Blessing: The Story of Israel's Occupation of the West Bank* (London, 1970).

THORPE, MERLE Jr., *Prescription for Conflict: Israel's West Bank Settlement Policy* (Washington, DC, 1984).

TORRELLI, MAURICE, *Le Droit international humanitaire* (Paris, 1985).

TOYNBEE, ARNOLD, and TOYNBEE, VERONICA (eds.), *Hitler's Europe*, iv: *Survey of International Affairs, 1939–1945* (London, 1954).

TRAININ, ILIA P., 'Questions of Guerrilla Warfare in the Law of War', trans. from Russian, reprinted in *AJIL* 40 (1946), 534.

UNITED KINGDOM WAR OFFICE, *Manual of Military Law, Part III, The Law of War on Land* (London, 1958).

UNITED NATIONS, *United Nations Treaty Series.*
—— *UN Reports of International Arbitral Awards.*
—— UN Economic Commission for Western Asia, *The Industrial and Economic Trends in the West Bank and Gaza Strip* (New York, 1981).
—— United Nations Relief and Works Agency (UNRWA), *Report of the Commissioner General of UNRWA*, 38 UN GAOR Supp. (No. 13), UN Doc. A/38/13 (UN 1983).
UNITED STATES OF AMERICA, Dept. of the Army, *Field Manual FM 27–10, The Law of Land Warfare* (Washington DC, 1956).
—— Dept. of State, *Country Reports on Human Rights Practices for 1987* (1988), 100th Cong., 2d Sess. 1189.
—— *International Law*, II, 27–161–2 (Washington DC, 1962).
—— US Military Tribunals, *Trials of War Criminals Before the Nuernberg Military Tribunals*, 15 vols. (1949–53).
VALTICOS, NICOLAS, *International Labour Law* (Deventer, 1979).
VAN ARKADIE, BRIAN, *Benefits and Burdens: A Report on the West Bank and Gaza Strip Economies since 1967* (New York, 1977).
VERZIJL, J. H. W., *International Law in Historical Perspective* IX–A: *The Laws of War* (Alhen, 1978).
VON GLAHN, GERHARD, *The Occupation of Enemy Territory* (Minneapolis, 1957).
—— *Law Among Nations*, 5th edn. (New York, 1986).
—— 'Obiter Dictum: An Unofficial Expression of Opinion on the VAT Case Judgment', *PYIL* 4 (1987–8), 210–21.
VON KOHLER, L., *Die Staatsverwaltung der besetzten Gebiete*, i: *Belgien* (Stuttgart, 1927).
VON LISZT, FRANZ, *Das Völkerrecht*, 12th edn., ed. Max Fleischman (Berlin, 1925), 491.
VON OPPEN, BEATE RUHM (ed.), *Documents on Germany under Occupation 1945–1954* (London, 1955).
VON SCHMOLLER, G., MAIER, H., and TOBLER, A., *Handbuch des Besatzungsrechts* (Tübingen, 1951).
WALDOCK, HUMPHREY, 'Human Rights in Contemporary International Law and the Significance of the European Convention', *ICLQ* 14, Supp. Pub. No. 11, (1965).
WATTS, G. TRACEY, 'The British Military Occupation of Cyrenaica, 1942–1949', *Transactions of the Grotius Society* (1951), 69–81.
WEILER, JOSEPH H., 'Israel and the Creation of a Palestinian State: The Art of the Impossible and the Possible', *Texas International Law Journal* 17 (1982), 287.
WEISSBRODT, DAVID, 'The Contribution of International Nongovernmental Organizations to the Protection of Human Rights' in Theodor Meron (ed.), *Human Rights in International Law: Legal and Policy Issues*, 403–38.
WHEATON, HENRY, *Elements of International Law*, ii, ed. A. Berriedale Keith, 6th Eng. edn. (London, 1929).
WHITEMAN, MARJORIE, *Digest of International Law*, i and x (Washington, DC, 1963 and 1968).

WHITTOME, CANDY, *The Right to Unite* (Ramallah, 1990).
WILL, D. S., 'Zionist Settlement Ideology', *JPS* 11(3) (1982), 37–57.
YAHIA, F., *The Palestine Question and International Law* (Beirut, 1970).
YINGLING, RAYMOND T., and GINNANE, ROBERT W., 'The Geneva Conventions of 1949', *AJIL* 46(3) (1952), 393–427.
ZINK, HAROLD, *The United States in Germany, 1944–1955* (Princeton, NJ, 1957).
ZOLLER, Elizabeth, *Peacetime Unilateral Remedies: An Analysis of Countermeasures* (New York, 1984).
—— *Enforcing International Law through US Legislation* (New York, 1985).
ZUIJDWIJK, TON J. M., *Petitioning the United Nations* (Aldershot, 1982).

OFFICIAL JORDANIAN DATA
Official Jordanian Gazette.
Jordan Development Board, *Five Year Plan for Economic and Social Development 1976–1980*.
Central Bank of Jordan, *Annual Report 1986* (Amman, 1987).

OFFICIAL ISRAELI DATA
The Civil Administration, Judea and Samaria, *Annual Report*.
Central Bureau of Statistics, Jerusalem, *National Accounts*
—— *Judea, Samaria and Gaza Area Statistics*.
—— *Statistical Abstract of Israel*.
Bank of Israel, *Annual Statistics of Israel's Banking System*
Israel Ministry of Defence: Coordinator of Government Operations in the Administered Territories, *The Administered Territories 1971/1972*, also issued in 1972/1973 and 1973/1974.
—— *Survey of the Administered Territories 1967–1975*.
—— *A Sixteen Year Survey (1967–1983)* (Jerusalem, 1983).
—— *An Eighteen Year Survey (1967–1985)* (Jerusalem, 1986).
—— *Judea, Samaria and the Gaza District 1967–1987: Twenty Years of Civil Administration* (Jerusalem, 1987).

Index

administration of justice:
  occupied territory, in 261–2
administration of occupied territories:
  belligerent occupation: legal framework of 242–50; situations outside 241–2
  changes in constitution or institutions, status of 245
  democratic structure 264–5
  existing structure, departure from 254–9
  express provisions 265
  geographical units, departures from 257–8
  human rights protection 249–50
  justice, of 261–2
  military government, by 253–4
  new bodies, creation of 256
  occupying power: armed forces and administration not subject to local law 248; demands on 250–1; duty of obedience to 251–2; elections and political activity, suspension of 257, 264, 266; existing law, respecting 47–9, 255; population, relationship with 252; requirement of 246–7; specific duties and prohibitions imposed by international law, constraints of 249–50; specific obligations 246–7; temporary authority, not sovereignty, acquiring 244–5
  occupying state, integration with 259–61
  population, whether required to obey lawful orders of occupant 251
  principles of 265–6
  prolonged occupations, in 262–5
  structure of 252–4
  treaties 242
  West Bank, see West Bank
Afghanistan:
  Soviet occupation of 32
Al-Haq:
  abuses of human rights, addressing 11
  closure of unions, taking up case against 335–7
  developments and precedents, making use of 485–6
  establishment of 11
  humanitarian law, working within framework of 11
  laws of war and human rights, research on 12–13
  mandate 11
  territories, monitoring treatment of 11
  violations of human law, writings on 13–14
Allon Plan 6, 286–7, 444
annexation:
  illegality of 245, 369n.
  ineffective to alter status 245
  occupation excluding 176–80
Arab Cement Factory:
  establishment of 406
Axis-occupied countries
  Allied resistance in 63

Bank of Palestine:
  vetoes on 407–8
Belgium:
  contributions to funds, imposition of 374–5
  German division of 258–9
  taxation: World War I, during 355–7; German occupation, under 363
belligerent occupation:
  administration of occupied territory, applicable to, see administration of occupied territories
  annexation, occupation excluding 176–80; illegality of 245, 369n.
  applicable laws 347–50
  application of law after end of hostilities 48, 192, 346
  character of 133
  civil laws, no alteration or suspension of 347–9
  civilian population, sincere and insincere concern for 201
  contributions to funds, imposition of: all occupants, on 375–6; German practices 374–6; Hague Regulations 373; specific limits on 373–4
  criteria of 171
  customary law, construction of 423–7
  development of law 192
  duration of, no limit for 73–4
  evolutive interpretation 423–7
  framework, point of 139
  general principles governing 420–1

belligerent occupation (*cont.*):
  government prevailing 8
  Hague Regulations, applicability of 344–7
  human rights, enforcement of 20–1
  inhabitant and occupying power, relationship between 146
  institution of 133
  international control, object of 203
  international law: framework of 16–18, 35–6, 242, 342; provisions, lack of precision in 238
  Israeli objections to applicability of 188–91
  juridical nature of 250–2
  law: codification of 188, 342–4; general considerations 170–1; lack of legal scholarship on 12; legislation by occupier 201
  lawful and unlawful acts of occupier distinguished 203
  legal institution, intrinsic character of 173
  occupant: powers, bias in use of 200; limitation of 187–94; prerogatives of 140; rights of 134, strict approach to 422
  occupied people, rights of, *see* occupied people
  Occupied Territories, status of 465–6
  organizations formed by population, hostility to 295
  prolonged 146
  right of peoples to self-determination 180–6
  rules applicable to, primary purpose of 348
  sovereignty, occupation not conferring 174–6
  taxation under, *see* taxation
  temporary circumstance, as 28, 134, 175, 244
  treaties protecting right to trade union organization, application of: displaced sovereign, of 305–6; occupant, of 307–8

Camp David Accords:
  autonomous Palestinian rights, provision for 145
  civilian administration following 8
  constituent parts 6
  interpretation by Israel 474–5
child:
  registration, place of 164
China:
  taxation under Japanese occupation 358–9

customary law:
  definition 113
  evolutive interpretation 423–7
  Fourth Geneva Convention as part of 111–14
  freedom of association as right of 296
  human rights norms as 485–6
  international treaties, reliance on 436
  legislative conventions distinguished 115
  modification in course of prolonged occupation 346–7
  trade union organizing: European Commission rulings 303–4; international instruments, practice reflected in 296–9; military occupant, customary human rights law binding on 300–5; norm protecting freedom of association 299–300; permitting 295–305; recognition of right to 296; State practice in exercise of military occupation 304–5; United Nations, State practice in 301–3
  Universal Declaration of Human Rights, position of 122–3
customs duties:
  belligerent occupation, under 354
  West Bank, in: Israeli occupation, under 386–7; prior to 1967 379
Cyprus:
  human rights violations in 303
  northern, Turkish occupation of 32

demonstrations:
  reasons for 125–6
  West Bank and Gaza occupations, against 125
deportation:
  appeals against 235
  Article 49, Geneva Convention, provisions of 109, 113
  Palestinians, of 127–8
  West Bank resident, of 95
Drobless Plan 6

East Jerusalem:
  annexation 41–2, 99n.; complaints about 79; non-recognition of 476–9
  boundaries, extension of 5–6
  foreign trade, security measures damaging 415–16
  legal status of 476
  Palestinian land, exploitation for Jewish colonies 444–5
  Palestinian property, pretexts or devices for seizure of 448–9
  trade unions: illegality 326; organization of 320–1

Index

emergency:
 derogation from human rights instruments in 310–12
emergency legislation:
 annulment of 107
Eretz Israel 6
European Community:
 vegetables and fruit, export to 414
expropriation of land:
 legality of 97–8

Fourth Geneva Convention 5
 actions of military government, opposition to: application of 106
 Additional Protocol, application of 190–1
 administration of occupied territories, principles of law on 242–3
 agreement, type of 121
 all circumstances, applying in 191–2
 alleged inapplicability of 130–6
 applicability to Occupied Territories 44–52, 130, 189, 244, 437; non-application, official Israeli position on 44–5, 101–3, 130–6; possibility of 121–2; revocation of article admitting 157
 application following agreement of State Attorney 108–11
 Article 49(6), discussion of 65–7, 95, 110, 113n., 249
 civilians, protection of 101–19
 Commentary on 193
 contractual international law, as part of 105–8
 customary international law, as part of 111–14
 declaratory or constitutive, whether 112
 demolition of room, whether prohibited 107
 deportation of West Bank resident, whether violated by 65–7, 95, 109–11, 113n., 249
 future post-surrender occupation, applicable to 30–1
 General Staff Orders, directions in 116–17
 Hague Regulations, distinction of 114
 humanitarian provisions: application of 103–5; Israeli government attitude to 137
 internal Israeli law, whether part of 105–6, 116
 internal law of Occupied Territories, as part of 119–22
 Israel's obligations extending beyond 468
 Israeli High Court, refusal of to apply 435, 495
 legislative convention, as 114–16
 Military Court, application by 188
 military occupation, rules relating to conduct of 35
 minimum rules of humanitarian conduct, prescription of 467
 missing reversioner argument 131
 obligatory Israeli law, part of 117–18
 occupation, applicability to 21
 occupation, nature of provisions relating to 190
 Occupied Territories, application in 45–9
 one year after provision 36–9, 192–3, 347
 prolonged occupations, rules on 36–9
 transfer of land, disregard for provisions as to 435–7
 West Bank local law, as part of 120
France:
 contributions to funds, imposition of 374–6
 occupation costs 376
 taxation under German occupation 363

Gaza Strip:
 area of 41
 citrus industry 413
 construction and alteration, prohibition of 422–3
 economic changes in 68–70
 Egyptian administration of 4
 fishing industry, demise of 408–9
 future status, transitional period to determine 7
 Jewish settlement in 7
 Palestinian population of 65
 taxation in 370–1
 vegetables and fruit, export of 414
 see also Occupied Territories of the West Bank and Gaza Strip
Geneva Conventions:
 Fourth, see Fourth Geneva Convention
 human rights law, concept taken into account 54
 Israel, obligation of to apply 189
 Jordan, accession of 121
 liberation struggles, legal constraints applicable to 64–5
 1977 Protocol, parties to 35
 taxation, no mention of 342
Germany:
 Allied occupation of 29–31
 occupation of, taxation under: American 365–7; British 363–5
Golan Heights:
 annexation: complaints about 79; non-

Golan Heights (cont.)
  recognition of 476
  Israeli law, extension to 41–2
Gulf of Suez:
  oilfields, development of 425

Hague Convention
  Fourth: military occupation, rules relating to conduct of 35
  Occupied Territories, application in 46
Hague Regulations 5
  administration of occupied territories, principles of law on 242–3
  Allied occupation of Germany and Japan, application to 30
  current circumstances, adjustment for 425
  customary value 189
  demolition of room, whether prohibited 100, 107
  existing law, respect for 211–15
  foundations of 68
  Geneva Convention, distinction between 114
  humanity and necessity, Article on 172
  imposition of value added tax, whether prohibited 96
  Israel, application by 91–8
  Israel's obligations extending beyond 468
  law of occupation, codification of 171
  local law, conflict with 99
  minimum rules of humanitarian conduct, prescription of 467
  Occupied Territories, applicability to 45, 88–91, 98–100, 189
  permitted deviation from 345–6
  practical non-application, justification of 100
  private land, legality of appropriating 97–8
  prolonged occupations, weakening in case of 345
  public order and safety, duty to restore and ensure 92–8, 197, 207–15, 246, 352–3
  ratification, application independently of 189
  seizure of private land, prevention of 95
  taxation: no mention of 342–3; principles on 350
  territories under belligerent occupation, applicability to 344–7
Head of Civilian Administration:
  administration by 275–7
  powers, exercise of 8
human rights:
  accords, Israeli view of 55
  emergency, effect of 310–12
  international law, development of 31
  law: citizen and own government, dealing with relations between 55; Geneva Conventions, taken into account on drafting 54; military occupations, applicability to 53–7, 78, 300–5; Nazi oppression, reaction against 53
  Occupied Territories, in: defence of: accurate documentation for 498–9, International Court of Justice, in 497–8, Israeli High Court, in 493–7, Israeli public opinion, appeal to 502–3, Jordanian law, under 490–2, other groups, implicating 501–2, public opinion 498–503, publicity, use of 500–1, tone and political conflict 499–500; domestic courts, advancement through 485–7; enforcement: annexations, by non-recognition of 476–9, Direct Enforcement Model 462–3, economic coercion, by 479–82, humanitarian intervention using armed force, prohibition of 481, Indirect Enforcement Model 463–8, international organizations, exclusion from 482–3; enforcement models for 462; minimum rules of 467; regime, classification of 464–8; Special Committee, investigation by 483–4; task of advancing 487; UN Charter, methods to secure protection under 475–84; violations of 489, Israel, by 462–2, as crime against humanity 147
  trade unions, right to form 296–9
  Universal Declaration of 122–3
  wartime, law applying in 301
humanitarian law:
  rules of 5
  West Bank and Gaza, provisions applied to 205
humanity and necessity: ambiguity of 197; application of criterion 136, 194–204; categories of necessity 197–8; exceptional measures 198; guiding principles of 194–7; military necessities 196–8

Indonesia:
  taxation under Japanese occupation 359–61
International Court of Justice:
  human rights, defence of 497–8
  legal status, advisory opinion on: acceptance of 471–3; effect of 473–5; response of Israel to 472–3; type of

Index

469–71; whether likely to be given 468–9
Occupied Territories, no consideration of issues arising 83–4
International Labour Organisation:
Conventions, applicability to Occupied Territories 484
right to association, recognition of 298–9
international law:
administration of occupied territory, applicable to, *see* administration of occupied territories
classic principles, interpretation of 185
continued occupation, challenged by 148
evolutive interpretation 423–7
lawful and unlawful occupant, no distinction between 243
long occupation, application to 2
powers of occupier, limitation of 187–94
international organisations:
prolonged occupations, role in 77
intifada:
internal front, development of 146
meaning 125
pervasiveness and durability of 143
reasons for 125–6
Israel:
Geneva Conventions, obligation to apply 189
Hague Regulations, application of 91–8
laws of war, interpretation of 1–2
liability of leaders 147
Palestinian resistance, suppression of 139
State of, declaration of 4
Israeli High Court:
appeals in 154
Fourth Geneva Convention: application in Occupied Territories, possibility of 121–2; Article 49(6), discussion of 110, 435; consideration of position in law 105–6; customary international law, as part of 111–14; internal Israeli law, as part of 116; refusal to apply 435, 495
Hague Regulations: applicability of 88–91; Article 43, interpretation of 92–7; attitude to 91; continued application of 98–100; judges, attitude of 99; local law, conflict with 99; practical non-application, justification of 100
human rights: protection of 493–7; use of to promote 487
humanitarian law, interpretation of 11–12

inefficacy of 92n., 237, 494, 496
international law, application of 87–8
Occupied Territories, available to 10; not a Court of Appeal for 154, 494
Palestinian use of 91n., 92n., 493
prolonged occupation, judgments on: general considerations 74–6; generally 70–1; international law rules applied 71; problems with 75–6; High Court cases 71–4
security, broad interpretation of 226–9, 233–6, 495–6
Supreme Court, sitting as 87
Universal Declaration of Human Rights, position of 122–3
West Bank cases, not a Court of Appeal 494
Israeli law:
international customary law, effect of 25
treaties, implementation of 25
Israeli occupation:
agreements covering 25–6
further prolonged, likelihood of 85
human rights law, applicability of 53–7
international community, views of: generally 57; Israeli settlements, to 65–7; level of interest 57–9; long-term economic change, as to 68–70; Palestinian deportations, to 65–7; resistance, legitimacy and treatment of 62–5; self-determination, favouring 59–62; territory, status of 59–62
international interest in 81–4
issues given rise to 26–7
law on occupations, abuse by adversaries 79–80
legality of 50, 136, 149
self-determination in 59–62
Israeli resident:
meaning, extension of 163
Israeli settlements:
administration of 158–60, 163, 282–5
illegal 66–7
Occupied Territories, in 5–8, 24–5, 66, 435–6
security, whether contributing to 66–7, 75, 226–9
High Court cases on 71–5, 226–9, 436
Israeli Supreme Court, *see* Israeli High Court
Israeli violation:
perception of 126–30
Italy:
taxation under Allied occupation 367

Japan:
Allied occupation of 29–31
Jerusalem, *see* East Jerusalem

Jewish homeland:
  opposition to 141
Jewish regional councils:
  establishment of 159, 282
Jordan:
  constitutional bodies 270–1
  Geneva Conventions, accession to 121
  human rights protection under law of 490–2
  judiciary 271
  lorries permitted to cross to 414–15
Jordan Rift:
  Jewish colonization of 444–5
Jordanian system of justice:
  Court of Appeal, appeal to 153

Kampuchea:
  Vietnamese occupation of 32
Karp Report 67n., 490–1

labour movement:
  West Bank and Gaza, in 316–21
land:
  acquisition of, military orders 158
  categories of ownership 450
  jiftlik 450
  mawat 450
  miri 450
  mudewwara 450
  mulk 450
  occupant's use of 427–32
  Occupied Territories, case-law on use of: doubts raised by 435–41; enemy property, whether public 437–8; Fourth Geneva Convention, disregard for 435–7; local population, whether actions serving interests of 439–41; requisition, appraisal of military necessity justifying 438–9; restraining impact of 441–2; Supreme Court, judicial review by 433–5
  Palestinian: cultivation of 162–3; exploitation for Jewish colonies 443–4, agricultural crops, destruction of 451, attempts to block 454–5, colonization policies, results of 447–8, development of 444–8, farmers, displacement of 452, Israeli Labour government policies 1967–77 444–6, Israeli Likud government policies 1977–84 446–7, National Unity Coalition Government policies 447, non-violent means to prevent 456, Ottoman laws, use of 455; expropriation of 214
  security reasons, requisitioned for 226–7

seizures, impact on Palestinian population 449–52
settlement, acquisition for 228
use, restriction of 162
West Bank, planning in 158–9, 221, 286–93
Landau Commission 232, 269
Latvia:
  taxation under German occupation 362–3
law:
  definition of 117
  military orders as part of 118
law of war:
  annexation incompatible with 179–80
  compromise of 170
  conditions for envisaging 169
  limits of belligerent conduct, delineation of 136
  military needs, balancing against humanitarian values 169–70
  proportionality, principle of 172–3

Mandatory authorities:
  responsibilities of 3
Mandatory Palestine:
  agricultural economy 399
military government:
  administrative structure 253–4
  Hague regulations, actions contravening 91
  structure, changes in 8
  West Bank, in: central command HQ, separation from 273; co-ordinator of activities 275; first restructuring of 273; government of Israel, interdependence with 274; internal security, responsibility for 273–4; powers exercised by 272–3; structure of 271–2; two arms of 273, 275
military law:
  experts on 12
military necessity:
  doctrine of, effect of 138, 194–204, 420
  plea of 136–42
  see also humanity and necessity
military occupation:
  conduct, rules of 35
  human rights law, applicability of 53–7
  international legal rules applicable to 25
  legal rules governing 419–20
  one year after provision 36–9, 192–3, 347
  trade unions, right to form, *see* trade unions
  variation in rules 39–40
military orders:

Index

acquisition of land, permitting 158
annexation, expediting 162
availability of 151
emergency regulations, power to make 160
first legislative phase, in 152–8
form, sloppiness of 166
fourth legislative stage 162–6
issue of 166
Jewish regional councils, establishment of 159
Jewish settlement: as to 222; emphasis on 158–9
judicial system, restructuring of 153–4
Labour Law, increase of entitlements under 165
local law, changes to 220
military jurisdiction, extension of 152
municipal elections, concerning 281
number of 151
objectives 165
officials, appointment of 163
organization of settlements, for 160
Palestinians, increase of authority over 163–4
permission from military, activities requiring 164
planting, restrictions on 222
pre-existing law, altering 212
printed matter, complete ban on 153
Proclamation No. 2 152
Proclamation No. 3 153
publication of 151–2
references to 151
rendering Territories annexed to Israel 156–7
second legislative stage 158–60
separate juridical area, rendering Territories as 155–6
taxes, no accountability for 154
third legislative stage 160–1
union elections, concerning 326–7
water, control of 221
welfare of local population, for 216
Morocco:
 Western Sahara, occupation of 32

Namibia:
 Opinion of International Court of Justice, history since 473
 South African occupation of 31–2

occupations:
 administration, international law principles, *see* administration of occupied territories
 belligerent, *see* belligerent occupation
 concept of 26
 existing law, respect for 247–9, 255
 illegal, concept of 49
 land and natural resources: exploitation, right of 426; land, water and oil, considerations applied to 430–2; principles governing use of 421–3; state-owned, use by occupant 427–30
 law on: abuse by adversaries 79–80; application to Occupied Territories: international agreements 43, international community, view of 52–3, official Israeli view 44–9, PLO views 49–51, viewpoints for 43–4; codification of 171; purposes of 27–8
 peacetime 34
 prolonged: administration during 262–5; bodies of law, special importance of 33; category, as 28–34; context of 32–3; customary law, modification of 346–7; decisions made during 33; definition of 29; ending of 84–5; existing law, concern with 77–8; formal international agreement on 77; generally 76–9; Germany and Japan, Allied occupations of 29–31; Hague Regulations, weakening of 345; international organizations, role of 77; Israeli Supreme Court judgments on 70–6; legal rules governing 419–20; Moroccan, of Western Sahara 32; peacetime, overlap with 34; permanent, not meaning 42–3, 85; powers of occupant, recognition of 34; Principal Conventions, in 35–40; purposes of law, relevance of 76; South African, of Namibia 31–2; Soviet, of Afghanistan 32; Turkish, of northern Cyprus 32; Vietnamese, of Kampuchea 32
 proportionality, principle of 139, 172
 resistance, legitimacy and treatment of 62–5
 sovereign power, displacing 131
 trustee, idea of 51
occupied people:
 existence, continuation of 174
 sovereign rights of, respect for:
  annexation, occupation excluding 176–80; criterion of, relation to principle of humanity 200; criterion of right of occupant, constituting 186; Palestinian peoples, of 182–6; present and past wars 173–4; sovereignty, occupation not conferring 174–6

Occupied Territories of West Bank and
    Gaza Strip:
  administration 18–20
  administrative acts, justification of:
    criteria applied 205; interpretations
    237; military orders, of 212; public
    order and safety, to restore and
    ensure 207–15; security 223–36;
    welfare of local population, for
    215–23
  administrative and legal framework
    8–10
  administrative orders, appealing 234–5
  Al-haq, role of, see Al-Haq
  annexation to Israel *de facto* 156–7, 162,
    260, 464
  Arab Cement Factory 406
  areas of 40–2
  Bank of Palestine, functioning of 407–8
  bilateral trade 411–13
  budget: components of 390; conclusions
    392, 394; development 390–2; foreign-
    aid support 392; military authorities,
    by 389; regular 392–3
  cheap labour from 317
  children and students, cleaning etc.
    efforts of 315
  colonization, policy of 443
  demography, changes in 65
  deportations from 65–7, 109–11, 113n.,
    249
  development planning 405–11
  disputed sovereignty, effect of 135
  economic policies: effect of 416;
    evolution of 399; responsibility for
    400
  economy of: economic growth 401–2;
    standard of living 402–3;
    transformation of 68–70, 400
  employment in 403–4
  export trade 413–16
  external sources of income 402
  fishing industry, demise of 408–9
  foreign trade, security measures
    damaging 415–16
  Fourth Geneva Convention: application
    following agreement of State Attorney
    108–11; humanitarian provisions,
    application of 103–5; non-application,
    official Israeli position on 101–3;
    as part of internal law 119–22;
    possibility of application of 121–2
  general considerations 79–81
  guidelines on administration of 206
  Hague Regulations, applicability of
    88–91
  human rights, enforcement of, *see*
    human rights
  humanitarian law, provisions applied
    205
  ILO Conventions, applicability of 484
  industrial goods, sale of 411
  International Court of Justice, no
    consideration by 83–4
  international interest in 81–4
  international law, application of 87–8
  international legal norms, applicability
    of 44–5
  international legal standards, relevance
    of 46
  Israel, legal position of 142
  Israeli and Palestinian compromise,
    working towards 61
  Israeli Supreme Court, availability of 10
  Israeli treatment of 22
  Israelis residing in, jurisdiction to try
    161
  Jewish settlement in 5–8, 66, 222, 435–6
  Jewish settlers: as local population
    165–6, 220–2, *see also* Israeli
    settlement
  Jordan, lorries permitted to cross to
    414–15
  judicial system, restructuring of 153–4
  labour force, 1985 316
  labour movement 316–21
  land in, *see* land
  law on occupations: abuse by
    adversaries 79–80; application of:
    international agreements 43,
    international community, view of
    52–3, official Israeli view 44–9, PLO
    views 49–51, viewpoints for 43–4
  legal status of 461; assessment,
    principles for 470; belligerent
    occupation 465–6; International Court
    of Justice, advisory opinion of:
    acceptance of 471–3, effect of 473–5,
    response of Israel to 472–3, type of
    469–71, whether likely to be given
    468–9; Israel, as part of 464; non-self-
    governing territory 466; sui generis
    465, 467; trustee occupation 465
  length of occupation, analysis of 43
  local population: best interests,
    respect for as principle of international
    law 420, determining 216–20, 439,
    welfare of 215–23, who is 202, 220–3
  mass-based organizations: activists,
    restrictions on 331–2; aim of 324;
    authorities, response of 339; bar
    association, establishment of 333; *bona
    fide* nature of 314; early organizing
    efforts 314–16; emergence and

growth of 314–24; first years of occupation, little activity during 314–15; Israeli authorities, view of 313; Israeli repression of 324–32; labour movement 316–21, see also trade unions; medical relief committees 323–4; meeting halls, closure to prevent meetings taking place 330–1; recourse against repression 332–9; women's movement 321–3; workers' bloc 319
military occupation, standards for judging 461
military orders, see military orders
non-residents, work permits for 156
occupation: Fourth Geneva Convention not applied to 5; Israeli view of 5; origin of 3; Six Day War, following 4
occupied territory, as 143
Palestinian inhabitant, subjugation of 142
Palestinian land, exploitation for Jewish colonies 446–7
Palestinian nationalism, growth of 60
Palestinian property, pretexts for seizure of 448–9
physical planning in 409–11
poultry industry in 406–7
presentation of occupation, changes in 166–7
prolonged occupation of 42–3
public expenditure 396–8
public order and safety, duty to restore and ensure 92–8, 197, 207–15, 246, 352–3
revenues collected 394–5
security: curfews, imposition of 225–6; for whom secured 229–31; broad interpretation of 495; justification of military actions on grounds of 223–5; land, requisitioning 226–7; military reliance on 236; needs, expanding scope of 225–9; powers, supervision of 231–6; responsibility for 231–3; settlers, of 229–31
security threat in 142
self-determination in 61
separate juridical area, as 155–6
sovereign rule, whether under prior to occupation 99
standard of living 402–3
taxation in 369–73
trustee-occupant, Israel as 132–3
United Nations: as concern of 466; preoccupation of 58
use of land, case-law on: doubts raised by 435–41; enemy property, whether public 437–8; Fourth Geneva Convention, disregard for 435–7; local population, whether actions serving interests of 439–41; requisition, appraisal of military necessity justifying 438–9; restraining impact of 441–2; Supreme Court, judicial review by 433–5
vegetables and fruit, export of 414
water, control of 221
water resources, see water resources
women's movement 321–3

oil:
Israeli relations with Egypt, relevance to 70
occupant's use of 430–2

Palestine:
Jewish immigration 3
land, exploitation of, see land
mandate, termination of 471
occupation, history of 180
partition of 4
Palestine Liberation Organization:
formation, acceptance of 181
law on occupations, views on application of 49–51
recognition of 63
unions alleged to be front for 333–4
Palestinian self-determination:
denial of 140
implementation, process for 144
legitimate exercise of rights 147
Palestinians:
bar association, establishment of 9, 305, 333
bilateral trade 412
employment of 403–4
expression of national sentiment, repression of 324
failure to treat justly 148
foreign rulers, living under 313
increase of authority over 163–4
labour movement 316–21
medical relief committees 323–4
people, legal existence of 180–1
sovereign rights of 182–6
trade unions, see trade unions
West Bank and Gaza, of: denial of right to self-determination 140; situation of 145
West Bank, low level of services in 397–8
worker, Deduction Fund 154, 317, 395, 404
workers in West Bank, rights of 317

planning:
  Jordanian law 158-9
  see also land
Poland:
  taxation under German occupation 361-2
political issues:
  legal terms, discussion in 26
property:
  Christian and Muslim Palestinian, seizure of 443
  confiscation, protection from 421
  Palestinian, exploitation for Jewish colonies 443-4; colonization policies, results of 447-8; development of 444-8; Israeli Labour government policies 1967-77 444-6; Israeli Likud government policies 1977-84 446-7; National Unity Coalition Government policies 447; non-violent means to prevent 456
  requisition of 421
  seizure, pretexts for 448-9
  state-owned immovable, occupant's use of 427-30
public order and safety:
  cost, payment for 352-3
  duty to restore and ensure 207-15
  economic and social affairs, including 209
  existing law, respect for 211-15
  far-reaching modifications to 210-11
  French text of 246
  meaning 348-9
  principles arising 244
  restore and ensure, whether read together 208

resistance:
  Geneva Convention, treatment in 64-5
  legal right of 147
  legitimacy and treatment of 62-5
  UN, involvement of 64
Rhineland:
  taxation during World War I 358

security concerns:
  Israel, of 137-8
  plea of 136-42, 198-9
self-determination:
  occupations, in respect of 59
  Palestinian 59-60, 183, how to implement 144
  right to, non-abuse of 184
  West Bank and Gaza, in 61
Serbia:
  taxation during World War I 357-8

Shin Bet:
  lack of control over 232, 269
  recommendations of 269
Sinai Peninsula:
  Israeli control, coming under 41
  oilfields in 70, 425
  withdrawal from 41-2
Six Day War 4
  riots preceding 125
South Africa:
  Namibia, occupation of 31-2
South Korea:
  taxation under American occupation 367-8
sovereignty:
  occupant not acquiring 244-5
  occupation not conferring 174-6

taxation:
  belligerent occupation, under: Belgium, in 355-7, 363; China, in 358-9; contributions, imposition of 373-6; conventional regulation, gaps in 341; customs duties 354; existing taxes, adjustment of 352; France, in 363; Gaza Strip, in 370-1; general considerations 350-4; Germany under American occupation, in 365-7; Germany under British occupation, in 363-5; Hague Regulations, principles in 350; Indonesia, in 359-61; interpretations of law 343; Israel's Occupied territories, of 369-73; Italy under Allied occupation, in 367; judicial decisions 343; Latvia, in 362-3; law, under 342-3; local 351; military manuals, rules in 355; new taxes, levy of 351-4; ousted government, collected for 351-2; Poland, in 361-2; public order and safety, payment for 352-3; Rhineland, in 358; Serbia, in 357-8; South Korea under American occupation, in 367-8; West Bank, in 369-70; World War I, in 355-9; World War II, in 359-68
  Gaza Strip, in 370-1
  VAT, introduction of, see value added tax
  West Bank, in 369-70; assessment and collection of 388-9; Israeli occupation, under 380, amended laws 383, bridge crossing tax 385-8, customs duties 386-7, income tax 381-3, purchase of foreign currency, on 388, security offences, fines for 388, stamp revenue tax 385-8, value added tax 383-5;

prior to 1967 377, customs duties and excises 379, education rules, under 379, exemption from 379–80, government services, fees and customs duties on 379, income tax law 378, land, on 379, property, on 379

taxes:
  accountability for 154
  income of settlers in West Bank, on 161
  new: introduction of 165; levy of 154
  taxation under belligerent occupation, *see* taxation

trade unions:
  East Jerusalem: illegality 326, organization of 320–1
  Gaza 320
  military occupation, organizing during: customary law obligation to permit 295–305; customary norm protecting freedom of association 299–300; European Commission rulings 303–4; extreme situations, restriction in 309–12; international instruments, practice reflected in 296–9; military occupant, customary human rights law binding on 300–5; national security, effect of threat to 309–10; public emergency, derogation in 310–12; public order, effect of threat to 309–10; recognition of right to 296; State practice 304–5; treaties protecting, application of 305–8; United Nations, State practice in 301–3
  Palestinian: first establishment of 314, role of 313
  West Bank: activities 320–1; arrests without charges 329; elections, military orders 326–7; employers, relations with 321; formal structure of 318–19; functioning 327; General Federation of 318–19; ILO Committee on Freedom of Association, complaint against Israeli government sent to 337–8; Israeli authorities, attitude of 332–4; Israeli repression of 324–32; Jordanian labour law, formation according to 317; justification for measures against 333–4; leaders, restraints on 329; meeting halls, closure to prevent meetings taking place 330–1; membership, estimates of size of 320; nationalist positions 319; number of 318; offices: army-ordered closure of 332, 335–7, break-ins at 328; PLO, as front for factions in 333–4; prohibited publications, possession of 328; recourse against repression 332–9; registration, application for 325; size of 318; towns and villages, in 318; travel restrictions on members of 330; violation of rights, protests of 339–40
  western and Israeli, alliances between 338

Transjordan:
  West Bank, administration and annexation of 4

trustee occupation:
  concept of 51

United Nations:
  General Assembly, utility of solemn declaration 468
  Israeli occupation, attitude to 52n., 82–3, 182, 465
  Occupied Territories, on economic policies in 69, preoccupation with 58
  resistance, on 64
  Resolution 181 471
  Resolution 242 4–5, 7, 60
  Resolution 338 5, 60
  resolutions, consistency and utility of 83
  Special Committee to investigate Israeli practices 58, 483
  Uniting for Peace Resolution 463

value added tax:
  customary international law, validity under 372
  imposition of 96, 213, 220
  introduction of 165
  Occupied Territories, introduction in 371–3
  West Bank, imposition in 383–5

Vietnam:
  Kampuchea, occupation of 32

water resources:
  occupant's use of 430–2
  Palestinian, exploitation for Jewish colonies 443–4; deep-bore well, drilling of 452–4

West Bank
  administration under Israeli rule: annexationist aims, revealing 293; bodies responsible for 268–9; civilian administration, establishment of 275–81; co-ordinator of activities 275, 279; decision-making 268; delegation of powers 278; Head of Civilian Administration 275–7; indigenous population, effects on life of 286–93;

West Bank (*cont.*)
  integration to own system 267; land planning 286–93; local authorities 281–6; military government, introduction of 271–5; pre-1967 structure, changes in 267–8; quasi-police functions 277–8; Shin Bet, role of 269; structure of 279–80; village leagues 278
  administration under Jordanian rule, 1948–67 270–1
  area of 40–1
  basic utilities, supply of 216–18
  budget: components of 390; conclusions 392, 394; development 390–2; foreign-aid support 392; regular 389, 392–3
  closed military area, as 156
  Companies Department 155
  Court of Cassation, no replacement for 9
  disuse, term falling into 167
  electricity supply to 217–18
  future status, transitional period to determine 7
  import on money into 165
  income of settlers in, taxation of 161
  Israeli citizens, influx of 160
  Jewish settlement in 7; funding for 284; plan for 6
  Jordanian government structure, identification of 268
  Jordanian seat of government, severance from 9
  land planning 162–3; Central Planning Department 290; District Planning Committee 291–2; Higher Planning Council 291; Local Planning Committees 292–3; Minister of the Interior, role of 290; physical 286–8; settlements, for 287–8; structure of 289
  land use, restriction of 162
  law prior to occupation 9
  local government: elections, postponement of 281; existing Jordanian law 281; funding 284–5; Israel and Jordan, functional partition between 282; Israel, established by 282; Jewish colonies 283–4; municipalities 281; regional and local councils 283–4

  military government: central command HQ, separation from 273; co-ordinator of activities 275; first restructuring of 273; government of Israel, interdependence with 274; internal security, responsibility for 273–4; powers exercised by 272–3; reorganization of 161; structure of 271–2; two arms of 273, 275
  Military Governor, validity of legislative acts of 94
  non-residents working in 166
  observance of Geneva Convention, order as to 119–20
  Palestinian workers, rights of 317
  renaming 11
  resident, deportation of 95
  road system 218–19
  services, low level of 397–8
  taxation in 369–70; assessment and collection 388–9; Israeli occupation, under 380, amended laws 383, bridge crossing tax 385–8, customs duties 386–7, income tax 381–3, purchase of foreign currency, on 388, security offences, fines for 388, stamp revenue tax 385–8, value added tax 383–5; prior to 1967 377, customs duties and excises 379, education rules, under 379, exemption from 379–80, government services, fees and customs duties on 379, income tax law 378, land, on 379, property, on 379
  Trademarks Registration Department 155
  Transjordan, administration and annexation by 4
  economic changes in 68–70
  Palestinian population of 65
  see also Occupied Territories of the West Bank and Gaza Strip
West Bank Data Base Project:
  work of 14–15
Western Sahara:
  Moroccan occupation of 32
women's movement:
  West Bank and Gaza, in 321–3

Zionism:
  Israeli territory, views on 141